VIKINGS

THE NORTH ATLANTIC SAGA

VIKINGS

THE NORTH ATLANTIC SAGA

Edited by
William W. Fitzhugh
and
Elisabeth I. Ward

Published by
SMITHSONIAN INSTITUTION PRESS
WASHINGTON AND LONDON

in association with the
NATIONAL MUSEUM OF NATURAL HISTORY

CONTENTS

V NORSE GREENLAND

VI VIKING LEGACY

Library of Congress Cataloging-in-Publication Data

Vikings : the North Atlantic saga / edited by William W. Fitzhugh and Elisabeth I. Ward.

        p.   cm.

       "An exhibition at the National Museum of Natural History, Smithsonian Institution, Washington, D.C., April 29, 2000–September 5, 2000"—P.

       Includes bibliographical references and index.

       ISBN 1-56098-970-x (cloth : alk. paper) — ISBN 1-56098-995-5 (paper : alk. paper)

       1. Vikings. 2. Northmen. 3. North America—Discovery and exploration—Norse. 4. Canada—Discovery and exploration—Norse. 5. Greenland—Discovery and exploration—Norse. 6. Vikings—Catalogs. I. Fitzhugh, William W., 1943– . II. Ward, Elisabeth I. III. National Museum of Natural History (U.S.).

DL65.V586   2000

970.01'3—dc21   99-057983

British Library Cataloguing-in-Publication Data available

Printed in Japan, not at government expense
07 06 05 04 03 02 01 00 5 4 3 2 1

∞The paper used in this publication meets the minimum requirements of the American National Standard for Information Sciences—Permanence of Paper for Printed Library Materials ANSI Z239.48-1984.

This publication has been prepared by the Arctic Studies Center, National Museum of Natural History, as part of the exhibition program of the same name.

Editors' Notes

1) Language and spelling: Viking studies conducted in Danish, Icelandic, Norwegian, and Swedish have precipitated a number of acceptable spelling variations. The editors of this volume have chosen to utilize in all cases the original Old Norse terms, but with concessions to the modern reader. Old Norse personal names were normalized by eliminating accent marks over a, o, u, and i and by adding u before the nominative marker r for most male personal names. Certain accent marks were also eliminated for terms and historic place-names, though á was retained in most cases. The special character Þ has been transcribed as th, and æ has been transcribed as ae. An exception to this standardization has been ð (a voiced th sound), which has been retained in all cases except certain place names that have modern appellations. The Scandinavian characters of ä, å, ø, ö have been retained in modern place and personal names.

2) The editors would like to thank Leifur Eiriksson Publishing and Penguin Classics for the permission to reprint extensively from their translation of the *Vinland Sagas.*

3) The illustrations of objects in this catalog are primarily pieces lent to the exhibition by their home institutions. For permission to reproduce illustrations appearing in this book, please correspond directly with the owners of the works, as listed in the Checklist. The Smithsonian Institution Press does not retain reproduction rights for these illustrations individually or maintain a file of addresses for photograph sources.

FRONT COVER: *Íslendingur*, replica Viking ship.
Photograph by Antonio Ottó Rabasca, courtesy of skipper Gunnar Eggertsson of the Vestmann Islands, Iceland

PAGE 1: Misty cliffs rise above the western side of Suduroy Island in the Faeroe Islands. Photograph by Símun Arge.

PAGE 2: Silver and bronze inlaid Viking Age swords, Norway (Universitetets Oldsaksamling, Oslo C1415, C257). Photograph by Peter Harholdt.

BACK COVER: Bishop, Queen, and Warder, from a cache of ninety-three chessmen found on the Isle of Lewis in the Outer Hebrides in 1831. (see Checklist, fig. 23.1)

PATRONS

Her Majesty Queen Margrethe II of Denmark

Her Excellency Tarja Halonen, President of the Republic of Finland

His Excellency Ólafur Ragnar Grímsson, President of the Republic of Iceland

His Majesty King Harald V of Norway

His Majesty King Carl XVI Gustaf of Sweden

The North Atlantic Saga

VIKINGS: THE NORTH ATLANTIC SAGA

has been made possible through the generous support

of the Nordic Council of Ministers

and Volvo

Additional support from

Phillips Petroleum Company Norway

The Barbro Osher Pro Suecia Foundation

Special thanks to

Icelandair

National Geographic Society

Ward Television Corporation

The White House Council on the Millennium

PREFACE

BY HILLARY RODHAM CLINTON

Historic occasions are few enough, and the arrival of a new millennium is certainly one of them! This millennium has special significance for us here in North America because it signifies the arrival of the first Europeans on the northeastern shores of this continent in A.D. 1000. In 1992 we had the opportunity to reflect on five hundred years of European settlement in America that began with the voyages of Christopher Columbus. Now the thousandth anniversary of Leif Eriksson's visit gives us reason to reflect upon a deeper strand in our history. The discovery in 1960 of what scholars believe is Leif Eriksson's base camp in northern Newfoundland proves beyond any doubt that Nordic peoples explored and at least briefly settled North America five hundred years before Columbus.

I am personally very excited about this exhibition and the information presented in this book because it is something that is long overdue. The kind of information and excitement that is being conveyed to readers and to visitors to this exhibition as it travels around the country will further understanding of the contributions made by Nordic peoples and culture to our North American heritage. I am particularly pleased because of the way *Vikings: The North Atlantic Saga* fits into the White House Millennium Council's celebration, which was created to help mark this historic passage. We knew this was not just a moment to watch a ball drop down in Times Square in New York or to greet the New Year with ephemeral frivolities, but an opportunity to really take stock of who we are, where we come from, what we hope and want for the future. This unique moment in history gives us an opportunity not just for a celebration but for a conversation—about history and science, culture and art, and the common values that bind us together as human beings. And that is particularly true for the United States—a nation that owes so much to so many cultures, and one that every day celebrates the diversity that makes it a unique and very special place.

In keeping with our theme for the millennium—"honor the past, imagine the future"—we have been encouraging Americans to look back at our history to appreciate how America became the society it is today. Certainly the story of Viking explorations can help us realize that goal, turning our attention to events that took place around one thousand years ago when two vastly different people met for the first time on the shores of North America.

When the Millennium Council began its work, we realized the exhibition the Smithsonian had planned about the Vikings and their pioneering and lasting role in creating the world we enjoy today provided many opportunities to broaden our understanding of the past and to link it to our aspirations for the future. The Vikings, after all, are more than an historical presence in North America; they also represent the spirit of discovery that Americans, especially, can relate to.

The Viking saga is not only about the past but suggests values that we can continue to learn from in creating our future. As we commemorate the courage of these seafaring pioneers, we honor the spirit of exploration that has fueled the progress of both the Nordic countries and the United States. And as we focus through the long lens of history, we can discover other common traditions that we will want to continue to carry forward with us into the new millennium.

I've been interested to learn, for example, that within Viking society women had a good deal of freedom to engage in trade and to become active participants in the political and religious lives of their communities. We've also been learning about the way that the Viking explorers sought to preserve their history and accomplishments through their beautiful poetry and sagas, new forms of literature that were developed in Viking and the medieval periods.

The experience of the Vikings can also teach us how to be mindful of our interaction with our environment. No one knows, I am told, exactly what caused the Norse settlers to die out or disappear in Greenland, for example; but scholars believe that environmental factors played a central role in their demise. That should be a very sobering reminder that each of us must do our part to protect and preserve our fragile environment for the generations of the next millennium.

This Viking Millennium project speaks to us in other ways. It is important to take this time and really contemplate our duty to the past, if indeed we mean to honor it. Preservation and restoration efforts like those represented by this exhibition and publication are models for such initiatives. If we don't preserve what we know of our past, if we don't continue to try to discover that past, we will lose countless treasures and a lot of information that perhaps could tell us about who we are and where we came from. This Viking exhibition will remind us that there are places on our own continent where you can see traces of human exploration and settlement that date back one thousand years.

Viking explorers navigated the rivers of eastern Europe as far as the Caspian Sea and brought back all kinds of treasures from surrounding lands, including silver and precious stones like lapis lazuli, to trade. Their fleets reached Constantinople and sailed into the Mediterranean. The Vikings traveled far and wide, and with them brought their own ideas and their own experiences. But because they were such restless explorers, the Vikings were among the earliest conveyors of information and experience and culture from one part of the known world to another. In a way, the Viking longship was the Internet of the year 1000, connecting places and people who themselves could not even imagine what lay beyond that wide sea or that mountain range.

Our children and grandchildren will only learn about the courage and ingenuity of these explorers who came to our shores one thousand years ago, and touched so many other shores as well, if we are prepared to help them learn. They will discover through these stories, perhaps, something about what happened in faraway places. They will hear about adventures and they will learn about the sagas. And perhaps—just perhaps—some young person will have his or her own spirit sparked. Because, after all, what the Vikings really convey to us over all these centuries is the power of the human spirit and the universal urge to find and cross new horizons.

The National Museum of Natural History was honored to have the First Lady present at the press conference announcing the Vikings exhibition program and tour. This Preface has been adapted from her remarks on that occasion.

Sva er vpundara ꝛ meli ꝼ
melt at engi maðr ſkal
haꝼa ꝛanga pundara eða
meꞇ kꝛollꞇo. Eñ ſa er vettꝛ puñ
daꝛi at .xx. merkꝛ ſe i ꝼiorðung hꝑꞇ
ok megi at vega ſ at viſi av ꝼior
dungi ok æ meira at vega eñ tuer
ꝛe ꝼiorðunga vettꝛ ſ æ er annar
puñdari er heꞇ hanðpundari. ſa
ꝑk viſa at haalꝼꞇ .ꝛ. ok æ meira
at vega eñ haalꝼan añan ꝼioꝛðuñg
ꝙ ꝑk vera tuñgu pundari. Stika
ꝑk giora .ij. alnar ſlikar ſem vꞇ
haꝼa. Eñ þeſſ ſko va meli kꝛollꞇo
til bu nꝑtiar ok ſꞇꝛa ſuꞇa er i kꝛoll
dum ꝑk mela. Er ſiav gꝑꝛſꞇ buſkio
ſa er i liggr haalꝼꝛamaꝛ ꝼioꝛðuñ
gꝛ. ſia er ꝼiorðungr er giꝑer at va
ag .xx. merkꝛ rugar ꝛ riſta tꝑſu
i kꝛollꞇoi ꝛ daga treꝑꝛ. kuen aꝛ
kar ꝼiol i ꝼiorðuñg. haalꝼꝛamañ
at kuen aſkr ꝛ kartaſk. Sko heꝼ
ſer pundaraꝛ ok meꞇ kꝛollꞇo liggꝛ
ia a ꝼꞇg uelli unð logmañ ſaꞇ ſ.
Skal þar eꝼt hiuꝛ ſiuꞇu maðr retta
ſina pundara ſꞇꝛu ꝛ meli kꝛollꞇo
eꞇ bende eꝼt ſia meꞇ kꝛolltuuꝛ
ꞇhuer ſiuꞇu. Eñ hiuꝛ ſem ett hu
ert i þeſſari grein heꝑer ꝛangt
ſekꝛ .ꝛ. uið kg eꝼ þ vett ok haꝼi

ꝼi mañ eꝼt ſiuꞇu mañꝛ puñda
rum marka. Eñ æ eru aller be
nðꝛ ſkꝑllꞇo meꞇ kꝛollꞇo at haꝼa.

Ver en
loghg þar
ꞇekna eꞇꞇ
eꝛ engi meꞇ
er i þioꝛd
ꝑk taka
ſkyr mañ i eða þ lꝑgligum v
ꝛoðſ mañni ꞇ vegna vꞇꞇni við
tuau eð ꝼleꝛi ok ſegi ſꞇ ꞇ aꝛꝛaꝼ
nar er þar ꞇoku. eñ ſiñ ꞇ legu
tiurðar er ſkiꝑ bꝑgg. Eñ eꝛ ſa
ꝼaſꞇꝛ at vm kaup maꞇa ſiꞇ. þa
haꝼi ſa ſiꞇ maal er uꞇꞇni gꝑlð
ok va ſꞇꝛ ſua ꞇ ſuua at uð heꝑꝛꝝ
oð ꝑkkꝛ beggia ok ſiꞇð vꝛuð
ſia ſaꞇð ꞇ ſamkaupa vñ þaꝛꞇeꝛꝝ
w ꞇð vm leſꞇ oꝛ legu. þa er ſ
uꞇꞇni ꞇꝑgleꝛꝝa beꞇꞇ ꞇar lꝑg ſuꞇ u
þar ꞇekit. eꝼt vꞇꞇð þar ñ lꝑgu.

Skiꝑ ſ er hꝛ ... ſiꝑ er
auſa þarꝛ þryſuar at .ij.
dꝝgrum ſ er alt þart i

PUFFINS, RINGED PINS, AND RUNESTONES

The Viking Passage to America

BY WILLIAM W. FITZHUGH

*S*ometime between A.D. *997 and 1003 the world suddenly became a smaller place, as Leif Eriksson, son of Erik the Red of Greenland, brought his ship to shore in a wooded bay along the central Labrador coast in far northeastern North America. He wanted to inspect the local timber and find some fresh meat and water, but he was curious— and apprehensive—about the column of smoke he saw rising from the forest near the mouth of a small stream. Until now there had been no sign of indigenous people in this new land, but he was not too surprised because relics of former inhabitants had been found near his home in Greenland. The prospect of encountering possible adversaries was not comforting. What kind of people could these be, and how would he fare with them?*

Leif had been following the coast south for a week after crossing Baffin Bay from Greenland, accompanied by flocks of Atlantic puffins and flightless great auks. The lands Leif passed matched the descriptions he had heard several years earlier from Bjarni Herjolfsson when he had been blown off course sailing from Iceland to Greenland. Bjarni had reported that after traveling many days, the weather lifted and he found himself off a wooded land far south of his destination. Turning north, he followed the coast on his left, and after seeing the trees give way to barren mountains, he regained the latitude of Greenland. Turning east across the sea he soon found himself with his countrymen.

Bjarni's tale kindled interest among Erik the Red and his sons, and several years later they planned a voyage to explore the lands Bjarni described. When Erik was riding down to join his ship, his horse stumbled, and taking this as an unlucky sign, he remained home, but Leif set out on his own. If these lands had good pasture and abundant timber, Erik and his family might find better lands than they had settled in Greenland and would prosper.

* * *

JÓNSBÓK (BOOK OF LAWS)
A page from one of the beautifully illuminated manuscripts created in Iceland in the thirteenth century that preserve information about Norse settlements in the western North Atlantic.

1. ATLANTIC PUFFIN
The Atlantic puffin was an ever-present companion to Viking voyagers in the North Atlantic. Its brilliantly colored bill and comical way of flying—with belly-flops and erratic flight paths—make it endlessly endearing to sea travelers. The puffin also signaled proximity to land, as did the presence of its relative, the flightless great auk. The migrations of the pelagic auk to breed on terra firma would have suggested to the Vikings that explorations to the west might reveal land.

Neither Leif nor the skraeling, *as the Norse called the Native Americans, had any inkling of the significance of their meeting. To Leif the tall, dark-haired people whom he found in wooded Markland and in areas further south, which he named Vinland (for the grapes his men found there) were similar to the Karelians the Norse had met in the arctic regions of Scandinavia and Russia; but to the* skraeling, *the Norse were a novel sight. They were tall and had blue eyes and blond or reddish hair; they wore multicolored garments made from the hair of an unknown animal; their weapons included powerful bows and arrows, glistening spears, swords, and axes*

of a material that could cut off a man's arm or head with a single blow; and they traveled like the wind in huge wooden ships with sails that made them look like giant seabirds. As the Norse and the natives stood nervously eyeing one another, neither group could sense the full import of their meeting; whatever it was, Leif knew that his people, after exploring and settling empty lands in the western ocean, were no longer alone.

✳ ✳ ✳

2. HELGE AND ANNE STINE INGSTAD
Credit for discovering the first and so far the only known Viking site in North America goes to Norwegian explorer and author Helge Ingstad, who found L'Anse aux Meadows during a survey of northern Newfoundland in 1960. In 1961 he and his archaeologist wife Anne Stine Ingstad returned and began the excavations that confirmed the site's identification.

Leif Eriksson's arrival in North America in the year A.D. 1000 and the subsequent explorations he and his countrymen made in the North American lands he called Helluland, Markland, and Vinland mark a momentous turning point in world history. Prior to this time the dispersive process of migration and adaptation had resulted in the spread of humankind out from Africa, Europe, and Asia to the farthest reaches of the globe, even to such distant places as Patagonia, the Hawaiian Islands, and north-ernmost Greenland. With humans in con-tact with each other virtually everywhere else, only one gap remained—closing the ring of humanity across the North Atlantic. Although there may have been others who succeeded in reaching America before him, at present their identity and ethnicity remains unknown, and so credit for completing this last stage of global exploration and settle-ment belongs not to Christopher Columbus or the other well-known European naviga-tors but to a Norseman whose voyage just happened to take place exactly one thou-sand years ago. Leif's accomplishment was not due to one man or one voyage but was the culmination of two hundred years of Norse exploration and settlement in the North Atlantic.

The dramatic story of the Viking ex-pansion west across the North Atlantic be-tween A.D. 800 and 1000, which resulted in the settlement of Iceland and Greenland and the exploration and brief settlement of northeastern North America, is a chapter of history that deserves to be more widely known (map, p. 13). Thanks to recent advances in archaeology, history, and natural science, the Norse discoveries in the North Atlantic can now be seen as the first step in the process by which human populations became reconnected into a single global sys-tem. After two million years of cultural di-versification and geographic dispersal, humanity had finally come full circle.*

Although their history is full of mystery and adventure, the Norse and their Viking ancestors are little known, misunderstood, and almost invisible on the American land-scape. For most Americans, knowledge of American history begins with the voyages of Christopher Columbus in 1492. Yet, although the information about Leif Eriksson's voyage as indicated by the *Vinland Sagas* has been known since the early 1800s, the absence of physical evidence of Vikings in the New World (outside of Greenland) rendered this information speculative, at best, or moot. Other than a small group of Nordic scholars and enthusi-asts, few people took seriously the possibil-ity that Norse explorers had reached the North American mainland five hundred years before Columbus or had a legitimate claim to New World history. Even the five hundred-year history of Norse settlement in Greenland has never been seen to have an American perspective despite its physical proximity.

For this reason the discovery of a Viking site in northern Newfoundland in 1960 by Helge Ingstad and subsequent ex-cavations by him and his wife, Anne Stine Ingstad (fig. 2), has to be considered a watershed event in New World history: for the first time physical evidence con-firmed a pre-Columbian European presence in the Americas. Although this settlement did not lead to permanent settlement, and no other Norse settlement sites have been found, scores of Norse artifacts have since been found in a dozen or more Native American archaeological sites scattered widely throughout the eastern Canadian arctic and subarctic, and a Norse penny has been found even further south, in Maine. These finds do not include spectacular

An exhibition entitled Full Circle, a Viking 1000 program of the Government of Newfoundland and Labrador, has been prepared for circulation in Canada to inaugurate this millennium.

WILLIAM W. FITZHUGH

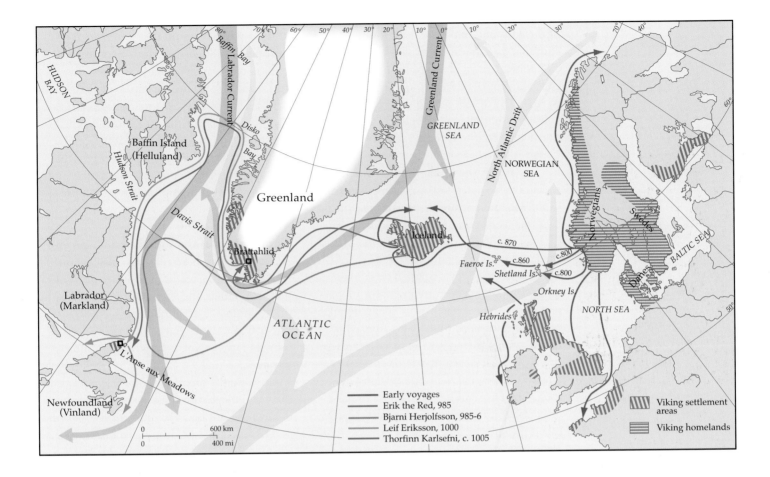

Norse voyages in the North Atlantic did not require open sea passages of more than four hundred miles. With favorable wind even the direct route from Bergen to Iceland could be sailed by Viking ships in three days. More problematic was the arctic pack ice, icebergs, contrary winds, and fog found in the western North Atlantic. Bjarni Herjolfsson was the first to sight Vinland after he was blown off course while traveling from Iceland to Greenland; many other Viking discoveries may have been accidental as well.

runestones and silver and gold hoards such as have been found Viking sites in Europe and Scandinavia (fig. 6); nor do they indicate that Vikings traveled deep into the heartland of America, as was proposed by many writers during the speculative stage of Viking studies in the New World from the 1830s to 1960. Nevertheless, when combined with new evidence from Norse settlements in the North Atlantic the knowledge recently gained from archaeology and natural sciences tells a story as significant and dramatic as that of Viking raids in Europe or Columbus's voyages for Spain. The question is no longer whether there was a pre-Columbian discovery of North America but rather how far south of Newfoundland the Norse explored and what impacts their contacts had on Native Americans, on their own societies in the Faeroes, Iceland, and Greenland, and on Europe. Not least is the question of whether Nordic knowledge of the northwestern North Atlantic and its lands and peoples was transmitted to Europe from its medieval manuscripts and tradition-bearers in Iceland and Scandinavia, what information this consisted of, and whether it influenced later European explo-

ration. For instance, was Icelandic knowledge of western lands passed to Christopher Columbus in his 1477 trip to Iceland? Some scholars believe that he or other European explorers such as John Sebastian Cabot, Jacques Cartier, Martin Frobisher, John Davis, and others (Stefansson 1942; Egilsson 1991; Quinn 1992; Seaver 1996) must have grasped the import of the Norse voyages. Columbus may have learned about the Vinland voyages from the Icelandic sagas or those who knew of them. The history of the West Vikings—those early Scandinavians who ventured west across the North Atlantic to seek their fortunes—need no longer be understood solely on the basis of sagas and conjecture. Scientific evidence allows us to substantially revise the history of the discovery of America by giving due credit to the Nordic people who for most of the past thousand years created and maintained a gateway between Europe and North America.

"VIKINGS" AND "NORSE"

By the latter part of the eighth century the Norse had largely mastered the challenges of making a living in their Scandinavian homelands and had developed a remarkable ship that gave them the ability to seek adventure, profit, and new lands beyond the coastal farms of western Norway. In doing so, the early Norse earned a new identity—Vikings—in the eyes of their European neighbors which followed them far across the North Atlantic.

To many, the term "Viking" has become indelibly associated with seafaring warriors, explorers, and entrepreneurs, despite the fact that this word was only sporadically applied directly to the Nordic peoples by the British; the latter used it to refer to the "curse of the north" who regularly despoiled their coasts after the famous first raid on Lindisfarne monastery in A.D. 793. That date is generally taken as the beginning of the Viking Age, which lasted two hundred and fifty years until the Normans, descendants of the Vikings, crossed the channel to invade England in 1066. The term Viking is thought to have originated from a place in southern Norway called "Vík," which became an early center of Viking raiding fleets. The name soon came to refer to Norse-speakers, called "Northmen" by their southern adversaries, who sallied forth from "viks" ("bay" or "harbor" in Old Norse, or "refuge" in Old English) seeking adventure and profit. Those "bay men" who went off raiding were said to go "a-viking" or were simply called "vikings."

The term Viking did not refer to the Nordic peoples who stayed home; those who shared a similar language (Old Norse) and cultural traditions that distinguished them from other linguistic or ethnic groups were known by various ethnic names, such as Goths, Svear, Norwegians, Danes. The pioneering Norse who discovered and settled lands in the Faeroes, Iceland, and Greenland were never called Vikings. In the early *landnám* (land-taking) years, the language and culture of these pioneers reflected their homelands—primarily southern and western Norway—but by medieval times the Norse began to form distinct societies and nationalities that reflected Faeroese, Icelandic, or Greenlandic character, despite having a common Old Norse language. Collectively these ninth- and tenth-century Norse are sometimes also called West Vikings, although their traditions and history are primarily those of Nordic seafaring farmers rather than

of the Viking marauders who terrorized Europe. Although the Norse ethno-linguistic term is much preferred and is especially appropriate for Nordic peoples of the North Atlantic, who derive primarily from Norway, the long history of the search for "Vikings" in North America and its modern popular use has made it the only term recognizable to a general North American audience, and so it is used here in a broad generic sense.

VIKINGS AT HOME

Until the end of the Viking period, circa A.D. 1050, most Norse lived as farmers on small plots or as retainers to kings or locally powerful chiefs and their supporters. Despite their reputation as shipbuilders, sailors, and warriors, the Norse identified themselves as farmers rather than as fishermen, hunters, trappers, or traders, even though individual Vikings might spend considerable periods of the year engaged in these tasks. Commercial fishing did not become important to Nordic peoples until the Middle Ages; hunting such sea mammals as walrus and whales was a seasonal rather than full-time activity. Even as late as A.D. 1000, except in a few trade centers such as Ribe in Denmark, Kaupang and Bo in Norway, York in England, and Dublin in Ireland, few Vikings engaged in specialized commercial production. On the other hand, carpentry and especially boat building were not trades; they were skills known to all Viking men, just as spinning, weaving, and clothes-making were known to all Viking women. But there were no activities more central to Norse identity than farming. Most farms occupied only a few thousand square feet of in-field pasture in which they grazed cows, horses, sheep, and goats, and if they were lucky, a small number of pigs. Farms varied in size according to geography and personal means, being larger in the fertile flat lands of Denmark and Sweden and smaller in the mountainous coastal terrain of Norway and the Atlantic islands. The majority of a family's time and energy went to nurturing their animals and tending crops.

The technological element upon which Viking expansion and influence depended was boat-building and maritime skill. Little was known about Viking ships until the late 1800s when a series of well-preserved finds were excavated from burial mounds in Oslo

Fjord. The most spectacular of these was found in 1904 at Oseberg, revealing a nearly perfectly preserved ship that contained the burial goods and remains of a Viking queen and a female servant. Recent excavations of late Viking Age ships in Roskilde Fjord near Copenhagen have given maritime historians and archaeologists more detailed information on Viking ship types and their development, allowing their sailing characteristics to be researched by use of replicas (Crumlin-Petersen 1978, 1997). Tree-ring dating has provided a precise chronology for their construction and repair.

Vikings perfected vessels constructed with a lapstrake hull built up from a mortised keel without a heavy internal structure of ribs and supports, making the vessel both skeleton and shell at the same time. Iron rivets and washers replaced lashings to fasten lapped planks, adding strength to the hull. The addition of oars and sails gave Viking boats

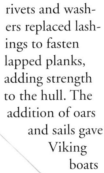

3. VIKING SHIP MODEL
This scale model recreates the features of the vessel found in the Gokstad ship burial in Oslo Fjord. It is shown rigged and set with sail but without the oars or shields that would have been mounted between the oar-ports when ready for battle. There would have been no Viking Age without the Viking ship.

an advantage over all other watercraft of their day in speed, shallow draft, weight, capacity, maneuverability, and seaworthiness. Viking boats were designed to be dragged across long portages as well as to withstand fierce ocean storms. Such ships (fig. 3) gave Vikings the ability to trade, make war, carry animals, and cross open oceans and at the same time provided sufficient protection and security for the crew (Brøgger and Shetelig 1951).

The magic ingredients that made Viking ships possible were iron, carpentry skills, and abundant timber. Iron was more accessible than bronze, and while it had the distinct dis-

advantage of rusting, especially in saltwater, the availability of iron for tools and fastenings meant that even moderately well-off farmers could muster the materials and manpower to build a ship. Thus mobility was no longer the exclusive right of powerful chiefs, as had been the case in the Bronze Age. Swarms of Viking boats could be produced, and during the long midwinter farming break, the northern seas came alive with Viking crews out for valor and profit.

VIKINGS AND THE VIKING AGE

The territorial expansion of the Vikings from their Scandinavian homelands that began in the last decades of the eighth century was the fundamental historical reality that created the Viking Age. This expansion started as seasonal raids on the northern and western British Isles by Norwegian Vikings, who first invaded the Shetlands and Orkneys and then used these as bases for staging raids on northern Scotland, Ireland, and the west coast of England (figs. 4, 5). Danish Vikings struck along England's eastern coast and along the northwestern shores of the mainland south of Denmark. Norse chiefs had already become familiar with these lands through trading activities, and within a few decades after the strikes began, the purpose of the raids became more economic and political. Soon, Vikings were trading and extorting money (called *danegeld*) more than they were raiding, although the raids continued sporadically throughout the British Isles and western Europe for the next two centuries, and even extended to Spain, the Mediterranean, and North Africa.

Over time Vikings who went raiding later returned to regions they had first visited as marauders and took wives and land and settled there permanently, leaving younger and more boisterous generations to go a-viking elsewhere. In this way Viking population and lands expanded rapidly during the ninth and tenth centuries, and soon farming, trading, and diplomacy became as common as raiding and pillaging for Vikings living abroad. Danish Vikings expanded enclaves along the eastern coast of Britain and on the continent, eventually founding Nordic population bases in these regions. Soon towns were established in Dublin and York, and Normandy became a Nordic territory. At the same time that these raids were beginning in western Europe, Vikings from Götland and Sweden were exploring, raiding, and building economic relationships to the east through the eastern European and Russian rivers systems leading to the Black Sea, the Caspian, and the eastern Mediterranean. Swedish Vikings became powerful traders, politicians, and mercenaries in these regions, and founded a dynasty that ruled Kiev.

Vikings who ventured west, primarily Norwegians and those who had resettled in the northern and western British Isles, embarked on a different course, settling the islands of the North Atlantic as farmers and hunters who supplied medieval Europe with such exotic goods as ivory, falcons, and precious fur, in addition to wool and other products. These hardy Norse farmers reached the Faeroes by 825 and Iceland, which may already have been sparsely occupied by reclusive Irish monks, by 870. By 930 a population of thirty thousand Norse had become established in Iceland and all of its arable lands were occupied in a process known to the Norse as *landnám* (land-taking). Thereafter, communication with Norway and the British Isles was maintained on a regular basis. By 930 the Icelandic Parliament was founded, and in 982 Erik the Red, outlawed from Iceland, set off to explore Greenland, returning to Iceland in 985 to lead a colonizing effort that founded Greenland's Eastern and Western Settlements.

On or about 1000 Leif Eriksson explored lands west and south of Greenland which he named Helluland (Rock Slab Land), Markland (Forest Land), and Vinland (Wine Land), and during the next decade or so other Vinland voyages were made by members of his family who remained on the western shores of the Atlantic for several years. Thereafter Vinland explorations ceased, and during the following three hundred and fifty years until the Greenland colonies were abandoned, about 1450, the Norse in this distant settlement remained oriented primarily to Iceland, Norway, and the British Isles.

Finds of Norse artifacts in Native American archaeological sites show that throughout this period, however, Greenlandic or Icelandic Norse occasionally visited Markland for timber and made sporadic contacts with native peoples in northwest Greenland and the Canadian arctic.

During this seven hundred-year period northern Europe, the British Isles, and Scandinavia underwent extensive technological, social, political, and religious change. At first these changes were instigated by the Norse, whose Viking raiders plunged western Europe and the British islands into chaos and terror, influencing the politics of nation formation in these regions. By the tenth century political and religious changes instigated by Viking contacts and activities in western Europe and the British Isles had begun to transform the social structure of the Viking homelands. The independence of individual Viking leaders and chieftains was curtailed as political and economic power became centralized in trade centers controlled by the kings and regional elites. Christianity was making inroads into the traditional pagan Norse religious base, and the lives of the average Norse at home were increasingly constrained. With the formal conversion to Christianity by the emergent kings of Denmark and Norway in the last decades of the tenth century, and about one hundred years later in Sweden, the Catholic Church began to exert major influence in economic and political affairs. The defeat of King Harold of England by William the Conqueror of Normandy in 1066 effectively ended the Viking Age; raids ceased and the political and economic integration of Scandinavia, Europe, and the North Atlantic settlements moved forward rapidly.

Although the Viking Age was officially over, the everyday lives of Norse settlers in the North Atlantic continued more or less unchanged, with strong ties to Norway and the British Isles. Fishing and hunting supplemented the farming economy, and few technological or farming innovations were introduced. As the climatic optimum waned and was replaced by colder, wetter, and more variable weather, the economic situation of the small Norse populations in the North Atlantic islands and Greenland declined. Further isolation occurred when Europe emerged from the Crusades. Trade routes to Africa and the Near East opened, undercutting the value of Greenlandic walrus ivory and dimming the lights of the Greenland Norse and their Norwegian and Icelandic trade partners.

In short, the West Viking story may be likened to a Nordic wave that surged out of Scandinavia and the northern British Isles at a peak period of the Viking Age and raced across the North Atlantic to Iceland, Greenland, and northeastern North America during a period of unusually warm, stable climatic conditions. By the time the western front of this wave attained its maximum reach during the Vinland voyages, Viking

4,5. RING AND PENANNULAR BROOCH This ornate ninth-century gold and silver brooch (above) was recovered at Hatteberg, in Hordaland, Norway. It may have been crafted in the Irish Sea region and came to Norway as loot, or possibly it is an example of Irish-influenced Norse craftsmanship. The tenth-century gold finger ring (left), which was found on the Isle of Skye, is a rare example of a gold Viking jewelry find in Scotland.

prospects had already begun to decline in Iceland, which by then had been occupied for one hundred and fifty years, and many of its *landnám* resources—its "natural ecological capital" (Cronon 1993)—were being depleted by overgrazing and human and animal population growth. Greenland would suffer the same decline in the fourteenth century as unstable weather and lower temperatures intersected with rising human population and intensified exploitation of this remote land's tenuous agricultural resources. By then the Nordic wave was about to retreat from Greenland to Iceland, where it would remain until the economics of fish replaced stock farming as the primary resource capital.

THE WEST VIKING EXPANSION

The North Atlantic *landnám* had an entirely different motivation than that pursued by

Vikings who sought opportunity through banditry, raids, or military or political action in the populated lands to the south. The latter activities produced profits at considerable risk; one had to defeat or displace the present owners. For this reason many Norwegian Norse found it more convenient to take their risks at sea. After having exhausted opportunities to settle lands in the marginal farming regions of upland or northern Norway, sea-savvy Norse farmers turned west, following the open horizons of the Atlantic. The Faeroes were only three hundred and fifty miles west of Norway, a two-day sail under favorable conditions, and a day or two further the gleaming 7,000-foot high dome of Vatnajökull Glacier rose above Iceland. Both provided the Norse with empty lands full of rich resources. News of these new lands must have spread quickly through West Norway as well as among the Norse settlers who had moved earlier into the northern British Isles. By 930 the richest Iceland farms had all been taken and newcomers were having to settle for poorer lands, often working as tenant farmers for immigrants who had preceded them to Iceland by only a decade.

Many theories have been advanced to explain the events that propelled Vikings outward from their northern homelands: developments in ship construction and seafaring skills; internal stress from population growth and scarce land; loss of personal freedom as political and economic centralization progressed; and the rise of state-sponsored Christianity over traditional pagan belief have all been cited. Probably all are correct in degrees; but the overriding factor was the awareness of the opportunities for advancement abroad that lured Norsemen to leave their home farms. By taking on lives as soldiers of fortune, Vikings who faced declining opportunities at home could dramatically alter their prospects: becoming wealthy, reaping glory and fame in battle, and achieving high status as leaders and heroes based on their own abilities and deeds, provided that luck—a crucial ingredient in every Viking venture—was on their side. With success abroad, one could advance rapidly to positions of prestige and power in the relatively open structure of Viking society; or, by the same token, an unlucky stroke might put a man in an early grave. In either case, in the worldview of the pagan Viking, one's fate was inevitable.

To the Norse the discovery of western lands and peoples was only an incremental addition to knowledge accumulated in the course of many previous voyages by earlier Norse explorers who, aided by remarkable advances in ship technology, had been venturing further and further out into the North Atlantic since the mid-700s. Although the Norse were the first to establish viable populations in these regions, they may have learned of these lands from Irish monks who in turn may have been preceded by such figures as Saint Brendan, the sixth-century Irish abbot whose semi-mythical voyage has inspired endless speculation. Even Brendan may not have been the first to venture into the northwestern seas: in 330 B.C. a Greek mariner named Pytheas reached the northern British Isles, if not the Faeroes or Iceland. As the Vikings sailed west new lands kept emerging from below the horizon: first the Shetlands and the Faeroes, then Iceland, Greenland, and finally North America. Navigating without instruments, by the winds and swells, by the movements of birds, and by keeping the height of the noonday sun at a constant altitude, they traveled from land to land in little more than a two- or three-day sail. As soon one land had been colonized, they pressed on to other uninhabited lands further west. The problem was not how to find these lands; it was how, as northern seafaring stock-breeders, they could use them.

The rapidity by which the western islands were populated was not merely a function of opportunity and motivation; these economic strategies and technology had been developed to a great degree along the fjords and islands of western Norway and in the earliest Norse settlements in the Orkneys and Shetland Islands. The West Norwegian agrarian economy, which was based on sheep, goat, pig, cow, and horse farming, was immediately transferable to the northern maritime climate of the North Atlantic islands with little loss except for the inability to grow grain in all but the most favorable locations; and the Norse economy was almost completely self-sufficient. Animals produced transport, food, and dairy products, and raw materials for nearly everything the Norse needed, including woolens for clothing and sailcloth. Woodworking, shipbuilding, and even iron smelting and blacksmithing were familiar home skills. What could not be produced at home could be obtained by local exchange or by trade. The latter provided such luxury goods as fine textiles, jewelry, glass, and precious metals, high-quality weapons, and exotic foods such as sugar, grain for bread and beer, and wine, which was associated with church ritual. Once leaving the mainland, however, most of these luxuries became very expensive, and in most cases were foregone. The lack of iron and timber for building ships and houses and for use as fuel was the principal constraint in offshore life. These drawbacks did not cause major disruption of Norse life in the remote Atlantic communities; rather they ensured that communication with the mainland was maintained regularly, at least partially to preserve social and political relationships. West Vikings were not about to be relegated to a cultural backwater, but the islanders had to find ways to pay for mainland luxuries, and it was here that life in the North Atlantic turned on a harsher edge.

Just as credit for the discovery of the Faeroes and Iceland may lie elsewhere, modern research suggests that the West Viking expansion may not have been exclusively a Norwegian enterprise. DNA studies show modern Icelanders to have a significant amount of Celtic ancestry, perhaps as much as 10 to 20 percent, explaining the dark eyes and curly hair seen in Iceland today. (Conversely, similar studies indicate that the Iceland and Norwegian mouse have identical DNA, suggesting that Norwegians owned the ships that carried most settlers westward.) Linguistic and oral history also reflects a strong Celtic strain in Icelandic language, making one wonder whether Celtic literary tradition may be partly responsible for Icelanders' prodigious creation of stories and sagas, which were probably not part of their Norwegian heritage. Icelandic language today is closer to the Old Norse of Viking times that any other Nordic language, partly as a result of its geographic isolation and partly from dedicated efforts, exerted over generations, to consciously maintain the language and alphabet, as well as personal naming traditions. Genetic isolation and breeding management have also preserved

WILLIAM W. FITZHUGH

old Icelandic breeds of horses, cattle, sheep, and dogs. It has been forbidden, for instance, to import horses into Iceland since the twelfth century. This law was stimulated by the flood of Arabian horses that appeared in Europe at the end of the Crusades, threatening to swamp the gene pool of the specially bred Icelandic horse, which was better suited to local conditions.

THE DECLINE OF "NATURAL CAPITAL"

For many of the early settlers, life in the northern islands must have begun with a rush of optimism: they saw the opportunity to obtain new lands, wild game, livestock herds, and become lord of the local manor. But the *landnám* process soon had powerful impacts on the local resources, which in these northern regions were easily perturbed and

6. A VIKING HOARD
Silver was the primary currency of the Viking Age, and much of it was brought into the Nordic region by Viking raiders and traders who obtained it in Europe, Russia, or the Near East. Arabic and European coins were usually melted down and formed into wearable money. Stashes such as this hoard, have been recovered periodically, but the reasons why they were hidden remain obscure.

adversely affected by human agency. Within a decade, the local forests—marginal by mainland standards in any case—had been decimated for wood and fuel. Analysis of pollen preserved in peat deposits and lake sediments record sudden changes in vegetation within decades of *landnám* in all regions. Animals were even more destructive than people in changing local vegetation and ultimately whole landscapes, reducing forest and shrublands to grasslands, and through time, by overgrazing, converting grasslands to wastelands. These ecological stresses grew more difficult to manage in the harsher climates to the northwest and accumulated over time, more rapidly as the climate deteriorated generally after 1350.

Research has also produced evidence of Norse *landnám* impacts in wild animal populations, especially among marine mammals and birds. A higher percentage of wild game is found in food remains from early *landnám* sites in Iceland than during later periods, when domestic animals dominate midden deposits. Marine and terrestrial birds declined in number, as did sea mammals such as polar bear and walrus, both of which were prized for the value of their hides and ivory. Although salmon and other ocean fish were also taken in considerable quantities, size of fish bones found in middens remained relatively large throughout the Viking period, indicating little human impact. By contrast, medieval-period middens contain larger amounts of fish bones, but their sizes decreased as fishing became an important part of the North Atlantic economy after 1400.

ERIK THE RED AND LEIF THE LUCKY

One of the most important legacies to be passed down from the Viking Age into modern northern civilizations was a local form of self-government known as the Thing (Assembly). Although known from both Scandinavian and North Atlantic communities, the Thing came to special prominence as a national system of governance only in Iceland, whose population never fell under the dominance of a single local secular leader as occurred in Scandinavia. The Icelandic Thing, established in 930 is frequently cited as the origin of the longest-lasting democratic parliament in history.

The role of the Thing assembly in the Norse discovery of America has been immortalized in the *Vinland Sagas*. In 982 the local Thing assembly in Breiða Fjord, northwest of Reykjavík, decided to banish an ill-tempered immigrant named Erik Rauða, or Erik the Red, who had arrived from Norway a few years earlier with little more than a boat, a band of followers, and a reputation as a hotheaded troublemaker. He had already been banned from Norway for an unjustified killing, and within a short time after his arrival in Breiða Fjord, where he had taken a small, poor plot of land and married, his ill temper erupted again. This time the ostensible cause was an argument with a neighbor over a cow and a set of wallboards Erik had loaned him. When Erik settled the dispute by more murders, the local Thing banished him for three years, and in 982 he set out with a small party to make a life in lands that had been reported several days sail west of Iceland in the vicinity of Gunnbjorn's Skerries, where Icelandic hunters had occasionally gone to hunt walrus, seals, and polar bears.

The events leading to the discovery and settlement of Greenland by Erik the Red and of the discovery and exploration of northeastern North American by Erik's son, Leif, are among the best-known stories surviving from Viking times. Two separate sagas, *Erik the Red's Saga* and the *Greenlanders' Saga*, describe how Erik returned to Iceland, organized a group of colonists, and departed in 985 for "Greenland," which he reportedly named to entice others to join his coloniza-

7. Viking Horizons: Approaching Greenland

Sailing west from Iceland, the southeast coast of Greenland rises above an ice-strewn sea in a view similar to that first seen by Erik the Red in 982 when he first sailed to Greenland after being banished from Iceland.

tion effort. Twenty-five heavily loaded ships set out, but only fourteen of them reached their destination safely. Erik established his base at Brattahlid, a lush grassy region at the inner end of one of the deepest fjords in southwestern Greenland across from what is now modern Narsarsuaq. Within a few years Erik's Fjord became the hub of a rapidly growing Eastern Settlement, while a second smaller settlement area named Western Settlement was centered in the present region of Nuuk (formerly Gothåb), capital of the modern Greenland Home Rule government.

As chief of the Eastern Settlement and the de facto leader of the Western Settlement, Erik prospered. He and his wife

Thjodhild raised a large family, including three sons, Leif, Thorvald, Thorstein, and a daughter, Freydis, herself a fiery hothead! The climate was warmer than the present and the animal stock had not reached the point of overgrazing the land. Wild game was abundant and walrus ivory, hides, and other goods from the Nordsetur hunting grounds around Disko Bay were exported for handsome profits.

By the year 1000, with farms prospering, population growing, and trade contacts with Iceland and Europe flourishing, Greenland was showing signs of becoming a thriving new center of Norse culture and society. Erik, who never converted to Christianity, begrudgingly humored his wife's interest in the new faith by building a small church; this tiny structure—eight feet wide and twelve feet long—became the first Christian church on the western side of the Atlantic (fig. 21.4). But Erik was growing restless: when Leif returned from a diplomatic business mission to the king of Norway, Erik announced that it was time to go to sea again to explore the lands Bjarni Herjolfsson had reported seeing when he was storm-driven southwest of Greenland. The stage was set for the next and final phase of Norse expansion.

Archaeology of Vinland

Leif Eriksson's voyage to Vinland and the subsequent voyages of his brothers, and of his former sister-in-law Gudrid and her husband Thorfinn Karlsefni, and his half-sister, Freydis are described in the *Vinland Sagas*. (The full stories of the North American Vinland Voyages, excerpted from the sagas, are reprinted on pages 220–225.) Where they traveled has been a long-standing mystery that has fueled more debate and controversy than any other subject in early North American history. Helge Ingstad's discoveries with his wife Anne Stine Ingstad of Norse houses, a ringed pin, and a soapstone spindle whorl at L'Anse aux Meadows on the northern tip of Newfoundland put an end to most of this speculation by demonstrating conclusively that this small site is Norse and is almost certainly where the Eriksson family established their base camp for explorations in the Vinland region. Ingstad was drawn to this location by a notation on a map prepared in the 1670s by Icelander Sigurður Stefansson reading

"Promontorium Winlandiæ." Although not a map in the true cartographic sense, the schematic Stefansson Map (fig. 15.3) gives tangible form to the saga reports, and according to Ingstad, it led him directly to the site. Leif may also have been led in this direction by the flocks of flightless great auks, extinct since the 1830s, that moved annually from their open-ocean fishing territory to their summer breeding grounds in Iceland, Greenland, and northern Newfoundland (fig. 1). The finds made by the Ingstads included house foundations, a soapstone spindle whorl, a bronze pin, and other articles that have been radiocarbon dated to the late tenth century and could only have resulted from an early eleventh-century Norse occupation.

While it has been impossible to prove that this was the camp Leif built and occu-

8. Leif Eriksson Sculpture by Stirling Calder
In 1930, for the millennial anniversary of the founding of the Icelandic Assembly, the United States presented Iceland with a large bronze statue of the first European to reach North American shores, which today stands in front of the National Cathedral in Reykjavík.

pied as described in the sagas, both the Ingstads and Birgitta Wallace, who expanded their excavations under Parks Canada direction in 1973–76, are convinced that this is so. Wallace's recovery of butternut husks and butternut wood has led her to refine Ingstad's interpretation, concluding that the site should be considered a "gateway" camp for explorations to the south, primarily around the island of Newfoundland and in the Gulf of Saint Lawrence. Wallace's ideas are elabo-

rated here in papers that discuss the site finds and her interpretations of the sagas based on consideration of archaeological evidence and the natural history of the Gulf region. Somewhat different views are presented by Gísli Sigurðsson, based on his textual analysis of the sagas themselves. His views are similar to those reached by many who have tried to interpret the saga evidence on its own merits, apart from archaeology, believing that Vinland was located well south of Nova Scotia and perhaps even as far south as Newport, Rhode Island, or New York (Bergthórsson 1999). Unfortunately there is no way to prove such an interpretation until evidence of more southern Viking sites appears. So far all of the purported Norse finds south of Newfoundland have been discredited with the exception of a single Norwegian penny found on the central coast of Maine which dates to the reign of Olaf Kyrre 1065–1080, at least sixty years after the Vinland voyages took place (see Cox sidebar, p. 206).

Although there is reason for speculation about how far the Norse traveled south of Newfoundland, recent archaeological research provides a solid basis for understanding more about Norse explorations and contacts further north. At the same time that the Ingstads were excavating L'Anse aux Meadows, archaeologists were beginning to find Norse artifacts in early Inuit (Eskimo) sites in the Canadian arctic and Greenland. That people of the Dorset culture had begun to replace their stone blades with metal after A.D. 1000 seemed curious, but an explanation was forthcoming when both late Dorset and Early Thule culture sites began to produce not only Norse iron and copper, but a host of other Norse materials. Soon Norse materials were reported from many eastern Canadian arctic and northwest Greenland sites dating to the Norse period (McGhee 1984b; Sutherland, Schledermann, Gulløv, this volume). Most of these objects and materials date to the twelfth and thirteenth centuries, and only one, the Maine penny, to the eleventh century. Peter Schledermann's finds from Skraeling Island in northern Ellesmere, the gateway to Greenland from Canada, include a spectacular array of Norse materials—chain mail, woolen cloth, iron tools, and even a Norse carpenter's wood plane. Such a trove suggests that a group of Norsemen may have met their end while exploring and hunting in this dangerous, ice-choked region, for Norse would never have traded such precious possessions. In total, these finds suggest that Native Americans interacted with Norse in a variety of ways: by casual contacts, scavenging Norse wrecks, or outright skirmishes. The broad scatter of thirteenth- and fourteenth-century Norse finds in Canada might even suggest some kind of informal trade with native Dorset and Thule people for walrus ivory or other products, an idea given tantalizing substance by a bronze balance-scale fragment (fig. 17.13) found in a Thule Inuit site in the Canadian high arctic. It is also possible, however, that all or most of the Norse materials recovered to date came from a single Norse wreck or military defeat.

9. MICMAC INDIANS

This anonymous mid-nineteenth-century oil painting shows a group of Micmac Indians from Nova Scotia or New Brunswick. Micmac ancestors are one of several Native American groups the Vikings met in Vinland. Although their bark canoes and tipis were probably similar to those seen here, almost everything else about their lives had changed by the early nineteenth century; guns, trade beads, woven clothing, tobacco, and Christianity are all seen in this painting.

These finds have required recalibrating ideas about the geography of Norse involvement in North America. With so many finds from the north and only a penny (which is believed to have originated from northern trade rather than direct Viking contacts in Maine) in the south, most archaeologists have come to believe that the Vinland voyages probably did not extend south of Nova Scotia or west of Hudson Strait, and that the primary contacts between Norse and Natives occurred in arctic regions during the later phase of the Greenland Norse settlement. The absence of Norse materials in native archeological sites in the south, even

in Labrador, diminishes the prospects for finding Norse sites on the scale of L'Anse aux Meadows south of Newfoundland. Had such sites existed, one would expect more Norse artifacts to have been found in Native American sites in these locations, as is the case in arctic regions. The large number of Indian groups living along the coasts of the southern Gulf of Saint Lawrence, the Canadian Maritimes, and New England at this time would have presented a formidable military challenge to the survival of small numbers of Vikings and their vulnerable vessels in these regions (fig. 9)—and the *Vinland Sagas* do not indicate that the Vinland explorers were adept politicians or negotiators!

THE GREENLAND COLONIES

The final chapter of the Norse story in the North American region concerns the history of the two colonies established by Erik the Red in Greenland. Much is known of life in Norse Greenland from the sagas and from nearly two hundred years of archaeological investigations that began when the Norwegian missionary Hans Egede and German Moravian missionaries initiated a recolonization effort on behalf of the Danish crown in 1721. Since then tales of the Norse and Greenland Inuit have been gathered by Rink (1875) and stories have been illustrated by the famous nineteenth-century Inuit artist, Aron of Kangeq (figs. 26.4–26.9). Essays by Lynnerup, Berglund, Gulløv, Arneborg, Petersen, and McGovern present views of the history of the Greenland colonies, the crucial economic and cultural links with Europe, relationships with the Inuit, and possible causes of extinction of the Western Settlement in the mid-1300s and of the Eastern Settlement in the mid 1400s. A voluminous literature now exists on the archaeology of the Greenland Norse by Aage Roussell, Knut Krogh, and others. In recent decades an early interest in architecture and artifacts has broadened to include investigations into the economics of Norse life at sites such as the Farm Beneath the Sand (Gård Under Sandet or GUS), where a farm that was occupied for three hundred years has been preserved in permafrost, including an entire door, a loom, and even whole animal carcasses. Such studies are bringing into sharper focus the major questions that still remain unresolved about how the Greenland colonies functioned and whether they died out as a result of the onset of the Little Ice Age, overpopulation and depletion of natural resources, isolation from Europe, raids by pirates, Inuit attack or territorial infringement, immigration to America, or simply gradual population loss. The truth may be found in some or all of the above, but for North Americans, who tend to look at Greenland as an icy high arctic wasteland, its thousand-year European history as a sophisticated Nordic society may come as a surprise.

VIKING AMERICA

After the disappearance of the medieval Norse from Greenland and the integration of the Iceland Norse into the broader European economic and political scene, little was heard of Vikings in North America until the early nineteenth century. Before the 1830s North Americans knew the Vikings only as the Europeans saw them—as raiders and pillagers of Europe. These views changed rapidly after 1837 when Carl Christian Rafn's *Antiquitates Americanae* (abstracted in English in 1838) published translations of the saga texts that indicated Leif Eriksson and others had explored and settled in northeastern North America. The discovery of literature describing Viking explorations that may have reached southern New England struck American antiquarians like a thunderclap. Rafn's case was greatly strengthened when American scholars like Thomas Webb, Secretary of the Rhode Island Historical Society, began providing him with information about mysterious rock engravings, a pagan burial containing "plate armor," and a conspicuous old stone tower in Newport, Rhode Island, that had baffled local antiquarians for years. All became grist for a new Viking craze in North America (Rafn 1844). The early American romance with Vikings was sealed when Henry Wadsworth Longfellow published his epic poem *The Skeleton in Armor* in *Knickerbocker Magazine* (1841). This tale of a love-struck Viking warrior who sailed to America, built the Newport Tower for his lost love, and came to an unhappy end buried in his armor in an unmarked grave became an indelible part of nineteenth-century American literary romance (fig. 10).

It was later discovered that the inscriptions and burial were Native American and dated to the colonial period and that the tower was built in the mid-seventeenth century by Governor Benedict Arnold.

Rafn's theories established the foundation upon which interest in Vikings in North America has grown for more than one hundred and fifty years. One of its most vigorous promoters, Ebenezer N. Horsford of Boston, lectured and published scores of books on his theories of Viking contacts in New England throughout the 1890s. Although his and many other claims of Viking finds have been dismissed by scholars (Haven 1856; Babcock 1913; Wallace 1982), the allure of a "Viking America" lives on and continues to motivate a small circle of advocates whose steadfastness in promoting evidence of Viking and earlier European Neolithic or Bronze Age finds in America have been termed "fantastic archaeology" (Williams 1991). Most of these finds are the result of innocent mistakes, but a considerable number are pranks or hoaxes based on finds of real Viking artifacts that came to America as heirlooms with Scandinavian immigrants. Even institutions like the Smithsonian (in the case of the Kensington Stone) or Yale University (in the case of the Vinland Map) have fallen prey to siren call of Viking America.

Understanding the history of this phenomena and its broader roots in popular attitudes about Vikings in European and American society (Wallace and Fitzhugh, Orrling, Ward, this volume) helps explain the enduring nature of the American public's romance with things "Viking." North Americans today associate "Nordic" with winter track events or episodes from the public radio show "Prairie Home Companion." The term Viking connotes a brawny, psychotic battle-crazed berserker from comic books or the Monty Python movies, but its only assured recall is the Minnesota Viking football team. All, of course, wear helmets with horns, despite the face that Vikings never had horns on their helmets; this persistent image seems to have originated as a nineteenth-century Wagnerian opera costume based on archaeological finds of Bronze Age and Vendel and Migration Period horned helmets (Orrling, this volume). Clearly America's romance with the Vikings is more than historical!

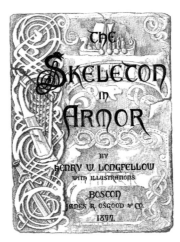

10. *THE SKELETON IN ARMOR* Nineteenth-century antiquarians believed a seventeenth-century Indian burial in Massachusetts containing metal plates was the grave of a Viking dressed in armor. The misidentified find inspired Henry Wadsworth Longfellow's romantic epic poem of 1841, *The Skeleton in Armor*, which was reprinted in this illustrated version in 1877. The poem helped establish an aura of authenticity for nineteenth-century Viking claims in New England.

THIS NEW AMERICA: A VIKING MILLENNIUM AND BEYOND

Following the Columbus Quincentennial, the Nordic Council of Ministers approached the National Museum of Natural History about organizing a Viking exhibition to inaugurate the new millennium and celebrate the Norse role in North American history. This presented the opportunity to explore a new and unknown chapter in the history of North America that has been emerging from evidence found at the Viking settlement at L'Anse aux Meadows and finds of Norse artifacts in Native American sites in northeastern North America. This new research confirms information related in the *Vinland Sagas* and extends the range of Norse contacts or influence in North America from

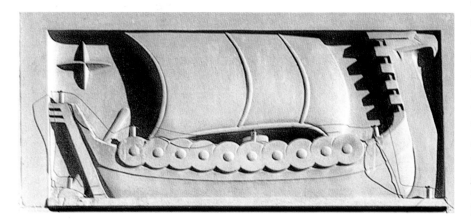

11. VIKINGS AND JUSTICE
The frieze around the top of the United States Department of Justice building at 10th and Constitution Avenue features a flotilla of Viking warships under sail beneath the polestar. A few novel "Americanizations" ahve been added: the dragon prow has become an American eagle, and the unmanned helm is misplaced on the port side—making it hardly a *stýraborð* (starboard).

Greenland to Maine. Even if some of these objects arrived at their destinations from other locations of original Norse-Native contact, the fact that these finds date from 1000 to 1360 also corroborates historical evidence that the Iceland and Greenland Norse continued to visit North America long after the Vinland voyages ceased, to obtain timber, and possibly ivory and other materials, throughout the duration of the Norse colony in Greenland (985–1450). Even though they did not establish long-term settlements in America, the continuing Norse visits ensured that a tradition of knowledge about these lands, resources, and peoples remained alive in Greenland until about 1450 and in Iceland at least until 1500.

The long-term impact of the Viking explorations and contacts in the North American arctic is difficult to assess without more archaeological evidence. Current information suggests that Native American people

of the Canadian arctic and subarctic were familiar with—and sought opportunities to obtain—iron, copper, brass, wool, and other materials from the Norse. On the other hand, there is no evidence that native groups learned new technologies such as ironmaking, shipbuilding, textile production, or stockraising; nor do they seem to have suffered from introduced European diseases that decimated many post-Columbian Native American societies. Perhaps the most important outcome of contact was the familiarity Native Americans gained about European habits, behavior, and materials which helped them take best advantage of future interactions. This information must have been passed down through time within native societies, for when later Europeans like Martin Frobisher and John Davis appeared in Labrador and Baffin Island (voyages of 1576–78 and 1586, respectively), Inuit groups were already familiar with people they called *kablunat* (white men) and their technology. Their interactions—trading, scavenging, hostage-taking, and skirmishing—with these explorers closely resembles their encounters with Vikings described in the *Vinland Sagas*. These contacts were not all one-sided, with Norse materials passing into Native hands: Inuit souvenirs have been found in Greenland Norse sites, and North American bison and grizzly bear fur has been found woven into wool recovered from Norse archaeological sites in Greenland. If there is one thing that archaeology teaches us, it is to expect that surprising finds will continually change our views of the past.

Finally, our investigation of the Norse North Atlantic saga also teaches us much about the Vikings and later Norse societies who opened this early northern bridge to North America. To date, the Scandinavian component in the history of the Americas is absent from the popular tradition and educational base of American history, which for most begins, "In 1492, Columbus sailed the ocean blue . . ." It is therefore useful in this millennium era to consider how another tradition—a northern European Nordic tradition—played a crucial role in the early American contacts, maintained this tradition through the Middle Ages, and passed this information on to others, perhaps even

12. A VIKING LAUNCH IN MAINE
The launching of the American-built Viking ship *Snorri* on Hermit Island near Popham Beach, Maine, in April, 1997, was cause for celebration by the local community. Built by Hodding Carter in the style of a small ocean-going knarr, the vessel was shipped to Greenland later that spring and sailed from there to the L'Anse aux Meadows Viking site in northern Newfoundland in 1998.

to Columbus himself. After a quiescent period between 1400 and 1800, when Norse economies were severely strained by the Little Ice Age, Nordic influence reemerged as a wave of immigrants to North America in the eighteenth and nineteenth centuries began making major new contributions to North American society. Although these more recent activities are not the focus of this book, they must be considered as part of the millennium-long roster of contributions made by Nordic peoples to the history of the Americas (figs. 11, 12).

Instead, this book and the exhibition it accompanies celebrate Leif Eriksson's epic voyage, which brought the first Europeans to the New World. In doing so he closed the ring of humanity that had spread in different directions around the globe for hundreds of thousands of years. Even though his was not the first—nor the last—voyage of Viking exploration and did not lead to permanent settlement in the Americas, Leif's voyage achieved an important and highly symbolic goal that made the world an infinitely smaller place. For this reason if for no other, A.D. 1000 stands as a notable date in world history and is an anniversary to be considered seriously as we enter a new millennium of even broader ethnic partnerships in this new America. To a great extent our next millennium will be shaped by the very same values that motivated the Vikings in their western push across the Atlantic—the need to explore new horizons, to test the human spirit, to seek opportunities wherever they exist. Such is the stuff of the Viking North-Atlantic saga!

The editors would like to dedicate this volume to Helge Ingstad and Anne Stine Ingstad, who discovered and conducted the first archaeological excavations at L'Anse aux Meadows.

VIKING HOMELANDS

INTRODUCTION

SCANDINAVIA IN THE VIKING AGE

BY PETER H. SAWYER

SCANDINAVIA IS THE GREAT PENINSULA that reaches from the Arctic Circle south to the Baltic Sea, forming the eastern border of the North Sea and the North Atlantic (map, p. 28); today it is occupied by the Norwegian and Swedish kingdoms. Though this peninsula is also inhabited by the Saami (also known as Lapps), the term "Scandinavian" is usually limited to the occupants of that geographic region who speak a common Germanic language. It is also generally extended on historical and linguistic grounds to include Denmark and even Iceland.

The term *Viking* is of disputed origin and meaning, but most likely it originally meant an inhabitant of Viken, that is, the area surrounding Oslo Fjord. The term was coined by the English during the Viking Age, the late eighth to eleventh centuries, to mean raiders or pirates, but it was only one among many terms used for these invaders. It began to be used in the nineteenth century in English and other languages in a wider sense to mean Viking Scandinavia and anything associated with the Viking Age. A third term, *Norse*, means Norwegian in its narrowest sense, although the language Old Norse includes all the early Scandinavian languages; *Norse* is also used for Viking settlers of Iceland and Greenland. Although the term *Vikings* is best reserved for warriors and not for (relatively) peaceful farmers and settlers, it is understood within the North American context to refer to the Norse explorers of Vinland.

The common use of the term *Viking* suggests that the Viking Age was a period of raiding and looting. More than that, it was an important transitional time for Europe and Scandinavia. Trade routes flourished, kingdoms emerged, and the Christian religion became dominant. These changes are rooted in the centuries before the Viking Age. During the last years of the seventh century trading increased between the Continent and England. One effect of this growing commerce was the development of several relatively large trading centers along the coasts of eastern and southern England—Hamwic (later Southampton), Fordwich (the port of Canterbury), London, Ipswich, and York—and in the northern Frankish Empire (the empire of Germanic speaking peoples occupying the western Roman Empire)—Dorestad on the Rhine and Quentovic near Boulogne (Sawyer 1998a: 223–5). This trade grew even faster after about 700, when the Frisians, the loose confederation that dominated the Low Countries, obtained a very large stock of silver from a source that has not yet been identified. They then produced a huge number of coins that quickly found their way to the Continent and to England.

Scandinavia and the lands around the Baltic Sea were soon affected by this development. Merchants could sail into the Baltic in the summer to buy furs, skins, and other products such as amber, eiderdown, and good-quality whetstones in trading centers that were established during the eighth century. By 705 such a center had been founded at Ribe on the west coast of Jutland, the mainland of what is now Denmark, and by the middle of the century there were others around the Baltic, the most important being Hedeby at the head of Schlei Fjord in southeast Jutland, Birka (fig., p. 30) on Lake Mälar in Sweden, and Wolin near the estuary of the Oder River in what is now Poland (Clarke and Ambrosiani 1991).

Most of what was offered for sale in such places had been gathered by the Scandinavians as tribute from the

---

FYRKAT: RING FORT OR VILLAGE FORTRESS?

Fortresses like this one at Fyrkat in Jutland, southern Denmark, appeared throughout much of Scandanavia in the tenth century. Originally these earth-mounded ring sites were interpreted as military strongholds, but excavation at Fyrkat and other sites indicate a wide range of domestic and village activities, including iron and jewelry making, storerooms, and domestic dwellings.

ETHNO-LINGUISTIC MAP OF NORTHERN EUROPE AND SCANDINAVIA

Saami, Finns, and Balts who inhabited some of the best fur-producing areas, and by the middle of the eighth century Scandinavians were already gathering similar tribute in Finland and north Russia, which continued to be the main source of high-quality furs in Europe for centuries. By 750 at the latest a base for this activity, with a mixed population of Finns, Slavs, and some Scandinavians, had been established at Staraja (Old) Ladoga on the Volkhov River in what is now Russia, some eight miles (thirteen kilometers) from its estuary in Lake Ladoga.

Those rulers and chieftains who were best able to exact tribute gained wealth and power, as did those who controlled the trading centers or the routes leading to them. The Danish kings, whose central territory was in south Jutland and the adjacent islands, benefited most, for they controlled the entrance to the Baltic Sea and could offer security to ships passing through the Great or Little Belts, the channels that separate the island of Fyn from Zealland and Jutland. They were thus able to attract merchants to Hedeby, which was conveniently close to the land route between Jutland and Saxony. The other channel into the Baltic, Øresund, was less attractive partly because of strong currents, but also because of the threat of piracy; it was not directly controlled by Danish kings until the end of the tenth century.

There are various indications that in the first half of the ninth century Danish kings were acknowledged as overlords by many of the local rulers and chieftains in the lands around Skagerrak and Kattegat, arms of the North Sea north of Jutland. What is now the west coast of Sweden, the provinces of Bohuslän and Halland, were in the late ninth century described as *Denamearc*, "the march or boundary territory of the Danes" (Lund 1984: 22). Any who were unable to resist Danish power and were unwilling to submit could choose exile, a prospect made more attractive by the opportunity to win fame and fortune by taking part in Viking raids. Many of the leaders of the raids on the Frankish Empire in the early ninth century were exiled members of Swedish royal dynasties.

The Danes were particularly eager to have hegemony over Viken, the land flanking Oslo Fjord, a district of great value in part for the iron that the Danes could obtain there. If, as seems likely, the word *Viking* originally referred to the inhabitants of Viken, it could explain why the English, and only they, called Scandinavian pirates Vikings, because England was the natural objective for men from Viken who chose exile as raiders rather than accept Danish overlordship.

These political developments prepared the way for the Viking raids. In addition, technological advances in boat building, brought on by increased familiarity with western European sailing ships, led to the adoption of sails in Scandinavia. It was the sail that allowed the sleek Viking ship to become a swift attack vessel. The contacts with western merchants enabled Scandinavians to learn about Europe's wealth and about the conflicts between, and within, the Christian kingdoms of western Europe from which they were later able to profit.

THE VIKING RAIDS

Late in the eight century small bands of Scandinavians began swooping down on northern Europe. Viking pirates preferred to attack undefended targets, especially churches or markets where they could hope to find rich booty. The Viking raids undoubtedly destroyed much and caused widespread disruption, but the historical accounts probably greatly exaggerated the scale of the destruction the raiders wrought. Some monasteries were damaged, but most survived. There is no reason to believe that Vikings were any more brutal and ruthless than other warriors in early medieval Europe (fig. 108). The Franks, English, Irish, and others behaved in much the same way against their neighbors or in their internal conflicts. There were, however, two important differences between the Vikings and their victims. First, they came by sea, giving them the advantage of surprise when attacking coastal regions. Second, the first generations of Vikings were pagans. Too much weight should not be put on this difference; churches were not immune from attack by Christians, and Christian kings and magnates could be as ruthless, cruel, and destructive as any Viking in their violent competition for the wealth on which their power depended.

Vikings normally operated in small bands numbering hundreds rather than thousands. The need for an adequate food supply was a decisive factor in limiting their numbers: a warrior needed three pounds (1.5 kilograms) of bread a day and a horse some twenty-two pounds (ten kilograms) of grain and fodder. A force of one thousand mounted Vikings would have needed more than eleven tons of food every day. It is not surprising that many of the raids made from their bases in western Europe were to search for food supplies (Abels 1997).

The frequently repeated argument that the main cause of the Viking raids was the pressure of increasing population in Scandinavia and the shortage of land is unsatisfactory. In Denmark and Sweden there is no hint of population pressure; in those parts of Scandinavia there was abundant unexploited land available for later internal colonization. In western Norway, however, there were few reserves of land and it is, therefore, not surprising that the Norwegians appeared as settlers in lands to the south and west earlier than other Scandinavians. There are good reasons for thinking that Orkney, Shetland, and the Hebrides, together with adjoining areas of mainland Scotland, were under the control of various Norwegian chieftains in the early ninth century and that by then the Norwegian colonization of those parts of Britain had begun. This colonization was, indeed, the first stage of the colonization of the North Atlantic islands described in Section III of this volume.

The Danes began to settle in England in the 870s, while the Swedish/Finnish settlement in north Russia began in the early tenth century (Jansson 1997). In both cases, opportunities abroad rather than pressures at home probably instigated this resettlement. The descendants of the Vikings who settled in England, Ireland, the Frankish Empire, and Russia were quickly assimilated, but in the previously uninhabited Atlantic islands Norwegian colonists and their descendants continued to speak their own language. Those who settled in Orkney, Shetland, the Hebrides and the Isle of Man did so too for many years. This was a huge and largely permanent extension of the Scandinavian world that remained in such close contact with Norway that much of it was eventually incorporated into the Norwegian kingdom.

Scandinavian settlers stimulated the growth of towns in both England and Normandy. It is indeed possible that the main Viking achievement in western Europe was to redistribute the wealth that was stored in the treasuries of churches, kings, and magnates. They stole it, shared it out, and spent it: a good example of Keynsian economics in action. It is no accident that some of the major towns of medieval England, including Lincoln, Norwich, Stamford, and York, began to expand shortly before or after the year 900, a few decades after Scandinavians had settled in their vicinity (Sawyer 1998a: 230: 178–80). Lucien Musset has noted a similar development in western France (Musset 1974). This urban development had wider consequences, for towns depended on their surrounding region to supply the food, fuel, and raw materials they needed.

Vikings were also responsible for many political changes. They created the duchy of Normandy in France, and in the ninth century they conquered two English kingdoms and dismembered a third, leaving only Wessex to survive under the rule of a native dynasty. Thanks to his successful opposition to the invaders Alfred, king of Wessex (848?–900), could claim to be the true representative of all Anglo-Saxons, thus preparing the way for his children and grandchildren to extend their authority and create the unified kingdom of England. Several of the bases the Vikings established on the coast of Ireland retained some measure of independence for awhile and were a complicating factor in Irish politics at least until the twelfth century (Byrne 1973: 268). In the tenth century several of these Viking bases became active trading centers as well as bases for raids by land and sea.

CHANGES AT HOME

There were also profound changes in Scandinavia during the Viking Age, some of which were a direct result of Viking activity. In the ninth century, Vikings who returned to challenge the power of the Danish kings caused much disruption and by the beginning of the tenth century contributed to the collapse of the Danish overlordship in south Scandinavia. This gave Harald Finehair the opportunity to create an independent kingdom in west Norway. Although it did not remain independent for long, this was a critically important first stage in the formation of the medieval Norwegian kingdom.

The most fundamental change in Scandinavia in this period, the conversion to Christianity, was at least partly

due to the Vikings themselves. They must have been impressed by the enormous wealth and elaborate rituals of the great churches in the Frankish Empire and the British Isles. When Viking leaders came to terms with Christian rulers, they normally accepted baptism. Although these conversions were not all permanent, some were, and by the early tenth century most descendants of Vikings who had settled in western Europe were as Christian as the natives. In tenth-century England some priests and monks were of Danish descent, including three archbishops. In Scandinavia there was no Christian infrastructure to support the faith of any sincere converts who returned, but such people certainly contributed to the toleration of Christianity in ninth-century Scandinavia. This prepared the way for the next stage of Christianization, the acceptance of the exclusive claims of the Christian god, which meant the abandonment of traditional beliefs or their reduction to mere superstitions. This dramatic cultural break required the support of powerful magnates and, above all, of kings, some of whom recognized that the new religion could bring them great benefits for it not only enhanced their status and prestige, it also brought missionary bishops with experience of royal government in Christian kingdoms. These men introduced new methods of government that eventually made the authority of Scandinavian kings more effective and enabled them to convert unstable hegemonies into relatively stable kingdoms.

THE END OF THE VIKING AGE

Without exaggerating the effectiveness of royal authority in eleventh-century Scandinavia, there is no reason to doubt that at least in Denmark and Norway the creation of new towns was largely the work of kings who, through their agents, could provide increased security for craftsmen and traders and grant the privileges that enabled fledgling urban communities to flourish. Towns were not only centers of royal authority—in many of them, coins were struck in the names of kings—by the year 1100 most of them also had cathedrals or other major churches, reflecting the close link between kingship and the church.

By the end of the eleventh century few if any Scandinavians could hope to find new homes in the British Isles or the Atlantic islands or realistically expect to repeat the exploits of their forefathers in gathering treasure in western or eastern Europe by force. They could, however, profit from peaceful trade, earning not silver but such useful products as cloth, cereals, flour, and beer, as well as ornaments and furnishings for churches and the residences of kings and wealthy laymen. The rapidly expanding medieval towns of western Europe needed huge quantities of timber and other raw materials as well as the preserved food that Scandinavia could supply. By the early twelfth century, and probably much earlier, Norwegians were exporting large quantities of what became their most important product, dried cod, which could supplement the food supply during the winter and spring months. The large numbers of twelfth-century stone churches, many of which must have been built by foreign craftsmen (there was no native tradition of building in stone), suggest that many landowners in Denmark and southern Sweden, as well as in Norway, benefited from the trade that continued to flourish after the Viking Age, as it had before.

1 | THE SCANDINAVIAN LANDSCAPE

The People and Environment

BY NEIL S. PRICE

He said that the land of the Norwegians was very long and very narrow. All that they can either graze or plough lies by the sea; and even that is very rocky in some places; and to the east, and alongside the culti-vated land, lie wild mountains.

THIS DESCRIPTION, FROM NOTES taken by a royal scribe of a lengthy discussion between the Anglo-Saxon king Alfred and a visiting Scandinavian merchant is one of the earliest—probably from the 880s—and full of significant detail. The king asked the visitor—whom the scribe called Ohthere (this was probably an English attempt to write the Norse name Ottar)—to talk about his home, its landscape, and inhabitants (Lund 1984). Alfred's interest was partly scientific—he was keen on geography and the general acquisition of knowledge—but more probably strategic: he wanted to know more about these foreigners who had plagued his kingdom in recent years, the people whom we know as the Vikings.

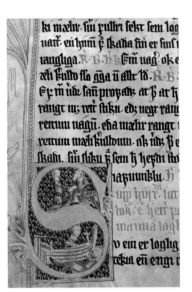

SHIPBUILDING, *JÓNSBÓK*

Ottar's description, which encompasses both the far north of Norway and the western Baltic, is a narrow window on a complex world, a land of great environmental diversity and home to several different peoples and cultures that each had individual adaptations and economic strategies. Archaeology and environmental studies supplement the scattered written descriptions, allowing us to reconstruct what Scandinavia was like at the beginning of the Viking period—its landscape and geography, and its inhabitants' ethnic and political groupings—and develop a rather different and more complex picture of the Vikings and their homelands.

GEOGRAPHY OF SCANDINAVIA

The Scandinavian peninsula itself, comprising modern Norway and Sweden, extends more than 1,200 miles (700 kilometers) from north to south (map, p. 32). This landscape was created by the mile-thick glaciers that covered most of the region until the end of the last Ice Age some thirteen thousand years ago. The later distribution of human settle-

ment was largely determined by the geological patterns set by the retreating ice.

The indented Atlantic seaboard of Norway, with more than 12,500 miles (20,000 kilometers) of shoreline, was directly formed by glaciers, which in moving westward had cut deep valleys into the chain of mountains at the spine of the Scandinavian peninsula; these valleys flooded at the end of the last glaciation and became the long, narrow fjords that characterize the coast. Extensive chains of offshore islands provided sheltered channels for hunting, fishing, traveling, and settlement. In the mountains the climate was harsh, with bitterly cold winters and deep snow lasting for many months of

1.1 A SOUTH SCANDINAVIAN FOREST
The forests of southern Scandinavia provided rich resources for the Viking peoples. In addition to agricultural lands supporting the crops and domestic animals that were the mainstay of the Viking economy, forests also yielded timber, game, amber, and useful minerals such as soapstone and iron ore.

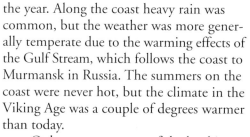

1.2 THE NORWEGIAN COAST

Norway's deeply indented coast gives it thousands of miles of shoreline. The many harbors and islands and the rich fisheries promoted the development of watercraft and maritime skills. As a result Norway's farmers, who lived along the narrow strip of arable land bordering the coast, always felt the tug of the sea and supplemented farming by exploiting marine resources.

the year. Along the coast heavy rain was common, but the weather was more generally temperate due to the warming effects of the Gulf Stream, which follows the coast to Murmansk in Russia. The summers on the coast were never hot, but the climate in the Viking Age was a couple of degrees warmer than today.

Only some 3 percent of the land in Norway is suitable for arable farming; in these areas the Viking Age towns of Oslo and Trondheim would develop. Beyond this, settlement generally focused on the coastal

areas and the green sides of the fjords, making use of the abundant marine resources (fig. 1.2); fish, which could be dried and salted for storage through the long winter, formed the staple food for these economies (fig. 1.5). Domesticated animals such as cattle, sheep, and goats were also kept. The edges of the fjords were dotted with coniferous forest, while the north of Norway (more than 300 miles [500 kilometers] of the country lies above the Arctic Circle) is and was a treeless zone of tundra. Sea mammals such as whales and seals could be hunted throughout the region and walrus were found off the arctic coast. The forests and tundra yielded elk, reindeer, and small game, which provided valuable furs.

The mountains form the natural border between Norway and Sweden, which lies to the east. The northern two-thirds of that country—Norrland—is dominated by hill country and vast coniferous forests, a landscape similar to the Siberian taiga. In the Viking Age the forests were virtually impassable to travelers except by means of the numerous navigable rivers that flowed eastward from the mountains to the Gulf of Bothnia: the fertile estuaries of these rivers formed the only centers of permanent settlement in the Swedish north. Like southern and western Norway, the southerly parts of Norrland are nonetheless rich sources of iron ore, a valuable commodity both at home and abroad in the Viking Age. In the Dalarna region of Sweden there were encampments almost entirely given over to ore extraction, serving the region's intense need for iron. Further south, the forests include a greater variety of deciduous trees and begin to open out into a landscape of lakes, waterways, and flat clay plains with occasional outcrops of granite

GEOGRAPHY AND RESOURCES OF SCANDINAVIA

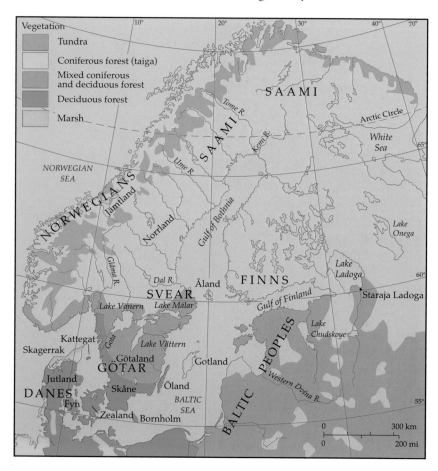

1.3 Birka, an Eastern Viking Trade Center

Numerous burial mounds are seen in the foreground of this winter photograph of Birka, Sweden's largest Viking trading site, which is located on an island in Lake Mälar. The flat topography, myriad lakes and watercourses, and cold winters not only gave Viking culture its distinctive northern flavor but facilitated transportation and trade.

RIGHT

1.4 Bronze Age Ship Burial

Scandinavian maritime tradition extends back to the Bronze and Stone Ages. By the Bronze Age ships had taken on a special meaning for the afterlife. The ship-shaped grave markers typical of this period throughout Scandinavia are seen here in the cemetery near Umeå in northern Sweden.

1.5 Fishing Gear

Today the coast of Norway is renowned for its fishing stocks, but in the Viking Age fishing and sea-mammal hunting supplemented farming. Bottom fishing with baited hooks weighted with grooved-stone sinkers was the most common method for saltwater fishing, while nets and harpoons were used to catch salmon and trout in the rivers.

rock and dotted with dense woodland. All of Sweden supported ample resources for settlement in terms of timber for building, game, and fish, but in the lake district (which spans the lower center of the country) lay the two agricultural heartlands of Sweden, which were the largest population centers in the Viking Age. To the west are the fertile lowlands of Götaland, focusing on the great lakes of Vänern and Vättern; to the east lies Svealand, dominated by Lake Mälar (fig. 1.3), which is connected to the Baltic by an extensive system of inland waterways. The broad Mälar Valley extended far to the north and south, where the rivers and watercourses were flanked by long gravel ridges that furthered lines of communication and settlement into the interior. This favorable geographical situation was instrumental in the later development of the Swedish state, which would expand from this region.

For the most part, the physical geography of Scandinavia has altered little since the Viking Age, but in some areas there have

been considerable changes in the coastline due to the lingering effects of the glaciers: this is especially the case in the eastern lowlands of Sweden. When the ice melted, the land was relieved of countless billions of tons of pressure, causing it to rise; the process was modified by the simultaneous release of huge quantities of meltwater into the sea. Parts of eastern Scandinavia and the far north have been slowly rising (at different rates) ever since and continue to do so today. The practical effect of this is that since the beginning of the Viking Age, the sea level in eastern central Sweden has fallen approximately sixteen feet (five meters), with progressively lesser amounts to the north, south, and west. The Viking harbors here were deeper, the rivers more accessible to boat traffic, and there were more islands in the lakes and archipelagoes. The winters here were almost as harsh as in the mountains, but especially on the central Swedish lowlands the summers were warm. The annual temperature scale could easily range from $-13°$ F$(-25°$ C) in the winter to $86°$ F $(30°$ C) at the height of the summer, giving rise to a life strongly marked by seasonal rhythms that continues today.

Since at least five hundred years before the Viking Age, the southern part of what is now Sweden had close connections with the Danish islands, and this relationship is reflected in every aspect of the region's material culture. As the early Danish state consolidated itself in the Viking period, its territory spanned the straits separating modern Denmark and Sweden, extending into the southern province of Skåne and parts of Blekinge and Halland. These southern settlements were separated from those of the central lakelands by a natural belt of

1.6 Iron Axe
The vast forests of southern Norway and Sweden provided abundant timber for construction of Viking longhouses, boats, and other materials. Axes such as this Swedish specimen were an important part of a carpenter's tool kit.

dense forest and hill country, largely preserved today in the form of the modern province of Småland. No Viking Age inhabitant of central Sweden would have considered the south to be anything but Danish: Sweden did not assume its modern borders until well after the Reformation.

Although not part of the Scandinavian peninsula, Denmark was one of the most prosperous and culturally influential regions of Scandinavia. The main part of the country consists of the Jutland peninsula, which is linked to the south with Europe and northern Germany, a vital route of communication; the northern tip of Jutland also guards the narrow approaches to the Baltic from the North Sea, another factor in Denmark's importance. To the east of Jutland are the two large islands of Fyn and Zealland, which together span the waters of the Kattegat to the coast of modern Sweden; in addition, hundreds of small islands dot the area. Unlike its northern neighbors, Denmark is a low-lying country, predominantly favored with light and fertile agricultural soils, now characterized by gently rolling farmland. In the Viking Age, however, much of the area was covered by deciduous woodland (fig. 1.1), and there were large areas of marshes, bogs, and sandy heaths. Here, too, the land is penetrated by several deep fjords, though without the mountainous valleys of their counterparts in Norway. The lack of large marine mammals and moose was more than compensated for by the abundance of fish and shellfish, which coupled with cereal production formed a mainstay of the Danish economy.

Beyond Scandinavia proper, the Baltic islands of Bornholm, Öland, Gotland, and Åland can also be considered integral parts of the Viking homelands, although each has a distinctive character and played particular political roles that were dictated by their strategic locations around the Baltic. Bornholm, Öland, and Gotland all support shallow, fertile soils suitable for farming and enjoy a temperate climate, while Åland—situated between Sweden and Finland, and now belonging to the latter nation—is essentially an archipelago of several thousand small islands, some of which are suitable for settlement.

It cannot be emphasized too strongly that Scandinavia at this time was the home of a coastal culture, most obviously so in Norway but also in Denmark and Sweden, with water transport oriented respectively to the North Atlantic, the North Sea, and the Baltic. The concept of *time-distance*—that is, focusing on the amount of time taken to travel from one place to another, rather than on the actual measured distance between them—is very important to understanding communications in early Scandinavia. Thus a major sea crossing from mid-Norway to southern Denmark might be faster (and therefore "nearer" in perceptual terms) than overland travel to a place comparatively close by. This concept underlies the importance of the region's sea coast and rivers and may illuminate why the Vikings were so willing to undertake raiding expeditions overseas. Throughout the Viking Age in Norway and Sweden, the coastal waters, fjords, rivers, lakes, and channels between the Danish islands were the main conduits of travel. Other than in the agricultural lowlands, inland journeys were most often made in winter, on skis, sleighs, and skates (figs. 1.8, 1.9) over the snow and on the frozen waterways.

Early Cultures and Peoples

The ultimate origins of the modern (and Viking Age) population of Scandinavia can be found some 14,000 years ago toward the end of the last Ice Age, when the geographical outline of northern Europe as we know it today was still forming. As the inland ice began to retreat, human beings began to migrate north from the German plains and colonize the new land. What is now the western entrance to the Baltic was covered by a land bridge, and by approximately 9000 B.C. people had moved into all of Denmark, southern Sweden, and perhaps even south-

1.8, 1.9 Bone Skates
Viking ice skates made from horse or cattle bones were secured to the feet with leather straps. Unlike modern skaters, Viking skaters (wearing skates like these from Birka) propelled themselves with the aid of an iron-tipped pole. This method was still common in the mid-sixteenth century when Olavus Magnus made the accompanying woodcut, which shows a hunter on skis.

1.7 Arrowheads
Besides being weapons of war, iron-tipped arrows were also used for hunting wild game, including mammals, birds, and even fish.

western Norway—first in seasonal visits and then gradually settling into a cycle of year-round exploitation. These settlers probably originally had their roots in the Magdalenian cultures of central Europe and France.

A series of distinctive cultural complexes—the so-called Hamburg, Federmesser, Bromme, and Ahrensburg people—developed successively in southern Scandinavia through the early Stone Age, representing thousands of years of slow adaptation to fluctuations in the environment and climate as the Ice Age drew to a close. Others appeared in the north of Scandinavia—among them the so-called Komsa and Fosna cultures—though their origins are unclear: the debate continues whether they migrated from the east, either overland or across the sea ice, or, as other scholars contend, moved slowly along the Norwegian coast from the area now covered by the North Sea and were followed by later newcomers from the southwest (see Larsson 1996 for a comprehensive overview of current research on the early settlement).

Through the five thousand years of the Middle Stone Age, or Mesolithic, settlement continued to spread further north along the coasts, lakes, and river valleys. Change came slowly: archaeologists examining developments in stone-working technology and other aspects of material life have isolated only three major trends in cultural traditions, evolving successively through the so-called Maglemose, Kongemose, and Ertebølle cultures, but each of these shows considerable regional variation. These first Scandinavians

all lived by hunting, foraging, and gathering. According to the season, they followed herds of reindeer and other game, fished the seas and waterways, collected shellfish in abundance, and picked berries and other edible plants. Some moved from one place to another as necessary, living in temporary encampments; others lived in centralized, permanently occupied sites and used seasonal camps at different times of the year.

The introduction of agriculture, an innovation that spread from the south starting around 4000 B.C., was the most significant development in early Scandinavia. With agriculture came an entirely new way of life that was to characterize much of the region for millennia. Beginning in the Neolithic period, or New Stone Age, and over the following two thousand years permanent farming settlements were established on the fertile soils that would also form the centers of population during the Viking Age. Coincident with these new village settlements, there is a massive expansion in the range of material goods produced, which alongside similarly sweeping changes in burial practices and religious expression (in the form of monumental structures) mark the transition from a mobile to a sedentary mode of existence.

At this period new cultures, which may reflect new population groups, begin to appear in Scandinavia. Some of these groups—in the south such as the Funnel Beaker (ca. 4000–2800 B.C.) and Battle Axe (ca. 2800–2200 B.C.) cultures—were primarily agrarian in their lifestyles, while others—such as the Pitted Ware culture (ca. 3500–2200 B.C.)—were largely hunter-gatherers, who were more sedentary. Several of these groups were active at the same time in essentially the same areas and showed a marked preference for agricultural or marine environments. In the north, beyond the areas with fertile soils, the hunting cultures continued to follow much the same way of life as they had for millennia.

Identified on the basis of excavated evidence—settlement form, pottery, burial rituals, rock art, and so on—it is far from certain what kind of ancient society lay behind all these artifact-determined "cultures" that archaeologists use today, and it is even unclear whether the obvious differences in their economic strategies and possessions really do mean that they were separate groups of people at all. An alternative theory is that

1.10, 1.11 OVAL BROOCHES

Viking women pinned their aprons to their dresses with oval brooches, and more than fifty styles of oval brooch have been identified (Petersen 1928). The differences may reflect changes in fashion, but more likely this enormous diversity shows an arcane language of class and regional affiliation we can no longer understand.

Agriculture, whatever its cultural associations, grew steadily in importance throughout the later Neolithic and into the Bronze Age, but the crucial role of hunting and fishing in household economy was maintained in many parts of Scandinavia until recent times (fig. 1.7).

The introduction of bronze—an alloy of copper and tin—came, like the agricultural revolution, from the south, reaching Denmark around perhaps 1800 B.C. Knowledge of the new metal spread north into Scandinavia during the succeeding centuries, but the cultural history of Scandinavia cannot be reduced to a series of technological leaps—from stone to bronze and eventually to iron—as all these developments came slowly and were inextricably bound to a continuously changing social context. Because both of its raw components had to be imported from abroad, the coming of bronze brought with it a major reorientation of Scandinavia's cultural outlook. In the Bronze Age (approximately 1800–500 B.C.) the region became part of a pan-European economic network of trade and exchange, albeit on its northern periphery. This system encompassed not only metals, finished goods, and produce, but also ideas—both social and political.

New practices, such as increasingly elaborate burial rituals (fig. 1.4) and the deposition of huge quantities of bronze objects in bogs and lakes, hint at new forms of social structure emerging in Scandinavia at this time. There have been attempts to demonstrate the rise of chieftaincies and increasing social stratification, and some archaeologists have detected hierarchies of settlements, linking villages and farmsteads in basic patterns of power and control. Certainly during the Bronze Age the first signs of the tribal societies that would dominate the centuries leading up to the Viking period become evident.

By the middle of the first millennium B.C. when ironworking technology (figs. 1.6, 1.9) found its way to Scandinavia, the settled areas of the region were dotted with small villages perhaps linked together in loose confederations. Cattle herding had come to be almost as important as arable farming in these economies, and the ownership of these animals also seems to have been understood in terms of personal status. In the north of Scandinavia, however, society developed at a different pace, particularly in terms of subsistence strategies. It was not until five hundred

their subsistence strategies varied through the year or according to where they were at any one time, and the seasonal change from one mode of life to another may have been bounded by such strict ritual codes that this entailed the use of a completely different type of material culture in each context. The processes by which cultural change came about are far from clear, and the ramifications of this dilemma continue to haunt Scandinavian archaeology today. Was one culture displaced, even conquered, by another? How are these groups related to the modern Nordic population? Archaeologists, geneticists, and even linguists continue to debate these issues.

1.12 ROUND BROOCH
Sometimes made in silver with detailed filigree ornamentation, round brooches were worn in the middle of the chest between oval brooches. This bronze brooch with low-relief ornamentation indicates it is the product of mass production. Multiple castings from a single mold led to less detail over time.

years later, for example, that farming began to be practiced in large parts of Norway. While the middle part of the region had developed metalworking through it close links southward during the Bronze and early Iron Age, in northernmost Norrland the period 800 B.C. to A.D. 200, known as the Early Metal Age, is characterized by continued reliance on hunting and fishing with a primarily mobile, nomadic population. There are clear indications of strong eastward connections with Finland and northern Russia, not least in the distribution of a type of pottery made of asbestos (probably used in ironworking). It has been suggested (Baudou 1995) that the "asbestos pottery people" are essentially the ancestors of the Saami, though use of this term would be inappropriate at such an early date; others would identify the pottery more with a function appropriate to a specific place, rather than with a particular ethnic group.

During the period from 500 B.C. to the birth of Christ, also known as the Celtic or pre-Roman Iron Age, southern Scandinavian society was increasingly linked to that of northwestern Europe. By the time of the Roman Empire, whose influence was felt in Scandinavia despite its distance from the imperial borders, there is evidence—massive weapon sacrifices—that this was a period of considerable social unrest: the political patterns that would develop into the petty kingdoms of the pre-Viking period were already beginning to form.

SCANDINAVIAN ETHNICITY: THE GERMANIC AND SAAMI PEOPLES

Few written sources directly describe the ethnic situation in Scandinavia at the eve of the Viking Age (Ottar's account, quoted p. 31, is one of them), but from notes in Continental chronicles, a cautious reading of the later medieval Icelandic sources, and the findings of archaeology we can attempt at least a basic reconstruction of the population structure of the region.

It is difficult to estimate reliably how many people lived in Scandinavia at this time, but probably the population was no more than a few hundred thousand. At the most basic level, there were two broad ethnic groups living in the Viking homelands— the majority population of Germanic origin and the Saami (pronounced "Sar-mee"), also known, though not to themselves, as the Lapps. The Slavic and Baltic tribes from the regions of modern north Germany, Poland, and the Baltic States also exerted cultural influence; some of these peoples had been present in Scandinavia since long before the Viking Age and added their own contributions to the ethnic melting pot.

The Germanics are sometimes referred to as the Nordic peoples or simply as Scandinavians. These are the people who can also be called the Vikings, but the popular use of this term to refer generally to anyone living in Scandinavia during the eighth to eleventh centuries is misleading. There has been much discussion of what *Viking* actually means, though there is no doubt that it carried a general connotation of piracy and peripatetic, seaborne violence. Although the term is found in non-Nordic sources—for example, the Anglo-Saxons used *wicing* to describe the northerners who raided their shores—it is also found on runestones.

There is no doubt that there were Vikings operating on the home front too. The word may derive from the Old Norse *vík*, meaning "bay," thus a Viking could originally have been someone who operated from bays and other appropriate locations for maritime ambush. Other scholars have seen its origins in the place-name Viken, the area around the Oslo Fjord in Norway, and perhaps the men from this district were known for their aggressive raiding. Other suggestions link the word to *wic*, an Anglo-Saxon term for a trading settlement, making Vikings the people who targeted such places for their attacks.

1.13, 1.14 RING BROOCHES
Men also displayed their status through jewelry. They fastened their cloaks at the shoulder with ring pins—the pin's length, ring decoration, and the value of the metal all announced a man's standing and worth.

Nordic people, as they do today, though then as now there must have been general bilingual communication between the two groups. The Vikings called the Saami "Finns," sometimes adding a prefix meaning "ski," which refers to their legendary abilities in this respect. One reference in a saga to some young men uses a compound noun incorporating a version of the word Saami, indicating that even at this early date the term was in use; probably, as in modern times, the Saami called themselves one thing while their neighbors referred to them as something else. The Saami have a conception of their homeland that crosses— and in practice ignores—national boundaries, a place called Saapmi that encompasses northern Norway, the inland areas of northern Sweden, northernmost Finland, and the Kola Peninsula in what is now Russia.

For centuries, scholars have debated the respective origins of the Saami and Germanics: where did they come from and when? Until relatively recently these arguments often had somewhat racist overtones, and the question of which people "arrived first" has been particularly divisive. Although outside Scandinavia the Saami are almost universally accepted as an indigenous population group (not least by UNESCO and the United Nations), within the region this is still the subject of intense and controversial debate of a kind familiar from many countries around the world. The "answer"—if indeed, such a thing is even worth seeking— is to be found far back in Scandinavian prehistory. By the time of the Vikings both groups were firmly established and had been so for millennia. A still-topical question, however, is exactly where in Scandinavia the Saami were living at this time. This concerns the extent to which they encountered and interacted with the Germanics and by extension the nature of the two groups' lifestyles. In a broad generalization, most of the Vikings followed a settled, agrarian way of life while many (but by no means all) Saami were nomads. This is not just a discussion of interest to historians, as archaeological evidence for early Saami settlement has been used in modern land-rights claims (Zachrisson 1994).

The Saami have often been neglected in studies of Viking Age Scandinavia, relegated to a far-northern periphery and seen alternately as subjects of the Nordic population or trading partners for their fur supplies, but

The reality may have been even more complex, with formalized warrior brotherhoods, perhaps with ritual dimensions. Despite its specific meaning, the general sense in which "Viking" is understood is now so ingrained that there is little point in attempting to revise its usage, and it is employed in this expanded sense throughout the present volume.

The Germanic peoples spoke a broadly common language during the Viking Age. While most people could probably understand each other throughout the region, there were regional dialects that intensified throughout the period as the medieval languages of the Nordic countries began to diverge from one another. The language of the sagas is usually known as Old Norse or Old Icelandic, but even this is a later, medieval development of the tongue the Vikings spoke.

The Saami people are of Finno-Ugrian origin, quite separate from the Indo-European Germanics and instead distantly related to the Finns, Estonians, and Hungarians. They spoke a language different from that of the

1.15, 1.16 GOTLANDIC JEWELRY
The people of the island of Gotland, off the Swedish coast in the Baltic Sea, had a distinct ethnicity in the Viking period that is readily seen in their unique jewelry. Box brooches, like the gold and silver one above, were worn by women; penannular ring pins, like that below, were worn by men.

this picture is now beginning to be reevaluated. The ethnic attribution of archaeologically recovered objects is not without its problems, but graves laid out according to Saami burial rites, together with campsites and stray objects of Saami manufacture, have been found as far south as the Viking heartlands of central Norway and Sweden, just north of Oslo and Uppsala (Zachrisson 1997). This suggests that at least in a trading capacity, and very possibly as nomadic pastoralists, the Saami were active far further south than has been previously understood and that large parts of "Viking Scandinavia" actually supported two quite distinct populations. There is no evidence of conflict: the Germanics and Saami seem to have lived relatively peacefully side by side, following different lifestyles. Scholars are only just starting to explore the implications of this peaceful coexistence, not least concerning the cultural exchange that is likely to have taken place on many different levels between the two peoples. The Saami contribution to Viking Age culture in Scandinavia is as yet poorly understood, but it is already the focus of several planned research projects.

IDENTITY AND SOCIETY ON THE EVE OF THE VIKING AGE

Within the broad ethnic category of the Germanic Scandinavians, or Vikings, there were many levels of identity and affiliation. Throughout Scandinavia an individual's alle-

giance might be to a local king or chieftain, to the senior farmer or magnate of a district, or simply to one's family, friends, and the people of the neighborhood. None of these identities were mutually exclusive, although they were not always without conflict; all relied on complex ties of duty, loyalty, and reciprocity expressed in varying degrees of gift-giving, hospitality, or basic tax. People could have simultaneously thought of themselves as, for example, Swedes, Upplanders, as coming from the Uppsala area, or from a particular group of farmsteads (figs. 1.10, 1.11). At the same time people had their identities as farmers, warriors, merchants, craftsworkers, or just as men and women, the old and the young. Just like ourselves, they brought different identities to the fore in different situations: in war or peace, when meeting strangers or representatives of officialdom in whatever form, when working or socializing, and so on.

The immense variation of the Scandinavian environment produced natural locations for settlement, and through their influence on communication and access these same factors also shaped social and political networks in the different areas. Traces of such regional or local groups have been found by archaeologists comparing the material culture from neighboring parts of the homelands. All over Scandinavia, people wore broadly similar types of clothes, with generally the same forms of jewelry and accessories (fig. 1.12); they lived in more or less the same sorts of buildings and settlements, and buried their dead within the same very generalized traditions (cremation predominated in Norway and Sweden, while inhumation was the general practice in Denmark). But there were crucial distinctions at a level of specific detail: in one area a particular type of brooch might have been fashionable, in another a certain kind of pottery, while in a third area women may have worn especially large numbers of beads (figs. 1.17, 1.19)—these differences can be detected in the archaeological record. Most often, these assemblages of objects are found in graves, deposited either for the use of the dead person in the other world or as indicators of social status (figs. 1.13, 1.14)—not only that of the deceased but also of their relatives or peers; these "grave goods" and the rituals for which they are evidence form patterns combining objects of different types used in

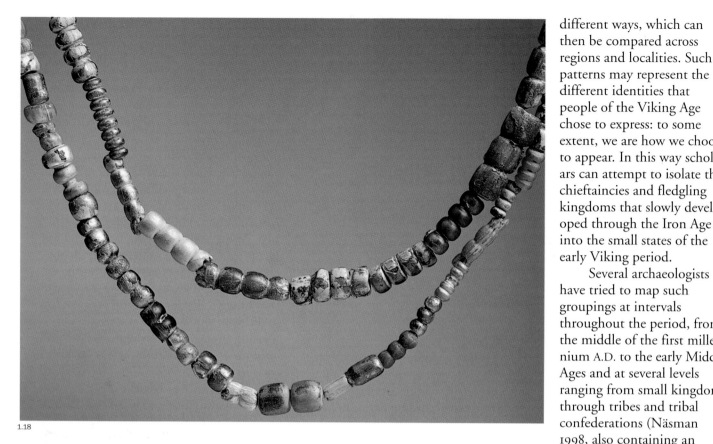

1.18

1.19

different ways, which can then be compared across regions and localities. Such patterns may represent the different identities that people of the Viking Age chose to express: to some extent, we are how we choose to appear. In this way scholars can attempt to isolate the chieftaincies and fledgling kingdoms that slowly developed through the Iron Age into the small states of the early Viking period.

Several archaeologists have tried to map such groupings at intervals throughout the period, from the middle of the first millennium A.D. to the early Middle Ages and at several levels ranging from small kingdoms through tribes and tribal confederations (Näsman 1998, also containing an extensive bibliography for these issues), right down to individual settlements and clusters of farmsteads (Callmer 1991). At about A.D. 500 perhaps seventeen or so small polities can be distinguished in the material culture around Norway's coasts, with thirteen or fourteen more in Sweden and another nine in the Danish part of the south. From an early date the island communities of Bornholm, Öland, Gotland, and Åland all had their own distinctive identities, for the most part—like the different ethnic groups of the mainland—represented by relatively minor variations in the dominant forms of dress and clothing, and especially in the specifics of burial ritual and its material culture. The numerous fortifications found on Öland suggest that this island was a particularly contested area and may have been where much of the interregional conflict was decided as these early state modules competed for power and influence.

Around the year 700 there may have been seven or eight small kingdoms along the Norwegian coast, and another in the province of Jämtland around Lake Storsjön (which in the Viking Age was culturally Norway, but is now part of Sweden). The territory of present-day Sweden was dominated by the two kingdoms of the Svear and the

1.17

1.17–1.19
BEADED NECKLACES
Glass and amber beads were a sign of status, prestige, and perhaps regional affiliation. These blue and foil-covered glass beads (figs. 1.17, 1.18) which were recovered at Birka, show the late imported styles. The string from Gryta has larger beads (fig. 1.19) in assorted sizes, shapes, and materials—including glass, crystal, and carnelian—characteristic of older, more traditional Viking styles.

Goths, in the fertile heartlands of Svealand and Götaland, respectively. The location of viable agricultural soils was a crucial factor in both the distribution of Scandinavia's population and in its political groupings, which tended to develop around the centers of farming. In Denmark, the density of settlement that the amount of arable land made possible, coupled with the small size of the country, led to a high level of sociopolitical cohesion and resulted in the formation of a unified kingdom considerably earlier than in other parts of Scandinavia. Even from the 500s Denmark was remarkably consolidated, but by 700 there is evidence of a Danish core area, centered on the middle island of Fyn, with an inner and outer periphery encompassing the area from Jutland to the settlements in the south of modern Sweden.

By 800, the beginning of the Viking Age itself, these groups had become so consolidated that Denmark appears to be a more or less unified kingdom, but the process by which this took place is little understood. Sweden and Norway were each dominated by a handful of competing protostates, and the uneven process of slow consolidation would dominate the domestic history of Scandinavia for most of the Viking Age and into the twelfth century. Both Bornholm and Öland had largely been subsumed in the broader political groupings that were developing, but Åland and Gotland remained independent. The people of Gotland, while clearly part of the greater Scandinavian cultural world, nevertheless boasted highly developed styles of accoutrement, jewelry, and dress accessories that were unique to

the island (figs. 1.15, 1.16); the same applies to such monuments as the famous picture stones (fig. 3.2), which are also found nowhere else. Despite its small size, Gotland should be recognized as another of the cultural complexes alongside those of the three larger Scandinavian societies that correspond to its modern countries. The island's strategic position made it a natural point of contact—and occasionally conflict—for all the peoples living around the Baltic littoral, and this is inevitably reflected in the material culture of the Gotlanders.

A similar pattern of diversity characterized the external contacts of the Scandinavian peoples, and control of trading centers and channels of economic access to the wider world was crucial in the formation of early political centers in the north. The kingdoms of northern Norway traded with their southern neighbors, with the Saami who inhabited the territories in the far north, and westward to the Faeroes, Iceland, and Greenland; the southern Norwegian kingdoms also traded westward, in addition being involved with Denmark and the western Baltic. The Svear kingdom of the Mälar region focused on the east, developing its contacts with the Baltic cultures and Russia, while the Goths were oriented more westward toward Denmark and Norway. Southern Sweden looked south and west, to the cultures of the Continent. These European contacts particularly enriched Danish culture, and through Denmark many innovations and ideas from the Continent—material, political, and spiritual—reached Scandinavia.

Despite the increasing centralization of power, all the way through the Viking Age the local and regional groupings never really disappeared; the old allegiances were still maintained, and royal authority was not universal, however much kingly propagandists might have it so. In the nominal kingdom of the Svear in eastern central Sweden, for example, it is possible to distinguish archaeologically at least half a dozen distinctive groups of settlements (Callmer 1992); but archaeology certainly fails to capture the finer nuances of these kinds of social constellations, and the real picture would inevitably have been even more complex. Such individuality and an emphasis on personal identity would be a hallmark of the Vikings until almost the end of the period—indeed, it is a defining characteristic of the age.

2 | FARMING AND DAILY LIFE

BY SIGRID H. H. KALAND AND IRMELIN MARTENS

THE POPULAR CONCEPTION OF VIKINGS
—that of a seafaring people who raided and traded in foreign lands and colonized the lands they found in crossing the North Atlantic—suggests a society adapted to coastal and maritime life. In fact, the Vikings were farmers. Although they usually lived near the sea (fig. 2.1), their economy was primarily based on agriculture and animal husbandry. When Viking men went "a-viking" (raiding or trading), their families at home went about their daily work tilling the soil and tending livestock, as their predecessors had for thousands of years. They raised grains and several kinds of vegetables, but the harsh northern climate and short growing season dictated that cattle, sheep, goats, and pigs and not food crops sustained the Viking economy. Horses provided power for farming, transport, and war. As the Vikings expanded their domain between A.D. 800 and 1050, it was animal husbandry that was the basis for their economy and made possible their colonization of the North Atlantic islands, of Greenland, and, for a brief period, northeastern North America.

CUTTING A WHALE, *REYKJABÓK*

THE ARCHAEOLOGY OF FARMING

The natural conditions for farming varied greatly throughout the Nordic region (Price, chapter 1). Farmers had adapted to local conditions and knew how to use the special resources of their local environment. They knew which products could be used for eco-

nomic exchange, for even though most of their needs could be produced on the home farm they nonetheless required goods from outside. A farmer in Denmark or Skåne, in southern Sweden, might have thought it impossible to farm a steep hillside in a Norwegian mountain valley, but he would certainly have been pleased to accept some of the iron made there or a grindstone from its quarries.

The remains of the farmhouses, infields, meadows, and grazing land provide the most valuable source of information about Viking farm economy. Unfortunately, farm remains are best known from marginal areas where they were abandoned in hard times. Even though large villages have been excavated in rich farming areas such as Denmark, they lie under soil that has been plowed and cultivated for hundreds of years, making it

rotted away or burned in funeral pyres. One of the most important implements was the ard or scratch plow, which was drawn by oxen or horses and was used to prepare the soil before sowing (figs. 2.2, 2.3). The ard had a wooden shaft tipped with iron that could cut the sod but could not throw it because it lacked a lateral blade. Turning the soil required a wheeled plow with a moldboard; Vikings used this plow on flat land, but the ard was easier to handle on small and rocky fields.

Barley was the most common grain, but even wheat, oats, and rye were grown where conditions permitted. Cabbage, onions, peas, and beans were raised, and the Norse also collected and used the seeds of several plants viewed as weeds today. They grew flax both for its oily seeds and for its fibers, and hops gave taste to beer, which was the favored beverage. Hemp was another important fiber plant; other plants were grown to color textiles—for instance woad (Isatis tinctoria), which gave a blue color.

THE FARM MICROCOSM

Vikings most commonly ate beef, but in some areas, mutton was of equal value. Bone remains show that the average size of cattle and sheep was fairly small; the bones also provide information on the age of the stock and on breeding customs. Coastal farms raised more rams, which produce more and better wool than ewes, indicating that wool production was important. Vikings kept sheep as much for the wool as for the meat, and sheep and goat milk were consumed and made into cheese. Although the bones of goats and sheep cannot be distinguished, goats certainly were kept in many areas,

impossible to identify the relationship of field to farm or farm to village (Roesdahl 1982). Valuable information also comes from the remains of livestock and food. Livestock were kept in stables during the winter, except for sheep, which stayed outdoors all year in the milder coastal areas. Cow stables and animal pens can often be identified; frequently the number of horses and cattle kept on a farm can be estimated from indications of stall divisions. When soil conditions permit, fragments of animal bones reveal which species of animal were kept and the kinds of grains and plants that were grown or consumed. Even weeds provide data on cultivation practices and farm management, while pollen analysis gives indispensable knowledge both about farm practices such as clearing land for grazing and fodder production.

Farming implements have been found in Viking graves. Most of them are fragments, as only the iron parts are preserved, while the wooden parts, mostly shafts, have

Borg: A Chieftain's Farm

Extensive excavation revealed that a large farm at Borg (fig. 2.1) in Lofoten, Norway, north of the Arctic Circle must have been the residence of a chieftain from the eighth to ninth century (Stamsø Munch et al. 1987). The farm had a protected location at the inner part of a fjord with a good harbor and a view of the surroundings. There was also arable land, pastures, and easy access to the sea, and three boathouses were found, with the longest being eighty-five feet (twenty-six meters).

The main dwelling house in the central courtyard was 272 feet (eighty-three meters) long and had been the chieftain's guildhall. Implements found inside the main

house show that farming and fishing were the most important activities. Most artifacts reflected daily life, but there were also some unusual finds, including shards of fine glass and pottery from the European continent and some gold fragments. This kind of outstanding material is usually found only at marketplaces and towns in southern Scandinavia (figs. 2.18, 2.19).

Could Borg have been some kind of a northern trading port? Perhaps, but it is more likely that it was a powerful chieftain's farm of the kind described by Ottar (p. 49) that gained its wealth by gathering resources from distant places using complex social and political networks.

2.4

2.3

especially where hillsides were steep. Pigs were important too; and pork was ranked as high-status food, as shown by its being the daily dish eaten by Odin's warriors in Valhalla, according to Snorri Sturluson's *Edda*. Cattle were used both as draft animals and as the main source of meat in most places. Denmark, in particular, exported cattle to the south (Hedeager 1988). Horses were the most important and highly valued animals on the farm and were used for riding and as draft animals for carts, sleds, and plowing. Cut marks on horse bones from middens indicate that horse meat was eaten frequently. Later, after the conversion period around 1000, this custom was strongly fought by the Catholic church, which considered eating horse a heathen practice. Finally, chickens and geese were all members of the barnyard family, as well as dogs and cats.

Most Vikings ate food produced on farms, supplemented with fish from the sea, lakes, and streams. Sea and land mammals were caught and eaten in all areas where they were accessible. In late summer and autumn, berries were plentiful in the forests and must have been popular with children as well as with grownups. Meat and fish, slaughtered and caught seasonally, must have been stored for use in other less productive seasons by drying, salting, and smoking, but these processes have left few archaeological traces. Butter and cheese were also important food-stuffs that were stored for the winter. Much daily nourishment came from wheat and other grains that were processed by grinding with small, hand-rotated querns (millstones).

HOUSING AND SETTLEMENT

Throughout the Nordic lands several construction techniques were common to farmhouses for centuries before the Viking period. Houses had an inner frame consisting of two parallel rows of interior posts placed in pairs and connected by transverse and longitudinal beams to a stable frame. The posts were placed in holes dug into the subsoil, making them easy to trace in archaeological excavations. Walls were built of various materials according to climate and availability of wood and other materials such as sod. Walls might be either straight or bowed outward, and those houses with bowed walls also had a curved roof ridge making the house resemble, at least symbolically, an upside-down ship. Such houses could be made to be very long

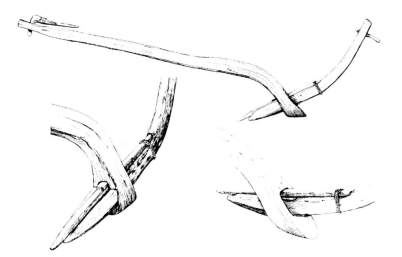

2.2–2.4 FARM TOOLS
Wooden plows tipped with iron and small scythes were essential Viking tools. Norse farmers grew oats, barley, rye, peas, cabbage, and beans. Rye and wheat were used for bread; oats and other grasses were stored for winter animal fodder; and barley was the crucial ingredient for making beer.

and were divided into several rooms that housed animals as well as people. As the Viking period progressed, houses became smaller, with separate structures for people and livestock and the interior posts were moved closer to the walls, thus giving more interior space. Between the posts and the walls were low benches where people sat while eating, talking, producing crafts, and sleeping. Daily life centered on the fireplace, which, because of its shape, was called a long hearth. New building materials and wall construction techniques also were introduced. Roofs were either thatched (covered with birchbark and grass sod) or made solely of

wood. Floors were of stamped earth, and their buried layers, when not destroyed by later plowing, often contain many finds from daily life, including spindle whorls, shards of soapstone vessels, and small metal objects.

The earliest preserved log house construction in Scandinavia is the burial chamber in the Gokstad ship from about 900. It is not known where this building technique was introduced from, but it probably came from the east. In the medieval period most houses in the coniferous forests of Scandinavia were of this type. Such buildings, which lacked postholes and foundations, left few archaeological traces. Because log house construction was better suited for small buildings, its use eventually resulted in the division of the longhouse into smaller structures.

Each farm had a variety of outbuildings used for storing food for people and fodder for animals. Pithouses were made by digging into the ground. Spindle whorls and loom weights found in many such houses indicate that spinning and weaving, as well as other craft productions, took place in these auxiliary buildings.

In Denmark and central Sweden most people settled in villages and hamlets (Welinder et al. 1998). Hamlets in eastern

Daily Bread

The Eddic poem *Rigsthula* deals with the Norse god Rig or Heimdall who visited three different homes. In the first one, a thrall's home, he was served a coarse loaf, heavy and thick, stuffed with bran, and a bowl of soup. In the second home, a farmer's wife served him a dish of stewed veal. (Unfortunately, the lines telling about the farmer's bread are lost.) In the earl's home, the table was laid with a linen tablecloth, and thin loaves of white grain were placed on it. He was served wine with the meal of roasted birds and pork.

This text provides some indication of the foods served by different social classes in Viking Scandinavia. People of all classes ate twice a day, a "day-meal" early in the morning and a "night-meal" in early evening when the day's work was over. Both archaeological and written sources provide evidence of cooking and foodstuffs.

Bread has been found in quite a few Swedish graves, and it is sometimes preserved when burned. Loaves vary in size and content, but barley was the most common ingredient, often mixed with other grains, pea flour, or linseed. Most breads were thin and many were unleavened, while others were leavened with yeast. The circular iron frying pans (fig. 10.4) found at several sites were probably used for bread making.

The daily porridge was probably just as common as

daily bread. Archaeological remains of soups and stews have been analyzed and have been found to contain flour and grits mixed with animal ingredients and vegetables. These dishes—in a variety of recipes—changed little down to our own time. The same goes for sausages, which are well documented in the medieval cities. Cooking pots of soapstone or iron were in common use, but cooking in pits filled with hot stones was not completely outmoded. Meat and fish would be wrapped in large green leaves, placed in the pit, and covered by sod and earth. Roasting spits indicate still another way of preparing meat and fish.

Several herbs and spices were known. The Oseberg grave contained seeds of cumin, mustard, and horseradish; of these, at least mustard was a rare import. Honey was the only sweetening agent known. Beekeeping is well attested in the medieval period, but it is uncertain whether this was practiced by the Vikings, or if honey for making mead was imported. Mead—whose basic ingredient is honey— and beer, made from malted barley and hops, were highly appreciated alcoholic drinks and were made at home. Wealthier families also were able to indulge in wine imported from the Rhine, judging from fragments of containers of German stoneware.

2.5, 2.6

HUNTING ARROWS AND PITFALLS
Standard arrow points were used for hunting mammals such as bear and reindeer; bifurcated points, which were less likely to pass right through the prey, were used for hunting birds and waterfowl. Moose and reindeer were hunted with pitfalls—pits camouflaged with branches that trapped prey below ground—as they had been since Stone Age times.

Sweden usually were smaller, typically consisting of three farms (Stibéus 1997). In the Viking period the village was made up of seven farmsteads placed along both sides of the village road. Each consisted of a fenced plot 260 feet (eighty meters) on a side with a gate to the road. The farm's structures were inside the fence, with a one-hundred-foot (thirty-meter) longhouse in the middle. These houses were divided into three rooms; the eastern one was a stable for twenty to thirty cattle, and the other two were for people. Smaller buildings, mostly placed along the fence, served a variety of purposes. It has not been possible to trace the outlying fields, but we can imagine that farmers cooperated closely in farm management activities like sowing, harvesting, use of grazing land, and repairing fences.

WEST NORWEGIAN COASTAL ECONOMY

People living on the coast always combined farming with fishing. In that way they obtained a very secure food supply, which made it possible for them to survive on rather small farms. In these locations men spent part of the year fishing and catching sea mammals and seabirds while the women had the responsibility of running the farm.

Along the western Norwegian coast the Gulf Stream produces a mild climate in which little snow falls at sea level during winter almost as far north as the Arctic Circle. This favorable climate made it possible to keep animals, especially sheep, grazing outside in the heath during the winter; it also made the construction of animal shelters unnecessary and lessened the time needed for collecting fodder during the summer. Excavations at a farm in Lurekalven in western Norway have shown the precise size of the fields, meadows, and outfields (Kaland 1987). This farm had two dwellings of sixty-five feet (twenty meters) and thirty-three feet (ten meters) in length, and a combined byre and stable with room for sixteen cattle, all around a small courtyard. The surrounding heath supported at least sixty sheep, and the sea provided fish, birds, and sea mammals.

In all of these farms, it is extremely difficult to determine exactly what the people's everyday lives were like and how they used natural resources. Even determining the relative importance of fishing, sea-mammal hunting, and bird catching from archaeological data alone is difficult (Helberg 1997). Fish, however, were always an important part of the diet and were caught everywhere along the coast and in lakes and rivers, both for private consumption and for commercial sale. During the Viking period the importance of commercial fishing increased dramatically, so that by A.D. 1100 fish and fish products had become the most important Norwegian export and supported large coastal villages and international markets.

In addition to farms, Norwegian Viking period people established fishing stations consisting of small buildings or huts along the outer coast. Traces of these buildings, which vary in shape from octangular to oval and range from ten to twenty-six feet (three to eight meters) in diameter, have been found close to the shore. Typical finds from these fishing camps include potsherds, fishing hooks, line sinkers, knives, and bones of haddock, cod, and saithe. In northern Sweden, where they were used between 800 and 1100, these houses served as seasonal bases connected with fishing, trapping, or sealing; in Norway they were used from around 700 into the medieval period (Broadbent 1987). Archaeological remains from such stations also record changes in the development of the fishery from single isolated structures in the early Viking period to groups of contiguous structures late in the Viking period. In some cases these stations seem to be part of the daily life of nearby local farms, whereas in others they may have been remote stations owned by distant farms. The chieftains sent their men out to the stations to fish, as stated in saga accounts.

This combination of fishing, sea-mammal hunting, and agriculture provided

S.S. KALAND AND I. MARTENS

2.7, 2.8 IRON PRODUCTION
Ore from mines and peat bogs in Norway and Sweden was smelted in charcoal-fired furnaces to produce iron "blooms" (fig. 2.8) by the direct-reduction process. As a bloom cooled, it was split with an axe to determine the quality of the iron. If the slag content was low, it was then forged into standard-sized bars, ready to be made into tools or sold on the market.

could be caught and dried or salted for winter use.

Cod, and particularly the Norse arctic cod, were caught in large quantities, especially in the Lofoten area of northern Norway. Fisherman caught cod in late winter and early spring, and dried the fish in the fresh, cold, and windy air until summer. By then the fish was so dry that it could keep for years. *Torsk*—meaning cod today but derived from the Old Norse for "dried fish"—could also be preserved by smoking or by salting followed by drying. An important by-product was fish oil. The fishery made northern Norway one of the richest and most powerful regions in the Nordic area. Its center in Vaagar, in the Lofoten Islands, is mentioned in the Icelandic *Egil's Saga* as the place where Egil had his men fish for cod. Accounts from the days of King Harald Finehair in the early tenth century tell of an Icelander who was advised to go cod fishing at Vaagar as a good way to earn money. By the end of the Viking period Vaagar had developed into an important market that supplied massive amounts of dried fish, through Bergen merchants, to much of northern Europe, where it had come into demand as a crucial food staple.

Nordic lakes and rivers also contained large stocks of fish, and salmon was the most important. An eleventh-century runic inscription from east Norway records the stocking of Lake "Rausjøen": "Eilif Elk carried fish into Rausjøen." By carving this inscription, Eilif Elk established his right to fish there. People had the right to exploit salmon, trout, and other inland fishes depending on whether they did it on common land or as part of their own private farm. It was illegal to block salmon or trout runs by nets or barriers; fish were caught by spear, net, or line. Many place-names attest to the value of this resource.

the economic basis for coastal settlements. Despite considerable local and regional variation, the coastal settlement pattern always included a twenty- to fifty-foot (six- to fifteen-meter) long structure, which combined storage for a boat and fishing gear, and farm buildings located farther from shore in the midst of the fields. The importance of fishing increased northward along the Norwegian coast; as fishing and hunting grew to be an important part of the economy, cattle and sheep breeding and grain cultivation declined. By fishing offshore with lines and nets for cod, saithe, halibut, ling, and other fish, ample amounts

HUNTING AND TRAPPING

Pits dug to trap large mammals produced some of the largest and most spectacular traces of Viking period culture that exist in the forests and mountains. Hunters constructed traps in different ways, but the most common technique was to dig rows of deep pits (fig. 2.6), numbering from just a few up to several hundred. They placed the pits where moose or herds of reindeer passed regularly and used them mainly in the autumn when the animals' fur and antlers were most valuable. These pitfalls were camouflaged

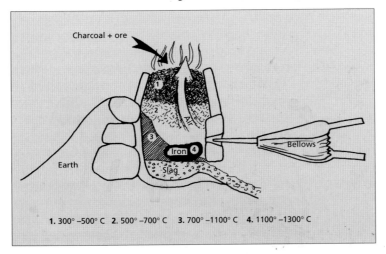

Charcoal + ore

Earth

Iron 4

Slag

Bellows

1. 300° –500° C **2.** 500° –700° C **3.** 700° –1100° C **4.** 1100° –1300° C

with branches and twigs and were so deep and narrow that the animals could not climb out. Reindeer were also hunted by driving them between long stone fences that led the herds to a lake or funneled them into enclosures made of poles. These systems required a large group of hunters to direct the herds and kill the animals in the water or at trap sites.

Many trapping sites also include remains of huts used by hunters and animal drivers, and the refuse heaps they left behind leave no doubt about the success of these enterprises. From the moose and reindeer they took meat, antler, and hides—the latter two as highly valuable trade commodities. Antler was used for making combs, handles, and other small objects. In medieval Scandinavian towns, moose and reindeer antler dominate workshop refuse, while craftsmen in southern Sweden and in Denmark used antler from red deer (Mikkelsen 1994).

Many of the Vikings trapped small fur-bearing animals such as ermine, marten, squirrel, and fox, and their furs have long been among the most valuable Scandinavian commodities. It is, however, very difficult to trace this activity archaeologically, because neither the traps nor the furs is preserved. In recent times, traps were made mainly of wood and other organic materials, and the remains of the animals trapped have rarely been found. In excavations at Birka, a Swedish trade site (fig. 1.3), leg bones of these fur-bearers have been recovered, suggesting that furs were brought to Birka with the paws still on for later removal when the fur was processed (Ambrosiani and Erikson 1994).

2.9–2.11

SHARPENING TOOLS

Large iron files and sandstone whetstones were used to give the primary edges to swords, scissors, shears, knives, iron-tipped plows, and scythes. Small hones, most of which were perforated for carrying, were constantly in use. The finest whetstones came from southern Norway and, like Norwegian iron, were exported as unfinished blanks to Europe. The cache illustrated here was recovered from a sunken trading ship.

S. S. KALAND AND I. MARTENS

OTHER RESOURCES

Trapping, iron extraction, and the use of other resources outside the farmland cannot be viewed merely as supplemental to the Nordic peasant economy. For many farms located in marginal farming territories, the income or sustenance derived from these resources were crucial to survival. While managing large trapping systems required collective activity, iron extraction and trapping of small fur-bearing mammals were largely family tasks well suited to small communities. In such places, farmers performed a variety of specialized activities in addition to the normal cycle of farm work. Some of these activities were seasonal, the best example being the large-scale communal trapping that took place when reindeer and moose moved from summer to winter pastures. Other tasks, especially working up raw materials into tools and clothes, were done mainly indoors in winter.

One premise was indispensable in this type of mixed economy: regardless of a farm's poverty, it had to be part of an economic system that was stable enough to secure the sale of its commodities. These goods had to be exchanged for necessities that could not be produced on the spot. Necessities included not only what was needed for physical survival, but other materials and activities that made it possible for people living in peripheral areas to share in the cultural values and practices of society in general.

HUNTING SEA AND COASTAL ANIMALS

In the ninth century a Norwegian called Ottar visited the court of the Anglo-Saxon king Alfred of Wessex, who recorded Ottar's visit in his annals. Ottar lived in far northern Norway where he took tribute from the *Finnas* (the Saami):

> That tribute consists of the skins of the [reindeer] herds, the feathers of birds, whalebone and ship rope made from walrus hide and sealskin. Each pays according to his rank. The highest in rank has to pay fifteen marten skins, five reindeer skins, one bear skin, ten measures of feathers, and a jacket of bear skin or otter skin, and two ship ropes. Each of these must be sixty ells long, one made from walrus hide, the other from seal.

Ottar looked upon himself as a man of rank, and his wealth came mostly from the sea: whalebone, seal and sealskin, walrus tusk, down and feathers from seabirds, and fish. He carried these products on his boat

2.12–2.14
IRON-WORKING TOOLS
During the Viking period nearly every farm had its own forge, and many smelted their own iron. Blacksmiths used tongs to hold iron bars while they were heated in a forge and shaped by hammering on a boot-shaped anvil (fig. 2.14). By late Viking times, blacksmithing became a specialized craft.

and sailed the entire length of the Norwegian coast to Denmark, stopping at various market centers. He then crossed over to England, where he presented King Alfred with a walrus tusk as a token of respect and to secure the king's protection during his visit.

Walrus inhabit cold water and are closely linked to arctic and subarctic regions that have seasonal pack ice. In Viking and medieval times walrus visited the northern coast of Norway often enough to have influenced place-names. Walrus were especially abundant northeast of Norway, around Murmansk. Ottar and Norwegian and Saami hunters sought them for their precious tusks and hides, from which strong ropes could be produced. The texts also indicate that Ottar traveled east along the arctic coast with the whale hunters.

Seals and whales were hunted both in northern and southern Scandinavia and were of great importance in Nordic subsistence. Like the walrus their importance is attested by place-names such as Kvaløya (whale island), Kvalvåg (whale bay), and Kvalvågnes (whale ness or cape). The old medieval laws contained detailed information—which must have originated in the Viking period—concerning the ownership of whales that had stranded or had been trapped or driven by men in small boats into shallow water. When in deep water, whales were caught by harpoons and tether lines. Whale meat was eaten either fresh or dried, and oil was used as food and fuel for oil lamps. The importance of whale products is evident in a number of grave finds, of which perhaps the most amazing is a tongue of a whale found in a Viking grave from North Cape, Norway. Other grave finds made of whalebone include weaving batons, decorated ironing boards (fig. 11.16), gaming pieces, decorated scrapers, and sword handles. Although it is difficult to assess the volume or profits from trade in whale and walrus products, it was sufficient to tempt Viking hunters to travel as far west as Greenland by 985 and as far north as Spitsbergen in 1194.

Seal hunting was also of major importance for all Scandinavian coastal populations, and unlike whales and walrus, this resource extended into the Baltic Sea. According to *Egil's Saga*, harp seal gathering places were looked upon as valuable property. The earliest known law in Norway—Gulathing's law—states that if a man finds other hunters sealing in his territory, he may claim the catch. Sealing was mainly carried out in spring and early summer by men hunting singly or as an organized enterprise by groups of men in small boats. The hunters would chase the seals into shallow water or onto the land, where they were clubbed, speared, or harpooned. Seal meat was considered delicious, and its blubber and oil was used as an alternative to butter. The blubber was rendered into lamp oil. Thickened seal oil was used to waterproof boats, and seal pelts were made into waterproof shoes, clothing, and bags. As in the case of walrus and whales, place-names derived from seal were common. So important were whale and seal as foods that even after the Vikings converted to Christianity, whale and seal meat were exempt when meat was prohibited on fasting days.

Seabirds of all kinds nest around the entire Scandinavian coastline, and many islands are named for birds. Down, feathers, and bird flesh had high economic value, especially in Norway, and were highly sought as materials of trade and export. Birds were hunted and eggs collected with a great variety of methods, according to the different species' habits. Hunters with nets and lines climbed cliffs where birds nested, raided nests in trees and burrows, speared birds and shot them with arrows (fig. 2.5), and caught them with hooks.

Peregrine falcons were tamed and taught to hunt ducks and seabirds. An Eddic poem makes mention of two men who rode out with their falcons and bows. The Swedish King Olaf hunted eider ducks with falcons, and such a hunt is recorded on the Norwegian memorial stone from Alstad, Toten, from around 1000.

Birds were used as fresh food and were also dried for winter use, and feathers and down were collected for insulation in clothing and bedding. Down materials were a mark of wealth and high status. The royal woman Queen Aasa, who is thought to be buried in a Viking ship grave at Oseberg, had a large supply of feather quilts, and the chieftain buried in the Gokstad ship wore a down jacket. An indication of the value of down is seen in Ottar's report that he received many of his taxes in down and feathers, while *Egil's Saga* notes that chieftain Torolv Kveldulvsson had down-collecting stations among his assets.

2.15 A BLACKSMITH AT WORK
This carving on a door panel from Hylestad Church in Setesdal, Norway, shows the blacksmith Regin making a sword on his anvil while Sigurd operates the bellows. This panel was carved to illustrate "Sigurd the Dragon-Slayer," a tale in which Sigurd uses this sword to slay a dragon.

SETTLEMENT IN FORESTS AND LOW MOUNTAIN AREAS

By late Viking times, around 1000, the population had grown to the point where farms and small communities had become established in higher or more northerly locations where climatic limitations made it impossible to farm as a self-sustaining occupation (Svensson 1998). Nevertheless, even in many of these locations small farms with plots of barley existed in the medieval period and may also have existed in Viking times. In such areas, animal husbandry dominated. Outside the small infields, farms had access to large stretches of forest and mountain where the animals could graze and winter fodder could be gathered. Such farms required a large resource area to provide sufficient fodder, and livestock had to be kept in stalls for long periods during the winter. Here, as in Iceland and Greenland, the task of collect-

ing winter fodder took much of the year's farm effort.

SHIELINGS

Use of shielings—upland pastures where livestock are transferred during the summer—has been widespread in large parts of the Scandinavian peninsula for the past thousand years. Cattle, sheep, and goats would be taken to pastures, sometimes at considerable distance from the farms, where the animals could graze on land that was not immediately accessible from the farm itself. Often family members and servants moved with the animals to the shielings for the entire summer. Such mountain pastures produced the highest-quality milk, and milk products were valuable trade commodities.

Archaeological evidence on the origin of shielings is scanty, but some sites thought to have been shielings have been excavated in western Norway, and pollen studies show that mountain pastures were grazed since before Viking times (Bjørgo 1986). Because the first Nordic settlers arriving in Iceland and the Faeroe Islands early in the eighth century used shielings, they must have brought this practice with them from their homeland. Shielings were also used in such lowland forest areas as Vaermland in Sweden during the Viking Age (Aquist 1992).

FOREST AND MOUNTAIN RESOURCES

In addition to grazing lands, forest and mountain regions were rich in many other resources, including moose, reindeer, fur-bearing animals, iron ore, and other minerals and rocks used to make whetstones and grindstones that were valued trade items. Forest game resources had been used since the first humans settled the Nordic countries about ten thousand years ago (Magnus 1986).

Mountainous areas of Sweden and Norway contained three kinds of rock that were very important to the Viking economy: slate, sandstone, and soapstone. Slate and sandstone were used as whetstones for the daily task of sharpening tools (figs. 2.9–2.11) and weapons. Whetstones and grindstones are frequently found in settlements and graves in the Viking homeland and abroad and were clearly mass-produced and exported from their quarries of origin (Resi 1990). A cargo of whetstones was recovered a ship wrecked in south Norway (fig. 2.11).

2.16

2.16, 2.17 Soapstone Pots
Vikings made cooking vessels and oil lamps of soapstone (steatite). Soapstone is easily shaped with iron tools, holds heat well, and is more durable than ceramics. Because good soapstone deposits are rare, vessels made from it were sometimes traded great distances. Cooking vessels like this Norwegian example were often made with handles (fig. 2.16); the bowl (fig. 2.17), made in Norway, was traded to Sweden and has been mended with an iron fastener.

Soapstone, a soft mineral that was easy to cut and shape, was used widely for cooking pots, loom weights, spindle whorls, fishing sinkers, lamps, and casting molds. Soapstone pots (figs. 2.16, 2.17) were chiseled directly from the outcrop in rough shape and were finished later at home. Such outcrops display large heaps of waste rock. An ordinary pot of ten inches (twenty-five centimeters) diameter usually weighs about eleven to thirteen pounds (five to six kilograms). Soapstone pots hold their heat for a long time after being heated over a fire. Fragments of broken pots were reused as spindle whorls, fishing sinkers, and loom weights. Chemical analysis shows that soapstone pots and whetstones were exported far beyond their production areas (fig. 2.17), and in some regions their extraction and production developed into a specialized industry.

Iron Extraction

Bog ore and other kinds of secondary sediment ores containing iron are quite widespread in Scandinavia, and iron extraction took place in all the Nordic countries. Such ores were especially abundant in forest and low mountain regions, and recent investigations have shown that most of the iron used in the Viking homelands was produced in these regions beginning early in the Christian era.

The "direct reduction" process of iron extraction was a time-consuming task that required extensive technical skill and detailed advance preparation. Iron ore had to be mined, dried, and roasted on an open fire, over charcoal prepared from wood. Small clay-lined furnaces powered by hand-driven bellows were preheated to 2000–2400° F (1100–1300° C). Furnaces were charged with charcoal and roasted ore. The slag resulting from the melting of nonferrous rock was drained through a small port, leaving the smelted metal behind as a soft lump, or "bloom," of malleable, low-carbon iron (fig. 2.7). One disadvantage of this simple reduction technique is that a considerable amount of the original iron was lost in the slag.

Managing the process required knowledge and technical experience that was widely available in local society. Finding the ore, judging its quality, and managing the air flow into the furnace to obtain the correct temperature during different stages of the extraction process were only some of the finer points that needed to be mastered (fig. 2.8). It is uncertain how much Norse ironsmelters knew about influencing the quality of the bloom, but they probably knew how to raise the carbon content to produce a low-grade steel (Magnusson 1986). Certainly, many producers and communities had their own secret methods and believed that their special procedure was the best one of all (figs. 2.12–2.14).

Iron extraction leaves many tell-tale traces in the terrain. Most obvious and numerous are the pits used to produce charcoal, followed by great numbers of slag heaps. Most of these sites are small, suggesting family production activities (Martens 1988). Structures with combined workshop and living quarters were often constructed at extraction sites, and these structures indicate periods of intensive work, probably taking place during the winter (fig. 2.15).

2.17

2.18

2.19

2.18, 2.19 VIKING CERAMICS
Vikings generally did not make ceramics, perhaps because they preferred more durable wares. Although some pottery was made locally, most fancy ware, such as this decorated bowl, were luxury imports. The pitcher (fig. 2.19) of French or Rhenish manufacture, inlaid with tin foil, was found in the grave of a high-status female at Birka.

Iron was traded over long distances, and hoards of iron blooms and specially shaped iron currency bars are numerous, but most of these bars predate the Viking period (Espelund 1995). Danish finds include iron goods that have been imported from Sweden and Norway, but we do not know the extent of such imports.

TRANSPORTATION AND COMMUNICATIONS

On many Swedish runestones, and even on a few Danish and Norwegian ones, bridge building is mentioned as one of the best and most memorable of deeds (Foote and Wilson 1980). Although such wooden constructions that were placed directly above marshy ground are not technically bridges, they were used as "boardwalks" in many places in the Nordic countries. The most impressive bridge was built by the Danish king, Harald Bluetooth, around 980 at Ravning. It crossed the Vejle valley a short distance south of the royal center in Jelling in Jutland (Sawyer 1988). This bridge was 2,300 feet (700 meters) long and 18 feet (5.5 meters) wide, and was made of solid oak timbers.

Travelers rode horses or walked. Remains of sunken roads, which resulted from the wear and tear of thousands of horses and men throughout the centuries, are found in many places. Carts and wagons, drawn by horses, were used in those areas where the terrain was favorable. Throughout most of Scandinavia, however, people had to rely on pack horses to climb hills and follow the long, stony glacial moraines, which in several regions formed the spine of important communication routes. Of course, boats were frequently used on lakes and rivers and along the coasts.

In many ways, transportation was easiest during winter, when horse-drawn sledges could be pulled over frozen and snowy rivers, lakes, and marshes. Horses could pull heavier loads on sledges than they could carry on their backs, and iron cleats ("frost-nails," fig. 7.14) were often fastened to their hooves to improve traction and prevent slipping. In medieval times, markets and fairs were often held in the winter, and it is likely that these customs had ancient roots. True metal horseshoes did not come into use until the early medieval period. Skis are also well represented in Viking period archaeological finds, having been in use for thousands of years. There are also many finds of "ice-legs"—skates made of cow and horse leg bones

"Too Weak, Too Weak is the King's Bow"

In the saga about Olaf Tryggvason, Snorri Sturluson tells about the final stage of the sea battle at Svolder waged by competing Viking forces (A.D. 1000). The bow of the excellent archer Einar Tambarskelver was splintered by an enemy arrow. Then said King Olaf, "What burst so loudly?" Einar answered: "Norway from thine hand, O king!" "So great a burst has not yet befallen," said the king, "take my bow and shoot with it." Einar took the bow and straightaway drew the point of the arrow beyond the bow. He shouted, "Too weak, too weak is the king's bow." After more hard fighting, Olaf lost the battle and was killed.

Bows and arrows were used both in fighting and hunting (fig. 2.5), with the same types being used for both purposes. Viking bows are not preserved, but finds from earlier periods and the lengths of arrows indicate that longbows, which could be nearly six and one-half feet (two meters) in length, were common (Farbregd 1972). Pine, especially yew tree, was preferred for bows. Picture stone engravings indicate that a shorter bow was used as well.

Arrowheads of iron are very numerous. They are found in graves in Scandinavia, and in addition the heads of arrows shot away by hunters are recovered every year in Norwegian mountains up to nearly 6,500 feet (2,000 meters) above sea level and in Sweden as well. Some arrows that landed in the expanding glaciers of the Little Ice Age were soon covered by ice. In the warmer 1930s, several completely preserved arrows were found in the receding glaciers of central Norway. They were about two and one-half feet (0.8 meters) long, and many, but not all, had fletch-ing feathers.

Most arrowheads have a sharp point and were used for large game such as reindeer, moose, and bear. Dispersal of arrowheads show that hunters moved around widely in their search for game. But, of course, wounded animals could bring the arrows far away from the places where they were shot. Blunt arrowheads were used for small, fur-bearing animals, so as not to damage the fur, and blunt or forked points were used for hunting birds.

(figs. 1.8, 1.9)—frequently found in old town sites, indicate that skating and sliding on the ice during the long Scandinavian winter was a common means of transport, and possibly a sport as well.

The homeland societies of the Vikings had a great variety of resources that they used and combined in various ingenious ways. The Viking period was a time of rapid population growth, expanding economy, and political integration. Markets and towns were being established in a countryside that had previously supported only family farms. All of these developments placed new economic strains and constraints on individuals and families. These changes also created new

opportunities for men to sail off and make their names and fortunes raiding, trading, or settling new lands, providing a new life for their families, and the lure was sufficient to initiate large-scale outward movements. When the people from all parts of Scandinavia began exploring westward across the sea, they were looking for a new life no longer available to all members of society at home. The lands they found were not unlike those they left behind, so it was relatively easy to adapt their Scandinavian farming, hunting, and fishing way of life to the North Atlantic lands. In the process they experienced and became part of a larger and more complex society.

3 RELIGION, ART, AND RUNES

BY ANNE-SOFIE GRÄSLUND

**VALHALLA AND *MIDGARDSORM*,
*SNORRA EDDA***

THE VIKINGS HAVE LONG BEEN admired for their ability as shipbuilders, mariners, explorers, traders, and warriors, as well as for their less-reputable history as raiders and plunderers. Unfortunately, the more constructive side of the Vikings is less well known. The spread of their material and intellectual culture demonstrates that they were not isolated from the outside world, as is sometimes presumed; on the contrary, the Vikings traveled widely and participated in large international economic networks. In addition to being successful farmers, traders, colonists, and craftspeople, Viking culture was rich in art, religion, and intellectual life, and these aspects of their society are documented archaeologically in material remains that have survived in such Viking monuments as burials, church art, and runestones. Although seemingly diverse, Viking religion, art, and runestone monuments were closely interrelated in Viking culture; religion was an important part of daily life that was expressed in both art and runic inscriptions. For this reason, an appreciation of Viking art and runestones begins with an understanding of pagan Viking religion.

RELIGION

The old Norse religion dating to before A.D. 1000 may be classified as an ethnic religion, meaning that it belongs to a specific people or group of people, in contrast to, for example, a religion like Christianity, which has become a universal or multiethnic religion. Traditional Scandinavian religion was polytheistic and comprised a large number of gods and goddesses, called *aesir* and *vanir*, as well as many other groups: mythic giants who struggle with the gods (but were not completely evil, as there are marriages between gods and giantesses); dwarves who worked as craftsmen, lived underground, and helped the gods; female *norns* who sat in the center of the world and held power over the fate and fortune of individuals, spinning each human's life thread; female *dísir* who were associated with objects and sovereignty; valkyries, female spirits who gathered the souls of dead warriors from the battlefield (fig. 3.3); and elves who had powers of fertility and were associated with departed ancestors and with cultivating the soil (Davidson 1969, 1993; Foote and Wilson 1980; Steinsland and Meulengracht Sørensen 1992; Page 1990; Turville-Petre 1975).

Since the Stone Age, religion has existed in the form of ideas about supernatural powers guiding people's lives. Religious belief allows people to communicate with these powers through rituals and cults. Bronze Age sites contain evidence of cult ritual documented in rock carvings as well as in a large number of sacrificial artifact deposits. These finds indicate that fertility was a central part of old Scandinavian religion; other archaeological

evidence supports the existence of a sun cult as well.

Another common theme in Scandinavian prehistory is the widespread use of sacrifices made in water or wetlands. Many sacrificial finds from the Stone Age through the middle of the first millennium A.D. have been discovered in springs and bogs, the most famous ones being the large bog finds containing booty, weapons, and other military equipment, dated mainly to the period A.D. 100–500. At the end of this period this religious cult seems to have changed: the old wetland sacrificial places were abandoned, and thereafter the rituals were mainly performed on dry land, in the halls of the big chieftains' farms. The change in venue also indicates social change, toward a more hierarchical society. Thereafter, if not even earlier, cults were organized on a regional basis at different levels within society: on a local level, in the farm; on a regional level, in the chieftain's farm; and, at least during the Viking Age, on a superregional level, for instance, as attested in the literature about Old Uppsala, Sweden.

In the Old Norse language there was no specific word for religion: the closest concept was *siður*, meaning custom, which hints at how integrated religion was in daily life. Unlike today when religion is often separated from secular life, it was then a natural part of all occupations. Viking mythology, which is best known from Old Norse literature, is comprehensive and shows that the Scandinavians had an integrated view of world processes, including its creation and its destruction.

Viking Age religion is known from a variety of sources. The written sources of Old Norse poetry and *Prose Edda*, which describe mythology, gods, and other supernatural beings, were compiled by Snorri Sturluson, the famous Icelandic saga writer, in the thirteenth century. The *Prose Edda* is a text book on poetics and provides Christians with an understanding of pagan mythology. The *Poetic Edda* was compiled later and includes earlier narrations. Other accounts were written by non-Scandinavians, such as Adam of Bremen's church history compiled around 1072 in Germany. Archaeological sources contain information about sacrificial sites, burial customs, and artifacts connected to religion.

Old Norse religion should not be regarded as a static phenomenon but as a dynamic religion that changed gradually over time and doubtless had many local variations.

3.1 MYTHOLOGY IN STONE
This ninth-century picture stone clearly illustrates the shape, rigging, and sail of a Viking ship including the spiral scrolls at the bow and stern and the clothing and weapons of its deceased crew. The upper panel probably illustrates life after death, with Odin riding his eight-legged horse Sleipnir, valkyries offering drinks, and Valhalla—the hall of valor—to the left.

3.2 PICTURE STONE
Vikings on the island of Gotland erected engraved limestone slabs known as picture stones to commemorate people and deeds of valor. This stone illustrates a common motif: a ship sailing deceased warriors into the afterlife and two Viking warriors with conical helmets and shields battling with swords in Valhalla, the warriors' heaven.

ANNE-SOFIE GRÄSLUND

These silver female figurines are thought to represent valkyries, female spirits of Norse mythology who gather the souls of dead warriors from the battlefield and escort them to Valhalla. They wear long dresses, large beaded necklaces, and elaborate knotted hairdos as they offer the dead a drink from a conical cup.

By the second half of the first millennium A.D. the influence of Christianity is evident, for by that time there were frequent contacts with western Europe and the British Isles. In particular, the myths about the end of the world, *Ragnarök*, have many features in common with the biblical treatment of the Day of Judgment.

GODS AND GODESSES

The most-quoted source concerning the mightiest gods in Old Norse religion is probably Adam of Bremen's description of the ceremonial site in Old Uppsala, Sweden. Adam, who was a German cleric, never visited Old Uppsala himself, but one of Adam's informants, the Danish king Sven Estridsen, had. About 1070 Adam wrote that the pagan temple of Old Uppsala had images of three gods: Thor, the most powerful god, occupied the center of the hall, flanked by Odin and Frey. The Swedes sacrificed to Thor when there was threat of famine or disease, to Odin if war was at hand, and to Frey if a wedding was to be celebrated.

Frey was the fertility god. According to *Ynglingatal (Accounting of the Ynglings)*, the Old Norse poem that Snorri Sturluson used for his summary of the Norse gods in the *Saga of the Ynglings*, Frey was the ancestor of the Ynglinga Viking dynasty of Uppsala and the Vestfold dynasty in Norway. Frey belonged to the *vanir* family, which according to Snorri was the original dynasty of gods in Scandinavia and was closely connected to the fertility cult. Other *vanir* gods known during the Viking Age were Freya (a fertility goddess who was the sister of Frey) and Njord (the father of Frey and Freya whose name means "earth"), though Njord was less important than Frey and Freya. Odin and Thor belonged to the dynasty of the *aesir*. One myth tells about the wedding between the *vanir* god Frey and the giantess Gerd, and their offspring Fjolnir, the first king of the Ynglinga dynasty in Uppsala. The *vanir* and *aesir* dynasties of gods are problematic in terms of religious interpretation. Some early religious historians thought the *aesir* gods were introduced in the middle of the first millennium A.D. and coincided with the arrival in Scandinavia of a new group of people who became the ruling class and oppressed those who believed in the old *vanir* dynasty. Most scholars today do not agree with this war-connected scenario and suggest instead that the two dynasties were complementary and that the importance of one or the other reflects different social status among competing groups in Viking society. Likewise, the relations between gods and giants are thought to mirror changing gender attitudes.

Thor ruled in the sky and governed thunder and thunderbolts, wind and rainstorms, sunshine and crops. He is often described as struggling with the giants, and there are many myths about his physical strength. In Viking cosmology the world was thought of as being like a flat round plate on which humans and other beings had assigned places. The gods lived in the center of the world in *Ásgarð*, around the tree Yggdrasil (fig. 3.8), with humans surrounding them in *Miðgarð*; giants lived in *Útgarð* around the outer edges (fig. 3.8). However, there was some vertical space as well, for the dwarves lived underground and the *norns* lived among the roots of Yggdrasil. Beneath the ocean lay *Miðgar«sorm* (Mid-Earth Serpent), whose body bound the world together. When Thor struggled against the giants, his task was to protect cosmic order and prevent the giants from intruding on the lands of gods or people, but his attempt to capture the world serpent as an act of strength and prowess endangered humans because without the serpent, the world would fall apart.

Thor was an extremely important and popular god, perhaps because weather was central to the productivity of Scandinavian agricultural society. His popularity is evident in the many Scandinavian place-names that include "Thor" (Tor) as the first element (Torslunda, Torsåker, Torsvi), especially in Sweden. Odin (Oden) and Frey (Frö) are represented also although not with

3.4 FREY, GOD OF FERTILITY
Frey was the Norse god of fertility and is usually depicted with a large erect phallus. In Old Norse poetry, he sails a magical ship called *Skidbladnir* and controls the wind, rain, and sun. Adam of Bremen, who received a first-hand account of the religious site of Old Uppsala in Sweden in the eleventh century from the Danish King Sven Estridsson, reported that Odin, Thor, and Frey were the major gods worshiped there.

such frequency (Odensö, Frösö). Thor is also the first element in many Scandinavian personal names and is still in common use today (male: Tore, Torbjörn, Torsten, Torkel and female: Tora, Torun, Tordis, Torgun).

Odin was the god of the upper classes—the elite, kings, poets, and warriors—and according to some Old Norse poems, also of seafarers. Other gods invoked by seamen were Njord and Thor. Old Norse literature often describe Odin as the mightiest god. He was the creator of the human race, for he gave life and breath to Ask and Embla, the first man and woman, whom he made from the trunks of trees. He was the god of wisdom and had the knowledge of runes. Odin possessed shamanistic powers, and through a special kind of magic called *seiður*, he had power over life and death, gained by his ritual hanging from Yggdrasil. Because he was also the god of royal power, the king was considered part of Odin's family. Odin is said to be the ancestor of the Danish royal Skjoldunga dynasty, and to judge from place-name evidence, he was especially worshiped in Denmark and southern Sweden.

Adam of Bremen's assertion that Thor is the mightiest god is both interesting and astonishing, as both Odin and Frey are equally likely candidates for this title. In the *Anglo-Saxon Chronicle* Odin is mentioned first in the Saxon royal genealogies, which

suggests that his warrior-king appearance was especially attractive in western European societies, while Frey, as a fertility god, was more important in the thoroughly agricultural societies of eastern Europe. It has also been argued that Thor might have been the ancestor of royal dynasties (Grønvik 1983: 132), and Adam's description of him sitting on the throne in the middle of the hall of the pagan temple supports such an idea. Different rankings for these deities—Odin was the god of the upper class and Thor the god of peasants—as well as local and temporal variations in religious and social beliefs may reveal origins of this confusing hierarchy.

The archaeological evidence of these gods in ancient material culture is limited to some small statuettes made of bronze, bone, and amber that are interpreted as images of Frey. The most famous is a figurine of a sitting man with an erect phallus, found in Södermanland (fig. 3.4); Adam of Bremen's description indicates that the image of Frey in the Uppsala temple displayed a similar condition.

BURIAL PRACTICES

Literature provides evidence of other specific attributes of the Viking gods: the spear was Odin's symbol as well as the *seiður* staff (fig. 3.5); the hammer was the symbol of Thor, and the sickle that of Frey. Miniatures of such objects are sometimes found in graves, indicating that the deceased or his or her family had a special relationship to the god in question. It has also been argued that burials in boat graves may indicate that the deceased were priests of the Frey cult, because boats are thought to be symbols of Frey's ship *Skidbladnir* (Schönbäck 1983; Crumlin-Pedersen 1992). Such an interpretation may also be considered concerning the type of burial monuments called ship settings (stones set in the ground making the shape of a ship, fig. 1.4). By analogy, the burial of women in wagons, also a transport vehicle, which was a tenth-century custom in southern Scandinavia, might be seen as indicative of the Frey cult. Another common religious motif that is frequently found in burials are small silver or iron "Thor's hammer" amulets (figs. 3.6, 3.7). Silver hammers are mostly found in silver hoards from late tenth and eleventh century. Iron hammers, fastened on wrought-iron neckrings, date slightly earlier and are found in cremation graves from the ninth and early tenth century in a very restricted area in the eastern Mälar area of Sweden, on the island of Åland in the Baltic, and in Russia (fig. 3.16). It is not known for certain that Thor's hammers were part of a cult of Thor, but because they are frequently placed on top of the incinerated bones in cremation graves, it seems likely.

Information about Old Norse beliefs in the afterlife is revealed by burial furnishings. An interesting account is given by Ibn Fadlan, an Arab diplomat who in 922 witnessed the funeral of a Rus leader (who was probably a Norseman) at the Volga River in Russia. The description is very detailed, both of the preparations and of the funeral itself. The dead person was cremated, and afterward Ibn Fadlan asked one of the Scandinavians why they burned their dead. The latter answered,

3.5 ODIN, GOD OF WAR
This horned-helmeted figurine is thought to represent a follower of Odin, the supreme deity in the Old Norse pantheon. Odin, a magical one-eyed god, seems to have been worshiped in shamanistic rituals by attendants dressed as horned animals; this figure holds a sword in one hand and two spears in the other. He possesses the knowledge of life and death, composes poetry, and rules over Valhalla and warriors.

"You take those you love and honor most and put them in the earth where the worms and earth devour them. We burn them in the blinking of an eye so that they go to paradise at that very moment." Viking Age cremation graves often contain symbols of rebirth—eggs, hens, and hazelnuts, for instance—together with more status-related and practical equipment (figs. 3.9, 3.10), all indicating a belief that the deceased would take up his or her worldly life in another place.

CULT PLACES

Records of pre-Christian cult houses in the Germanic area are of questionable value as ethnographic sources and were probably influenced by Christianity. Likewise, archaeologists have little confidence in Adam of Bremen's description of an opulent pagan temple in Old Uppsala. Archaeological evidence reveals settlement remains under the medieval church in Old Uppsala, from around A.D. 200 onward, but nothing justifies the interpretation that is was built on an earlier square pagan temple. It has been suggested that what Adam had heard about was a ritual ceremony that had been carried out in a royal hall (Gräslund 1996). In attempting to describe that ceremony, Adam may have based his imagined temple on the small Celtic house-shaped shrines; one such shrine, which was recovered archaeologically, has an inscription in Norwegian runes, and another has a gold roof and a gold carrying chain similar to features in Adam's description.

Such terms as *vi*, *harg*, and *hof* in Nordic place-names help identify the presence of cult places (Nilsson, 1992). *Vi* seems to be an outdoor ritual site that was presumably enclosed with stones or poles. *Hof* and *harg* refer to some kind of cult building. *Hof* seems to be the name for a big central farm that was probably the local chieftain's dwelling. Place-name research shows that after northern Sweden converted to Christianity, the churches were often built on land belonging to big, central farms bearing the name Hov, which may indicate continuity in the locus of important ritual and ceremonial life with pre-Christian religion. An incontestable example of such cult-place continuity has been found on Frösö (Frey's island) in Jämtland, northern Sweden. Under the chancel of the medieval church in Frösö, which is on land belonging to a farm named Hov, excavation revealed a Viking Age sacrificial site with numerous animal bones, mostly bears, lying around a charred birch stump, indicating that animals had been sacrificed or hung on the tree.

Harg is described in Old Norse literature as a cult place where images of the gods were kept on a stone pile, perhaps a kind of altar, that sometimes had wooden walls and a roof, or just a roof and four corner posts. Two recent Swedish excavations have reenergized the investigation of *hargs*, a concept that had been founded solely on literary

3.6, 3.7

THOR'S HAMMER AMULETS

Odin's son, Thor, possesses incredible physical strength and
wields a hammer, called Mjölnir,
which may identify him as the
god of blacksmithing, an essential
technology to Viking Iron Age
society. His popularity is seen
by the large number of hammer-
shaped pendants found in
Viking burials.

3.6

3.7

evidence. On two Swedish Viking Age chieftains' farms, remains of small, simple constructions—in one case of stone, in the other
of wood—regarded as possible buildings,
were found on the outskirts of the farm.
Excavations at both revealed deposits containing amulet rings, pig bones, and hearths;
both cases have been interpreted as *hargs*.

Like other people, the Norse created their
own cultural landscape with their settlements,
cemeteries, cult places, and other monuments,
such as runestones and bridges, that were
adapted to local topographic conditions and
must have had special meaning to the inhabitants. The most striking examples are in royal
settings such as Jelling in Denmark, Borre in
Norway, and Old Uppsala in Sweden, where it
is still possible today to get an impression of
the Old Norse cultural landscape.

CONVERSION

Viking Age religion cannot be dealt with
without some words on Christianity and the
conversion process (Gräslund 1987a; Nilsson
1992, 1996). Conversion precipated important changes in society, as Scandinavia then
became more integrated into western European Christian culture, but it was not a sudden event. Rather it was a long process of
contacts between Scandinavians and continental and insular (British Isles) people that
continued for hundreds of years and is
clearly distinguished in archaeological evidence, especially in burial customs. Burial
customs in Scandinavian countries changed
over time and place: pagan cremation graves
with rich grave goods give way to animal burials over inhumation graves, still richly furnished (fig. 3.11). Later, inhumation graves
without furnishings but clearly oriented to the
east are often found. Finally, burials at conse-

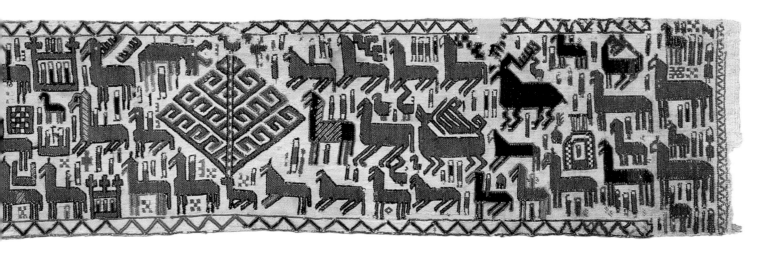

3.8 ÖVERHOGDAL TAPESTRY
This linen textile embroidered in colored thread dating to the Viking Age was found in the attic of a parish church in northern Sweden. Elements of Old Norse cosmology are the World Tree, Yggdrasil (which holds together heaven, earth, and hell), and an eight-legged horse, perhaps Odin's steed Sleipnir. Christian elements include squares, presumably buildings, with crosses on top.

crated churchyards become most common. These changes mark the progress of the conversion because Christianity discouraged the practice of burying grave goods with the dead.

For example, the conversion of Iceland, which was decreed at the Althing (the annual political assembly that served as the governing body for most early Nordic societies) in the year 1000 or possibly 999 must be regarded as the result of a long Christianization process that had reached a certain ripeness. Of course, the kings' conversions were of great importance and well noted in history books and on runestones because they brought the Scandinavian kingdoms into the European fold. On the big stone erected around 960 in Jelling, Denmark, Harald Bluetooth claimed that he was the one who Christianized the Danes (fig. 4.2). In Norway the inscription on a runestone in Dynna, Hadaland, decorated with Christian symbols confirms the literary evidence that Christianity was accepted as the official religion in the 1020s. The rune-stone must have been dedicated to the bridge mentioned on the stone, and the bridge's construction has been established by radiocarbon dating. For Sweden, the evidence is less clear, but runic inscriptions in the Mälar area indicate that conversion occurred during the first half of the eleventh century. In the last decade of the tenth century royal coinage with Christian symbols, on the pattern of English coinage, was issued in the three Scandinavian countries. But it also must be remembered that the conversion at the highest levels did not mean the conversion of the entire society; while it hastened the process, old ideas continued in force in some areas for centuries. Finland, for instance, which is not a part of Scandinavia but is part of the Nordic community, was not converted until the

twelfth century, but archaeological evidence of Christian graves and remains of early church buildings from the eleventh century suggest an earlier date.

The Viking Age is characterized by overlap of Old Norse religion and Christianity, which was marked by extensive mixing of old and new ideas and peoples and syncretism or blending of rituals and beliefs (fig. 3.13). Because the domestic religion was polytheistic, adding Christ as a new god was not a problem. In grave material of the Viking Age this mixture of the two religions can be discerned, with some pagan elements together with elements connected to the new beliefs occurring in the same grave (fig. 3.12). In Old Norse literature we encounter characters such as Helgi the Thin, who believed in God but who invoked Thor when there was bad weather at sea. Through the work of missionaries and international contacts the Scandinavians gradually came to understand that Christianity meant that Christ/God should be the only god, but they probably could recognize many of their old gods and mythic beings in the Christian saints. The Anglo-Saxon stone cross from Nunburnsholme in Yorkshire, England, containing an image of Sigurd, the dragon slayer, is an extremely interesting piece of sculpture because of such composite iconography. It shows Sigurd, wearing a bishop's gold ring on his hand, above a priest holding a chalice and paten, a composition that must be regarded as the Vikings' interpretation of the Eucharist, the moment of salvation (Lang 1976a, 1976b). Relict concepts of the domestic religion lasted for centuries, and even folklore collected in the nineteenth century contains tales of dwarfs and giants that were remnants of old pagan beliefs.

ART

Religion permeated life in the Viking Age and was especially important in Viking art. Artists and craftsmen certainly would have been important people because in prehistoric times art was generally created not for its own sake but as a mark of social prestige, often commissioned by the upper levels of society. Even though much of its meaning is lost to us, we can be confident of our interpretations at least in cases where myths known from Old Norse literature can be identified. Elements of Viking mythology are present in artistic ornamentation, and that religious content would have been obvious to contemporary viewers. This may explain the ambiguity seen in renderings of some beastly or transformational animal forms, such as the Oseberg burial carvings (fig. 4.15).

Knowledge of Viking art derives mainly from archaeological evidence, and as such suffers from the vagaries of preservation. Organic materials such as wood, textiles, leather, and bone are highly perishable and are preserved only in especially favorable circumstances, while materials such as metal and stone have been much more stable (fig. 3.14). A large part of the preserved material consists of handicrafts, metal objects such as jewelry, and various kinds of utility goods, but seldom includes objects of wood, leather, or cloth (fig. 3.17). Many Viking artworks, including objects, houses, and runestones (fig. 4.2), were painted, but little evidence of this medium survives other than traces of red, white, and black paint, and occasional suggestions of brown, yellow, green, and blue. Compensating for this bias in source material is a constant dilemma for the archaeologist.

Sometimes literary evidence provides important clues, when descriptions of artworks and figurative representations exist in the Old Norse literature. Norse pictorial art, either carved in wood or stone or woven into tapestries, often seems to reproduce mythological tales found in Old Norse literature, such as the popular tales of Sigurd the dragon slayer. The most prominent examples of pictorial art are the stones found on Gotland Island (Nylén and Lamm 1988), which include scenes showing people, ships, weapons, and gods (figs. 3.1, 3.2). Many of these are representations of myths: for example, the scene (fig. 3.1) of a rider being welcomed by a woman who offers a drinking horn probably depicts a valkyrie greeting a fallen warrior on his arrival at Odin's Valhalla.

In a few fortunate circumstances ornamented textiles and tapestries have been preserved. The Norwegian Oseberg tapestry (fig. 4.14) depicting a ceremonial procession, perhaps a bridal train, is from the early Viking Age; the transition from the Viking Age to the early Middle Ages is represented by the Swedish Överhogdal and Skog tapestries depicting animals, people, gods (possibly), and a church with a bell tower (fig. 3.8). Icelandic saga literature indicates that tapestries were used as wall hangings in the Scandinavian halls on the big farms, and this custom still existed on prosperous farms in southern Sweden until the end of the nineteenth century.

ORNAMENTATION

Viking art, as known from preserved remains, consists largely of the so-called Nordic animal-style ornamentation (Wilson and Klindt-Jensen 1966; Karlsson 1983). This style of art is one of Scandinavia's truly original contributions to global art, but Nordic animal-style art is neither original nor is it limited to the Viking Age. As early as the Roman Iron Age (during the first four centuries of the present epoch) the Scandinavians had been depicting animals on their jewelry and utilitarian goods. This rather simple usage presaged the development of full animal ornamentation, which probably began in southern Scandinavia in the beginning of the Migration period (A.D. 375–550) through influences from Scythic, Oriental, Celtic, and Roman art. This period of mass migrations throughout Europe also affected Scandinavian culture. The style uses an animal body or its parts to create the design, and in the process the animal form becomes lost and is totally suppressed under the ornamentation. The treatment is often so stylized that the animal body and its parts lose any ties to biological reality, and the line itself (rather than the animal it nominally delineates) creates an effect across the entire surface of the object being ornamented. Although the style changed over several centuries, the band-shaped, stylized animal seen in profile remained the style's central motif until the Middle Ages, when it was abandoned in all but folk art genres.

During the Migration period and the following Vendel/Merovingian period (ca. 550–800), times that were fond of splendor,

3.9, 3.10 BENT SWORD AND
PUNCTURED SHIELD BOSS

Pagan burials provided Vikings with
the tools for a proper afterlife. The
deceased's possessions were deposited in graves and were often
"killed" to release their spirits for
travel to the next world. An alternative explanation holds that weapons
were killed to ensure that the spirits
of the dead who returned to earth
could do no harm to the living.

different stylistic variants of animal-style
ornamentation appeared in rapid succession.
Gilded bronze mountings for horse equipment, weapons, and jewelry were frequently
decorated with these designs. These objects
were often so small and the ornamentation
so intricate that it is the line play rather than
the motif that creates the dominant visual
impression. This ornamentation was often
made with a special technique called "chip-
carving," which derived from wood-carving
but was adapted to metal-casting. The raised
technique is enhanced by light creating contrasts that would be particularly effective as
ornamentation on an object such as a horse
bridle that was always in motion (fig. 3.15).

At the turn of the twentieth century, the
Swedish archaeologist Bernhard Salin divided
the Migration- and Vendel-period animal-
style ornamentation into Styles I, II, and III
(Salin 1904). The changes in lines and curves

from one style to the next were found to follow a strict chronological sequence, and so
they were used to date objects and the sites
in which they were found. Salin's classification is still used today, although with some
refinement because it is now recognized that
stylistic change is not always indicative of
chronological change, as it can also result
from regional or personal artistic variation.

At the beginning of the Viking Age,
about 800, Style III (or Style E, as it is
known in another classification system),
which had originated in the previous Vendel
period, continued to be popular. Its basic
motif was the band-shaped animal seen in
profile. This style is characterized by animal
bodies of various width, openwork shoulders
and hips, and tendril-like outgrowths. The
composition often consists of two animals
arranged in the form of a lyre. This very
elegant style is believed by many experts to
be the most refined expression of animal-
style ornamentation (chart, p. 66).

As Vikings journeyed to the east and
west and brought Scandinavians into contact
with other societies and their artistic styles,
new ideas began to appear. These foreign
styles were seldom assimilated directly into
indigenous Nordic art but were transformed
to fit Scandinavian taste. An example of this
process of innovation may be seen in the western European (Frankish) plant-ornamentation
style, which begins to appear in Scandinavia
in the ninth century but did not become
attractive to Scandinavians until the eleventh
century. At first when they tried to imitate
it, as on the trefoil brooches, the result was
a lifeless, uninteresting spiral decoration.
(Trefoil brooches themselves are an interesting example of contact history: they originated as Frankish sword mounts that were
brought to Scandinavia as Viking loot and
were then adapted as brooches.)

Perhaps the most important Viking art
style of all was the so-called gripping-beast
style. The style, which first appeared at the
beginning of the Viking Age and is related to
Style III, is no longer an animal seen in profile but *en face* with a round face, huge round
eyes, and a neck tendril. Its thin ribbonlike
body is set off by large muscular shoulders
and hips, and its legs end in paws, which
grip tight to everything—to the edge of the
ornamentation border, to neighboring animals, or to its own body. The tigerlike beast
appears filled with energy and seems to cling

3.11 BIRKA CRUCIFIX
This silver pendant is the earliest Scandinavian crucifix discovered; it was found in a rich female grave at the ninth-century trading site of Birka. It marks one of the first indigenous steps toward conversion to Christianity in Scandinavia, a process that took more than two hundred years and transformed Viking society.

3.12 HOLY WHITE STONE
This stone may have marked a cremation burial—some Viking Age peoples cremated and buried the ashes of the dead with their possessions. Stones, sometimes laid out in the shape of a ship, and ship-shaped mounds also marked Viking graves. Grooves cut into the stone contain the remains of red paint.

"harder" style is called Oseberg Style III, named after the famous Norwegian ship burial from the first half of the ninth century (fig. 4.15).

The most popular style during the middle Viking Age was the Borre style, which developed from the gripping-beast style and is named after another large ship grave found in Borre, in the Vestfold region of Oslo Fjord. The animal now has a triangular cat-like face with distinct eyebrows, ears, and neck tendrils. The body consists, as before, of heavy shoulders and hips with ribbon-shaped links between them, and the legs end in the typical gripping paws. Sometimes the ornamentation consists solely of Borre-style heads and ribbons. One of the important innovations to appear in this style is a motif made of a chain of rings with inserted rhomboids. This probably reflects an influence from the British Isles, but the ring-chains there have a different construction. The Borre style is an interesting example of the wide extension of Viking culture during the middle Viking Age. In addition to the many objects decorated in this style found in Scandinavia, several such objects have also been found in Russia and in the British Isles.

Another important style, one that overlaps chronologically with the Borre style, is named Jelling, after the site in Jutland where the Danish Viking kings, Gorm and Harald Bluetooth, had their royal estates. The town has given its name to the famous Jelling Stone (fig. 4.2), the runestone on which Harald proudly announced that he had unified and Christianized Denmark. The site also has a twelfth-century church and Denmark's two largest grave mounds (fig. 4.3). A chamber grave in the North mound, dated by tree-rings to A.D. 958–959, contained a small silver cup (probably a chalice) decorated with animal-style ornament that has become identified with the Jelling style (fig. 4.1). Jelling style is not as common as the Borre style and seems to indicate a return to the styles of the pre-Viking Vendel period in which a ribbon-shaped animal is seen in profile. Characteristic traits of the Jelling animal are the head with a round eye, open mouth, a rolled-up nose tendril, and a neck tendril, as well as a ribbon-shaped and usually patterned or striped body, and sometimes spirals at the shoulders and hips. The animal is often laid in a **S**-shaped loop. An interesting phenomenon is the mix between them:

to the assemblage at all costs. In contrast with the earlier Style III, the gripping-beast style is more fluid and plastic.

The different art currents in early Viking Age ornamentation, represented by Style III and the gripping-beast style, occur separately but are also found melded together in the so-called Broa style where a latticework motif plays an important role in the design. When such a lattice is laid on animal-style ornamentation it creates an openwork grid in which the ornamentation, either Style III or gripping beast or a combination of both, appears through the lattice holes. The contrast between the regular, geometric latticework and the underlying curvilinear motion of the animal-style ornamentation creates a striking effect. The gilded bronze mounts for a horse bridle from a famous grave find on Gotland are the finest example of this combination Broa style. A similar, somewhat

3.13 Hedging One's Bets

Both pagan Thor's hammers and Christian crosses could be made from this steatite mold, indicating that pagan and Christian beliefs coexisted at least to the tenth century. This piece was found near Jelling, the Danish royal administrative center. King Harald Bluetooth converted the Danes to Christianity around 965, the first Viking king to take this revolutionary step.

3.14 Decorated Walrus Skull

Norwegian Viking sites have yielded several examples of decorated walrus skulls. Their function remains mysterious but may be related to pagan ritual. Vikings doodled on wood, slate, and clay, and skull decoration may fall into that tradition of experimentation. Given the economic importance of the walrus in northern Scandinavia, these designs probably have more serious significance.

3.13

3.14

3.15 Rangle, a Magic Rattle

Vikings used rattles made of iron to frighten away evil spirits. This one is particularly simple. Others could be quite complex (fig. 7.17) and were attached to horse bridles and transportation equipment. Many circumpolar cultures including the pagan Norse used jangling metal to attract or repel spirits.

there are objects decorated with both styles and even a single animal with traits from both styles, a Jelling animal with gripping paws! It is obvious that these two styles were in use at the same time for a considerable period.

Beginning in the mid-tenth century a new motif appeared in Viking art: a large quadruped struggling with a snake. This motif has been interpreted as an influence from Christian art, symbolizing the struggle between good and evil. Ultimately of Oriental origin, the motif became common in Scandinavia in the late tenth and eleventh centuries. Sometimes this late Viking Age art is called the "great beast's style" because the central element is a large quadruped.

The large three-sided memorial stone in Jelling is one of the most magnificent monuments of the late Viking Age, partly because of its important inscription, but also because of its majestic triangular shape and its beautiful ornamentation, which includes representations of the great beast on one face of the stone and of the bound Christ on another. The third side is covered with runes. The representation of the great beast—a lion with the head of a bird (a griffin) fighting a snake—is a classical example of another Viking art style known as the Mammen style, named after a grave in Mammen, Jutland, and identified with the silver-inlay style found on an iron axe (fig. 4.9). The Mammen style is characterized by the double contour line, spiral-shaped shoulders and hips, and by the development of neck and tail lobes into luxuriant acanthus-shaped crests, which were probably intended as plant ornamentation.

The related Ringerike style, named for

the Norwegian province that was the source of stone used to make runestones, is very close to the Mammen style but gives an even more powerful impression. Neck crests, tails, and wings end in leaves, palmettes, and richly ramified tendrils. By this time the influence of plant ornament, an introduction into Viking art from the south, is quite obvious and elegant, whereas its early use had been notably unartful. The Ringerike style was also popular in England and above all in Ireland, especially in areas connected with the Vikings.

The last of the Scandinavian animal-form ornamental styles is called Urnes after the decoration on the doorway of a stave church in Urnes, western Norway. The planks on which this art was found had been reused from an older stave church that had been built on this location. The Urnes style is characterized by an extremely elegant motif including the great beast, rendered as a graceful deer with a long neck and a slender head, that incorporates snakes laid out in soft figure-eight loops and coils. Most of the Swedish Upplandic runestones are rendered in this style, so the term "runestone style" was sometimes used in Sweden instead of Urnes style. Runestones in Södermanland, Sweden, are to a high degree decorated in Mammen and Ringerike styles. A Swedish archaeologist has argued that this difference is geographic (Christiansson 1959), but in my view it is chronological. The Urnes style occurs not only as architectural decoration and on runestones but also in crafts, jewelry, and other metal items where the slender shape of the head and the almond-shaped eye are easily recognizable (fig. 12.10). Like the Mammen and the Ringerike styles, the Urnes

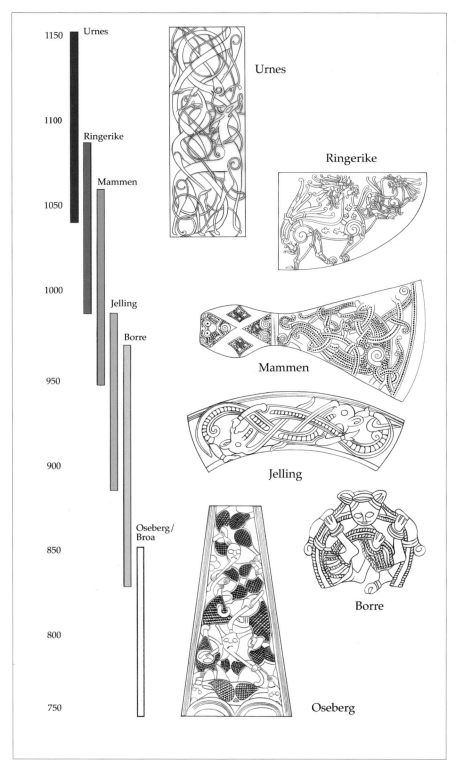

VIKING ART STYLES

Curvilinear animal-style decoration dominated Viking art as diverse as jewelry, runestones, and ship burial furniture. Its evolution from 750 to 1100 is identified stylistically with sites where objects were found—Broa/Oseberg, Borre, Jelling, Mammen, Ringerike, and Urnes. Some styles had ties with Celtic art, others with circumpolar art.

style also occurs in England and Ireland.

Animal-style ornamentation becomes less prevalent at the end of the Viking Age but it does not disappear completely or in an abrupt way. Some of the oldest ecclesiastical objects in Scandinavia, which date to the beginning of the twelfth century, are fine examples of animal-style art: the famous Lisbjerg altar in Jutland, Denmark; in Sweden, a baptismal font from Ytterselö in Södermanland, and a church bench from Kungsåra in Västmanland; and the Urnes stave church in Norway. On the Lisbjerg altar and on the Kungsåra bench, the native style appears in combination with Romanesque elements. Later in the Middle Ages, animal art seems to have been regarded as pagan and therefore unsuitable for ecclesiastical use, but for many centuries animal-style ornamentation continued to be used to decorate utensils in peasant society. A revival of animal art occurred in the nineteenth century as part of nationalistic movements in literature and art, and at the turn of the twentieth century this style was frequently used in architectural decorations, home furnishings, furniture, and on textiles and book covers (Orrling, this volume).

RUNES

When Christianity, with its Latin script and bookish culture, came to Scandinavia a writing system—based on runes—was already present there (Jansson 1987; Page 1987). The origin of the runes has been much debated, but most scholars today agree that runic writing was probably created in the second century A.D. somewhere in the Germanic area under influence of Greek and/or Latin alphabets. The oldest runic inscriptions that have been found on artifacts in Scandinavia as well as on the continent are datable to the beginning of the third century, although it is not until the Viking Age that runic inscriptions become frequent. Runes, carved in wood, bone, stone, or metal, consist of a main staff from which one or more lesser staves point diagonally up or down. One explanation for why the lesser staves are almost never horizontal may be to avoid conflicts between carving of the runes and the grain of the wood. Before circa A.D. 800 there was a twenty-four-character rune series, called the old Germanic or primitive Norse *futhark* (after the phonetic values of its first six letters: f, u, th, a, r, k), that was once used by all Germanic people (fig. 3.19). About

3.16, 3.17

ART FOR ART'S SAKE

Objects as different in prestige value as a bone pin and a fancy silver ring pin have equally fine decoration. An interlacing Urnes-style beast graces the former, while gold filigree animal figures occupy the ends, and animal band motifs are etched into the silver and filled with niello inlay on the pin and ring shafts of the latter.

scription, *Harald had this stone erected in memory of Gorm his father and Thyra his mother—that Harald who won all Denmark and Norway and made the Danes Christians,* is usually seen as the starting point for the flourishing of runestone creation in late Viking Age Scandinavia. The custom of erecting memorial stones may have been a continuous tradition. Ibn Fadlan concludes his description of a (probable) Norseman's funeral in 922 as follows:

> Then they built on the place…something like a round mound. In the middle of it they raised a large post of birch. Then they wrote the name of the man and the name of the king of the Rus on it.

Even if this was not a real memorial inscription, it indicates a related tradition.

The province of Uppland, situated in eastern Sweden along the Baltic and immediately north of Lake Mälar, has the greatest number of runestones: about 1,300 Viking Age runic inscriptions have been discovered, carved on stones, boulders, and rocks. They were created mainly in the eleventh century, although some were carved probably during the later part of the tenth century and others in the beginning of the twelfth century. The primary function of runestones was for memorial purposes, but their use to record missionary work or document inheritance has also been suggested.

Several rune carvers are known by name, as they sometimes signed their work; the three most famous are Asmund, Fot, and Öpir. It has been much debated whether one carver made the ornamentation and another the text, as well as why runestones are sometimes so similar, appearing almost as copies. Similarities have been explained as a result of a close relationship between stones; those who commission the stone carvings; or perhaps it was a sign of loyalty to raise a stone with ornamentation similar to that used on a local chieftain's stone.

The question of whether the Norse in general could read the runic inscriptions has been much debated. As runestones were erected in such public places as along roads, at bridges, in cemeteries, and in other places

A.D. 800, at the beginning of the Viking Age, a new, sixteen-character rune series appears; philologists believe this was the outcome of conscious reforms intended to make the rune script conform more closely to spoken language, although every rune had to cover more than one sound.

In early studies the magic component in rune writing was always emphasized. According to mythology, Odin, the god of wisdom, received knowledge of runes by passing the threshold of death when he hanged for nine nights from Yggdrasil pierced by a spear. He later gave the knowledge of runes to humans. Modern runology, however, stresses that runes were a functional tool to write down spoken language and were used for everyday messages as well as for religious incantations. The magical power of runes is suggested by situations where the runes are hidden, as for instance underneath a metal buckle, or where the runic inscription relates to the maker's name, as a kind of owner's mark (fig., p.100).

RUNESTONES

In total, between five thousand and six thousand runic inscriptions are known today, and more than three thousand of these are found in Sweden, mostly on runestones from the late Viking Age (fig. 3.18). The monumental Jelling stone from circa 965 with its in-

3.18 Commemorating the Dead

Runestones bring together art, religion, and language into a single medium expressing the vibrant Viking culture. Such stones were not grave markers but honored the life, death, and status of the deceased. This runestone was erected in Morby, Uppland, Sweden, and says: "Gullög made the bridge for her daughter Gillög's soul, who was the wife of Ulf. Öpir cut the runes."

but runic inscriptions from many parts of Sweden, even from the Mälar region in east Sweden, commemorate men who took part in the Viking attacks against England. A monument consisting of two runestones in Yttergärde, Orkesta parish, was raised by two sons in memory of their father, about whom they say: *And Ulf took in England three gelds. The first was paid by Toste. Then Torkel paid. Then Canute (the Great) paid.* This indicates that Ulf got his share of the money paid to the Vikings by the Anglo-Saxons—the famous *danegeld,* payments made by local authorities in England to Viking invaders to keep them from attacking their villages.

Runestones may also be seen as tokens of conversion, but very few can actually be connected to the Old Norse religion: one or two in Västergötland and one or two in Södermanland, but none in Uppland. A majority of the Upplandic stones are decorated with a large central cross and/or have a Christian prayer included in the text. Through the inscriptions we see something of the language used by the missionaries: for example, the inscription on a stone from Risbyle, Täby parish, raised by two sons to the memory of their father, concludes, *may God and God's mother help his spirit and soul, and grant him light and paradise.*

It is generally believed that males raised most runestones and that both the subjects they described and the most common type of inscription are male oriented. Such inscriptions as *Ulf had this stone made for Sven, his father,* are the most common. But a closer look at all inscription material from Uppland reveals that women are mentioned fairly often in the texts, either as the raisers or the ones commemorated, either alone or together with men (Gräslund 1988–89). The inscription on a stone from Morby, Lagga parish, reveals that it was raised by a mother for her daughter: *Gullög had the bridge made for her daughter Gillög's soul, who was the wife of Ulf. Öpir cut the runes.*

These inscriptions also show that the families who raised runestones had many sons; sometimes as many as six sons are mentioned in a family but surprisingly few daughters, only one or two. One possible explanation may be that female infanticide was practised, as was done in continental Europe in the Middle Ages. Killing female offspring was common also in Iceland at the time of conversion; as one of the precondi-

where many people would see them, it seems likely that most people could read them, or there would have been little sense in putting them up. Judging from medieval urban archaeological material, for instance, from Bergen in Norway, rune writing incised in small pieces of wood was used for all kinds of messages and transactions (fig. 20.11). It seems likely that such writings were also used in the Viking Age but have not been preserved.

Runestones constitute fascinating archaeological and philological source material for the late Viking Age: archaeological when they are regarded as monuments in the landscape, including their connection to settlements and arable land, and as art objects and philological when the language is analyzed. The content of the texts gives a rare and fleeting glimpse of historical Viking society and is an invaluable aid to Viking Age research. The inscriptions recount raiding expeditions and trade journeys, both to the west and the east. Sometimes they actually correct erroneous literary sources: for example, in the *Anglo-Saxon Chronicle* the invaders in England are described as Danes,

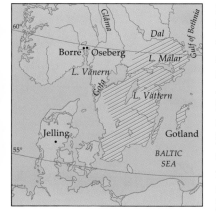

ᚠᚢᚦᚨᚱᚲ᛬ᚺᚾᛁᛁᛋ᛬ᛏᛒᛗᛚᛦ

f   u   th   å   r   k   :   h   n   i   a   s   :   t   b   m   l   R

ᚠᚢᚦᚨᚱᚲᚼᛁᛁᛁ᛬ᛏᛒᛚᛚ

3.19 FUTHARK,
THE VIKING ALPHABET

Runes developed along the northern fringe of the Roman Empire, styled in part after the Latin alphabet. Their simplified straight lines made it easier to carve symbols into stone and wood. Most runic inscriptions convey short messages about ownership and also had religious significance. The runic alphabet is often found on the backside of objects, suggesting some sort of incantation. The first six letters of such strings, F U TH A R K, give the alphabet its name. Shown above are the Danish (top) and Swedish versions of the *futhark*.

tions to accepting Christianity the Icelanders demanded that this practice be allowed—and the Church agreed! This strange permission—and permission to continue with sacrifices (if hidden) and to eat horse meat—was only valid for a few years, however.

RUNESTONES AND CHRISTIANITY

One of the most common purposes for raising a runestone was to dedicate a bridge or a road. In such cases the inscription might indicate that Gullog had a bridge made for her daughter's soul, and "bridge" could mean either a span over open water or a pavement over a boggy or wet area. An inscription on the rock of Ramsund in Södermanland, with a beautiful depiction of the myth about Sigurd, the dragon slayer, provides evidence for a real bridge over water: *Sigrid, Alrik's mother, Orm's daughter, made this bridge for Holmger's soul, her husband, father to Sigröd.* The most famous bridge stones are probably those raised by a powerful man named Jarlabanke at either end of a long causeway in Täby, north of Stockholm. Probably two pairs were erected because two of them still stand in situ, bearing similar texts: *Jarlabanke had these stones raised in memory of himself in his lifetime, and he made this bridge for his soul. And alone he owned the whole of Täby. May God help his soul.* To promote the building of public works such as roads and bridges, the Catholic Church at an early stage had included sponsors of such construction in its system of "indulgences"—actions for which the Church offered intercession for the soul of the dead and/or absolution. To build a bridge was an act commensurable to giving

alms, donating to churches, or going on pilgrimage. The formulation "a bridge for her/his soul" expresses clearly the Christian meaning that this act implied. Another inscription says that the bridge was made "for the pleasure of God."

Runic writing did not disappear with the end of the Viking Age or with conversion to Christianity. A rich body of material from medieval towns in Scandinavia includes merchants' labels, personal letters, even love letters, and amulets made of wood with incantations written in runes (fig. 23.3). There are also examples of a mixture of Latin script and runes in medieval Scandinavian manuscripts. In the province of Dalarna in central Sweden the tradition of writing and carving runes survived without a break into the nineteenth century and may have a role in the history of the famous Kensington Stone found in Minnesota (Wallace and Fitzhugh, this volume).

Today's fascination with the Vikings is heavily biased toward the stereotyped image of the Viking warrior and plunderer. By contrast, archaeological and literary research has begun to expose a deeper and more meaningful picture of early Scandinavian culture and society, one whose indigenous roots have been influenced in many ways by the peoples, societies, and institutions with whom they interacted. The surviving myths, art, and material culture have much to reveal about Old Norse religion, and through the study of burial customs and runestones, we are beginning to understand more about the Scandinavians' gradual conversion to Christianity.

Shamanism and the Vikings? BY NEIL S. PRICE

"Odin had the skill which gives great power and which he practiced himself. It is called *seiður* [magic], and by means of it he could know the fate of men and predict events that had not yet come to pass; and by it he could also inflict death or misfortunes or sickness, and also deprive people of their wits or strength, and give them to others. But this sorcery is attended by such wickedness that manly men considered it shameful to practice it, and so it was taught to priestesses" (Snorri Sturluson describing Odin in the *Saga of the Ynglings,* translation from Hollander 1964)

The abilities described here are all recognized features and functions of shamanism in the circumpolar region. The pre-Christian religion of the Vikings has generally been interpreted as primarily a product of the northwest European cultural sphere, and many of the Norse divinities have direct counterparts in the areas bordering the North Sea and the Baltic.

They are related to the Greek and Roman pantheons and there are distant links to the Indo-European religious heritage. There are also indications of other, perhaps even older, traditions in the Norse belief system, however, some of which suggest connections more with the circumpolar hunting cultures than with the Germanic world. For instance, the *Saga of the Ynglings* describes how Odin could change his shape into that of an animal and in that form travel to far-off places "on his own or other men's errands." This latter comment is especially important, as one of the defining characteristics of a shaman is that such an individual does not work alone but rather within the context of a community and its needs. Snorri also notes that while Odin "himself" (perhaps his soul or spirit?) was journeying in this animal form, Odin's physical body "would lie as if asleep or dead." Both a shaman's flight and trances, in which the performer enters an ecstatic state while his or her spirit travels to other worlds, are defining descriptions of a shaman. There are also references to what appear to be animal helping spirits, such as Odin's ravens Huginn and Muninn; their names mean "thought" and "memory," and they seem to have been in some way extensions of the god himself.

SAAMI HOARDS

The Saami (Lapp) peoples, who occupied the mountainous regions of Norway and Sweden as well as arctic Finland, Russia, Sweden, and Norway, interacted closely with their Viking neighbors. The axe-shaped pendant found with this silver votive offering is of Estonian-Baltic design; the remaining pieces were acquired by the Saami from Vikings and Finns, quite likely in exchange for furs.

several descriptions of "seiðr staffs," although their precise function is unclear. The use of such staffs may be supported by archaeological record; decorated iron and bronze staffs have been found in the graves of apparently high-status Scandinavian females—perhaps the burials of women who practiced this kind of magic. Similar staffs also appear, together with a sword, in the hands of dancing warriors depicted on textiles, metalwork, and silver pendants; these have been interpreted as images of Odin.

Perhaps the most striking direct parallel with circumpolar shamanism is the steed on which Odin rides to other worlds: the eight-legged horse called Sleipnir or "sliding one." Such a creature has been called the "shamanic horse par excellence" (Eliade 1964: 380) and occurs in Siberian and Saami religion in exactly the same form as in Norse mythology as the shaman's means of transport to other worlds. Eight-legged horses are depicted on Viking Age picture stones from Gotland and on textiles (figs. 3.1, 3.8). Even the form of the Norse cosmology itself is paralleled in circumpolar shamanism, with several levels of worlds connected by a tree or pillar. The Viking "World Tree" was called Yggdrasil (the name means "steed of Ygg," an alternative name for Odin), and it was from this tree that the god hanged himself, apparently experiencing a kind of ecstasy in which he grasped the runes for writing for the first time.

Among the human practitioners of seiðr (magic), women seem to have been dominant. Snorri's observation that seiðr was thought shameful for men to practice is echoed in many other sources, and some scholars have speculated that the rituals were partly sexual in nature; the contradiction of Odin, a male god, as the master of the "female" magic of seiðr is a fundamental source of his power. More than fifteen different terms for female sorcerers are recorded, implying that there were different types of practitioners with specific functions and skills. Seiðr among humans seems to have been mainly for divination, but there are also descriptions of its use in bestowing good or bad fortune, manipulating the weather, attracting game animals or fish, causing injury or death to people and animals, and communicating with the unseen.

The material culture of seiðr includes a single, but much-discussed, reference to what may be the use of drums. Ritual platforms are also mentioned, and there are

But if the Vikings did practice some form of shamanism, how did it fit into the overall pattern of Norse religion? We know from studies of numerous shamanic cultures that such beliefs never exist in isolation, but rather form the basis of a whole worldview. In addition to the shamanic character of the Norse cosmos, already mentioned, the link between seiðr and the supreme god, Odin, is crucial and may imply that the rituals were deeply embedded in his worship (see Hedeager 1997).

At some level these elements of Viking pre-Christian religion were connected with similar beliefs among the Saami people with whom they shared the Scandinavian peninsula (see Rydving 1990). Many aspects of Norse interaction with the Saami have yet to be explored, and it is clear that large areas of "Viking Scandinavia" supported two ethnically distinct populations. The study of Viking Age Scandinavian society in the context of the circumpolar cultures promises to be one of the most exciting research fields of the future.

SAAMI HUNTER IN REINDEER SLED
One of the many interesting woodcuts by Olavus Magnus in his *A Description of the Northern Peoples* (1555) shows a Saami hunter being pulled in a sled drawn by a doglike reindeer. "The Lapps...find their sledges amazingly useful...so that they can accomplish long journeys to the places appointed for bartering goods."

4 | POLITICAL ORANIZATION AND SOCIAL LIFE

BY LARS JØRGENSEN

In this year [793] terrible portents appeared in Northumbria and miserably afflicted the inhabitants: these were exceptional flashes of lightning, and fiery dragons were seen flying in the air, and soon followed a great famine, and after that in the same year the harrying of the heathen miserably destroyed God's church in Lindisfarne by rapine and slaughter.

(from the ANGLO-SAXON CHRONICLE*)*

ACCOUNTS LIKE THIS ENTRY IN the *Anglo-Saxon Chronicle* from A.D. 793, one of the most frequently quoted descriptions of the Vikings' notorious sea raids, appear often in English, Irish, German, and French monastic annals and chronicles of the age. The chronicles depict the Scandinavian Vikings as small, aggressive groups of wandering pirates or disorganized army units that spontaneously attacked and plundered coastal areas in Europe. The Vikings concentrated on plundering the treasures of churches and monasteries, and when one area had been pillaged, they went looking for new treasures. Their capacity for more positive communication with foreign population groups seems—to put it mildly—to have been rather limited.

Counter to the stereotype, the Scandinavian Vikings had well-developed social, cultural, and military structures with roots far back in the preceding centuries. The Vikings were experienced actors on the international political stage, and this required more talents than brute force. They had gained this experience from cultural, political, and military contacts and exchanges with other population groups in central and northern Europe since the fourth to fifth centuries A.D. South Scandinavia in particular had maintained close connections throughout the first century A.D. with the changing powers on the continent.

PRELUDE TO THE VIKING AGE: THE MILITARIZED SOCIETY

The power base of the early Scandinavian kings in the sixth to eighth centuries was a high-ranking warrior aristocracy, which formed the core of the king's retainers. It included magnates who already had prominent status in their local areas and their own retinues. By forging these personal alliances the king built up his position like a spider in its web. The loyal magnate protected the king's interests in an area he would otherwise have had no opportunity to monitor. Such personal alliances meant obligations for both the king and his retainers. The magnates

HARALD THE FINEHAIR, *FLATEYJARBÖK*

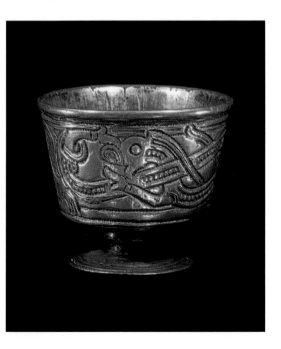

4.1 JELLING CUP

This small silver cup was one of the burial goods found in King Gorm's grave mound. The distinctive decoration on this cup—the head of the beast seen in profile and its ribbonlike body—was the first example of the Jelling art style and gave it its name.

supported the king with both political and military power, and they administrated the king's policies locally. In return for these services, the king granted benefits in the form of costly gifts and/or lands.

Several archaeological finds in Scandinavia illustrate the oaths sworn between the king and his retainers. Costly jewelry (figs. 4.4–4.5) and swords, some with oath symbols on the hilts consisting of two rings forged together and symbolizing the alliance between the king and his warrior, have been recovered in graves and as isolated finds. The king always had to own enough resources to hold the magnates to their alliance agreements; if the king's revenues failed, the magnates would not be so motivated. To ensure a stream of new resources, a king might, for example, subjugate other areas. The Frankish kings did this extensively in the sixth to eighth centuries, and the same situation probably motivated many of the Vikings' raids and conquests in the neighboring areas.

Several graves reflect the resources at the disposal of the monarchy and the highest aristocracy in this early Viking period. In central Sweden the first generations of the kings of the Svear from the sixth century are buried at Old Uppsala (just north of Stockholm) in three monumental barrows (Lindqvist 1936). In the graves, archaeologists found burned traces of magnificent furnishings of gold, ivory, and gems, only matched by finds in royal graves on the continent. The retainers of the Svea kings were buried

4.2, 4.3 JELLING, DENMARK
The eight foot (2.43 meter) high Jelling Stone is one of the most important monuments produced during the Viking Age in Scandinavia. It was erected by King Harald Bluetooth around 965, and bears this inscription: "King Harald ordered these memorials to be made to his father Gorm and his mother Thyra. It was this Harald who won for himself all Denmark and Norway and made the Danes Christian." It is believed that the Danish King Gorm and possibly Queen Thyra were buried in the north mound (far right) before their bodies were removed by Harald Bluetooth, presumably to be reburied at the first Christian church constructed at the royal site of Jelling.

4.4, 4.5

RINGS OF ALLEGIANCE

Kings and chieftains maintained the allegiance of local magnates and retainers by bestowing valuable gifts. In the *Prose Edda*, Snorri Sturluson notes that Old Norse poetry often referred to kings as "givers of rings."

at a number of sites in the Mälar valley, the best known of which are Vendel and Valsgärde (Lamm and Nordström 1983; Graham-Campbell 1994). At each site lie the members of a magnate family, buried in mounds with boats and many rich grave goods, with all the accoutrements of war—ornamental helmets, swords, shields, lances, and horses. Often several horses and sets of weapons were laid in one grave. Weapon fittings and harnesses in gilded bronze were finely decorated with the period's characteristic Norse animal ornamentation. Objects in these central Swedish graves are rife with power symbols and warrior ideology. Among the magnificent helmet decorations, for example, are depictions of warrior heroes, battle scenes, and processions.

Throughout southern Scandinavia, other archaeological finds show that there were similar potentates in Denmark, Norway, and Finland, but no similarly prestigious furnished graves have been discovered there. In Denmark settlement sites and rich hoards reveal the nature of the early monarchy. At Gudme on Funen a large, rich settlement of the third to sixth centuries has been excavated. A central feature of the settlement was a royal residence—an impressive nearly 1,650 square foot (165 square meter) hall (Sørensen 1994). The absence of animal sheds and other utility buildings suggests that the magnate's economy was based on tributes from thirty to fifty ordinary farms nearby. On these farms craftsmen worked, including gold and silversmiths, and their products were traded along the coast. A similar but smaller artisan settlement has been found on the island of Helgö in Lake Mälar, central Sweden (Graham-Campbell 1994). There too, especially in the third to sixth centuries, a fairly large number of craftsmen lived and produced a wide range of products for sale in central Sweden and the Baltic area. Another magnate's hall has been found on Helgö, with many fragments of expensive imported Frankish drinking glasses from western Europe and other luxury products (fig. 8.28). Helgö was later to be superseded by the famous Viking period trading site of Birka (on the island of Björkö a little to the west of Helgö). Gudme and Helgö both show how in this period powerful people began to concentrate trading and

4.6 Neckring
Ibn Fadlan, the early tenth-century Arab diplomat who described Viking life, noted that a silver neckring was a fine gift for a man to give his esteemed wife. They were made from melted Arabic coins and were worn by women as signs of wealth.

craft activities at their residences, which became the first generation of Scandinavian trading places. The magnates aimed to control and profit from this trade, among other ways by levying tribute. In return he offered protection and peace for traders in the market, which was guaranteed by his army.

Kings and Aristocracy of the Viking Age

The king and the aristocracy held power in Viking society, which consisted of two population groups: freemen and bondsmen. According to the customary laws, the local Things (or courts) regulated social interactions; above these was the national assembly Thing, which constituted the highest authority (Fenger 1992). Historical records indicate that the collective made decisions, solved problems, and settled disputes. The Thing debated and attempted to resolve disputes between villages and settlements. At the Things all free, adult, able-bodied men had the right to speak and vote, and the most important function of the Things was to keep the peace in their respective areas. Higher-level policy decisions were in the hands of a far narrower circle of people: the king and the magnates. Their military power and

wealth meant that the Things had to accept the dispositions of the higher powers. That a freeman was free was a qualified truth; some were freer than others, and at the top of the pyramid sat the king and the mightiest magnates of the kingdom.

In the centuries before the Viking period the foundation was laid for a social structure in which the king and the aristocracy gradually assumed greater control over land, production, and trade. In the eighth century the second generation of centrally regulated trading places was established this time with a clear international aim. Such sites as Ribe and Hedeby in Schleswig in old Denmark (present-day Germany) and Birka in Sweden developed in the ninth century into the first Scandinavian towns as a result of the monarchy's growing economic interests.

Archaeologists suspect that several other sites may be royal burials. At Borre, slightly south of Oslo, lies Scandinavia's largest grave field, with nine large mounds and a row of smaller ones (Myhre 1992). The biggest are one hundred to one hundred fifty feet (thirty to forty-five meters) and sixteen to thirty feet (five to seven meters) high. The oldest seem to have been built between A.D. 600 and 650. Because most had been plundered, little is known about the mounds' contents, but in 1852 a ship burial was found in Barrow I with, among other things, prestigious gilded horse trappings from about 900. Borre was thus a dynastic burial field belonging to one of the powerful families in Vestfold.

At some point the family lost its grip on power. The great barrows at Borre were all plundered in the Viking Age, and the people buried there and their most important equipment taken out of the graves. This may have been done as a demonstration of power by a new ruler in Vestfold. The two large Norwegian mounds with ship burials at Oseberg and Gokstad in the Oslo Fjord areas and not far from Borre were also plundered in the Viking Age. There must have been fierce competition among several dynasties: on the one hand among several Norwegian petty monachies, but perhaps also between Norwegian Vestfold kings and the Danish kings. Much of southern Norway, including Vestfold, belonged to Denmark in the ninth century, and the Frankish annals tell us that the Dane Harald Klakk and his brother were sent to Vestfold to put down a rebellion in 813. The more or less permanent competition

Mammen, where a wealthy loyalist to one of the Danish kings was buried in 970 or 971, lies not far from Jelling. The burial chamber contained traditional pagan grave goods—axes, a cauldron, buckets—but a large wax candle showed Christian influence.

among the families in this period led to a constant need to mark and legitimize power and status, and this may explain the many large barrows in the Oslo Fjord area.

OSEBERG

The richest of all the Scandinavian royal graves is the magnificent ship burial at Oseberg, Norway, which was excavated in 1904 (Brøgger, Falk, and Shetelig 1917; Graham-Campbell 1994). In the autumn of 834 a seventy-two-foot (twenty-two-meter) long Viking ship was drawn ashore from Oslo Fjord and placed at the bottom of a half-finished burial mound (fig. 5.8). A burial chamber was built on the deck of the ship, and there a noblewoman and her female

slave were laid to rest. The exact date of the burial is known thanks to dendrochronological dating of the wood used for the burial chamber and to finds of pollen from autumn flowers in the chamber. In the same way it was established that the ship had been built of oak timbers around 820. It was a luxury vessel with fifteen pairs of oars and magnificent carvings on the stern and bows (figs. 4.15, 5.11–5.13), but it would have been unsuitable for sailing on the open seas. The burial goods were sumptuous, worthy of a queen (fig. 4.17). Some goods, unfortunately, including the woman's personal jewelry, had been robbed from the burial chamber. The remaining grave goods are extremely impressive: one ornamental carriage (fig. 4.16), three magnificent sledges for driving in winter (fig. 5.10), one working sledge, one riding saddle, at least twelve horses, three ornate beds and two simple beds, one chair, chests, two tents, wooden buckets with fittings decorated with brass and enamel (fig. 4.14), troughs, cooking vessels, oil lamps, many kitchen utensils, looms, tablets for tablet-weaving, spindles, and food in large quantities. Among the finds were numerous remains of fine textiles—the largest body of textile material from a Viking Age grave (fig. 4.13)—many of which were tapestries and silks, some decorating the walls of the burial chamber.

HEDEBY

Four years after the find of the Oseberg grave, another rich ship burial was excavated just outside the Vikings' great trading center at Hedeby (Müller-Wille 1976). In the Viking Age the area belonged to the Danish king, and Hedeby was situated at the southern border of Denmark (today it is in Germany). Just before 850 a ship around sixty-six feet (twenty meters) long had been sunk in the barrow. Amidships, but below the ship, was found an eight by fifteen foot (2.5 by 4.5 meter) plank-built burial chamber almost seven feet (two meters) high. The bones of the deceased had almost completely disappeared, but rich weaponry shows that the grave had held a prominent man and two warriors of high standing. Three horses were found in a grave below the bow of the ship. The chamber was divided into two rooms with a transverse plank; in one lay the magnate with his magnificent accoutrements, and in the second the two warriors, who had evidently accompanied their lord in death.

4.8 GOLDEN HARNESS BOW

Two harness bow mounts were found in the refuse of a bronzesmith's workshop on what may have been a chieftain's farm not far from the Mammen Church. Such mounts guided the reins across the back of a carriage horse. Both mounts are decorated in Jelling style with gilded animal heads, each of which holds a gripping beast in its mouth.

4.9 MAMMEN AXE
This axe with silver inlay defined the Mammen style and is one of the treasures of the Viking Age. Both sides are decorated, one with a stylized bird, the other with plant ornamentation.

Their weaponry and riding harness show that they were both high-ranking men, and objects among their equipment suggest that they were the dead magnate's cupbearer and marshal. The magnate's grave goods are of far higher quality than those of his two companions. The hilt of his Frankish dress sword is silver-plated and decorated in niello inlay with Christian symbols: doves, snakes, a cross, and the tree of life, which suggest that this was a converted Viking. The sword belt has filigree silver fittings, and harness and saddle for his horse were also finely decorated. He also had spurs, a sheaf of hunting arrows, a shield, a drinking glass, a brass-ornamented wooden bucket with cross motifs, an iron-bound wooden chest, a washbasin of bronze, a knife, a comb, a board game, and food. Sword, belt, spurs, harness, glass, arrows, and the metal-ornamented wooden bucket were not made in Scandinavia; they came from the Frankish kingdom, in what is now Germany; the presence of so many Frankish objects is another remarkable feature of this grave (Wamers 1994, 1995).

JELLING

The royal grave site at Jelling Church in central Jutland, Denmark, is the most impressive burial monument yet recovered. By the village church lie Denmark's two largest burial mounds (fig. 4.3), around 230 feet (70 meters) in diameter and forty feet (ten meters) high, with two runestones and the biggest "stone ship" setting in Scandinavia—an alignment of stones set into the surface of the ground in the shape of a ship—of 560 feet (170 meters). This is one of the rare cases in which a contemporary runic text on two stones describes the monuments. Jelling is such a remarkable site that

UNESCO has designated it as one of the monuments of world culture.

In the tenth century, the Danish kings lived in Jelling, and shortly before 950 one Danish king erected a runestone in memory of his queen, Thyra. His intention is revealed in runes carved on the stone: "King Gorm made these monuments in memory of his wife Thyra, the adornment of Denmark." Among the monuments is a huge ship-shaped stone setting, of which the runic stone may have formed a part. A few years later according to dendrochronological dating of its wood, in 958–959, a large barrow was raised north of where the church now stands, on top of a mound from the Bronze Age. In the newer mound a very large burial chamber of 8.5 by 22 feet (2.6 by 6.75 meters) was built. Shortly after the north barrow had been completed, the building of a similar large barrow south of the church began. This took several years, and one can trace several interruptions in the work. The mound eventually covered the south end of the large stone ship setting. Its purpose remains an enigma, however, because the mound has no grave, but tradition has it that it is the burial mound of Queen Thyra.

The second runic stone at Jelling (fig. 4.2) was erected by King Harald Bluetooth, son of Gorm the Old and Thyra, in the years around 965 to 985. It has been called "Denmark's certificate of baptism," because bringing Christianity to his people is one of the deeds in which King Harald took pride: "King Harald ordered these memorials to be made to commemorate his father Gorm and mother Thyra. It was this Harald who won for himself all Denmark and Norway and made the Danes Christian." Harald was baptized around 960. The occupant of the north mound burial chamber was very likely King Gorm, but after his Christian baptism, King Harald ordered his father be removed from the heathen grave and reburied in the church. Today, the remains of Harald's first wooden church lie under the present Romanesque church. Below the floor a grave chamber has been found, containing the bones of a middle-aged man. Because the bones were not found lying in an anatomically correct position, the body had obviously been reburied. A few pieces of fine belt mountings in gilded silver recovered from this chamber grave are stylistically so similar to other rare goods from the chamber in the north mound that

4.10

Pieces of carved and painted wooden panels from furniture and decorations of very high quality were also recovered from the burial chamber. The circumstances in which the burial chamber was investigated in 1820 were unscientific, and so invaluable cultural information was lost forever.

The monumental ship burials, the royal mounds in Jelling, and the rich furnishings illustrate that the Vikings thought it essential to emphasize the military caste of the deceased and their feudal rule and their absolute power over the life and death of their immediate retinue, including their slaves. The material evidence of their lifestyle shows their far-flung connections with the Frankish empire, or the British Isles, itself a mark of their extraordinary military prowess. At the center of this new Viking military caste was the ship, which made such a lifestyle possible, and which then as now was the symbol of the Viking Age (Wamers 1995: 156f).

Burials of individuals whose status was below that of the people buried in monuments such as Oseberg and Jelling have also revealed brilliant artifacts of Viking Age material culture. At Broa on the Swedish island of Gotland a rich man's grave from about 800 has been found: he had been buried with an ornamental sword, gilt harness, and a stringed instrument. The latter find bolsters evidence in skaldic poetry that music and singing were important social elements in the aristocratic environment. Among the three thousand burials in the grave fields of the Swedish trading town of Birka by Lake Mälar, a number of rich graves have been found (Arbman 1940–43). The grave fields can be divided into a number of groups, and the rich graves, often found clustered together, belonged to the leading families in Birka.

Grave 750 from the mid-tenth century is a good example of Birka's elite graves. Beneath a mound was a wooden chamber grave that contained a man and a woman. The man had been given a sword and a Frankish sword belt with silver fittings, a lance, and a shield. A ring-headed pin of silver fastened his cloak. At the head of the grave was a tool chest with an axe, file, hammer, fire steel, whetstone, and other tools. Beside the chest lay a Frankish drinking glass and a leather bag with Arab silver coins. A game board with twenty-six pieces in colored glass, a wooden bucket, and a bronze wash basin lay

they must have belonged to the same furnishings. King Harald thus probably removed his father from the barrow and on this occasion a ceremony was held to purify the heathen burial chamber.

When the barrow was opened in 1820, a wax candle that must have come from this ritual was found above the burial chamber. Although King Gorm's grave was much damaged during the reburial, as well as by the opening in 1820, the remains of the grave goods show that he had been laid to rest with full honors. Gilded silver fittings from a costly harness and the remains of gold-brocaded textiles testify to his wealth. A fine silver goblet originally had niello inlay in the elaborate animal ornamentation on the outside. The ceiling and walls of the chamber were lined with woolen materials, and by the end wall stood a wooden coffin, which collapsed when the chamber was opened in 1820.

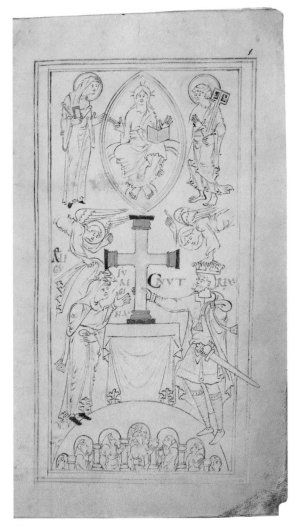

4.11

at the foot of the grave. The woman, who lay close to the man, was wearing a dress and a complete set of jewelry consisting of the Vikings' characteristic oval-shaped brooches and a third, circular brooch—all in gilt bronze. Around her neck she wore amulets: a Thor's hammer and a Christian cross pendant. The couple's draught horse with a harness with gilded and silvered bronze fittings lay on a ledge at the end of the grave. The grave contained many more furnishings, which together indicated that the magnate couple was fully equipped for their journey and their stay in the next life. They would arrive with their magnificent trappings in a fashion appropriate to their rank.

MAMMEN

A fascinating magnate grave was found in Mammen in Jutland (Iversen 1991). In the year 970–971 a powerful magnate was buried in a 6.5 by ten foot (two by three meter) plank-built chamber, and a mound was then raised above the grave. In 1868 the grave was found when workers removed the mound. The preservation conditions were very good, and when it was opened the workers could still see the impression of the buried man in the down pillows on the chamber floor. He was dressed in a fine costume of gold-brocaded silk and embroidered woolen cloth with fur trimmings (figs. 4.10, 4.12). At his feet lay a magnificent axe (fig. 4.9) with silver and brass inlay, as well as a simpler battle-axe. Above the chamber a bronze cauldron had been laid, as well as two wooden buckets and a tall wax candle (fig. 4.7).

The Mammen grave furniture is typical of the magnate graves of the latter half of the tenth century in southern Scandinavia. The quantity of furniture had decreased, but the

few fine objects indicate the high status of the deceased. Christianity has begun to win converts among the elite, as the wax candle, a Christian symbol, found in this grave and several others from the late tenth century suggests (fig. 4.11). Mammen has also contributed another important find from the time around 950: a chest that contained a craftsman's stores of metal, consisting of several gilded-bronze fittings for guides (which regulated the reins to the animals pulling a fine carriage, fig. 4.8) and several bronze dishes and a punch for making jewelry. Perhaps this was a storage place for a craftsman who was affiliated with the magnate's residence in Mammen.

THE ESTATES OF NOBLES

The splendid burials of people belonging to the highest social strata of the Viking Age had a very deliberate aim: to mark and legitimize the nobles' rights to their property and social position. The same signals were sent by the elite's large residences.

New excavations at the central Swedish burial sites Vendel and Valsgärde have revealed magnate residences near the grave fields. Although they were established as early as about 600, the dating of the graves shows that these estates continued far into the Viking Age. This very long lifetime for these estates is by no means uncommon. At the Norwegian grave field near Borre, the large barrows were built between 600 and 900, and the same family probably lived in the related house throughout that period. In Denmark the excavations of the two biggest magnate seats at Old Lejre and Tissø in

4.12

Zealand show that they were both established around the year 600 and continued to be used without interruption until around 1000 to 1050. For four hundred years the same powerful families seem to have had their impressive seats here.

In the Viking Age there were two systems whereby the aristocracy

have been excavated in their entirety. At Old Lejre, Tissø, and Strøby, all in Zealland in Denmark, and at Borg (fig. 2.1) in northern Norway, the extensive excavations reveal the milieu of the estate. The archaeological finds show that besides particularly large halls, there are hoards of precious metals; gold, silver, and gile bronze jewelry of high quality; imported objects; and coins. This testifies to great resources and high consumption compared with the more ordinary farms where one often finds only a little pottery and iron. Raw materials are not found in large quantities in the residential areas of the magnate estates, which indicates that metal was not cast in these splendid halls: manufacturing was done far from the central buildings.

The hall was the prestige building of all Viking estates. This was where the magnate received and entertained guests with great feasts and ceremonies. The Old English epic *Beowulf* from the eighth century and the later Icelandic sagas give detailed accounts of the magnates' and kings' great feasts and banquets, which was one of the social duties of the aristocracy. The power and status of the magnates were measured by how many guests they could entertain. These occasions provided a perfect opportunity for the lord of the estate to show his generosity and economic capacity, perhaps with costly gifts or land, because many prominent persons would be invited and new loyal supporters could be won.

The recently found magnate's seat on the banks of Lake Tissø, Denmark, was a residence belonging to a dynasty at the highest levels of society (Jørgensen n.d.). The seat, begun around 600 and closed down sometime between 1000 and 1050, was rebuilt and expanded several times. This has given archaeologists unique insights into the temporal development of a magnate estate. Around the year 700 it covered an area of 32,700 square feet (10,000 square meters). It grew to about 50,000 square feet (15,000 square meters) around the year 800 and to nearly 60,000 square feet (18,000 square meters) around 900. In the last phase,

4.13, 4.14 BURIAL GOODS FOR A QUEEN

Although some of its jewelry was robbed, the A.D. 834 boat burial at Oseberg, perhaps the resting place of Queen Aasa, is still the most informative archaeological find from a Viking grave. In addition to its wood carvings (figs. 4.15–4.17, 5.13) and the fine buckets decorated with brass and enamel (fig. 4.14), the Oseberg burial also yielded silk and woolen tapestries. This embroidered textile (fig. 4.13) reconstructs the royal procession that probably accompanied the Oseberg queen to her grave.

could procure great wealth: *tribute* from independent people and farms in the form of goods in kind, crafts, prestige objects, precious metals, and rents and *direct farming* of a major estate system by their own retainers. The two systems were not necessarily mutually exclusive, and the tribute system could also have involved the direct farming of large land areas. The economic basis of each estate was manifested in different structures: estate based on tribute had only a few prestigious buildings and generally lacked cattle and storage buildings; estates engaged in direct farming had some prestigious buildings, connected cattle and storage buildings, workshops, and smaller dwelling houses for the work force. Both types of magnate estate are known archaeologically, and much evidence indicates that the slightly older tribute system was gradually superseded by the system of direct farming in the course of the late Viking Age.

The largest magnate estates found hitherto cover areas of as much as 120,000 square feet (40,000 square meters), but very few

around the year 1000, it reached an area of 140,000 square feet (40,000 square meters). Throughout the period monumental halls occupied the central part of the complex.

Among the four thousand metal objects from the Tissø complex is a large body of weapons and riding gear in the form of arrowheads, sword mountings, spurs, and bridles. The aristocratic setting is further underscored by the many magnificent ornaments of gilded silver and bronze, as well as a few of gold. Fragments of Frankish drinking glasses from the area around the central halls confirm that this was where the feasts were held. At a safe distance from the halls lay the smithy and the estate's workshops, where model jewels and bronze punches were found, suggesting that jewelry was crafted at the farm itself. Enameled Irish chest mountings, gilded Frankish belt fittings, and Frankish coins also bear witness to the international connections of the estate. Heathen

4.15 Detail of Cart Drag
The intricate woodworking found on Oseberg pieces, such as this cart drag carved with mythical beasts in a bold roiling style, indicate that professional woodcarvers of the highest caliber prepared the Oseberg queen's funeral entourage. Some pieces reveal traces of painted decoration in red, reddish brown, black, yellow, and off-white.

miniature amulets in the form of Thor's hammers, fire steels, and lances were recovered from the central hall area. A separate enclosed area with only one smallish building connected to the halls may have been a heathen cult area, a so-called *hof*. Next to this enclosure the jaw bone of a three- to four-year-old child was found, something not normally found in ordinary settlements. Support for the idea of a heathen cult site can also be found in the name Tissø, which means literally Tirs' Island, named after the Vikings' war god Tyr (Tir). On the lake bottom near the magnate residence swords, axes, and lances have been found—probably offerings to the war god Tyr.

In 1977 Denmark's finest treasure from the Viking Age was found just outside the gate of this residence—a neckring of four and a half pounds (two kilograms) of gold. It must have been hidden away by the lord of the estate at some time in the tenth century. It represented a fortune, with a gold value corresponding to the price of five hundred head of cattle. The costly ring was probably a king's gift to his loyal supporter on the magnate estate. Because there were not large numbers of stalls for animals, the Tissø magnate's seat was probably not an agricultural estate, and the food was supplied by the dependent farms in the area. Outside the magnate's estate a five to seven acre (two to three hectare) market area was found with pithouses and workshop areas. Goods were traded in this market under the protection of the magnate's army. The magnate levied taxes on the market activities in return for protection and his guarantee of market peace.

Tissø shows that the magnate of the Viking Age had several functions in society. He was responsible for the military protection of the area, he controlled the trade and crafts at the marketplaces, and he was responsible for the heathen cult ceremonies, including the great ritual meals held in the hall. As a leader he was multifunctional: general, priest, great landowner, trade administrator, and social guarantor for his dependents.

Peasants, Craftsmen, and Slaves

Viking Age society did not consist exclusively of kings and magnates, although they have left the most striking archaeological monuments. Most of the free population consisted of peasants, small traders, and craftsmen, who have left far more modest archaeological

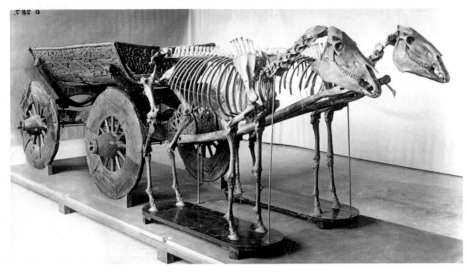

4.16 OSEBERG HORSES AND CART

Although the Oseberg burial is famous for its ornate Viking ship (fig. 5.11), it reveals more than boatbuilding techniques. Its three decorated sleds, carriage with twelve sacrificed horses, and four sleds made a procession fit for a queen entering the afterlife. The wide range of transport vehicles shows that she was equipped for all seasons and would not lack for spares.

RIGHT
4.17 OSEBERG ANIMAL POSTS

Four ornate animal-head carvings were found in the Oseberg burial. Each beastly form was carved by a different artist, some working in an older and more traditional eighth-century style, while others anticipated later stylistic developments. The "academic" artist executed post 3 in a more traditional style, while the "baroque master" executed post 1. The replica of the baroque master's work seen here approximates the look of the original.

traces. The great social differences within this group of freemen is most evident from their graves and farm complexes. Most of the population's economic resources were limited and life must have been a constant struggle, so independent farms would attach themselves to the elites in return for their services.

The farms of the age were not occupied by what we understand today as a nuclear family with parents and their children. These were extended households consisting of the couple owning the farm and their children, grandparents, unmarried brothers and sisters of the owners, foster sons and daughters, and servants. The more prosperous farms probably had slaves in the household. The pagan burial places reveal the hierarchy within the individual family: usually, only the couple owning the farm had relatively prestigious grave furnishings (figs. 4.6, 4.18, 4.19); other members of the household were given fewer furnishings, and many had hardly anything in their graves.

The frequent references to slaves in the Icelandic sagas suggest they were a significant segment of the society, but archaeologically it is difficult to get any impression of their numbers. Did all free Vikings have slaves on their estates, or was this the privilege of the most prosperous? The last is undoubtedly closest to the truth. Although the presence of slaves is not demonstrated at most sites, they do appear in a few special grave finds. At a burial site near Stengade on the island of Langeland in Denmark, a large chamber tomb from the tenth century revealed a prosperous farmer who had been accompanied to the grave by a decapitated man with no furnishings. We must assume that this was a

master and his slave. The Arab diplomat Ibn Fadlan, who went on a journey in 920–922 to the Volga Bulgars in Russia (Foote and Wilson 1980; Jesch 1991), gives a detailed description of the funeral of a Scandinavian Viking chief in a ship. In this ceremony a female slave was executed so that she could accompany her deceased master. Ibn Fadlan's account also has several parallels with the ship burial at Oseberg, where the noble lady was also accompanied by a woman.

The Scandinavian rural population lived in villages of three to ten farms or in settlements consisting of loosely grouped single farms, which permitted a more strategic deployment of the work force for field work. Rural populations quickly established cultivation collectives at the village or settlement level. Many villages in southern Scandinavia are known: Vorbasse, Saedding, Trabjerg, and Omgård, all in Jutland, Denmark (Jørgensen and Skov 1979, Nielsen 1979, Stoumann 1979, Hvass 1993). Farther north in Sweden, Norway, and Finland, rural settlements of scattered farms begin to appear later in the Viking Age.

The structure of the ordinary farms differed in several respects from that of the magnate residences. The main building, or hall, is far smaller than that of the magnate estate and often incorporated stable sections. The large farms have more stable buildings and cattle pens for the large stocks of domestic animals. There are generally few metal finds, which indicates scanty economic resources. Although luxury goods in the style of the magnate estates are not found, these peasants were not poverty-stricken: at many ordinary farms buried hoards have been found with silver coins and silver fragments—from just a few grams to several kilograms of silver. The amount put away against hard times clearly depends on the size of the farm and probably represents the accumulated fortune of the farm.

1

Finely made keys, such as these, once hung from a woman's belt to indicate that she was the mistress of the farm. While men were away, women managed the finances, ran the farm, and kept the keys to the chest where valuables were stored. Evidence of women's social position includes this silver amulet (fig. 4.19), whose elaborate hairdo and jewelry indicate high status.

4.18

The well-investigated villages in Denmark show surprising stability over several hundred years, in the number of farms, which suggests that the so-called free peasants were not all that free. The establishment of new farms and villages was probably controlled by the magnate of the area. In the Viking Age, particularly in the Danish villages, the farms began to have standardized dimensions for their toft, that is, paddocks or enclosed farm areas. This standardization of the paddock size is evidence of centralized control and the existence of a taxation system. One finds whole, half, and quarter farm sizes, where the smaller sizes may have been due to the divided inheritance of whole farms. The toft area would be proportionate with the cultivated area, and on this the

From Warrior to Trade Economy BY LOTTE HEDEAGER

Wealth in the Viking world was not the passive accumulation of gold and silver, hidden away in the ground or in the bottom of a chest, but rather richness in position, alliances, and connections. The Scandinavian societies of the Viking period were open systems in which every single member or individual family had continually to defend his or their position against others, theoretically of equal rank.

Gold and silver were the weapons required in this battle for social position. In skaldic poetry, in the *Poetic Edda*, and in the sagas, gift-giving is described with great precision: fine weapons, gold and silver rings, various items of jewelry, splendid ships, and so on. Gifts were the axis around which the upper stratum of society moved; by means of the gift and the reciprocal gift social systems were continually recreated and status achieved.

The kings and chieftains in this warrior society with its gift economy were not only lords but, above all, open-handed distributors—of weapons, gold, silver, ships, and great feasts. But they were also warlords, for the treasures that entered into the circulation of gifts could not simply be obtained through the fruits of the earth. War, plundering, and piracy, together with great land-holdings, formed the basis necessary for keeping this stream of gifts in motion (left); the chieftain's goal was to secure his reputation so that he could win the best men to his retinue and the most powerful lords as his allies.

European and Arab merchants, who sold goods for money often to complete strangers, entered into transactions that were fundamentally different from the Viking gift economy. A merchant sells goods for money that is used to buy other goods that can be sold for yet more money and so on. But the Vikings who sailed to Staraja Ladoga or Kiev in the land of the Rus or Bulgar on the Volga were not looking for goods that they could buy for resale back in Scandinavia for a certain profit. They were there to get just those goods they needed—Arab silver coins (p. 85). For the Arab merchants, the coins were money, the media of their transaction; for the Vikings these were the object, the commodity itself (Samson 1991b:125–7). Ibn Fadlan, the Arab merchant who wrote about the Vikings he met in Bulgar, states that every single coin they took from the Arab merchants was weighed, and a heavy silver neckring was made for every 10,000 dirhams acquired, which the Vikings gave to their wives as a mark of their wealth (fig. 4.6). Viking weapons, dress accessories, and jewelry were made, often of exceptional artistic quality, from gold and silver coins.

HACKSILVER

Viking warriors and traders returning home with booty and profits converted the silver coins they had collected into armbands, rings, and neckrings. Whole pieces of this jewelry were given as gifts to valued allies or retainers, but these objects were often cut up into pieces to bestow lesser awards or to purchase goods and services.

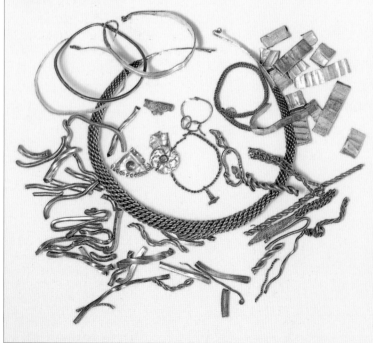

4.19

farmer would have to pay taxes to the local magnate. The same taxation system is known from the Middle Ages, and it clearly existed far back in the Viking Age.

The great trading towns of the Viking Age show that artisans gradually came to form a larger group in society. Their status was not high, and the majority belonged to the group of freemen who, like the peasants, were subject to magnates and the king's taxes. The ablest goldsmiths and armorers may have been slaves, permanently attached to the milieus around the kings and magnates, where they had the opportunity to cultivate their art to perfection (fig. 4.19). Contemporary Frankish legal texts mention compensation sums for the killing of goldsmiths, silversmiths, and smiths with slave status. But many craftsmen were probably part-time farmers or perhaps a combination of trader and artisan, and took up crafts for varying periods with a view to selling their products at the markets.

By the end of the Viking Age in the mid-eleventh century, society was changing in many ways. The monarchy had become far stronger than in the ninth century, and the control of the economic structures of society was becoming better and better organized. A new power that had gained its full strength by the eleventh century was the Christian church, which with sound political sense and broad economic perspective, began a collaboration with the kings and magnates of society that was to last through the subsequent centuries.

VIKING MINT COINS

The earliest coins minted by Vikings, such as those struck in the eighth and ninth centuries, imitated Frisian, Carolingian, and Arab coins. Late tenth-century coins, which imitated Anglo-Saxon coin style, bear the name of the Viking king who had them minted. The faces of the three coins shown here bear the first name of the king who struck it, followed by REX.

During the Viking period the first real trade and production sites—real towns—came into being, such as, for instance, Ribe and Hedeby in Denmark; Birka in Sweden, and Kaupang in Norway. The origin of the earliest Scandinavian towns seems to have been related to a new political order. Any ruler who was able to control such markets could hope for increased wealth and prestige (Sawyer 1982: 73).

The very first towns, whether in Denmark, the Baltic area, or along the North Sea coasts, show evidence of a planned layout organized, protected, and controlled by the king. Maintenance of international contacts, trade in foreign staple goods and raw materials, and production of a wide range of necessities was systematized and concentrated at particular sites by royal instigation. To these ends, kings had coins struck (above) and, by enforcing a monopoly that required weighed silver and foreign coin to be exchanged for the king's own coinage, kings also secured a certain profit, in addition to income from trading fees and tolls (Andrén 1985: 78). The towns, besides securing royal control of the goods necessary to the prestige economy, also provided an income that did not require expensive raiding expeditions to foreign coasts.

Long-distance trade was brought under a royal monopoly, and from their very beginnings the towns were regarded as nodes for an exchange of goods that was meant to secure the best trading goods from abroad for the king (Andrén 1989: 174). The valuable objects had to be purchased either through the conversion of local products or in exchange for other objects obtained by long-distance expeditions. The process fostered an economic valuation of the goods. The result was a gradual separation of the economy from the social ties that drove the system of gift-giving. In other words, the economic system was socially neutralized; it was monetarized and commercialized at the same rate as the gift-giving Viking society decayed. Two widely differing social systems are represented here, one running back into prehistory, the other looking forward into the future.

Adapted from an article published in Journal of European Archaeology (vol. 2, no. 1, 1994:130–148); reprinted with permission from Sage Publications.

ISLAMIC COINS

More than 85,000 Arab coins dating to the ninth and tenth centuries have been found in Scandinavia. Some of this wealth came to Scandinavia through Viking mercenaries who served as bodyguards to the Byzantine emperors, the so-called Varangian guard; others came from Viking traders. The coins were often melted to create wearable wealth or incorporated as ornaments in jewelry and clothing.

5 | SHIPS AND NAVIGATION

BY ARNE EMIL CHRISTENSEN

AT THE BEGINNING OF THE VIKING era, around A.D. 800, shipwrights in Scandinavia were working in a shipbuilding tradition that can be traced to before the birth of Christ and is still being practiced by rural boatbuilders all over Scandinavia. In western and northern Norway, the tradition has changed so little over the centuries that it is possible to ask a living boatbuilder questions about vessels made more than a thousand years ago and get relevant answers. There is a clear continuity in basic techniques, use of materials, detail solutions, terminology, and even some of the hand tools (fig. 5.16). This rare repository of knowledge that extends back a millennium, along with the large number of boat-related finds spread over Denmark, Sweden, and Norway (figs. 5.3, 5.4), has given Scandinavian archaeologists a unique opportunity for understanding and interpreting the technology and art of Viking shipbuilding.

The Vikings sunk ships and boats as gifts to the gods in holy lakes that have turned into bogs, preserving the wood to this day. Before the Christian era, some Vikings were buried in vessels, and in a few lucky cases wood has been preserved. Usually only the iron nails and rivets are left (fig. 5.6), but they are sometimes found in undisturbed rows, permitting a reconstruction of the lines of the lost vessel. With the adoption of Christianity around .D. 1000 this practice, and thus this source of ships, disappears. Archaeologists have also recovered ships from the end of the Viking Age and early Middle Ages that were used to block harbors and wrecks, which are valuable for the study of a continuing shipbuilding tradition. Norse poems and sagas, written down in the early medieval period when ships had not changed much since the Viking Age, provide valuable sources, as do the pictures of ships that were carved on wood or bone or cut into stone.

The basic principle used by shipbuilders was to shape a watertight shell of overlapping planks, fastened together at the overlaps (fig. 5.1). When the builder had finished the shell, he stabilized the shape and added some stiffness to the construction by inserting ribs inside the planking. This technique, named shell building, was the only way ships were built in northern Europe until the late Middle Ages, when a new method was adopted from the Mediterranean. In the new southern technique, a skeleton of keel, stems, and ribs was erected first, and then covered with planks that did not overlap and were fastened not to one another, but only to the ribs.

The oldest Norse vessel built of planks in the shell technique is a third-century .. boat from Hjortspring, Denmark. A broad bottom plank, which is curved both across and along the hull, forms the backbone of the vessel. Two side planks and two top planks (or sheerstrakes) were sewn to ribs to form the shell. Heavy blocks of wood standing on the bottom plank close the hull

5.1 VIKING SHIPBUILDING

The Bayeux Tapestry, which commemorates the Norman invasion of England by William the Conqueror in 1066 and was completed about 1077 for the consecration of the cathedral in Bayeux, contains the only contemporaneous illustration of Viking ship construction. Carpenters are seen felling trees, trimming timbers, and building up the hulls of two vessels that were destined for the Norman invasion fleet.

5.2 SAGA SIGLAR AT SEA

Much has been learned about sailing characteristics of Viking ships by using replicas such as the *Saga Siglar* (Saga Sailor) modeled after archaeological finds. Surprising results of these sailing tests show that oceangoing Viking ships could sail within 70 degrees of the wind.

at both ends, giving the boat a profile that closely resembles ships seen in Bronze Age and early Iron Age Scandinavian rock art. The Hjortspring boat is built of lime, a light and soft wood that is easy to work, while Viking shipbuilding is based on stronger, heavier, and more sturdy woods such as oak and pine. Pine dominates the northern parts of Scandinavia, where oak does not grow, but the Viking finds indicate that oak was the preferred wood for shipbuilding in those parts of Scandinavia where it was available. Lacking oarlocks, the Hjortspring boat was propelled by about twenty men who paddled rather than rowed.

From the beginning of the third century A.D. some boatbuilders started to use iron rivets instead of lashing the planks together. A third-century ship sacrificed in a bog at Nydam in southern Jutland (near the present-day border between the Danish peninsula and Germany), has many of the characteristics still found in Norse clinker vessels, whose planks overlap like clapboard on a house (Crumlin-Pedersen and Rieck 1993). On the Nydam vessel, sturdy curved stems have replaced the end blocks of the Hjortspring ship. The ribs are made from naturally curved timbers instead of thin bent rods, and the fastenings in the planking are of iron (fig. 5.6). The boat is built on a sturdy bottom plank and has five planks of enormous size on each side. Thirty men were needed to row the nearly ninety-foot (twenty-three-meter) ship. Its oars rested in hook-shaped oarlocks of a type still used in Scandinavia. The earliest example of such oarlocks, which were found in a bog at Mangersnes in western Norway, are a few centuries older than the Nydam ship; this suggests that the change from paddling to rowing took place around the birth of Christ.

Scandinavians were surprisingly late in adopting the sail (fig. 5.5). Although the sources are admittedly limited, they strongly indicate that until around 700, ships were rowed. The early seventh-century vessel from Sutton Hoo in East Anglia, part of a Saxon-style princely burial that was preserved only as an impression in the sand, and the early eighth-century Kvalsund ship from western Norway, may both have set a sail (Shetelig and Johannessen 1929). Their hull shapes indicate, however, that they can only have been efficient when sailing downwind.

Scandinavians may have been so late in adopting sails, which had been in use for centuries in waters as close as the English

5.3 BRONZE WEATHERVANE
Illustrations of Viking ships on picture stones and on a scrap of wood from Bergen show some ships carrying a triangular vane at the prow. This decoration in the eleventh-century Urnes style is made of gilded copper. Such vanes may have functioned as wind indicators in Viking times, but their elaborate design suggests they also had social and ritual meaning.

5.4 VIKING FLEET GRAFFITI (REPLICA)
A remarkable piece of casual Viking art was recovered during the excavation of medieval Bryggen Harbor in Bergen, Norway. The memory of Viking ships and perhaps tales of the great battles that raged between rival Viking kings in early times may have inspired this elegant bit of graffiti showing fleets of Viking ships in receding perspective.

Channel, because the Nordic type of hull was not well developed and strong enough to withstand the stresses set up by sail and rigging until around 800. It is tempting to suppose that the Viking Age did not start until the sail was in use and sailors had mastered this new invention (fig. 5.3).

BOAT GRAVES

Viking Age belief, which was based on older Germanic and circumpolar beliefs, called for well-equipped graves. The nature and quantity of what was deposited in the grave differs within Scandinavia, but most Viking Age graves contain some grave goods, with much of the same equipment used by the living interred for the next life after death. A rich burial probably raised the prestige of the heirs as well as that of the dead person. Along the coast and inland waterways, boats are often part of the burial. This may reflect a

belief that the land of the dead lay across water. Another theory is that the boats indicate that the dead person was active in the cult of the fertility god Frey, who was associated with transportation themes. Other scholars argue that the presence of a boat, which was a necessary tool for living life in the other world, suggests that ancient people expected life in the other world to resemble that of the living. The custom of burying a boat in a grave mound precedes the Viking Age by many centuries, but the use of really large ships is extremely rare before around 800. We know of two instances, one at Sutton Hoo in East Anglia, England, which is based on the Germanic Saxon model, and one at Karmøy in western Norway. The use of boat graves continued in northern Russian and Baltic countries into the nineteenth century and is still practiced by some Siberian peoples today.

In most cases only lines of iron rivets indicate that a ship or boat was part of the funerary equipment. Some burials are cremations, in others all wood has rotted. In the outer Oslo Fjord area, where the subsoil is blue clay, the clay formed a hermetic seal on a few grave mounds (fig. 5.8a), including those at Gokstad, Oseberg, and Tune and preserved wood, textiles, and leather remarkably well (fig. 5.9). The ships found at Oseberg and Gokstad are nearly complete, that from Tune is less well preserved (Bonde and Christensen 1993; Brögger and Shetelig 1951; Nicolaysen 1882; Shetelig 1917 a,b). In all three graves, rich equipment was loaded on board the ship for the funeral, but the graves were later robbed. The wood, leather, and textiles did not interest the robbers, but fine arms and jewelry that were probably part of the grave goods are gone (fig. 5.10). Very little was left in the Tune ship (fig. 5.7), whose condition was originally as good as the two other ships. The ships were dated to the ninth century by comparing the wood carvings of Oseberg and Gokstad with other Viking art. Recently, the year-rings of the wood have been studied and more precise dendrochronological dates have been established. The Oseberg ship (fig. 5.11) was built around 815–820 and those found at Gokstad (fig. 5.12) and Tune shortly before 900. In the case of Oseberg, timbers from the burial chamber had the outermost year-ring intact, giving a remarkably precise date for the burial (fig. 5.8b).

This scene from the Bayeux
Tapestry shows Viking ships and
armed warriors under full sail.
The tapered sails are likely an
artistic convention: Viking sails
were square and were made of
oiled woolen cloth. The steering
oar (*styri*) was mounted on the
right-hand (*styrbord*) side of the
vessel, and this term has persisted
into modern nautical language,
as starboard.

The logs were cut in the summer of 834, and
as timber was certainly used straight from the
forest, this dates the burial to that year.

The three ships are housed in the Viking
Ship Museum in Oslo, together with the rich
equipment found in the graves. The oak of
the ships was so well preserved that slow drying and several coats of linseed oil was the
only conservation necessary. After 1,100 years
buried in clay, the oak is brittle but has still
retained enough strength for the ships to
carry their own weight with sufficient support. Other finds from Oseberg, made of
less-durable wood than oak, had to undergo
lengthy conservation after the excavation in
1904. The Gokstad ship was less damaged
than that found at Oseberg and could be
taken out of the mound in two large fragments when excavated in 1880. It was exhibited for nearly fifty years with no restoration.
After being moved to its present location in
1929, the ship was dismantled and rebuilt,
using the technique developed for Oseberg.
Not enough was left of the Tune ship for a
complete and certain reconstruction, and
stands as it came from the burial mound
in 1867.

All three ships are of the same general
type, and it is believed that they are the
personal traveling ships of royal owners.
Men were buried in the graves at Gokstad
and Tune, but the fragmentary skeletons of
two women were found at Oseberg, the richest Viking grave ever recovered. The amount
and quantity of equipment included in the
grave is a strong indicator of the high status
of women in Viking Age society.

The Oseberg ship is the earliest sailing
vessel found in Scandinavia (figs. 5.11, 5.13).
Many improvements to the rowing vessels of
earlier centuries have been introduced: the
bottom plank has developed into a true keel;
the seats of the oarsmen have changed function and become crossbeams, firmly fixed to
an extra strong strake at the waterline. The
beams form transverse braces that can withstand the stresses set up by wind pressure in
the rigging. The ship's sides are higher, supported by knees on the crossbeams. In order
to set the oars at the optimal distance above
the water, oar holes have been cut in the top
strake instead of using oarlocks. The mast is
stepped in a keelson, a longitudinal oak
structure resting on the keel, and additional
support is given by a "mast partner," a sturdy
block of oak resting on the crossbeams. The
mast partner has a long opening facing aft,
so the mast could be lowered and raised at
sea by the crew. In contemporary pictures
the mast is shown supported by ropes.

Earlier ships had rounded bottoms
while the bottom of the Oseberg ship has
a pronounced V-shape. Together with the
deeper keel, this gives the hull better sailing
qualities, especially when beating against
the wind. The planking is about one inch
(2.5 centimeters) thick, not much for a ship
eighty-five feet (twenty-two meters) in
length. The light planking and the lashing
holding them to the ribs make a light, flexible hull. The woodworkers of the Viking
Age did not use saws (fig. 5.1). Huge oak logs
were converted to planking by splitting the
log in first two, then four, then eight, and
finally sixteen wedge-shaped planks, which
were axed to shape and finished with scrap-
ing tools. Before the planks were riveted
together, a tarred string of wool was placed
in the overlap to ensure that the hull did not
leak. It is difficult to split long trees, so each

5.6 Ship Rivets

Lapstrake or shell-type hull construction did not require heavy framing; the strakes were both skeleton and shell, making for lightweight boats. Planks were riveted outboard of the plank below, producing a vessel that "rode up" in the water, reduced spray, and could be assembled rapidly. This form exposed iron fastenings to saltwater, so they rusted quickly and needed to be replaced frequently.

5.7 The Tune Burial

Unlike the Oseberg and Gokstad vessels, the vessel recovered from Tune in 1867 was poorly preserved and has not been completely restored. This was the first Viking ship to be excavated from a burial mound in Oslo Fjord, and it is presented in the Viking Ship Museum exactly as it came out of the ground.

5.8 a

plank was scarfed (joined) from several pieces to make up the length of the hull. The two fitting pieces had their ends worked to a feather edge and were then riveted together. To avoid leaks and damage to the thin edge, all scarfs open aft; this rule is so universal that it can be used to decide whether a fragment of planking belongs to the starboard or port side of a ship.

Axes seem to have been the primary tool for working wood, but the shipwrights needed large and small augers for boring holes, scrapers for finishing and making decorative moldings along the planks, and a hammer for riveting. The repetition of certain measurements in preserved vessels indicates that an "ell," a measuring tool of about 18 to 21 inches (47 or 55 centimeters), may have been used in Norway. The ells are known from medieval sources, and the 55-centimeter ell is still used for building small boats in western Norway.

Viking Sailing Ships

The Oseberg ship was probably a royal yacht for inshore use because it is less seaworthy than the more utilitarian ships found at Gokstad and Tune. The year-ring dates suggest another reason for the differences in design, which had become more sophisticated as the result of three generations of intense shipbuilding activity on the North Sea. Oseberg is the oldest true Viking ship found to date and is probably typical of the vessels used for the early Viking raids around 800. Certain design elements of a sailing ship are still rather undeveloped: the Oseberg ship could have been sailed successfully from Norway to Britain or Ireland in summer, but she is a much less seaworthy ship than the younger vessels (fig. 5.15). Many vessels were lost during the early period of sailing ships, and some crews must have barely reached home after narrow escapes. The Gokstad vessel has a hull shape that is much more seaworthy than Oseberg, with a higher freeboard and sturdier support for the mast.

At that time, the art of sailing was not old in Scandinavia, but the sailing ship, even in its early form, must have been a tool that gave the Norsemen a tactical advantage over Anglo-Saxon, Frankish, and Irish opponents, who did not use sailing ships. One reason for their success is that the crew of a sailing ship

5.8 b   5.9

5.8 a, b OSEBERG BURIAL MOUND
The famous Oseberg ship burial was
excavated from this mound in the
Oslo Fjord. The blue clay of the
burial site, impermeable to air, preserved the vessel and its contents for
more than one thousand years (fig.
5.8 b). The local place-name of the
site, Oseberg ("Aasa's mounds"),
suggests linguistic continuity from
Viking times, for this is thought to
be the final resting place of Viking
Queen Aasa.

5.9 THE OSEBERG EXCAVATION
This photograph, taken in 1904
while the Oseberg excavation
was underway, speaks eloquently
about the social context of
archaeology in Norway at the
turn of the century: the all-male
crew is attired in fine dress and
standing at the bottom of a clay
pit. Dendrochronology has revealed that the ship was built in
815–820 and was last repaired
in 834, probably for the burial.

5.10 OSEBERG SLEDS
The burial ritual at Oseberg
included elaborate preparations for
transport to the afterlife. In addition
to an ornate cart (fig. 4.16), several
highly decorated sleds were found.
Such carving would not have been
done simply for prestige or aesthetic
reasons. The Oseberg art probably
played a role in protecting the deceased from harm in the unpredictable journey ahead.

would have arrived in much better fighting
shape than a crew tired from rowing; another
is that because the Viking ships had shallow
drafts they could land on any suitable beach,
well away from defended harbors. The ships'
ability to tack against the wind gave the
Vikings a third tactical advantage: it was
possible to make a quick raid and get away
before a defense could be organized, even if
the wind was not blowing away from the land.

The development of sailing ships did
not do away with rowing all together: the
Gokstad ship has oar holes for thirty-two
crew-members and the Oseberg ship for
thirty. Oar-ports seem to have been standard
equipment for as long as Viking-type vessels
were used for warfare. All Viking ships have a
side rudder or steering oar mounted on the
right side aft. The Old Norse name for a rud-

der is *styri*, and that side of the ship where the
rudder was fastened hundreds of years ago is
still *stýraborð* in the Scandinavian languages
and starboard in English.

Experiments with replicas of Viking
ships in recent years show that they are remarkably fast and tack well against the wind
(fig. 5.2). We know little of the ships of the
Irish, Franks, or Anglo-Saxons. Irish seafaring
seems to have been based on skin-covered
curraghs, which must have been easy prey for
the larger wooden ships of the Norsemen.
When Alfred of Wessex established a navy to
counter the Viking attacks around 890, the
chronicle states that he did not build ships on
either the Norse or the Frisian model, but as
the king himself thought they would be most
efficient. This report suggests that there was
no obvious Anglo-Saxon model for building
warships. The Carolingian empire had a navy,
but it seems to have played a minor role in the
defense against the Vikings. The Viking ships
were troop transports rather than warships.
The ram, a favorite naval weapon in classical
Mediterranean ships, was not used in the
north, and sea battles were fought with infan-
try tactics, generally by lashing several ships
together to make stable fighting platforms.
The maritime supremacy of the Vikings is
probably best demonstrated by the fact that,
as far as we know, no attempt was ever made
by Franks or Anglo-Saxons at striking back
across the sea. There are no sources indicating
that Frankish or Anglo-Saxon troops ever
sailed north across the sea to plunder the
coasts of the Viking homelands in revenge.

5.11

5.11, 5.12
VIKING SHIP DESIGN

The Oseberg vessel, with its low sweeping hull and soaring prow scroll, has few rivals for simplicity and elegance of nautical design (fig. 5.11). Those inclined toward open ocean sailing find more nautical security in the Gokstad ship's lines (fig. 5.12), with its greater beam and deeper hull. The beauty of both ships is matched by their display in the Viking Ship Museum.

5.13 OSEBERG PROW

Parts of the Oseberg prow did not survive one thousand years of burial. However, fragments of the terminal scroll bearing the image of a serpentine beast were drawn for the scientific record, and later the drawings were used to reconstruct the vessel for public exhibition.

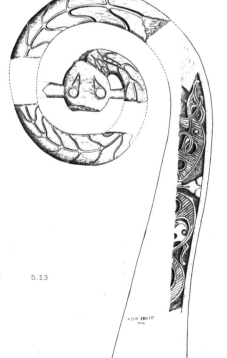

5.13

DIVERSITY FOR WAR AND TRADE

During the tenth century, society in the Viking homelands changed. Central kingdoms became more powerful, and trading centers developed into towns. About this time the old all-purpose vessels like that found at Gokstad were developed along two lines (fig. 5.14). Long, slender warships, propelled by sail and oars and intended only to carry men and arms, were built for the king and chieftains. People who traded to the towns or went abroad to find new land used the broader-beamed sailing ships, which were seaworthy and capable of carrying more cargo.

Twice in the eleventh century the channel leading to the town of Roskilde in Denmark was blocked to prevent enemy ships from entering. Old ships, stripped of all equipment, were filled with stones and sunk. A large-scale excavation in 1962 rescued the ships, which have been restored and are exhibited in the Viking Ship Museum, Roskilde (Olsen and Crumlin-Pedersen 1968). While the museum was being enlarged in 1997, more ships came to light in the old harbor of Roskilde.

The preserved material of recovered ships is so small that they do not document for certain when more specialized ships for war and trade were developed, but the tenth century is the most likely period. The eleventh-century find from Skuldelev in Roskilde Fjord shows that the two subtypes had become firmly established. Warships are long and slender, extremely so, judging from the cases of the fragmentary ships found in the harbors of Hedeby and Roskilde. They retain the oar-ports all along the side, in part because warships were staffed with a large crew to row the ship in a calm or contrary wind, and the narrow ships had high potential for speed. The Skuldelev wreck 5 (fig. 5.14b) is a small warship, much repaired and built with some planks recycled from an older ship. The excavator Ole Crumlin-Pedersen has suggested that this was one of the ships that farmers along the coast were obliged to build for defense purposes and which the king could commandeer for military purposes. The other warship (fig. 5.14a)—originally believed to be two ships because of its length—has been shown to have been built from Irish oak, but in all probability it is the work of a Norse shipwright working in Dublin. To take a ship as slender and low on the water as this one across the Irish and North

seas, even in summer, is a feat for daring and clever sailors.

The merchant ships—Skuldelev wrecks 1 and 3 and the small freighter wreck 6—show another picture. Wreck 3 is built of oak and shows many similarities to the small warship (fig. 5.14d). They may both have been built near Roskilde. Wreck 3 is a small coaster, less slender than the warships, but with elegant lines and good workmanship. It has an open hold amidships for cargo and small decks fore and aft for working the ship. It can carry about 4.5 tons of cargo and can be sailed by five men. In and out of the harbor, or in a calm, a few oars can be used fore and aft. The large merchantman, wreck 1, and the small freighter or fishing vessel 6 are both built of pine from western Norway. There was no lumber trade at that time, as far as we know, so these ships must have been built in western Norway. Wreck 1 is a sturdy, broad vessel, well suited to the rough seas of the North Atlantic (fig. 5.14c). It has the same open hold amidships and small decks fore and aft as number 3, but the cargo capacity is much larger, about twenty-four tons. Five to six men can sail the ship, but in the Viking Age, no sensible merchant would risk his cargo with so small a crew, because pirates might wait behind the next island. A few rich men of the upper class might have goods to fill such a ship, but the general trading pattern was probably the one described in the Norwegian medieval laws, where it is stated that when a ship-owner wants to travel to a market, he should make his intention known. People with goods to sell would then hire space for their wares by working as crew members. The possibility of overloading is regulated, and "a ship which requires bailing three times in twenty-four hours will be declared seaworthy for all kinds of travel; but if they so wish, the crew can entrust themselves to a ship which requires more frequent bailing." The *Grágás*, or Icelandic lawbook, even stipulates a plimsoll mark, a technical measurement of ship draft, which requires that two-fifths of the ship's height amidships be above water.

In comparing the Oseberg, Gokstad, and Tune ships on one hand with the Skuldelev ships on the other, we see that hull shape and technical solutions have changed somewhat. The Norwegian ships still have the traditional solutions of ribs

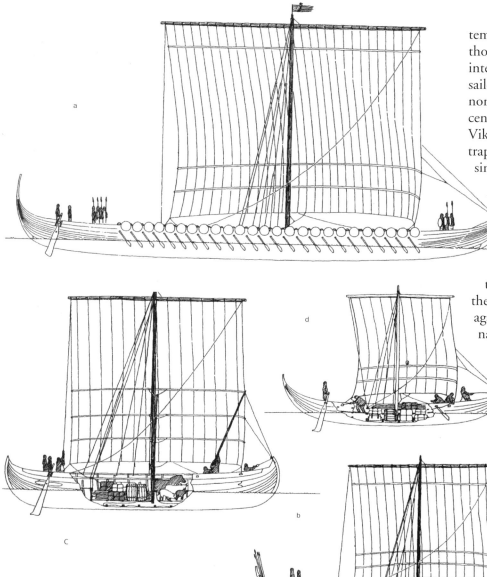

temporary record of rigging and sails, although it is often a complicated source to interpret. More informative are the square-sailed fishing boats used in western and northern Norway until the beginning of this century whose hulls have changed little from Viking times. The sails are rectangular or trapeze-shaped and controlled by fairly simple rigging. A yard stretches the sail along the upper edge, and a halyard to hoist the sail runs from the middle of the yard, through a hole near the top of the mast and down. From the bottom corners of the sail ropes (known as sheets) run aft to control the sail when the ship is sailing with the wind from behind. When tacking against the wind, the sail is stretched diagonally across the vessel.

Replicas of the nineteenth-century fishing boat rig have sailed well, using the potential of the hull for speed and tacking ability. Written sources and fragmentary finds show that wool was used for sailcloth, which people accustomed to the thin, light sailcloth of today find surprising. The breed of sheep raised by the Scandinavians produced wool different from that of modern sheep that was more suitable of wool for sailcloth. The outer hairs of this sheep are long and straight, well suited to spinning strong yarn, and if the wool was not washed, as the custom is today, it contains sufficient lanolin to be water repellent. In the Viking Age, spinning was done with a spindle, a much slower process than using a spinning wheel. Weaving was done on an upright loom where the warp was stretched by clay or stone loomweights. The weavers worked standing, beating the weft up. The effort used to collect and sort wool and spinning and weaving sailcloth must have been equal to that of building the ship. More than 930 square feet (one hundred square meters) of cloth was needed to make a sail for the Gokstad ship, enough to make a set of clothes for a crew of about forty. Textile work was clearly a female responsibility, so a Viking shipmaster must have had the support of women to sail.

Much Viking seafaring took place within sight of land, and the pilots' knowl-

5.14 VIKING SHIPS DIVERSIFY
During the past twenty years several well-preserved late Viking boats recovered from the mud of Roskilde Fjord in Denmark have given Viking ship experts new information. Reconstructions revealed large (a) and small (b) warships (Skuldelev 4 and 5), an oceangoing vessel (c) (Skuldelev 1), and a coastal merchant vessel (d) (Skuldelev 3). One had the construction of the oceangoing vessels that sailed the North Atlantic; its higher sides, second deck, and extra trusses could withstand heavy seas and provided minimal shelter for cargo, animals, and crew.

lashed to cleats on the planking, while the ribs of the Skuldelev ships are fastened by wooden dowels called treenails. The mast support of the merchant ships is simplified: instead of the mast partner resting on the crossbeams, additional crossbeams steady the mast. The Skuldelev warships are long and slender, with seats for many oarsmen. The merchantmen are broader for taking more cargo, and they rely mainly on sail. These changes most likely took place during the tenth century.

SAILING AND NAVIGATION

On the island of Gotland in the Baltic, richly carved picture stones (figs. 3.1, 3.2) were raised in memory of the dead. On many other stones from the Viking Age a ship is depicted, providing the most detailed con-

edge of good landmarks was important. The rocky coasts of Norway and parts of the Baltic have an abundance of natural landmarks that were often enhanced by stone cairns (piles). The low coasts of Denmark may have given navigators problems, and this is where some of the oldest man-made landmarks were built in the Middle Ages. In Norway the landmarks, mainly characteristic mountains, are featured in fairy tales that explain them as petrified trolls and giants, who in the old days had their quarrels and friendships. The stories told on board not only passed the time but instructed young crewmen in the art of navigation: such tales helped the sailors remember the landmarks.

On the high seas ships sailed day and night. The Old Norse name of Polaris, the north star, *Leiðarstjarna*, clearly indicates that its position was known and probably used. In summer the northern skies of the North Atlantic are too light for stars to be seen, but early and late in the sailing season stars may have been used for navigating. Few people sailed in open water during winter when the best fishing often occurs, but inshore fishery probably took place also in winter. Around 1230 a father in Norway wrote a book of instructions for his son, including this advice about the life of a merchant:

> If you prepare for trade across the sea and own your ship, tar it well in the autumn and let it stay tarred over the winter, if possible. But if your ship is beached so late in autumn that it cannot be tarred, tar it early in spring and let it dry well. Own shares in good ships, or none. Make your ship pleasant, you will then get good men as crew members. Get ready in early summer and travel at the height of summertime. Have sturdy gear, and do not

stay at sea late in autumn, if possible. When setting out, take with you two to three hundred ells of wadmal suitable for mending sails, plenty of needles, twine, and rope for reefpoints. You need nails, axe, gouge, auger and all other tools for shipbuilding.

There is little reason to doubt that the Vikings followed similar rules.

Navigating the Open Sea

The techniques of coastal sailing are fairly well understood, but there has been much debate about how people navigated in the Viking Age when they were out of sight of land. The *Hauksbók* (an Icelandic manuscript) gives directions for sailing from Norway to Greenland. The starting point is Hernar, on the coast north of Bergen, with a course set to the west. On a clear day the Shetland Islands would be visible; the next landmark is the Faeroe Islands. The sailor would meet whales and see seabirds south of Iceland, but never sight the land before arriving at the southern tip of Greenland. This description is highly instructive because it adapts coastal sailing techniques—moving from landmark to landmark—to the high seas. Including start and landfall, it identifies five landmarks to navigate across the North Atlantic Ocean. No landmark on Greenland is mentioned, but later medieval sources tell of a characteristic snow-clad mountain that could be seen from far out at sea. The same source gives sailing time between important places in Norway, Iceland, and Ireland: four to five days from Norway to Iceland was normal. When Leif Eriksson set out from Greenland to find the land Bjarni Herjolfsson had seen

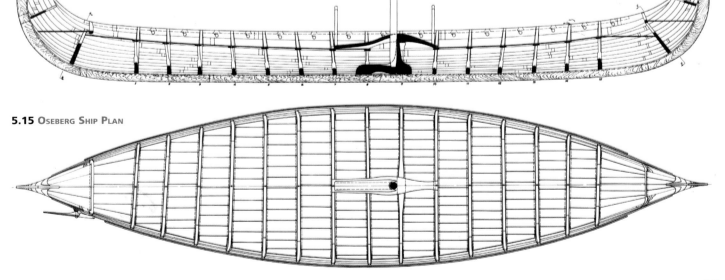

5.15 Oseberg Ship Plan

when he was blown off course while voyaging from Iceland to Greenland, a set of landmarks were described for him to find his way. The question is, was there really nothing else to help sailors cross the ocean?

Traveling from Denmark, ships could have contact with the coast all the way to Gibraltar and into the Mediterranean. When going to England from northern Denmark or eastern Norway, a course set *útsuð* would cross the North Sea in two to three days. The traffic from western Norway to Scotland or the Irish Sea probably went by the Shetland and Orkney islands, so the stretches of open sea would be fairly short. The Baltic and the Russian rivers could be sailed by landmarks. Only the voyages from Norway or Ireland to Iceland and Greenland called for sailing out of sight of land for many days. In the description of the voyage from Norway to Greenland no mention of tools used for navigation can be found in the text; apparently the sailor had to learn how to use nature as a guide.

Some researchers, many of them navigators and sailors, have maintained that Viking Age navigation was very advanced and based on a sophisticated knowledge of astronomy. Most of the written sources are Icelandic and date well after the Viking Age. Some of the Icelandic sagas tell of men who were knowledgeable about stars. About a century after the Viking Age, a gifted astronomer known as Star-Oddi lived in northern Iceland. It is not known if he was literate himself, but some of his astronomic observations have been written down and preserved. He seems to have had no connection with the astronomy practiced by the church, which was mainly aimed at establishing the right dates for moveable feasts. Oddi used the diameter of the sun as his measuring unit and seems to have been ignorant of degrees. We do not know if he used instruments. Although his work has been cited as evidence for astronomic navigation in the Viking Age, in the opinion of this writer, he was an astronomer on land, not a navigator at sea, and when he lived, the Viking Age was already history.

Some men of the church took the interest in astronomy further than what was necessary for establishing feast days. Another Icelander, bishop Nicolas of Tverá, went on a pilgrimage to Jerusalem around 1150. He reports that when he lay on his back near the river Jordan, bent his knee, and placed his fist on the knee with outstretched thumb, the polestar "rested" on the thumb. This clearly proves that the bishop knew that different latitudes could be deduced by the height of stars above the horizon, knowledge that was necessary for "latitude" sailing.

One possible latitude observation is described in the *Greenlander's Saga.* It notes that on a certain day, the sun set at a named point on the horizon, which showed that Vinland was far south of Greenland. Neither the day nor the point on the horizon can be identified with full certainty, however, and the observation has been used to place Vinland in widely different places on the east coast of North America. The observation was made on land and offers no proof that similar observations were used for navigation at sea.

In the light northern summer nights, stars are not visible for use as navigational aids. Polaris was known and could be used to find north when it could be seen. On clear days, the sun would help in establishing directions, but the combination of fog and calm caused problems. The condition was known as *hafvilla* in Old Norse, meaning to lose your way at sea. One saga tells of a long debate in the ship's council on where to set a course when the sun was again visible after some foggy days.

There is general agreement that the magnetic compass was not known in northern Europe in the Viking Age. The sea chart and the log are also later inventions. The *St. Olaf's Saga* includes a story of a man who claims to know the cardinal points even when the sun is not visible. The king checks this out on a snowy winter day with the help of his "sunstone." Some readers assert that the saga passage is a reference to a feldspar, a crystalline mineral that polarizes light and shows where the sun is, even when it is below the horizon. Although the double-refractive feldspar found in Iceland has this property, no such stone has been found in a Viking Age context. Such crystals may have been the prized secret of a few people, but it is highly doubtful that it was a common navigation tool.

One much-discussed artifact is a fragmentary disc of wood found in the ruins of a Norse farm in Greenland. This has been interpreted as a bearing dial, or a kind of shadow compass, which uses the sun for orientation(fig. 20.5). It is a fragment, a little more than half a circular disc of pine with a diameter of two and one-half inches (seventy to seventy-two millimeters). Triangular

5.16 Vittangi Boat

Viking ship construction continues today in Scandinavia, including production of Viking replicas, small homemade utility vessels, and vessels used by native Saami such as the one shown here from Vittangi in northernmost Sweden. Perhaps someday it will be shown that the design of Viking ships did not originate in the southern Baltic and Europe, but from boatbuilding traditions of the northern boreal forests, which also survive today.

notches are cut around the edge, and several straight and curved lines mark the surface; in the middle is a hole. The first to identify it as a navigation instrument was the maritime historian and navigator Carl V. Sølver (1954), who built a reconstruction as a bearing dial with a central sighting pin, a pointer, and thirty-two points, like an old-fashioned marine compass. The reconstruction came under heavy criticism as idealized mainly because triangles on the points of the original are far less evenly spaced than the reconstruction. The object has later been reinterpreted not as a bearing dial, but as a sun compass (Vebæk and Thirslund 1992). The shadow from a central pin would be measured against the lines scratched on the surface: on a westerly course, a shadow that was too long would indicate that the ship was too far north; too short a shadow meant the ship was too far south. Although modern computer-calculated shadow compasses do work, the lack of precision in the points around the edge makes this interpretation just as doubtful as the bearing dial theory. Again, there is no proof that either instrument was known or used by the Vikings.

Understanding the prevailing wind and wave systems of the North Atlantic may have been important to navigation; recognizing flight patterns of birds, the migration of whales in coastal waters, and the tendency of clouds to form over land could also have assisted sailors in establishing bearings. The first man who settled in Iceland is said to have brought ravens with him on board the ship. When they were let loose, one of them rose to a great height before flying straight ahead; the ship followed and found land. This method of finding land is possible, but the legend is probably a literary loan from the Old Testament and the story of Noah's dove. Shipwreck was far more common than it is today. When Erik the Red set out to colonize Greenland, less than half of the ships reached their destination, and the rest were driven back to Iceland or wrecked.

From the early-ninth-century Oseberg ship to the mid-eleventh-century Skuldelev wreck 1, we see great changes in the hull shape of the Viking ships. The basic concept of a fairly light and flexible clinker-built shell with no permanent deck is unchanged, but there is more weight on seaworthiness and sailing ability. Generations of experience in sailing the North Atlantic ocean produced ships capable of reaching Iceland, Greenland, and North America. The Viking expansion, in Europe as well as across the North Atlantic, was possible first and foremost because of superb shipbuilding.

II VIKING RAIDERS

INTRODUCTION

THE VIKING AGE IN EUROPE

BY CHRISTOPHER D. MORRIS

MOST PEOPLE ASSOCIATE THE BEGINNING of the Viking Age in Europe with the oft-quoted accounts of raids by Scandinavians on the coasts of the British Isles in the last decade of the eighth century, the most famous being the sack of Lindisfarne in 793, which is recorded in the *Anglo-Saxon Chronicle*. The *Royal Frankish Annals* record the first raid on the Frankish empire in 799, and shortly thereafter, the Franks began organizing coastal defenses against North Sea Viking pirates (map, p.101). What most distinguished Vikings in the minds of the chroniclers was that they were not Christian and were therefore not subject to the taboos of Christian society; "harrying heathens" is how the *Anglo-Saxon Chronicle* describes the attackers of Lindisfarne.

To the pagan Norse, the undefended wealth of the churches and monasteries in Europe were an obvious source of rich pickings. Their predilection for attacking holy places made it appear that the Vikings were particularly antagonistic toward monastic establishments, a view reinforced by the monastic clerics who recorded yearly events at religious sites in the British Isles, such as Lindisfarne (off the northeast coast of England) and Iona (off the west coast of Scotland). But within the broader perspective of the times, the Vikings were perhaps not particularly violent in what was, after all, a violent age.

Unfortunately, these biased historical sources have formed the basic understanding of Viking activities in Europe. However, as more information has become available from archaeological studies of Viking hoards, burials, and settlement sites, a different side of Viking culture, one that is not known from historical accounts but which shows how Vikings functioned and related to other groups, including monasteries and trade centers, has come to light.

The presence of silver hoards attests to the accumulation of wealth in Scandinavia during the Viking Age. Large hoards containing coins, hacksilver—cut up pieces

of jewelry and metal work—silver neckrings, bracelets, and massive ingots have been found in both Scandinavia and the British Isles. In addition to vast quantities of Arab silver, the hoards also contain many silver coins from western Europe. Most of these are probably from *danegeld*, literally "Danish tax," the protection money levied on parts of France and Anglo-Saxon England by Vikings who then promised not to initiate raids. While some hoards may have been buried by local peoples as insurance against Viking raids, others were made by Vikings who used this technique as "security banking." In both cases, the hoards provide archaeological evidence of the breadth, impact, and success of the Viking raids in Europe.

Hoards often contain broken or reworked pieces of Insular (British Isles) metalwork including shrine mounts and jewelry, which has been interpreted as archaeological corroboration of Viking raids. However, the presence of loot in Scandinavia does not necessarily support concerted Viking attacks on ecclesiastical centers. Beautiful pieces of Insular metalwork such as Ranvaig's casket (p. 100) could have arrived through legitimate trade and exchange, or through the activity of Christian missionaries at such places.

Monastic centers were not the only recorded targets of Viking raids; such wealthy trading sites as Dorestad were hit, often repeatedly, and a raid is even recorded on the Swedish trading center of Birka. Recent investigations help explain why these trade sites would have been attrac-

TREASURE FROM ABROAD
Important prestige items in Viking culture, such as this piece known as "Ranvaig's casket," were likely acquired as loot. This copper-plated and red-enameled box served as a reliquary in a Scottish monastery before it was acquired by a Norwegian Viking woman named Ranvaig, who carved in runes on the bottom, "Ranvaig owns this casket."

tive targets. Archaeological excavations at trading sites in Hedeby and Birka have revealed an extensive trade network, which indicates that North Sea and Baltic trade links began prior to the Viking Age (Sawyer 1982). Frisian coins or *sceattas*, which were produced in large numbers circa 700 and after, have been found, for instance, at Ribe. Trading centers or *wics* of the Channel and North Sea areas, which facilitated commerce between England and the Continent, had been growing since the seventh century. The growth of such trading centers encouraged Scandinavians to exploit their natural resources, including goods and materials obtained through neighboring Saami and Baltic tribes, as trade items for goods from farther afield in northwest Europe and the east (Clarke and Ambrosiani 1991). Familiarity with the worth and availability of these products at trading sites could have been instrumental in instigating the Viking raids. Such evidence has led some archaeologists to advance the date of the beginning of the Viking Age well before the conventional historical date of A.D. 800. Peter Sawyer sees the Viking raids in the west as a direct consequence of economic development in northwest Europe, Scandinavia, and the Baltic region; such commercial links may have inspired Viking raids, rather than raids evolving into trade.

But evidence of Viking raids resulting in growing trade networks is also found: the Viking takeover of the monastic centers at Noirmoutier (near the mouth of the Loire at the southeastern tip of Brittany) and lands such as Normandy and York gave the Vikings bases from which to control commercial activity further south into the Frankish Empire and down to Spain and the Mediterranean (Bates 1982). For instance, the takeover of York by the *micel here* (great heathen army), which marched across England in 866–867, resulted in a flourishing trade town.

Eventually the Viking tactic of raiding and trading resulted in a vast trade network that they controlled—and that greatly expanded the areas of Viking influence. The linchpin in this network were strategic towns which the Vikings established or took over, such as Dublin, York, Hedeby, Birka, and Staraja Ladoga. The Viking trade network spread from Scandinavia to Spain in the west and to Kiev and the eastern Mediterranean. Staraja Ladoga was key to the eastern trade routes down the rivers of Russia to the Black Sea and Mediterranean, while Dublin became the major international place of exchange for the western Irish seaboard, with the result that distinctive Irish artifacts, like ringed pins, spread throughout the North Atlantic area, even as far as Newfoundland (Clarke et al. 1998). The sack in 870 of Alt Clut (modern Dumbarton Castle) may have provided some of the hundreds of captured Britons and Picts arriving in Ath Cliath (Dublin) in 871; Vikings clearly required slaves to support the vast Viking trade and economic network.

Scandinavians not only stimulated the growth of towns in the British Isles and the Continent, they also influenced a redistribution of wealth and produced new populations that emerged from mixing between Scandinavians and local populations in the regions they occupied. So-called Viking towns such as York cannot have been ex-

clusively Viking settlements; these towns were based on preexisting population centers. Whether these towns were established by Vikings, or merely taken over by them, is difficult to determine; debate about the role of the Vikings in the development of Novgorod, Kiev, and other Russian towns has escalated as new evidence has come to light that more Scandinavian material exists in archaeological collections than was previously acknowledged. But it is still likely that Kiev cannot have been exclusively Scandinavian during the Viking Age; more likely it was under the control of princes and rulers of Scandinavian descent (Graham-Campbell 1994).

While some of these commercial centers may have been implanted Scandinavian settlements, they could hardly have existed without affecting and being affected by their respective rural hinterlands. Evidence for Scandinavian influence on the countryside derives from various sources, but is most notable in place-names. Viking place-names abound in many regions where Vikings settled, but the question remains whether they result from large-scale immigration, as suggested from historical sources, or whether they owe their origin to a less-dramatic process that did not entail armies and navies, but well-directed, highly mobile forces that numbered in hundreds rather than thousands. Most scholars today are inclined toward the latter, seeing Viking farm and village names as representing linguistic changes in local speech resulting from political dominance by Viking military or aristocratic elites. Certainly in Normandy, the Danelaw in eastern England, and in Kiev it was primarily the Scandinavian

role as a ruling group that effected changes in speech patterns and place-names. In both Normandy and Brittany, evidence for Scandinavian rural settlement is entirely lacking from an archaeological perspective, despite Scandinavianized place-names. This was also the case until recently in Wales, where now a single site, Llanbedrgoch, has been identified.

Burials most clearly reveal the Scandinavian material culture of the Viking Age, and they provide evidence of the number of Vikings which lived, died, and were buried in foreign areas. For a culture that was so attuned to both mastering the sea and exploiting it, it is hardly surprising that the Viking boat graves represent the highest level of pagan burial practice. Outside the Nordic region, the most spectacular European ship grave is the chieftain's burial on the Ile de Groix in Brittany (Price, chapter 7). Few others exist in Europe on this lavish scale (Sutton Hoo belongs to the pre-Viking period). Well-furnished burials, such as those from the Isle of Man or the Hebrides and the cemeteries from Orkney and outside Dublin, also attest to a period of Scandinavian pagan burial practices as part of the mainstream culture; there are other examples scattered across England, but very few in Normandy. Two particular sites in England, which date from the late ninth century, merit mention here: the Ingleby cemetery, with a number of cremations and even cenotaph mounds, and nearby Repton, with an enormous charnel-pit, apparently a burial of warriors (Richards 1991). The burials outside Dublin might represent not merely a Norse military elite, but one engaged in commerce in the late ninth century.

To the east, there continues to be a dearth of reliable information about the nature of the burials associated with the traditional settlements of the Rus Vikings, and perhaps the Scandinavian contribution has been downplayed in past reports. There can now be little doubt, however, that cemeteries such as those at Staraja Ladoga demonstrate considerable Scandinavian influence and should be given serious attention.

Further north, in the Earldom of Orkney-Caithness-Shetland, settlement evidence has been more forthcoming. Here archaeologists have found not just burials, but whole Viking-style farms and towns. Jarlshof in Shetland has long been seen as a Viking-type site; it has excellent farming and its access to the sea provided additional natural resources and a safe harbor. Other Viking and late Norse sites—Freswick in Caithness, Birsay and Orphir in Orkney and survey work elsewhere—might soon lead to a more comprehensive view of the Viking settlement patterns (Graham-Campbell and Batey, 1998). In Ireland, as elsewhere, it has been difficult to identify any Scandinavian rural settlement at all, to the extent that some have denied that the Scandinavians had any perceptible influence on the Irish countryside (Clarke et al. 1998).

The transplanted Scandinavian communities in the different lands were quite prepared to adapt to particular circumstances in which they found themselves. Whether they were raiders, traders, or settlers, the activities they engaged in varied not only according to particular geographical and topographical circumstances but also to the nature of the native communities they came into contact with. When Vikings went to Christian lands, they do not seem to have been aggressively pagan—if anything, it was quite the reverse. York, the center of the Kingdom of Northumbria, was taken over in 867, and in 876 its lands were shared out. As early as 886, however, there was a Christian king in York, and by the tenth century it is likely that those of Scandinavian origin in English communities would also have been Christian.

Stefan Brink and others have suggested that a number of chieftains in various Nordic regions moved toward an informal adoption of Christianity significantly earlier than written sources suggest. The written records have always indicated that the adoption of Christianity occurred at different times in the different Nordic countries, with Denmark officially converting during the reign of Harald Bluetooth in the tenth century, followed by Norway under Olaf Tryggvason circa 1000, and Sweden lagging behind as a bastion of paganism especially at such places as Lund (if we are to take the words of Adam of Bremen at face value) until the twelfth century (Roesdahl 1992). Even in Sweden, however, there are indications of earlier Christian influences at such trading sites as Birka (fig. 3.12). Perhaps the sources refer not to the beginning of the process of acceptance of Christianity but to the formal acceptance of this religion on an exclusive basis.

The general lack of large numbers of pagan burials in England seems to reinforce the view of an early conversion. There is little doubt that the Norsemen were prepared to accept the Christian god into their pantheon: for instance, the Gosforth cross, in Cumbria, one of the most spectacular of all Viking Age sculptural monuments, has a Christian crucifixion scene amid a plethora of Scandinavian mythological scenes. The degree to which incoming Scandinavians were prepared to adopt the native religious tradition is demonstrated by the largely Christian form of Anglo-Scandinavian sculptures found in northern England. Conversely, the native Christian communities accepted Scandinavian decoration onto their own distinctive monument forms and even adopted elements of Scandinavian mythology.

Ultimately, Scandinavians adopted the Christian ethic and ideology and became part of the mainstream medieval European Christian community, thereby in some measure losing their earlier Viking identity. Similarly, the Viking settlements along the Viking trade routes lost their Scandinavian flavor by the end of the Viking Age. In both Normandy and Brittany, there was a remarkably quick assimilation of the Viking invaders into the local French populations. In England, the Danelaw, partitioned off from Saxon areas of England with its own Scandinavian law and administration, retained its Scandinavian flavor longer, but it became the target of West Saxon advances in the tenth century, ending the hegemony of Scandinavians in the area. Northumbria survived a little longer as a Norse offshoot of the Dublin Vikings, but only until 954. In many areas Scandinavian control persisted until at least 1066, when the Battle of Hastings in southern England and the Battle of Stamford Bridge in Yorkshire took place, if not even later. Although William the Conqueror, who was victorious in the Battle of Hastings, came from Scandinavian stock from Normandy, allowing some historians to argue that his was the last Viking invasion of England, in reality by then Normandy had shaken off its Norse roots.

6 THE EASTERN ROUTE:

Finland in the Viking Age

BY TORSTEN EDGREN

VIKINGS IN SEARCH OF RICHES AND fame were undoubtedly aware of the fabulous wealth of the Byzantine Empire, which occupied present-day Turkey and much of the Middle East during the Viking Age and prior. Several runestones in Sweden speak of Vikings who served as mercenaries for the Byzantine rulers, who would richly reward their loyal warriors. To reach this desirable destination, the Vikings did not circumnavigate all of Europe and sail across the Mediterranean. Instead, they followed an inland water route, consisting of connecting rivers and lakes, which went from the Baltic through the heart of modern Russia where a local population and an economy sufficient to sustain the crew existed. There is documentary and archaeological evidence that the kingdom of Kiev was established by Viking raiders who decided to settle there. The account of the Arab diplomat Ibn Fadlan who met in 922 along the Volga people whom he called the Rus—who were undoubtedly Vikings— is further indication of the Viking infiltration southeastward from their homelands in Sweden. Evidence of the Norsemen appears in many places along the water routes to the Black Sea, and grave mounds of Scandinavian type and containing Scandinavian grave goods are found, for instance, at Gnezdovo near Smolensk, an imposing cemetery containing more than 4,500 grave monuments.

One of the two most important routes to Russia and Byzantium led across the Baltic to the Duna River in present-day Latvia, while the other, mentioned in medieval sources, led via Åland and the sheltered archipelago of southwestern Finland to the Hanko Peninsula and Porkkala on the southern Finnish coast (fig. 6.2). It is possible either to sail south from Porkkala to Lindanes (present-day Tallinn in Estonia) and then eastward along the Estonian coast or follow Finland's south coast from Hanko onward (map, p. 105). In either case, the objective was the Neva River at the head of the Gulf of Finland, which led to the open waters of Lake Ladoga (Edgren 1995), Europe's largest lake. From Lake Ladoga one could either follow the Svir River to Lake Onega or take the Volkhov toward the south and the heartland of present-day Russia. From the Volkhov one could reach the source of the Dnepr via Lake Ilmen and continue via Kiev to the Black Sea, where the town of Berezan evolved into an important trade center. From Lake Ladoga it was also possible to follow smaller streams to the Volga. This led down to Bulgar, the capital of the realm of the Volga Bulgars with its contacts to the Silk Road, and onward to the Caspian Sea. These many possibilities are too broad to treat here; this chapter will focus instead on this eastern route and its effect on Sweden's non-Nordic–speaking neighbor, Finland, through which Vikings traveled and, along trade routes, settled.

6.1 TRAVELER'S SCALE
The two half-spheres hanging from the chains of this scale fit together to form a compact ball in which the suspension chain and lead weights are stored; the balance arm also folds in half for transport. Folding scales are found in burials throughout the Viking area, from Russia to the British Isles (and arctic Canada, fig. 17.13). Weights came in a variety of shapes, sizes, and materials.

FINNS AND VIKING SCANDINAVIANS

The Finns were ethnically distinct from the Viking Scandinavians, though they shared with them an agricultural, late Iron Age base economy. Their language was not Germanic, but rather Finno-Ugric, related to Hungarian and the language of the Saami. This ethnic difference can be seen in the archeological record in several ways, most notably in house types and religious practices.

The remains of late Iron Age (circa A.D. 900) settlements are almost invisible above ground, which makes them difficult to locate and consequently rare. Our knowledge of late Iron Age house forms is scant and was limited for many years (Kivikoski 1964), but later research has shown that the houses were usually constructed of wall panels woven from branches and fastened between upright posts that formed the actual load-bearing frame. The space between the posts could also be filled with a tight row of split saplings, and in all cases the walls were caulked with clay daub and the floor was of hard-packed earth. Log houses, which came into use later, were presumably much smaller than the large Scandinavian halls.

One prerequisite for the Viking Age Nordic expansion and trade was the double-ended clinker-built ship known from the famous Nordic ship finds. Viking Age boat graves show that large ships with oars and sails were also built—or at least used—in Finland. A different and more specifically Finnish boat-building technique was used in the inland area. These vessels were smaller and instead of being fastened together with iron rivets, the planks were sewn together with spruce roots. Sewn boats, known from a number of bog finds, were especially flexible and well adapted for running rapids, the epitome of an old Finnish tradition and technique.

The dominant form of burial was in cremation cemeteries, a signature Finnish phenomenon and unlike Viking burial practices, which had been introduced late in the seventh century and remained in use until around 1000. Mixed stone/earth cairns also appear with extensive paving of stone; in between, under, and on top of the stones lay the remnants of the pyres of the dead: burned bones, ashes, and grave goods. It has been presumed that whole villages used the large cremation cemeteries, but many villages had several cemeteries, which apparently belonged to individual farms. Cremation cemeteries sometimes contain boat graves, burials in which the deceased were burned in their boats. This form parallels the Scandinavian boat graves, although the latter were not cremations. So while the Finns shared a few characteristics with the Scandinavian Vikings, they were a distinct people worshiping their own gods.

BIRKA AND STARAJA LADOGA

The eastern route was sustained by two major trade centers, Birka, in Sweden, and Staraja Ladoga, in what is now Russia (fig. 6.1). At the mouth of the Volkhov there arose in the seventh century the trading center of Staraja Ladoga, called *Aldeigjuborg* in Old Norse, which became in time one of the

8°
12°
16°
20°
24°
28°
32°
36°
72°
64°
56°
Laksefjorden
Tana R.
Varanger Fjord
Tenojoki R.
Inari
Lotta R.
Tuloma R.
Kola R.
Voron'ya R.
Nota R.
Ounasjoki R.
LAPPLAND
Luleälven R.
Piteälven R.
Skellefteälven R.
Vindelälven R.
Torneälven R.
Kemijoki R.
Strel'na R.
NORWAY
SWEDEN
FINLAND
OSTROBOTHNIA
Oulujoki R.
White Sea
Kemi R.
Ångermanälven R.
Indalsälven R.
Ljungan R.
GULF OF BOTHNIA
Vroijoki R.
SATAKUNTA
KARELIA
RUSSIA
Åland
Lake Mälar
Eura
HÄME
SAVO
FINLAND PROPER
Lake Onega
Hittinen Is.
UUSIMAA
Lake Ladoga
Karjaa
Porkkala
GULF OF FINLAND
Staraja Ladoga
Tallinn
Gotland
BALTIC SEA
ESTONIA
Pasha R.
Suda R.
Volkhov R.
Gulf of Riga
Gauja R.
Velikaya R.
RUSSIA
Wenta R.
LATVIA
Lovat' R.
Volga R.

Finland in the Viking Age
Finland lay between the Viking territories in Scandinavia and the eastern trade route, which passed through Russia as it headed south to the Black and Caspian seas. Because few Vikings settled in Finland, their impact varied from region to region.

most important towns on the Eastern Route. Staraja Ladoga, which is first mentioned in the *Nestorian Chronicle* from 862, had been protected since the 860s with a log fortification; in 882 this was replaced by a defensive structure of stone, erected by Prince Oleg. According to Snorri Sturluson's *Heimskringla Aldeigjuborg* was taken by the Norse in 997. The town is also mentioned in *St. Olaf's Saga* in connection with the fact that Ingegärd, daughter of King Olaf of Sweden, was given in marriage to Prince Yaroslav the Wise of Kiev, probably in the 1020s. The ethnic background of the townsfolk of Staraja Ladoga, who included merchants, craftsmen, and civil servants, has been widely discussed. The present view is that the population was polyethnic and included Scandinavians, Baltic Finns, Balts, Slavs, and perhaps Frisians. The Scandinavian contingent was at its strongest in the ninth century, while finds from the following centuries have a more Slavic character.

The eastern trade route began in Sweden at a trade town on Lake Malär. Just prior to the Viking Age, the trade site of Helgö on the shore of Lake Malär had been important, but during the Viking Age, Birka, which was located on an island in the center of the lake, was established under the protection of the king and became the most important point of departure for trade voyages via the eastern route, which commenced somewhat later than the Viking raids in western Europe (figs. 6.3, 6.4). The strategic importance and wealth of Birka can be seen in its fortification, several large cemeteries, and impressive burial goods (fig. 1.3). Excavations have revealed about seventeen acres of the so-called black earth, a settlement site with a thick culture layer. At some phases, the area of the actual town may have been significantly larger than what has been found; after the year 923, a semicircular dike with several gates surrounded the settlement. Among the 1,100 graves excavated in Birka so far, more than half are ordinary cremations under mounds; the rest consist of large wooden chambers that contain rich inhumation burials. On the basis of the graves, the population of Birka has been estimated at five hundred to six hundred people.

At least during the trading season, Birka must have been a meeting place for many nations, a polytechnic center. Its favorable location, from both a regional and a trans-Baltic viewpoint, gave Birka a central role in the Baltic trade and the Nordic fur trade—although it was abandoned toward the end of the Viking Age. It also served a large local district, the densely populated Malär region, which in turn provided a basis for the town's industry of combs (figs. 9.13, 9.14), pottery, wool, and jewelry products. Birka probably also handled a large part of the Swedish iron exports, goods that came originally from production centers in the north.

EXTENT OF FINNISH PARTICIPATION

Finland lies between Birka and Staraja Ladoga, so it is natural to assume that Finns participated in this eastern trade. But such evidence has been hard to come by in the archaeological record. Aside from a few Finnish round brooches, no finds of Finnish character are known from the Russian water routes. One reason for this may be that Viking Age eastern trading voyages were undertaken primarily by men; Viking Age male costumes were almost identical all over the Baltic area and Finnish men also followed this fashion, while the women were more conservative as far as dress was concerned. Because the weapons found in graves also represent common types, it is difficult to say with certainty whether a Viking buried somewhere along the Eastern Route was a Finn or not (fig. 6.5).

Evidence in their homelands of Finns participating in Viking voyages is also hard to interpret. One reason for this is that Vikings settled in parts of Finland, so it is difficult to determine if Viking goods found in Finland represent Finns going on Viking raids or Vikings living in Finland. For instance, the Viking Age hoards from Åland consist exclusively of Islamic coins (fig., p. 85), which were presumably obtained by the local people themselves on voyages to the east. The Islamic coins found in western Finnish graves and hoards were probably brought to Finland by Viking voyagers, who need not necessarily have been Finns but could have been Viking settlers. Likewise, coin finds from the northern coast of the Gulf of Finland are best characterized as traces left by the Vikings passing through. Certain finds are considered evidence of direct contacts with the east. These include the so-called Permian belt mountings and bronze-handled strike-a-lights (both first described from finds in the region of Perm in the southern Urals) found on the northern coast of the Gulf of Finland (fig. 6.12). These fire-starters were widespread in the Nordic countries and known, for instance, from Hedeby and Birka (Lehtosalo-Hilander 1982), which indicates that the strike-a-lights were valued trade goods, not that they were brought to Finland by Finnish voyagers. The fact that the Finns were a separate people who spoke a different language than the Vikings may be one reason why the Finns did not take part in the Viking voyages to any notable extent.

EFFECTS AT HOME

Though the Finns were probably not major, active participants in trade, their culture at home was significantly affected by the eastern trade of the Vikings. Its effects included cultural blending, new settlement patterns, a greater emphasis on fur trapping and iron production, and a notable increase in wealth and population.

The Åland archipelago, Finland's westernmost province, received a strong influx of immigrants from central Sweden in the sixth century A.D. and formed a part of the Scandinavian culture area throughout the Viking Age. Both the material culture and the graves—cremation burials in earth mounds—are totally Scandinavian in character, but objects imported from Finland are also present. The latter consist primarily of women's jewelry, possibly indicating that at least some of the local men obtained wives from Finland (Kivikoski 1964). The culture of Åland also shows connections to the east, especially Russia. One special category of finds that points to Finnish contacts to the east is the so-called clay paws (fig. 6.6), which are common in Late Iron Age graves on Åland. The Åland paws have no parallels on the Finnish mainland, but similar objects are common in central Russia and are likely connected with a particular beaver cult that appeared among Finnic tribes in eastern Russia. There is, however, no other archaeological evidence of close contacts between the two areas.

The most important Finnish trading center during the Viking Age was a harbor located on the island of Hiittinen in the southwestern Finnish archipelago (fig. 6.2), which lies right on the eastern route of the Vikings (Edgren 1993, 1995). It has been suggested that the great trade route to the east, which followed the southern coast of Finland, was actually detrimental to settlement near the coast, because the lively traffic along the route made the coast a dangerous place to live. This could explain why the previously rich Iron Age villages in Karjaa, western Uusimaa, were abandoned around 800, but the new finds from Hiittinen show that the coastal farmers could also form productive relationships with the voyagers on the eastern route. Both parties were astute enough to take advantage of the Viking Age economic boom. This led to a western Finnish culture that was heavily influenced by Viking Scandinavian culture.

6.2 Kyrksundet Harbor
The archipelago off the southern coast of Finland provided safe harbors and a protected passage for Viking ships on the eastern trade route. Some of the stone beacons Viking navigators erected to mark their sailing route through the maze of islands and shoals still stand. Kyrksundet, shown here, was not only one of the main harbors, it had a Viking trading post.

The culture of Ladoga Karelia, the ethnically Finnish province of Russia that stretches from the eastern edge of the Baltic Sea to the northwestern shore of Lake Ladoga, was also affected by the Viking Age eastern trade (Uino 1997), taking on a decidedly more western Finnish character. Their intermediate position—between the Baltic peoples and those of the Russian arctic coast on the one hand and the rivers providing transport to the Black Sea, Near East, and Mediterranean on the other—assured them an important role in provisioning and transport, as guides, translators, and intermediaries. Because their services were important to Viking traders, their culture flourished during this period.

FUR TRADE

Furs, seal products, and skins—not to mention beeswax, which was an old household commodity among the Baltic Finns—were unquestionably among the most important trade goods of the Viking Age. The fur trade required intensive hunting, which took place primarily in the deep forests that surrounded the Finnish Viking Age villages. Only a small portion of present-day southern Finland was permanently settled during the Viking Age.

The rest of the country was a vast wilderness that offered excellent hunting, fishing, and trapping, the latter being economically the most important of the three. The most important game animals were beaver, moose, wolf, lynx, and brown bear.

Skis were particularly important for winter hunting. More than one hundred skis have been discovered in bogs, where the preservation of wood is exceptionally good; one-third of these have been dated by pollen analysis and radiocarbon to before the year A.D.1200. The skis were all carved of pine, an elastic and hard material that had good sliding properties due to its natural resin content. Finnish skis were slender, up to ten feet (three meters) long, and were often decorated with grooved lines or artistically executed band patterns. They also made asymmetrical-paired skis, which consist of a long left ski with bottom channel and a notably shorter right ski. The bottom of the latter was covered with stiff-haired hide, the hairs pointing backward for traction. The skier slid along on the long left ski while kicking with the shorter right ski and maintaining balance with a ski pole. At least during the historical period, and

6.3

6.3, 6.4 EXOTIC EASTERN IMPORTS
This bronze statuette of Buddha from northern India, found in the eighth-century site of Helgö, is evidence of trade between Sweden with Russia and the Near East that existed even before the beginning of the Viking Age. Eastern beads, such as this rock crystal (quartz) string (opposite), which probably originated in the Caucasus, reached Swedish Viking trade sites like Birka through the eastern trade route.

probably in the Viking Age, asymmetrical-paired skis were used primarily for moose hunting.

As the market for furs grew with the increased trade contracts, and the hunting grounds near the villages were depleted, hunting trips became longer and longer. The hunting grounds were now frontier wilderness areas hundreds of miles from the core villages. While the number of western Finnish farms, villages, and cemeteries increased during the Viking Age in the old core southern settlement areas of Finland Proper, Satakunta, and Häme, the Finnish population also expanded into areas that had formerly been sparsely inhabited (Kivikoski 1964, 1967; Edgren 1993). A number of new cemeteries appeared along the coast while former population centers shrank. Both trade and subsistence considerations directed the inhabitants' interests toward the sea, while the river valleys were first-class conduits to the inland with its boundless hunting grounds.

In the province of Häme (Tavastia) settlement expanded beyond the borders of the old core area located around the lake region of southern Häme; cemeteries appear in several districts outside the actual core cluster, including the eastern part of the province. As a rule, finds that originate from outside the core settlements come from male graves, apparently those of trappers. But a sign of the increased pressure to settle the inland and eastern areas is seen in a well-furnished female burial found in a cairn in Pertunmaa. The burial contained a full range of western Finnish jewelry, including round brooches, a large twisted-bar neckring, heavy, massive bracelets, finger rings, and an iron knife. A necklace with a double row of beads and two Islamic coins dates the grave to the tenth century. The grave lay adjacent to the Mäntyharju route, which—along with the Greater Salpausselkä ridge—formed one of the most obvious natural highways between Häme and the Savo region of eastern Finland and was an important route for supplying fur.

A new settlement area arose during the Viking Age in Savo (around the present-day city of Mikkeli), which became a provincial population center over the following centuries. Both the grave types and the artifact forms of the early period were clearly western Finnish in origin, which indicates that the region was colonized by settlers from Häme

6.4

(Taavitsainen 1990). Contacts with Ladoga Karelia intensified during the eleventh century and became predominant during the following centuries. The development of permanent settlement in Savo and Karelia seems to have been primarily related to a notable increase in the market for frontier products, especially furs.

The numbers of archaeological finds dating to the Viking Age also rise in northern Finland, northern Ostrobothnia, and Lappland. Most of the archaeological finds come from the northern region between the Gulf of Bothnia and the White Sea—Kainuu, Kuusamo, and Salla—which were important centers in the Lappland fur trade with the Saami, native peoples of northern Scandinavia, Finland, and northwestern Russia. The White Sea, with its rich opportunities for

6.5 FINNS OR VIKINGS?
The presence of a sword and spear usually indicates a warrior's grave in southern Finland. Because both Finns (who were culturally and linguistically distinct from Vikings/Norse) and Vikings used similar armaments, it is difficult to determine the affiliations of a particular grave. Excellent preservation conditions have left Finland with a remarkable collection of Viking Age weaponry.

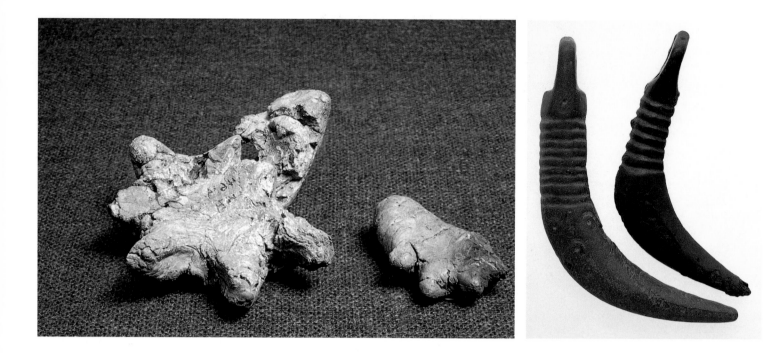

6.6, 6.7 ANIMAL AMULETS
Clay models of animal paws, probably representing either beaver or bear, have been found in Viking graves in Finland and Russia but not in Scandinavian Viking burials. Both real bear-tooth pendants and bronze bear-tooth amulets, which were worn from a woman's belt, have been found in Finland. Such belts were also worn by shamans in northern Siberia.

productive fishing and maritime seal hunting, played a major role in the economy of the region. It was connected to the Gulf of Bothnia by several major water routes, which traders from northern Norway originally used when traveling the five hundred miles to the White Sea, but in the ninth century the trade traffic shifted to the sea route around the North Cape. This route was discovered by Ottar (Othere) of Halogaland, a Viking chieftain who lived near present-day Tromsø on the northwest coast of Norway; Ottar described this route to the Anglo-Saxon king Alfred around 875 (p. 49).

IRON PRODUCTION

Ready access to ore and unlimited supplies of charcoal for smelting made Finland a strategic center of north Baltic iron production. Iron was extremely important in Nordic society both for weapons and subsistence activities. The large amounts of slag discovered in Finnish settlements and mixed earth/stone cairns indicate that iron was produced in quantity. Merely replacing the iron tools, weapons, and other objects that were taken out of circulation by being deposited in graves would have required a sizable output of iron. The raw material was the readily available iron ore found in bogs and lake sediments, which has been used up to the present day. We do not know in what form the iron was distributed, and other details of the apparent large-scale iron manufacturing activities are also unknown. Because com-

merce and distribution technology required that the iron be refined into products of a standard form and weight, we assume that some form of ingots was used in Finland. Present data suggest that simple blacksmith's jobs were taken care of at the farm and professional blacksmiths handled more complicated work. Folk poetry indicates that the blacksmith was a central and powerful figure in the community.

Raw iron from Finland was important for making weapons, especially the two-edged sword (fig. 6.5), the long-handled axe, and the spear. The sword was primarily a striking weapon, and strength was required to wield it as the heaviest examples weighed some four and one-half pounds (two kilograms). The length of the whole sword including the grip was around thirty-three inches (one hundred centimeters); the longest sword found in Finland measures forty inches (121 centimeters). Sword blades were made from Finnish iron in the Frankish kingdom of western Europe and were then exported to the Nordic countries as half-finished goods, the grips being provided by Nordic craftsmen. Sword blades were on average some five inches (twelve centimeters) wide and two and one-half feet (seventy-five centimeters) long. Running along the middle of the blade is a shallow channel, half an inch (two centimeters) wide, referred to as the blood groove. The blades might be damascened, a Near Eastern technique in

Cupric salts from bronze-wire
embroidery preserved portions of
aprons found in a women's graves in
Luistari (Eura), Finland, allowing
garments to be reconstructed like
the one seen here (fig. 6.10). Cold
soil conditions and frequent use of
bronze have preserved textiles in
Finland better than in other parts of
Scandinavia, where information on
dress has come primarily from the
study of illuminated Icelandic
manuscripts.

6.10

been found in women's graves (fig. 6.16).

Perhaps the most common weapon of
the Viking Age was the spear, which measured around six and one-half to ten feet
(two to three meters) in length, including
the eight- to twenty-four-inch (twenty to
sixty centimeter) metal point with its socket
tube. The most common form, known as
the **E**-type, is of central European origin but
is found all over Scandinavia and Finland
and is usually damascened. The socket tube
of later spear types may be handsomely
decorated with silver inlay and gilded looped
animals in the style of the late runestones
(fig. 6.15). Most of these spear points, like
the most artistically silver-inlayed sword
grips, may have been manufactured on the
island of Gotland (Lehtosalo-Hilander
1985). Another common and effective
weapon was the battle-axe, which was made
in both wide and thin-bladed forms.

6.8

6.9

which iron and steel layers are repeatedly
folded and hammered together, producing a
hard but flexible blade (fig. 6.13). While
damascened blades are typical of the early
Viking Age, the practice of furnishing the
blades with signs, symbols, and texts was introduced in the tenth century (fig. 6.14).
Trademarks of certain workshops and smiths
(Leppäaho 1964) appear repeatedly:
"Ulfbert," a master's name, appears over a
period of around 150 years. During the late
eleventh century the finest blades might be
decorated with Christian symbols or text in
silver or gold wire that was hammered into
grooves on the blade. These were luxury
swords, but the majority were plain swords
intended for use. Finnish finds have produced a large number of swords, close to 330
examples, which are similar to other Scandinavian Viking swords. Rarely, swords have

WEALTH FROM TRADE

Seen as a whole, the Viking Age can be characterized as a period when the Finnish population had access to a higher standard of
living than ever before. The internationaliza-
tion of trade and the economic boom stimulated the community and created resources
for the production of domestic fine handicrafts. One area of exceptional affluence is
the region known as Vakka-Suomi, south of
the present town of Uusikaupunki, which
had closer ties with central Sweden than with
the other settlements in southwestern Finland. One reason for this might be the area's
geographical location, another, the fact that
the rich farming villages in Kokemäki, Eura,
and Köyliö maintained their ties with the
Baltic world via Vakka-Suomi. Because the
area is not known for having exceptionally
productive fields, its affluence in the Viking

6.11 FINNISH BROOCH WITH CHAIN
More than 500 inhumation graves
have been excavated in Eura,
Satakunta. Although soil conditions
were not ideal for organic preservation, copper and copper alloys, such
as this brooch assemblage from
Grave 35, were preserved. Worn in
the same position on the body as
the oval brooches of Scandinavians,
round brooches were a Finnish ethnic
specialty.

Age may be derived from its fame for the
manufacture of wooden containers, particularly the bushels (in Finn, *vakka*) that gave
the region its name. During the Viking Age
with its growing village clusters, there was
great demand for storage vessels of all kinds.
Containers were also required on trading
voyages, both for storing the merchandise
and for packing provisions.

Another important handicraft was jewelry making (fig. 6.11). Coins furnished the
most important raw material for jewelry, but
because silver was rare during the ninth and
tenth centuries, bronze was used and highly
valued for such objects (fig. 6.17). Silver
coins were frequently used as is, either perforated or furnished with a loop for hanging
on a necklace or chain assembly. Arabian
dirhams were especially popular, which is
evident from the fact that "counterfeit"
dirhams were manufactured specifically for
use as jewelry hangings. A large number of
coins mimicking Byzantine silver miliaresion
have also been discovered in Finland. Numis-
matists have identified five different types
among these imitation coins, four of which
have not been found elsewhere. Many of the
copies have identical stampings and are
therefore probably of Finnish manufacture
(Talvio 1980a) and date to 1025–1050. The
coins were not used as currency: they are all
perforated and have been used as hanging
jewelry. The fact that the Byzantine coins
were larger than other coins of the period
appears to have attracted the western Finns,
as did the Byzantine designs.

Viking Age silver apparently came to
Finland from two different directions. During the early part of the period silver was
obtained on voyages to the east, later on it
came from western Europe (Talvio 1980b,
1982). The oldest Finnish hoards, which
contain only oriental coins, come from
Åland and date to the ninth and tenth centuries. The others, which also include various
other kinds of silver objects, are from Finland proper and Häme and date to the latter
part of the eleventh century. Thirty-eight
separate coin hoards from the Viking Age,
totaling about 1,600 Islamic, 1,000 Anglo-
Saxon, and 4,000 German coins together
with a few Scandinavian, Irish, Bohemian,
Hungarian, Spanish, and Byzantine pieces,
have been found in Finland. These numbers
are minuscule compared with the great coin
hoards of Gotland. The silver hoards of the

6.12 GRAVE 348
A highly ornamented dress pin, Islamic coins dating to before 927, weights, and a strike-a-light ornamented with two bronze horsemen were found in a rich male grave in Eura, Satakunta. Similar strike-a-lights have been found from the Western Urals to Trondheim, Norway, but their greatest concentration is in southwestern Finland.

Viking Age have generally been interpreted as evidence of war and troubled times: when danger threatened, people hid their silver in the ground. Another possibility, suggested first by the thirteenth-century Icelandic chronicler Snorri Sturluson, is that this was a religious custom: he asserts that Odin had laid down laws whereby anything one buried away during one's lifetime could be enjoyed in the afterlife.

Another example of bringing one's riches to the grave has been seen in the Luistari cemetery in Eura, southern Finland (fig. 6.11). This is not only the largest Viking Age cemetery in Finland, with more than 1,300 excavated graves (Lehtosalo-Hilander

1982), but it is an inhumation cemetery (rather than a cremation cemetery), which is also unusual. The dead were interred dressed in their best clothes and finest jewelry. Organic materials such as cloth are rarely preserved in graves, but small spiral tubes of bronze wire used to decorate Finnish costumes, which eventually oxidized and preserved the surrounding cloth, were recovered (figs. 6.8, 6.9). Because of this, it has been possible through painstaking studies in the field and laboratory to reconstruct a number of women's costumes (Appelgren-Kivalo 1907; Lehtosalo 1984). Ironically, the clothing found in the Eura graves provides the most complete examples of Viking Age

6.15

6.14

clothing, despite the fact that it is not Scandinavian in type but rather Finnish. The best-preserved Eura dress (fig. 6.10) includes a wealth of jewelry: spiral bracelets with ten turns, two finger rings on each hand, and a necklace with thirty-four glass beads, ten Arabian and two western European coins, and two punched and embossed pendants of silver sheet were found adorning the woman. The chain assembly includes two typical round brooches and an equal-armed brooch; on the side chains hang links with sleigh bells and other objects.

On the belt hangs a handsomely decorated knife sheath of bronze, which was found in many Finnish Viking Age women's graves. Unlike most Scandinavian Viking jewelry, which was predominantly made of silver, the pieces of Finnish jewelry that appear in grave finds from the ninth and tenth centuries are predominantly heavy and massive bronze objects (Kivikoski 1973). Bronze, which seems to have been the precious metal of choice for Finland during this period, was imported from central Europe in the form of ingots and was worked locally (fig. 6.17). Although Viking jewelry styles are found, usually in rather unornamented and basic versions, most Finnish jewelry reflects northern and eastern traditions not found in the Nordic regions or Europe.

6.15 SILVER SPEARHEADS
During the eleventh century, iron spearheads with silver plating and decorated sockets were popular; more than seventy examples have been recovered from southwest Finland. This socket bears an Urnes-style beast similar to carvings on runestones from Gotland, where this spearhead may also have been decorated.

6.14 "ULFBERT MADE ME"
Swords in the late Viking Age were often inscribed with the maker or owner's name. The mark of the master swordmaker "Ulfbert" appeared on blades for 150 years. Latin inscriptions like "Beno Me Fecit" also identify the maker, and by the late Viking Age phrases like "In Nomine Domini Amen" reflect the gradual conversion to Christianity.

6.13 DAMASCENED SWORD BLADES
Repeated folding and hammering of hot iron turned it into damascene steel, so named because the technique was first perfected in Damascus. If done well, the process also left an attractive linear pattern, still seen on these thousand-year-old blades. Damascened swords were light, beautiful, strong, and highly prized.

6.13

6.16 A Woman's Sword
This sword, one of two found in a woman's grave in Suontaka (Häme), Finland, is evidence of international influence on Finnish culture, which may have led to redefining the roles of women. Iron blades were usually imported from Europe, but hilts were usually made in Finland to personal tastes. This copper hilt is decorated with Viking beasts.

Conclusion

Although Finland lay on the northern fringe of Viking society and had different linguistic and cultural traditions, as did the Saami people in northern Finland and Scandinavia, the Finns participated in the Viking world as trading partners and facilitators of the Viking eastern trade. Probably their greatest, and least known, contribution was in providing such northern products as fur and iron from northern Finland and the White Sea region. In this process they became increasingly tied culturally and economically to the Nordic regions and Europe, which helped secure Finland's Baltic, and western, orientation.

Although the eastern trade routes of the Vikings did influence the economy and settlement patterns in Finland, the flourishing economy cannot be explained solely through foreign contacts and trade relationships. On the contrary, the changes appear to emanate from the evolution of the domestic economy, which included a change from shifting swidden agriculture to the use of permanent fields and the birth of village communities (Meinander 1980). Finnish Viking Age grave finds do not reflect the stratified society of the Merovingian period, but point instead to an egalitarian society of the type that usually characterizes affluent farming communities. None of the graves differ from the others—whether in construction, location, or grave goods—to the extent that they could be thought of as belonging to leaders with exclusive political power. This does not mean, of course, that there were no affluent landowners or merchants who could afford to buy expensive swords, nor that there were no paupers and slaves. Throughout this period, Finland maintained its own, more egalitarian social structure and identity. In this regard, the Finnish Viking period does not reflect the hierarchical social structure that is the hallmark of other Viking Age societies in Scandinavia and northern Europe.

6.17 Bronze Hoard
The most valued metal in Finland during the Viking Age was bronze, not silver as in Scandinavia. This hoard, consisting of jewelry from the eighth to the tenth centuries, was found in Hattemala, Häme. It probably belonged to a bronze molder who had scavenged these items from a burial ground.

7 "LAID WASTE, PLUNDERED, AND BURNED"

Vikings in Frankia

BY NEIL S. PRICE

FOR MANY SCHOLARS THE VIKING Age begins with the first recorded raid on England—the attack on Lindisfarne monastery in A.D. 793—and takes its tone from the ninth-century plundering expeditions in Britain and Ireland. This focus overlooks the fact that the same fleets, armies, and individuals that were active in the west also spent much of their time on the mainland continent of Europe in the lands of the Franks. Throughout most of the ninth century the monasteries, towns, and villages of the Frankish empire endured a sustained assault of looting and destruction unparalleled in their history. While this did not ultimately culminate in the kind of political transformations seen across the English Channel, the dislocation in the cultural life of Europe is hard to overstate. Some of the Vikings' most lasting achievements were grounded on the continent: short-lived adventures like the brief colony in Brittany were balanced by the establishment of such stable polities as the duchy of Normandy, which by the end of the eleventh century had expanded to conquer one of the most powerful kingdoms in all of Europe, England.

FROM CONTACT TO CONFLICT: THE EARLY RAIDS ON THE CAROLINGIAN EMPIRE

During the Viking Age western Europe was dominated by the Frankish empire of the Carolingians, the dynasty descended from Charlemagne the Great (reigned 768–814). The empire reached its greatest size during the early Viking period and the reign of Charlemagne's son Louis the Pious (emperor 814–840), when its territory included all of modern France, the Low Countries, Germany, Switzerland, Austria, most of the Italian peninsula, and extending south into Spain as far as Navarre. From approximately 800 onward, the empire's main administrative seat (effectively its capital) was the imperial palace at Aachen, then called Aix-la-Chapelle, in the modern Netherlands. The essential sources for the period are the court records of the empire, the *Royal Frankish Annals* (Scholtz 1970) and the so-called *Annals of St.-Bertin* (Nelson 1991), with an eastern perspective from the *Annals of Fulda* (Reuter 1992; useful recent overviews together with further references can be found in McKitterick 1983; Price 1989; Graham-Campbell and Batey 1994; Nelson 1992 and 1997; and Coupland 1995).

The empire was a complex political entity in a constant state of tension with its neighbors—a legacy of the prolonged military actions by which Charlemagne had forged his kingdom. Of key importance in the context of the Viking raids was the province of Frisia, a region of low-lying coastal plains and offshore islands that stretched from southern Denmark to the western Netherlands. The sea route to Frankia was a natural one from the Scandinavian homelands, and by the late eighth century many

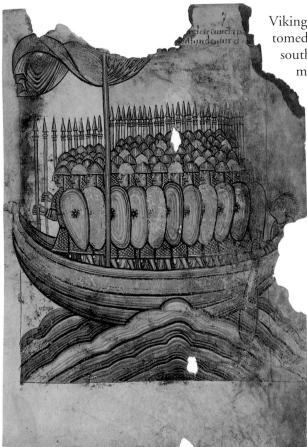

7.1 Viking Invasion

A Viking invasion of the French coast witnessed by Saint Aubin, who became the ninth-century Bishop of Angers, was recorded in the *Life of Saint Aubin*. The artist, who illustrated many other manuscripts at Saint Aubin Abbey, made several errors in the details, including the position of the steering oar and the shape of the shields, but the image of countless invades captures well the fear that Viking raiders instilled.

Vikings were quite accustomed to following the coast south-southwest from Denmark into northern Frankish waters. Long before the commencement of large-scale plundering expeditions, Scandinavians had traded with the rich mercantile centers of Frisia and the Low Countries: in flourishing emporia like Dorestad on the lower Rhine the Vikings witnessed the wealth of the empire's markets and especially its mints.

The transition from traders to raiders is not hard to understand, as it became increasingly clear to the Scandinavians how much portable wealth was to be had for comparatively little effort. The shock that monastic chroniclers recorded at the first Viking attacks should therefore be seen not as expressions of surprise at the sudden appearance of seaborne Scandinavians, but rather as incomprehension and dismay that their former (albeit rather irregular) trading partners had taken up arms to obtain what they had previously acquired through barter (fig. 7.1).

Although the first recorded attack on Frankia was in 799, in the Vendée region, it is unlikely that the raids began as a "bolt from the blue." In all probability, northern pirates were a not uncommon feature of the Frankish coasts in the last years of the eighth century, though as yet they posed no significant threat to the security of the realm. Over the next two decades the main focus of Viking attention was on Ireland, and Scandinavian attacks on the empire were mainly confined to raids on the Frisian islands.

By the 830s the raids on Frisia had begun to escalate alarmingly and were better organized. There is no doubt that at least some of the Viking commanders were well informed on the disorganized political situation in Frankia. The emperor's sons had begun to openly oppose their father, leading to dissent and several outbreaks of rebellion. The chronicles hint several times at Viking involvement in such conspiracies, noting for example that a bishop who had plotted against the emperor in a failed coup made his escape "with the help of certain northmen."

The trading settlement of Dorestad was burned and looted by Danes every year between 834 and 837. By the time of the fourth and most ambitious of these assaults, the imperial annalist wrote cynically of the Vikings' "usual surprise attack" and observed that civil disobedience and breakdowns in the military command structure were making resistance to the raiders impossible. While the Franks disagreed about what to do, the Scandinavians felt free to establish a temporary base on the island of Walcheren, now in the Netherlands. Matters were finally resolved by the arrival of an army led by the emperor in person, as much to suppress revolt among the Frisians as to drive off the Vikings, who left immediately.

Given that the Carolingians monitored developments in external spheres in general and Scandinavian domestic politics in particular, it is ironic that a series of events that temporarily destabilized the Frankish empire from within gave the Vikings the opportunity to establish themselves on the continent of Europe in a manner quite different from the hit-and-run operations that characterized the early phase of raiding. In 840 when emperor Louis the Pious died, the already simmering tensions within the realm gave way to full-scale civil war; in the three years of conflict that followed, the empire was crucially divided.

THE FRANKISH CIVIL WAR: VIKINGS AND OTHER POLITICIANS

In the turmoil that preceded Louis's death, a significant indicator of the second phase of Scandinavian attacks on Frankia had passed almost unnoticed: in 819 a small Viking force had established a temporary camp on the island of Noirmoutier at the mouth of the Loire. Noirmoutier was an ideal point from which to command both Brittany to the north and the southern Atlantic coast, as well as the river route inland to the Frankish heartlands. A monastery housing the relics of Saint Philibert was situated on Noirmoutier, which the Vikings used initially as an intermittent base, but by 836 the monastic com-

7.2 GLASS FROM THE RHINELAND
During the Roman Iron Age (A.D. 200) Scandinavian chieftains used glass drinking vessels as a sign of prestige, and this tradition continued through the Viking Age. Familiarity with prestige goods available in Europe and the desire to acquire them certainly motivated the Viking raids. This glass beaker decorated with reticella yellow and blue trails was found at the trade site of Birka in Sweden.

7.3 LOOTED FASHIONS
Fine sword mounts made of gilded silver, which were popular in the Carolingian empire, caught the eye of Viking raiders. This nearly complete sword mount with a three-pointed center piece may have been acquired as payment. Copies of such sword mounts became popular as Viking women's jewelry.

munity had abandoned the entire island to the Scandinavians. The establishment of the Viking base at Noirmoutier signals the creation of what scholars call the Army of the Loire, the first of three major Scandinavian forces that were to remain in the empire more or less continually for several decades.

While the base at Noirmoutier was being set up, the strife between Louis and his sons was intensifying. Four years later when the emperor died, the Vikings were firmly established on the continent as new players in a complex political game that had been ongoing essentially since the collapse of the Roman Empire. In the war for imperial succession following Louis's death, the main factions were represented by his sons and their respective supporters: Lothar, who had control of the Italian territories; Louis the German, whose power base lay east of the Rhine; and Charles the Bald, who had been the most loyal of the emperor's sons and who after the latter's death controlled most of France and the Low Countries. The situation was complicated by various groups of disaffected Carolingian nobles, renegade army commanders and administrators, independent warlords and their mercenaries, a range of provincial and ethnic factions, and even elements of the church, all struggling for control of the trappings of empire.

The Vikings operated in this context not simply as a destructive external force, but also as a significant factor in Frankia's internecine conflicts, choosing and changing sides at many different levels as it suited them. The undifferentiated mass of "Vikings" that we may perceive today, perhaps blunted by the relatively bland terms used in the contemporary sources (such as *nordmanni*,

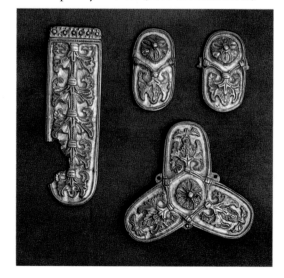

"northmen"), conceals an extremely complex reality. We can trace many different fleets and Viking forces operating on the continent in the ninth century, each with their own commanders, motives, and objectives. Some of the groups, or perhaps only specific elements in them, had more fluid command structures, with decisions made by committee or even by drawing lots. All these different kinds of forces could combine on occasion, or fragment into other, different groups; it was also not unknown for Vikings to fight each other, either on their own account or for pay. A particularly controversial issue is the size of the fleets in question (Gillmor 1988; Nelson 1997: 35–42; Sawyer 1971; Brooks 1979), and most current estimates acknowledge a range of forces from small flotillas of three or four ships up to major fleets of several hundred vessels.

For three years the Frankish territories were riven by conflict, and while the Carolingians fought each other, the Vikings raided as never before. In 841, Lothar allied himself with a commander called Haraldur and granted him possession of the island fortress at Walcheren that the Scandinavians had earlier used as a temporary base. The long-term effect of this was the establishment of the second of the three Scandinavian bases on imperial soil: the so-called Army of the Somme.

The third base was set up the same year when the largest Viking fleet yet seen in Frankia sailed into the Seine and moved upriver, burning monasteries at Rouen and Jumièges, sacking settlements, and taking captives; they were only stopped when they tried the same tactics on the Loire and were met by the forces of Charles the Bald. This fleet, known as the Army of the Seine, appeared regularly on the continent for many years, although unlike the Loire Vikings they did not overwinter in Frankia until the early 850s. The Seine Vikings variously operated independently of their compatriots on the Loire and Somme, in cooperation with them, or occasionally on opposing sides.

The attacks grew worse in 842 when Frisia again came under heavy assault. The long-sought end of the Frankish civil war came in 843, when the empire was partitioned into three kingdoms each ruled by one of Louis the Pious's sons: Lothar received the broad corridor of lands between the Rhine and the Scheldt; Louis the German was granted the territories east of the Rhine;

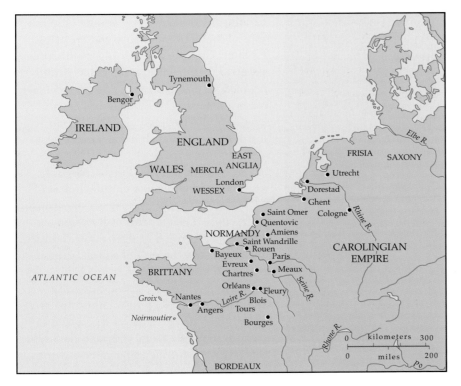

RAID LOCATIONS IN FRANKIA

The raids of the following years were too numerous to recount here in detail. Every summer the long ships would leave their winter bases or arrive from Scandinavia, returning to familiar places on the coasts or harrying up and down the great rivers. The same settlements, monasteries, and trading centers were attacked again and again; the Vikings carried off everything portable in the way of loot and supplied themselves with the crops and produce of the region. Taking captives for sale into slavery (or, more often, ransom) was a constant feature of these raids that has been somewhat underplayed by historians; numerous nobles of both sexes, together with churchmen, nuns, and layfolk were taken prisoner, and their freedom had to be bought back by the Frankish rulers for sometimes vast sums of gold and silver (see Nelson 1997: 28–29, 37).

Aquitaine and its settlements were hit in 845, 848, 849, and throughout the 850s. The Seine Vikings wintered on the river for the first time in 851–852, and established bases on the islands at Oissel and Jeufosse. In 856 Paris was attacked again, and for a whole decade thereafter the Seine basin was raided every year, without intermission. The blitzkrieg-like effects of the Viking advance are clear, and for much of the mid-ninth century it must have seemed to the ordinary people of Frankia that their world was ending. The monasteries, villages, and towns of the interior burned, as the river valleys that had once been arteries of commerce became highways for the raiders to strike deep into the heartlands of Charles's kingdom. The sense of unstoppable calamity is vividly conveyed by the monastic commentator Ermentarius of Noirmoutier, who around 860 penned a memorable list of disasters:

> The number of ships grows: the endless stream of Vikings never ceases to increase. Everywhere the Christians are the victims of massacres, burnings, plunderings. The Vikings conquer all in their path and nothing resists them: they seize Bordeaux, Périgeux, Limoges, Angoulême, and Toulouse. Angers, Tours, and Orléans are annihilated and an innumerable fleet sails up the Seine and the evil grows in the whole region. Rouen is laid waste, plundered and burned: Paris, Beauvais, and Meaux taken, Melun's strong fortress leveled to the ground, Chartres occupied, Evreux and Bayeux plundered, and every town besieged.

and Charles ruled the rest of the empire as far south as Spain, including most of modern France. The end of the civil war did not bring peace, however, because the three Viking armies on Frankish soil began the coordinated assault on the empire in earnest.

THE VIKING ASSAULT ON FRANKIA

It is hard to judge whether at first the Carolingians were aware of the extent of the crisis that faced them. For the first time the Scandinavians spent the whole winter in their base on Noirmoutier, "in something like a permanent settlement," as the *Annals of St.-Bertin* worriedly noted in their record for 843. Raiding was constant thereafter, and within two years the Vikings were at the gates of Paris—to the evident disbelief of the monks of St. Germain-des-Prés, whose description conveys both the unusual nature of the situation and its gravity: "In the year of our Lord 845, the vast army of Norsemen breached the frontiers of the Christians. This was something that we never heard or read of happening before." The Viking army was bought off from destroying the city by a massive payment of nearly six tons of silver and gold bullion, in the first of what would become a regular series of such extortions, known as *danegeld*. Over the next decades towns, monasteries, and sometimes even individual house owners would frequently pay the raiders to leave their property untouched.

7.4 HON HOARD

This extraordinary hoard containing a gold trefoil brooch from Frankia, a large golden neckring from Russia, Arabian, Byzantine, and English coins, and other items of the finest craftsmanship, which may have been collected in Paris as insurance against future Viking raids, was deposited in a bog in Hon, Norway. It is not understood why hoards were buried; was it an offering to the gods, insurance for life after death, a method of storing precious goods that were never retrieved, or an attempt to hide them from raiders? The number of hoards indicates that they were part of Viking religious or social practice, not just accidental leftovers.

The attacks took a steep economic toll on the Franks; the spoils of the Vikings' endeavors have been found by archaeologists all over Scandinavia in the form of Carolingian jewelry, decorated mounts from book covers or other objects, reliquaries and ecclesiastical objects, other kinds of metalwork in silver or gold, glassware, and so on (Arbman 1937). Particularly spectacular examples, which illustrate the richness of the loot that Viking raiders obtained in Frankia, include Danish finds such as the silver liturgical cup from Fejø and the strap-end from Als; Swedish finds such as the Frankish glass from Birka (fig. 7.2) and the sword mounts (fig. 7.3); and finds from Norway such as the trefoil mount from Huseby (Graham-Campbell 1980: 92–4; Roesdahl and Wilson 1992: 258). The largest and richest hoard from the Viking Age, which was found at Hon in Norway (fig. 7.4), included a gold trefoil brooch of the very finest

Carolingian workmanship among objects from all over western Europe and even Russia (Graham-Campbell 1980: 143); it has been suggested that the deposit represents part of the *danegeld* paid in Paris in 858 (Roesdahl and Wilson 1992: 234). Hundreds of Frankish coins have also been found, either in buried hoards or sometimes reused as parts of necklaces and other jewelry.

It was not until 862 that Charles the Bald was at last able to gain full control of his domain and take decisive action against the Vikings. The emperor ordered the construction of fortified bridges across the Loire and Seine, which were linked to fortresses that could block the passage of a Viking fleet along the waterways (see Gillmor 1989; Coupland 1991). As part of his campaigns against the Vikings, Charles was forced to resort to more desperate measures, including sometimes submitting to the raiders' demands for "protection money" and even entering into alliance with specific groups of Scandinavians in an effort to play them off against each other.

By 865 the new difficulties they had encountered in Frankia persuaded many of the fleets to try their luck in England, and the Vikings success there had the effect of shifting their attention from the continent for over a decade, during which time the Franks consolidated their defenses but were once more weakened by internal conflicts. Twenty years later, just as they had after the death of Louis the Pious in 840, the Vikings took advantage of the Franks' disorganization following the emperor's passing and returned to Frankia from England in 879, again launching probing attacks in Frisia and Flanders. In 881 another fleet cruised the Rhine and its tributaries, taking more than fourteen towns and even the royal palace at Aachen; the Vikings used the imperial chapel as a stable for their horses.

By 884 the scale of the destruction resembled scenes familiar from modern warfare. The *Annals of St. Vaast*, written in the monastery at Arras in northern Flanders, records the signs of the times that year:

> The Norsemen continued to kill and take Christian people captive, destroy churches, tear down fortifications and burn towns. Along all the roads lay the bodies of clergy and laity, nobles and commoners, women, children and infants. There was no highway or village where the dead did not lie, and all were filled with torment and grief to see the

7.5, 7.6 Gjermundbu Helmet
The only complete Viking helmet found to date was reconstructed from fragments discovered at a chieftain's cremation burial in Gjermundbu, Norway. Pieces of chain mail (fig. 7.6) hung from the back of the helmet; other fragments, which were likely a chain mail shirt, were also found. The apertures for eyes gave the wearer a fierce catlike appearance like illustrations in the Bayeux Tapestry, but the helmet has no horns!

devastation of the Christian people, driven to the point of extermination.

In 885 half the Viking forces turned once more for England, while the remainder sailed south to the Seine and resumed their activities. The fleet pushed deeper and deeper up the river, until finally a Viking army stood before the gates of Paris for a third time (figs. 7.5, 7.6). The initial attack failed after fierce fighting on the walls; as did an attempt to set the defenses on fire, which has come down to us in an extraordinary eye-witness account of a monk watching from the cathedral precincts who describes how the glow from the flames turned the sky over the city "the color of copper." For more than a year Paris was encircled by the Scandinavians, until Charles the Fat finally arrived with a relief force and brought food to the starving inhabitants.

After Charles was deposed in 887, the division of the empire gave rise to two leaders of great military skill whose experience and tenacity halted the final phase of the Viking assault. In the west, the Franks were led by the newly crowned king Odo, who had ably commanded Paris during the long siege of 885. Over the next two years Viking fleets were driven from the Seine, and the area was secured. In the east, an equally tough resistance campaign was launched by the new king Arnulf. The Scandinavians were met with heavy resistance everywhere, and the Franks reinforced their position with fortifications and defenses. By 890 a large part of the Viking force had withdrawn, and in 891 the Franks won a decisive victory at Louvain.

The time of the great raids was over, but the damage to the empire had been immense. According to the continental sources, the *danegeld* payments made by the Franks during the ninth century amounted to around twelve tons of silver, most of it in cash: seven million silver pennies was paid in protection money to the Vikings over a period when the estimated total output of the Frankish mints was fifty million coins (Nelson 1997: 36–37). Even without reckoning the supplies of grain, livestock, produce, wine, cider, horses, and other commodities frequently demanded in addition to the payments of bullion, that sum was equivalent to 14 percent of the entire monetary output of the western empire for most of the century. To this we must add the cost in towns and villages burned, monasteries sacked, and markets looted: at least 120 named settle-

Image caption text within tapestry: **HIC HAROLD REX INTERFECTUS EST**

7.7 NORMAN VIKINGS
The Bayeux Tapestry was created in 1077 to commemorate the Norman invasion of England, which was led in 1066 by William the Conqueror, a descendent of the Viking chieftain Rollo. The 230 foot (70 meter) embroidery includes detailed and accurate depictions of the warriors' material culture. The "cartoon strip" narrative form includes captions like the one that accompanies this scene, "Harold dies after having been shot in the eye with an arrow." With Harold's death, the major Viking raids in Europe ceased and The Viking Age ended.

ments were attacked in this way (some many times over) between 830 and 890 alone, not including those in Brittany, and not including the numerous references to the unspecified devastation of whole regions (see Hill 1981: 32–41). Lastly, the most basic cost, the lives lost and people physically removed to foreign slavery, may best reveal the catastrophic effects of Viking raids.

The fact that Frankish political institutions survived intact and with minimal administrative dislocation testifies more to the nature of Viking motivations (cash not conquest) and the disparate nature of their forces than it does to the heroic efforts of the imperial troops. Indeed, civil strife was the main factor leading to the division of the empire; politically, the Scandinavians functioned more as agents than catalysts. Nevertheless, the Franks had held their own and not gone under like some of the Anglo-Saxon kingdoms. When the Vikings returned to Frankia, it would not be to plunder and profit, but to cultivate opportunities for permanent settlement.

THE CREATION OF NORMANDY

By the end of the ninth century the Franks had at last built up sufficient defensive systems to withstand all but the most concerted Viking attacks. As a result, coordinated

Viking raiding activity largely ceased on the continent in the later 890s, to be replaced over the next few decades by a different kind of attack intended to secure permanent settlements that could serve as bases for continued raids. The majority of these were in northern and eastern England, Scotland, and Ireland, but two Viking colonies were established in Europe during the early tenth century.

In 896 a small fleet appeared on the Seine, which for five years had completely been free from attack; these Vikings laid the foundations of what would eventually become the Duchy of Normandy (its creation and early years are discussed in detail by Bates 1982; Searle 1988; and most thoroughly by Renaud 1989). The new Frankish king, Charles the Simple, spent the first decade of his reign fighting repeated Viking incursions on the Seine, although none were on the scale of the great ninth-century assaults. An intriguing object found in the late 1980s at La Grande Paroisse in Seine-et-Marne bears witness to the raids from this period: a piece of clay daub, originally part of a wall, scratched with the image of a Viking ship under sail (Roesdahl and Wilson 1992: 317). A more graphic reminder of the Viking incursions are the numerous swords that have been dredged from all along the lower Seine, together with a single Scandina-

7.8, 7.9 STRIKING WEAPONS
Swords and "weapon knives" were used when locked in close combat. Swords were on average two feet (.6 meters) long (or a bit more), which made them effective striking weapons. Sword blades were usually imported from Frankia (the same area the Vikings were invading!); hilts were often made in Scandinavia and decorated with inlaid silver and copper wiring. The smaller knives were jabbing devices, quick and deadly. Even with the handle missing, this knife measure over a foot (34 centimeters).

7.10 TERROR FROM THE SKY
The sagas often mention *skothrí* (shower of arrows) when describing battles; and the memorable sound arrows made when hurtling through the sky was referred to as "Odin's wind" in Old Norse poetry, after the god of war.

vian axe (Arbman 1969; Price 1989: 82).

By the end of the first decade of the tenth century the two forces, Carolingian and Viking, seem to have fought themselves to a standstill (figs. 7.6– 7.12). The Scandinavian control of the lower river was unbreakable, but a major Viking outbreak seemed equally containable, and it appears that a negotiated solution was sought on both sides. The exact details of the arrangement made between Charles and the Seine Vikings are unclear from the fragmentary and contentious sources that have come down to us, but in 911 a treaty was signed at St. Clair-sur-Epte between the king and the Viking leader Hrolfur, who is usually known by his Frankish name, Rollo. The Scandinavians were granted land around Rouen on the condition that they cease their expeditions inland and protect the Seine against other raiders.

This may have been intended by the Franks as nothing more than a temporary measure of the kind taken on several occasions in the ninth century, but the Vikings clearly had other ideas. Rollo and his followers began to parcel out the land between the Epte and Risle rivers and settled there with a de facto capital at Rouen.

The Scandinavians "protected" the Seine for a short time, but soon Rollo was lead-

ing his own raids again—though now from the security of a settled homeland rather than a mobile fleet and island fortresses. Rollo, who had expanded his lands as far west as the Vire River, handed power to his son, William Longsword, before dying in 927. William was not an idle ruler and launched a concerted campaign to conquer the Cotentin peninsula to the west of the Vire. When this was achieved in 933, William controlled a geographically contained area along the northern seaboard, with a defensible inland border against the Franks. Through his single-minded ambition—offset by a combination of Frankish weakness and negligence—a new polity had been formed, with defined borders fixed by treaty and ruled by dynastic succession: *Nordmannia*, "the land of the Northmen," or Normandy (fig. 7.7).

It is remarkable that by the early tenth century Normandy had acquired the boundaries that it retains today as a French province. Its population was not stable, however, and showed considerable ethnic complexity. Scandinavian place-names, scattered throughout Normandy, testify to the breadth of settlement, although they may reflect the fact of administrative control in Viking hands rather than a large number of colonists. Rollo, though a Norwegian, seems to have led a following comprised mostly of Danes, which is reflected in the place-names of eastern Normandy, the area granted in the first treaty of 911. The names in the western part of the region show a marked Celtic influence, which strongly suggest that Irish-Norse immigrants, relocated here from the Viking colonies in Ireland, along with others from Scandinavia itself, England, Orkney, and the Hebrides (see Price 1989: 39–40). The colony and its population were clearly built up over some time, with repeated influxes of new settlers from different parts of the Viking world.

The Scandinavian newcomers seem to have been quickly assimilated into the local Frankish population. There are very few obviously pagan graves, which implies either a fairly rapid adoption of Christianity by the

7.11, 7.12 WARRIOR'S WEAPONS
The most common weapons used by Vikings were broad-bladed battle-axes and spears. Silver inlay in this spear socket shows the care given to creating some warrior's weapons.

Seine Vikings or, at least, that they followed local burial customs regardless of their actual beliefs. At Pîtres near Rouen, a woman's grave has been found with a complete set of what is definitely Scandinavian jewelry, including two fine oval shoulder brooches. There is no doubt that the immigrants included people of both sexes, but we cannot be sure that the Pîtres woman was a Viking, only that she wore clothes and ornaments of Scandinavian style. Historian Janet Nelson put it elegantly, "She may have been a Dane who had embraced Christianity . . . she may have been a Frank who had embraced a Dane" (1997: 47).

By the time of William Longsword, a second-generation Viking who took command of his father's domain in 927, the use of the Norse language seems to have declined rapidly; it probably died out completely in Normandy in the early eleventh century. Because the Norman rulers were keen to establish themselves on an equal footing with their Frankish peers, adopting the appropriate trappings of European lordship quickly became more important than maintaining a redundant Scandinavian identity. Through this kind of political adaptation and rapid integration with the native populace, the idea of a Frankish reconquest became ever more distant. By the very beginning of the eleventh century the Norman rulers were already referring to themselves as *dux*—"Duke"—and their duchy was an established principality in the cultural sphere of literate, Christian Europe.

THE CONQUEST OF BRITTANY

In addition to the area that became the duchy of Normandy, the Vikings attempted the conquest and semipermanent settlement of one other region of the European mainland: the small, independent province of Brittany in northwestern France. The Bretons were a Celtic people who had much in common with the British population of Devon and Cornwall across the English Channel: indeed, Brittany may originally have been settled by refugees fleeing the successive Roman and Saxon invasions of Britain. They spoke their own language, elected their own rulers, and maintained distinctive cultural traditions, including a Breton church whose liturgy and practices were unique to this area (Galliou and Jones 1991). There was little enthusiasm in the province for the trappings of Frankish power.

Before the early 840s Brittany seems to have been relatively untroubled by raiding, though the Viking base at Noirmoutier was uncomfortably close. The opportunistic attacks that were launched during the Frankish civil war also reached the Bretons. In 843 a large fleet arrived at Nantes: after heavy fighting in the city, the Vikings took the cathedral, killing the bishop, all the priests, and many others before continuing down the Loire. Nominoë, the Carolingian-appointed leader of the Bretons who had later rebelled to lead an independent Brittany, fought and repulsed the same Scandinavians the following year. Like Frankia, Brittany suffered continual raiding for much of the 840s, including a massive attack in 847 when the Bretons lost three pitched battles to the Vikings (figs. 7.13–7.15).

For thirty years Brittany experienced the familiar pattern of Viking raiding in combination with Breton and Frankish political maneuvering. In 886 a huge force of Scandinavians descended on Brittany, after having been slowly forced back from Frankish territory following the relief of Paris, and Nantes was captured with its surrounding territory. Since 874 Brittany had been divided between two parallel governing houses, which could not cooperate efficiently, and in 888 western Brittany was overrun by raiders. The last descendant of Nominoë was killed in battle against the Vikings that year, and therefore Brittany once more had a single ruler, Alain of Vannes. He united the Bretons and led them to a major victory, which drove the Loire Vikings back to Noirmoutier and freed the province of Scandinavians. Between 889 and 891 a series of attempts were made on the province by the Seine Vikings, who were defeated by the Bretons in collaboration with the Franks. From 892 until his death in 907, Alain maintained peace and stability in Brittany, rebuilt its institutions, and kept his land free from Viking attack; his achievements are reflected in the name by which he became known to his people, Alain the Great.

The establishment of Viking Normandy was to have dire consequences for Brittany, which by 911 had become the only target in western Europe for those Scandinavians who had no intention of abandoning the Viking life and settling (figs. 17.13–17.17). With a relatively stable border with Normandy and Rollo's followers effectively protecting the Seine, the Franks were more than happy to see the Viking problem concentrated beyond their borders in the lands of their old enemies: the Bretons were politically isolated, alienated from the expedient alliances of the ninth century.

In 912 and 913 Brittany's coasts were hit by the worst raiding in the province's history: several monasteries were completely destroyed, and the roads filled with refugees. In 914 the situation began to deteriorate seriously when a new fleet of Danes arrived from the Severn in south Wales. This group of Vikings stayed in Brittany for four years, and under commanders Ottar and Haraldur effectively ruled the province, although there are no indications that they actually settled down like their countrymen on the Seine; instead they lived more or less as an army of occupation. By 919 Ottar and Haraldur's Vikings had returned to England and Wales, but in the same year a new and even more powerful group of Norwegians arrived in Brittany from the Loire. Their commander, Rognvaldur, had come to stay.

First to fall was Nantes, which the Vikings took and occupied, apparently using it as a capital for their operations. The thoroughness of the Viking campaign is shown by the mass exodus of Bretons, including the son-in-law and infant grandson of Alain the Great, who took refuge in England. The remaining records from this period describe how shiploads of nobles, administrators, and clerics sailed into exile, while others fled to Frankia; the peasants were left to endure Viking rule, and large parts of the country are described as being virtually depopulated . After 920 there is an almost complete absence of documentary records from Brittany, eloquent testimony to the fact that no one seems to have been left to write them.

By 921 Rognvaldur's takeover of Brittany was complete; and the Franks, having failed in an attempt to dislodge the Vikings and claim the province for themselves, even recognized him as the legitimate ruler. The tide turned against the Vikings in Brittany during the 930s and their situation worsened in 935 when the Normans made a solid alliance with the Franks, thus leaving the occupying forces as politically isolated as the Bretons had been before the invasion.

In 936 some members of the Breton clergy who had remained behind sent letters to the exiles in England requesting their help for another rebellion. During the Viking occupation the grandson of Alain the Great—also called Alain and nicknamed Twisted-Beard—had grown up as a favorite at the court of the English king. When the request for aid came in 936, Alain was provided with a fleet and auxiliary troops by the Anglo-Saxons and crossed safely to Brittany with an army of his exiled countrymen. The landing seems to have taken the Vikings completely by surprise, and Alain moved around northern Brittany fighting group after group of Scandinavians. His army grew, swelled by Bretons who had remained after the Viking invasion, and quickly drove the Vikings back to the area around Nantes, where they built a fortress for protection. After a whole day of intense fighting in blazing sun, Alain's army stormed the ramparts and the Vikings fled, retreating down the Loire by ship. By 939 Brittany, liberated after more than twenty years of occupation, would see no more major Viking activity until the late eleventh century when the Bretons would find themselves drawn increasingly under the domination of Normandy.

Where the Norman settlements had succeeded, the occupation of Brittany had failed: so what kind of colony was this? In effect, Brittany seems to have been a very large and very long-lived Viking base. The Scandinavians forced the local people to pro-

7.15

7.14

7.13

7.13–7.15 A Vikings' Companion
Horses voyaged with Vikings on raiding expeditions, rode into battlefields, labored on the farm, and were sometimes buried with their owners. Most Viking equestrian equipment is similar to what is used today: stirrups, spurs (fig. 7.15), bits, and grooming tools (fig. 7.13). Vikings did not shoe their horses; instead, when conditions were icy and slippery, spikes (fig. 7.14) were driven into the horses hooves.

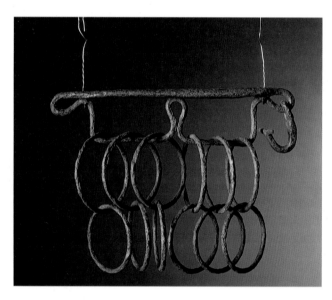

7.16, 7.17 SOUNDING THEIR
PRESENCE

A variety of noisemakers including
rattles, like this one made of three
layers of interlocking rings (fig. 7.17),
and chain-link whip mounts were
attached to the horse's saddle or to
the carriage. The noise they generated
was intended to strike fear into the
enemy, whether the foe was evil
spirits of the forests
or opponents on the battlefield.

vide their means of support, but the Vikings in Brittany do not seem to have developed the region's trading potential, as they did in other colonial settlements such as York and Dublin.

If they neither revived the Breton trading networks nor made their mark on the linguistic map, the Vikings did leave other material signs of their presence, all appropriately militant in nature. A circular fortification near Saint-Brieuc seems to have been either occupied or attacked by Scandinavians in the early part of the tenth century. Another similar fortification has been excavated at Trans, the site of the last battle with the Vikings in 939, and several others have been surveyed elsewhere in the province (see Price 1989: 55–63); the size of these other fortifications suggest that they could hold a force of perhaps one thousand men at most (Price 1991). Like the Seine, the Loire has given up numerous Viking swords and other weapons from the period

of Scandinavian contact (Arbman 1969; Price 1989: 72–75).

Perhaps the most representative archaeological find related to the Vikings in Brittany is also the most unique, and the most fitting with which to close a discussion of the Scandinavian adventure in Frankia. The magnificent ship burial constructed on the small island of Groix off the south Breton coast is one of the most spectacular finds outside Scandinavia from the entire Viking Age, and the only European burial of its kind (Price 1989: 64–72; Müller-Wille 1978). Sometime during the first half of the tenth century, a forty-three-foot (thirteen-meter) long ship was dragged up onto a rocky headland overlooking the sea and laid out on a prepared site surrounded by standing stones. In the ship were laid the bodies of an adult and an adolescent—the latter may have been a human sacrifice of a kind found in other Viking graves—together with a great variety of objects that strongly imply that the burial was that of a man; these included two swords, a quiver of arrows, four lances, two axes, up to twenty-four shields, riding equipment, a gaming set, a variety of metalworking tools and agricultural implements, and a large assortment of household vessels, bowls, and cauldrons. The dead man was dressed in fine-quality clothing, with gold appliqués and jewelry of precious metals, and was accompanied in the ship by the bodies of sacrificed dogs and birds. The entire ship and its contents had been set on fire, and the ashes covered with an earthen mound.

Who was the Groix warrior? The date of the burial suggests that he died during the Viking occupation, and the immense wealth of the grave implies that he had attained the highest status in his society; no certain identification is possible, but it is tempting to speculate that he may have been one of the army commanders mentioned in the sources, and perhaps even Rognvaldur himself. The grave is certainly an anachronism, an extravagant pagan gesture in the grand manner, belonging to an age that had already passed. As such, it connotes the image of the Vikings in Brittany, as in many ways the last of their kind, the final flourish of the European raiding tradition.

VIKING EXPANSION AND CULTURAL BLENDING IN BRITAIN AND IRELAND

BY COLLEEN E. BATEY AND JOHN SHEEHAN

MONK IN SCRIPTORIUM, *HAMBURD MANUSCRIPT*

THE ARRIVAL OF THE VIKINGS IN England is recorded in the *Anglo-Saxon Chronicle* under the year 793:

> In this year dire portents appeared over Northumbria and sorely frightened the people. They consisted of immense whirlwinds and flashes of lightning, and fiery dragons were seen flying in the air. The great famine immediately followed those signs, and a little after that in the same year, on 8 June, the ravages of heathen men miserably destroyed God's church on Lindisfarne, with plunder and slaughter.

The graphic description of this event, which was probably not the first of its kind on the British Isles, has set the tone our understanding of the Vikings (fig. 8.2). Although the reported actions undoubtedly took place and were not isolated or unique events, it is only the beginning of the story of a people and their expansion westward. This expansion dominated the political and social history of parts of the British Isles for six hundred years or more and was to have a profound effect on the Viking movements northward and westward, ultimately to Vinland, in North America, for the British Isles provided a stepping stone toward the North Atlantic and, perhaps most significantly, provided some of the people who traveled to the new colonies of the North Atlantic.

THE EARLY VIKING RAIDS ON BRITAIN AND IRELAND

Although the attack on Lindisfarne in 793 is the best known of the Viking raids, the *Anglo-Saxon Chronicle* announced the arrival in 789 of three ships carrying Scandinavians at Portland in southwest England. The killing of a royal officer of the Wessex crown may

well have been a misunderstanding rather than a premeditated action, but it was in character with events that followed in subsequent years. Following the Lindisfarne raid, the eminent cleric Alcuin of York, who was an official at the court of Charlemagne at Aachen, wrote to the king of Northumbria:

> Never before has such terror appeared in Britain as we have now suffered from a pagan race, nor was it thought that such an inroad from the sea could be made. Behold the church of St. Cuthbert, spattered with the blood of the priests of God, despoiled of all its ornaments; a place more venerable than all in Britain is given as prey to pagan peoples. (Whitelock 1979: 842)

Subsequent Viking raids are frequently recorded: in 794 a second Northumbrian monastery came under attack (possibly Jarrow/Monkwearmouth or Tynemouth). Massive raiding attacks on Ireland and west Britain occurred in the following decades with renewed interest in English targets from the 830s (map, p. 131). Iona, off the west coast of Scotland, founded by the Irish ecclesiastic Saint Columcille in the sixth century, was subjected to three separate raids between

8.2 LINDISFARNE STONE

This ninth-century engraving is one of the most famous icons of the Viking Age. The carving on one face is thought to commemorate the dead lost in the first Viking raid in 793 at Lindisfarne Priory on the northeastern English coast, an event considered to mark the beginning of the Viking Age. The other face (opposite) shows the Day of Judgment.

8.1 THE CHESTER HOARD

A hoard of 522 silver coins mostly from Anglo-Saxon mints in Chester, Canterbury, Norwich, Winchester, and York, with two coins from France and one from Italy, was found in 1950 buried in a plain ceramic jug in the town of Chester. Accompanying this English coinage were 142 pieces of Viking-style silver (bracelets, silver rod, etc.) and more than eighty complete or fragmentary silver ingots. The coinage dates suggest that the hoard was hidden in the 970s, possibly by a cautious Viking trader as he approached a Saxon town.

795 and 806. This latter attack, which resulted in the deaths of sixty-eight members of the monastery, led to the relocation of some of the religious community to Ireland.

Ireland saw its first attacks in 795, according to the *Irish Annals*, when the offshore islands of Rathlin, Inishmurray, and Inishbofin were attacked. Many other important monastic centers, particularly in the coastal regions of the northern half of Ireland, were plundered during the first forty years or so of the Viking Age. Armagh, for instance, was raided on no less than three occasions in the year 832 alone. Such attacks were not motivated by any form of anti-Christian feelings by the pagan Vikings; rather they focused on the monasteries as the main repositories of economic and cultural wealth in a country otherwise characterized by relatively small dispersed farmsteads .

The magnetic effect that the monasteries had for the Vikings is clear; these were centers of manufacturing of fine metalwork made to adorn holy books and reliquaries. For the Vikings these were attractive and highly portable—loot in the simplest sense—and many items found their way back to Scandinavian Viking graves (fig. 8.28). Other pieces remained in the British Isles in the hands of Viking settlers, as in the case of the shrine mounts from Carn a' Bharraich on Oronsay (fig. 8.5) that were modified to make brooches and the horse-harness equipment from the Viking burial at Navan in Ireland. The simple view of looting and destruction is not accurate however; the case of Ranvaig's Casket (p. 100), for example, cannot be so simply dismissed. This

and depredations of the Viking raiders are known. Consequently, it is difficult to gauge the actual effects of early Viking activity on Irish society at this time. Undoubtedly the Vikings took slaves, and the many finds of metalwork stylistically linked to the British Isles recovered from graves in Norway are testimony to the losses suffered by the Irish church. Apart from these looted items, however, remarkably few monastic centers in the British Isles have yielded evidence of the violent raiding of the Scandinavians.

The early raids, limited in geographical extent, probably had little real impact on England, Scotland, or Ireland as a whole. The fact that some monastic centers suffered repeated attacks can be interpreted as an indication of their resilience, and it is clear that in both social and economic terms, Ireland was a wealthy, well-populated country capable of surviving this type of marauding.

reliquary may have passed from a monastery in Scotland or Ireland, presumably through the hands of a Viking, to a Viking lady in Scandinavia by the name of Ranvaig. Her name was carved in runes on the casket that she may have used to hold personal items. Later in its history it held late medieval holy relics wrapped in silk. Whether Ranvaig valued it as a holy item is unknown, but it was sufficiently attractive in its complete form to prevent its being broken up for elaborate jewelry. In the case of fine book mounts found in Viking contexts, presumed to have originally been attached to leather bindings, it is much harder to judge whether the book was given in good faith to a visiting Viking rather than stolen, dismantled, or split between raiders after an attack.

From a historical perspective, raids on these relatively easy monastic targets certainly had a long-lasting effect on the subsequent record. For in these centers of learning, the very clerics who were victimized had the strongest weapon of all—their written testament. It is through the writings of the victims that the scale of the attacks

VIKINGS SETTLE IN

The nature and frequency of Viking raids increased during the first half of the ninth century. The *Irish Annals* report the presence of larger fleets and, in the early 840s, they note that the Vikings began to overwinter in Ireland for the first time. Some form of defended ship harbors, termed *longphorts* by the annalists, were built at Dublin and elsewhere. These events appear to testify to more organized Viking intent against Ireland, which is supported by the range of raiding recorded in historical documents. The cemeteries at Islandbridge and Kilmainham almost certainly contain residents of the Dublin *longphort*, which was in existence until 902. The cemeteries contained at least eighty burials, and the majority of them were occupied by males accompanied by weapons and, to a lesser extent, the paraphernalia of trade (balance scales, weights, etc.). The evi-

8.3, 8.4 ARM RINGS

Arm rings were worn as tokens of allegiance by those who received them as gifts from benefactors. Made from silver coins, they were also likely to be cut up and given out as coin of the Viking realm. Irish-Viking arm rings of this type are specific to the Irish Sea region and were probably made by Norse settlers in Dublin in the late ninth and early tenth centuries.

dence suggests that these Dublin graves, dating to the second half of the ninth century, were those of a Norse military elite who also engaged in commerce (O'Brien 1996).

This intensification of Viking activity from the 840s galvanized an Irish response, and resulted in Irish victories in several important battles. At about this time the historical sources begin to record the development of alliances—political, military, economic, personal—between the Irish and the Scandinavians: these events marked the beginnings of long-lasting linguistic influence. A gradual process began whereby the Viking populations of the *longphorts* became more integrated with Irish ways. The best archaeological evidence of this process is the large amounts of silver acquired by the Irish from the Vikings, presumably mainly through trade and tribute, during the later ninth century. Many hoards of this precious

commodity have been found on Irish settlement sites, such as the find of ingots and hacksilver (cut-up pieces of silver) from the ring-shaped fort—a classic type of Viking defensive site—at Carraig Aille, County Limerick (O'Riordain 1949).

In southern England the first overwintering is dated to 850 with a settlement on the Isle of Sheppey, but the years from 835 to that time had been hard on the kingdom of Wessex on the coastal fringes of southern England. Presumably, Viking interest in the lands of the Frankish empire, a short sea journey across the English Channel, occasioned attacks on London, Rochester in Kent, Dorset, and Southampton, as well as on the east coast kingdom of Lindsay and into Northumbria, which are described in the *Anglo-Saxon Chronicle*.

In 866 the largest Viking army ever seen arrived in East Anglia, the districts northeast of present-day London. The presence of what is known as the Great Army marked the change from sporadic small-scale attacks to massive army campaigns with the goal of permanent settlement. The Great Army reached a temporary peace with the East Angles that year and moved north the following year into Northumbria, where they overpowered local rulers and established a base at York. Surrounding kingdoms were attacked in seasonal forays until the Vikings controlled the whole of north and east England; only the southeastern district of Mercia, in central England, and the southwestern region, Wessex, held out. Sustained and bloody battles ensued between the Vikings and the West Saxons (fig. 8.8), with the Saxons under King Alfred achieving a temporary respite in 871 when the Vikings retreated to London. From that base the Vikings turned to securing Mercia, which encompassed all the districts surrounding the city. The major excavations at Repton in Derbyshire may have revealed the defended camp the Vikings built for their army to overwinter in 873–874 during this campaign. The vast charnel deposit of burned human bones found there may contain the remains of warriors from the Great Army.

To the north, the *Anglo-Saxon Chronicle* records in 876 that "Halfdan shared out the land of the Northumbrians, and they proceeded to plough and support themselves." This became the Vikings' first permanent settlement in England, and farming was a

VIKING BRITAIN

line to Bedford, then up the Ouse to Watling Street." The lands north and east of this border and well into Northumbria, at its northern limit, were to be under Viking control and became known as the Danelaw (Jones 1984).

Between 892 and 900 there were several Viking raids and battles over Danelaw lands. By 927 Aethelstan, the Anglo-Saxon king, was ruling a kingdom concentrated in northern England with York as its focus. In 937 at the battle of Brunanburh, Aethelstan was victorious over a combined force of Vikings, but on his death in 939 the Viking kings of Dublin reestablished power in York and controlled it with the use of puppet kings. The Viking kingdom could not be sustained, however, and it disintegrated on the death of the last Viking king, Erik Bloodaxe, who was murdered in 954.

VIKING TOWNS

The Danelaw can clearly be identified today by the striking distribution of place-names of Scandinavian origin. Place-name elements such as -by, meaning a settlement or village, may have been the most obvious group of Viking-influenced place-names. Examples include Aislaby, Balby, and Selby, most commonly associated with a Scandinavian personal name as the first part of the place-name. Names ending in -thorpe seem to indicate marginal lands, for instance, Bishop-thorpe or Towthorpe. The loose confederation of settlements known as the Five Boroughs within the Danelaw—Derby, Stamford, Leicester, Nottingham, and Lincoln—were all fortified centers that were to become towns. Recent excavations at Norwich, a principal center in the Danelaw, show that the settlement that began in the ninth century grew steadily to become a major urban area. Excavations in Lincoln have revealed the far-reaching contacts of such mercantile centers: material imported from Scandinavia as well as farther afield has been recovered. However, the most thoroughly investigated town in the Danelaw to date is York, and this provides a yardstick for our current understanding of the nature of Viking town life in England.

YORK

Extensive excavations have been undertaken in York over several decades, beginning with a series of small-scale investigations and stray

novel development in the British experience of Viking activity, as the astounded chronicler attests. Shortly after this, the Viking commander Guthrum led his army to attack Wessex, and battles raged between him and Alfred until Guthrum was forced to make peace at Wedmore. He withdrew to East Anglia where the Vikings began to farm, and soon the armies crossed the Channel to garner the rich pickings of the Frankish Empire.

ESTABLISHMENT OF THE DANELAW

In 885 Guthrum unsuccessfully attempted to break the peace of Wedmore, and Alfred, strengthened by a few years without Viking attack, renewed the terms of the peace and defined the frontier of the Scandinavians— "up the Thames, and then up the Lea, and along the Lea to its source, then in a straight

8.5 ORONSAY SHRINE MOUNTS
These ornaments were once part of a looted reliquary shrine that had been broken up by Vikings for reuse as brooches in the style of Scandinavian Viking women's fashion. They were recovered in 1891 from the grave of a woman at Carn a'Bharraich, Oronsay, Scotland.

from the current street line (fig. 8.9). The plots were of equal size, and the plan remained throughout the Viking Age, possibly indicating some formal planning process. The Coppergate site included four of these plots, with the buildings erected gable-end onto the street frontage and barrel-lined wells, cesspits, and storage pits in the backyards. In the buildings, craft industries were carried out, producing copper and lead alloy debris, as well as silver, gold, and iron. Craftsmen must have occupied these houses. In addition to local craft production (figs. 8.15, 8.16, 8.18–8.20), there is also widespread evidence of imported material from areas near at hand, such as jet from Whitby, but also further afield, such as amber from the Baltic (figs. 8.13, 8.14), ceramics from the Rhineland, and silk from the Far East (fig. 8.17).

About 975 these structures were demolished and replaced by plank-built buildings with sunken floors, but they remained the focus of craftworking activities. Waste material was deposited faster than it could be removed from the buildings, although attempts were clearly made to clean out the interiors and dump the waste outside. It is evident that this urban environment would have been both congested and unpleasant to live in; it may well have compared quite negatively with living conditions in the surrounding countryside—where, unfortunately, we seldom have such good organic preservation.

Life outside the towns of the Danelaw or those of the Irish coast is less well documented. Remarkably few pagan Viking graves have been identified, although there is a clear concentration in the northern Danelaw area, in modern Cumbria for example, such as Hesket le Forest, Aspatria, and North Yorkshire, particularly a small group from the cemetery at Kildale.

Only a few Viking dwelling sites have been excavated and published, and these are difficult to ascribe to a date within the Viking era or indeed to the Scandinavian cultural orbit. Although the Isle of Man was the locus of exceedingly rich area of Viking contact, only a few settlements have been identified. Both silver hoards (found, for instance, at Douglas) and several impressive pagan graves with rich grave goods, such as Balladoole and Ballateare (Fell et al. 1983; Graham-Campbell 1983) indicate the great wealth of

finds and including extensive recent work at the site of Coppergate in the heart of Viking York. The Viking settlement was bounded on the north and west by the Roman defenses, refurbished around 900, and by the rivers Ouse and Foss to the south and east. The area of Viking York in its early stages was some eighty-seven acres (thirty-six hectares), larger than even Hedeby or Birka, major trading towns in the Scandinavian homelands (fig. 1.3).

At Coppergate the damp ground gradually slopes down to the banks of the river Foss, which produced excellent organic preservation and a unique opportunity to learn about perishable archaeological remains (Hall 1984; 1994). A series of long narrow tenements were laid out sometime early in the 930s with wattle fences running away

8.8

8.7

8.6–8.8 Vikings in Scotland and the Isle of Man
This woman's skull was part of a skeleton found in a Viking male grave at Ballateare on the Isle of Man. She died from a sword blow to the head, probably a ritual murder of a slave. The shield boss (fig. 8.7), the only remaining part from a wood and leather shield, was found on the chest of a pagan Viking warrior buried at Caithness, Scotland; the spear (fig 8.8), found in Sweden, is typical of Viking weaponry.

8.6

the Isle of Man during the Viking period (fig. 8.6).

Excavations at Ribblehead in North Yorkshire revealed a small complex made up of a longhouse with a smithy and field system. At Simy Folds, also in northern England, five building groups were identified, which included a longhouse and two adjacent smaller structures surrounding a yard and set within fields. At Bryants Gill in the Lake District and Green Shiel on Lindisfarne similar structures have been located, but ascribing a Scandinavian ethnic origin to the inhabitants is difficult (Richards 1991). Recent excavations at Cottam in East Yorkshire have revealed extensive material spanning the eighth to tenth centuries, including Anglo-Scandinavian metalwork. Its proximity to York makes it a feasible prototype for the locations and type of sites the farmers and settlers who used York as a market base may have occupied.

The impact of the Viking settlers in the area of York can be seen in the legacy of sculptured stones that remain in many local churches. The combination of Scandinavian wealth and art styles—most particularly the distinctive Jelling style, with its sinuous beasts—and a strong stone-carving tradition in the areas of Anglian settlement blended to produce a new tradition. Many stones found at Brompton and Sockburn in north Yorkshire, for example, stylistically complement carved stones found in excavations beneath the Minster at York and the Coppergate carved stones. The spread of distinctive types of monuments such as hogbacks (fig. 8.26), which can be seen as a characteristic if unusual type of Viking sculpture, partially mirror the expansion of carved stone crosses with combined Christian and pagan iconography. Examples of these include Thorvald's Stone (fig. 8.24) from the Isle of Man. These stone carvings epitomize more clearly than anything else the cultural blending that

8.9 JORVIK, AN ENGLISH VIKING URBAN CENTER

The York Archaeological Trust began excavations in 1972 at the eleventh-century Viking town of Jorvik in the northeastern English city of York. The well-preserved Viking materials from the waterlogged riverside site were incorporated within an innovative program of public education and have helped revolutionize knowledge of Viking trade and economy.

the presence of a settled Norse population. The Norse were the catalyst for growth that could not have happened without their presence. The wealth of Chester becomes obvious with the deposition around 965 of the savings hoard from Castle Esplanade (fig. 8.1), which comprised hacksilver, ornamental metalwork, fragments of Irish-Norse armrings, ring money, ingots, and several hundred coins including continental, local, and Viking copies of English coinage (Webster et al. 1953).

IRELAND'S VIKING TOWNS

In Ireland, many of the Viking *longphort* settlements did not endure, and in 902 the Dublin settlement appears to have been totally destroyed by the Irish (Wallace 1985). Those of its inhabitants who survived appear to have migrated across the Irish Sea to settle in northwest England. The massive silver hoard from Cuerdale, Lancashire (Graham-Campbell, ed. 1992), which was buried shortly after this event, may indicate the great wealth that was generated by the raiding and trading activities of the Dublin *longphort* before its sudden demise.

The Dublin Vikings in exile in England during the opening years of the tenth century may have realized that they would never have the manpower necessary to colonize Ireland to the same extent as they had the Scottish Isles. They may also have reflected on the difference in commercial potential between their *longphorts*, which were essentially nonurban in character, and the urban centers they observed close at hand in England. It is evident that when Scandinavians returned to Ireland from around 915 onward, and refounded bases in Dublin, Wexford, Waterford, Cork, and Limerick, a gradual shift toward urbanization and commerce was initiated. This urban nature of Viking settlement patterns in Ireland is unlike those found in Scotland, Iceland, and elsewhere in the North Atlantic region.

Ireland's Viking towns, all located on the coast, were primarily orientated toward the sea and beyond rather than inland. They served as important links in the international trade network that joined the Scandinavian homelands with their North Atlantic colonies and western Europe. The most important of them, Dublin, became heavily involved in the politics of the north Irish Sea region, including the Isle of Man and the

took place between the Vikings in northern England and the local population.

Smaller-scale excavations and reevaluation have brought attention to the city of Chester, located near the west coast, along the present-day boundary with Wales. Its orientation on the Irish Sea links activities in Dublin with those of the Danelaw. The amount of silver hoards and coins found around Chester has a considerable importance: the rapid growth of the Chester mint in the period 920–940 "was a revolutionary rather than evolutionary change," according to recent scholarship (Griffiths 1992). The growth of a series of urban markets around the Irish Sea as a whole, of which Chester and Dublin were part, derived partially from

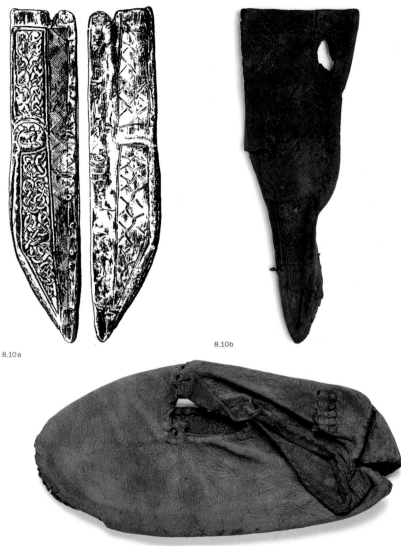

8.10a

8.10b

8.11

8.12

8.10–8.12 LEATHER CRAFTS
Among the many organic remains recovered from the Coppergate site in York were leather and leather-working equipment, including knives, whose sheaths carry complex patterns embossed in leather (drawing, fig. 8.10a). Many Viking shoes were recovered, all of simple construction (fig. 8.11).

Hebrides, and a Dublin Viking king seized control over the kingdom of York for a time. Within Ireland, the Viking rulers of Dublin and the other towns participated in the dynastic and tribal rivalries that characterized the politics of early medieval Ireland (Clarke et al. 1998).

Much is known about the form and layout of the Viking town of Dublin from extensive excavations. Large numbers of well-preserved wooden buildings were uncovered within fenced yards or plots that faced onto streets. The houses were smaller than the Viking Age types found throughout the North Atlantic settlements, but shared certain characteristics with them such as central hearths and benches. Many of them served as workshops where such crafts as smithing, amberworking, woodcarving, and leather working were carried out. Some of the products identified with Viking Dublin, such as the characteristic ringed pins (fig. 11.12), have been found in graves and settlements in the Scandinavian countries and across the North Atlantic colonies (map, p. 172). One of the most notable finds from the Viking settlement at L'Anse aux Meadows, Newfoundland, for instance, was such a Dublin pin (fig. 14.5).

The artifactual evidence for contact between the Irish Viking towns and the North Atlantic colonies may be supplemented by other sources. Local forms of Irish personal names—such as Brjan (Brian) and Tadkr (Tadg)—appear in the Icelandic sagas, for instance, and may be evidence of Irish-Norse involvement in the settlement of Iceland, as is suggested in *Book of Settlements* (Kristjánsson 1996). This Icelandic source contains several Irish or Gaelic names of settlers, such as Bekan, Kalman (Colman), Kjaran (Ciaran), and Melbrigdi, suggesting a sizable Celtic component in the early settlers. There is also literary evidence that Ireland and Iceland fostered close cultural relationships, mediated through Dublin, during the eleventh and twelfth centuries. It seems likely, for instance, that *Brian's Saga* was actually written in Dublin, although it was preserved in Iceland.

The tenth- and eleventh-century Viking occupation of Ireland, being largely urban in character, clearly distinguishes it from Viking settlement elsewhere. In Scotland, for instance, rural settlement was the norm. Nevertheless, there is historical, place-name, and

8.13, 8.14 Jet and Amber Production

Coppergate shops produced jewelry from amber and jet. Amber was available in small quantities from the English east coast but may also have been imported from the Baltic; jet came largely from Whitby in Yorkshire. Amber was used primarily for beads, pendants, and gaming pieces, whereas the more durable jet was fashioned into bracelets and finger rings. Artifacts nearly identical to these finds from York have been found in Viking sites as far west as Greenland (figs. 11.9–11.13, 23.21).

other evidence for Viking influence in the hinterlands of their Irish towns. Political and economic control of these areas and their resources was vital to sustain the towns on a daily basis, and it is likely that a mixed Irish-Scandinavian population settled these surrounding areas. Coastal bases would also have been necessary along the sea routes that linked the towns. The recovery of a rune-inscribed stone from the remote island settlement of Beginish, County Kerry, suggests this to have been a Viking way station on the treacherous southwest coast between Cork and Limerick (O'Kelly 1956).

Scotland

These sources indicate that Viking activity in England and Ireland was rather different than in Scotland. Although the Vikings raided Scottish lands, their political influence lasted longer than elsewhere in the British Isles. Whereas the settlement of England and Ireland was dominated by the development of towns as trading centers, in Scot-

8.15 Bone Skate

This bone skate from Coppergate is nearly identical to skates recovered from Birka in Sweden (fig. 1.8). Although its sliding surface is highly polished from use, England's mild winters during the Viking Age suggest that it could not have been used as often as similar objects in northern climates.

8.16 Wood Cup

Coppergate had an active woodworking industry that produced lathe-turned bowls, plates, and cups. Attention to style is evident in decorative rims and attractive wood grain. The site's name probably derives from the Old Norse words, *koppari* (a wood-turner or cup maker) and *gata* (street).

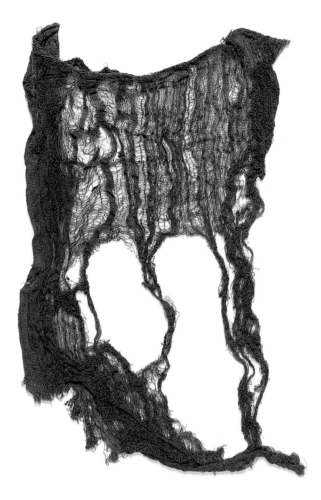

8.17 SILK CAP

Silk garments, mostly limited to caps and scarves, were found fairly frequently at Coppergate and have also been recovered in excavations in Viking Dublin. Silk, including that for this remnant of a cap, was imported, sometimes as yarn but also as finished cloth, from Asia or the Near East. Silk garments are common enough that they were not only for the well-to-do, although most Vikings wore only wool. Traces of multicolored dyes indicate that Vikings appreciated colorful accents on their clothing.

land the overwhelming evidence is that the Vikings established rural settlements, some lasting over six hundred years, as was the case of the Shetland Islands. The only site so far examined that may have a more urban nature is Whithorn in the southwest of Scotland. Both the manufacturing evidence and the building forms there show the main influence of the Irish Sea area, particularly Dublin and its environs; this cultural amalgam sets it apart from the rest of Viking Scotland (Hill 1997). The archaeological evidence of the Scandinavian impact on Scotland is predominantly rural, which indicates clearly that the Scottish situation is more comparable to settlements in the rest of the North Atlantic route to Vinland than it is to either England or Scandinavia (Graham-Campbell and Batey 1998).

The early raiding on the Scottish Isles was related to raids in Ireland; raiding through the 830s followed plundering in the Hebrides in the west in 798. Although most targets were ecclesiastical (as with the repeated attacks on Iona), secular sites were no doubt also targeted, although evidence for this is lacking in historical sources. There are references to raiding in 871–872 on nonecclesiastical centers at Dumbarton Rock on the Clyde by Vikings based in Ireland and interesting observations in *Saga of the Orkneys* to the use of raiding bases in northern Scotland:

> One summer Harald Finehair sailed west to punish the Vikings, as he had grown tired of their depredations, for they harried in Norway during the summer, but spent the winter in Shetland or the Orkneys (Taylor 1938: 874).

The locations of bases from which Vikings launched their raids are difficult to identify, but recent discoveries on Barra in the Western Isles of Scotland may indicate one such a site.

Buckquoy in Orkney provides the best example of the impact of the Vikings on the Picts, the native population of much of Scotland. Located in the northwest corner of Mainland, the largest of the Orkney Islands, this site has a series of cellular Pictish houses that underlie rectangular buildings commonly identified as Viking. The forms of buildings that the Picts constructed is undergoing close scrutiny at the moment, and it is quite possible that the earliest rectangular structure at Buckquoy may in fact be late Pictish rather than Viking (Ritchie 1977; Graham-Campbell and Batey 1998). The cultural traits present in the buildings at Buckquoy can be interpreted as an integration of cultures, probably spurred by intermarriage and trading rather than a violent takeover.

Although the ecclesiastical records of the first meetings with the Vikings record the shock and disruption that the incoming Vikings caused, in some areas the archaeological record is more ambiguous: at Skaill in Deerness, Orkney, and at the Udal in North Uist in the west, it seems more likely that the cultures merged over time and through personal and economic ties rather than through confrontation.

The date of the arrival of the Vikings in northern Scotland is currently under debate (Morris 1996). Excavations at Pool, Sanday, have suggested a late eighth- to early ninth-century date, which may be supported by the evidence from a magnificent Viking boat burial at Scar on Sanday where three people were buried with grave goods including swords, combs, and a whalebone plaque, as

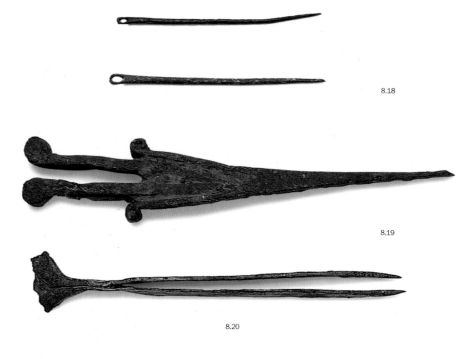

8.18

8.19

8.20

8.18–8.21 **IRON SMITHING**

Iron smithing at Coppergate produced a plethora of consumer items like these sewing needles (fig. 8.18), tweezers, and a wall-mounted candleholder. In addition to finished objects, production tools like anvils, tongs, rough rotary grindstones (fig. 8.21), and small hones for sharpening needles and blades have been recovered.

8.22, 8.23 **BONE CLEAVER AND PINS**

Bone was an important resource for Vikings especially in the Orkney and Shetland islands. These bone pins and a fishgorge were recovered from a small Viking house excavated in 1956 from Drimore on South Uist, Hebrides. Whalebone which was used for this cleaver from South Uist, was a serviceable and readily available substitute for iron.

8.21

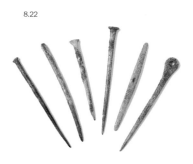

8.22

8.23

well as a north Norwegian-type brooch. We cannot currently judge whether this was the arrival date even in Orkney, or whether the wealth of Sanday's rich agricultural lands was an early focus of Viking occupation. It is clear that Orkney's wealth in the Viking period was great: one of the largest Viking hoards from Scandinavian Scotland was found at Skaill in Orkney, deposited around 950–970, and weighed more than seventeen pounds (eight kilograms).

The Viking presence in Scotland was not confined to Orkney and Shetland (figs. 8.29–8.31), although their geographical proximity to Scandinavia made them an obvious and easy target for settlement. These islands were also a suitable stopping point for Vikings traveling to the western Scottish islands and beyond to the Viking town of Dublin. In the Western Isles, Viking settlement is scant: the Udal in North Uist, Drimore Machair in South Uist (figs. 8.22–8.23), and the newly identified sites at Bornish on South Uist, and Bosta on Lewis and Barra. Viking settlement on mainland Scotland is hard to find as yet; there is evidence for late Norse presence in Caithness (fig. 8.7), as indeed there is Pictish evidence, but the early Viking picture is obscure. Possibly Caithness was settled from an Orkney base and then only after the initial settlement had been consolidated in the island, as suggested in the *Saga of the Orkneys*.

As in England and the Isle of Man, pagan Viking graves in Scotland, albeit numbered in tens rather than hundreds, provide a range of Viking cultural material and an insight into the people themselves. The small number of pagan graves, presumably due to a relatively swift conversion to Christianity, is more than made up for in the spectacular nature of their contents. At Westness on Rousay, a major Viking cemetery has yielded rich pagan male and female groups, including two furnished male boat graves (fig. 8.25) and one particularly wealthy female buried with an elaborate brooch presumed to be an heirloom but possibly a looted item from the west.

In the early 900s the expulsion of the Dublin Vikings had a far-reaching effect in the locality of the Irish region including movements to north Wales. This expulsion from Dublin also provided an impetus for movement to the new Viking colonies in Iceland.

8.24 THORVALD'S STONE

This fragmentary tenth-century slate cross-slab from Andreas, Isle of Man, dramatically illustrates the Insular Viking transition from Old Norse religion to Christianity. One face depicts the famous scene of *Ragnarök*, the last great battle of Norse mythology in which the god Odin, seen with a raven on his shoulder, is devoured by the Fenris wolf. On the other side is a belted figure holding a book and cross trampling a serpent; the Christian fish symbol underscores the message that Christ now reigns instead of Odin.

8.25 WESTNESS VIKING BURIAL

When Vikings moved on to the British Isles and the continent they carried their pagan burial traditions with them, as seen in this boat burial from Westness in the Orkney Islands. The deceased lies with his weapons and tools inside the remains of a small boat, whose outline archaeologists traced by carefully following the rows of iron boat rivets in the soil.

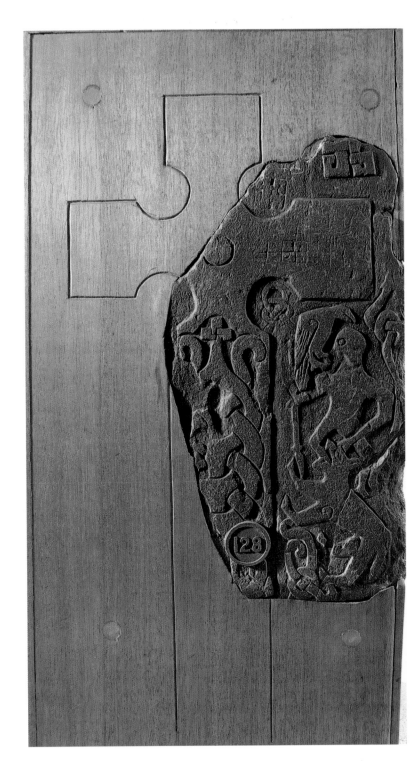

8.26 BROMPTON HOGBACKS

Stone monuments known as hogbacks were used by Vikings in northern England and Scotland to mark graves. They are five feet long (nearly two meters) and their form imitates the shape of Viking longhouses, with bow-sided walls showing paneling or ornamented exterior decoration and gabled, shingle-covered hog-backed roofs. Bearlike beasts clasp the structure's ends, an iconographic form that remains mysterious. This set of three comes from Brompton in Yorkshire.

8.27 PENANNULAR BROOCH

This replica of an early ninth-century gold and glass brooch, which has the ruptured circle form identified as penannular, was recovered from near a large Viking cemetery at Kilmainham Island Bridge. Beautiful jewelry like this was one factor that contributed to the early Viking raids on Ireland. Similar pieces, taken as loot, have been found in the Viking homelands.

8.28 HELGÖ CROSIER

This enameled bronze mount was found at Helgö, a large Swedish Viking trade site near Birka. Its early eighth-century Irish style suggests it originated as a crosier head that came to Sweden with some of the earliest loot of the Viking Age.

THE LEGACY

Direct Scandinavian influence continued in northern Scotland into the fifteenth century, when the Shetland Islands were formally ceded to the Danish crown. Strengthening political ties within these colonies also heightened the cultural impact. The soft-spoken people of the Northern Isles today express themselves with accents that derive from Scandinavia.

The role of these Late Norse people in the extensive fishing industry that dominated the economy of the later eleventh to thirteenth centuries and beyond laid the foundation for the basic economy of these lands. Excavations at Freswick Links in Caithness have identified large-scale fishing activity, concentrating on cod and ling. It is clear that the activities at Freswick were not isolated, although perhaps they were unprecedented in the scale of activities occurring there. A mixed economy with stock farming and cultivation activity, but dominated by massive fishing activity, was the basis of the late Norse economy in Caithness, Orkney, and Shetland. Norway and the lands further west in the North Atlantic went through a similar economic transition to a fishing-dominated life by early medieval times.

The long period of close contact with Scandinavia created a legacy of linguistic influence in some areas. In Yorkshire many dialect words are still recognizable as Scandinavian in origin. In the Northern Isles, where direct political influence continued into the fifteenth century, Norn, a Scandinavian dialect with Scottish influence, could still be heard into the eighteenth century. In Ireland, it is known from historical sources that the Scandinavians began to form military alliances with the Irish and became absorbed into Ireland's political framework from the mid-ninth century onward. Cultural assimilation went hand in hand with this process, and intermarriage became common. The interchange of personal names between the two groups is indicative of this, with many Old Norse names being used today by Irish (for instance, Ivar, Ragnall, and Sitruic). The conversion of the Scandinavians to Christianity is another likely effect of this assimilation. Other types of linguistic borrowings such as *long* (ship), *margad* (market), and *pingin* (penny) testify to the commercial activities of the Scandinavian townspeople.

8.29, 8.30 JARLSHOF GRAFFITI
A number of engravings scratched quickly on fragments of slate were found during the excavations at the large Viking site of Jarlshof on Shetland. They include this ninth- or tenth-century image of a rigged Viking ship and a curly-haired Viking (or their Pictish neighbors) in profile. See also fig. 5.4.

8.31 JARLSHOF
Jarlshof is the most spectacular archaeological site in the Shetland Islands. Occupied since the Bronze Age, its ancient history is evident in the maze of superimposed ruins, among which Viking Age longhouses are clearly defined. The name "Jarlshof" is a bit of historical nonsense: this romantic name, meaning "earl's mansion," was given to the medieval ruins by Sir Walter Scott.

In Ireland, Old Norse elements are found in place-names, particularly in the hinterlands of Scandinavian towns. In the Dublin hinterland, for instance, this is reflected in such place-names as Ballygunner (Baile Gunnair) and Rathturtle (Rath Torcau), which incorporate Scandinavian personal names. Purely Scandinavian place-name forms are rare in Ireland, however, and this reflects both the limited geographic extent of Viking settlement and the degree of cultural assimilation that took place. Examples are usually confined to coastal locations and include Smerwick, County Kerry; Arklow, County Wicklow; and Carlingford, County Louth.

Even though the Icelandic sagas extol and celebrate the Norse achievement of discovering and settling the islands of the North Atlantic, to some extent the Vikings seem to have been repeating the voyages of earlier Celtic hermit monks. According to the Irish ecclesiastic Dicuil, writing in 825, monks explored the North Atlantic from about the year 700 and settled on certain uninhabited islands. The later sagas record that the earliest Viking settlers encountered such monks—they refer to them as *papar*—both on the Faeroe Islands and in Iceland.

While no unequivocal archaeological evidence has been discovered to support an early Celtic presence either on the Faeroes or in Iceland, the limited historical evidence and some place-names combine to suggest that such a presence did exist. Indeed it is possible that the first Scandinavian settlers may have discovered these islands by using geographical knowledge and tradition acquired in Ireland and Scotland. The Celtic form of the surname of Grim Kamban, the individual identified in the *Saga of the Faeroes* as the first Scandinavian settler on the Faeroes, suggests that he may have been from one of the Scandinavian settlements in Ireland or the Hebrides rather than from Norway. The various strands of evidence derived from Celtic and Icelandic sources suggest that Ireland and the Scottish Isles may have served as more than just stepping stones for the colonization of the North Atlantic by the Scandinavians. Indeed, it is conceivable that they provided part of the impetus and inspiration for these Scandinavian voyages.

III VIKINGS IN THE NORTH ATLANTIC

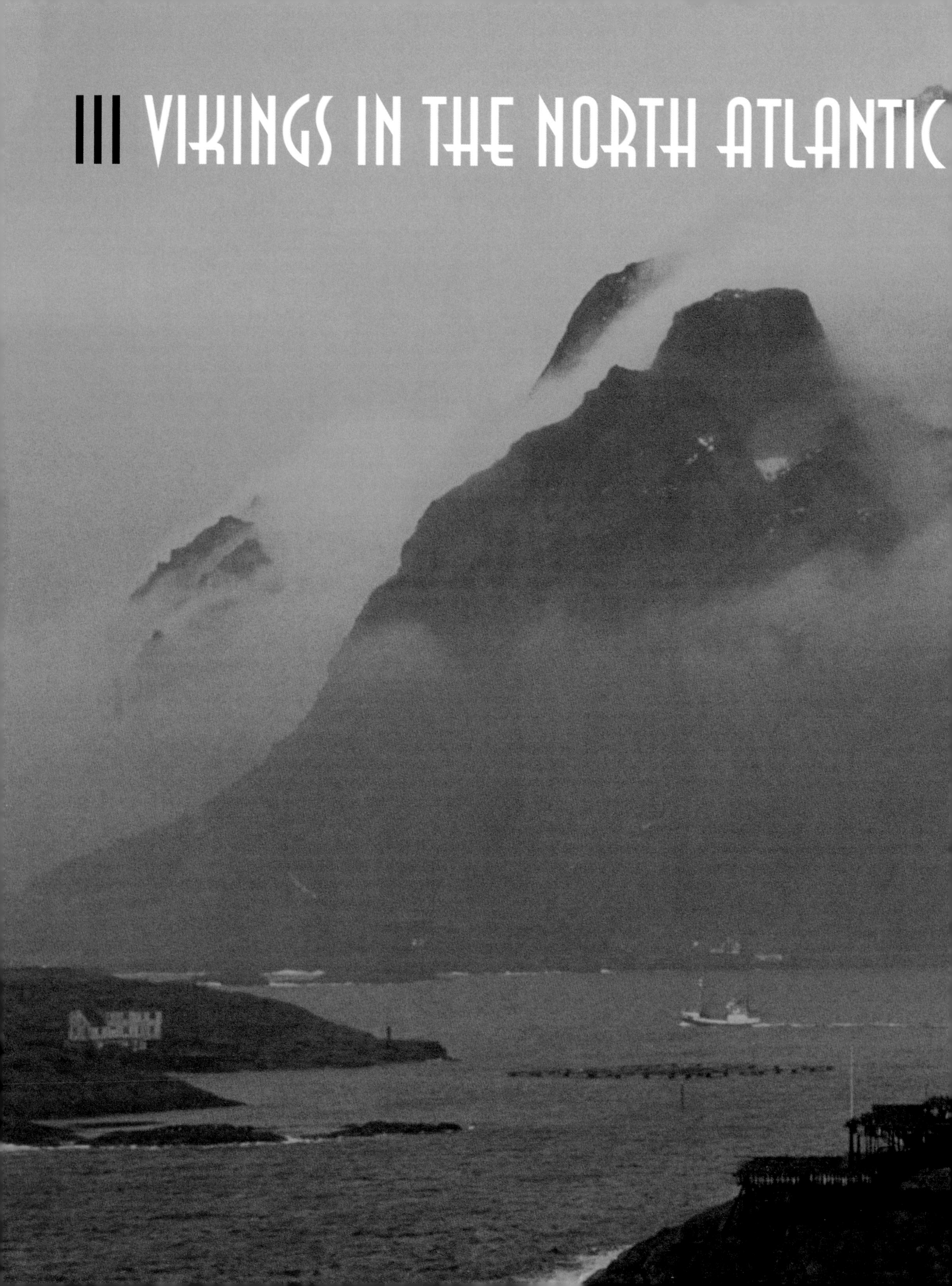

INTRODUCTION
SAGAS OF WESTERN EXPANSION

BY HARALDUR ÓLAFSSON

BEGINNING IN THE NINTH CENTURY the seafaring Vikings colonized Iceland and the Faeroe Islands and enlarged their world with the establishment of two settlements in Greenland; this expansion culminated, in about the year A.D. 1000, with the discovery of the east coast of North America. A new world was opened up as the North Atlantic regions were brought into contact with Europe, and a large part of the globe suddenly became known to Europeans (map, p. 144). When the seafarers from Greenland and Iceland arrived at the American east coast and met the native peoples, the circle around the northern world was finally completed. For the first time in recorded history, east and west met on the rugged shores of North America. Although Nordic people did not succeed in making a permanent settlement on the American mainland at this time, Icelandic chroniclers spread the knowledge of these new lands to Europe. It is likely that Columbus knew about this discovery when he sailed west expecting to find the continent of India on the other side of the sea.

It is possible that other European people, such as the Irish, had landed even earlier than the Norse on the shores of the American mainland, but if so they may not have survived the return trip. The only clear accounts of the discovery of a landmass on the other side of the Atlantic Ocean are records Icelanders kept of the exploits of their forefathers and kinsmen.

These sagas, written in Iceland in the thirteenth and fourteenth centuries, are the best sources of what is known about this remarkable Viking expansion into territories to the north and west. Although they were written more than two centuries after the discovery of Greenland and the American mainland, they preserve a believable account of this discovery.

The sagas, such as *Erik the Red's Saga, Greenlanders' Saga, Egil's Saga,* and the various sagas of the Norwegian kings, give a vivid account of the western expansion during the Viking Age. They not only describe the life and culture of the people in Iceland, but depict the entire northern and western region known at this time. Our understanding of the history of the Viking Age would be very different if the Icelandic sagas had not been written.

Who were these Vikings as portrayed in the sagas? In addition to being warriors and seafarers, they were (perhaps primarily) farmers and traders. In the Old Norse poems like *Hávamál* (Sayings of the High One), for example, the values of farming and a peaceful life are stressed. Farmers and/or their adult sons regularly spent several months each summer in foreign countries, combining plunder with trade. According to the sagas, the same applied in Iceland. In the first decades of the Icelandic Commonwealth many of the young men went to Scandinavia and took part in Viking raids. These men were not all Vikings in the usual sense of the word, but some clearly took part in sporadic raids; the majority were farmers with considerable power in their home countries.

On the basis of the records and chronicles written by the English and French monks, the Viking expansion in the late ninth and tenth century might seem to be merely a series of raids involving robbery and violence. This was true in many cases, but the large-scale migration of people

LOFOTEN ISLANDS, NORWAY
Its steep coast limited Norway's capacity for absorbing population as much as it encouraged the development of ships and maritime skills. By the eighth century these conditions led some Norwegians to seek new opportunities abroad, while others developed fisheries and trade at home.

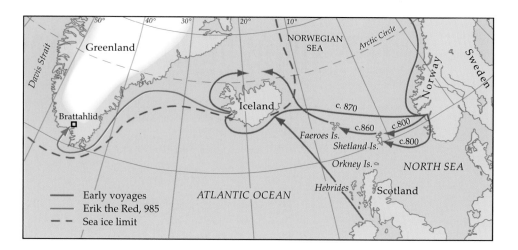

from the Scandinavian countries at this time was much more than just a barbaric invasion. It was part of fundamental changes in political and social structure that were taking place in northern Europe when the growth of markets and consolidation of power by kings and courts stimulated the colonization of new lands.

Expanding Viking territories west from Scandinavia was only possible because of the excellence of the Norse ships. The ships found in Oseberg and Gokstad in southern Norway and Roskilde in Denmark bear witness to the fine construction of these vessels. One of the design innovations of these ships was their keels, which made them both strong and easy to handle in a rough sea. Light enough to be hauled over short stretches of land, these vessels were so well built that they could withstand the storms and waves of the North Atlantic, which is notorious for its heavy weather. The crews, however, needed both knowledge and courage to sail one of the most dangerous sea routes in the world. Knowledge of the movements of the sun and the stars, for instance, was necessary if they were to find their way; so, too, they had to be physically and psychologically fit.

What brought about these expeditions to new and unknown lands? In the early eighth century numerous so-called kings or chieftains of small districts, who functioned more or less as heads of tribal families, ruled Scandinavia. Laws and rules were laid down by local assemblies, which functioned as law courts. In the middle of the ninth century some of these local kings began consolidating their power, trying to drive out rival chieftains and make themselves monarchs over the whole country. Conflicts in Norway established the conditions that precipitated the Viking Age and had much to do with the initial migration to Shetland, Orkney, Scotland, and Ireland. The rise of the Norwegian kings was one of the main reasons for the next stage of the migration, to the Faeroe Islands and Iceland, during the late ninth century. Local conflicts were not the main reason for Norwegian chiefs to migrate to Iceland, although they did have some effect. This expansion to the east, north, and west in the ninth and tenth centuries was essentially a response not only to political difficulties in Norway, Denmark, and Sweden,

but also to growing economic and social problems. After the middle of the ninth century, overpopulation and the need for new land was driving people—especially the people of mountainous and crowded western Norway— away from these countries to new lands. Considerable means, many relatives, and a good supply of workers were required to undertake this sort of movement. The most important resource was their ships, capable of taking them over the ocean along with everything else that was needed to make a settlement in the new lands.

It is not known exactly how many came to Iceland as settlers during this period, but twelve thousand is a common postulate. What is most remarkable, however, is that it was possible in just a few years to ferry over all these people along with everything that they needed to begin daily life in a virgin country. All farm animals, such as sheep, cows, horses, pigs, and chickens, had to be taken with them, along with all equipment, including tools, timber, and metals. Food and grain needed to be provided for man and beast on the long journey over the ocean. All this depended on ships that were big enough and strong enough to transport all this cargo.

The sagas contain long, detailed accounts of the first settlers, noting where they came from and why they left their home country. Most came from Norway, although some were from Denmark and Sweden. Many had stayed for a while in Shetland, Orkney, northern Scotland, or Ireland before sailing to Iceland. The founders of the new Icelandic society were therefore a mixture of Nordic and Celtic folk, which had some influence on the shape and culture of the new nation. Celtic and Irish culture in particular left clear traces—in both tales and religion—on the Icelandic culture of the Middle Ages. The Celtic languages, however, had very little, if any, real influence on the Icelandic language, except for a few loan words.

The remarkable Icelandic *Book of Settlements,* written in the thirteenth century and perhaps based on earlier manuscripts, tells of about four hundred settlers (*landnámsmenn*) who came to Iceland over six decades, from 870 to 930. Most came in the years between 890 and 910; only a few settlers arrived in Iceland after 930.

Like many of the Icelandic sagas, the *Book of Settlements* begins by providing long genealogies and narrating the events that lead to the departure from Norway or the British Isles. The descriptions of battles and great events in all these works are vivid and fantastic, but daily life in the peasant society is given very few words. The common people were of little interest to the writers of sagas.

These emigrants founded a new society that was adapted to the local geography and ecology of Iceland. It is not easy to enter a new and unknown land where the unexpected and unforeseen are commonplace. After their dangerous trip over the ocean, the settlers had to find their way around the island, to discover what was behind the mountain ranges, to find fords to cross the rivers. They had to divide the land equitably among the settlers or at least to carve out functional parcels that could support the homesteaders. It was of utmost importance that laws and rules of conduct be made. In many cases, people had to accept totally new rules, quite different from those they had known in their former homes.

The building of the new society in Iceland is one of the most remarkable events in the history of the Nordic people. This new society was a diverse cultural amalgam, with men and women from Norway, Denmark, Sweden, the Saami regions (Lappland), Scotland, and Ireland. It was a society that not only preserved the social structure of the immigrants' homelands but also created a rule of laws that was adapted to the new demands of a specific, virgin environment.

The religion of Icelandic society from the age of settlement to the acceptance of Christianity in the year 1000 was likewise diverse. Most of the Nordic people accepted the existence of the gods of the Germanic mythology; others, particularly the Scots and the Irish, were Christians.

The new Icelandic society was relatively peaceful and harmonious, although strife and disputes were known. The *hreppur,* a remarkable social service institution, expressed the compassion of the new society by providing a guarantee for people who lost their property because of fire or some other catastrophe, replacing some of the former familial safeguards in a society where families had become dispersed by migration.

Once Iceland had been populated, the timetable for the discovery of both Greenland and America was accelerated. Clues such as the migration of birds and sightings of land by mariners blown off course led navigators to discover Greenland and then America. The population that moved from Iceland to Greenland in around the year 1000 attempted to maintain the lifestyle they had known in Iceland, keeping herds of sheep and cows and even horses. The extreme climatic conditions in Greenland, however, were very different from those in Iceland. Greenland is enormous, but only a small strip along the southwest coast is inhabitable. The various settlements were isolated, and the settlers had to be totally self-sufficient in most matters. Although some of the valleys in the deep, long fjords in southern Greenland were fertile and would support sheep and cows, any small change in temperature could have tragic consequences. Only in the core settlement of Brattahlid-Gardar, where the bishop lived, was there a sense of a community and social organization like that which existed in Iceland.

The western migration of the Viking Age was far from easy, but the men and women of northern Europe faced these extreme challenges and difficulties and built a new society. The Vikings, or rather the people of Viking stock, were not merely warriors; they were highly cultured and in close contact with European civilization. Their most lasting achievement was to alter totally the picture of the world held by other Europeans through the knowledge they gained on the northern reaches of the Atlantic.

The Viking Age is a period full of contradictions. The Vikings plundered and destroyed, but they were also effective merchants and colonizers. These complex people were mercenaries who fought for the kings and dukes that paid the highest salaries, while at the same time they were peaceful peasants who settled after their battles in foreign countries, married, and became citizens of new states. Feared because of their barbarism and their raids on churches and monasteries, they brought knowledge of Christianity to their homelands. They were the best sailors in Europe at that time, fearlessly steering their tiny vessels across the Atlantic, traveling sometimes thousands of miles without seeing land, finding their way without compasses to the farthest corners of the north. The world would be a totally different place today if they had not dared set sail.

9 | THE NORTH ATLANTIC ENVIRONMENT

BY PAUL C. BUCKLAND

I N AROUND 825 AN IRISH MONK, Dicuil, who lived at the court of Charlemagne's successors in France, wrote a description of the world. In it he refers to a group of islands that are located at a two-day sail from the coast of "Scotia" (Scotland) and had been settled by Irish *culdees*, monks in search of solitude (Dicuilus 1967). These islands had since been deserted, according to Dicuil, because of attacks by Norsemen and were then occupied only by birds and sheep. It is generally accepted that these islands were the Faeroes, *Faeringeyar,* the islands of sheep (Jones 1986; Marcus 1999), although the Irish presence there has been much debated (Jóhansen 1979; Buckland 1992; Buckland and Dinnin 1998; Buckland et al. 1998). Dicuil's further comment—that this was a place where at midnight at midsummer it was sufficiently light to pick lice from a man's shirt— suggests not only a slight knowledge of Iceland but also the first hint that the Vikings must have been very familiar with this local environment.

CUTTING A WHALE, *JONSBÓK*

Wherever preservation in the archaeological record is good, in the organic sediments of Anglo-Scandinavian York (Kenward and Hall 1995), the farmhouse floors of Iceland (Buckland et al. 1992), or the frozen farms of the Western Settlement in Greenland (Sveinbjarnardóttir and Buckland 1983), human lice, *Pediculus humanus,* abound. Such external parasites, however, are not the only fossils preserved in the deposits, for many sites provide rich assemblages of plants and animals, ranging from the deliberately introduced domesticates—oats and barley, cattle, sheep, goats, pigs, horses, dogs, cats, and chickens—to less-welcome guests, both vertebrate and invertebrate (fig. 9.6). Native biota are also preserved, allowing one to hazard a picture of the landscape at the time of settlement (*landnám*) in Iceland and compare it to statements by Ari the Wise that when the Norsemen arrived the landscape was forested from mountaintop to seashore.

LANDSCAPES AT *LANDNÁM*

The first Norsemen, sailing westward in search of new lands (fig. 9.1) to farm, may have encountered a few lonely monks, but the scale of their impact was slight. The *landnám*—in the eight and ninth centuries in the Faeroe Islands and Iceland and at the end of the tenth in Greenland—caused profound change in most areas that is recorded in the nature of sediments. A European farming system—based on hayfields, grazing, and a little crop cultivation—was introduced to islands that had previously been inhabited by few, if any, people. Iceland's first Viking settler, Flóki Vilgerðarson, found such a wealth of bird life that he spent the summer hunting and failed to gather sufficient fodder for his domestic animals to overwinter. When the migrant birds left and the seabirds returned to the sea, he and his crew were in deep trouble, and the name Iceland reflects the nature of his problems.

9.1 SAKSUNARDALUR, FAEROE ISLANDS

Farming in the Faeroe Islands is confined to lowland coasts and valleys where agricultural practices today are similar to those of the Viking period. The landscape and soils, however, have changed; centuries of intensive use have caused soils to deteriorate and erosion rates to accelerate. Trees and shrubs once present are gone, and fields that once produced both hay and grains today support only grazing and hay production.

9.2 VEGETATION HISTORY IN ICELAND

Historical changes in regional vegetation can be studied by analyzing the types and quantities of pollen deposited over time in lakes and bogs. This diagram shows the species present in a sediment core taken from Vatnsmýri, near Reykjavík. Radiocarbon dates and chemically distinctive ash falls (known as tephra) allow the levels to be dated accurately. The decline in birch and expansion of grasses and sedges are dramatic during the *landnám* (original settlement) period, 870–900, and this trend continues until the present day. Juniper also declines, but more gradually.

Whether Flóki's story is foundation myth, didactic folktale, or history, the need to gather sufficient edible materials for farm animals is a constant in all ecosystems that largely shut down for the winter. The number of animals kept was strictly dictated by the amount of fodder—grass and leaf hay, seaweed, even fish offal—obtained over the summer and tempered by estimates of how long and severe the winter was likely to be. Too little fodder and starvation followed. All landscapes can look deceptively productive in the right season, and Iceland is littered with the remains of farms lying out in that overly optimistic pioneer fringe, which was good for some years but not others (Sveinbjarnardóttir 1992). In southern Iceland many animals were left outside through the winter and fed only occasionally on surplus hay; in some years these animals would have had to be slaughtered as supplies ran out. Jon Jónsson of Hlíð in Mývatn District recounts (1877) his desperate search for early-spring growth and enough twigs of willow and birch to keep his animals alive, an experience that must have been a fact of life, or death, for many northern farmers in many years. Although the initial settlement phase may have coincided with a run of good years in terms of climate, the introduction of domestic animals grazing in a land previously used only by swans and geese inevitably led to landscape degradation, soil loss (Dugmore and Buckland 1991), and decreasing productivity. When these effects coincided in the occa-

sional runs of bad years, farms were abandoned, sometimes to be reoccupied in better, more optimistic times. Halldor Laxness's novel *Independent People* (1946), satirical or tragic depending on your viewpoint, chronicles such a story in the nineteenth century, but it could equally have had a medieval setting.

At *landnám*, the Faeroes had little forest cover: birch was probably restricted to the few more sheltered areas away from salt spray (Mahler 1991) and willow scrub was probably more extensive. One impact of the initial settlement would be to destabilize this landscape (Buckland and Dinnin 1998) as colonists and their animals sought to exploit the natural resources (figs. 9.3–9.5). Thereafter, the remaining soils had to be conserved by walling and terracing small handworked fields around the occupation sites, and both grass hay crops and limited barley cultivation needed careful management if settlement density was to be maintained. In a rapidly filled landscape, survival was underpinned by the use of marine resources. Seaweed provided both compost and fodder; protein and fat came from fish and seal (Williamson 1948).

Iceland presented a different set of problems to Viking farmers bent on maintaining a northern dairying economy (fig. 9.7). Unlike the Faeroes, where no farm could lie more than a kilometer or so from the coast, Iceland offered extensive coastal plains and inland valleys, remote from the sea. To a settler whose mindset was fixed upon grass hay for his stock, however, the first sight of continuous birch and willow forest, broken only by areas of glacial outwash sands, where glacial rivers had washed out the trees and evidence of recent lava flows was abundant, would not have been appealing. Initial settlement in these areas may well have been where trees gave way to lush natural bird meadows because nesting birds would provide extensive nutrient enrichment. As the pollen record shows (Hallsdóttir 1987), the fate of the forest was sealed (fig. 9.2). Even on the small offshore island of Papey in eastern Iceland, cuts through peat bogs show a peak of charcoal (Buckland et al. 1995a) immediately below a volcanic ash layer, the so-called *landnám* tephra, which was widely spread across the Icelandic landscape in around A.D. 868 (Larsen 1984). Humans' most effective tool, fire, was widely used to replace woodland with pasture

Vatnsmyri I, Reykjavík.

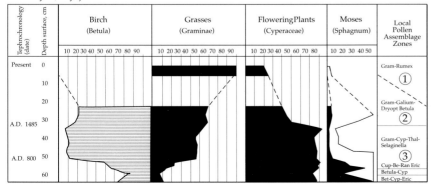

analyst: Margrét Hallsdóttir -1975

9.3

9.4

9.5

9.3–9.5 *LANDNÁM* IMPACTS

The Faeroes, like other areas of Viking settlement in the North Atlantic, experienced rapid and drastic change soon after Vikings arrived. Cutting timber and clearing land for agriculture and animal husbandry quickly depleted fragile ecosystems. Axes, plows (represented here by an ard-blade that was fitted to the end of a wooden plow, fig. 9.3), sickles (fig. 9.5), fire, and livestock were the major agents of change.

and hayfield. Nowhere in the North Atlantic region is there forest that is unaffected by human remains, and it is difficult to envisage the nature of the landscape that was destroyed. The paucity of decomposer species in the Icelandic invertebrate fauna is a consequence of its "sweepstake origin"— many species arrive but few survive—at the end of the last glaciation (Buckland 1988); because of this, forest litter layers would have been exceptionally deep, having accumulated over several hundred years without much disruption. Those fragments of Iceland's forest that were not removed by fire and grazing were heavily exploited for their leaf and twig fodder and, by coppicing (cutting of new shoots), for a regular, managed supply of timber (figs. 9.3–9.5). The small amounts that are left, in places like Hallormstaðir in the east and Thórsmörk in the south, reflect this management technique in their birch trees with multiple stems. The accidental destruction of woodland by fire is the cause of one feud in an Icelandic saga (Pálsson 1971), and it is evident that the remaining woodland rapidly became a much valued and conserved commodity. In northern Iceland and at higher altitudes, birch forest gave way to low-lying dwarf birch and willow scrub. Much of this was also converted to grassland by a combination of fire and grazing pressure, as farmers sought to recreate the conditions with which they were familiar.

To the poor and small farmers of Iceland, which was already close to, or perhaps past, its land capacity for self-sufficient farms, the exploration of Greenland in 984 by Erik the Red provided an opportunity for survival. All available sites for farms in both the Eastern and Western Settlement of Greenland were rapidly occupied, and even the inner fjords of Greenland with their warmer, if shorter, summers would have seemed preferable to the more maritime areas of Iceland. Birch and willow dominate woodlands in the south, and in the valleys of the Western Settlement those species are joined by alder (Fredskild 1981). The mindset of the settlers included grass hay, however, and the Norse *landnám* is again marked by a thin layer of charcoal in the stratigraphy, where forest was made to give way to grassland (fig. 9.2). Six hundred years after such cultivation was abandoned, much of this grassland is still evident in the landscape. Despite their evident commitment to long-range maritime hunting for walrus and polar bear, to procure skins and ivory for European trade (Arneborg 1998), there is little fish in Greenland middens, and sealing appears to have been restricted to clubbing and perhaps netting in the breeding season. The Greenland Norse were essentially farmers who relied upon obtaining sufficient hay to overwinter their dairy animals and balanced their diet with seal, bird, and caribou meat.

The wave of Norse expansion finally washed up against the eastern shore of North America in 1000. The short-lived settlement at L'Anse aux Meadows had little impact on the local vegetation (Davis et al. 1988), and the fodder needed for the livestock, as mentioned in the *Greenlanders' Saga,* would not have led to changes in the land over such a short occupation.

THE NORSE FARM

The overall picture of land rapidly converted from forest and scrub to grassland and coppice is well supported by the palynological (pollen) evidence (fig. 9.2), but the more immediate environments of the farms are more effectively reconstructed from the macrofossil record, particularly that of insects, whose habitat requirements are often very specific and so allow detailed reconstruction of past environments (fig. 9.6) (see Buckland et al. 1993; 1994a). Along with the ectoparasites traveling on their bodies, the Norse emigrants also inadvertently loaded a broad range of other insects onto their boats (Sadler 1991). As well as fodder to sustain livestock

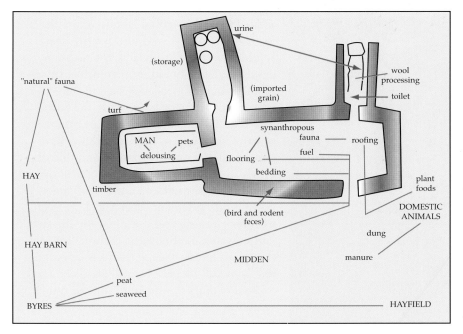

9.6 Ecology of a Norse Farm

The turf and peat longhouse used by the Norse in the North Atlantic was more than a dwelling place for people; its dirt floors, middens, and surrounding barns and stables sheltered a rich ecology of humans, animals, and uninvited guests. This ecology is being explored by analyzing the middens, which preserve remains of food and other materials, as well as fleas, lice, and the ever-present Viking house fly. Although few artifacts are recovered from such excavations, these inventories provide information about Viking life that help explain how people survived—or didn't—in their new surroundings.

9.7 Soapstone Pot

Soapstone was a prized material for making bowls, pots, and lamps in Norway (see fig. 2.10). Raw soapstone occurs in the Shetlands and Orkneys, but not in the Faeroes or Iceland. To maintain this part of their traditional culture, Vikings in the Faeroes and Iceland had to import soapstone. The heavy wear on this pot, found at Snaehvammur in eastern Iceland, indicates the value its owner placed on it.

during the crossing, dunnage would have been necessary to protect the thin planking of the ships from the hooves of the animals and other items of cargo, and ballast would also have been needed to trim the ships (Buckland and Sadler 1990). As Carl Lindroth's (1957) classic study of post-Columbian faunal and floral introductions to North America shows (see also Buckland et al. 1995b), these items would all have contained animals and plants, from dung beetles to weed seeds. In both the Faeroe Islands and Iceland, the earliest trace of human occupation is the wide dispersal of the dung beetle (*Aphodius lapponum*) into the landscape (Buckland 1988), exploiting the droppings of introduced cattle, horse, sheep and goat. Either because of biogeographic accident, the nature of the climate, or availability of dung, *A. lapponum* did not flourish around the farms of Norse Greenland. Because grass formed the basis of survival for the domestic animals, it is hardly surprising that fauna found in stored hay and associated with its fungi decay dominate in samples from farm buildings. Present-day collecting in hay barns in Iceland has produced similar beetle (Coleoptera) faunas (Buckland et al. 1991).

The suite of fungal feeders—*Lathridius minutus* (grp.), *Corticaria elongata*, *Mycetaea hirta*, *Typhaea stercorea*, and *Cryptophagus* spp.—is present in both modern and fossil faunas. In addition, the

fossil assemblages from Iceland contain large numbers of *Catops borealis* (=*fuliginosus*), a kind of beetle that has been recently recorded in the lush vegetation around puffin burrows at Vík at the southernmost point of Iceland (Lindroth et al. 1973; Buckland et al. 1991). Once a significant element in hay-barn fauna, this beetle is now found primarily in areas where other native animals create an enriched environment, reflecting the modernization of farming in Iceland. Large fields of grass and clover have replaced the small scythe-cut fields of sedge and grass exploited by the Vikings and supplemented by material collected wherever it was available. No suitable sites have yet been examined in the Faeroe Islands, but Greenland barns have provided slightly different faunas, with the indigenous *Corticaria linearis* replacing *C. elongata*, and no *M. hirta*, *T. stercorea*, or *C. borealis*. With these fungal feeders occur a range of predators, of which the rove beetles (*Xylodromus concinnus* and *Quedius mesomelinus*) are common to the Faeroe Islands, Iceland, and Greenland, and *Omalium rivulare* occurs in both the Faeroes and Iceland. These differences in synanthropic (animals that live in close association with humans) beetle faunas reflect the sweepstake nature of accidental transport of species across the Atlantic rather than differences in hay storage. Some species in these primary ballast and dunnage faunas failed to establish themselves. The water scavenger beetle *Cercyon analis* and spider beetle *Ptenidium punctatum* appear in the deposits of the Norse farm at Toftanes on Eysturoy (Edwards et al. 1998); neither are currently recorded from the Faeroe Islands, although *C. analis* is present on Iceland in similarly synanthropic situations.

Hay also provided useful material within rooms intended for human purposes, and so fauna endemic to hay spread throughout farms as well as ending up in middens (fig. 9.16). In addition, peat and material from the surface of fields was widely employed not only as fuel but also as animal litter; the turf used for walls would contain insect fossils of varying ages. At Ketilsstaðir in Mýrdalur, southern Iceland, peat exploitation can be dated by the infilling of cuttings with tephra from an eruption of the volcano Katla circa 1357 (Buckland et al. 1986). It is often difficult to determine the various sources of material incorporated in samples

Life in the windy, timber-less North Atlantic required new materials and methods of house construction. Adopting techniques used in the Shetlands and Orkneys, Vikings began building longhouses with rock foundations and peat-block walls, and used imported timber or driftwood for roof trusses, which were covered with brush and finished off with turf. Peat and turf were mined in blocks and were laid up in horizontal or herringbone courses that provided strength and insulation.

9.9, 9.10 NEEDLECASE AND COMB

Viking women kept their needles in various types of needlecases. This cast-metal specimen derives from Stöng (fig. 9.10), a Viking chieftain's center in southern Iceland, but it is a rather unusual find because it is an eleventh- or twelfth-century east Scandinavian type. Its circle-and-dot decoration, a common element of Viking ornament, is also found widely in circumpolar native art. The comb, a type dating to the mid-twelfth and early thirteenth centuries, was also found at Stöng.

from house floors and middens, but the presence of larval water beetles and caddis fly (*Trichoptera*) in otherwise man-made deposits usually indicates the presence of peat, rather than the utilization of wetland vegetation, although the latter undoubtedly occurred.

On many sites, this fauna is supplemented by the external parasites of sheep, the fleece louse, *Damalinia ovis*, and the ked, *Melophagus ovinus*, a wingless fly that sucks blood and spends its entire life cycle on the animal, giving birth to a live maggot, which pupates immediately and attaches itself to the wool. Occasional examples of these parasites probably reflect loss from individual sheep, but larger numbers, as at Stóraborg in southern Iceland (Buckland and Perry 1989), are more likely to reflect the processing of fleeces, an activity that would otherwise be invisible in the archaeological record. Primitive breeds of sheep shed their fleeces in a single unit during the spring, and these are pulled off the animals, together with their collection of parasites, dung, dirt, and lanolin. An alkali, which

reacted with the natural lanolin of the fleece to create soap, was used to clean the fleece. In the absence of artificial soaps, an abundantly available liquid, human urine, substituted. Barrels of urine, collected through the year at a convenient location on the farm, may have indicated the large-scale processing of wool. At Stöng in Thjórsárdalur, a farm destroyed by a twelfth-century eruption of Hekla (figs. 9.9, 9.10), three barrels of urine found in an outbuilding and sealed tanks down either side of another may have been used for cleaning and dyeing of the finished fabric (wadmal) (Buckland et al. 1993)—although to ignore the alternative suggestion that some of the barrels may have been used for food storage would be to impose modern values on the past.

The scatter of keds and lice through most rooms on farms probably derived from the carding of wool before spinning, although the occasional hand-reared lamb might also have been a source (fig. 9.15). Human parasites are similarly distributed, although one sample from a room in postmedieval Reykholt in Iceland, with more than a hundred *Pediculus humanus* and one crab louse, *Pthirus pubis* (Buckland et al. 1992), is clearly the residue from delousing, once a popular pastime (for example, Busvine 1976). Human fleas, *Pulex irritans*, are recorded from Anglo-Scandinavian York (Kenward and Hall 1995), Viking Dublin (Rothschild 1973), and in abundance from Norse Greenland (Buckland and Sadler 1989; Buckland et al. 1998a). The North American origin of this genus has been discussed by Buckland and Sadler (1989), but *P. irritans* had clearly reached the Old World long before Leif Eriksson landed in Newfoundland, given that it appears in Pharaonic Egypt (Panagiotakopulu 1999) as well as Late Neolithic Orkney (Buckland and Sadler 1997). Sheep lice and the occasional goat louse occur in samples from the Norse farm at Gård Under Sandet (Farm Beneath the Sand) in Greenland (Berglund, this volume); these are not only present in the hay fauna but human lice and fleas are also found in rooms that are clearly animal stalls. This commingling indicates that the herders lived with their animals through the winter, perhaps to force-feed their weakened charges with a marginally palatable mix of hay, twigs, seaweed, and other materials.

In contrast to the Faeroe Islands and

9.11–9.14 VIKING HYGIENE

Life in a turf house with dirt floors, animals underfoot, and no running water presented challenges to personal hygiene. Lice were an ever-present nuisance, as the large number of discarded combs with broken encrusted teeth attest. Combs were often beautifully decorated with resin-filled engravings. The comb from York (fig. 9.12) shows one of the craft specialties that evolved in early Viking towns: plates of antler were cut with tiny saws into thin teeth that were ganged up and fastened onto a bone or ivory bridge. "Ear spoons," also highly decorated, were used to remove wax (fig. 9.11).

9.15 SHEEP SHEARS AND WOOL COMB

A set of iron sheep shears and wool comb were found at the core of every Viking North Atlantic farm. Early settlers produced wool primarily for home use, but in late Viking and early medieval times, wool became a major Norse export to Europe, in exchange for iron, wood, and other scarce materials. The form of sheep shears has hardly changed since the Viking Age.

Iceland, where scattering hay or turf would have been sufficient to absorb moisture and hide food and other debris accumulating on the floors, the farms of the Western Settlement in Greenland lay over permafrost. To prevent collapse of the structure from melting of the ground (Buckland et al. 1995a), a carefully prepared surface was necessary. Floors consisting of layers of twig, wood chip, hay, and moss also provided a suitable habitat for a range of insects, including the fly *Heleomyza borealis*, which Skidmore (1996) has christened the "Viking house fly" (fig. 9.18). In the wild, this species exploits accumulations of guano on cliffs, but it is equally at home in human feces. Its presence along with another fly, *Telomarina flavipes*, which is capable of breeding in large numbers in carrion and human and carnivore excrement, in what are clearly living rooms indicates the squalid nature of the farms—although similar species are found in contemporary Oslo, York, and Dublin. Along with many of the hay and dung fauna, the ectoparasites of man and beast, and a range of weeds, several species of true fly (Diptera) were introduced to the Atlantic islands by the Norse farmers (Skidmore 1996). Several, like *T. flavipes,* are only capable of maintaining breeding populations in the artificially warmed environments and trash middens created by the farmers, but the Greenland and some of the Icelandic midden faunas show a significant absence of species associated with fat and marrow, a contrast with samples from the Eskimo midden at Qeqertasussuk. This absence implies that every last piece of flesh had been removed from the bones before disposal, and the full utilization of the marrow is further indicated by the degree of fragmentation of much of the animal bone. This feature is not restricted to the latest levels on farm sites, before starvation forced abandonment, but is evident throughout the middens; in both northern Iceland and Greenland, farmers lived on the edge of their resources throughout the medieval period and beyond.

Dung, the clearings of human and animal houses, and turf-building debris all provide excellent manure that thrifty farmers would use, and so the accumulation of substantial mounds of this material around farms in Iceland and Greenland is unusual. Bertelsen (1979) has argued that the failure to exploit this resource in northern Norway

9.16 FOSSIL FAUNA

Norse archaeology today involves more than excavating artifacts and recording architecture. These microscopic insect remains extracted from middens at an old farm site at Stóraborg in southern Iceland include hay fauna, dung, ground beetles, and fly puparia. The appearance or disappear-ance of various species helps scientists deduce climate and environmental changes. Climate-sensitive data like this may eventually shed some light on mysteries like the Norse disappearance from Greenland.

reflects a net labor deficiency during the spring, when men are occupied with fishing; the situation may have been similar in Iceland, where most mounds begin in the late medieval period (Buckland et al. 1994). In Greenland, males involved in hunting expeditions in Nordsetur (Arneborg 1998) may similarly have been absent from the labor force in the spring, but both sealing and a prestige hunt for caribou may also have been involved. Marine resources were utilized but to differing extents. The *grind*, an organized hunt for pilot whales, took place in Shetland and Faeroe, but not in Iceland or Greenland. Seals were hunted throughout. There is little evidence for fishing in Greenland, whereas Iceland rapidly responded to the need for additional sources of protein to sustain urban life in mainland Europe and became involved in the cod fisheries (Carus-Wilson 1967). Large mussels appear in Greenland and Iceland, where they reached the inland site of Hofstaðir, along with less palatable species. Their main use may have been as bait or additional animal fodder. Charred seaweed, flies associated with trash, and a hydroid (a marine invertebrate) that lives attached to seaweed appear on both coastal and inland sites; the latter, *Dynamena pumila*, is present at Norse sites from Orkney to Greenland and probably reflects the feeding of seaweed as fodder to stock (Buckland et al. 1993). Charred seaweed, however, more likely results from burning *Fucus* to provide ash as a source of salt used for preserving meat, for which there is a good ethnographic parallel (Buckland et al. 1998a).

TRADE

Fossil insect faunas not only provide a detailed picture of conditions within the farms and the use of natural resources they occasionally also provide evidence of other connections. Fridriksson has argued (1960) that the weed flora associated with charred barley from sites at Berþórshvöll in Eyjafjall District and Gröf in Öraefi in Iceland indicates local cultivation of cereals, but some weeds including the lesser stinging nettle, *Urtica urens*, are more likely to have been brought in with imported grain. The local cultivation of cereals is attested for both the Faeroes (Jóhansen 1979) and Iceland (Thórarinsson 1956), but Greenland lay beyond the limit of successful annual cultivation. Both the declining length of the growing season in the Little Ice Age (Ogilvie 1984), which undoubtedly reduced the viability of cereal cultivation, and the ease with which locally caught cod could be exchanged for barley are likely to have driven out local cultivation. The frequency of the grain weevil, *Sitophilus granarius*, and the saw-toothed grain beetle, *Oryzaephilus surinamensis*, in the midden at Bessastaðir (Amorosi et al. 1992) suggests that grain was regularly imported, because neither species would find the necessary habitat continuity or temperatures high enough to maintain breeding populations in the small stores of Icelandic farms. These species, which appear only occasionally in deposits from other sites in Iceland, support the theory that the Bessastaðir farm, later to become the residence of the Danish governor, was from its earliest occupation a particularly rich and high-status site. *S. granarius* is not recorded by Larsson and Gígja (1959) in the modern fauna of Iceland, although it is listed by Ólafsson (1991). The Bessastaðir faunas also include the dung beetle *Oxyomus sylvestris*, whose present northern limit lies in the English Midlands and southern Scandinavia. Its presence in Iceland must reflect a casual introduction as a result of trade with Europe. Two other dung beetles not native to Iceland, species of *Aphodius*, also appear in a sample from Stóraborg in Eyjafjall District (Coope 1986). Much later, in postmedieval Reykholt, the ant *Hypoponera punctatissima* suggests an even more southerly connection, perhaps with Iberia or the Mediterranean (Buckland et al. 1992); the species is now a common pest of heated buildings (Ólafsson and Richter 1985).

INSECTS AND CLIMATE

The major swings in temperature that characterize the end of the last glaciation have been well defined by studying the changes in insect faunas (Atkinson et al. 1986), but the more subtle variations of the last two millennia are less easily differentiated from changes resulting from human impact or simply from the inadequate nature of modern collecting data from remote areas (Buckland and Wagner n.d.). Local extinctions and extirpations of some insect faunas are apparent on all the North Atlantic islands, and these are not restricted to species whose habitats, like those in the farms of Norse Greenland, disappeared with their hosts. The water beetle *Coelostoma orbiculare* from early Holocene deposits on Streymoy, Faeroe, may have succumbed to the widespread modification of wetlands (Buckland et al. 1998b), and the small rove beetle *Ochthephilum omalinus* from the same island disappears about the time of the *landnám*, perhaps also a victim of pollution of waters by humans and animals (Buckland and Dinnin 1998). A similar argument could be advanced for the disappearance of the small water beetle *Hydraena britteni* from southern Iceland, but it survives until the beginning of the Little Ice Age and Perry has convincingly demonstrated (through an elegant playing of the Mutual Climatic Range model backward in Buckland et al. 1983) that a 1°C decline in summer temperatures would be sufficient to extirpate it from the Icelandic fauna. This also suggests that, because of the lack of mechanisms to reintroduce the species during the Holocene, the coldest part of the present interglacial, at least in Iceland, has been within the last five hundred years.

Two other beetle species, in addition to those casualties associated with the Norse farmers in Greenland, appear to have disappeared. Jens Böcher (1998) recorded the small rove beetle *Euaesthetus laeviusculus* from the Sarqaq site at Asummiut in the Disko region in deposits of circa. 2500 to 500 B.C. and the leaf beetle *Phratora* (= *Phyllodecta*) *polaris* from two sites of the sixth millennium B.C. in northwest Greenland (Böcher and Bennike 1996). Both occur in samples from the Norse farm at Gård Under Sandet in the Western Settlement.

On balance, the faunas do suggest a colder end to the medieval period, which taken with other evidence (Barlow et al. 1997b), implicates climate change in the loss of the Greenland farms during the fourteenth and fifteenth centuries. At Nipaitsoq in the Western Settlement, Skidmore (1996) was able to show how the fly faunas changed as the abandoned farm became too cold for the indoor fauna. A similar pattern is emerging from Gård Under Sandet, where, by the time the abandoned goat crawled into the building and died, the synanthropic elements in the insect fauna had also disappeared (Buckland et al. 1998a); as the human occupants and their domestic animals left, artificially warmed habitats suitable for the faunas, accidentally introduced with the first settlers, also faded away.

CONCLUSION

Waterlogged and frozen sediments on the North Atlantic islands provide an ideal opportunity to examine in minute detail the living conditions of both humans and domestic animals from the time of Norse immigration onward. The fossil invertebrate faunas include everything from the parasites of people and animals to elements able to exploit the accumulation of food debris, excreta, and other debris on house floors. The transformation of natural woodland to landscapes heavily eroded by overgrazing (Dugmore and Buckland 1991) is documented in the sedimentary, floral, and faunal record. The faunas and floras also contain evidence for trade, and there is some hint of a deteriorating climate. Using this data, in combination with that from the archaeological, artifactual, and animal-bone assemblages, more is perhaps known about living conditions for the Norse farmers than any other contemporary group. In the words of Hobbes in *Leviathan* (1651) life must have been "nasty, brutish, and short," but not that different from contemporary sites elsewhere in northern Europe, and perhaps slightly better than in urban centers where epidemic disease frequently returned to collect its tithe.

9.17, 9.18 FLEAS AND FLIES
One of the most common finds from middens and house floors is the fly *Heleomyza serrata L.*, informally christened the Viking house fly. Like fleas and many other animals, this species accompanied Vikings when they moved into the Atlantic region. The same was true of the human flea, figured above. None of these species was present in these areas prior to the Norse arrival.

10 | VIKINGS IN THE FAEROE ISLANDS

BY SÍMUN V. ARGE

CUTTING A WHALE, *SKARÐSBÓK*

SINCE THE BEGINNING OF THE nineteenth century the traditional view of the settlement of the Faeroe Islands has held that Irish monks arrived about A.D. 700 to live as hermits, and it is supposed that they in turn were driven out when Norwegian settlers arrived and established farms about A.D. 825. The idea of such an early Irish settlement is based on a literary source: Dicuil's *De Mensura Orbis Terrae*, written about 825, which contains information about sea voyages made by Irish clergy to lands north of Ireland and Scotland where they sought refuge to pursue their religious beliefs in peace. Although Dicuil's brief description of the islands and sailing distances from the British coast is not conclusive, scholars have nevertheless generally accepted the idea that the lands described were the Faeroes. By contrast, the evidence for early Norse settlement is more substantive, coming from written records, place-names, oral tradition, and relics found in early settlement remains.

Although new research has not greatly modified the traditional view and has not confirmed the presence of early Irish monks, botanical studies revealing changes in the natural vegetation resulting from human settlement and land use suggest that human impact began even earlier than supposed from historical sources, perhaps as early as A.D. 600 to 650 (Jóhansen 1985). The most substantial body of new data, which is archaeological, provides the basis for the following outline of Viking and early Norse settlement culture and history in the Faeroes and its relationships to contemporary societies in the British Isles and the North Atlantic region (Arge 1991).

LITERARY SOURCES

Dicuil's work was relatively unknown until it was printed in 1807, first in Latin and later in English (Dicuilus 1967). The relevant passage states:

There are many other islands in the ocean to the north of Britain which can be reached from the northern islands of Britain in a direct voyage of two days and nights with sails filled with a continuously favorable wind. A devout priest told me that in two summer days and the intervening night he sailed in a two-benched boat and reached one of them. There is another set of small islands, nearly all separated by narrow stretches of water; in these for nearly a hundred years hermits sailing from our country, Ireland, have lived. But just as they were always deserted from the beginning of the world, so now because of the Northman pirates they are emptied of anchorites, and are filled with countless sheep and very many diverse kinds of seabirds. I have never found these islands mentioned in the authorities. (Diciulus 1967: 75, 77)

Evidence for the early Norse settlement comes from the *Saga of the Faeroes.* This

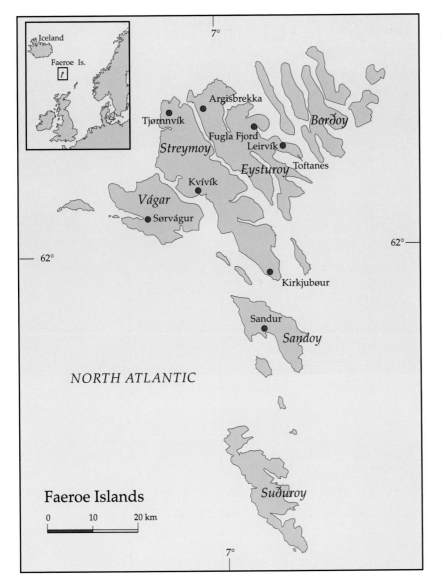

THE FAEROE ISLANDS

Faeroe Islands

0   10   20 km

islands such that one cannot be certain to which islands or societies he is referring. The history of the Faeroes must therefore be studied through archaeological material and evidence from natural science. Beyond the literary sources and recent studies of vegetation changes caused by humans and animals that began in the seventh century (Hannon 1999), the archaeological studies have, to date, provided no evidence for existence of pre-Viking or "early" Viking settlement.

GEOGRAPHY AND ENVIRONMENT

The Faeroe Islands are located in the North Atlantic at 62 degrees North Latitude 7 degrees West Latitude (map, left). The islands lie almost midway between Norway, Iceland, and Scotland; the closest land is Shetland Island, 180 miles (300 kilometers) to the southeast. The Faeroes consist of eighteen islands separated by narrow sounds and fjords.

The climate and weather of the Faeroes are both strongly determined by the archipelago's situation midway in the North Atlantic. Here there is a continuous confrontation between the warm, humid air masses associated with the Azores anticyclone and much colder air masses originating from the Arctic region. At the boundary between these two air masses the North Atlantic polar front develops creating depressions characterized by dense cloud cover, widespread precipitation, and strong wind, to which the islands are fully exposed. Two other factors are of major importance to the climate. The high northerly latitude means that the length of the day varies considerably throughout the year. The strongly developed topography causes rain clouds to strike the mountainous islands, and the humid air above the sea is forced upward, increasing condensation and precipitation.

Geologically, the islands are essentially a dissected basalt plateau belonging to the North Atlantic Basalt Area, consisting of three main series of flood basalt lavas with intervening layers of volcanic ashes, tuff, slate, and basaltic sandstone. Today, the ungrazed areas give an impression of how the island vegetation looked before human beings arrived with their sheep and cattle. The islands never became naturally forested after the last glaciation, but copses of willow, juniper thickets, and a profusion of herbaceous plants made up the climax vegetation. Species such as arctic willow and tea-leaved

work describes events that took place mainly in the Faeroes in the decades before and after the year 1000, most of which were connected to the introduction of Christianity to the islands. These texts mention a man named Grim Kamban who settled in the Faeroes after Harald Finehair came into power in Norway in the 880s. Before the saga's compilation in 1832 the texts relating these events were found scattered in many different versions of the Icelandic sagas. It is presumed that these texts were written about the year 1200 and were based on traditional Faeroese stories. The accounts may therefore contain a grain of historical truth, but it is impossible to verify events that took place two hundred to four hundred years prior to the time of writing. More or less the same must be said about Dicuil's work, which is quite ambiguous. He speaks of several different islands and groups of

Sandur was one of the important harbors and settlements in the Faeroe Islands during the Viking Age. The Viking hero Sigmundur Brestisson, a major figure in the *Saga of the Faeroes* who reportedly introduced Christianity to the Faeroes, lived at Skúvoy, visible in the distance.

willow were once common but are now rare. Creeping dwarf juniper is still found in one location, but elsewhere it has disappeared (Guttesen 1996).

Norse *Landnám*

The Faeroe Island population mainly derives from west Norwegian farmers who set out in the ninth century to find and take new lands (*landnám*) in the North Atlantic. Although use was made of what could be caught from the sea or along the shores and from the bird cliffs, the early Norse economic base was agricultural and was based primarily on the cultivation of crops and the raising of domestic animals. These farms were established along the coasts and fjords following the same models that had been developed in their Norwegian homelands (figs. 10.4–10.7).

A typical Faeroese *bygd* (farm) consisted of several distinct physical areas, each with a specific function. Of primary importance was the distinction between enclosed cultivated infields and uncultivated outfields (fig. 10.11). Infields were immediately adjacent to the farms and were used for growing grain and hay needed for winter fodder; outfields were used for pasture, for turf and peat cutting, and for exploiting a range of other natural products. Turf was an important building material, and peat was widely used

as hearth fuel, for the Faeroes had no trees. Shielings—pastures that were located some distance from the farms, usually up in the highlands—were used for seasonal summer grazing and were established at propitious places in the outfields. By all appearances the early settlers applied this economic model to their new farms successfully and made rapid adjustments to the new conditions of life in this unforested, maritime island setting (fig. 10.2).

According to the structure of the so-called old agricultural society that persisted in the Faeroes until the end of the nineteenth century, the Faeroese village could consist of several settlements called *býlings* (settlements in Faeroese) or *fyrndarbýling* (old settlements). A village might consist of several of these settlements, each again consisting of a single or several farm units. Records of such farms are found in the oldest surviving land survey books, which date as early as 1584. Often the village's old church site was established in one of these settlements, usually erected on the most prosperous *landnám* farm—that is, belonging to one of the original settlements—in a given region (Thorsteinsson 1981).

The actual core of the farm was located at a specially defined area called a *heimrúst*, where the buildings, farmhouses, outhouses, enclosures for storage of hay, angelica plant gardens, and refuse piles were located (fig. 10.11); parts of the *heimrúst* were also used as a grazing area for young cattle and other small animals. Usually this settlement core was separated from the outlying infield by a stone fence and a *geil*, a stone-walled cattle passage that connected the settlement core with the outfields. Many Faeroese *heimrúst* have been occupied continuously since the early settlement period, and gradual accumulations of *heimrúst* deposits over time have created so-called farm mounds. These areas therefore contain a valuable archaeological record of Faeroese history. Excavations at several settlements have demonstrated that such sites often have been occupied continuously since the Viking Age.

SETTLEMENT ARCHAEOLOGY AND ECONOMICS

Given the paucity and problematic nature of the few early records, knowledge of early Faeroese history comes largely from archaeological remains of buildings, farm complexes, outfield structures, and burials. Remains of ancient human activities are often most visible in the outfield, for the landscape contains visual signs of stone livestock shelters and pens, locations for storing peat fuel, cairns marking old roads, and different kinds of stone and turf walls. Many of the dwelling remains—walls, floor layers, hearths, and implements of daily life—have, however, through the centuries disappeared below the surface.

Viking remains have been excavated at a number of farm complexes and farmsteads in the old settlements. Even though interest in Faeroese history predates the establishment of the first museum in 1898, professional archaeological excavations in the Faeroes did not begin until 1941, when the site in the village of Kvívík on Streymoy was excavated (fig. 10.10). This site still remains the classic example of a Faeroese Viking farm, with a longhouse measuring seventy-eight feet (twenty meters) in length and containing a central hearth, benches built of earth along the long walls, long curved lateral walls made of stone with an earthen core, and a roof supported by two parallel rows of posts on either side of the central axis of the structure. Beside the dwelling there was a smaller building, a byre, or barn, with stalls along each side and a drainage trench running down the middle.

During the 1950s and 1960s Viking settlements such as Kvívík were mapped and excavated in the villages of Fugla Fjord and Sørvágur. Research has also been conducted at outfield sites that have been identified from place-name studies and where archaeological excavation has provided details of outfield structures and economy. Finally, in the village of Tjørnuvík, a Viking burial site has been investigated.

One fine example of an old settlement with its central *heimrúst* core that has revealed Viking remains is the site of Toftanes in the village of Leirvík, Eysturoy (fig. 10.3). This Viking Age farm excavated between 1982 and 1987 gives an even clearer picture of everyday Viking life than at Kvívík (Hansen 1991). The longhouse was seventy-eight feet (twenty meters) long and nineteen feet (five meters) wide. The long walls, curved outward, were nearly four feet (one meter) thick and had been constructed with an outer and an inner wall of drystones covered with turf for windproofing. A fireplace in the center of the western half of the

10.2 RINGED PIN

Three examples of Irish-Norse ringed pins have been found in the Faeroe Islands, two at Toftanes and another, illustrated here, from a woman's grave excavated at Tjørnuviik in 1956. Similar pins have been found in Norway, Iceland, and at L'Anse aux Meadows, Newfoundland. All were probably made by Vikings in Ireland following Irish pin styles. The distribution of these finds (fig. 11.13) clearly illustrates Irish connections with the North Atlantic.

10.3 TOFTANES

Excavations in 1982–87 at Toftanes showed that its dwellings, while similar in shape to those at Kvívík, were essentially of wood construction surrounded by a substantial stone and earth outer wall. Its several houses and related structures provided information on the organization of an entire Faeroe Island Norse farm.

building was nineteen feet (five meters) long. Five pairs of roof-supporting posts had been set in stone-reinforced holes in this section of the house, and the remains of benches along the side walls could be detected. A paved staircase marked the main entrance near the middle of the long north wall. This entrance led to an adjacent house to the north, while an opposite entrance in the southern wall led to two adjacent structures. The eastern part of the longhouse was not so well preserved but may have contained a byre. A drainage channel was recorded under the east gable, and another entrance in the northern wall close to the east gable end was connected with a staircase leading away from the building. Excavations revealed a number of other structures. As in other farmsteads from this period, the buildings were basically constructed of wood but had thick insulating outer walls of stone, earth, and peat. Even though building timber was scarce, the wooden stave-building tradition based on the Norwegian model was employed with modifications to suit local conditions. This architectural tradition continues in use in the present day.

Excavation of outfield sites has produced an equally detailed picture of early shielings, where farmers transferred their animals during the summer season to preserve the infield crop for winter. To date, two shieling sites have been studied. One of these, Argisbrekka, near the village of Eiði on Eysturoy, was excavated totally in 1985 to 1987 (Mahler 1991) and revealed the remains of eighteen buildings, of which seventeen can be dated to six or seven different phases in the Viking Age. The houses were found in eastern and western settlement areas, each containing seven and ten houses, respectively. Within each of these two settlement areas there were two to three smaller settlement units, each consisting of a dwelling house and one to two outbuildings. Three types of buildings could be identified: dwelling houses, work houses, and storage buildings. During the tenth century two shielings seem to have used the area simultaneously. Regardless of function, all the buildings were constructed with walls of turf, sand, clay, and gravel. Although turf houses are often found in Iceland and

Greenland, Argisbrekka is the first Faeroese settlement where all the buildings were constructed entirely with this technique. Most of these buildings show evidence of having been constructed or altered in several phases. Alterations, additions, and replacements usually indicate a long period of use. Some of the buildings are rather small, with inner rooms measuring only fifteen feet (four meters) long and ten feet (three meters) wide.

The settlements at Argisbrekka seems to indicate that the *landnám* settlers brought with them a farming system very similar to the Celtic and Norwegian shieling sites such as those known from the Sogne Fjord area. Work at the shielings necessitated the full range of summer production, including milking, processing, and preparation of dairy products. These activities were normally supplemented by a range of activities varying from the collecting of winter fuel, peat cutting, iron production, fishing, and the preparation of wool, depending on local conditions and resources at each site. This shieling economy of the Viking Age was replaced in the eleventh and twelfth centuries by more intensive use of the outfield regions for sheepherding, which by then had become the centerpiece of the Faeroese economy (Mahler 1998).

Place-name studies have provided much impetus for archaeological studies of outfield

activities. For instance, several sites have such place-names as "Lambhagi" or names including the word "Lamb-" (Thorsteinsson 1977). Remains of stone and turf walls are frequently found, which along with the place-name evidence, indicates the practice of sheep milking. This is not known in the prevailing sheepherding tradition and is not mentioned in written sources.

ARTIFACTS AND CULTURE

Archaeological excavations over the years have resulted in the recovery of many Viking artifacts from floor levels and middens of sites (fig. 10.2). These artifacts provide a glimpse of everyday life in the Faeroe Islands during the Viking Age; they also reveal something about their contacts with other people and provide crucial information about the actual dating of the sites. Unlike most archaeological collections in which the materials found have been produced locally, the limited resource base of the Faeroes necessitated the import of many items. This also required the Faeroese to find ways to meet the costs of imported materials and goods. Eventually these economic forces drove the Faeroe economy into the export business in woolen products, homespun, and, later, in fish.

During the Viking Age the most essential imported artifacts included wood and minerals. Wood was required for everything from building boats and houses to the pro-

duction of everyday tools and equipment (fig. 10.9). Unfortunately, to date, relatively little work has been done to trace the origins of imported wood in the Faeroes. We may presume that most of this material came from Norway, supplemented by hardwoods from the British Isles.

Mineral materials have been more readily preserved as archaeological finds and include a variety of materials. Soapstone, a dense, heavy, and heat-resistant material that could be carved easily with iron tools, was used for making different types of cooking vessels as well as for spindle whorls or weights that women used with wooden spindles when spinning wool into thread (figs. 25.14, 25.15). The latter were frequently made from broken fragments of steatite vessels; such fragments were also used to make line sinkers for fishing (fig. 10.8) and for tuyeres (nozzles for bellows). All the soapstone implements found in sites on the Faeroes must have been imported because this material is not found locally in the Faeroes and occurs as artifact types that are identical with those found in Norway (figs. 10.8, 1.5). The first Norse who settled in the Faeroes must have brought soapstone and many other materials with them. Later on, continuing requirements for items and materials that were unavailable locally must have resulted in the establishment of regular trading relationships with Norway, the Shetlands, Orkney, and the British Isles, as well as Iceland and perhaps even Greenland.

A similar situation existed with regard to mica schist and sandstone whetstones, used for sharpening iron tools that were the basis of Norse weaponry and agricultural technology. The export of Norwegian mica schist whetstones is well documented in the Middle Ages, and it is assumed that trade with England in whetstones began as early as the Viking Age. Norwegian overseas whetstone trade is also documented to North Sea regions in the period between 900 and 1100 (fig. 2.10). It is also presumed that the soft mica schist stone needed to made querns for grinding grain were also imported from Norway. Quern quarries in west Norway were worked in the Middle Ages and, judging from Viking grave finds of this material, must have been worked in Viking times.

Despite evidence that many materials were brought in, not everything used in the Faeroes was imported. Among the articles of

10.8 Line Sinker

In the Faeroes, which lacked local soapstone deposits, fishing sinkers were made by cutting grooves into naturally rounded river or beach cobbles.

10.9 Juniper Cordage and Barrel Parts

Juniper roots, strong and flexible, were used widely by the Vikings to make barrel hoops and other types of cordage. As a result juniper was one of the first local species to decline drastically after *landnám* in the Faeroes about 830. These barrel parts are of pine, most likely Scotch pine, the dominant coniferous wood identified in the Toftanes collections, which probably arrived in the Faeroes as driftwood from Scotland.

Faeroese origin are local earthenware goods, spindle whorls of the local tuff and basalt, line and net sinkers made of beach pebbles, and lamps and pots of volcanic tuff or other soft stones.

One category of locally produced material that has special significance for Faeroese archaeology is pottery. Faeroese earthenware is unglazed and was shaped by hand without a potter's wheel. It was fired with low heat and has a rough unfinished texture resulting from the inclusion of small stones. Sizes and shapes vary widely and include bowl-shaped, hemispherical, and bucket-shaped forms. Although the archaeological excavations have revealed a considerable amount of pottery, this class of material has not been analyzed in detail and its chronology and typology is still provisional (Arge 1991).

The origins of Faeroese pottery are equally unknown. Excavations at Toftanes, a settlement in Leirvík dated to around the year 900 have brought this problem to the fore because it is completely devoid of ceramics. For this reason and based on observations from other sites, it has been argued that

the earliest settlement of the Faeroes occurred during an a-ceramic horizon, as is true also for the Viking settlements in Norway, and at early Viking settlements in the British Isles (Hansen 1988). Although people in Norway had used earthenware in pre-Viking times, ceramics were abandoned during the Viking Age and the early Middle Ages and not reintroduced until the twelfth and thirteenth centuries, from the continent, south Scandinavia, and England.

The same trend apparently occurred in the Scottish region, where local production of earthenware ceased with the arrival of the Norsemen, after which soapstone use increased considerably. The situation in the Shetlands and Orkney appears to be similar. Shetland, as well as Norway, had local soapstone outcrops. At Jarlshof, where it has been possible to investigate Norse settlement over a long time span, earthenware vessels first came into use in the twelfth and thirteenth centuries (Arge 1991; Hansen 1988).

Excellent preservation conditions for organic material in the Faeroes have preserved considerable numbers of domestic implements such as bowls, spoons, buckets, and barrel staves, which have been recovered archaeologically. In addition, a special group of wooden items commonly found are ropes made of twisted juniper branches or roots (fig. 10.9) (Larsen 1991), which probably served as barrel hoops and ropes for constructing houses. Juniper is almost absent in the Faeroes today, but fossil pollen studies indicate that it was abundant during the early settlement period and declined rapidly thereafter. As one of the most useful of the scarce wood products, juniper seems to have been overexploited by the initial Viking settlers, and agriculture and animal grazing practices prevented its regeneration.

The most important wood resource for the early settlers, however, may have been Siberian driftwood, especially *Picea* and *Larix*, which would have been found on the beaches and was used for houses and artifacts and probably also for boats and ships. Such reserves, accumulated over centuries, would have been quickly depleted, and so the settlers must have had to begun importing new stocks to satisfy their constant need for wood. In addition to its shortage, wood was also used selectively; for instance, local alder wood was selected regularly for bowls and other small items, as occurred also in Iceland

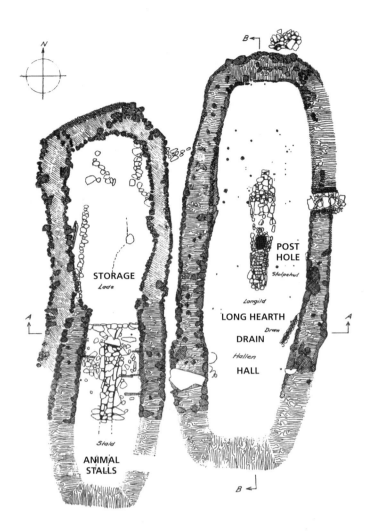

Labels within figure:
STORAGE
Lode

POST HOLE
Stolpehul

Langild

LONG HEARTH

DRAIN
Drœn

Hallen
HALL

Stald

ANIMAL STALLS

10.10 Longhouses at Kvívík
Excavations at the large Viking farm site at Kvívík revealed modifications in the classic homeland Viking dwelling to accommodate the lack of wood and the harsh climate. The major change was the replacement of the lower wooden wall with a three foot (one meter) high earth-filled stone foundation wall (right). In addition, cattle sheds (left) were located closer to the dwelling hall to provide easier maintenance of animals during the dark, stormy winter months.

and Greenland where forest wood was not available (Malmros 1994).

Excavations have also revealed objects reflecting leisure activities such as games and toy boats and horses (figs. 10.13, 10.14). At Toftanes archaeologists found half of a twenty-eight inch (seventy centimeter) long piece of oak board inscribed on one side with the old Norse game known as *hnefiafl* and on the other with nine men's morris, identical with the game called *mill* that is played today in Scandinavia. A similar game board was found in the early tenth-century Norwegian boat grave at Gokstad.

Personal items such as combs, beads, buckles, and jewelry have also been recovered from Faeroes sites of the Viking Age. At Toftanes two tenth-century ring-headed pins of bronze belonging to a type whose distribution is linked to the western part of the Viking world were found. Another example was found earlier in a grave at the Viking burial site in Tjørnuvík, Streymoy (fig. 10.2). Toftanes also produced a tenth-century circular bronze brooch decorated in the Borre

style with latticework and three animal heads. Parallels are known from such Scandinavian sites as Birka in Sweden, Trelleborg in Denmark, and Hedeby in northern Germany; a jet bracelet, possibly originating from the jet or lignite quarries in Viking York or Dublin, has been found. Finally, a number of glass and amber beads, many of the segmented type, have been found at Kvívík and at Toftanes.

BELIEF SYSTEMS

Little is known about the religious beliefs of the Faeroese people before the introduction of Christianity. Even though place-names and traditional oral history refer to pre-Christian burials, only two grave sites of the Viking Age have been documented archaeologically, one at Yviri í Trøð in the village of Tjørnuvík in northernmost Streymoy and another at Við Kirkjugarð in Sandur, on Sandoy (fig. 10.1, 10.12).

The Yviri í Trøð site included twelve graves, most containing individuals lying on their backs while one was lying on his left side (Dahl and Rasmussen 1956). The skeletons were in a very poor state of preservation, and only in one case could gender be determined, a mature woman, twenty to forty years old, with a stature of about four foot, eleven inches (150 centimeters). Four adults, two infants, and a teenager over fifteen years of age were identified, but the other remains were indeterminable. The graves, which faced in different directions and had more or less been encircled with cobbles, had been excavated to about one and one-half to two feet (fifty to seventy centimeters) below the surface. No traces of wooden coffins were found, but in one case it was possible to determine that the body had been dressed in woven garments. Of the few burial artifacts found the most interesting was a ring-headed, polyhedral bronze pin of a type dating to the tenth century, similar to a pin found at Toftanes (fig. 10.2).

Excavations conducted since 1969 in and around the church in Sandur have revealed information about settlement and burial activity in the Viking Age (Arge and Hartmann 1989). Around 1000, about the time when the Faeroese were becoming Christians, this settlement was important enough to warrant the erection of a church. After a period, however, the settlement site was abandoned, leaving the church and its

churchyard as the only surviving focus of activity. During the settlement phase, the dead seem to have been buried near their houses; after the erection of the church, the old settlement area that had existed here previously continued to be used as a cemetery in the churchyard.

The graves uncovered in 1989 are situated to the south of the old churchyard and are believed to be part of an extensive ancient burial ground (fig. 10.12). The burials extended northward into the churchyard. The burial layout gives the impression of an organized, well-managed cemetery in which bodies have been placed end to end in more or less parallel rows so that none of the graves overlap. All graves are aligned east-west and all the excavated skeletons were found with their heads to the west. It was possible to tell that four of the bodies were interred in extended position on their backs; three others were interred on their side, two of which had flexed legs. It is provisionally believed that these burials are pagan burials dating to the Viking period. In all, eleven graves were found, of which seven were excavated. Five graves were marked by set stones visible on the surface; two were placed in a stone coffin; and one seems to have been buried in a wooden coffin. Among the identifiable remains there were three women, one man, and one child; in the two other burials the determination of gender was impossible.

Grave goods are a common feature in pagan Viking burials, and in this case the objects recovered were the personal belongings of the deceased rather than gift deposits. One of the most interesting graves was J6B, that of a male about eighteen years old and five feet, eleven inches (180 centimeters) tall. The grave had been marked on the surface with a boundary of larger stones enclosing a spread of smaller stones. The west (head) end of the grave was clearly marked with a large stone, and the body seems to have been buried in a wooden coffin nearly two feet (thirty centimeters) below the surface stone markers. The grave goods included an iron knife with a handle decorated by windings of silver wire; a bronze finger ring; a pouch or a purse containing seven circular and rectangular lead weights; a bronze belt ornament decorated with an animal head; a fragment of a cast-bronze ornament bearing an interlace motif of Irish origin; and some small silver fragments. Finds from other graves included

10.11 KOLTUR

Viking farms in the Faeroes and other regions of the North Atlantic, like this modern farm at Koltur (top), used an infield/outfield pasture system. The infield (or home field) immediately adjacent to the farm was cultivated and used for growing crops and hay for winter fodder. Outfields some distance away were used for summer pasture, and for cutting turf, peat, and shrub wood.

10.12 VIÐKIRKJUGARÐ

Excavations at this Viking churchyard in Sandur, on Sandoy, have provided information on Faeroese burial practices dating to the late pagan and early Christian period. Excavations of the existing church, built in 1839, revealed the long history of church development that took place here: the foundations of five earlier churches built over the past thousand years have been found, including the earliest, an eleventh-century Norwegian-style stave church.

10.13, 10.14 TOY HORSES
AND BOAT

Wooden toys have been found in
several sites on the Faeroes and in
Viking sites throughout Norway. This
boat, found at Argisbrekka and
carved from willow, models clinker-
built Viking vessels. The stallion
(center), carved from fir and found at
Kvívík, represents its species fairly
well, as does the Norwegian carving
(bottom). The first livestock all had to
be imported into the North Atlantic
colonies by boat.

small single-aisle stave church similar to eleventh-century churches from Norway. To have
such a record of one thousand years of
Christian church building at one location in
the Faeroes is quite remarkable.

Christianity came to the Faeroes circa
1000, and the first churches were erected
apparently at the leading village farms. These
churches seem to have been of the same
Norwegian types as found at Sandur. By the
early twelfth century the Faeroes had its own
bishopric, which became subject to Trondheim in 1152 or 1153. This institution was
centered at the village of Kirkjubøur on
Streymoy, which was the cultural center for
the Faeroes throughout the Middle Ages.
The historical remains of this center, which
includes three medieval stone churches and
the foundations of the bishop's residence,
primarily illustrates the importance of outside influences and reflects little of the local
Faeroese traditional medieval culture.

CONTACT AND COMMUNICATION

History and archaeological research show
that the inhabitants of the Faeroes always
depended on close communications with
the surrounding world. This requirement is
clearly reflected in the frequent recovery of
imported goods found during the excavations throughout the islands. Much of these
materials—for instance, soapstone, schist,
and wood—have been identified as having
origins in the settlers' homelands in western
Norway. On the other hand, many of the
luxury goods recovered from Viking period
sites in the Faeroes seem to have come from
the south, through Faeroese participation in
the western Norse sea trade with the British
Isles, especially with Viking Dublin, and the
Norse societies in the North Atlantic
(Hansen 1996).

Both the Catholic church and the
Norwegian crown had strong interests in
the Norse settlements in the Atlantic. After
Christianity was adopted about 1000, the
Faeroes were probably forced into a tributary
relationship with Norway in the eleventh
century. By the early Middle Ages the church
and the Norwegian crown strengthened
Norwegian control over the North Atlantic
region as a whole, and the Faeroes became
linked with the broader economic and cultural network of the North Sea and North
Atlantic region.

finger rings; beads of bone, glass, and amber;
knives; and in one case, a fragment of an Arabic coin. This is the first and only coin of this
type found in the Faeroes and dates to the
period 750 to 775; it may have been deposited into the grave between 850 and 900.
There is also a possibility that the coin was a
later imitation dating to about 880.

Coins are fairly rare finds in the Faeroes;
for this reason, it is interesting that the only
Viking coin hoard known in the Faeroes was
found in the Sandur churchyard by a grave-dig-
ger in 1863. This hoard consisted of ninety-
eight silver coins whose dates ranged from
about 1000 to 1090 and whose origins included Germany, England, Ireland, Hungary,
Norway, and Denmark. For reasons we only
can guess at, the owner wished to hide these
coins and buried them sometime around 1090.

Sandur is a remarkable site for other
reasons than its early cemetery. When the
first archaeological work began here in 1969
and 1970, excavations inside the existing
church, which was built in 1839, revealed the
foundations of five earlier churches at this
site (Krogh 1975). The oldest of these was a

11 | THE ARCHAEOLOGY OF *LANDNÁM*

Early Settlement in Iceland

BY ORRI VÉSTEINSSON

I N A.D. 871—GIVE OR TAKE A YEAR or two—a large volcanic eruption started in southern Iceland (Grönvold et al. 1995). The volcanic debris, or tephra, that was thrown up into the atmosphere was carried by winds over most of the country and settled on it like a blanket (graph, right). Judging from the thickness and extent of the ash blanket, this eruption lasted for a long time, perhaps several months. We do not know if there were people in Iceland at the time. If there were, they were recently arrived and they must have been surprised by the flames bursting from a rift in the earth, illuminating the night sky, darkening the sunlight by day, and filling the air with irritating dust. Coming from northern Europe these people would never have encountered such a phenomenon and must have had second thoughts about colonizing such a strange land.

TWO HORSES FIGHTING, *HEYNESBÓK*

If there were settlers, they were nevertheless undeterred, for in the years following this eruption a colony of Norse settlers was established in Iceland (map, p. 165). We can date the beginning of this process to the volcanic blanket, called the *landnám* tephra, which can still be found buried under a foot or two of soil in most parts of the island. The earliest traces of human occupation at archaeological sites in Iceland are found just above the *landnám* tephra. In places as far removed from each other and in as disparate environments as Bessastaðir on the southwestern coast and Hofstaðr in the northeastern highlands people had begun to build houses in a matter of years after the eruption of A.D. 871. Apart from a single pollen profile close to Reykjavík, indicating that barley cultivation had begun just before the eruption (Hallsdóttir 1996), no unambiguous traces of human activity have been found below the *landnám* tephra; conversely, the high number of sites just above the *landnám* tephra where such traces have been observed suggest that

the colonization of Iceland did not begin until the last quarter of the ninth century. It is, however, very likely that people had reached Iceland earlier in the ninth century and some scholars have postulated that there was an initial phase where early colonists explored the country and lived principally from hunting and fishing (Kjartansson 1997) before the arrival of farming colonists. Because such groups would have been small and would not necessarily leave identifiable traces in the archaeological record, we have no way of verifying their existence.

The same holds for the possible presence of *papar*, or Irish hermits. The Irish scholar Dicuil writing at the Frankish court in the 820s mentions in his *De Mensura Orbis Terrae* that a group of Irish hermits had sailed north from Ireland and found a land where the summer nights were bright enough to pick the lice off the shirt of one's fellow (Dicuilus 1967). The account is clearly authentic and the land to which Dicuil refers is further away than the Faeroe Islands—which he also mentions—

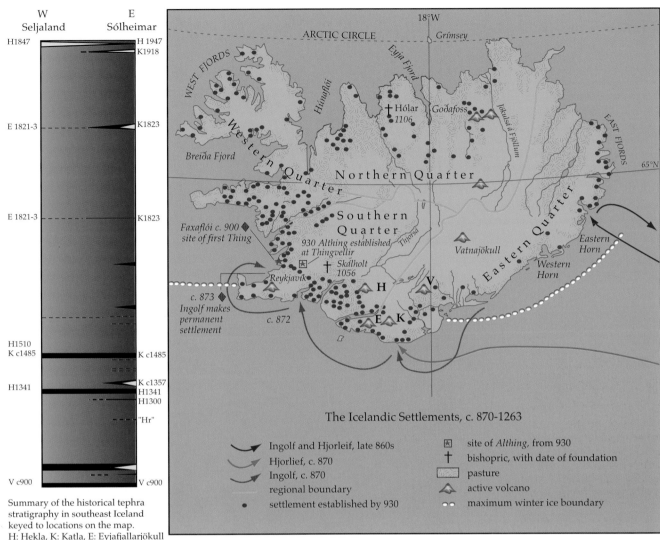

The Icelandic Settlements, c. 870-1263

Ingolf and Hjorleif, late 860s

Hjorlief, c. 870

Ingolf, c. 870

regional boundary

settlement established by 930

site of *Althing*, from 930

bishopric, with date of foundation

pasture

active volcano

maximum winter ice boundary

Summary of the historical tephra
stratigraphy in southeast Iceland
keyed to locations on the map.
H: Hekla, K: Katla, E: Eyjafjallarjökull
V: Veiðivátn. After Buckland et al, 1991.

so it must be Iceland. Dicuil refers to only one expedition and those hermits returned the same year, so that there is little foundation to the belief that there was a permanent settlement of Irish anchorites in Iceland before the arrival of the Norse settlers. The Norse do, however, seem to have had some inkling of the Irish presence, indicated by a few *papar* place-names and the writings of Ari the Wise, who reports in the beginning of the twelfth century that when the Norsemen arrived they found Irish books, bells, and crosiers, which they concluded had been left by Irish hermits. A concentrated effort to verify the presence of Irish monks in Iceland archaeologically has not turned up any new evidence (Eldjárn 1989), and so we have at present to content ourselves with Dicuil's testimony that some Irish monks did make their way to Iceland and stayed there in the summertime. Their impact on later developments was clearly negligible.

ADAPTING TO A NEW ENVIRONMENT

Before the arrival of Norse people in the 870s Icelandic lowland vegetation was dominated by birch. The woodlands were separated by swathes of wetlands—bogs and river estuaries—and at higher altitudes dwarf birch, willow, grasses and moss took over where the forest ended. Although Iceland is a large island—it is larger than Ireland by a third—it for the most part consists of uninhabitable deserts, mountains, and glaciers. The inhabitable lowlands are principally along the coast and in a number of small plains and valley systems stretching into the interior. To a farmer from western or northern Scandinavia, Iceland would have seemed a prosperous land, with plenty of fish and seal, good and extensive meadows to provide fodder, and enormous tracts of pasture. In the south and west barley could also be grown, providing the conditions for the

11.1

These cartoons illustrate changing human-environmental interactions during the Viking and medieval periods. This sequence applies primarily to Iceland, but the process was similar in other North Atlantic regions such as the Faeroes and Greenland.

A. *LANDNÁM* **(850–1000)**

During the initial settlement period the climate was warmer than today; grass grew higher on the hillsides and trees grew at lower elevations. Walrus, seals, and seabird colonies were present. A chief (sword) has established a farm with cows, pigs, and sheep. Slaves and tenants (neckrings) live in the woods, highlands, and on islands, consuming wild resources and farming sheep and goats. In a separate settlement (right) a less powerful but independent man (axe) runs a farm with mixed cattle and sheep.

B. **ESTABLISHED ECONOMY (1250)**

Weather is more variable: the snowline is lower on the mountains; grass has moved down the hillsides; and trees have been eliminated. By now, many farms are independent, and few small-holdings exist under the chief's control. A church has been established by the chief, and a rival chief has emerged. Local vessels have been supplanted by foreign traders. Wild game is still important, but walrus have been hunted out. Most farms keep a mix of cattle and sheep; goats are gone, and pigs are rare.

C. **HARD TIMES (1350–1550)**

Weather has turned cold, the ice cap grows, grass retreats, and soil erosion accelerates. Many upland farms have been abandoned or are run by tenants. The chief controls tribute and rents and runs local trade and fishing. The church has a bishop. The few independent farmers who remain have to supplement their diets with fish. Drift ice brings harp seals, and English and Hanseatic merchants control the intensified export fish trade.

11.2, 11.13 SEWING AND MENDING

Women were responsible for turning cloth into clothing, and bronze, iron, or bone needlecases and iron scissors were worn by a woman on a chain with her keys (fig. 9.9). Most clothing was made from wool cloth, but linen undergarments were common. Men wore trousers under a long shirt, while women wore a long shift covered front and back by a full-length apron, which was held in place by brooches.

11.4 WOOL INDUSTRY

Sheep-wool thread was woven on an upright loom, usually not more than four feet (one meter) wide, to form bolts of cloth. The weaving baton was used to beat the thread as it was laid in, ensuring a tight weave. By the twelfth century, church tithes were collected in wool. Wool cloth known as wadmal became Iceland's major export, and oiled wool cloth was also used for ship sails.

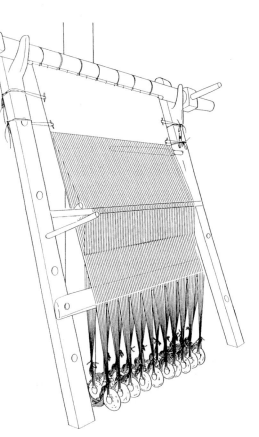

same sort of lifestyle the settlers knew from their homelands (figs. 11.5, 11.6). The obstacles—the long distances between habitable areas and the rugged terrain that made travel difficult and dangerous—would have been a source of as much security to the first settlers as inconvenience. The relatively small size of the habitable landscape and its definite natural borders would have allowed a small group of men to undertake reconnaissance in a matter of days. The first settlers could therefore quickly make sure that their new land was not infested with hostile natives or evil spirits, and they could lay claim to sizeable chunks of land without the risk of running unexpectedly into other groups of settlers.

The available archaeological evidence indicates that once the settlement of Iceland by Norse farmers got started it progressed quickly: most of the habitable areas were occupied within a few years, definitely in less than a few decades. There are sites, like Granastaðir in the interior of Eyja Fjord, where some soil had accumulated between the eruption of A.D. 871 and the building of the earliest structures, indicating that they were occupied quite late in the process. This does not mean, however, that the landscape in question had not been occupied much earlier. The very early presence of humans at a site like Hofstaðir in Mývatn District, some thirty miles (fifty kilometers) inland and 825 feet (250 meters) above sea level, in an environment not at all ideal for cattle-based agriculture, suggests that the best land had already been claimed as early as the 880s. An even more dramatic piece of evidence comes from the south where pollen analysis shows a sheer drop in birch pollen immediately after the eruption of A.D. 871 (fig. 9.2); the presence of birch continues to decline, becoming marginal in the profile before another eruption in A.D. 920 deposited another layer of tephra (Hallsdóttir 1996). This suggests that in the south (at least) the forest was cleared off prime coastal land within fifty years of the arrival of the first settlers; thereafter forest was relegated to the mountainsides and highland margins where it survived down to early modern times (fig. 11.1). The forest was cleared by burning (Thórarinsson 1943; Smith 1995), and the large scale of the clearances suggests that the earliest settlers were intent on occupying the land completely. They were not

small, single-family groups eking out a living in isolated groves or small clearings; rather, settlement was a highly organized affair, with powerful individuals laying claim to large tracts of land and occupying them systematically.

When a group of settlers had chosen a site to build a farm, they seem as a rule to have built a pithouse as a temporary shelter. The pithouses were the simplest kind of building: a hole was dug into the ground and a roof erected over it. These houses vary in size from very small (43 square feet [about 4 square meters] in Stóraborg) to quite large (around 325 square feet [30 square meters] in Hofstaðir) but apart from a fireplace they do not have elaborate furnishings. Only occupied for a very short time, they were left to collapse or

to provide a more peripheral function. The pithouses were soon replaced by longhouses as the main dwelling of each farm (fig. 11.7).

The longhouses have the characteristic shape of Scandinavian houses in the late Iron Age to Viking Age, that is, slightly curved walls with a doorway on one end of one long wall and a long hearth in the middle of the house. A characteristic of the early Icelandic sites is the presence of more than one longhouse at each site (Vésteinsson 1998b). In Bessastaðir, Reykjavík, and Herjólfsdalur two longhouses have been found; in Hvítarholt there were three. The houses at each site seem to be contemporary, suggesting that more than one family (or at least very large and complex groups of people) started off occupying each site. In later times the predominant settlement pattern in Ice-

11.5, 11.6 KEEPING UP APPEARANCES
The common stereotype of Vikings as unkempt is untrue: Vikings were concerned about their physical appearance, as the many items related to hygiene and dress indicate. The heavy green-glass smoother (above), imported to Norway from the continent, was used to flatten seams on boards like this decorated one (right) made of whalebone. Whalebone plaques are known primarily from western Norway, while smoothers are found in female graves all over the Viking area. Vikings who emigrated to Iceland maintained these dress codes.

11.7 Stöng Reconstruction
The eruption of Mount Hekla in 1104 threw so much ash into the air that the nearest inhabited area, Thjorsá Valley, has still not recovered. Once a vibrant community with several chieftain's estates and excellent grazing land, it is now an archaeological treasure. The longhouse at Stöng, for example, was sealed in volcanic ash, and its sod walls are still largely intact. In 1974 this reconstruction opened to the public in a nearby area less damaged by the ash.

11.8 Lava Lamp
Because timber was scarce and later almost nonexistent throughout the North Atlantic islands, except as driftwood, Vikings had to find other fuel sources. Burning peat, which had long been used in the British Isles and Ireland, was quickly adopted for heating; but oil lamps fueled by sea-mammal fat were often the only way to cook and light windowless sod houses. Oil lamps were often made of soapstone, but soft volcanic rock was substituted in the Faeroes and Iceland, as in this case. A similar style lamp was found at L'Anse aux Meadows in Newfoundland (fig. 14.4).

land was single-household farms, with separate sites being occupied even when they belonged to the same property. It also seems clear that the early multihousehold farmsteads were a short-lived phenomenon. In Herjólfsdalur and Hvítarholt the sites were abandoned completely after a short period of occupation, presumably as a result of reorganization of land use when the individual households parted ways. In Reykjavík and Bessastaðir, on the other hand, occupation of the sites continued, but only with a single household according to present research.

These multihousehold sites indicate that in the first years of settlement, there was a large degree of cooperation between groups who were otherwise distinct enough to build separate dwellings for themselves. Banding together to explore and clear the land makes good sense, but the brevity of this arrangement suggests that the underlying social structure was based on single-household farming units, which are still dominant in Iceland in this century.

Material Culture

All the early settlement sites are characterized by limited numbers of small finds, rarely

exceeding two hundred items recorded for each site. The objects suggest that there was a shortage of raw materials and that the tool-making industry was of a low caliber (fig. 11.8). Preservation of organic materials is poor in most of the early sites excavated so far, but inorganic remains suggest that iron was a scarce commodity and heavily reused and that attempts were made to produce cutting and sawing tools from local stone, primarily obsidian. Evidence for iron working is found at all the sites and in some of them smelting slag has been found, indicating that iron was being produced from local bog iron. Although iron is usually the largest part of registered finds in each assemblage, the majority of the iron finds are pieces of slag, rust, or unidentifiable scraps; identifiable objects—broken or whole—are quite rare. Setting aside the iron, which was either made locally or imported, local materials dominate the find assemblages. Stone implements make up the largest group, but most of the sites also have some bone and horn objects. The imported objects are, in order of frequency, steatite, schist, glass beads, copper alloys, antler, lead, jet, and amber (figs. 11.9–11.13). Of these materials steatite is the only one commonly found. It does not occur naturally in Iceland but is found in great quantities in other Norse colonies all over the North Atlantic. In Iceland access to steatite seems to have varied considerably: in Hvítarholt steatite objects make up 17.7 percent of the assemblage and around 13 percent in Grelutóttir and Herjólfsdalur, whereas in Hofstaðir in Mývatn District, Granastaðir, Isleifsstaðir, and Goðataettur the percentage is less than two. It is difficult to determine whether these significant differences indicate cultural choices or differential access to trade.

The grave goods support the general impression of material poverty among the first generations of Icelanders. Some three hundred pagan burials are known in Iceland, but judging from the forty-seven that have been preserved completely, the Icelanders were very much the poor cousins, compared with Norway, when it came to personal objects taken to the other world (Eldjárn n.d.). Many of the graves are adequately furnished, the men's graves with a weapon or two and the women's graves with pairs of oval brooches as well as the less gender-specific glass beads, knives, and whetstones (figs. 12.6, 12.7); compared with graves in Norway, the wealth range

11.9 INTERNATIONAL CONTACT
This jet bracelet from a woman's grave in southeast Iceland speaks to the international contacts Icelanders maintained, as this raw material derives from western England.

in Iceland is much narrower. A large number of furnished graves are poor, a small number of graves have some jewelry and/or weapons, and none can be termed rich. Four boat graves are known in Iceland but they all contained small rowing boats—a far cry from the longships of Oseberg or Gokstad. Large burial mounds are not known in Iceland; in general, graves seem to have been simple constructions that were not very visible in the landscape. The grave material does not therefore give an impression of social or political stratification; although there were clearly some who were richer than others, there are no signs of political or economic power being expressed in rich and visible burials.

Two other differences are worth mentioning. In contrast to Scandinavian sites, tools are very rare in the Icelandic graves. Horses, however, were deliberately slaughtered and interred in one-third of the Icelandic graves, a much higher proportion than elsewhere in the Nordic world. If there was a shortage of raw materials, possibly aggravated by a lack of expertise in their manufacture and repair, it makes sense that tools were preserved. Horses, however, may have been more plentiful and therefore more readily disposed.

In sharp contrast to the rather poor and small assemblages found in Viking Age contexts in Iceland, the dwellings are often quite large and apparently well made. Longhouses like those at Hvítarholt III, Skallakot, or Hofstaðir—with inside dimensions of about 62 by 20 feet (19 by 6 meters), 85 by 16 feet (26 by 5 meters), and 118 by 26 feet (36 by 8 meters), respectively—required considerable resources of labor to cut and stack the turf, transport the timbers, and erect the frame. How difficult it was to obtain the wood for buildings like these is not easy to assess. It might have been bought in Norway—and literary evidence tells us that this happened as early as the high Middle Ages—or it might have been driftwood collected on the shores. Such collection may not have been simple, especially for inland households that did not own land on the seaboard.

These difficulties were, however, clearly overcome and the considerable width of some of the longhouses suggests that the early settlers did not have to economize in their construction work. Apart from the timber, skill and labor were needed to build one of these rather substantial longhouses. (If they had turf roofs—and this is by no means certain—the cutting of the turf alone will have taken one man weeks if not months.) Given the rather short Icelandic summers, it seems most likely that the building of the large longhouses was accomplished by large groups of people.

These fragments suggest that the new society was operating on a lower technological level and at a lower level of social complexity than the culture in which it originated, because it lacks specialized skills and material symbols of wealth and power. The early Icelanders seem on the other hand to have enjoyed good nutrition: food was plentiful, and the households were large and in good health. Hardly any nutritional deficiencies were discovered in a study of the population at Skeljastðir in the eleventh and twelfth centuries; and the population seems not only to have been remarkably healthy but markedly more so than contemporaneous groups on the continent. This is surprising because vitamin C would have been in short supply in a diet based almost entirely on meat and dairy products. Some researchers have suggested that the stability of this diet compensated for its limitations—that is, even if it provided much less vitamin C than that of other Europeans, the supply of it was steady. The plentiful supply of clean water and the isolation of the population, which may have impeded the spread of infectious diseases (Gestsdóttir 1998), also contributed to the Icelanders' good health.

Although it is difficult to determine the quantity of food available, the composition of the animal-bone assemblages studied so far suggests that food sources were remarkably varied, with animal husbandry an important resource and a large nutritional component coming from hunting and fishing. All the assemblages that have been analyzed have large quantities of cattle and sheep bones, and some goat, pig, and horse bones. In Hofstaðir, where the chronological development of the settlement is known, pigs and goats decrease in proportion to cattle as the tenth century progresses. Pigs and goats,

which are sturdy animals that could forage and fend for themselves in the forests, were soon replaced by less hardy but more productive cows as the forests disappeared and hay-making became established. There is more variation between sites in the kinds of wild fauna represented. In Reykjavík and Herjólfsdalur, great auks and other seabirds dominate, whereas in Hofstaðir salmonid bones and the bones and eggshells of freshwater fowl are more common. In Hofstaðir and Granastaðir, both on the highland margins more than thirty miles (fifty kilometers) from the sea, a surprising amount of bones from saltwater fish, seabirds, and mollusks have been recovered. Although marine resources are not dominant, they were clearly significant to these households (Amorosi and McGovern 1995; McGovern et al. 1998).

The economy of these earliest Icelandic farms was clearly based on animal husbandry, but archaeofauna suggests that each household also managed to fully exploit the surrounding environment—even to distances of about six miles (ten kilometers). This implies that the labor force was both considerable and organized and begs the question of what sort of social structure the settlers brought with them to Iceland.

THE MAKING OF A NEW SOCIETY

Although the cattle component of the bone assemblage in Hofstaðir is smaller in the earliest layers than it became later, it is nevertheless clear that from the very outset the economy was based on cattle raising. This is suggested by the bone assemblages as well as the number and size of byres found at many of the early sites (Vésteinsson 1998b). The apparently heavy emphasis on cattle is slightly surprising because cows need to be kept indoors most of the year in Iceland and must be supplied with quality fodder if they are to produce milk. Even if climatic conditions were somewhat more favorable in the Viking Age than they became in later times (Ogilvie 1991), the Icelandic environment would have been more suitable to an economy based on sheepherding and the exploitation of marine resources. The bone assemblages and settlement patterns established in the Viking Age show that while sheepherding, fishing, and seal and bird hunting were important components in the economy of each farmstead, it was the need to procure fodder for the cows that determined the basic economic structure.

In Iceland the settlement pattern is characterized by scattered farmsteads; the distance between each two is determined by the fodder-producing capabilities of the intervening tracts of land. The largest and richest farmsteads were, as a rule, situated where quality fodder could be mowed in meadows and where there is ample winter pasture. Summer pastures and direct access to the sea were clearly secondary considerations when farmstead sites were chosen. This simple observation can help us understand the settlement process and how the society we know from the medieval sagas took shape.

The early settlers to Iceland exhibited a cultural preference for dairy products, and so those regions that offered quality fodder—that is, fodder rich enough to keep cows milking—were preferred in the initial settlement patterns. That individual sites were occupied continuously has also been shown by excavations of the farm mounds of Bergþórshvöll, Stóraborg, Videy, and Bessastaðir, where successive layers of occupation can be traced from the Viking Age to modern times (Eldjárn and Gestsson 1952, Snæsdóttir 1991, Kristjánsdóttir 1995, Olafsson 1991). This indicates that the patterns observable in the high Middle Ages are those that were established in the settlement period, and they can therefore be used as evidence for the *landnám* process.

The first groups of settlers who came to Iceland were intent on establishing permanent farmsteads and a way of life similar to what they knew in their homelands. They therefore sought out places where fodder could be procured before winter fell and where hunting and fishing could be relied on to provide subsistence until the domestic animals had multiplied. There is a variety of such places in Iceland, primarily on river estuaries where seasonal flooding produces rich meadows and where seal and fish could be caught with ease. In the south and west cereal cultivation is possible as well, a consideration that was no doubt important when sites were first selected for permanent settlement. Selecting wetlands or wetland borders for the initial settlement sites also precluded clearing forest, which would have grown mainly in drier soils.

Once the best coastal sites had been occupied—and possibly jealously guarded by the pioneers—the exploration of the hin-

11.10, 11.11 INTERNATIONAL STYLE

An openwork Jelling-style chape found in northern Iceland (below) is remarkably similar to metal mountings of scabbards and sheaths found in York, England (above) and along the Baltic into Russia. Even Vikings in the western Atlantic were keeping up with international fashion.

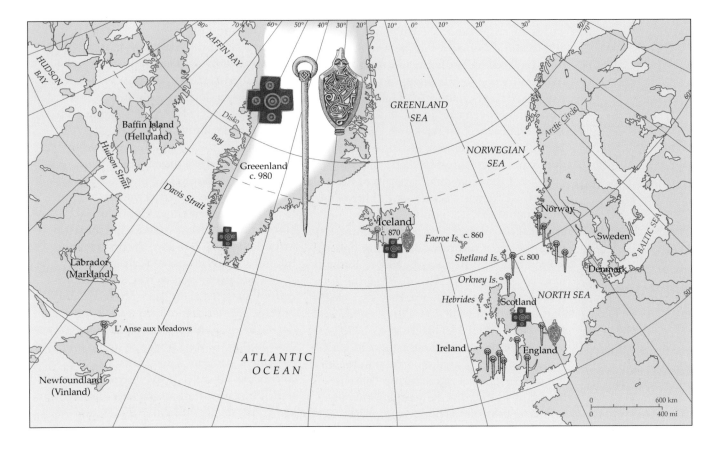

11.13 RINGED PIN ARCHAEOLOGICAL FINDS

11.12 RINGED PINS:
A WEST-VIKING MARKER

Iceland was settled not only by Vikings, especially Norwegian Vikings, but also by people from the British Isles. Place-names referring to *papar*, thought to be Irish monks, and Irish and Scottish names are listed in the *Book of Settlements*. Archaeology also confirms this mixed Norse-British (especially Irish) heritage; similar ringed pins, probably made by Viking craftsmen in Dublin after Irish styles, have been found in Norway (b), Faeroes (fig. 10.2), Ireland (c), Iceland (a), and Newfoundland (map, above).

terland commenced. Subsequent waves of settlers traveled inland along the major rivers, where conditions similar to those on the coast prevail, with flooded meadows on the riverbanks and fishing in the river itself. As a result, all the richest estates from medieval times are located along the principal rivers or in and around major wetland areas bordering on the coast (Vésteinsson 1998b).

Those who brought their own livestock needed to find a ready and dependable source of fodder the same summer they arrived to prevent the animals from dying of starvation in the first winter. Bringing one's own livestock would have been a stressful and cumbersome undertaking, with risks at every stage during the first year—in the spring voyage from Europe and throughout the following winter. It is therefore unlikely that people continued to bring their own animals once the pioneers had established herds large enough to allow the sale of animals to new arrivals. This would only have taken a few years for sheep, goats, and pigs but longer, perhaps a decade or two, for cattle. After the initial struggle for survival, the successful groups—those who managed to establish herds of cattle and sheep and to use the natural resources around them to the

11.14 POWERFUL
CHIEFTAINS, STRAINED ECOLOGY
Icelanders imported fine weaponry
like these high-status silver-inlaid
swords, which provide evidence
of social roles and stratification.
Unlike the homelands, Iceland's
ecology could not sustain the
pressure of intensive exploitation and with the degradation
of the landscape, power became
concentrated in fewer and fewer
hands over time.

maximum—were therefore in an excellent
position to capitalize on their hard-earned
success. It is unlikely that there was stiff
competition for land in the very early stage
of the *landnám*, when even large and well-
organized groups had to struggle for survival. Once these pioneers had established
viable settlements, it can, however, be assumed that new settlers began to
arrive in ever-increasing numbers.
The easily occupied land became
scarce, and conflict between the
pioneers and the new arrivals and
competition for land—or more precisely for control over land—will have
set in (fig. 11.14).

At the point when the trickle of settlers
had become a flood, the pioneers would
have to protect their favorable position and
prevent the newcomers from benefiting too
much from their hard work. There are natural limits to how much land a single household, or even a group of households
working as a single unit, could actually use, and defending land that was
not being used would not have been
viable in the long run. The best way for
the pioneers to maintain their senior position was to people the landscape around
them with their own dependents.

The settlement patterns in areas that
were forested when Iceland began to be
settled suggest that a considerable degree of
planning was necessary to occupy such
lands. In those environments the properties
tend to be spaced at even intervals and to be
more or less equal in size and value, normally considerably smaller and with more
restricted access to resources than the wetland estates (Vésteinsson 1998b). It seems
therefore that there was a second stage in
the *landnám* process, in which already established parties made available less-desirable
lands—those that needed extensive forest
clearance to be farmable, for instance—to
the newcomers.

Those who had already established
themselves would naturally try to influence
or control settlement in the land around
them. It may also have been imperative from
a political point of view once there were
enough pioneer groups established for competition to arise, for resources, prestige, and
power. When one pioneer group started to
grow faster and occupy more land than another one in the next fjord or valley, the lat-

ter group would have had to respond if it was not to fall under the shadow of their neighbors. Bringing in new people to settle their own hinterlands would be one strategy that may have been fed by established recruitment programs in the Scandinavian homelands, probably among relatives and their dependants. The pioneers could also try to catch those who came to Iceland on their own and offer them lands and assistance. Accepting land from another party, even if the receiver was to be the owner, put him in a dependent position vis-à-vis the pioneer. A more tangible way of establishing ties of dependency during the high Middle Ages when the majority of householders in Iceland were tenants was to rent livestock along with the land (Kjartansson 1997). This system originated as a consequence of conditions in the settlement period, when late arrivals had no option but to rent livestock from the pioneers who had already established herds of sheep, goats, pigs, and cattle.

The sagas of Icelanders, written mainly in the thirteenth and fourteenth centuries, and the *Saga of the Sturling Family*, which described contemporary society of the twelfth and thirteenth centuries, depict a society dominated by a small group of chieftains, each ruling over a loosely defined group of householders. These householders had considerable legal rights, which supports the view that early Icelanders were free in both a political and economic sense, but detailed records of land tenure and land ownership, which are available from the fourteenth century on, reveal that the majority of the householders were tenants, and real political power lay in the hands of a small aristocracy. One theoretical model suggests that this social system did not evolve over many centuries but was established at a very early stage in the *landnám* period of the late ninth and early tenth centuries when the successful pioneers managed to control the settlement of the majority of the island. Basing their authority and political power on the rental of livestock and land, the first arrivals became an upper class.

CONCLUSION

Our understanding of the settlement of Iceland until quite recently derived from the written accounts of twelfth-century chroniclers—Ari the Wise's *Book of the Icelanders* in particular—which established a date for the *landnám* and provided a rough sketch of constitutional developments in the tenth and eleventh centuries. These sources do not throw much light on the initial shaping of Icelandic society. Although archaeological evidence for the settlement period has been available for some time, our understanding of it was changed in 1995 with the secure dating of the *landnám* tephra to A.D. 871, making it possible to view the archaeological data in context and to build a coherent picture of the *landnám*.

The settlers may have had to forego some of the technological advantages of their culture of origin and no doubt found themselves in a situation that was much less complex socially and politically; their poverty was expressed in simpler tools, cheaper art, and less ostentatious displays of wealth and power. Their nutrition seems to have been good, and while the fare was no doubt monotonous and simple, there seems to have been plenty of it.

Social and political differentiation seems to have been established at the outset with wetland estates, or settlements in locations favored by the pioneers, dominating scores of farmsteads founded in forest clearings. This basic structure remained well into the late Middle Ages with changes only in political consolidation among the aristocracy. In the early eleventh century there were some seven hundred estate owners in the whole country ruling over some twenty-five hundred dependent households. In between there was a class of up to one thousand economically independent householders who may have occupied an intermediate social position as well. Between the eleventh and thirteenth centuries there was stiff competition for power among the estate owners, with ever fewer families dominating the political scene and increasing complexity of the political structure, leading eventually to the incorporation of Iceland into the Norwegian state in the late thirteenth century. The first traces of imported pottery appear in the archaeological record in the thirteenth century (Sveinbjarnardóttir 1993), marking the stage, in terms of technological and political development, at which the Icelanders had caught up with the lands they had left in the late ninth century.

12 THE ICELANDIC COMMONWEALTH PERIOD

Building a New Society

BY HELGI THORLÁKSSON

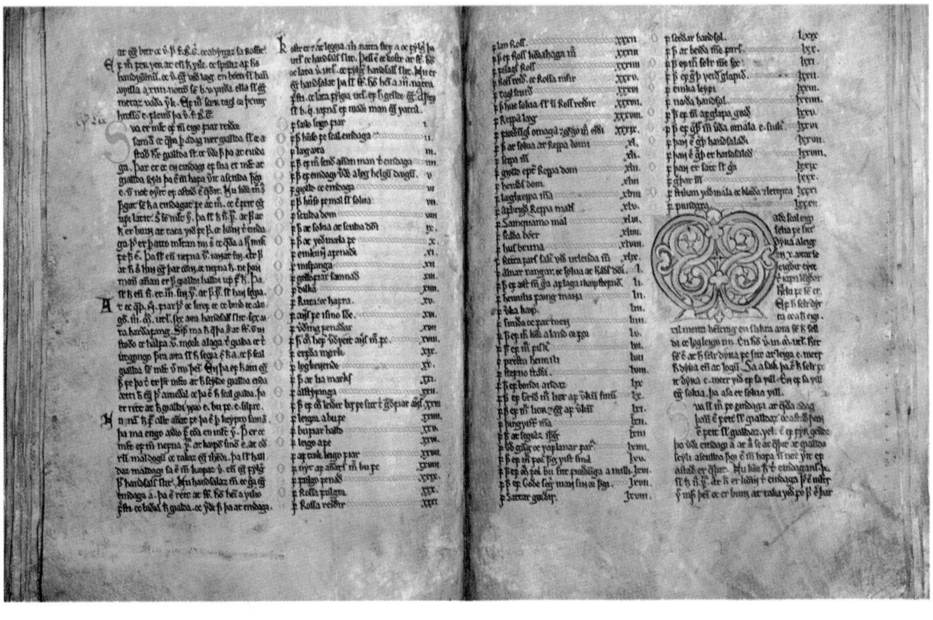

WRITTEN LAWS

The laws of the Icelandic Commonwealth were originally recited orally by *lögsögumaður*, a "law speaker," and only later written down. The earliest manuscript of these laws, now lost, was known—for reasons no longer understood—as *Grágás*, the *"Grey Goose."* The table of contents of this copy from around 1260 lists the laws.

THE FOUNDING OF THE ASSEMBLY (Althing) at Thingvellir in Iceland in the year A.D. 930, or thereabout, marked the beginning of the Commonwealth, the social formation that existed in the period around 930 to 1262 and ended with the imposition of Norwegian rule. In 1930 the thousand-year anniversary of this event was commemorated at Thingvellir (fig. 12.1). Distinguished foreign guests addressed an eager and enthusiastic congregation in the open and told the audience what it wanted to hear: the U.S. representative noted that their ancestors had been seeking freedom and democracy and had established a fine system of justice and equal rights. The delegate from Canada called the Althing the oldest legislative assembly in the world, at least of a free nation, and the British delegate sent by the House of Lords identified the Althing as the grandmother of parliaments, the English parliament being the mother. The representative of the House of Commons did even better and called the Althing the mother of all known parliaments. Those sweet and friendly words were no doubt inspired by the much-acclaimed sagas of the Icelanders.

For people in 1930 the Althing represented a democratic institution of popular politics, excellent laws, justice, entertainment, and education (Stefansson 1939). All were free and equal. This view can be traced back to the age of romanticism in the nineteenth century (see Orrling, this volume). At that time Thingvellir was considered the place where the nation was born, where the Commonwealth was composed of democratic, law-abiding, peace-loving parliamentarians. At several occasions in the nineteenth century politicians held meetings in Thingvellir to seek inspiration and combine forces against the Danes who ruled in Iceland. The idea lived on that in Thingvellir truly Icelandic politicians would recognize the trivialities of their disputes and clashes

12.1 THINGVELLIR

A national assembly was held annually at Thingvellir at a dramatic site beside the Axe River (at right) whose name may refer to an opening ritual in which an axe was thrown into its waters, perhaps to signify that no weapons were allowed. In the eleventh century, the Norwegian king had a church built where Axe River meets the lake; today a modern church stands near that location.

and elevate themselves over their nagging debates and frivolous conflicts. In spite of strife, the Icelanders would in Thingvellir always perceive themselves as a whole, as a nation.

After a persistent indoctrination for some one hundred years, who could resist such a splendid and powerful interpretation of the Althing and its importance? Certainly very few if any could resist the interpretation at the time of the fight for independence, which ended in 1918. This version prevailed for decades afterward, however, because it is what people wanted and expected to hear.

In the last two or three decades this picture has been altered because it did not fit all the facts: people were not so equal in the Commonwealth and its democracy could be called in question. Slaves had almost no rights, and laborers on the farms and women had few (Aðalsteinsdóttir and Thorláksson 1983). Only farmers who possessed a minimum amount of property could participate freely at the Althing, probably only some forty-five hundred men at A.D. 1100 out of a population of up to sixty thousand.

The natural beauty also draws the Icelanders to Thingvellir (Foote 1987). It is a natural spot for Sunday outings, not least for

the people of the capital, Reykjavík, some thirty miles (fifty kilometers) away. When events of national importance are being celebrated Thingvellir, not the capital, is the chosen location and the reason is the same as it was in 1930. It is the place for the nation to unite, to elevate the minds, and to forget temporary and mundane problems and disagreements. In 1944, the festival celebrating the founding of Iceland as an independent republic was held in Thingvellir; in 1974, the national festival to commemorate the eleventh centenary of Iceland's original settlement took place there (fig. 12.2); and in 1994, the fifty years of the republic were celebrated there (Foote 1987; Thórðarson 1945; Thorláksson 1981; Margeirsson 1994). To Icelanders Thingvellir is a holy place with a secular meaning.

ORIGIN OF ALTHING

What was Thingvellir to the Viking settlers? Or were the settlers farmers rather than Vikings? One would imagine that the ones who set out deliberately for Iceland in the ninth century were experienced seafarers—in other words, Vikings—because the Vikings were the great nautical experts of the time.

12.2   12.3

12.4

Undertaking long voyages across the open ocean was no easy task and quite dangerous; it is therefore probable that the first settlers were capable outlaws and unruly roughnecks. That is the picture given in the *Book of Settlements,* which was composed in the early twelfth century but is only preserved in some late thirteenth- and early fourteenth-century redactions. According to this source, the first settler, Ingolf, fled from Norway as a culprit. People in the twelfth century clearly saw this as a logical reason for anyone to risk his life for a new home in a distant country of uncertain whereabouts. The same goes for Erik the Red and Greenland, and this might be true. These men led the way, others took after

them, and gradually the land was settled. Most of the settlers were probably peaceful farmers, hungry for land.

In the twelfth century most (or even all) of the leading families in Iceland traced their ancestry back to one Björn Buna. Some of this genealogy is fictional but clearly it was important to be able to register Björn as a forefather. It is claimed he lived in Norway, but there are reasons to believe that his was a leading family of Norse origins in the Hebrides and that he had to flee from there. Men of his family must have been rather successful in their struggle for power in Iceland in the early tenth century. Some prominent members of that family, grandchildren of Björn, seem to have settled down in Iceland in the last decade of the ninth century but the first settlers (like Ingolf in Reykjavík) might have come as early as the 850s. Men of the Björn Buna family must therefore have driven out or subdued some farmers who were already there. They must have been a warlike family and Iceland was a tempting option for them.

The only written source that seems worthwhile when it comes to the founding of the Althing is the *Book of the Icelanders,* written by Ari the Wise between 1122 and 1133. His information on Ingolf is limited, but he has more to say on how the Althing came about. The leaders were the men of Kjalarnes, the descendants of Ingolf in collaboration with some chieftains who, according to the *Book of Settlements,* were some of the most important members of the Björn Buna family.

Was the founding of a general assem-

12.5 A Sword from Hrafnkel's Valley

The most complete sword from Iceland is this silver-inlaid specimen found in Hrafnkel's Valley in eastern Iceland. This valley was named for a powerful leader who wielded the sword far too often against the men in his district. In the Commonwealth period, every free man was responsible for enforcing the law, even by taking violent action when necessary. The Althing would then review such actions, but there was no executive branch to enforce their rulings. In that situation, some leaders took advantage.

bly—at which the entire country would meet every year—a clever move of the Björn Buna family, who were scattered all over the country and wanted to meet to strengthen their position? General assemblies did occur among the Norse people on the Isle of Man and the Faeroes; in Norway, the Gulathing was taken over as a general assembly from some irregular minor gatherings. The Althing in Iceland was therefore not an absolute novelty, but it did cover an unusually large area.

Ari the Wise explains why Thingvellir was chosen as the site for the assembly: the land had been confiscated because the owner had committed a murder. It therefore became common land and was dedicated to the Althing. Ari even reports that the grandson of the murderer killed his own brother by arson. That such heinous crimes and the people who committed them had to be stopped by an effort like the Althing seems to be the purported message in the *Book of the Icelanders.*

The modern scholar cannot help noticing that the location of the Althing was, however, convenient for people traveling from three—southern, western, and northern—of the so-called quarters of the country. The passage through the middle of the country, called Kjöl (keel), which is barren today, was then covered with soil and vegetation and gave a direct thoroughfare from the north to Thingvellir, even on horses without shoes. Around 930 it was easier to travel in the highlands than the lowlands because of the birchwood forests. Thingvellir is on the outskirts, close to the highlands.

The reasons for the establishment of the Althing must therefore have been something other than urgent problems arising from heinous crimes. The interests of the Björn Buna family and communications both played a role. Iceland was well suited for sheepherding and the making of the much-needed cloth wadmal. In medieval times flocks of sheep were grazing in the Icelandic highlands and early on this probably necessitated some talks and rules for the roundup of sheep, control of boundaries, and owner's marks. The leaders must also have realized how practical it would be to sort out different laws and customs into one corpus for all. The most obvious way to do this was to gather all the influencial men of the country. For all these reasons, people met in Thingvellir in 930 or close to that year to found the Althing.

Natural Features

The topography of the place is of considerable interest. Travelers foreign and domestic like to visit Thingvellir and try to imagine what the place was like in the Commonwealth period. Where did they meet, where did they stand? There is a ravine, and a river cascades into this ravine making a fine waterfall. This river is called Oxa, the river of the axe, since one of the settlers supposedly left an axe in the river. Whether historically accurate, the story probably means that he was establishing the boundaries between his land and that of his neighbors (fig. 12.2).

Geologically, the lake and the plain are growing, because Iceland sits astride two continental plates that are drifting away from each other. The gap forming between them is seen as a great cleft at Thingvellir, which is filled with some (geologically) "new" lava (Jónasson 1992). In fact two landmasses are departing in Thingvellir, the continents of Europe and North America (fig. 12.9). The land is very much alive here; in 1789, for example, an earthquake shook the place, some new ravines were formed, the land sank, and the lake at Thingvellir came closer to the site of the Althing.

The central point of Thingvellir prior to 1262 was the *lögberg* (law rock), but we do not know for certain where it was. It used to be the place where the *lögsögumaður* (law speaker), the only official of the Commonwealth, had his seat. He would recite the laws from there, every year (weather permitting). This is where the Althing would be inaugurated, its boundaries defined, and the session declared open (fig. 12.5). Announcements were made there and the sessions formally closed. This is the place where the *lögsögumaður* rang his bell and led the chieftains and the judges from there in a procession to the sites where the courts were held. *Lögrétta*, the law council or the legislative court, seems to have been east of the river and to the east of *lögberg*. A fenced site with three benches, it probably formed three rings, around which people stood to watch and listen. When Iceland came under Norwegian rule in 1262, there was no longer a need for the place; within a decade or two it fell into disuse and passed into oblivion.

In the eleventh century, the kings of Norway wanted to make their presence felt in Thingvellir and a church intended for the Thingmen was their donation. If there ever

12.6

12.7

12.6–12.8 Eastern Contacts
These bronze brooches and glass, bronze, and amber-bead necklace were found in Dadastaðir, northeastern Iceland. The sagas assert and cultural similarities suggest that the movement from Norway to Iceland originated in southwestern Norway. But other evidence, including this unusual Saami-influenced brooch (fig. 12.8) suggest that arctic Norwegians also had an impact on early Icelandic Viking society.

was a pagan temple in Thingvellir, its remains have not been discovered. No pagan temples have ever been found in Iceland. There seem to have been two churches simultaneously, one at the farm in Thingvellir close to the site and another within the Althing's boundaries, built twice at the instigation of two kings of Norway out of materials provided by them.

Heroic Events of Icelandic Past

Did the founding of the Althing in the tenth century help make the Icelanders a nation at that time? Hardly, because the idea of a nation in the modern sense must have been unfamiliar to them. By at least the twelfth century, however, the Icelanders realized that they were different from the Norwegians. The people in Norway at that time probably felt they were one with the Icelanders, but the islanders probably saw that to a great extent they were sharing the same culture with their neighbors, customs not shared by the Norwegians.

The Althing without doubt contributed considerably to unifying the inhabitants and giving them their own customs and culture and some sort of conformity. Around 1100 at least some five hundred farmers were obliged to meet in Thingvellir, which all farmers of a certain economic status were

supposed to do in turns. The number of people present each year must have been at least around six hundred and probably on the average close to a thousand—twice as many participants as horses must have been brought (figs. 12.3, 12.4).

For a fortnight in June each year Thingvellir was the universal focal point of Iceland, its capital so to speak. There were no towns in Iceland, but Thingvellir became a town in a way and offered the rustic Icelanders a taste of some cosmopolitan pleasures. There were some merchants and peddlers there and craftsmen such as carpenters, cobblers, sword-whetters, and brewers. Ale was sold and cooks are mentioned and so are clowns and beggars. Most of the booths probably had walls made of turf and stones and wooden frames covered with blankets of wadmal (which is homespun, rather coarse domestic stuff) but this has never been thoroughly investigated by archaeologists. Saga reports and archaeological remains suggest that some booths seem to have been quite large and comfortable.

According to *Njal's Saga*, the most acclaimed of all the family sagas, Thingvellir

12.8

is the place where Gunnar and Hallgerd met. One day when Gunnar was going from *lögberg*, he passed below the booth of the Mosfell men, and then he saw some women in fine dresses approaching. The best dressed of all was walking in front and when they met, she at once spoke to Gunnar. Replying with some polite words, he asked her who she was. She said her name was Hallgerd and named her father. She spoke up frankly and asked him to tell her about his travels and he said he would not refuse. Then they sat down and talked. She was wearing a red dress with much lace on it and a cloak of fine cloth, ornamented with lace all the way down. Gunnar was in the ceremonial dress King Harald Gormsson in Denmark had given him and had on his arm a bracelet that he had received as a present from Earl Haakon in Norway. For a long time they

12.9 THINGVELLIR GEOGRAPHY
Below the lava crags and sparkling waters of Lake Thingvellir lie the shearing forces of the Mid-Atlantic Ridge, a geologically active zone running north and south through the middle of the Atlantic Ocean. Iceland sits astride this ridge, and its effects are clearly visible at Thingvellir. As the North American and European continental plates move apart, Lake Thingvellir and the lava cliffs around it widen almost half a centimeter a year.

talked in normal tones. Then came a moment when he asked her whether she was married.

This is how people of the late thirteenth century, when *Njal's Saga* was put to parchment, saw things happen at Thingvellir some three hundred years earlier. Even though we do not know the actual location where Gunnar and Hallgerd first met, the account seems authentic; Thingvellir was the place for prominent travelers to turn up and tell their stories (figs. 12.10, 12.11). When Magnus, a newly consecrated bishop of Skálholt, returned to Iceland in 1135, he arrived at the assembly when men were in court and at odds over some lawsuit:

> But then someone came to the court and said that bishop Magnus was on the way to the assembly. And they were so glad at this news that they immediately went back to the booths. And afterwards the bishop went onto the paving in front of the church and told the whole gathering of events in Norway while he was abroad and everyone was greatly impressed by his eloquence and spirit. (Karlsson 1967)

Some of his news from Norway was sensational enough: King Magnus Sigurdarson had been blinded and castrated and shut up in a monastery and now King Harald Gilli ruled with Danish backing.

Eloquent men were highly esteemed and people seem to have enjoyed their public talks (fig. 12.15). Ambitious chieftains sought opportunities to make their presence felt at Thingvellir. The big man Sturla, already a conspicuous character, was eloquent and practiced the art of rhetoric and political persuasion to make a name for himself and extend his influence. In 1181 he was at the Althing "and one day when most of the assembly participants had come to *lögberg*, Sturla came forward . . . for it was often his way to embark on long speeches concerning his affairs, being a clever man with a supple tongue" (McGrew 1970–4). Sturla was the father of the well-known chieftain and author Snorri Sturluson, an influential chieftains at the Althing in the 1220s who discharged the office of *lögsögumaður*.

COMMONWEALTH LAW AND THE SOCIAL CONTRACT

What was the Althing and what was it for? What kind of political jurisdiction and power did it have? The answers used to be that the *lögrétta* was the governing body of the country, not only in charge of legislation binding all the people but also the mouthpiece of the nation in foreign matters. It also had some central and binding function for the whole of the country with its four quarter-courts and the High Court, called the Fifth Court, where cases could be appealed.

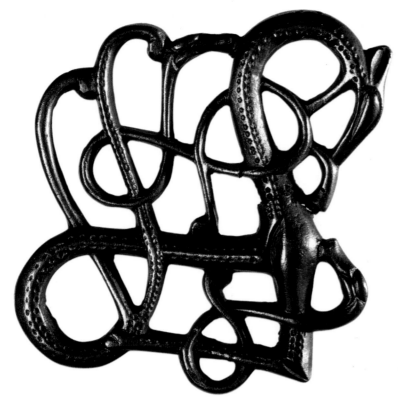

12.10 ORNATE JEWELRY
This Urnes-style silver brooch, found in Iceland and one of the finest known anywhere in Scandinavia, would have been a prestigious import.

This seemed to be straightforward and simple and earlier in this century schoolchildren had to learn by heart that there were thirteen spring assemblies in the country, each sending three chieftains (*goðar*, singular *goði*) to sit in the *lögrétta* and the members of that body were, all in all, 144 with the advisers of the *goðar* and supplementary representatives included. These were the core of *lögrétta*, all sitting on its middle bench, as it was called.

The main sources for the old governing system has been the law book *Grágás*, meaning the "grey goose" (p. 175). Preserved in two redactions, it is a collection of rules and norms, not an actual book of laws. It is difficult to find out which of its clauses were accepted, which were only suggestions but never accepted, and which were simply learned reflections and speculations. Scholars nonetheless accepted its prescriptions for the governing system. In many cases there was only general agreement concerning how to interpret some of its more important clauses; for instance, the number of judges who sat in the quarter-courts. Were there thirty-six in each or only nine? Most scholars have opted for thirty-six, given that there is evidence

other assemblies used multiples of twelve to determine the number of representatives. There are many problems related to interpreting the clauses and the functioning of the system. Verdicts at the four quarter-courts had to be virtually unanimous it seems or there was legal deadlock. This difficulty was largely removed by the creation of the so-called Fifth Court, circa 1005, probably an effective court of last resort in which verdicts depended on a majority decision.

There are even more problems with the laws and the legislation. Scholars have lately been realizing that the legislation was conditioned by the rule that no one was obliged to abide by laws he had not accepted (Líndal 1990). How would this have worked in practice? Many scholars think that the rule in *lögrétta* was that laws were accepted if they enjoyed the majority of votes among the forty-eight men on the middle bench. Another possibility is that a veto from anyone outside *lögrétta* was sufficient. At least this was the rule when someone applied for an exception from the laws. It does not seem very likely, however, that this also applied to the legislation. If the majority did rule, what happened if, for instance, all the *goðar* from a particular spring assembly voted against a decision? Did the law then not bind them?

Iceland in the Commonwealth period was without any direct executive power (Byock 1988). There was no king, no central authorities, and no police. It is possible that scholars have not fully grasped the meaning of this and have been trying to turn the Althing, or rather *lögrétta*, into something like a central governing body, which it clearly was not. What then did the Althing's function imply?

In studying the terse prose of the family sagas, scholars feel there must be some law clauses that are not in *Grágás* but with which the original storytellers were familiar. Furthermore, the laws and the courts at the Althing were often ignored. While the sagas are not factual in a strict historical sense (see Sigurdsson, this volume), the social circumstances they relate could have taken place around 1200 and in former times, as far as people of the thirteenth century knew. They are therefore very important sources of social history, evidencing how the society functioned in the twelfth century and earlier. Therefore they have to be taken seriously when they show people shunning the laws and the courts

Meetings of the Althing were also an opportunity for socializing, deal making, courtship, and good times. These game pieces were used in a game called *hneftafl*, a form of chess where the pieces line up in an inner circle and at the outer corners rather than across from one another. Back-gammon (fig. 23.7) and proper chess pieces (fig. 23.1), which became more popular in the Middle Ages, are also known from the Viking Age.

(Hastrup 1985; Durrenberger 1989).

The Commonwealth was a society of feuds that could turn into blood feuds, and that is what the family and the so-called contemporary sagas are mainly about. A comparison shows that the main subject matter of the contemporary sagas, those that relate events in the twelfth century, is also feuds (Miller 1990). And they are corresponding in the sense that the processes are very similar, conflicts turn into feuds, which in turn lead to more and more violence. At a certain point some intermediaries are bound to step forward and try to bring about a truce and thereby peace. The usual solution turns out to be arbitration, both parties agree to heed what the arbitrator decides, usually on some conditions that were stated beforehand. The laws and the courts are not mentioned, wounds and damages are meted out, and there are no sentences and no culprits. Both of the parties come out with their honor intact, which seems to be the main point.

If the laws and the courts in the Althing could be shunned in this way, what was their role? First, it has to be remembered that there were men who were sentenced by the courts, some into exile and some even made outlaws. At least three of the main characters of the family sagas are outlaws, who were antisocial in their dealings with their enemies and therefore lost all social support. No arbitration could be considered and the courts dealt with their cases. Erik the Red is one who was exiled. Gunnar in *Njal's Saga* went too far in his pride and was also sentenced. Hrafnkel Freysgodi was haughty and had to pay for his arrogance with a sentence of outlawry (figs. 12.3, 12.5).

Second, many of the cases that were sent to the courts were never finished because the parties were willing to negotiate or submit to arbitration. In such cases the courts functioned very well as a deterrent, since the laws were merciless. It has occurred to some scholars that the stipulations of the laws were made severe to force some unruly and stubborn parties to negotiate.

Since there was no executive power in Iceland everyone had to take care of his own affairs and exact his own redress. When parties having feuds or quarrels decided to negotiate or turn to an arbitrator, there were no authorities to complain and no king who was offended and felt deprived of a fair share of the fines.

The courts were therefore not as important as the scholars used to think, or rather they were important in a different way. Thingvellir was more a place for negotiations and less a place for prosecutions and sentences. This was probably the most important aspect of the whole business: negotiations and power balance. The quarreling and feuding parties would usually sooner or later turn to the chieftains with their cases. Two chieftains usually took over and continued the feud and more and more people became entangled. The cases could take on large dimensions with other chieftains becoming involved and the factions meeting at the Althing where they would eagerly seek support among the other chieftains. Often some chieftains could take the support of others for granted which made them strong in their home district. The biggest chieftains could usually settle the matter but when these were feuding, the negotiations could be very diffi-

2 NORWEGIAN RULE

Iceland joined the Norwegian kingdom
...62, Icelandic laws were revised and
...led in *Jónsbók* (c. 1350). The formal
...ion of the Norwegian crown marked
...nd of the Commonwealth period in
...d. Iceland remained under the Danish-
...egian crown until 1918 and became an
...endent republic in 1944.

cult. In Christian times the bishops often turned out to be the only ones with authority enough to negotiate and arbitrate. Althing then was a gathering where the chieftains would seek support and forge coalitions.

It has been said that the absence of any central executive authority was in keeping with the love of independence that had brought influential settlers to the country in the first place. According to Foote and Wilson: "The early period economic forces and the constitution the Icelanders adopted worked together to ensure a reasonably stable and not grossly inequitable society" (1980: 58).

CONVERSION TO CHRISTIANITY

Many of the most historic events of the Commonwealth took place at the Althing in Thingvellir. In 995 Olaf Tryggvason ascended the throne in Norway, and he is credited with the conversion not only of Norway but also of the communities in Orkney, Shetland, the Faeroes, Iceland, and Greenland. His eagerness to save souls has caused scholars to speculate whether he believed the world would end in the year 1000—an idea that

was around on the Continent at the time.

King Olaf sent a priest, Tangbrand, to Iceland, to work on the Icelanders. He spent one or two winters in the country and baptized a number of chieftains in the south and southeast but met such general hostility that he returned to the king and said it was hopeless. Angered, the king proposed taking reprisals on Icelanders who were in Norway at the time. Our oldest source concerning the conversion is Ari the Wise's *Book of the Icelanders*. He begins by saying emphatically that "King Olaf Tryggvason got Christianity accepted in Norway and Iceland," (Dennis et al. 1980) but then speaks of Tangbrand and the king's anger. He continues by telling how Gizur the White Teitsson, who was among the converted chieftains, went to Norway and persuaded the king (with whom Gizur could claim kinship) that a fresh attempt to change his countrymen's ways should be made. He returned to Iceland and after a series of events the Althing elected to accept Christianity as the national religion, although "the old laws concerning the eating of horseflesh and the exposure of infants"

12.13, 12.14 CHRISTIANITY COMES TO ICELAND

Thorgeir the *lögsögumaður*, shown here in a stained glass window (fig. 12.14) created by Finnur Jónsson in Reykjavík's Bessastaðir Church, was personally responsible for deciding at the Thing assembly of A.D. 1000 that the nation should convert to Christianity. Thorgeir allowed some pagan practices to continue, a fact that is reflected in this church panel in the Viking Ringerike-style from the eleventh century. The panels (fig. 12.13) were originally displayed in a church, possibly Hólar Cathedral, and were discovered during the demolition of the last surviving turf farmhouse in Flatunga.

(Foote 1987) should stand. These concessions were soon removed.

Ari tells us that the two factions in Thingvellir, the Christian and the pagan, declared themselves "out of law" with each other. This was in effect a declaration of a civil war but the problems were solved by investing the *lögsögumaður*, Thorgeir, with deciding whether the Icelanders should accept the new religion or continue to be heathen (fig. 12.14). The *lögsögumaður* was pagan at the time but made up his mind and decided that the most sensible thing to do was to turn Christian. And so they did.

Before he announced his verdict, Ari says Thorgeir went to his booth and lay down under his cloak and did not speak for one day and one night. Why he did this Ari does not say, but the Icelanders like to speculate (Aðalsteinsson 1978). Whether historically accurate or not, Ari's tale about Thorgeir is convincing because charging es-

teemed arbitrators with settling disagreements and conflicts was an efficient solution for Icelanders.

When Olafur Haraldarsson came to the throne in Norway, there followed much activity to promote the new faith in Iceland. Missionary bishops were sent to Iceland as well as some timber and a bell for a church in Thingvellir. King Olaf made a pact with the Icelanders that guaranteed some notable reciprocal rights to Icelanders in Norway and Norwegians in Iceland.

Friendly and peaceful relations with Norway must therefore have been very important to the Icelanders—partly because it was from Norway most of the settlers came and the Icelanders still felt they had their roots there and partly because they were dependent on the Norwegians for ships. There were no woods in Iceland for providing timber for oceangoing vessels; driftwood, which was abundant in many places in the country, was not suited for shipbuilding. Vessels and usable timber had to be provided by Norway. The Icelanders probably felt that it was impossible for them to stay pagan when the Norwegians had become Christian.

At the end of the eleventh century the Icelanders possessed a fleet of oceangoing vessels but in the second half of the twelfth century they were very few and around 1200

12.15 THINGBREKKA AT THINGVELLIR

This watercolor of a meeting of the Althing during the Viking Age was painted in 1897 by W. G. Collingwood after he completed extensive travels in Iceland. Collingwood was familiar with the sagas and incorporated details from them, such as the two lovers secretly conversing behind one of the "booths" (foreground). He shows the *lögsögumaður* (law speaker) standing on the *lögberg* (law rock), but his placement of that landmark is different from where scholars today think it was.

there were none. All transportation over the ocean was in the hands of the Norwegians and men from the Orkney and Shetland islands. One motivation for foreigners to make the journey was the increasing demand for Icelandic wadmal, the homespun cloth that was both cheap and practical and that the Icelanders could produce in abundance. Fish only became a coveted article of export in the fourteenth century. Wadmal was the main currency in Iceland and other commodities were valued in wadmal.

Foreign merchants could come across wadmal in Thingvellir. One of the miracles of St. Thorlak concerns some wadmal that a man promised to pay to the bishop's seat in Skálholt, not far from Thingvellir, if his wounded son would live (Thorlaksson 1991). Thorlak helped him and the son lived and became well. The man went to the Thing—without much doubt the Althing—and before he had handed over the wadmal to the representatives of the bishop, as he intended, he spent it on a kettle he bought there, which fell off a horse on his way home and broke into pieces. The following year the man brought the same amount of wadmal he had promised to the Thing and told his story.

The interventions of the kings of Norway continued after the death of King Olafur Haraldarsson in 1030. His brother, King Harald the Hardruler, had great interest in Icelandic affairs, but after his death at Stanford Bridge in 1066 we seldom hear of Norwegian kings dealing with Icelandic matters. There was a civil war in Norway in the twelfth century but when peace prevailed anew in the 1170s, the rulers in Norway showed some new interest in Icelandic affairs.

Political influence became concentrated in fewer hands in the second half of the twelfth century, partly for economic reasons and partly because there were ruthless and ambitious individuals who were able and willing to exploit the imbalance caused by new economic conditions. The new sources for income were a few estates that had been donated to churches but were in the hands of the secular chieftains. These estate-churches were exempt from payment of tithes and secured considerable income from tithes paid by others, probably because they could provide some services for the smaller churches. These estate-churches grew richer during the twelfth century, as did the chieftains who administered their income and seem to have been free to a great extent to enjoy it themselves.

This development meant that chieftains became fewer and in the early thirteenth century a few families had gained all power in the country. Some of these families were quite ambitious and kept on seizing power, causing civil war, which was complicated by the interventions of the archbishop and the king of Norway. The Althing became a scene for repeated strife. The chieftains traveled with men of arms and often were on the verge of pitched battles at Thingvellir itself. Such battles were usually averted but many skirmishes took place there and men were wounded and killed. After 1235, a civil war raged in Iceland. This time of trouble led to submission to the Norwegian crown in 1262 to 1264, when the Icelanders unwillingly gained that service which the Scandinavian kings had provided for their own people for centuries, the service of an umpire with loyal officers to ensure that his decisions were kept (fig. 12.12). In this way, the Althing of the Commonwealth period came to an end.

Eddas and Sagas in Medieval Iceland By Gísli Sigurdsson

The sagas of the Icelanders came from a flourishing literary tradition. Medieval Iceland produced a vast number of literary documents that contain both mythic and legendary material from the Viking period, as well as numerous historical sagas about Scandinavia, the British Isles, the Faeroes, Iceland itself, and Greenland. These works are the major source of information about Scandinavian history in the Middle Ages; they have also, at times, been a major source of Icelandic national pride and played a central role in shaping that country's national identity during its struggle for independence from Denmark in the nineteenth and early twentieth centuries.

These Eddas and sagas were all written in Icelandic vernacular, a language that can still be read without much difficulty by modern Icelanders because Icelandic has not changed significantly over the centuries. The fact that Latin was not used for this literary production puts these works in the same class as the Irish sagas, the only other secular heroic prose literature in this part of the world that was written in the vernacular.

THE CHURCH AND LITERARY ACTIVITY IN THE TWELFTH CENTURY

As the church became established within Icelandic society, its influence increased. One outcome of this was that the oral transmission of knowledge, which was traditional in Viking society, was supplanted by the writing of books. Law texts were among the first secular materials to be put in writing in the early twelfth century (p. 175). A little more than a century after the coming of Christianity, the professional status of the orally trained *lögsögumaður* had been undermined; he could no longer decide which law was applicable but had to consult a book of law that was kept by the bishop. The direct transfer of power from the secular chieftain to the church is evident in this transition as well as the evolution from oral to written culture, and from the pagan heritage to the Christian world where the book had a central function.

Book of the Icelanders, written in the third decade of the twelfth century by Ari the Wise, is the second major achievement in the history of Icelandic letters. It is the earliest major

source on the first ages of life in Iceland as well as the Icelandic settlement in Greenland, but regrettably it is told from a very clerical standpoint, focusing on the coming of Christianity and the history of the church rather than more secular and perhaps more interesting matters, for example, the Vinland voyages.

By the twelfth century secular chieftains had also begun to realize the power of the book, and probably around that time started to compile the *Book of Settlements*, which describes the *landnám*, or original settlement around the country, in every firth and valley. This rendition probably reflects how the ruling families of the twelfth century wanted to remember the history of their ancestors, so it also served their purposes at that time, as is common practice in oral cultures. This book is unusual because it describes the beginning of an entirely new nation and because it was written at such an early date. It was probably extremely influential in creating a shared sense of identity among the people who lived in Iceland and could all trace their origins into this single book.

THE TWO EDDAS: *PROSE EDDA* AND *POETIC EDDA*

The mixed population that settled Iceland created from the very beginning a culture different from that of its neighbors and the countries of origin of most of its citizens—Norway, Scotland, and Ireland. It is often called "the first new society." Early on, while most of the population was still pagan, people from Iceland soon made a name for themselves at the royal courts in Scandinavia and in the British Isles as poets, composing mostly prose poems in exceptionally complicated meter, called skaldic meter. In addition to the intricate rhyming rules of skaldic meter, this poetry created special terminology and phrases, called kennings (literally, way of naming), for the terms most frequently used in the genre: kings, warriors, battles, swords, spears, bows, arrows, ships, sails, oars, women. For example, instead of using the noun "king" in a line of poetry, the phrase "giver of rings" would be used, a reference to the king's reward to his loyal retainers. Many of these kennings are based on Old Norse mythology and refer to characteristics of the gods and events in the mythology.

When these works were initially composed in the Viking period, the audience would have understood the references, but once Iceland converted to Christianity, this knowledge began to be lost. The art of this poetry is studied in a book compiled by the most renowned writer of the thirteenth-century literary golden age, Snorri Sturluson. He gathered in a single book, called variously *Snorra Edda*, *Younger Edda*, or *Prose Edda*, all the oral traditions that professional poets had to master to compose verse in skaldic meter. Because this learning consisted mainly of pagan myths, this book forms the basis of what we know about Old Norse mythology.

EGIL'S SAGA

Snorri Sturluson (1179–1241), the foster son of the wealthiest family in southern Iceland, became a prolific writer of the sagas. He wrote the Edda concerning poetry of the pagan gods and recorded the history of Norwegian kings in *Heimskringla*. He is also believed to be the author of *Egil's Saga*, which tells the adventures of an Icelander in Europe.

EGIL SKALLAGRÍMSSON

Strong as an ox, a gifted poet, and notoriously difficult to get along with, Egil Skallagrímsson is one of the most vivacious saga characters. The saga bearing his name recounts the troubles he and his extended family had in dealings with the Norwegian kings, including the banishment of his father to Iceland. Egil returned to Norway to antagonize King Erik Bloodaxe, until they settled on a truce, agreeing never to cross each other's path again.

More traditional oral poems, containing many pagan myths and heroic lore, some of which were common to Scandinavia and the old Germanic cultural area of northwestern Europe, were kept alive in Iceland much longer than elsewhere and eventually written down in the thirteenth century. Most of these Eddic poems are preserved in one of the most precious manuscripts from the Middle Ages: the *Poetic Edda*. Written around 1270, the poems are presented systematically, beginning with mythological poems about the creation and cosmic structures and proceeding to more general stories about individual gods, some very humorous. The second half contains heroic poems with the Nibelungenied, a race of dwarfs in Germanic legend, which also served as a major source for Wagner's operas. Pictorial evidence from runestones also shows that this legend was widespread all over the Germanic cultural area.

The Eddic poems and Snorri's book on the myths, usually referred to as the Eddas, would alone make Iceland's name stand out in the history of world literature because they caught the old pagan oral heritage in writing untainted by deep-felt Christian influence.

The Dawning of the Saga Age around 1200: Secular Kings' Sagas

Icelanders also translated historical chronicles from continental Europe into the vernacular recording histories of the Jews, the Trojans, the Romans, and the British. What followed was the dawning of an entirely new literary age, the saga age, which many see as the golden age of Icelandic letters. This format has also been called the forerunner of the modern novel, which influenced, for example, such writers as Sir Walter Scott and others who developed the historical novel. The first sagas were written about Norwegian kings. These gradually expanded and grew, and at the height of the development of the saga genre known as Kings Sagas, the same Snorri Sturluson compiled the best collection of them all in his *Heimskringla* (Circle of the Earth). He recounts tales about kings from the mythological past through King Harald Finehair, the founder of the united Norwegian state in the Viking Age, and down to Snorri's own time. It reflects the thirteenth-century view of many Icelanders that their forefathers had not been too happy with Harald's union and had therefore taken off to Iceland, which is the source of the

popular notion that Icelanders had self-selected as independent, cantankerous, literary individualists. The prototype of this characterization is Egil Skallagrímsson, whose saga was written in the first half of the thirteenth century, again possibly by Snorri Sturluson. Snorri was not alone in compiling sagas about kings; others were writing original works and constantly adding to what had already been written. These additions from the medieval period reflects its fashion, with short stories about Icelanders who had some connection with the different kings, not infrequently as poets. The high point of this additive process is found in a manuscript from the end of the fourteenth century, *Flateyjarbók*, in which Norwegian kings' sagas are told more elaborately than elsewhere and with more added material concerning Icelanders than elsewhere, including the only existing version of the *Greenlanders' Saga*.

Icelanders thus became the writers of royal history for Scandinavia. Around 1200 the earls in Orkney also got their saga as did the people of the Faeroes and Greenland, about whom the Icelanders wrote sagas along the same literary lines as about themselves. Other sagas are more legendary treating Viking heroes who were probably widely known and celebrated in poetry all over Scandinavia in former times but now are only remembered in these Icelandic sagas.

The Sagas of Icelanders: The Problem of the Oral and the Written

The *Book of the Icelanders* recounts the first centuries of settlement, often identifying the main characters in Norway and then following them across the Atlantic to Iceland where they face the difficulties and hardships of life in a new country. The coming of Christianity, which is regarded in a very positive light in these sagas, is depicted as bringing a peaceful solution to long lasting blood-feuds and internal family struggles that pit kinsmen in deadly opposition to the laws of duty. Despite the Christian perspective, the pagan forefathers are in no way condemned for their religion. These fascinating sagas are not only exceptionally well-composed pieces of literature, but more easily accessible to the modern reader than the medieval literature known from most other countries. The world that the sagas describe is so coherent and often so realistic that many readers are tempted to regard them as descriptions of real life even though they were supposed to have taken place two or three hundred years before they were written. Genealogies in one saga match those in another, and the same chieftains appear in various sagas; the same laws and customs appear in unrelated sagas, which reinforces the impression that they are describing a real society that can be reconstructed by using the sagas as field reports. Characters from the sagas are also not only literary prototypes, as is often the case in heroic literature, but more like people of flesh and blood who seem as familiar as our old schoolmates. Many are family friends in Icelandic homes today and are quoted for their wit and profound expressions of sorrow and joy.

IV VIKING AMERICA

A.D. 1000: EAST MEETS WEST

BY PETER SCHLEDERMANN

FOR THE NORSE INHABITANTS OF ICELAND it was an auspicious beginning to the new millennium. Among the hundreds of men and women attending the annual parliamentary assembly, or Althing, at Thingvellir during the summer of A.D. 1000 the tension must have been palpable. For years the Norwegian king, Olaf Tryggvason, had tried unsuccessfully to persuade the Icelanders to accept Christianity. Now on the eve of a new millennium, one Icelandic leader, Gizur the White Teitsson, promised the king that he would convert his fellow Icelanders to the true faith. Thorgeir, the Icelandic *lögsögumaður* (law speaker), the person who carried legal conventions for this society based on oral traditions, spoke for the heathens. At stake was the division of the Icelandic free state into two political and religious realms, an event that could, with very little effort, immerse the fledgling nation in civil war.

Thorgeir listened to the arguments, then retired to his *buðir* (literally "booth," seasonal dwellings) where he contemplated the troublesome issue of the people's religion. Not surprisingly he took his time, stepping out to face the tense crowd a full day later. In a remarkable show of political awareness and diplomatic cunning, the heathen law speaker announced that from that day onward Christianity would be the governing law in Iceland while certain heathen practices, such as infanticide, were allowed to continue albeit as covertly as possible (Hastrup 1985).

When news of the Icelandic proclamation reached the pioneering settlers in Greenland, Erik the Red's wife, Thjodhild, must have been pleased. Her earlier conversion to Christianity could now be further sanctioned by the building of a small church on the Brattahlid estate, even if it had to be erected at some distance from the eyes of her heathen husband. Erik may have grumbled, wondering how long decisions made at the Icelandic Althing would interfere in his life. Only fifteen years had passed since the same court had

banished him from Iceland. The ambitious Erik transformed what might have been severe punishment into a marvelous opportunity: he eagerly set sail for lands sighted to the west by voyagers driven off course on their way to Iceland. During his three years in exile Erik explored the southwestern portion of a magnificent country he referred to as "the green land." Some have suggested that he coined the name Greenland as a means of enticing other chieftains into leaving Iceland. There may have been some element of salesmanship involved, but essentially Erik used a name that reflected accurately the lush growth of the inner fjord areas and the vast uplands that he explored, which offers a sharp contrast to the overexploited, barren Icelandic countryside. Before returning to Iceland Erik carefully chose the location of his own farm, Brattahlid, in Erik's Fjord (Nørlund and Stenberger 1934).

The discoveries in Greenland catapulted Erik up the Icelandic social ladder; now he would have little difficulty convincing disgruntled chieftains, eager for new lands and opportunities, to load their vessels and follow him to Greenland. To be in on the first Greenlandic *landnám* (parceling out of new lands among the settlers) was most important; those who participated in the first Icelandic *landnám* had all secured high social status. According to the *Greenlanders' Saga*, one year after his return to Iceland Erik

---

ÍSLENDINGUR AT SEA

The Viking sailing tradition that swept beyond Iceland, first to Greenland and then to North America, has been revived in recent years by Nordic shipbuilders and sailors. Sailing ships such as *Íslendingur*, a replica built in the late 1980s in the south of Iceland and captained by Gunnar Eggertsson, have provided a means for recapturing knowledge of these lost traditions.

led a fleet of some twenty-five ships destined for Greenland. Of these only fourteen survived to reach their destination, a good indication of the dangers involved in crossing the often turbulent and ice-filled seas between Iceland and Greenland (Dupont 1970). The potential gain of being on the scene early was clearly thought to outweigh such risks. Leading the Greenland *landnám* had provided Erik the Red with far more than a new farm in Erik's Fjord. From ordinary farmer in Iceland he had become a most powerful chieftain and one of the voices listened to when Greenland's national assembly, the Althing, was convened. For all we know he may have served as the first *lögsögumaður* in Greenland.

In many ways the Greenland *landnám* could not have taken place at a more opportune time; the Northern Hemisphere was enjoying the Medieval Warm Period, a prolonged interval of warmer conditions that lasted from about the tenth to the thirteenth century A.D. (Hughes 1994). The extent and duration of pack ice moving down the east coast of Greenland was considerably less menacing than it is today. When Erik and the first settlers arrived, the inner fjord areas supported large stands of dwarf willow and birch. (Even today these areas are impressively lush in the summer compared with the eastern Canadian Arctic.)

The lands claimed by the first chieftains constituted what became known as the Eastern Settlement in southeast Greenland. For those who came slightly later, but still wanted to construct their longhouses in virgin territory, Erik could recommend another region about 120 miles (200 kilometers) to the north that he had investigated. The Western Settlement, which became the second-largest Norse settlement, was not as extensive as the Eastern Settlement, but the more northerly settlement had plenty of good farmland, luxuriant growth of grasses, and groves of dwarfed trees. Lakes and rivers were teaming with fish and migratory harp seals passed in large numbers; caribou were plentiful in the

vast uplands. The Western Settlement's location also turned out to be more convenient to the northerly hunting region, Nordsetur, where walrus were plentiful.

One advantage to Greenland for the pioneering *landnámsmenn* was that the land Erik had explored was uninhabited. History has recorded that not even the occasional reclusive Celtic monk was there to be chased away. Remains of old camps, even boat parts, were supposedly seen, but no people. There was no one to resist the newcomers, no competition for resources and hunting rights.

Not long after the first longhouses and byres were erected in Greenland, stories began circulating of discoveries of land even farther to the west (map, right). From the *Descriptio insularum aquilonis* in Adam of Bremen's *Gesta Hammaburgensis Ecclesia Pontificum* from A.D. 1075 (Jones 1986: 85), we know that three new lands to the west of Greenland had been named: Helluland, Markland, and Vinland. The Stefansson Map (fig. 15.3), drawn in 1590, shows a stretch of land labeled "Promontorium Winlandiae" (Vinland Promontory) which resembles the northern peninsula of Newfoundland Island. Among Norse scholars there is reasonable agreement that Helluland corresponds to the southeastern part of Baffin Island and perhaps includes the northern part of Labrador. Markland is thought to incorporate central and southern Labrador. Vinland undoubtedly denotes a region that includes Newfoundland and a good part of the Gulf of Saint Lawrence.

If Erik was growing a little weary of long journeys, his progeny were eager to continue the tradition of discovery he had established. Serious planning must have taken place within the sod and turf walls of the longhouse at Brattahlid. Though details vary between the *Greenlanders' Saga* and *Erik the Red's Saga* (Jones 1986; Wallace, Sigurðsson, this volume), the basic story line is that Erik's son Leif was the first to head for the new lands, followed

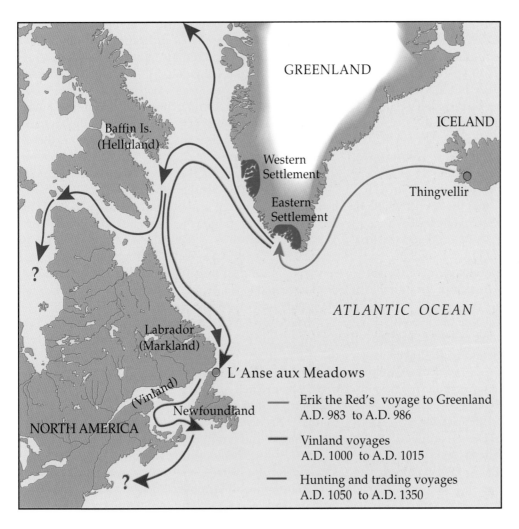

GREENLAND

ICELAND

Baffin Is.
(Helluland)

Western
Settlement

Eastern
Settlement

Thingvellir

?

ATLANTIC OCEAN

Labrador
(Markland)

L'Anse aux Meadows

(Vinland)

Newfoundland

NORTH AMERICA

?

— Erik the Red's voyage to Greenland
A.D. 983 to A.D. 986

— Vinland voyages
A.D. 1000 to A.D. 1015

— Hunting and trading voyages
A.D. 1050 to A.D. 1350

by his brothers Thorvald and Thorstein and sister Freydis.

It is quite possible that when the Icelandic law speaker Thorgeir made his historic announcement at Thingvellir, Leif Eriksson had already organized the construction of work sheds and a longhouse at L'Anse aux Meadows, located on the tip of the northern peninsula of Newfoundland. A series of radiocarbon dates indicate that the Norse occupation of Leifsbuðir, as the site is called in the sagas, took place around A.D. 1000. Birgitta Wallace, after more than twenty years of archaeological investigations at the L'Anse aux Meadows site, has suggested that Leifsbuðir was strategically placed at the gateway to Vinland and that its occupation spanned fewer than ten years. To this day L'Anse aux Meadows is the only accepted Norse settlement location in the New World (Wallace 1991).

According to the sagas, the Norwegian merchant and explorer Thorfinn Karlsefni, who was married to Gudrid (the widow of Leif's brother Thorstein), organized and led one of the last major attempts to settle the new territory. His expedition had the most contact with the native population of North America, whom the Norse called *skraeling*, a derogatory term that is likely to have referred to many different peoples. Karlsefni established an amicable relationship with the native peoples, but this came to an end when some of the *skraeling* were killed. Following additional skirmishes

Karlsefni headed for home, but not before an extraordinary historical event had taken place: his wife Gudrid gave birth to their son, Snorri, the first European born in North America.

The experiences of Karlsefni help answer why Leifsbuðir was occupied for such a short time. The pioneering Norse explorers in Markland and Vinland came up against a challenge they had not faced in Greenland or Iceland, where the small number of Celtic inhabitants were easily killed, enslaved, or chased away. The native people who confronted the Norsemen in the new land were different from anyone they had ever encountered. It was truly a momentous meeting between two worlds, east and west, the Old World and the New; a coming together of human beings separated at a distant and forgotten point in the history of human evolution. The Indians facing the Norse voyagers were descendants of people who had migrated through northeast Asia, crossed the Bering land bridge, and pushed south and east as the vast ice sheets melted away. They had come in several waves and adapted themselves to new environments with enough efficiency to survive and prosper. Over a period of fifteen thousand to twenty thousand years they had spread throughout the New World, separated into a dizzying variety of linguistic groups, and explored nearly every conceivable ecological niche including tropical jungles, arid desert landscapes, the rugged shores of Tierra del Fuego, and the rich coastal regions of the Northwest. Some relied on local shamans and simple religious rituals for their spiritual and physical well-being, while others put their trust in elaborate hierarchies of priests and complex ceremonies. When the first Norsemen stepped forward to meet these people they called *skraeling*, a somewhat mocking term for someone perceived as a scared weakling, the Maya civilization was already in decline and the Aztecs were but a nomadic tribe in Mesoamerica waiting to take their place in history alongside Columbus and his men.

Although the area of Vinland may have seemed uninhabited when Leif Eriksson and his party arrived, aboriginal populations were not far away. Archaeological evidence indicates that Indian populations associated with a prehistoric complex known as Point Revenge inhabited many of the coastal regions of Newfoundland and south-central Labrador between A.D. 700 and 1500 (Fitzhugh 1978: 166). The people may have been Algonquian speakers, ancestors of historic Montagnais and Naskapi Indians and possibly related to the now-extinct Beothuk Indians of Newfoundland.

In northern Labrador, along the Ungava coast of Hudson Strait and in southeastern Baffin Island, Norse landing parties would have encountered a very different people: Dorset Paleo-Eskimos, descendants of a people associated with an archaeological tradition known as the Arctic Small Tool tradition (ASTt). People of the ASTt were part of the last major human migration into the New World and the first human occupants of the Canadian High Arctic and Greenland. By 2000 B.C. the Paleo-Eskimos were well established throughout most of the North American Arctic and had penetrated far enough south along the coast of Labrador to displace Indians of the Maritime Archaic tradition (Cox 1978). Between 2000 B.C. and A.D. 1000 the Paleo-Eskimos responded to changing environmental and ecological conditions by adjusting their technological and social adaptations to different geographical regions. Dwellings, hunting methods, and tool types took on new forms that are recognized archaeologically and form the basis for designating such complexes as Independence I, Sarqaq, pre-Dorset, and Dorset. The year 1000 was the final stage of the Paleo-Eskimo presence in the Arctic, represented by the Late Dorset culture. If and when the first Norse explorers made landfall in southern Baffin Island, Ungava Bay, or northern Labrador, they most likely would have encountered Late Dorset people. The Norsemen probably established contact both with descendants of the earliest aboriginal groups to enter the New World, the Paleo-Indians, and descendants of the latest arrivals from northeast Asia, the Paleo-Eskimos. In the eyes of the Norsemen they were all *skraeling*.

Indian and Eskimo populations had long been rivals for the rich sea-mammal–hunting areas along the Labrador coast. By 500 B.C. Paleo-Eskimos had pushed as far south as Newfoundland where they continued to leave traces of their activities as late as A.D. 500. Then, once again, Newfoundland and southern Labrador became the domain of aboriginal Indian groups. By the time Leif Eriksson established Leifsbuðir, Late Dorset hunters frequented only the northern part of Labrador (McGhee 1984; Firhugh 1994). Why the Dorset people departed from more southerly regions we do not know. In other parts of the Arctic they pursued their way of life most successfully, becoming the first people to reenter the High Arctic and northern Greenland after a prolonged absence of Paleo-Eskimos in those regions. When the first Norse *landnámsmenn* staked out their holdings in southern Greenland, Late Dorset people were exploring sea and land resources in the Canadian High Arctic and northern Greenland (Schledermann 1990, 1996; Appelt et al. 1998). It is unlikely that the two peoples ever met in Greenland. By the time the Norsemen ventured into the far north, the Thule people had already displaced the Dorset people, and they would eventually displace the Norsemen in Greenland.

Many unrecorded voyages no doubt took place between Greenland and Markland/Vinland during the centuries of the Norse presence in Greenland; as late as A.D. 1347 a small ship drifted off course after having visited Markland and eventually reached Iceland (Gad 1965). Timber for boat construction and house building would have motivated some in Greenland to make the voyage because the only other source, aside from driftwood, would have entailed sailing to Norway. There was not, however, to be a New World *landnám* for the Norse Greenlanders. Karlsefni's return to Greenland probably dampened dreams of a successful *landnám* in Vinland. No one could doubt that the *skraeling* in Markland and Vinland were quite capable of holding their own in a fight, and by numbers alone they could overwhelm a sizable contingent of Norsemen. Metal swords provided no particular advantage against well-aimed arrows. Even so, the rich timber resources in Markland must have remained an attraction worth the occasional skirmish with hostile *skraeling*. From a European point of view, successful colonization of the New World would have to wait until the Europeans could marshal new weapons and technologies and take advantage of an even more powerful tool, disease.

13 SKRAELING: FIRST PEOPLES OF HELLULAND, MARKLAND, AND VINLAND

BY DANIEL ODESS, STEPHEN LORING,
AND WILLIAM W. FITZHUGH

One morning, as spring advanced, they [Karlsefni and his companions] noticed a large number of hide-covered boats [paddling] up from the south around the point. There were so many of them that it looked as if bits of coal had been tossed over the water, and there was a pole waving from each boat. They signaled with their shields and began trading with the visitors, who mostly wished to trade for red cloth. They also wanted to purchase swords and spears, but Karlsefni and Snorri forbade this. They traded a dark pelt for the cloth and for each pelt they took cloth a hand in length, which they bound about their heads. (Erik the Red's Saga Hreinsson 1997)

THE NORSE ARRIVED IN THE NEW World in A.D. 1000, a time of diverse social and political landscapes for the peoples living on the western shores of the North Atlantic. Members of several different ethnic groups—the Dorset people of the eastern Canadian Arctic and northern Greenland, the ancestors of the Labrador Innu, the Newfoundland Beothuk, and the Maliseet and Micmac of the southern Gulf of Saint Lawrence and Nova Scotia—had divided this territory into a multicultural region of discrete homelands where their ancestors had lived for many generations. After A.D. 1200 another people, the Thule—ancestors of the Inuit—would also arrive on the scene. Despite the cultural and linguistic differences that divided them, archaeological evidence shows that members of these groups were linked by trade relationships that involved the movement of goods, ideas, and people over hundreds, or even thousands, of miles. They were no doubt accustomed to meeting strangers in their territories and were adept at negotiating these encounters to sustain mutually beneficial interactions over time. In boundary areas at least, many were probably bilingual or even trilingual.

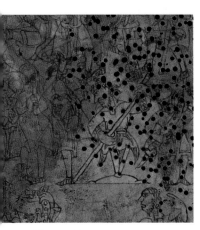

UNIPED, *PHYSIOLOGUS*

The degrees of cultural difference between these peoples varied, with the greatest similarities to one another characterizing the ancestors of the Micmac and Maliseet, on one hand, and the Beothuk and Innu, on the other. There were few cultural similarities between any of these Indian peoples and the Dorset people, or between the Dorset and the Thule. The following discussion introduces these peoples, as they are known from archaeology and by extrapolation from historical ethnography, during the time when the Norse were probing the margins of northeastern North America. Understanding the interrelationships, geographic distribution, demography, and cultural features of these peoples reveals the dynamics of contact and may also underscore the significance of a quote in *Erik the Red's Saga* attributed to Thorfinn Karlsefni on his departure from Vinland: "a rich and fruitful land, but one that we cannot safely inhabit."

THE DORSET: *SKRAELING* OF HELLULAND AND NORTHERN MARKLAND

Dorset, the name given to a cultural tradition that flourished in the eastern North American Arctic for more than fifteen hundred years before the Norse arrived in Greenland late in the tenth century, derived from a location on southern Baffin Island where that culture's remains were first iden-

13.1 DORSET HARPOON HEADS
The Dorset people made harpoons in different sizes depending on the animal being hunted. The harpoons were attached to a seal- or walrus-skin line and designed to turn sideways and toggle under the skin after it had pierced the animal's hide so the animal could not pull free. Stylized human faces, possibly the hunters' helping spirits, are incised on the tips of these harpoons.

13.2 SHULDHAM ISLAND FIGURINE
Small carvings, such as this soapstone figure from a Dorset site in northern Labrador, show that Dorset parkas had a high collar instead of the hood characteristic of Thule culture and modern Inuit parkas. The absence of hooded parkas in Dorset culture is as puzzling as Dorset peoples' lack of bows and arrows and dogs, which were used by earlier and later arctic peoples.

tified (Maxwell 1984; McGhee 1978). One of the two northernmost groups of *skraeling*, they were descendants of earlier pre-Dorset people who migrated east from Alaska more than four thousand years ago, colonizing the Canadian Arctic and Greenland for the first time. They eventually displaced Maritime Archaic Indians from territories they had occupied in coastal Labrador since about 6000 B.C. Dorset people generally lived in settlements of one or two houses—skin tents in the summer and sod-walled and snow houses in the winter—and changed their place of habitation with the seasons to match the movements of the animals on which they depended for food, fuel, and shelter.

Dorset people were consummate hunters who ate nearly all the birds, fish, and marine and terrestrial mammals available in their country. While they were adept at capturing sea mammals, including seals and walrus, they did not hunt the great baleen whales (fig. 13.1). In some locations, ducks, geese, and pelagic waterfowl were a major part of their diet; at others, the bones of the arctic fox dominate their trash middens. Everywhere they hunted caribou with lances, eating the meat, fashioning tools from the bones and antlers, and using the skins for clothing, bedding, and tents. They were also successful polar-bear hunters.

The Norse arrived in Greenland during the time when Dorset artistic traditions were at their zenith. At sites where perishable materials are preserved, archaeologists have found small, meticulously rendered animal figurines, some of which suggest transformation between human form and that of a polar bear. Amulets carved

in the form of a caribou's hoof, polar bears, seals, falcons, stylized animal-figured harpoon heads, or shaman's "teeth" were used in ceremonies, attached to clothing, or worn as necklaces (fig. 13.5). There are rare occurrences of human images: masks (fig. 13.6), individuals wearing parkas with high collars instead of hoods (fig. 13.2), and antler and wood batons carved with multiple human faces (figs. 13.7, 24.7), each so varied and detailed that they probably represent individuals known to the artist. Dorset artists also enjoyed making ivory and soapstone carvings of bird's eggs and other mundane subjects, as well as indulging fantasies or holding fertility rituals with carvings of phalli and copulating humans.

At the beginning of the eleventh century, Dorset interaction networks seem to have been more active than at any time in the previous thousand years. Perhaps as a reflection of the increased flow of ideas and information, the form of their tools, which previously had exhibited regionally distinct styles, suddenly became uniform, so that tools from the northern edge of their country in the High Arctic are very similar to those found at the southern margins of their territory on the coast of Labrador. There is other evidence for interaction as well: distinct types of stone and other materials were being traded hundreds of miles from their sources. Musk-ox hair shed in the High Arctic was collected and twisted into string and rope that was traded as far south as Frobisher Bay and northern Labrador, while Ramah chert from Labrador quarries found its way north to Frobisher Bay sites that also contain chert from Southampton Island, 360 miles (600 kilometers) to the west. This interaction was not limited to trade with fellow Dorset people; Ramah chert was traded between Dorset people in northern Labrador and ancestral Innu people and also appears in Indian sites as far south as Maine.

Although we know much about the Dorset people, there is much of their culture that remains enigmatic. Because they did not possess writing and are not ancestral to any living peoples, nothing is known of their language. McGhee (1984) has suggested that they probably spoke one of the Eskimoan tongues, but it seems equally possible that they spoke unrelated Paleo-Asiatic languages that have since disappeared. In addition, the paucity of Dorset skeletal remains recovered to date makes it difficult to establish their biological relationships with other arctic populations. They may have been quite similar in appearance to modern Inuit, but they could also have resembled Native Americans or any of several northeast Asian populations, including the Ainu. To add to the mystery, their artistic traditions are distinct from those of other peoples in the circumpolar world and show greater similarity to Yup'ik Eskimo traditions of western Alaska and the Bering Sea than to those of their closer geographic neighbors, the Canadian Inuit and Inupiat Eskimos of northern Alaska (Fitzhugh 1988). Certain aspects of their culture also seem counterintuitive: unlike the pre-Dorset people who were their ancestors and the Thule people who later replaced them, the Dorset peoples did not use dogs or the bow and arrow, both potentially useful items when dealing with polar bears and the notoriously irascible Norse.

As *skraeling* go, the Dorset were probably the least threatening of the peoples the Norse encountered in the New World. Dorset settlements of the Viking period were generally limited to one or two houses of perhaps eight to ten people each (fig. 13.3). For this reason, it is unlikely that the Norse would ever have encountered them in large groups. Even comparatively small Norse hunting parties of six to eight men would likely have had a numerical and military advantage when the two peoples met.

Ungava Longhouses

Thomas Lee has claimed (1968) the longhouses that he excavated, following their initial discovery by archaeologist William E. Taylor, Jr., in northern Ungava on Pamiok Island were made by Norse explorers. This idea has since been publicized in a delightful if rather fanciful reconstruction of northwest Atlantic history by Farley Mowat (1998). Lee supported his ideas with additional "Norse" evidence in the form of large stone *inuksuit*, stone cairns built by the Inuit, which he interpreted as "hammers of Thor," and other large stone constructions. Since then archaeologists have found longhouses throughout much of the Canadian Arctic and have securely identified them as being made by Dorset people from A.D. 600 to 900 (Maxwell 1984; Schledermann, chapter 18). While their function remains uncertain, it appears that

Dorset people occasionally gathered in large groups for social, ritual, or hunting purposes, building low rock walls to enclose a row of Dorset family groups. Linear structures are not unique to the Norse and have been found in Dorset, Maritime Archaic, and early historic Innu cultures in Labrador and Ungava. Patrick Plumet (1985) demonstrated conclusively that Lee's "Pamiok longhouses" were made by Dorset people circa A.D. 700 (fig. 13.3).

An iron axe, reputedly of "Norse" type, found at Pamiok by a native Inuit is lost and has never been analyzed. Despite confidence in the dating and Dorset interpretation, some scholars continue to promote the idea of a Norse connection involving iron smelting in northern Ungava (Seaver, chapter 20).

13.3 A Dorset Longhouse
Dorset people who lived in eastern Ellesmere Island about one century before the Norse arrived in Greenland made mysterious longhouselike structures. This one, measuring 148 by 6 feet wide (50 by 2 meters), served as a foundation for adjacent family tents erected at a summer gathering place. When these houses were first discovered in northern Quebec, they were mistakenly thought to be Norse (Lee 1972; Mowat 1998), but excavations produced only Dorset artifacts (Plumet 1982).

13.4 Willows Island, Frobisher Bay

Fog, ice, and rocky shoals, as well as strong winds and currents, make navigation in the eastern arctic challenging for even the most skilled mariners. Native hunters successfully navigated these waters in skin boats long before the arrival of the Norse.

13.5 Animal Figurines

Dorset artists carved small figurines from wood, ivory, antler, and soapstone to represent the animals in their world. The skeletal or X-ray motif is common in Dorset art. Dorset people carved exquisite polar bears, some of which are seen in the act of transforming to or from human form. Much of Dorset art is thought to be related to shamanistic beliefs.

For reasons that are poorly understood, the area occupied by Dorset people gradually began to contract shortly after A.D. 1000, even as the climate in the area would seem to have been improving with the onset of the Medieval Warm Period. It appears that they withdrew first from northern Ellesmere Island and Greenland, then from areas northwest of Hudson Bay. In the thirteenth century Dorset people continued to occupy northern Labrador, Ungava, eastern Hudson Bay, Frobisher Bay, and the western side of Baffin Island. By the beginning of the fifteenth century, the only Dorset people who remained appear to have been in Ungava, and they probably vanished about the same time that the Norse disappeared from Greenland.

What might contact between the Norse and the Dorset have entailed and how would Dorset people have responded to encounters with the Norse? Given that the sagas probably underrecord the number of voyages west of Greenland, we might expect the Dorset, whose settlements were scattered throughout the eastern arctic regions that were most accessible to the Norse, to have occasionally traded with them. If the Norse were seen as a reliable, or potentially reliable, source of trade goods, Dorset people might have actively sought contact with them. Conversely, if they had experienced hostilities like those described in the sagas, Dorset people would have come to hear of the unpleasantness through their extensive social networks. Given their inferior weapons and numbers, the Dorset would probably have chosen avoidance as the most sensible way to deal with the Norse.

In all likelihood, incidents of contact varied from one to the next. It seems likely that iron, cloth, ivory, walrus skin, and fur would have been the materials of interest in any sort of trading relationship. As consummate walrus hunters, Dorset people were in a position to accumulate surplus ivory and walrus skins. In return, they most likely would have desired iron and, possibly, cloth (see Sutherland, this volume). While the Norse probably never had a surplus of iron, the small scraps from broken or worn-out tools probably would have satisfied the Dorset, who were already acquainted with meteoritic iron from northwest Greenland, which they used when available for knives,

13.6 DORSET MASK

Dorset masks, such as this example from Avayalik Island in northern Labrador, often have a simple form. Their visages are haunting but rarely benevolent. This rough-hewn two thousand-year-old mask recovered from permafrost was probably made for a shamanistic ceremony and was discarded after use.

13.7 ANTLER WAND

Dorset artists sometimes decorated pieces of antler, ivory, or wood with a dozen or more faces, each unique and so expressive that they probably depict individuals known to the carver. Clues to the personality and ethnicity of the subjects appear on some; for instance, carvings with long-nosed images may depict Europeans. Similar pieces have been found in Greenland (fig. 24.7).

harpoon blades, and tools for working bone and ivory.

It is also possible that Norse hunting parties were occasionally stranded in Dorset territory when their boats were damaged by sea ice or storms. How Dorset people would have reacted to finding a stranded Norseman probably varied. If relations were good, they might have taken him (or her) in or rendered assistance. If they were not good, the Dorset might have left him to die or killed him outright and taken his possessions.

As McGhee (1984) has noted, the direct evidence to date for Norse-Dorset contact is sparse. Most of these finds come from sites in the Canadian High Arctic and northwestern Greenland, and only a few are from south of Hudson Strait. A smelted copper amulet (fig. 17.14) has been found in a Dorset site in Richmond Gulf on the east coast of Hudson Bay (Harp 1974–75). To date no Norse materials have been found in Dorset sites in Labrador (Cox 1978; Fitzhugh 1994), Frobisher Bay (Odess 1998), or Ungava (Plumet 1994), but the presence of a Late Dorset–style soapstone lamp (fig. 14.20) in the L'Anse aux Meadows "smithy" and the fact that the spindle whorl (fig. 14.18) recovered from one of the Norse houses there appears to be made from a fragment of a Dorset soapstone vessel suggest Dorset contacts or Norse scavenging from Dorset sites seen in northern Labrador, where a small Dorset population existed when the Vinland voyages took place.

The question of what ultimately caused the Dorset to disappear is both complicated and controversial. Most explanations have centered on their relationship with the Thule people who arrived from Alaska a century or more before the Dorset demise. Theories on contact between Dorset and Thule include everything from peaceful coexistence and gradual assimilation to a demise owing to adverse competition from the Thule people or outright warfare with them. Park's suggestion (1993) that there was no potential for contact between the two peoples because they never overlapped in the same areas at the same time seems untenable in light of the evidence for contemporaneity in Greenland (Gulløv, this volume), Frobisher Bay (Odess 1998), and Labrador (Fitzhugh 1994). It has also been suggested that the Norse might have precipitated Dorset decline by introducing European diseases (McGhee 1994).

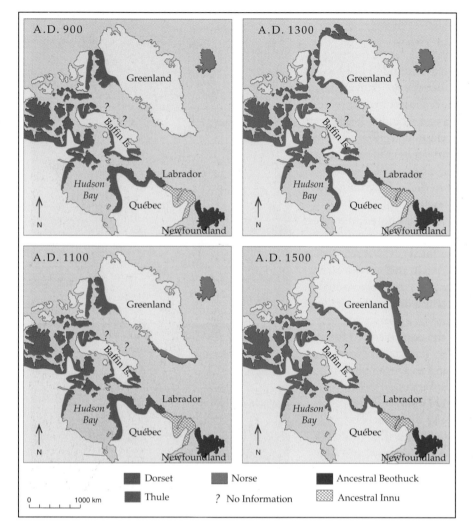

A.D. 900 · A.D. 1300 · A.D. 1100 · A.D. 1500

Greenland · Baffin Is. · Hudson Bay · Québec · Labrador · Newfoundland · N

| ■ Dorset | ■ Norse | ■ Ancestral Beothuck |
| ■ Thule | ? No Information | ▨ Ancestral Innu |

0   1000 km

CULTURAL AREA CHANGES

panied the Medieval Warm Period allowed the bowhead whale, a mainstay of their economy and social system in Alaska, to penetrate the rich waters of the High Arctic from both east and west (McGhee 1969–70).

Living along the northern coast of Alaska and on Saint Lawrence Island, these people had gradually developed sophisticated tools and techniques for taking bowhead whales, including the umiak—a multi-passenger skin-clad boat—and large toggling harpoons attached to inflated sealskin floats (fig. 13.9). They also had a complex social structure in which whaling boats were owned by the heads of large families who marshaled and coordinated the efforts of many individuals in pursuit of whales and other goals such as military action or the accumulation of surplus goods for trade.

The richness of the environment and their success in exploiting it allowed Thule people to live in permanent villages of up to a few hundred individuals in some areas. Competition for the best whaling locations was intense: Alaskan villages were sometimes fortified, and organized warfare with other Alaskan and Siberian groups was common. Thule social organization, their tradition of organized warfare (which included the use of the Asia-derived recurved bow), and their use of large boats and dogsleds (which provided rapid transport capabilities for large groups of people) would have made them a formidable force upon appearing in areas occupied by Dorset people and visited by the Norse.

There are interesting parallels between the situation in Iceland at the time of Erik the Red's exile and that in northern Alaska during the same period: desirable habitation areas were filled to capacity, and pressure for new lands and resources had become intense. Under these conditions, it is not surprising that as the yearly whale migrations expanded eastward into Canada, Thule people followed, bringing their complex social structure and sophisticated adaptation to the arctic environment into new lands.

Our current understanding of prehistory suggests that the initial movement of the Thule into the western Canadian Arctic was a migration into unoccupied territory. As they continued on to the central and eastern Canadian Arctic, however, the Thule would have encountered occasional settlements of Dorset people. The nature of contact between these peoples remains an unresolved

While disease clearly did not wipe them out completely, it may have eliminated them from some areas such as northwestern Greenland and eastern Ellesmere Island and reduced their ability to withstand the onslaught of Thule people from the west.

THE THULE:
SKRAELING FROM THE WEST

Approximately one thousand years ago, as Leif Eriksson was sailing west from Greenland, another group of pioneering explorers departed from northern Alaska for points east. These people, whom archaeologists call Thule, are the ancestors of the modern-day Inuit (fig. 13.10). Within a century or two—the problems of radiocarbon dating in the Arctic make it difficult to be more precise—they had colonized much of the Canadian Arctic and the Thule District of Greenland (Morrison 1989). This migration, like that of the pre-Dorset people three thousand years earlier, was accomplished during a period of climatic amelioration. For the Thule people, the reduced sea-ice cover that accom-

13.8 THULE WINTER HOUSE

The Thule people built winter houses from sod and earth to provide snug shelters from arctic winters. While temperatures outside hovered around 40° C below zero, human body heat and oil lamps kept the temperature inside above freezing. Ruins of their small, dome-shaped houses are seen at Kamaiyuk in Frobisher Bay as depressions within rock walls; these structures were more suitable than drafty high-roofed Viking longhouses in arctic regions.

question in the archaeology of the region, but over the next three centuries, the Thule settlement areas expanded and the Dorset gradually disappeared from most of their former territories.

Early Thule settlements in the Canadian Arctic were located in areas well suited for hunting the large whales that came north each summer (figs. 13.11, 13.12). They consisted of several houses and were probably occupied by thirty to forty or more people. Thule winter dwellings were pithouses made from stone, turf, and whale bones (fig. 13.8). Each was dug down below the ground level and had an entrance tunnel, which served as pantry and closet and helped to conserve heat. The entrance tunnel of the house was set lower than the floor, allowing the denser, cold air to settle into this cold trap. Burning of seal oil in soapstone lamps provided heat and light, an appliance the Thule people may have learned how to make from the Dorset. Elevated sleeping platforms, arrayed around the interior margins of the house, were covered with caribou skins for padding and insulation.

The numerous whale bones used in constructing Thule houses in the treeless arctic environment reflect their success at whaling during the twelfth to the fourteenth centuries. But then conditions began to change: the climate grew colder and fewer whales were able to reach areas that then remained choked with ice for years on end. A lifestyle dependent on whales was no longer possible in some places, particularly the central Arctic and the far north. In the Norse settlements in southern Greenland, these changes were felt as well. The increased sea ice meant that travel between Greenland and Iceland became more hazardous, and the lower temperatures reduced the productivity of Norse farms. These changes probably made travel to the north and west of the Norse settlements more difficult. Nevertheless, the presence of Norse materials in numerous Thule sites dating from 1200 to 1350 suggest that Norse-Inuit contacts continued, if not increased, during this period (see Sutherland, this volume).

Unlike the Greenland Norse, the Thule adapted to the onset of the Little Ice

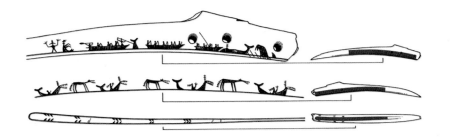

13.9 WHALING

In this pictograph carved on an ivory boat hook, crews of Alaskan hunters in large skin boats are shown pursuing whales and walrus. Cooperative hunting from boats allowed Thule Inuit in Alaska and the eastern Arctic to take enough food to sustain their villages through the long arctic winter. Dorset people did not hunt whales.

13.10 INUIT DRAWING

This drawing depicts a stylishly dressed Inuit woman leaving offerings at a monument erected in the 1570s by members of the Martin Frobisher expedition, the first Europeans to visit the Canadian Arctic. The rendering was made for explorer Charles Francis Hall by an Inuit in the 1860s.

Age (A.D. 1500–1750). Their economy had always been flexible, with char, caribou, birds, seals, and walrus providing dietary diversity and raw materials. The cooling trend that reduced the bioproductivity and accessibility of resources in some areas—for example, northernmost Greenland—forced the Thule people to abandon them, and they have remained unoccupied to this day. In other areas, when whales ceased to be a dependable resource, the Thule shifted to those species that remained. For some groups, this meant an increased emphasis on seals, particularly the ringed seal, which they hunted at breathing holes in the ice and at the edge of open water. This was facilitated by adopting another Dorset innovation, snow houses, that allowed Thule groups to establish seasonal villages on the sea ice for better access to ring seals.

The Thule people also told stories of a variety of human and humanlike beings that populated the land. These included stories about Dorset people and members of other Thule societies, but also about dwarfs and giants and other mythical peoples. They probably interpreted the Norse from this perspective when they first encountered them, but no such records exist except perhaps in western Greenland, where they were recorded in the stories collected in the eighteenth century by Henrik Glahn and in the nineteenth by Henrik Rink (Kleivan 1996).

The Thule have received the bulk of attention in discussions of contact between the Norse and the native peoples of North America, and the specific evidence of contact has been discussed at some length (see McGovern 1979 and other chapters in this volume). But what might that contact have been like?

At some point during the period of Norse occupation in southern Greenland, Thule people established settlements in northern Greenland, and on Ellesmere, Devon, and probably eastern Baffin Island,

as well as much of the central and western Canadian Arctic. Current evidence suggests these settlements were in place by the end of the thirteenth century. This means that while Thule people may not have been present in some areas during initial Norse exploration and hunting voyages to the north and west of their settlements, at some point these two peoples would have encountered one another and possibly the Dorset as well.

The conditions of contact and interaction were probably broadly similar to those previously described for Norse-Dorset contact, at least with respect to the resources and desires each side brought to any potential encounter. The Thule people had access to ivory and could have harvested walrus in greater numbers than the Dorset *if* they viewed production for trade with the Norse as worthwhile. In addition to iron the Thule obtained from the Norse, they also used iron from the Cape York meteorites to make small knives and to tip their harpoons. Thule people may have learned where these meteorites were located from the Dorset, and some have suggested that the presence of iron in the east was an additional motivating factor in their decision to colonize the area (McGhee 1984; McCartney and Mack 1973). If their acquisitiveness with regard to iron during the early twentieth century (Jenness 1928) is any indication, they might have been eager to trade for that material with the Norse; or, they might also have decided to take Norse iron and other possessions by force. Such a scenario may be represented by the trove of varied and valuable Norse materials found in a Thule village on Skraeling Island in eastern Ellesmere, if it does not result from scavenging a wrecked Norse ship (Schledermann, chapter 18).

ANCESTRAL INNU AND BEOTHUK PEOPLES

Once the Norse longships passed the imposing mountainous facade of Baffin Island and northern Labrador, the eyes of different *skraeling* would have observed their every move. As they made their way southward into the Markland and Vinland territories, Norse mariners would have passed a succession of Native American groups whose lives, like those of the Dorset and Thule, were also closely linked to the sea and its resources. These *skraeling* were ancestors of the Innu (Naskapi-Montagnais), Beothuk, Micmac, Maliseet, and Abenaki. Like the Dorset and

13.11 THULE ARROWHEADS
Like the Dorset, Thule hunters took seals and walrus with harpoons, but they also hunted caribou and musk ox with sinew-backed bows and arrows tipped with polished slate or jadeite points, or with ivory and bone arrowheads like these. Similar weapons would have been used in hostile encounters with the Norse.

13.12 THULE NEEDLECASES
Thule women made tailored clothing from the skins of birds, fish, and mammals using delicate needles of bone and ivory and thread made from animal sinew. The similarity of these Skraeling Island Thule needlecases to Alaskan prototypes confirms radiocarbon dating evidence that the Thule migration from Alaska occurred in less than one hundred years.

Thule peoples to the north, they were skilled mariners. In a variety of skin, bark, and wooden craft, the Indian peoples of the northern Atlantic coast were at home on the seas as much as they were in the forested interior. In addition to its food resources, the coastal waters provided an arena where young men sought prestige by trade and travel to distant lands.

Around two thousand years ago, a new group of Labrador Indians began expanding their settlements northward and started using the quarries of Ramah chert in northern Labrador. The exact circumstances that prompted this movement are not certain, but it coincided with the disappearance of Dorset settlements from the forested coastal regions south of Okak (after A.D. 500) and the onset of the Little Climatic Optimum (A.D. 1000–1250).

The ancestral Innu groups who occupied Labrador during this period are known archaeologically as the Daniel Rattle (circa A.D. 200–1000) and Point Revenge (circa A.D. 1000–1500) complexes (Fitzhugh 1978; Loring 1988). Daniel Rattle sites (fig. 13.13) are found mostly near the inner ends of the bays where they had ready access to caribou hunting in the interior. The later Point Revenge sites are found in similar locations but also occur on the outermost islands, suggesting a greater orientation toward coastal travel and maritime resources. In general, sites found on the coast appear to correspond with summer occupations while those on the interior seem to have been occupied in fall or winter.

Ancestral Innu lived in small, family-oriented bands scattered widely along the central Labrador coast. Their settlements usually consisted of a single skin-and-bark–covered structure with a central interior hearth (fig. 13.14). Occasionally, after an especially favorable hunt, several families would join together to build a *shaputuan*, a longer, multihearth wigwamlike structure of bark or skin, in which they passed the winter months in the shelter of the forest (fig. 13.13).

Like the historic Labrador Innu, most of the tools used by Daniel Rattle and Point Revenge people for hunting, fishing, and skin preparation, as well as for clothing, snowshoes, canoes, and toboggans were made of perishable materials such as animal skins, bone, wood, and bark. Because these

13.13 DANIEL RATTLE SITE
Indians living on the central Labrador coast from A.D. 800 to 1400 used both round tipi-like tents and elongated dwellings with long hearths in their centers. The historic descendants of these Indians, known as Innu, continued to use longhouses, which they called *shaputuan*, during certain seasons and for ceremonial purposes.

materials do not survive well in acidic sub-arctic soils, our understanding of ancestral Innu material culture is poor and relies heavily on what can be learned from their descendants and from documentary sources.

Furthermore, the deep respect and spiritual relationships that linked humans and animals required special disposal techniques for animal bones. In most cases animal remains were burned or were thrown into the water to keep them from being profaned by dogs or other creatures (Armitage 1991; Loring 1997). These ways of disposing of animal remains were practiced by many northern Indian groups. Nevertheless, the small amounts of calcined animal bones that have been recovered from early Labrador Innu sites have yielded walrus, black bear, caribou, and other species, which provide some inkling of their economy at the time of the Viking voyages (fig. 13.16). This lack of organic preservation also makes it difficult to determine much about ancient Indian technology and subsistence, but site locations on the outer islands and fragments of walrus and seal bones indicate a capability to hunt these marine mammals. The absence of gouges, which often indicate the building of dugout canoes, suggests that early Innu used bark- or skin-covered boats.

The sites known from this period are small and widely dispersed, suggesting a relatively small population that used coastal regions primarily during the summer season. Similarities in stone tools, widespread use of

Ramah chert from northern Labrador, and the presence of exotic southern raw materials, including pottery, all suggest a highly mobile population with wide-ranging trade and social contacts.

Site distributions provide important information about the relationship between these early Indian groups and their northern Dorset neighbors. Daniel Rattle and Point Revenge sites are most prevalent on the central coast south of Nain, whereas contemporaneous Dorset sites are found primarily north of Nain and encompass the area of the Ramah chert quarries. While Dorset people would have been eager to protect their access to this important lithic resource, the corner-notched Point Revenge projectile points that form an ad-hoc "trail" between Nain and the Ramah quarries suggest that Indian groups made periodic trips into Dorset territory to obtain this valuable material (fig. 13.15; see Cox, p. 207). Most of these points are solitary finds from obscure, even hidden, locations, that could be interpreted as evidence of clandestine chert-collecting forays into Dorset lands, but the reality might have been quite different. The huge amount of Ramah chert used by Daniel Rattle and Point Revenge groups, and the fact that blocks of this material and points made from it occur at Indian sites far south of Labrador, raise the possibility of systematic trade between early Innu and Dorset peoples.

This possibility is strengthened by the fact that the earlier Daniel Rattle sites are literally paved with Ramah chert. This apparently flagrant disregard of conservative stone-usage practices is dramatically reversed during the late Point Revenge period. By 1300, Indian sites became smaller and the amount of lithic materials was much reduced, suggesting that Ramah chert had become expensive and difficult to acquire. While Ramah chert remained linked to Indian cultural identity, whatever social mechanisms that had existed to facilitate its transportation and distribution to the south appear to have broken down when Dorset people were re-placed by the more powerful and aggressive Thule people after about 1350. After this date, in a period of climatic cooling, the Thule expanded rapidly south into former Indian-held territories and took possession of most regions of the northern and central Labrador coast. While the Innu retreated from many of their former coastal regions, they maintained settle-

D. ODESS, S. LORING, AND W. W. FITZHUGH

13.14 INNU TIPI

Innu also used conical spruce-framed tipis, which they covered with caribou hides. Spruce boughs served both as fuel and cushioning material to insulate them from the ground. The Innu rarely left the shelter of the forest, where tent poles were always available, and so they could easily move camp as hunting conditions in the northern forest required.

ments in many of the inner bays south of Nain, as well as on the Labrador interior, an area they continue to use today.

INNU-NORSE CONTACTS

One morning Karlsefni's men saw something shiny above a clearing in the trees, and they called out. It moved and proved to be a one-legged creature, which darted down to where the ship lay tied. Thorvald, Erik the Red's son, was at the helm and the one-legged man shot an arrow into his intestine. Thorvald drew the arrow out and spoke: "A fat paunch that was. We've found a land of fine resources, though we'll hardly enjoy much of them." Thorvald died from the wound shortly after. The one-legged man then ran off back north. They pursued him and caught glimpses of him now and again. He then fled into a cove and they turned back (Hreinsson 1997).

The presence of small Indian parties scattered along the central Labrador coast, from the outermost islands to the innermost sheltered bays, suggests that little in the way of Norse coastal movements would have gone unnoticed, especially as the Norse must have come ashore occasionally for water and food, to explore, or seek shelter in storms. Even if they chose to sail off the coast their passage around prominent headlands would have been easily observed.

A tantalizing suggestion of Norse contact with the Indians of Labrador or Newfoundland is hinted at by a pair of Indian projectile points, stylistically identical to Newfoundland-Labrador specimens, which were recovered from Norse sites in western

Greenland (Berglund 1981; Meldgaard 1961; Rowlett 1982). One made of chert was found in 1930 at Sandnes in the Western Settlement (fig. 17.2); the second, made of quartz, was a stray find recovered from rocks on the shore below the Norse ruins at Brattahlid, the very site from which Thorfinn Karlsefni left on a Vinland expedition in about 1003. Were these projectile points from stray arrows lodged in the deck of a Viking boat or in one of the Vikings themselves? Were they trophies gathered from a raid on a *skraeling* camp or were they gifts cautiously exchanged?

It would not have been until midsummer that the pack ice cleared off the Labrador coast sufficiently to enable the Norse voyagers to make their way south. Borne along by the two- to three-knot Labrador current and accompanied by the still massive icebergs from Greenland, Norse mariners would have passed the bleak, stony coastline of Baffin Island and northern Labrador and moved south along the wooded coasts of central Labrador and across the Strait of Belle Isle to Newfoundland. In Newfoundland the air was warmer; there were forests close at hand; and berries, birds, and fish were abundant. It was here that the Norse established at least one short-lived settlement in North America. While they may have made their initial landfall in quiet seclusion, it would not have been long before their presence was known to the native inhabitants of Newfoundland.

At the time of the Vinland voyages, Newfoundland was the home of an Indian people who were probably ancestors of the Beothuk. The Beothuk have the dubious distinction of being perhaps the first Indian people encountered by Europeans, as well as among the first to be exterminated: the last known member of their society died in captivity in 1829 (Howley 1915; Marshall 1996). Like the Innu, the Beothuk lived in small, dispersed family bands pursuing a seasonal round that included salmon fishing and caribou hunting in the interior of the island and seal hunting, fishing, and birding on the coast. Communal hunts in which the Beothuk drove caribou into elaborate systems of fences and traps would have been the occasion of much celebration and enabled large groups to spend the winter season together (fig. 13.16). The archaeological culture that occupied Newfoundland at this

13.15 POINT REVENGE ARTIFACTS
Point Revenge Indians, who lived in Labrador at the time of the Vinland voyages, made knives and points from Ramah chert, a translucent stone found north of the forest boundary in northern Labrador. These points are very similar to the arrow point (fig. 17.2) found at the Norse cemetery in Sandnes, Greenland.

time is known as the Little Passage Complex (Pastore 1992), but to date no archaeological evidence has been found in their sites that indicates contact with the Norse. Their way of life and technology were similar to the late prehistoric Indians of Labrador, and they sometimes made tools from Ramah chert, indicating contacts with mainland peoples to the north.

Farther south in the Canadian Maritimes and along the Gulf of Maine dwelt a succession of other Indian groups, the ancestors of the Micmac, Maliseet, and Eastern Abenaki (Bourque 1989; Prinns 1996; Sanger 1987). All these peoples were skilled hunters and fishermen whose populations were generally larger and more settled than that of their neighbors to the north. An abundance of shellfish, rich inshore fisheries, and the possibility of growing garden crops such as maize and squash provided resources for substantially larger populations than were possible among the hunting societies of the northern coasts (fig. 13.17). Norse voyagers appearing in any of the territories south of the Gulf of Saint Lawrence during the summer boating season would have discovered these coasts to be filled with Indian villages in nearly every bay and river mouth. Had they traveled west toward the mouth of the Saint Lawrence River they would have encountered an even more formidable force than the coastal Algonquians—the Iroquois, who were then aggressively expanding eastward into Algonquian territories.

Throughout the maritime northeast all coastal peoples shared a common focus on the sea as a provider of foods, material goods, and social exchange. It is through such an elaborate system of exchange, perhaps linked

to ritual celebrations and gatherings, that materials and objects traveled great distances. The one unequivocal Viking artifact to be recovered south of Newfoundland is a Norwegian penny minted between 1065 and 1080 that was excavated from the Goddard site, a fourteenth-century Late Woodland Indian encampment near Naskeag Point on the central Maine coast (Bourque and Cox 1981). Because the coin (p. 206) was perforated for use as an ornament or pendant and because the site also contained artifacts (a Dorset graver, jadeite knife, and flakes of Ramah chert) from Labrador, it is thought that the coin may have been traded south to Maine together with these other exotic northern materials (see Cox, sidebar, p. 206).

CONCLUSION

The sagas tell of battles fought, of enemies slain, of lands discovered, and heroes fallen. But the peaceful encounters and successful trade, if they occurred, seem not to have been epic events worthy of song and scribe. It was only the unusual, the extraordinary, superlative, and noteworthy events that the Norse recorded. And even then, it was sometimes a century or more before these oral histories were committed to paper, their details fading from memory and lost or embellished as tales were told and retold. While the sagas tell of great men and women and their deeds, they provide surprisingly little information about those whom the Norse met on the shores of North America, though some interpretation suggestive of distinctions derived from Indian and Inuit ethnography is possible (Collins 1970). While archaeology has given us a good sense of who the *skraeling* were, we are left to wonder how and to what extent they interacted with the newcomers from Greenland.

In the North Atlantic, as in other parts of the world, popular imagination has sought to distill the drama of contact between members of different cultures into simple themes—hostility or peace, trade or conquest—but the reality is doubtless more nuanced, contingent on the vagaries of circumstance, the idiosyncratic personalities of individual actors, and on their perceptions of those they encountered. The on-the-ground reality is that individuals, rather than entire cultures, came into contact during the Norse visits to the New World. When they met, each sought to make sense of the situation through refer-

13.16 INNU CARIBOU HUNT

Innu hunters in birchbark canoes took caribou when the animals crossed the lakes and rivers in Labrador during their annual migrations. This drawing was made by an Innu for William Duncan Strong in Labrador during the winter of 1928 to illustrate their method of hunting caribou.

13.17 INNU LEAVING CAMP

Birchbark canoes could carry several people or hundreds of pounds of cargo. Their lightweight design allowed the Innu to travel the rivers and lakes of interior Labrador and portage the canoes with relative ease. The *Vinland Sagas* do not mention bark canoes, but they note *skraeling* (natives) used hide boats and double-bladed paddles—cultural elements that are more descriptive of Inuit than of Indian watercraft.

ence to what he (or she) knew from firsthand experience or had heard of the other. As they negotiated these encounters, each person probably sought some self-perceived advantage as defined in their own cultural terms. In some instances, these advantages would have been material—for example, the acquisition of ivory, iron, or strips of red cloth. At the same time, they may have been geopolitical, involving the earliest attempts by native people to control access to European goods.

Over the four centuries or so that they remained in Greenland, the Norse continued to make periodic trips to the west, occasionally encountering native peoples. Whether these ventures were planned in part to take advantage of trading opportunities is not known, but the growing number of Norse objects being found in Dorset and Thule sites during the past three decades suggests that contacts between these groups were not uncommon (Sutherland, this volume). Like

the Maine penny, most of these finds or the sites in which they have been found postdate the period of the Vinland voyages. For the native people living along the shores of the North Atlantic, the Norse were only one of several ethnically distinct peoples who traveled along the coast to trade or make war.

While much remains unknown about the frequency and particulars of Norse voyages to the shores of North America, it seems apparent that their presence west of Greenland was never more than ephemeral. Incidents of contact may have had profound effects on individual lives on all sides of the cultural divide but in the aggregate, their arrival does not seem to have altered the history of native peoples or changed their cultures in any way. One thing it certainly did do, however, was to acquaint Native Americans with the ways and means of Europeans with whom they would be dealing more extensively in future centuries.

A Norse Penny from Maine BY STEVEN L. COX

On the morning of September 13, 1956, Guy Mellgren and Ed Runge, two avocational archaeologists from Massachusetts, were digging in a shell midden at Naskeag Harbor in the town of Brooklin along Penobscot Bay on the central Maine coast. One of the onlookers, DeWitt Goddard, mentioned that he thought there was an Indian site on his property at the tip of Naskeag Point and invited them over to look.

The two men started digging into the very black soil, and as soon as they stripped off the sod they were rewarded by the sight of a thick concentration of flakes, artifacts, and pottery sherds in a rich black-soil midden. By the time they had to leave Maine two days later they had collected about 375 artifacts, exclusive of pottery fragments, from the Goddard site.

Mellgren and Runge had stumbled on the richest site in coastal Maine and perhaps in New England. Not only was it tremendously rich in artifacts from a variety of time periods, it was situated at one of the most beautiful locations on the Maine coast, overlooking broad expanses of both Penobscot and Blue Hill bays. To the north lies the rich fishing and shell-fishing grounds of Blue Hill Bay, with the mountains of Mount Desert Island looming in the distance; to the southeast are the islands of Penobscot Bay; and to the southwest, the islands surrounding Deer Island, with Isle au Haut in the distance. Virtually all waterborne traffic along this section of the coast travels within view of the site, and during the summer it is a rare day when large yachts or sailing schooners are not in view.

Mellgren and Runge returned to the Goddard site in March of the following year, digging in still-frozen ground, and every year for the next twenty-two years, spending a

MAINE PENNY

This small coin, minted in Norway between 1065 and 1080 during the reign of King Olaf Kyrre, was excavated on the coast of Maine in 1957. It probably arrived at the Goddard site from Newfoundland or Labrador by way of native trade networks. A small hole had been drilled on one edge, suggesting it had been worn as a pendant or a clothing ornament.

week or two of their vacation time. By the end of their last visit to the site in 1978 they had dug more than 2,400 square feet (225 square meters) of the site and had amassed a collection totaling some fifteen thousand stone artifacts and thousands of pottery sherds from more than one thousand prehistoric vessels.

Following their spring trip in 1957, the two men returned again in both July and August. They established a grid and began digging. On August 18, Mellgren found a small silver coin about five inches deep in the midden. He did not think much of the coin at the time, only marking its location on his square map with a "C" but not noting it in his daily journal. Mellgren brought the coin to the American Numismatic Association for identification and was told that it was a British coin dating to the reigns of Stephen and Henry I (1135–1154). This identification was published in a 1958 article on the Goddard site by Mellgren and Runge and in a short 1978 article on the coin by Bert Farmer. Fortunately, a copy of Farmer's article, which included pictures of the coin, was sent to British coin dealer Peter Seaby through the good offices of Riley Sunderland of Bar Harbor, Maine. An expert on British coinage, Seaby immediately recognized that the coin was not British at all but was probably an eleventh-century Norse coin. With this news, the Maine State Museum arranged to have the coin examined by Kolbjørn Skaare, curator of the coin collection at the National Museum of Norway and a leading authority on medieval Norse coinage. Skaare's analysis, including neutron-activation testing of a small piece of the coin, confirmed the coin's identity as a Norwegian penny minted during the period A.D. 1065 to 1080 (Skaare 1979).

Not surprisingly, this news generated a great interest in the Goddard site, and funding was obtained from the Maine state legislature and the Maine Historic Preservation Commission for further studies (Bourque and Cox 1981). Inspection of the amateurs' collection indicated that the major occupation dated to the Late Ceramic Period, circa A.D. 900 to 1500 and was characterized by side-notched points, small end scrapers, and pottery decorated by a cord-wrapped stick. Particularly striking in this component was a large number of stone artifacts made of materials foreign to Maine.

We now know that eight centuries or so ago, at the time of the Norse coin's arrival at the site, Naskeag Point was very likely the largest seasonal village in Maine. Occupied yearly from late spring to early fall, the village was an important hub within a broad-ranging native trade network extending northward to Labrador, eastward to Nova Scotia, westward to the Great Lakes, and south at least as far as Pennsylvania (map). The site's strategic location, controlling access to the resources of the Penobscot drainage as well as coastal travel routes, put it in a central and probably controlling position within a regional exchange network, which would help explain its large size and rich cultural remains.

Many of the unusual stone artifacts in the collection are from the north, including more than thirty tools and several hundred flakes of Ramah chert, an unusual translucent quartzitelike stone that outcrops only in northern Labrador and was used widely by native coastal peoples

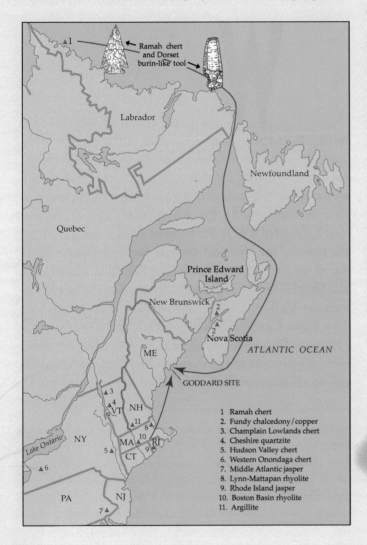

1 Ramah chert
2 Fundy chalcedony / copper
3 Champlain Lowlands chert
4 Cheshire quartzite
5 Hudson Valley chert
6 Western Onondaga chert
7 Middle Atlantic jasper
8 Lynn-Mattapan rhyolite
9 Rhode Island jasper
10 Boston Basin rhyolite
11 Argillite

north of Newfoundland. In addition, one the artifacts found by Mellgren was a Labrador or Newfoundland Dorset-culture burinlike tool that had been reworked into an end scraper. The artifact, a tool type used for bone and ivory working by the Dorset people (whose early Eskimo-like culture dates to circa 500 B.C. to A.D. 1200 in Labrador), has highly polished faces and edges. A second possible Eskimo (most likely, Dorset) artifact, a small polished jade knife, was recovered recently during a field school conducted at the site by the Maine State Museum.

It is unlikely that a Dorset Eskimo could have kayaked down to the end of Naskeag Point, and so these artifacts were almost certainly obtained through Indian trade channels that must have extended north to Newfoundland and Labrador, where Dorset people lived side by side with Indians. We suspect the Norse coin, which had been perforated for use as a pendant or a clothing ornament, arrived at the site in a similar manner. There are no other Norse artifacts from the site, and no evidence of a Norse settlement here or elsewhere south of northern Newfoundland. Certainly the Norse could have visited the site; indeed, it would have been a logical place to stop if the Norse were in the region and were interested more in trade than conquest. Perhaps someday the Goddard site on Naskeag Point or some other site in the Maine or Canadian Maritimes region will shed additional light on the events of eight centuries ago, when there must have been rumors of blond or red-haired strangers with pale skin and unusual, dazzling artifacts, fearsome weapons, and huge wooden ships with wings.

GODDARD SITE TRADE CONTACTS

The Goddard site on the northeast coast of Penobscot Bay, Maine, was one of the most important trade centers in northeastern North America in the centuries before Columbus arrived in the New World. In addition to its famous Norse penny, excavations recovered Labrador or Newfoundland Dorset tools and artifacts made of Labrador Ramah chert, as well as objects traded from the Great Lakes, Pennsylvania, and Nova Scotia.

GODDARD SITE ARTIFACTS

Woodland (Ceramic) period occupation of the Goddard site was contemporaneous with the Point Revenge occupation in central Labrador, and its tools (axes, points, scrapers, knives, and harpoons) show a close cultural relationship. In addition to corner-notched points made from local materials, specimens of translucent Labrador Ramah chert (bottom center) occur as well.

14 | THE VIKING SETTLEMENT AT L'ANSE AUX MEADOWS

BY BIRGITTA LINDEROTH WALLACE

WHEN THE NORWEGIAN WRITER and explorer Helge Ingstad announced in 1961 that he had found the remains of Norse buildings in Newfoundland (p.190), few believed him. Most expected the famed Vinland of the sagas to be located further south and argued that Helge Ingstad had simply located a Native American or early colonial site. Subsequent excavations from 1961 to 1968 under the direction of his wife, Dr. Anne Stine Ingstad, showed that this was no fanciful claim (A. S. Ingstad 1977; H. Ingstad 1986). For the first time Norse ruins dating from the time of the Vinland voyages had been unearthed in North America. The site was placed on the roster of Canadian National Historic Sites and shortly thereafter became the first UNESCO World Heritage Site. To understand the precise role of the site vis-à-vis the Vinland expeditions, further excavations were undertaken from 1973 to 1976 by Parks Canada (Wallace 1991), the Canadian agency governing the National Historic Sites. Almost all of the immediate site area has been excavated as well as about 25 percent of the surrounding area. Neighboring coves have been surveyed for additional features, but so far, they have yielded only aboriginal sites.

The idea that Norse ruins were most likely to be found in northern Newfoundland originated with native Newfoundlander William F. Munn, a businessman with a deep interest in history. In 1914 Munn published a series of articles in the *St. John's Daily Telegram* in which he laid out his theory that Leif Eriksson had landed at L'Anse aux Meadows and settled in the area of Pistolet Bay. The articles were later collected into a little book titled *Wineland Voyages*, which was published by the newspaper. Many years later, in 1946 and 1947, the book

SHIP UNDER SAIL, *REYKJABÓK*

inspired an American engineer, Arlington H. Mallery, to search the shores of Pistolet Bay for evidence of the Norse. A great enthusiast for things Viking, Mallery believed he had found evidence of Vikings throughout eastern North America. He felt he had uncovered ample and appropriate support for a Viking presence at L'Anse aux Meadows and published his findings in *Lost America* (Mallery 1951), but the evidence has not held up. Danish archaeologist Jørgen Meldgaard was the next to pursue Norse sites in Newfoundland, conducting a test excavation in 1956 at the mouth of Western Brook at the southeastern corner of Pistolet Bay, twelve miles southwest of L'Anse aux Meadows (map, right). Although nothing was found, Meldgaard considered the area prom-

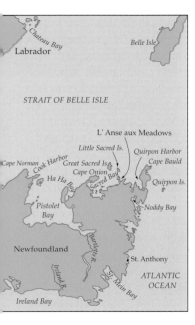

14.1 L'ANSE AUX MEADOWS

In 1961 Norwegian explorer and writer Helge Ingstad and his wife Anne Stine Ingstad came to the village of L'Anse aux Meadows, seen in the distance, while searching for Norse sites that he believed must exist somewhere in Labrador or northern Newfoundland. Local residents took them to the grassy field (foreground) on Epaves Bay and pointed out low foundations in the ground. Excavations provided conclusive proof in architecture, artifacts, and radiocarbon dates that the site had been occupied by Norse from Iceland or Greenland (or both) around A.D. 1000, as described in the *Vinland Sagas*.

ising and intended to return for a more extensive investigation. Because the expected funding did not materialize, the project never took place, but Meldgaard had let it be known locally what he was looking for, describing grassy ridges that would be the likely remains of Norse buildings. When Helge and Anne Stine Ingstad arrived in L'Anse aux Meadows, a small fishing village at the northern tip of the Newfoundland Peninsula, in 1960 people had taken the time to reflect on local features that might fit Meldgaard's description (R. Elliott, pers. comm.). The Ingstads were shown the "Indian camp" in a neighboring cove on Epaves Bay (a French-English hybrid meaning "Wreck Bay") half a mile south of the village, where in the past, Indians from Labrador had come to catch seals in the spring. Visible in the tall grass were the outlines of eight structures that looked much like Viking Age ruins in Iceland and Greenland. When a small test excavation on the spot by Anne Stine Ingstad showed promising results, extensive excavations were initiated. Over the following years, they proved that the ruins were indeed the remains of Viking Age buildings (fig. 14.2).

The setting for the Norse ruins at L'Anse aux Meadows is spectacular: a wide grassy cove on shallow Epaves Bay overlooking the Strait of Belle Isle (fig. 14.7). The Labrador coast forms a hazy outline in the distance. A low flat cape juts out to the northwest, separating the Norse area from another grassy cove on a deeper bay, Medée Bay, where the modern village of L'Anse aux

Meadows is situated. Originally a French seasonal fishing station, it was named for Medea, the murderous enchantress of Greek myth. L'Anse aux Meadows thus does not derive its name from the surrounding meadows—which were not here a thousand years ago when ancient balsam firs, poplars, and larches dominated and a thick snarl of softwood forest and brush edged the site. L'Anse means bay or cove in French, and Meadows is a corruption of the French name of the Greek enchantress. Offshore are five small islands; the largest is Great Sacred Island, which forms a distinct landmark as one approaches the site from the sea. To the south, a steep sandstone ridge separates the site from yet another cove. About half a mile inland is a small lake, Black Duck Pond, from which a small brook winds its way among the Norse ruins to the sea.

The ruins are situated on a narrow curving terrace about 320 feet (100 meters) inland, the only dry ground between a funnel-shaped sedge-peat bog and a tussocky, raised sphagnum-moss bog. There are eight buildings of which seven are grouped into three complexes. The complexes are lined up in a north-south direction on the narrow terrace, evenly spaced about one hundred feet (thirty meters) from each other (fig. 14.2). Each complex consists of an imposing multiroomed hall flanked by a small, one-roomed hut. The southernmost complex also has a third structure, a small, one-roomed house, larger than the huts but significantly smaller than the halls. The eighth building is a small hut away from the others, on the other side of the brook, closer to the shore. This settlement offers a peek into the lives of the Vinland explorers in North America: this is Leif Eriksson's base in Vinland, Straumfjord of *Erik the Red's Saga,* and, in part, Leifsbuðir of the *Greenlanders' Saga,* the base from which Vinland was explored. From L'Anse aux Meadows, expeditions were launched to explore areas farther away. We have proof that they went south to warmer, more hospitable areas where butternuts grew on large trees and grapes grew wild, for the archaeological evidence is unequivocal.

The silent ruins of the L'Anse aux Meadows site tell a fascinating story of the people who built them, when they were there, what they did, and why they were there. The early eleventh-century date for the settlement is based on radiocarbon dates,

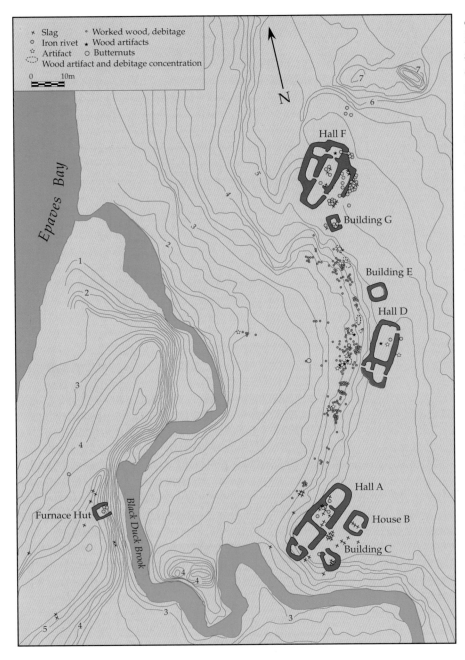

N

Epaves Bay

Hall F

Building G

Building E

Hall D

Furnace Hut

Black Duck Brook

Hall A

House B

Building C

14.2 L'Anse aux Meadows Site Plan

The layout of the Norse settlement along the terrace east of Black Duck Brook gives clear evidence of a planned community. Outbuildings associated with each of three dwellings, and a furnace hut dug into the bank of the brook, indicate three social groups that were probably organized around three vessels.

artifacts, and the style of architecture. Of 141 radiocarbon dates from L'Anse aux Meadows, most are associated with native occupations, but about fifty pertain to the Norse occupation. Their time spread is a good illustration of why radiocarbon dates cannot always be taken at face value. A stake of balsam fir within the Norse deposits had a date of A.D. 980 (1070±75 BP converted to calendar years and midpoint of Stuiver calibration, lab. no. S-1093). Right next to it, and demonstrably from the same time, was a plank of spruce, which had a date of A.D. 640 (1410 BP; converted to calendar years and midpoint of Stuiver calibration; lab. no. S-1092). The two dates illustrate how the age of the wood itself affects dating. Spruces

can become very old, living a thousand years in parts of Scandinavia. The inner part of such an old tree is several hundred years older than its outer part, which will be reflected in the radiocarbon analysis. In this case, the plank was cut from the very core or heartwood of the tree, and the radiocarbon dating confirms that the submitted sample was taken from its oldest part. The stake of balsam, on the other hand, was a young tree or branch, only about an inch in diameter, and so its inner and outer parts would have been almost the same age. Ideally, only such young wood should be used when dating a site. Seven additional radiocarbon dates on young wood from L'Anse aux Meadows allow us to date the site with a confidence level of 95 percent, to some time between 980 and 1020 (Lindsay n.d.).

Dating the settlement of L'Anse aux Meadows by the style of artifacts recovered there is less precise than the radiocarbon dates and covers the period from the late tenth to the early twelfth centuries. The large halls are distinctly Icelandic, and such specific details as number of rooms, their placement, the type of interior walls, and the placement of roof-support posts, doors, and fireplaces indicate that the time of building was the eleventh century (fig. 14.13).

The construction of the buildings indicates that they were made for year-round use rather than as the seasonally occupied *buðir* (booths). Such seasonal booths consisted of walls only; the buildings at L'Anse aux Meadows had permanent roofs and were solidly built. Considerable effort had been spent to construct them. All the buildings had thick sod walls and roofs over a frame of wood, and the living areas of the halls appear to have been paneled inside. About 35,000 cubic feet (1,000 cubic meters) of sod would have been required to construct each of the big halls plus eighty-six large trees for support posts and beams and vast quantities of branches to be woven in between the rafters to form the base for the sod roof. Additional wood was needed for the paneling and for the wooden platforms built along the side walls that formed the basic furnishings. It was an enterprise that required substantial labor and time.

The size of the living areas in the buildings suggest that about seventy to ninety people could have lived here: between thirty-six and fifty-four in the two largest halls,

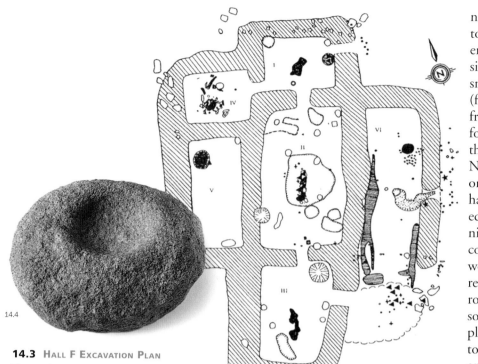

14.3 Hall F Excavation Plan

The northernmost structure, Hall F, was the most complex of the three dwellings discovered. Its six rooms include a kitchen/sauna (IV) and a storage room (V) to the west of the main dwelling rooms (I, II, III) with their central hearths and a work shed to the east (VI) containing the remains of a forge. Among the artifacts found here were iron rivets, a stone lamp, a bone needle, a soapstone spindle whorl, and several jasper strike-a-lights, or fire-starters. The explanation of the symbols of this plan appear on the map on p. 210.

14.4 Stone Lamp

Stones with hollows pecked into their tops are known from many Norse sites in the North Atlantic (fig. 11.8). Most are oil-stained and charred from use as oil lamps.

14.5 Ringed Pin

One of the early finds made by the Ingstads was a badly corroded ringed pin of high-leaded tin bronze from the forge pit in Hall A. This type of pin has a distinct West Norse design common in the tenth century. This type of pin originated in Ireland and the western British Isles (fig. 11.12c), and thirteen examples have been found in Iceland (map, p. 172).

about twenty-four in the smaller one, and anywhere between seven and fourteen in the small house and huts. There is some indication that at least two of the huts were workshops, but it is not certain whether people also lived in them, although they could have because all the huts have fireplaces. A stone arrangement reminiscent of that in a smithy at Gjáskógar in Iceland (Eldjárn 1961: 38) suggests that one hut had been used for iron working. Another hut had a stone oven similar to ones found in Icelandic weaving huts in one corner and nineteen fist-sized stones, which could be loom weights, in another corner. Unlike the other huts, which were square, the third hut was irregularly round; there were no signs that any specialized form of work was conducted and domestic debris, which had been cleaned out of the fireplace, suggests that it was used for housing.

Inside each hall was a workshop. In the southern hall, the workshop was a smithy where iron was forged. The middle hall had a small carpentry shop opening toward the sedge-peat bog, and hundreds of pieces of carpentry debris were found outside it (figs. 14.6–14.9). Broken pieces of larger objects had also been discarded here, presumably to be replaced with

new ones. At least a couple of pieces appear to be associated with boat repair. The northern hall had a lean-to added to its eastern side and here a heavy concentration of snipped and discarded boat nails were found (fig. 14.14). Of the total of ninety-nine nail fragments found on the site 78 percent were found in the northern complex, and more than 60 percent came from the shed. At West Norse sites, such quantities of iron nails are only found on sites where boats and ships have undergone repairs, which is undoubtedly what took place here. Buildings and furniture would have been held together with compressed wooden treenails, pegs that would swell to seal a hole. Rusted nails, which required replacing, have been cut and their roves (washers) have been split with a chisel so that they could be removed from the boat planks. Such cuts are revealed in X-ray photographs of all the L'Anse aux Meadows nails and roves.

The distribution of the buildings at L'Anse aux Meadows signals immediately that this was not a typical Norse settlement. In Iceland and Greenland dwelling complexes lay at great distances from each other. They were never grouped into villages or towns. The only other known instance of Norse houses being built together side by side in a tight cluster is from an early settlement in Iceland (Vésteinsson, this volume), and in this case they were part of a farmstead complex with byres and outbuildings, which are absent at L'Anse aux Meadows. The dwellings were always surrounded or joined by barns, byres, stables, and animal pens and a "home field" where vegetables and hay were grown. The larger the dwellings, the bigger and more numerous were the outbuildings. The only places where dwellings formed clusters were specific landing areas where markets were held when trading ships arrived from abroad. At these centers, however, the accommodations were simple and seasonal, consisting of *buðir*, which were a cross between tents and houses, with permanent walls of sod but only temporary roofs of tent cloth or skin. Typically at sites with large halls such as those found at L'Anse aux Meadows, outbuildings would have been substantial, but no byres, animal pens or corrals were built at the New World settlement. If domestic animals had been brought here, they must have been left out in the open or slaughtered before stabling was required.

14.6

14.7

14.8

14.6–14.9 WOOD OBJECTS

Many of the artifacts recovered during the Parks Canada excavations, which followed the Ingstads' work and were directed by Birgitta Wallace, came from wet areas where wood was preserved. These finds include a fragment of a small notched bow, a pedal-shaped object, a decorative finial made of pine, and a (ship?) patch with a hole and a peg. All were worked with iron tools.

14.9

The lack of such outbuildings and the location of the structures indicate the settlement at L'Anse aux Meadows was not a colonizing, self-sustaining venture depending on farming for its livelihood. In Iceland and Greenland, farms were not built on the outer coasts but in protected inland spots or at the heads of fjords; the L'Anse aux Meadows site, by contrast, is one of the most exposed locations in the entire area.

In the small hut away from the other buildings the first iron was manufactured in the New World. The equipment was modest but identical to that used in Iceland and Norway. A small stone frame, made airtight with a cover of kaolin clay found on the site, was set over a shallow pit in the ground to form the simple furnace in which the iron was produced. The raw material was bog-iron ore, which forms in formerly glaciated areas where water containing iron and manganese percolates through acidic bogs. The acids, in combination with bacteria, precipitate into lumps of impure iron. Such bog iron occurs at L'Anse aux Meadows. To make usable iron, the ore is first roasted, that is, its water content was burned off on a bed of fresh wood, and then packed into the furnace with alternating layers of charcoal. Charcoal, which had been produced in a

pit-shaped kiln near the furnace, was needed rather than raw wood because it burns at a much higher temperature than wood. A temperature of 2,282° F (1,250° C) was reached in the L'Anse aux Meadows oven, sufficient to make the ore fluid. The iron separates, however imperfectly, from the other materials contained in the ore and drops to the bottom of the pit in the form of a sponge; the impurities collect around it in the form of slag (figs. 14.13, 14.14). As in Iceland and Norway, the furnace was inside a hut, which was set into the bank and open to the brook. The bank itself, shored up with posts and sod, formed the back and side walls. Once the firing was complete, the stone frame of the furnace was smashed open and most of it was thrown down the brook bank. The slag was removed and also raked down the slope. The iron sponge was then retrieved, reheated, and hammered into a bloom at a high temperature to get out more impurities. Only after this was it ready to be forged. The iron production at L'Anse aux Meadows was limited to one smelting episode; only a very small quantity of iron was produced, which was most likely used to make new boat nails. Metallurgical analyses show that all the discarded cut-up nails had been made elsewhere. Although only one nail was found that had been made from the locally produced iron, it was also the only whole nail found on the site. Away from the others in the middle of carpentry debris, it had probably been accidentally dropped.

An intriguing aspect of the buildings is that they reveal that not everyone on the site was equal. The layout of the two largest halls confirms that they were not regular houses but manors of the kind used by chieftains and important people. In addition to two large communal living rooms, each of these two halls has a small, private living room of the kind used by the lord of the manor for himself and his wife or close associates. Of the two halls, the northern one was the largest and most complex, and its living quarters showed a more intensive use, with more artifacts and occupation refuse than the corresponding rooms in the southern hall. One may conclude that the leader of the expedition who built and owned L'Anse aux Meadows resided here with his crew. An interesting fact is that fire-starters found in this northern complex were made of jasper from western Greenland, while those from

14.10

14.11

14.12

14.10–14.12 CONTAINERS AND
SPRUCE ROOT ROPE

The bog areas of the site produced a
number of specimens related to
containers and storage, including a
barrel top, fragments of spruce root
rope used for barrel hoops and
cordage, and a small birchbark
container sewn with spruce root.

the other complexes on the site were made of jasper from Iceland (see Smith sidebar). Another prominent person and his crew occupied the southern complex. Although the third (center) hall was large, it had no private chamber, only a large communal sleeping/sitting area, which was probably used as quarters for a third crew, perhaps hired especially for the expedition. That relatively well-to-do people were present on the site is also evident from the artifacts found, which included a small fragment of a brass suspension loop from an ornament or piece of jewelry. The loop had been gilded, which would have made it relatively precious. Someone had also lost a glass bead, which was by no means rare, but finery would probably not have been worn by a laborer or domestic servant in the wilds of the New World.

The small house next to one of the large halls was the kind of dwelling used by subordinate people such as day workers or domestics. The small huts, especially the rounded one, which is the smallest structure on the site, may have been for slaves. According to the sagas, a few well-respected house slaves were brought along on the Vinland voyages. Such chores as cutting sod for house building and collecting bog iron were considered tasks fit only for slaves, so we may surmise that some were present at L'Anse aux Meadows as well.

There is little evidence of domestic activities and certainly no indication of normal family life (figs. 14.10–14.12). The traces indicate the presence of a male work force performing tasks such as carpentry, iron manufacture, boat repair, and exploration. The sagas indicate that on such expeditions women participated to perform traditionally female chores such as cooking, cleaning, and clothes maintenance. Women were also present at L'Anse aux Meadows as shown by the trio of textile implements found: a spindle whorl, a bone needle used for *nålebindning* (a form of knitting using a single needle), and a small whetstone of the kind used by women to sharpen needles, small knives, and scissors (figs. 14.16–14.18).

The Norse were not the only people who made L'Anse aux Meadows their home, but they never met *skraeling* (Old Norse word for native peoples) there. There were Indians on the site five thousand years before the Norsemen arrived, and evidence suggests that Dorset Eskimo groups also preceded them (fig. 14.19). Although Indians occupied this site in the thirteenth century and later, there is no evidence of native groups on the site in the tenth and eleventh centuries.

Sometimes the most exciting find on an archaeological excavation is not a treasure but something very ordinary. At L'Anse aux Meadows, for instance, finding butternuts—two whole nuts and one fragment—was a discovery that revealed much about the Norsemen's travels (fig. 14.21). Butternut trees are a North American walnut species, also called white walnut, which are not indigenous to Newfoundland and have never grown there. The area closest to Newfoundland where butternuts grow is the Saint Lawrence River valley, just east of Quebec City in northeastern New Brunswick, a bit inland from the Bay of Chaleur, the Miramichi, and other river estuaries. The nuts were found among the Norse deposits in the sedge-peat bog, along with a butternut burl that had been cut with a metal tool and must have been brought to L'Anse aux Meadows by the Norse. The significance of the nuts is that they indicate that the people who lived at L'Anse aux Meadows made excursions to regions farther south. Butternuts grow in the same areas as wild grapes, so whoever picked the nuts must have come across grapevines as well. This was the first archaeological proof that the saga stories of the Norse encountering wild grapes are not myth but based on reality. Both butternuts and grapes can be found farther to the south, in New England and farther south yet, but the distance from L'Anse aux Meadows to New England is many times greater than to New Brunswick. The location of L'Anse aux Meadows, near the northern apex of Newfoundland, provided convenient access into the Gulf of Saint Lawrence. The Strait of Belle Isle leads into the Gulf, which forms an inland sea that can be circumnavigated, beginning and ending at L'Anse aux Meadows.

Although it is not possible to tell how many years the site was occupied, it could not have been very long. Telltale evidence includes the small size of garbage middens, the lack of a cemetery, and the meager cul-

14.13, 14.14 Iron Production and Ship Repair
The furnace site on Black Duck Brook contained scorched earth and considerable amounts of iron-rich slag, proving that the Norse found bog iron ore and smelted it to produce small amounts of iron. Corroded rivets from the houses and middens indicate that vessels were repaired at the site.

14.19 Site Occupation History
Archaeological research at L'Anse aux Meadows has produced evidence not only of Norse occupation but of many other groups who left material traces here, beginning with Maritime Archaic Indians almost six thousand years ago.

tural deposits. Abandonment of the site was well planned and orderly. All equipment and tools were removed and brought back with the temporary inhabitants. The only objects left on the site were either small personal things that had been lost during the stay, such as a bronze pin (fig. 14.5), the spindle whorl, the bead, and the needle hone, or things that were broken and discarded (figs. 14.4, 14.6–14.12). The large halls had been in good condition when the move took place, but at least two halls were subsequently burned, either as the people left, or shortly thereafter. It is tempting to conclude that the fires had been deliberately set by the Norse themselves. The two halls are sufficiently far apart that an accidental fire would probably not have spread from one to the other, and none of the small huts were burned. Nor is there any indication that native people came to the site at that time. One can only speculate why this burning took place. Perhaps it was a token of complete abandonment, an open acknowledgment that the halls would never again be needed.

Putting all the evidence together, we find that L'Anse aux Meadows was not a colonizing venture but a base at which a large group of people, perhaps three ship crews, stayed for a short time (fig. 14.15). The occupants of the base were mostly men, from many walks of life, some with particular skills such as ironworking, carpentry, and boat repair. A few women were there, but there was no family life with children and regular households. In summertime, some of the occupants left the base and explored regions farther south where they came upon good hardwood lumber including butternut trees, and such exotic food as butternuts and grapes. Lumber, butternuts, and, presumably, the grapes were brought back to L'Anse aux Meadows and stored over the winter to be taken back to Greenland when the expedition returned home the following summer. The parallels with the *Vinland Sagas* are striking. Straumfjord (Current Fjord), the settlement described in *Erik the Red's Saga,* has the same kind of occupants and the same function. It was a base where some of the expedition members stayed year-round, but where most were absent on extended expeditions during the summer, both in northerly and southerly directions. In the south, in an area called Hóp (Tidal Pool) in the saga, the occupants of Straumfjord found lumber and grapes, which they harvested and brought back with them. At Hóp they also found lagoons locked off from the sea by sand barriers, shallow bays where the ship could not enter except at high tide, fine meadows, forests, and, unfortunately for the Norse who had hoped to colonize this land, large aboriginal populations using skin canoes. All these features are found in the Chaleur Bay and the Miramichi region of New Brunswick. There is little doubt that L'Anse aux Meadows is the Straumfjord of the sagas and that Hóp lies in northeastern New Brunswick. In the southern part of the Gulf and around the Saint Lawrence River in what is now northwestern New Brunswick, a landscape totally different from that of Newfoundland and northerly areas unfolds. Here are big hardwood forests, resources such as wild grapes and butternuts, and an extensive lagoon system along the coast. I have come to the conclusion that the Vinland of the sagas encompasses all the coasts around the Gulf of Saint Lawrence, and L'Anse aux Meadows was the base from which it was explored, the gateway into Vinland.

Why did the Norse need a gateway like L'Anse aux Meadows? The short navigational season in northern latitudes coupled with the long distance from Greenland to resources worth pursuing limited their explorations unless they overwintered in Vinland. Safe navigation in and out of Greenland would have been restricted to the months between

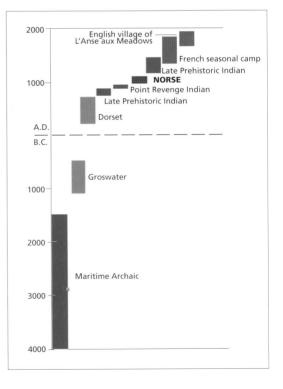

14.15 L'ANSE AUX MEADOWS RECONSTRUCTION

This reconstructed sod house approximates how the community looked during the Norse occupation. The relatively mild climate of northern Newfoundland allowed residents to work outside during much of the year. Archaeological finds indicate that woodworking, in particular, was conducted outside.

14.16–14.18 NEEDLE, HONE, AND SPINDLE WHORL

Among the finds recovered during the initial excavations were a bone needle, a whetstone, and a soapstone spindle whorl—all objects that could not have been left by any Native American group. One side of the spindle whorl has an old surface that is flat and encrusted with seal oil; apparently the Norse made it from a Dorset pot they found on their explorations.

June and September. The sailing distance from Brattahlid to L'Anse aux Meadows is two thousand miles (thirty-two hundred kilometers) if one sails much of that distance within sight of shore. The voyage would have required a minimum of two weeks in one direction only and, as has been learned from the voyage of the replica ship *Snorri* in 1998, it could have taken four to six weeks or longer. Thus a month or more would have to be set aside for the voyage alone. This would leave two months, at the most, for exploration. By establishing a base, the time available for exploration could be doubled. Ships could be out until October and the long trip back to

Greenland postponed until the following summer. This is the schedule described in the sagas.

Is L'Anse aux Meadows Vinland? No, for Vinland is a region; L'Anse aux Meadows is merely a place in Vinland. Grapes grew only at Hóp in southern Vinland; L'Anse aux Meadows was at the northern edge of Vinland, its port of entry. From what we know of the social structure of Norse society at the time of L'Anse aux Meadows, we can deduce that L'Anse aux Meadows was built and operated by Leif Eriksson. At the time, only a chieftain or king could found and own a gateway. Such a gateway was usually operated by a deputy. When the Vinland voyages began, Erik the Red was paramount chief of Greenland. While he was still alive, Leif served as his deputy for the Vinland exploration. After Erik died, Leif succeeded him and no longer went to Vinland, but it was Leif who authorized the subsequent expeditions and allowed the participants to use his buildings. The deputies were all siblings and close relatives: Thorvald, Karlsefni (by virtue of his marriage to Leif's sister-in-law Gudrid), and Freydis (Leif's sister) and her husband. In return all of them would have been required to bring Leif a share of the riches they brought back from their journeys. We do not know if the site was called Leifsbuðir (Leif's Camp) or Straumfjord; possibly both names applied. What is certain is that L'Anse aux Meadows was the base from which Leif and the others explored Vinland.

Why could not L'Anse aux Meadows be an unnamed location, from the voyages not named in the sagas? The answer is simple. At the time L'Anse aux Meadows was built, the total population in Greenland numbered only four hundred to five hundred (Lynnerup 1998: 115), including women, children, and elderly people. Even if one expedition crew was Icelandic, L'Anse aux Meadows was inhabited by more than 10 percent of the entire Greenland colony, and this group comprised mostly men in their prime working age. The size of L'Anse aux Meadows is also consistent with the number of people who accompanied Karlsefni and Freydis on their expeditions. As we have seen, great

14.20 SOAPSTONE LAMP

A complete Late Dorset soapstone lamp dating to A.D. 1000–1350 may be evidence of a Norse visit to a Dorset camp, but its interpretation is problematic because it was found in the roof turf and not on the hut floor. Because no Dorset people were living in southern Labrador or Newfoundland at this time, the lamp was probably collected by Norse from a northern Labrador Dorset site they had visited during their voyage. It is also possible that the lamp was left at L'Anse aux Meadows after the site was abandoned; perhaps it was visited by a Late Dorset group who were far from their northern Labrador home.

14.21 BUTTERNUTS!

An important piece of evidence from the Parks Canada excavations was the discovery of butternut shells and husks. Butternuts do not presently grow in Newfoundland, and even in the warmer conditions of A.D. 1000 were not found north of the Gulf of Saint Lawrence. The nuts must have been brought to the site by Norse returning from southern explorations.

JASPER FRAGMENTS

A number of small fragments of jasper, a red or yellow flintlike rock used with iron fire-sarters, were found during the excavations at L'Anse aux Meadows. The five pieces on the right are Icelandic jasper. Four pieces in the center came to L'Anse aux Meadows from western Greenland. The piece at the upper left is a jasper fire-starter fragment from north-central Newfoundland. The object at the bottom left is a thinning flake from a prehistoric Native American occupation at L'Anse aux Meadows made from western Newfoundland jasper.

quantities of material and labor went into the construction of L'Anse aux Meadows. Both L'Anse aux Meadows and the settlements described in the *Vinland Sagas* lasted only a short time. It is unthinkable that the Greenland Norse would have had sufficient human resources to construct—and, equally important, to operate—a series of posts such as L'Anse aux Meadows and Straumfjord.

The Vinland episode and with it the occupation at L'Anse aux Meadows was short. As we now under-

stand the nature of the Greenland colony (Arneborg 1996; Buckland et al. 1996; Keller 1989; Lynnerup 1998; McGovern 1992; Bigelow 1991), this is not perplexing. The exploration voyages to North America took place in an era when all of Greenland was being explored as well. These explorations were the natural consequence of settlement in unknown territory. First, the new environment and resources were evaluated; subsequently, their exploitation was confined to what would be profitable (McGovern 1980–81: 293). The resources of L'Anse aux Meadows were not sufficiently attractive to be pursued. The desirable resources—prime hardwood, grapes, and walnuts—lay at such a distance from Greenland that their pursuit was too arduous, especially as the same things could be brought in from Europe at less expense and the choice of commodities was much wider there. At the time of the Vinland voyages, there was no shortage of land and pastures in Greenland, and so there was no economic incentive to go farther afield. The only people in Greenland who might have had an incentive were poor tenant farmers and slaves, but they had no access to ships or the means to supply a fledgling colony. It takes a critical mass of people to set up a new colony in a totally new environment, if there are no other inhabitants on whom to piggyback until they become self-sufficient and increase their numbers. The first English settlements in North America, which were much larger, failed (McGovern 1980–81: 300). With only a few hundred inhabitants, the Greenland colony barely met the requirements of the minimum critical number for any colony (Lynnerup 1998: 118). Either they all had to go to Vinland to stay, or none of them. The fact that there were already large unfriendly populations in Vinland (who may have been responsible for burning the site after the Norse departed) may have been another incentive for the Norse to leave L'Anse aux Meadows after a few short years and abandon Vinland.

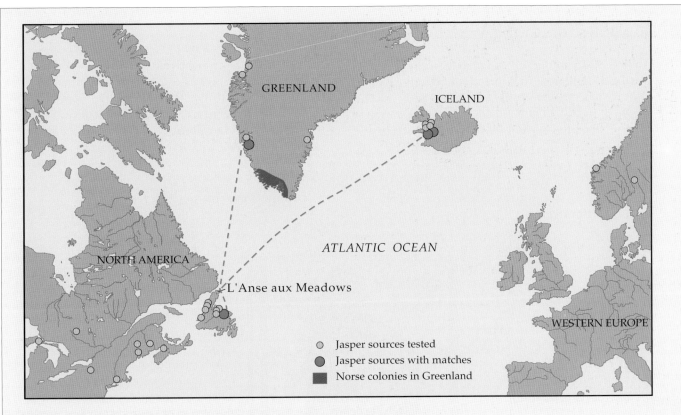

Who Lived at L'Anse aux Meadows? BY KEVIN P. SMITH

Where did the people who lived at L'Anse aux Meadows come from? Where else did they explore and what routes did they take to reach those places? What relationship does this site have to the voyages described in the Icelandic sagas? Raw materials used to make the tools found at L'Anse aux Meadows may help to answer these questions.

Ten jasper fire-starters from the site were recently analyzed using a technique called Instrumental Neutron Activation Analysis (INAA). Jasper is a flintlike stone that Vikings struck with steel to make sparks and start their fires. The places where these tools were made can be identified by comparing trace elements found in the artifacts and in raw material collected from regions where jasper occurs naturally. INAA measures these trace elements to develop geochemical fingerprints of the artifacts and geological samples.

The jasper tools from L'Anse aux Meadows were compared with geological samples from nearly sixty different source areas in Norway, Iceland, Greenland, Newfoundland, Nova Scotia, New Brunswick, New England, Pennsylvania, and the Great Lakes region. These analyses indicate that four objects came to the site from western Greenland. Five fragments were made from western Icelandic jasper. Although no jasper occurs naturally near L'Anse aux Meadows, one fragment from the site appears to have come from north-central Newfoundland, approximately 155 miles (250 kilometers) to the southeast.

These analyses suggest that the Vikings who settled at L'Anse aux Meadows came from Iceland and Greenland. Halls A and D—where only Icelandic jasper was found—may have housed two crews of Icelanders. Hall F may have been home to explorers from both Iceland and Greenland. The Newfoundland jasper fire-starter fragment found near Hall D suggests that these crews explored southeastward from the site.

The Icelandic sagas describe four voyages to the New World. One of these expeditions is said to have been undertaken by three crews: two from Iceland and one with both Greenlanders and Icelanders. Under the leadership of the Icelander Thorfinn Karlsefni, these men and women settled at a place they called Straumfjord and from there explored the coasts southeast, southwest, and north of their base. The presence of jasper tools from Iceland, Greenland, and Newfoundland at L'Anse aux Meadows suggests that Straumfjord may well be the place where Europeans first arrived in North America, where the first European child in the Americas was born, and where Old World and New World cultures first met, traded, and clashed.

JASPER TYPES IN THE NORTH ATLANTIC REGION

The jasper fire-starters from L'Anse aux Meadows were compared with jasper samples from more than sixty geological source areas around the North Atlantic and eastern North America. Trace-element "fingerprints" of the Viking artifacts matched geological samples from Iceland, Greenland, and Newfoundland.

An Introduction to the Vinland Sagas BY GÍSLI SIGURÐSSON

The Vinland Sagas comprise two separate works that were written down independently in Iceland in the early thirteenth century: the *Greenlanders' Saga* (p. 219) and the *Erik the Red's Saga* (p. 222). They contain accounts of several voyages across the North Atlantic that were undertaken at the height of the Viking Age (800–1050) by people from Iceland and Greenland. These journeys to North America around the year 1000 are the first authentically documented voyages across the Atlantic Ocean leading to the first meetings of the peoples of America and Europe.

There are earlier existing references showing that the Vinland voyages were well known in Iceland and on the European continent before these two sagas were written. The earliest reference to Vinland is to be found in a history of the archbishops in Hamburg written by Adam of Bremen in Saxony in about 1075. He reports information he had received in 1068 or 1069 from the king of Denmark, Svein Ulfsson, about an island in the ocean named Vinland where both grapes and wild wheat grow. Adam's description would be just another story about legendary islands in the Atlantic if it were not for the more reliable saga accounts from Iceland about the same Vinland.

A much shorter reference to Vinland appears in the *Book of the Icelanders*, the first written history of Iceland, compiled by Ari the Wise between 1122 and 1133. Ari tells us that Erik the Red had found remains of human habitation in Greenland that identified the people who had been there as similar to the people who lived in Vinland—whom the Norse called *skraeling*.

WRITTEN ACCOUNTS FROM ORAL TRADITION

The sagas are not written accounts by eyewitnesses, but transcriptions from oral tradition, containing stories and information about exceptional events—voyages undertaken more than two hundred years earlier. The stories about these voyages thus changed and were reformed in the tradition, kept alive both by descendants of the people who took part in the voyages as well as by other people, notably seafarers who told each other stories and exchanged information about faraway places, how to get there, and how to recognize landmarks. The tellers of the sagas were skilled seafarers who were able to take and give sailing directions and follow landmarks. Details of that kind are likely to be passed from man to man in oral tradition—preferably as integral parts of stories, which are often used to store information in traditional cultures. Because of their oral background they cannot be treated as contemporaneous historical documents. They cannot be discarded by historians, however, because archaeological data confirms that they are right about many general historical facts, such as the dates of settlements in Iceland (in the last decades of the ninth century) and Greenland (around the year 985) and the Norse encounter with North America around the year 1000 (Wallace, chapter 14).

The *Vinland Sagas* must be recognized as real sources of information in their own right. Without the straightforward accounts in the sagas, no one would ever have dreamed of going out to look for remains of Viking Age people from Greenland and Iceland in North America. It is, however, very unlikely that the sagas tell the full truth. They are a collection of what people remembered of bygone times and put in writing into a coherent order for the first time in the thirteenth century. The sagas are a mixture of fact and fiction, memories kept alive in an oral culture for several generations before they were committed to parchment.

Even though the *Vinland Sagas* are literary products, they are based on the oral tradition of people in Iceland and are therefore not of a similar fictive nature as creative literature. They are not made from nothing and certainly do not belong in the same category as myths and legends. There is no doubt that the *Vinland Sagas* contain memories about real characters and events, although they may not have occurred exactly as we are told in the sagas. The two sagas also disagree on certain details and contain material we would now classify as fanciful and supernatural but which medieval people believed to be part of the real world. All in all the sagas are our best proof that about one thousand years ago the people of Greenland and Iceland went on several voyages to the North American continent.

ERIK THE RED IN ARMOR

In this drawing of Erik the Red, included by Arngrímur Jónsson in his description of Greenland in 1688, the founder of the Greenland Norse colonies is inappropriately attired in late medieval armor! The saga descriptions of a hot-tempered redhead may give a better sense of his appearance.

Greenlanders' Saga

These excerpts from the *Greenlanders' Saga* were translated by Keneva Kunz and published in the first volume of the five-volume set *The Complete Sagas of the Icelanders* (Leifur Eiríksson Publishing, Reykjavík, 1997); also to be published in the *Saga of the Icelauders*, preface by Jane Smiley (Viking Press). The passages were chosen for their relevance to the Viking discovery of North America and for their relationship to *Erik the Red's Saga*, which follows this. The story begins with the trader Bjarni voyaging to visit his father in Greenland.

Bjarni spoke: "Our journey will be thought an ill-considered one, since none of us has sailed the Greenland Sea."

Despite this they set sail once they had made ready and sailed for three days, until the land had disappeared below the horizon. Then the wind dropped and they were beset by winds from the north and fog; for many days they did not know where they were sailing.

After that they saw the sun and could take their bearings. Hoisting the sail, they sailed for the rest of the day before sighting land. They speculated amongst themselves as to what land this would be, and Bjarni said he suspected this

was not Greenland....The land was not mountainous but did have small hills, and was covered with forests. Keeping it on their port side, they turned their sail-end landwards and angled away from the shore. They sailed another two days before sighting land once again.

They asked Bjarni whether he now thought this to be Greenland. He said he thought this no more likely to be Greenland than the previous land "since there are said to be very large glaciers in Greenland." They soon approached the land and saw that it was flat and wooded. The wind died and the crew members thought it advisable to put ashore, but Bjarni was against it....He told them to hoist the sail and they did so, turning the stern towards shore and sailing seawards. For three days they sailed with the wind from the southwest until they saw a third land. This land had high mountains, capped by a glacier. [Bjarni said] "this land seems to me to offer nothing of use."

They...followed the shoreline until they saw that the land was an island. Once more they turned their stern landwards and sailed out to sea with the same breeze. But the wind soon grew and Bjarni told them to lower the sail....They sailed for four days.

Upon seeing a fourth land they asked Bjarni whether he thought this was Greenland or not. Bjarni answered, "This land is most like what I have been told of Greenland, and we'll head for shore here."

There was now much talk [in Greenland] of looking for new lands. Leif, the son of Erik the Red of Brattahlid, sought out Bjarni and purchased his ship. He hired himself a crew numbering thirty-five men altogether....One of the crew was a man called Tyrker, from a more southerly country.

Once they had made the ship ready they put to sea and found first the land which Bjarni and his companions had seen last. They sailed up to the shore and cast anchor, put out a boat and rowed ashore. There they found no grass, but large glaciers covered the highlands and the land was like a single flat slab of rock from the glaciers to the sea. This land seemed to them of little use. Leif then spoke: "As far as this land is concerned it can't be said of us as of Bjarni that we did not set foot on shore. I am now going to name this land and call it Helluland [stone-slab land]."

They then returned to their ship, put out to sea and found a second land. Once more they sailed close to the shore and cast anchor, put out a boat and went ashore.

GREENLANDERS' SAGA

This inconspicuous tale, hidden among longer sagas with only a decorated Þ (thorn) to mark its beginning, contains one of two sagas telling of the Norse discovery of North America. It is only preserved in *Flateyjarbók*, a vellum manuscript of sagas concerned primarily with the Norwegian kings, which dates to the mid-fourteenth century.

This land was flat and forested, sloping gently seaward, and they came across many beaches of white sand. Leif then spoke: "This land shall be named for what it has to offer and called Markland [forest land]." They returned to their ship without delay.

After this they sailed out to sea and spent two days at sea with a northeasterly wind before they saw land. They sailed towards it and came to an island, which lay to the north of the land, where they went ashore. In the fine weather they found dew on the grass, which they collected in their hands and drank of, and thought they had never tasted anything as sweet.

Afterwards they returned to their ship and sailed into the sound, which lay between the island and the headland, which stretched out northwards from the land. They rounded the headland and steered westward. Here there were extensive shallows at low tide and their ship was soon stranded, and the sea looked far away to those aboard ship....

Their curiosity to see the land was so great that they... ran ashore where a river flowed into the sea from a lake. When the incoming tide floated the ship again they...moved it up into the river and from there into the lake, where they cast anchor. They carried their sleeping sacks ashore and built booths. Later they decided to spend the winter there and built large houses.

There was no lack of salmon both in the lake and the river, and this salmon was larger than they had every seen before. It seemed to them the land was good, that the livestock would need no fodder during the winter. The temperature never dropped below freezing and the grass only withered very slightly. The days and nights were much more equal in length than in either Greenland or Iceland. In the depth of winter the sun was aloft by midmorning and still visible at midafternoon.

When they finished building their houses, Leif spoke to his companions: "I want to divide our company into two groups, as I want to explore the land. One half is to remain at home by the longhouses while the other half explores the land.... This they did for some time. Leif accompanied them sometimes, and at other times remained at home by the houses. Leif was a large, strong man, of very striking appearance and wise, as well as being a man of moderation in all things.

One evening it happened that one man, Tyrker [the German], was missing from their company.... [Tyrker returned and] he spoke in Norse: "I had gone only a bit farther than the rest of you. But I have news to tell you; I found grapevines and grapes...[I am sure because] where I was born there was no lack of grapevines and grapes...."

The following morning Leif spoke to his crew: "We'll divide our time between two tasks, taking a day for one task and a day for the other, picking grapes and cutting *vínviður* [wine wood] and felling the trees to make a load for my ship." They agreed on this course.

It is said that the boat which was drawn behind the ship was filled with grapes....

When spring came they made the ship ready and set sail. Leif named the land for its natural features and called it Vinland [wineland]. They headed out to sea and had favorable winds, until they came in sight of Greenland....

There was great discussion of Leif's Vinland voyage and his brother Thorvald felt they had not explored enough of the land....

In consultation with his brother Leif, Thorvald now prepared for his journey with thirty companions. They made their ship ready and put to sea, and nothing is told of their journey until they came to Vinland, to Leifsbuðir [Leif's camp] where they laid up their ship and settled in for the winter, fishing for their food....

Several men took the ship's boat and went to the west of the land and explored there during the summer. They thought the land fine and well forested, with white beaches and only a short distance between the forest and the sea. There were many islands and wide stretches of shallow sea.

Nowhere did they see signs of men or animals. On one of the westerly islands they did find a wooden grain trough, but discovered no other works by human hands and headed back, returning to Leifsbuðir in the autumn.

The second summer Thorvald headed north around the land aboard the large ship and explored the country to the east. They ran into stormy weather around one headland, and they were driven ashore, smashing the keel of the ship. They stayed there a long time, repairing their ship. Thorvald then said to his companions, "I want us to raise the broken keel up on this point and call it Kjalarnes [keel point]."

They then left to sail to the east of the country and entered the mouths of the next fjords until they reached a cape stretching out seawards. It was covered with forest....Upon coming closer they saw there were three hide-covered boats [on the beach], with three men under each of them. They divided their forces and managed to capture all of them except one, who escaped with his boat. They killed the other eight and went back to the cape. On surveying the area they saw a number of hillocks further up the fjord, and assumed them to be settlements....

A vast number of hide-covered boats came down the fjord, heading toward them...After the *skraeling* had shot at them for awhile, they fled as rapidly as they could....Thorvald [was] wounded under the arm. Thorvald then spoke: "bury me...and mark my grave with crosses at the head and foot, and call the spot Krossanes [cross point] after that."

The group did everything as Thorvald asked, then left to meet up with their companions. Each group told its news to the other and they spent the winter there loading the ships with grapes and grapevines. In the spring they made ready for the voyage back to Greenland...and had plenty of news to tell Leif....

That same summer a ship from Norway arrived in Greenland. The skipper of the ship was named Thorfinn Karlsefni...a very wealthy man. He spent the winter with Leif Eriksson in Brattahlid. He was soon attracted to Gudrid and asked her to marry him....Their wedding took place that winter.

The discussion of a voyage to Vinland continued as before, and people strongly urged Karlsefni to make the journey, Gudrid among them. Once he had decided to make the journey he hired himself a crew of sixty men and five women....

They then put out to sea in their ship and arrived without mishap at Leifsbuðir, where they unloaded their sleeping sacks.

Karlsefni had trees felled and hewn for his ship and had the timber piled on a large rock to dry. They had plenty of supplies from the natural bounty there, including grapes, all sorts of fish and game, and other good things.

After the first winter passed and summer came, they became aware of *skraeling*....They set down their packs and opened them, offering their goods. The [Norse] women brought forth milk and milk products....

Karlsefni next had a sturdy palisade built around his farm, where they prepared to defend themselves. At this time, Gudrid, Karlsefni's wife, gave birth to a boy, who was named Snorri. Near the beginning of their second winter the *skraeling* visited them again, in much greater numbers...one of the *skraeling* was killed by one of Karlsefni's servants for trying to take weapons from them, and they quickly ran off.

"We have to decide on a plan," said Karlsefni, "since I expect they will return for a third time, hostile and in greater numbers...."

The *skraeling* soon came to the place Karlsefni intended for a battle. They fought and a large number of the natives were killed.... After that the *skraeling* fled into the woods at top speed, and they had no more dealings with them.

Karlsefni and his companions spent the entire winter there, but in the spring Karlsefni declared that he wished...to return to Greenland. They made ready for their journey, taking with them plenty of the land's products—"wine-wood," berries, and skins. They set sail and arrived safely in Erik's Fjord.

Discussion soon began again of a Vinland voyage, since the trip seemed to bring men both wealth and renown. The same summer...a ship arrived in Greenland from Norway. The skippers were two brothers, Helgi and Finnbogi, Icelanders from the east fjords.

Freydis, daughter of Erik the Red, met with the two brothers to propose that they make the journey to Vinland...they agreed to this. From there she went to her brother Leif and asked him to give her the houses he had built in Vinland.

They put to sea....The brothers arrived slightly earlier, however, and had unloaded their ship and carried their belongings to Leif's houses when Freydis arrived.... Freydis then said, "Leif lent me the houses, and not you." Helgi then spoke: "We brothers will never be a match for your ill-will." They removed their things and built themselves a longhouse further from the sea, on the bank of a lake, and settled in well. Freydis had wood cut to make a load for her ship.

When winter came the brothers suggested that they hold games and arrange entertainment. This went on for awhile, until disagreements arose. The ill feelings split the party so that the games ceased....

Freydis had each one of [Helgi and Finnbogi's] men... killed. Only the women were left, as no one would kill them. Freydis then spoke: "Hand me an axe." This was done, and she then attacked five women there and killed them all.

Early in the spring they loaded the ship, which the brothers had owned, with all the produce they could gather and the ship would hold. They set sail and had a good voyage, sailing their ship into Erik's Fjord in early summer....

In time [news of Freydis's wickedness] reached the ears of Leif, her brother, who thought the story a terrible one....As things turned out, after that no one expected anything but evil from Freydis's offspring.

To return to Karlsefni: he purchased land at Glaumbaer, Iceland, and established a farm there, where he lived for the remainder of his days. He was the most respected of men.... He and his wife Gudrid had a great number of descendants, and a fine clan they were.... After Karlsefni's death Snorri [who had been born in Vinland] married [and] Gudrid traveled abroad, made a pilgrimage south...[and] became a nun and an anchoress....There are a great number of people descended from Karlsefni, who founded a prosperous clan. It was Karlsefni who gave the most extensive reports of anyone of all of these voyages, some of which have now been set down in writing.

GUDRID THE WIDE-TRAVELED

A statue of Gudrid—who traveled to Greenland and Vinland, made a pilgrimage to Rome, and then settled in Iceland—was erected near Glaumbaer, the farm she lived on in Iceland. Gudrid, one of the central characters in the *Vinland Saga*, was married to Thorstein Eriksson, the son of Erik the Red, and when he died, she married a wealthy Icelandic trader, Thorfinn Karlsefni, with whom she traveled to Vinland. Their son, Snorri, was born in Vinland; he stands atop his mother's shoulder in this statue.

Erik the Red's Saga

Excerpts from *Erik the Red's Saga*, also from the translation by Keneva Kunz, reveal even in a casual reading the similarities and differences between this version of events and the *Greenlanders' Saga*. The excerpt below begins after Erik the Red has settled Greenland, and just after his son Leif has gone to visit the Norwegian king who has asked Leif to convert the Greenland Norse to Christianity.

Once he had made ready, Leif set sail. After being tossed about at sea for a long time he chanced upon land where he had not expected any to be found. Fields of self-sown wheat and vines were growing there; also, there were trees known as *mosur* [maple?; alt. trans., knotty wood], and they took specimens of all of them.

Leif also chanced upon men clinging to a ship's wreck, whom he brought home and found shelter for over the winter. In so doing he showed his strong character and kindness. He converted the country [Greenland] to Christianity. Afterward he became known as Leif the Lucky....

The suggestion that men go to seek out the land, which Leif had found, soon gained wide support. The leading proponent was Erik's son, Thorstein, a good, wise, and popular man. They made ready the ship which Thornbjorn had sailed on to Greenland, with twenty men to go on the journey. They took few trading goods, but all the more weapons and provisions....

They were tossed about at sea for a long time and failed to reach their intended destination. They came in sight of Iceland and caught birds from Ireland. Their ship was driven to and fro across the sea until they returned to Greenland in the autumn....

There was a man called Thorfinn Karlsefni, the son of Thord Horse-head who lived in north Iceland, at Reynisnes in Skaga Fjord. Karlsefni was a man of good family and good means. His mother was named Thorunn. He went on trading voyages and was a merchant of good repute. One summer Karlsefni made his ship ready for a voyage to Greenland... [and] sailed into Erik's Fjord that autumn....

After Yule Karlsefni approached Erik to ask for Gudrid's hand, as it seemed to him that she was under Erik's protection, and both an attractive and knowledgeable woman. Erik answered that he would support his suit, and that she was a fine match.

There was great discussion that winter in Brattahlid of Snorri [Thorbrandsson, co-owner of Karlsefni's ship] and Karlsefni setting sail for Vinland, and people talked at length about it. In the end Snorri and Karlsefni made their vessel ready, intending to sail in search of Vinland that summer. Bjarni and Thorhall decided to accompany them on the voyage, taking their own ship and their companions.

A man named Thorvard was married to Freydis, who was an illegitimate daughter of Erik the Red. He went with them, along with Thorvald, Erik's son, and Thorhall who was called the Huntsman. They had the ship which Thorbjorn [Gudrid's father] had brought to Greenland and set sail with Karlsefni and his group. Most of the men aboard were from Greenland. The crews of the three ships made a hundred plus forty men.

They sailed along the coast to the Western Settlement, then past the Bear Islands with a northerly wind. After two days at sea they sighted land and rowed over in boats to explore it. There they found many flat slabs of stone [*hellur*], so

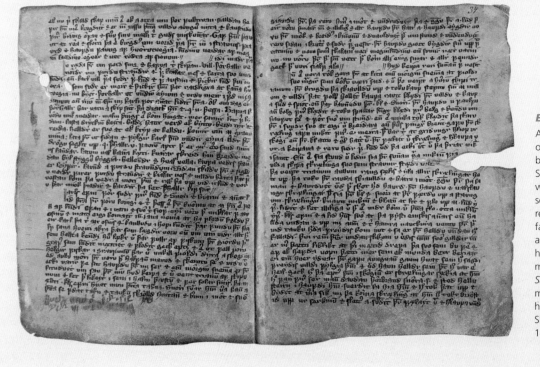

ERIK THE RED'S SAGA

Although it bears only the name of Erik the Red, this saga might be more aptly named "Gudrid's Saga." Only one chapter deals with Erik the Red's discovery and settlement of Greenland; the rest of the text focuses on the family of Gudrid Thorbjarnadottir and the travels she and her husband, Thorfinn Karlsefni, made to Vinland. *Erik the Red's Saga* is preserved in two manuscripts; the one illustrated here is from the bishopric at Skálholt and dates between 1420 and 1450.

large that two men could lie foot to foot across them. There were many foxes there. They gave the land the name Helluland [Rock Land].

After that they sailed with a northerly wind for two days, and again sighted land, with large forests and many animals. An island lay to the southeast, off the coast, where they discovered a bear, and they called it Bjarney [Bear Island], and the forested land itself Markland.

After another two days passed they again sighted land and approached the shore where the peninsula jutted out. They sailed upwind along the coast, keeping the land on the starboard. There were large harborless stretches, long beaches and sand flats. They rowed ashore in boats and, discovering the keel of a ship there, named this point Kjalarnes [Keel Point]. They also gave the beaches the name Furðurstrandir [wonder beaches] for their surprising length. After this the coastline was indented with numerous inlets which they skirted with their ships.

After sailing the length of the Furðurstrandir beaches, they put two Scots [slaves Haki and Hekja] ashore and told them to run southwards to explore the country and return before three days time had elapsed....After three days had passed the two returned down to the shore, one of them with grapes in hand and the other with self-sown wheat. Karlsefni said that they had found a good land. After taking them on board once more, they sailed onwards, until they reached the fjords cutting into the coast. They steered the ships into one fjord with an island near its mouth, where there were strong currents, and called the island Straumsey [Current Island]. There were so many birds there that they could hardly walk without stepping on eggs. They sailed up the fjord, which they called Straumfjord [Current Fjord] unloaded the cargo from the ships and began settling in.

They had brought all sorts of livestock with them and explored the land and its resources. There were mountains there, and a pleasant landscape. They paid little attention to things other than exploring the land. The grass there grew tall. They spent the winter there and it was a harsh winter....In the spring they moved further into Straumfjord and lived on the produce of both shores of the fjord: hunting game inland, gathering eggs on the island and fishing at sea.

They then began to discuss and plan the continuation of their journey. Thorhall wanted to head north, past Furðurstrandir and around Kjalarnes to seek Vinland. Karlsefni wished to sail south along the shore, feeling the land would be more substantial the farther south it was, and he felt it was advisable to explore both. Thorhall then made his ship ready close to the island, with no more than nine men to accompany him. The rest of their company went with Karlsefni.... They then separated and Thorhall and his crew sailed north past Furðurstrandir and Kjalarnes, and from there attempted to sail to the west of it. But they ran into storms and were driven ashore in Ireland, where they were beaten and enslaved. There Thorhall died.

Karlsefni headed south around the coast, with Snorri and Bjarni and the rest of their company. They sailed a long time, until they came to a river which flowed into a lake and from there into the sea. There were wide sandbars stretching out across the mouth of the river and they could only sail into the river at high tide. Karlsefni and his company sailed into the lagoon and called the land Hóp [Tidal Pool]. There they found fields of self-sown wheat in the low-lying areas and vines growing on the hills. Every stream was teeming with fish. They dug trenches along the high-water mark and when the tide ebbed there were *helgir fiskar* [flatfish such as halibut] in them. There was a great number of *dýr* [deer, caribou, or wild animal] of all kinds in the forest.

They stayed there a fortnight, enjoying themselves and finding nothing unusual. They had taken their livestock with them.

Early one morning they noticed nine hide-covered boats and the people in them waved wooden poles that made a swishing sound as they turned them around sunwise. Karlsefni then spoke: "What can this mean?" Snorri replied: "It may be a sign of peace; we should take a white shield and lift it up in return." This they did.

The other then rowed toward them and were astonished at the sight of them as they landed on the shore. They were short in height with threatening features and tangled hair on their heads. Their eyes were large and their cheeks broad. They stayed there awhile, marveling, then rowed away again to the south around the point.

ERIK'S FARM IN ICELAND

The effort to verify details in the sagas through archaeology has sometimes been frustrating in Iceland. Local tradition in Haukadal, where *Erik the Red's Saga* says Erik first settled, held that certain small ruins were the remains of Erik's farm. Archaeological excavations have revealed that the site has the correct date and size—given that Erik was newly arrived and living on his father-in-law's land—to be his farm, but no significant artifacts have been found in several excavations undertaken there.

The group had built their booths up above the lake, with some of the huts farther inland, and others close to the shore. They remained there that winter. There was no snow at all and the livestock could fend for itself out of doors.

One morning, as spring advanced, they noticed a large number of hide-covered boats rowing up from the south around the point. There were so many of them that it looked as if bits of coal had been tossed over the water, and there was a pole waving from each boat. They signaled with their shields and began trading with the *skraeling*, who mostly wished to trade for red cloth. They also wanted to purchase swords and spears, but Karlsefni and Snorri forbade this. They traded a dark pelt for the cloth....This went on for some time....At this point a bull, owned by Karlsefni and his companions, ran out from the forest and bellowed loudly. The natives took fright at this, ran out to their boats and rowed off to the south. Three weeks passed and there was no sign of them.

After that they saw a large group of native boats approach from the south, as a steady stream. They were waving poles counter-sunwise now and all of them were shrieking loudly. The men took up their red shields and went towards them. They met and began fighting. A hard barrage rained down and the natives also had catapults. Karlsefni and Snorri then saw the natives lift up on poles a large round object, about the size of a sheep's gut and black in color, which came flying up on the land and made a threatening noise when it landed. It struck great fear into Karlsefni and his men, who decided their best course was to flee upriver....

Freydis, who moved slower because she was pregnant, came out of camp as they were fleeing. She called, "Why do you flee such miserable opponents, men like you who look to me to be capable of killing them off like sheep? Had I a weapon I'm sure I would fight better than any of you."...She came across a slain man, Thorbrand Snorrason, who had been struck in the head with a slab of stone. His sword lay beside him and this she snatched up. Freeing one of her breasts from her shift, she smacked the sword with it. This frightened the natives, who turned and ran back to their boats and rowed away....

The party realized that, despite everything the land had to offer there, they would be under constant threat of attack from its prior inhabitants. They made ready to depart for their own country. Sailing north along the shore, they discovered five *skraeling* sleeping in skin sacks near the shore. Beside them they had wooden vessels filled with *dýr* marrow blended with blood. They assumed these men to be outlaws and killed them.

Then they came to a headland thick with *dýr*. The point looked like a huge dunghill, as the *dýr* gathered there at night to sleep. They then entered Straumfjord, where they found food in plenty. Some people say that Bjarni and Gudrid had remained behind there with a hundred others and gone no farther, and that it was Karlsefni and Snorri who went further south with some forty men, stayed no more than two months south at Hóp and returned the same summer.

The group stayed there while Karlsefni went on one ship to look for Thorhall. They sailed north around Kjalarnes point and then westwards of it, keeping the land on their port side. They saw nothing but wild forest. When they had sailed some distance they reached a river flowing from east to west. They sailed into the mouth of the river and lay to near the south bank.

One morning Karlsefni's men saw something shiny above a clearing in the trees, and they called out. It moved and proved to be a one-legged creature which darted down to where the ship lay tied. Thorvald, Erik the Red's son, was at the helm and the one-legged man shot an arrow into his intestines. Thorvald drew the arrow and spoke: "Fat paunch that was. We've found a land of fine resources, though we'll hardly enjoy much of them." Thorvald died from the wound shortly after....

They soon headed northward where they thought they sighted the Land of the One-Legged, but did not want to put their lives in further danger. They saw mountains which they felt to be the same as those near Hóp, and seemed to be equally far from Straumfjord in both directions.

They returned to spend a third winter in Straumfjord. Many quarrels arose, as the men who had no wives sought to take those of the married men. Karlsefni's son Snorri was born there the first autumn and was three years old when they left.

They had southerly winds when they left Vinland and reached Markland, where they met five *skraeling*. One was bearded, two were women and two of them children. Karlsefni and his men caught the boys...and taught them their language and had them baptized....They said that kings ruled the land of the natives; one of them was called Avaldamon and the other Valdidida. No houses were there, they said, but people slept in caves or holes. They spoke of another land, across from their own. There people dressed in white clothing, shouted loudly and bore poles and waved banners. This people assumed to be the land of the white men, Hvítramannaland.

They then came to Greenland and spent the winter with Erik the Red....The following summer Karlsefni sailed for Iceland and Gudrid with him. He came home to his farm at Reynisnes....

Karlsefni's son Snorri had a daughter, Hallfrid, who was the mother of bishop Thorlak Runolfsson. Karlsefni and Gudrid had a son named Thorbjorn, whose daughter Thorunn was the mother of bishop Bjorn. Thorgeir, Snorri Karlsefni's son, was the father of Yngvild, the mother of the first bishop of Brand.

And here ends the saga.

15 | AN ARCHAEOLOGIST'S INTERPRETATION OF THE *VINLAND SAGAS*

BY BIRGITTA LINDEROTH WALLACE

E XPERTS FROM MANY DISCIPLINES have analyzed the *Vinland Sagas*, including historians, literary historians, manuscript experts, navigators, geographers, astronomers, meteorologists, and philologists. My perspective is anthropological and draws upon evidence from archaeology. How has recent archaeological and anthropological work in Iceland and Greenland, and especially the discovery of the L'Anse aux Meadows Norse site in northern Newfoundland, influenced our interpretation of the *Vinland Sagas*?

THE SAGAS AS EVIDENCE

Both the *Greenlanders' Saga* and *Erik the Red's Saga* are transcriptions of oral histories, which explains why the historical events they describe seem to be compressed and stylized and not always recorded in chronological order. As in a stream-of-consciousness narrative, one association leads to another, incorporating later experiences before the saga teller gets back on the chronological track. The *Greenlanders' Saga* and *Erik the Red's Saga* complement each other; information encountered in one is elaborated on in the other. There are two variants of *Erik the Red's Saga*, the *Skálholt Book* and *Hauk's Book*, which represent different redactions of the same original, *Hauk's Book* being the most heavily edited version (Jansson 1945: 99).

The major difference between the *Greenlanders' Saga* and *Erik the Red's Saga* is that the four successful expeditions described in the *Greenlanders' Saga* (hereafter GS) have been combined into one in *Erik the Red's Saga* (hereafter ES). Thorfinn Karlsefni has assumed Leif Eriksson's role as the actual explorer, the major expedition leader, and the person who names Helluland and Markland. Leif has been reduced to the accidental dis-

coverer and does not figure in the expeditions at all. Otherwise the events are almost identical.

Ólafur Halldórsson, in a 1992 lecture, convincingly demonstrated that the two sagas had different purposes: the GS was written to provide a historical record of the Vinland explorations, whereas the ES was intended to pay homage to Gudrid, Karlsefni's wife, and to support the canonization of their descendants, Bishop Bjorn Gilsson of Hólar and Bishop Brundur Saemundarson. This probably explains the magnification of Karlsefni's role in the ES version of the Vinland expeditions. The editor of *Hauk's Book*, Hauk Erlendsson, was a direct descendant of Karlsefni and Gudrid, which may have affected how their roles were presented.

SOCIAL ORGANIZATION AND PURPOSE OF THE EXPEDITIONS

A chieftain or other person of distinction, sometimes in partnership with ship-owning traders, led each expedition. Most of the expedition members were men; all were adults. Sometimes the leaders' wives accompanied their husbands, and a few women were brought to perform domestic duties. The

THOR AND *MIÐGARÐSON, SNORRA EDDA*

only child was Snorri, the son of Gudrid and Karlsefni, who was born during their three-year stay. The expeditions were as socially stratified as life in Greenland or Iceland, although on a less complex scale. Next in rank to the chieftains were their business partners, shipowners with their own crews. The Icelandic brothers Helgi and Finnbogi were in partnership with Freydis and Thorvard; Karlsefni was allied with Snorri Thorbrandsson with whom he owned a ship, and with Bjarni Grimolfsson and Thorhall Gamlason, who had their own ship and crew. Crews were hired for a specific voyage for a share in the profits. Some members of the leaders' estate with special skills participated in the expeditions, for instance, Thorhall the Hunter, who had long been with Erik the Red's family and who was valued for his special understanding of unexplored regions. Finally, at the bottom of the social ladder were slaves such as Tyrker the German.

Logic might suggest that when new lands are discovered, people will inevitably rush to fill them. On the contrary, migration research has shown that the situation is far more complex (Anthony 1990). Colonization is always preceded by exploration. New resources are discovered, and the first settlements are usually simple posts situated at widely dispersed points in locations suitable for exploitation. People come to work and perform specific tasks but not to settle. Outposts are expensive ventures that have to be supplied from the homeland. Most of the early migrants are men who are hired for a period of time and who leave their families at home. Only as the individual outposts prosper and expand is the viability of settlement confirmed and an actual transfer of people begun. Archaeological evidence suggests that the Norse presence in Vinland is typical of the exploration phase of migration.

Colonization was not an immediate goal of these voyages of exploration, but it was held out as an incentive, which in this case did become a realistic option. The fact that there were no real families in the expeditions also indicates that their purpose was not to settle. Leif's brother Thorvald found a place where he wished to have a home, but he died before that plan was realized. Karlsefni's expedition intended to colonize the country "if they could," but the purpose that all the voyages shared was profit and honor. In the Norse's nonmarket economy, power and influence were enhanced by ventures such as these, provided they were successful, and especially if they led to attractive material goods. The profit motive is highlighted throughout both sagas and is the only one mentioned in ES: "They...looked around at what the land had to offer."

VINLAND: WINE OR PASTURE LAND?

The meaning of the name *Vinland* has always been a major issue. There are two words *vin* in Norse languages. One is *vin* with a short " i," the other is *vín* with a long "i," the accent indicating a double vowel. The double vowel affects the "i" in a way similar to "lot" and "loot" in English, with equally diverse meanings. *Vin* with a short "i" occurs in Old Germanic and it means "grasslands," but it does not exist in Old Norse. *Vín* with a long "i" meant "wine" in Old Norse. Some of the saga manuscripts including *Flateyjarbók,* spell Vinland with two "i's," indicating that wine is the proper meaning (Crozier 1998: 39). The idea that Vinland should be translated as "pasture land" was given prominence after the first excavations at L'Anse aux Meadows, when it became obvious that grapes had never grown there. However, in Old Norse "pasture land" would be *vinjaland* or *vinjarland*.

Because butternuts, which grew wild in the same area as grapes, were found at L'Anse aux Meadows, it is no longer necessary to explain away the wine from Vinland (fig. 14.21). Grapes had been imported into the Nordic countries from Italy and the Rhineland for at least a millennium by the time the Vinland voyages took place. Although wine was not available to everyone, it played an important role in Viking society, where a chieftain derived power in part from his ability to impress others. In addition to wearing elaborate clothes, living in a large hall with many household hands, and offering generous gifts, sumptuous feasts with delicacies imported from the continent—such as walnuts, spices, and wine—helped chieftains sustain their power and influence. Ostentatious rituals, feasting, and wine consumption reinforced the status of a chieftain. For Leif and Karlsefni, the prospect of controlling their own wine supply would have been a true bonanza for maintaining their power.

LOCATIONS IN THE SAGAS

In naming three areas that he had explored as Helluland, Markland, and Vinland, Leif

15.1 SNORRI OFF LABRADOR
Off the shore of Labrador, *Snorri*, a replica of a Viking boat built by Hodding Carter in Maine, rides the swells typical of the western North Atlantic. The land in the distance would also have been seen by Vikings, who "speculate[d] amongst themselves what land this would be," according to *Greenlanders' Saga*. Scholars are still trying to determine exactly which areas of northeastern North America Vikings visited a millennium ago.

Eriksson laid claim to whatever resources these areas might yield. He also laid down the gauntlet for scholars who nearly a millennium later still debate exactly where the Norse visited.

ES describes two settlements, Straumfjord in the north and Hóp in the south. Straumfjord is a year-round settlement from which expeditions were launched in the summer and to which everyone returned in the winter. No grapes grew there. Hóp is a camp used in the summer in southern Vinland where the Norse cut lumber and found *mosur* (burl) wood. It is a wonderful place where there is self-sown wheat, and grapes grow wild. Hóp was named for its tidal lagoons on river estuaries inside sand barriers, so shallow that a ship could enter only at high tide.

The GS describes only one settlement, Leifsbuðir. Leifsbuðir incorporates elements of both Straumfjord and Hóp. Its physical description is close to that of Hóp, but its function is that of Straumfjord. What is clear is that both Straumfjord and Leifsbuðir are gateways to Vinland. Resources were sought from a vast hinterland and brought back to

the base to be shipped to Greenland.

More developed forms of such gateways existed in Norse society where they become markets and towns. Gateways and markets were always controlled via a deputy by a king or chieftain who received a share of the goods. As the supreme chieftain of Greenland, Erik controlled the initial voyage and establishment in Vinland, with Leif as his deputy. When Erik died, and Leif succeeded him, Leif no longer went to Vinland, but he retained his control.

We no longer need to speculate whether the sagas record voyages that really took place. We know that the Norse had at least one substantial base at L'Anse aux Meadows (fig. 15.2). Far from a being small, temporary camp, L'Anse aux Meadows was a well-planned and rigorously structured outpost capable of housing up to ninety people. This was not a frivolous venture, considering the total population of Greenland was only four hundred to five hundred people (Lynnerup 1998: 115). It is not likely that such a vast construction project would be attempted more than once, and the GS indicates clearly that all expeditions used the same base.

Although ES uses different names for its settlements, the descriptions and events have so much in common that it is clear that they are different recollections of the same places. For instance, in both versions, Thorvald dies somewhere north of Kjalarnes. The two sagas must refer to the same spot, as Thorvald cannot have died in two separate locations.

L'Anse aux Meadows is too large and complex to have been a station forgotten or overlooked by the sagas; it is in fact Straumfjord. L'Anse aux Meadows corresponds well to the physical reality of Straumfjord. The site dates from around 1000 and its architecture is Icelandic. Like Straumfjord, it was occupied in winter, but some of its inhabitants traveled south in the summer, and like Straumfjord, the site functioned only for a short time. The buildings were substantial and were inhabited by a large and socially mixed group of people and included both large halls and smaller dwellings. The number of occupants was smaller than that given for Straumfjord, but it is about the same as the largest expedition to Leifsbuðir. The buildings and their layout indicate that the social composition of the occupants match those indicated in the sagas. There were prominent leaders, labor crews, domestics, and slaves. The inhabitants were not families but predominantly men engaged in specialized activities. There are no barns or byres. The proportion of storage facilities is much larger at L'Anse aux Meadows than at a normal farmstead, and like Straumfjord and Leifsbuðir, it is a typical gateway in terms of purpose, structure, and location.

Even the geophysical descriptions of Straumfjord and Leifsbuðir have certain resemblances to L'Anse aux Meadows. Entered from the north, the Strait of Belle Isle can well be seen as a fjord as one suddenly finds oneself with land on two sides, on a body of water that becomes increasingly narrow. At the mouth is Belle Isle, a large island eleven miles (seventeen kilometers) long, with more

15.2 Identifying L'Anse aux Meadows

Looking east from the shore of Epaves Bay, the outlines of the sod house reconstructions at L'Anse aux Meadows rise above the grassy fields. Was this the location of Leifsbuðir of the sagas? Or Straumfjord? Or some other unnamed location? How far beyond it did they explore? L'Anse aux Meadows is the only key so far found for unlocking the Vinland mystery. Will there be others?

islands beyond it. Currents in the strait are strong, in places up to four knots, as the south-running Labrador Current meets north-flowing currents from the Gulf of Saint Lawrence. There are large colonies of birds in this area and some offshore islands are covered with nests. Although the snow has been heavy over much of the past century, the mild winter of 1998 showed that with just slightly warmer temperatures, there is little or no snow, so winters are likely to have been snow-free in the warmer climate of the eleventh century. At that time there was forest behind the site, but the site itself would have been covered in tall grass, much as it is today.

Identification of Helluland and Markland

The sailing distances mentioned in the sagas have been one of the main sources of controversy. Páll Bergþórsson, who has made detailed studies of speeds achieved under a variety of wind conditions, obtained an average of seventy-five to eighty nautical miles (150 kilometers) covered per day (1997: 126–131). Missing from his equations are situations when there was no measurable wind, which would reduce the average considerably. The *Snorri* experiment, in which a replica of a Viking ship sailed from Greenland to Canada in 1998 (fig. 15.1), showed that this contingency must be considered: 1998 was one of Labrador's windless summers. The *Snorri*, which was undermanned and depended entirely on wind and oars, took eighty-seven days to make the journey from Erik's Fjord in Greenland to L'Anse aux Meadows.

The relative distances are easier to judge. If it takes four days to sail between the Eastern Settlement in Greenland and Helluland and two days from Helluland to Markland, the latter distance should be about half of the first. The records state that it took twelve days to sail between Bergen (Norway) and Greenland's Eastern Settlement, which is a distance of about 1,700 nautical miles (3,150 kilometers). Thus the distance to Vinland, which was eight or nine days, should be about 1,130 or 1,275 nautical miles (2,090 or 2,350 kilometers). In fact, L'Anse aux Meadows is 1,190 nautical miles (2,200 kilometers) from the Eastern Settlement.

Markland was two days north of Vinland, which by the same accounting would represent 280 nautical miles (520 kilometers). As the crow flies, this would take us to the vicinity of Cape Harrison, just north of Hamilton Inlet. From there another 280 nautical miles takes us to the area between Ramah Bay and Saglek Bay. This supports the identifications of Markland in central Labrador and Helluland in northern Labrador and the area north of it.

Today few dispute that Helluland is the area of the eastern seaboard closest to Greenland: Baffin Island and the northern point of Labrador, Cape Chidley to Saglek Bay. Along the Labrador coast the northern timber-rich forest limit lies at 55 degrees north latitude in the vicinity of Davis Inlet between Nain and Hopedale. This is about 200 nautical miles (380 kilometers) south of the actual vegetative treeline. A transitional vegetation of stunted trees and tundra separates the two zones. The southern segment of the Labrador coast 200 nautical miles south to Battle Harbor must be Markland of the sagas. Three distinctive features mark this coastline: the first is Hamilton Inlet, which runs 130 nautical miles (240 kilometers) inland to a thickly wooded, highly protected area. This is probably the place of Thorvald's death where English River, the location of the largest timber on the central Labrador coast that would have been immediately accessible to Viking boats, runs more or less from east to west, as pointed out by previous writers (Jones 1986). Another major inlet, although considerably smaller, is Sandwich Bay, 70 nautical miles (130 kilometers) south-

15.3 STEFANSSON MAP
The "Skálholt Map", whose first version dated to 1570, was printed in a 1590 book by Sigurður Stefánsson; the copy shown here was made in 1669. It is the earliest attempt to combine cartographic knowledge of North America with the stories conveyed in the sagas. The coastline represented on this map was the principal clue that attracted early theorists like William F. Munn and later archaeologists such as Jørgen Meldgaard and Helge Ingstad to the northern tip of Newfoundland in their search for Vinland.

east of Hamilton Inlet, which leads into dense woods of larch, fir, spruce, and birch.

Between the English River and Sandwich Bay is Porcupine Strand, a fifty-mile (eighty kilometer) stretch of white sandy beach backed by coniferous forest (fig. 16.1). Many writers (Hovgaard 1914: 199; Meldgaard 1961: 18) familiar with the Atlantic coast have suggested that this is Furðustrandir (Wonder Strand). At a speed of eight knots, it would have taken five hours to sail by it. Although there are similar beaches along the northern shore of the Saint Lawrence, in Prince Edward Island, and in-

side the sand barriers along eastern New Brunswick, none are that length. Nova Scotia has some lovely sandy beaches both along its northern and southern shores, but there, the longest one measures only about one and one-half miles (two and a half kilometers).

KJALARNES AND HÓP

In ES, Kjalarnes is a cape north of Straumfjord and two days' south of Markland, close to Furðurstrandir. In GS Kjalarnes is "eastward and north along the land" from Leifsbuðir. There is little land east of L'Anse aux Meadows, but north of it is the long and rugged Labrador coast. Another indication in ES places Kjalarnes north of Straumfjord; together they suggest that the cape is one of the many peninsulas near Sandwich Bay.

The area closest to L'Anse aux Meadows that meets all criteria pertaining to Hóp is northeastern New Brunswick, the Chaleur Bay and Miramichi area. At Hóp the Norse encounter *skraelings* (as they called the Native Americans) in skin boats, which establishes a southern parameter for its location. Birchbark canoes were rarely used south of Kennebec River in central Maine (Salwen 1978: 164) and never south of Massachusetts Bay (Snow 1978: 68), but they were extensively used in Atlantic Canada. Prior to the seventeenth century, the Micmac Indians in Nova Scotia, Prince Edward Island, and eastern New Brunswick had skin canoes:

> We have had our canoes, Father, from time immemorial...In olden times, instead of the birchbark we use now, our ancestors used moose skins, from which they had plucked the hair, and which they had scraped and rubbed so thoroughly that they were like your finest skins. They soaked them in oil and then placed them on the canoe frame.... (Arguimat to the Abbé Maillard, circa 1740, Whitehead 1991: 20).

One wild grass that grows in North America and has a striking resemblance to Norse wheat is lyme grass (*Elymus virginicus*). A shore plant, it prefers low-lying moist areas and is found from Newfoundland to British Columbia and south to Florida (Zinck 1998, 2: 1149).

Dýr are encountered both at Hóp and in an unspecified area north of Straumfjord. The Old Norse word *dýr* has often been translated as "deer," which might suggest a southern locale where these animals are commonly found. However, the word has a much wider meaning—"animal" or "beast"—and can equally well mean moose or caribou, even bear or any mammal.

There is no doubt in my mind that Hóp was in eastern New Brunswick. Ólafur Halldórsson (1986, 1992) suggested that if it were not for the fact that the sagas are demonstrably older than Cartier's account of his 1534 travels in the Gulf of St. Lawrence, one would swear that accounts of Hóp in the *Vinland Sagas* were patterned on Cartier. The similarities are indeed striking:

> We went out in our longboats to the cape on the north and found the water so shallow that at the distance of more than a league from shore there was a depth of only one fathom... a bay... ran back a long way; and so far as we could see the longest arm stretched northeast. This [Miramichi] bay was everywhere skirted with sandbanks and the water was shallow.... The land on the south side of it is...full of beautiful fields and meadows... and it is as level as the surface of a pond... on the north side is a high mountainous shore, completely covered with many kinds of lofty trees... near the water's edge... were meadows and very pretty ponds (Cook 1993:18-19).

I suggest that the similarities exist because they both describe the same area.

IDENTIFICATIONS OF THE *SKRAELING*

If these locations of Helluland, Markland, and Vinland are correct, it is possible to identify the *skraeling* the Norse encountered at Hóp and Markland. The sagas do not mention any encounters with *skraeling* at Straumfjord, which corresponds with the archaeological evidence that the area around L'Anse aux Meadows was not used by any natives during the time the Norse stayed there.

The first indication for the Norse that this land was inhabited did not entail a direct encounter. When Thorvald sailed west from Leifsbuðir in the first summer, he came upon a forested land where the woods extended almost to the shoreline, which were covered with white sands; many islands lay in the shallow waters offshore. They met no people, but saw a *kornhjallur*. *Korn* means cereal; *hjallur* is a frame of wood; and the word has been translated as grain holder (Jones 1986: 194). In the eleventh century there was no Native American agriculture east of the mouth of the Saint Lawrence or along the Atlantic coast north of New England. Thus this observation would have to have been

made west of the Saguenay River or on the New England coast. The vicinity of Quebec City location is the likely source. Eastern Quebec was sparsely populated whereas New England had large native populations, and it would have been virtually impossible for the Norse to stay a whole summer there without encountering people.

The largest number of *skraeling* were encountered at Hóp, which suggests these were the ancestors of today's Micmac, who have inhabited the rivers and lagoons of New Brunswick ever since the lagoons were formed 2,500 to 3,000 years ago. The Oxbow area, twenty miles (thirty-two kilometers) up the Miramichi River from the bay (today the Red Bank First Nation), was a prominent gathering place to fish for salmon and hunt sturgeon. The Micmac had skin canoes, arrows, and slings for shooting stones. ES tells us that the *skraeling* had staves, which they swung clockwise ("sunwise") when they were friendly and the opposite direction when they planned an attack. Staves in the hands of Micmac were reported in Cape Breton in the sixteenth century by Richard Hill of Redrife in England who wrote in 1593 that, "Thereupon nine or tenne of his fellowes...came towardes us with white staves in their handes like halfe pikes" (Hakluyt 1589-1600, 6: 95). ES also tells of a formidable weapon consisting of a big blackish object mounted on a pole, which they shot off toward the Norse, scaring them greatly. This could have been a throwing weapon known from other Algonquian tribes, a large boulder wrapped in skin and mounted on a pole (Schoolcraft 1851, I: 85).

Both sagas record the same first encounter with *skraeling* in Markland: Thorvald was shot by an arrow fired by a native. In GS, this happens after the Norse have killed eight *skraeling* while the *skraeling* were asleep under skin boats. In the eleventh century, the only natives present in central Labrador (Markland) would have been the Indian ancestors of the Innu (Montagnais and Naskapi). Archaeologists refer to them as the Point Revenge prehistoric complex in Labrador, but knowledge of their traditions is limited. The people were Algonquian-speaking. Their weapons included corner-notched stone-tipped arrows. Dwellings were conical and oval skin-covered tents in summer, occasionally for more than one family. They exploited coastal resources for sustenance in the

summer and spent winters hunting in the interior forests (Fitzhugh 1972: 127, 1978:146-174, 1979: 146-174). On the return trip to Greenland, Karlsefni's expedition again came upon five *skraeling* in Markland—one man, two women, and two boys. They capture two boys whom they abduct to Greenland where they are baptized and taught the Norse language. The boys told the Norse that their people had no houses but lived in caves or holes. This is consistent with the earlier Norse observation that the *skraeling* "sank down into the ground" when they entered these huts.

The *skraeling* boys also told the Norse that there was another nation on the other side of their land where people wore white clothes, whooped loudly, and carried poles with flags. The Norse, and many modern writers, have assumed that this was Hvítramannaland, "land of white men," or "Albania." I suggest that the boys referred to Dorset people, who then inhabited most of northern Labrador (Cox 1978:111; Fitzhugh 1978:166) and the central Arctic, especially if their clothing, like that of the later Thule Inuit, included polar-bear fur and sealskins with the fur side in. The Thule culture arrived in eastern Canada from Alaska about A.D. 1100–1200 but did not appear in Labrador or Greenland until around 1250 (Fitzhugh 1994: 253; Schledermann 1996: 113).

ABANDONMENT OF THE VINLAND SETTLEMENTS

ES is explicit that the Norse felt that they would never be safe in Vinland because of the many native inhabitants. The time to settle this splendid country had not yet come. Manuscript AM 770c states that the newly discovered places were abandoned by Karlsefni because it was beyond his power to fight the numerous people who already lived there and that these places were never again found. A millennium later, we have rediscovered them through the archaeological findings in Greenland and the New World.

16 THE QUEST FOR VINLAND IN SAGA SCHOLARSHIP

By Gísli Sigurðsson

THE SAGAS ABOUT VINLAND CONTAIN the oldest written descriptions of the North American continent and have been the subject of many learned studies. Numerous contradictory theories about the voyages described therein have been developed with these sagas as their major source. The progress made in Vinland studies in the past decades, both on the archaeological front as well as in the minute philological analysis of the texts and in the studies of oral storytelling traditions around the world, suggest new answers to the old problem of the whereabouts of Vinland.

LOCATING VINLAND

We cannot aspire to find any accurate locations with the sagas as our only source. They are of such a general nature that the exact locations they refer to cannot be found. Many descriptions in the saga nevertheless match the east coast of North America. Endless attempts have been made to navigate the Viking ships into several harbors on the east coast, and the nature of the sources is such that we shall never arrive at any consensus in these matters. When dealing with the sagas all the commentators have either stated their preferences in terms of which saga to rely on or else they have made some emendations to the texts to make them fit the suggested locations. These preferences and emendations have naturally determined the scope of their interpretations.

Over time, historians became more and more skeptical of the sagas as sources and made fewer attempts to locate the destinations of the various saga voyages. Literary critics focused on the role of the learned authors in the writing of the sagas, their sources, and the textual relations between the sagas rather than the kernel of truth they might contain. Some historians even claimed

that the sagas were not based on real memories about real voyages from Greenland and Iceland to North America. This was the situation in the early 1960s when the Ingstads confirmed that the L'Anse aux Meadows site had been inhabited by people from Greenland and Iceland for several years around the year 1000.

When Helge and Anne Stine Ingstad found L'Anse aux Meadows in Newfoundland and identified it somewhat speculatively as Leif's "Vinland" of the sagas, Helge operated on the theory that *Erik the Red's Saga* was a rewriting of the *Greenlanders' Saga*, which is no longer believed to have been the case. The sagas were the victims of a scholarly methodology in philology that explained all vaguely similar instances in medieval texts as examples of literary borrowings. This method led to the conclusion by Jón Jóhannesson in the early 1950s that the *Greenlanders' Saga* was older and more reliable than *Erik the Red's Saga,* which he claimed had been written with *Greenlanders' Saga* as a source. Nineteenth- and early twentieth-century scholars either preferred *Erik the Red's Saga* or else used both sagas. The Icelandic philologist Ólafur Halldórsson

THEORIST / LOCATION	Rafn 1837	Storm 1887	Babcock 1913	Hovgård 1914	Steensby 1918	Gathorne-Hardy 1921	Thóðarson 1929	Hermansson 1936	Ingstad 1969	Morison 1971	Wahlgren 1986	Bergthórsson 1997
Helluland	Labrador/Newfnld	Labrador	Labrador	Baffin Is./Newfnd	Labrador	Labrador/Newfnld	Labrador	Labrador	Baffin Island	Baffin Island	Baffin Island	Baffin Island
Markland	Nova Scotia	Newfoundland	Newfoundland	Labrador/Nova Scotia	Labrador	Nova Scotia	Labrador	Labrador	Labrador	Labrador	Labrador/Newfnld	Labrador
Vinland	Cape Cod	Nova Scotia	Nova Scotia	near Cape Cod	Saint Lawrence Valley	Cape Cod	New England / New Brunswick	New England	L'Anse aux Meadows	L'Anse aux Meadows	in Bay of Fundy	Saint Lawrence Estuary
Leifsbuðir	Mount Hope Bay			on Cape Cod					L'Anse aux Meadows	L'Anse aux Meadows	in Bay of Fundy	L'Anse aux Meadows
Krossanes	Cape Cod	Cape Breton Is.		Marblehead	near Hóp		in St. Lawrence River			W. Coast Newfnld	in Bay of Fundy	on Cape Breton Is.
Kjalarnes	Cape Cod	Cape Breton	Cape Breton Is.	Cape Cod/Cape Bauld	Point Vaches	Cape Cod	on Gaspé Peninsula	East Point Anticosti			Cape Porcupine	Cape Breton Is.
Bjarney	Cape Sable N.S.		Avalon Peninsula		Great Northern Peninsula	Off Nova Scotia	Belle Isle	Belle Isle				Asticosti
Furdu-strandir	Cape Cod	Cape Breton Is.	Nova Scotia	South Labrador	South Labrador	Cape Cod	South Labrador	South Labrador	South Labrador	South Labrador	South Labrador	Nova Scotia
Straum-fjord	Buzzards Bay	Strait of Canso	Bay of Fundy	Sandwich Bay	Saint Lawrence Estuary	Long Island Sound	Northumberland Strait	Chaleur Bay	Strait of Belle Isle	Strait of Belle Isle	Strait of Belle Isle	Bay of Fundy
Staumsey	Martha's Vineyard		Grand Manan Is.	Earl Island	Hare Island	Fisher's Island		Heron Island		Belle Isle	Belle Isle	Grand Manan Is.
Hóp	Mount Hope Bay	S. Nova Scotia	Mount Hope Bay	Sop's Arm E. Newfnld	Rivière du Sud	Hudson River	New England	New England	L'Anse aux Meadows	E. Coast Newfnld	South of Newfnld	Hudson River
One-legged Land			West Cape Breton Is.	Bonne Bay, West Newfnld			North of St. Lawrence Estuary	Saint Lawrence Estuary		West coast of Newfnld	Miramichi Bay	Saint Lawrence Estuary
Distance Mountains	Blue Hills			Great Northern Peninsula	Gaspé Peninsula		Appalachian Mountains	Gaspé Peninsula		Great Northern Peninsula		

has scrutinized the evidence and has come to the conclusion that verbal similarities between the texts are not of such a nature that we can talk about literary borrowings or a written link between the sagas. He therefore confirms that they were written down independently of each other, drawing on the same or similar traditional material, which was circulating in oral tradition.

Today we read the *Greenlanders' Saga* and *Erik the Red's Saga* as independent accounts taken from oral tradition, which allows us to look at them from a broader perspective, taking into account the varying nature of oral traditions as well as what we know from the L'Anse aux Meadows site in particular. It seems clear from recent research (Wallace, chapter 14) that this location was used as a staging post for exploring the lands further south, a place where the explorers repaired their ships and gathered strength before and after the crossing from Greenland. L'Anse aux Meadows, at the extreme northern tip of Newfoundland, is hardly a place that would create impressions such as the ones preserved about Vinland, the land of wine and grapes, in the sagas.

The initial response to the archaeological proof provided by the Ingstads was to accept that everything had been found and that there was no need to look any further: this was Vinland and the saga descriptions should fit this single location. All descriptions that did not fit were simply the creation of tradition and exaggerations. Some even went as far as to doubt that Vinland had anything to do with wine at all (as the written evidence unanimously tells us) and made a case for the word being a mistranscription of the archaic word *Vínland* meaning "land of grass" (instead of *Vínland*, "land of grapes").

Even though these suggestions are contradictory, we are not dealing with different interpretations of the saga texts but rather with different ideas about the nature of the texts, the relation between them, and their reliability. Scholars have had opposing views in these matters, and these views have in turn affected their reading of the texts.

16.1 *Furðustrandir*

"They also gave the beaches the name *Furðustrandir* (Wonder Strand) for their surprising length." (*Erik the Red's Saga*). Porcupine Strand, which stretches for thirty miles along the Labrador coast south of Hamilton Inlet, is believed by most scholars to be the inspiration for the Furðustrandir described in the sagas, but the most recent publication on the matter (Bergthórsson 1997) suggests another location: Nova Scotia.

16.2 Baie Trinité, Québec

Vinland was a good place in the imagination of the Norse who heard the sagas late at night in chilly Iceland and Greenland. Where precisely it was may not have mattered to them; in the Gulf of Saint Lawrence and northern Nova Scotia, any number of islands and rivers, bays and inlets, such as this one near the mouth of the Saint Lawrence River in Quebec, would have been inviting places for the Norse to explore.

When there is contradictory information in the sagas between navigational directions and information about vegetation and climate, many have also been tempted to rely more on the descriptions of the land quality (such as the warm winter experienced by Leif in Vinland) rather than the sailing directions. We must acknowledge that the sagas have very concrete stories to tell, contradictory in many respects but also supplementary, and they have to be analyzed in their own right.

Calculations of Latitude

To understand these various interpretations (see table) it is important to realize which details from the sagas have been commonly used by scholars to match the geography of the east coast of North America. Apart from general sailing directions, considerable attention has been focused on a single reference to the length of day around winter solstice and several descriptions of the different qualities of the land.

The detail that should be the most authentic and which many have tried to make minute calculations from is what appears to be an accurate reference in the *Greenlanders' Saga* to the measuring by Leif and his men of the length of day at winter solstice. The saga says that "the days and nights were much more equal in length than in either Greenland or Iceland. In the depth of winter the sun was aloft by midmorning and still visible at midafternoon" (ch. 2, *Greenlanders' Saga*).

But how should this be interpreted? There have been very contradictory results about the exact latitude that may be referred to here; everything from 31 degrees north to about 50 degrees north have been suggested. The difficult part has been to interpret the Icelandic words used in the chapter:

eyktarstaðir for the time or location on the horizon when the sun sets and *dagmálastaðir* for the sunrise. Gustav Storm and the astronomer Hans Geelmuyden made an attempt to solve the problem late in the nineteenth century and their conclusion pointed to about 50 degrees north, that is, through the northern part of Newfoundland—which was considered to be far too north for the current scholarly consensus at the time. It was therefore not taken as seriously as it should have been—not even by Storm himself. Most recently Páll Bergþórsson has taken up the question and with his expert knowledge of the Icelandic terminology for time calculations and nature observation he has been able to show that the reference is exact enough to be referring to the latitude of L'Anse aux Meadows at 50 degrees 30 minutes.

Flora, Fauna, and Natives

The description of the qualities of the land, the natives, the vegetation, and the type of fish encountered by the characters of the sagas have also been used to locate Vinland. Assuming that the grapes of the sagas are meant to be wild grapes *(Vitis riparia)*, the saga lands could not have been located farther north than southern Nova Scotia and the southern regions of the Gulf of Saint Lawrence. "Self-sown wheat" probably refers to wild rye *(Elymus virginicus)*, which occurs in roughly the same area and also coincides with the northern limit of the butternut *(Juglans cinerea)*, a form of walnut that was found at the L'Anse aux Meadows site and most likely was brought there by the Norse. Leif's men found more and larger salmon in Vinland than they had seen before, and the Canadian archaeologist Catherine Carlson (1996) has shown that in the eleventh cen-

16.3 "A View near Point Levy opposite Quebec with an Indian Encampment"

In 1788 Thomas Davies painted this scene of what is probably an Algonquia Micmac village along the Saint Lawrence River. The Micmac were one of several native groups the Norse encountered, but the ethnographic descriptions in the sagas are confusing. An amalgam of traits known from different native groups, including Dorset and Thule Inuit and Woodland Indian, are attributed to skraeling. Though the saga accounts are not ethnography, they are the only pre-Columbian descriptions of Native Americans.

tury there were no salmon in Maine or further south due to the warmer temperatures at the time. The rivers in the southern regions of the Gulf of Saint Lawrence, however, abounded with salmon. The fish enter the rivers after two years at sea rather than just after one as in Newfoundland, further narrowing Leif's Vinland to that general area. Other qualities, such as the timber collected (*mosur* wood can refer to several types of trees in the area) by all the seafarers in the sagas, a stranded whale, and the flatfish (sometimes translated as halibut in English but the Icelandic word, *helgir fiskar*, can refer to any type of flatfish) caught by Karlsefni and his men in Hóp could all be pointing to similar regions with similar resources. However, when Karlsefni sailed south to Hóp from Leif's Vinland (his Straumfjord), he did not find any salmon in the rivers there.

The description of natives in the sagas provide other, more contradictory clues. The *skraeling* seem to have been hunters and gatherers; they did not grow maize or trade in furs (fig. 16.3). These features suggest a location north of southern Maine. It is also noteworthy that the bark containers that *skraeling* used for food were common all over North America, whereas birchbark ones are only known from sites north of New York. References to skin boats, canoes, double-bladed paddles, and bullroarers, however, suggest northern culture contacts to some researchers.

EXPLORATORY VOYAGES

The quest for Viking archaeological remains in North America, which was finally successful on the northernmost tip of Newfoundland in the early 1960s, provides at least one fixed point with which to evaluate information in the sagas. Some of the Viking explorers—but not necessarily all—set up camp at L'Anse aux Meadows. The assumption that everything in the saga texts has to fit what we know from L'Anse aux Meadows will

only yield frustration. Although people from Greenland and Iceland may have sailed regularly to North America once the area had been explored, the limitations of Viking Age navigational technique may have made their routes erratic. Before these people had found the most convenient route and which places could be frequented without running the risk of meeting too many hostile natives, they could theoretically have traveled widely because the sagas tell us that they spent several years on each voyage. And if they had a whole summer to sail south from the northernmost tip of Newfoundland, their curiosity likely would not have been satisfied after just one day's sailing along the east and west coasts of Newfoundland and the south coast of Labrador, as Samuel Morison (1971) would like us to believe.

We know that Erik the Red spent three years exploring Greenland from south to north and covered it so well within that period that he chose absolutely the best farming area in this vast country. Accounts of early exploration in Iceland as they are remembered in the *Book of Settlements* suggest a similar procedure: first several people visited the country, sailed around it, and only after several such voyages did the first settler arrive, exploring about one hundred twenty miles (two hundred kilometers) of the coast for three years before he settled in Reykjavík—again an ideal location from his perspective. This suggests that people did not regard building temporary winter camps as a major obstacle; they expected to spend several years in such camps exploring new territories before they decided where to settle.

FITTING THE PIECES TOGETHER

Having realized the nature of all these difficulties and disagreement we can suggest that some sequence of events is more likely than others and some places are more likely than others in view of the threefold advances made in Vinland studies since earlier this century: 1) Our knowledge and understanding of the oral tradition has improved immensely; 2) We have found one Viking site in North America; 3) We know that both sagas were written independently from an oral tradition, thus making them both of equal value as sources but at the same time allowing for varying preferences. Analyzing the detailed descriptions the sagas contain, preferring the more detailed accounts and believing those

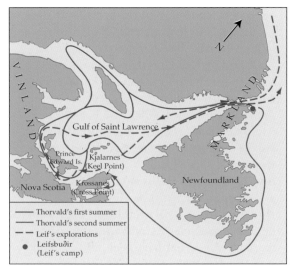

16.4. Explorations According to the *Greenlanders' Saga*

Gísli Sigurdsson has reconstructed the explorations of Leif, Thorvald, and Bjarni as told in *Greenlanders' Saga* in this illustration.

16.5. Floor plan of Erik the Red's farm in Breiða Fjord

Excavated by the National Museum of Iceland.

who have more to tell rather than less, it is possible to suggest the following locations for the places mentioned in the sagas.

According to the *Greenlanders' Saga*, Leif's brother Thorvald stayed the winter in a camp called Leifsbuðir (fig. 16.4). The location of this camp matches L'Anse aux Meadows on the northern tip of Newfoundland. The saga describes a voyage of exploration on the western side of the land in the first year; and the year after, they go north around the land and down the eastern side, crossing open sea before they break their ship on a peninsula, possibly Cape Breton Island, which they name Kjalarnes (Keel's Point).

Thorfinn Karlsefni and Gudrid lead three ships on a major voyage, two from Iceland and one manned by Greenlanders, all in all carrying 160 people (both sagas describe this voyage but *Erik the Red's Saga* has the more detailed description). They do not stop at Leifsbuðir but sail until they reach a peninsula with a broken keel; the text indicated already that Kjalarnes is south of Thorvald's camp; now it appears that it is also north of Straumfjord, which Karlsefni reaches later in his journey. This may also suggest that there was more than one base camp. From here Karlsefni and his men sail south with the land on the starboard, along what they

call Furðurstrandir (Wonder strand) (fig. 16.1) and beyond, where they find wild wheat and grapes. Finally they come to a fjord with very strong currents and an island at its mouth, which they name Straumfjord (Current Fjord). Karlsefni then goes south until he finds a river that flows into a sea lake with sandy bars and shallow waters at its mouth, which he calls Hóp (Tidal Pool). Karlsefni stays in Hóp through the very mild winter. He then returns north to Straumfjord and eventually heads north around the peninsula at Kjalarnes.

These very general descriptions fit the facts rather well nevertheless and give us a strong feeling that Leif's Vinland was in the Gulf of Saint Lawrence and that Karlsefni and Gudrid ventured south along the eastern coast of Nova Scotia, possibly as far south as the Bay of Fundy and perhaps even further. The Bay of Fundy can rightly be called a Straumfjord as it has more tidal difference, forty-nine to fifty-two feet (fifteen to sixteen meters) on average, than any other place on earth. The saga description of the qualities of Vinland, as well as the island and the strait explored by Leif, cannot possibly be made to fit the reality of L'Anse aux Meadows without severe text emendations or allowances for major literary embellishments of geographic facts. This shows us that the Leifsbuðir in later expeditions cannot both be referring to Leif's Vinland and L'Anse aux Meadows.

We can deduce from a close reading of the descriptions in the *Greenlanders' Saga* of Leif's voyage navigational directions that can be used to navigate a Viking ship from Newfoundland across the Gulf of Saint Lawrence or the Cabot Strait, to Prince Edward Island and into the Northumberland Strait. First they go ashore on the island and drink the sweet dew from the meadow, but after they have entered the strait it is not clear from the text whether they are supposed to go ashore on the island or the mainland. The saga therefore leaves open the possibility for the description to fit the Miramichi Bay on the coast of New Brunswick shortly after one comes out of the Northumberland Strait on the western side. And in this general region all the Vinlandian delicacies are to be found except for the mild winter referred to in the saga, which would then be the only misfit in all these descriptions.

If this reading is accepted we can also explain all the directions given in ES about Karlsefni's voyage when he and his mates are referred to as sailing north from their

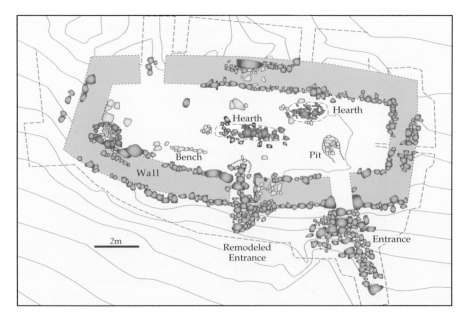

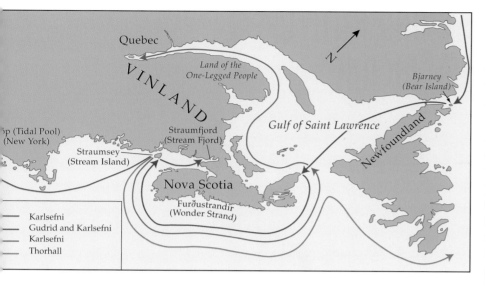

Quebec

V I N L A N D

Land of the
One-Legged People

Bjarney
(Bear Island)

Gulf of Saint Lawrence

Newfoundland

ɔp (Tidal Pool)
(New York)

Straumfjord
(Stream Fjord)

Straumsey
(Stream Island)

Nova Scotia

Furðustrandir
(Wonder Strand)

N

— Karlsefni
— Gudrid and Karlsefni
— Karlsefni
— Thorhall

EXPLORATIONS ÁCCORDING TO ERIK THE RED'S SAGA

Thorfinn Karlsefni is given credit in *Erik the Red's Saga* for exploring Vinland. Gisli Sigurdsson has suggested these routes for his voyages.

Straumfjord to round a peninsula and then turn west with land on their port side to find the Vinland of Leif Eriksson. These directions make sense if Straumfjord was located in the southern regions of Nova Scotia. It also makes sense that Karlsefni did not find any salmon in Hóp—as Leif did in his Vinland according to GS — but only some kind of flatfish—bearing in mind the southern limit of the salmon in the Middle Ages.

How far south from Straumfjord to Hóp Karlsefni may have gone is impossible to tell but reasonable suggestions have been made for anywhere along the coast of New England, even as far south as New York (Berg þórsson 1997). If they went that far south, however, these northerners would have experienced wind and water conditions that required different navigational techniques that what they used.

Because the sagas were written from oral accounts many generations after the actual events took place, they cannot be used to prove the exact location of any of the sites described

therein. In spite of these uncertainties the overall picture of the voyages that emerges from the texts is reasonably clear: around the year 1000 people from Greenland and Iceland went on several voyages along the eastern coast of North America, into the Gulf of Saint Lawrence and farther south. In more than one location they built camps in this area and spent from one winter up to a few years in them. They came into contact with natives, partly on friendly commercial terms, but they also fought battles with them. Internal conflicts as well as attacks from the natives eventually led to their departure. After that it is unlikely that the Greenlanders continued to go as far south as the sagas tell, but judging from a casual reference in an Icelandic annal it is probable that Greenlanders went to Labrador on a regular basis to get wood all through the Middle Ages.

Many lived to tell of these early adventures in Iceland when writers compiled surviving stories several generations later and preserved them in the written sagas. And where do you go if you are in L'Anse aux Meadows around the year 1000 with your Viking ship in the spring? Where do you go if you have a whole summer ahead of you to explore new lands and gather goods to bring home to Greenland? You are bound to go south and into the Gulf of Saint Lawrence. You hunt for the fruits and vegetation Greenland lacks, and you may even try to settle in some places. Finding the land already crowded with native people, you end up going back home. You spend the rest of your life boasting of the great time you had with your mates when you spent the summers sailing across the seven seas and finding new and previously unheard of lands … just like the Icelandic sagas tell us.

17 | THE NORSE AND NATIVE NORTH AMERICANS

BY PATRICIA D. SUTHERLAND

SKRAELING WAS THE DEROGATORY Old Norse word for the aboriginal peoples they encountered in Greenland and further west. During the centuries that the Norse occupied southwestern Greenland and made occasional ventures to the northeastern coasts of North America, that portion of the continent was occupied by three discrete aboriginal populations. The forested coasts extending northward from New England to central Labrador were the homelands of several distinct Indian peoples. These groups were ancestral to the Innu of Labrador, the Beothuk of Newfoundland, and the Micmac, Maliseet, Penobscot, and other Algonquian-speaking peoples of the lands to the south of the Saint Lawrence River. Iroquoian-speaking communities who occupied the Saint Lawrence Valley upstream from the present location of Quebec City may have made summer visits to the Atlantic coast, as did their sixteenth-century descendants.

OFFERING A DRINK, *HEYNESBÓK*

The treeless tundra of northern Labrador and the Canadian Arctic islands was the home of a Paleo-eskimo people known as the Dorset culture, ancient inhabitants of the Arctic whose ancestors had pioneered these lands more than four thousand years ago. It may have been the remains of Dorset settlements that Erik the Red discovered during his initial exploration of southwestern Greenland, but archaeological evidence supports the saga statements that native people no longer occupied southwestern Greenland between A.D. 1000 and 1400. Dorset people, however, continued to live in northwestern Greenland, perhaps in pockets along the Greenlandic east coast, the Canadian Arctic islands, and the tundra of northern Labrador and the Ungava Peninsula between the Labrador Sea and Hudson Bay. The Dorset people and their way of life disap-peared from the Arctic some time between the thirteenth and fifteenth centuries.

At about the same time that the Norse reached Greenland, another aboriginal people known as the Thule culture were moving eastward across Arctic Canada from their homelands in Alaska. During the eleventh or twelfth centuries, these ancestors of the Inuit reached the western shores of Baffin Bay. Here they flourished, gradually displacing the Dorset occupants of the area. By the time the Norse colonies disappeared, the Inuit were in possession of all of Greenland and Arctic Canada.

Norse accounts of contact with aboriginal peoples in North American and Greenland are few and vague (McGhee 1984b, Arneborg 1997). The saga accounts were recorded in writing at least two centuries after the events they report, so we cannot be confident that the brief descriptions of

17.1 "Bishop of Baffin"

The small wooden doll found in a thirteenth- or fourteenth-century Thule Inuit site on southern Baffin Island depicts an individual wearing a long split-fronted robe or tunic with edge trim that closely resembles Norse clothing of the period. A faintly incised cross on the chest has led some to suggest this may be an Inuit depiction of a priest, a missionary, or even a Teutonic knight.

17.2 Sandnes Arrow Point

This chipped-stone arrowhead was found near the cemetery at Sandnes, the location in Greenland's Western Settlement from which the Eriksson family staged their Vinland voyages. Of a type of stone unknown in Greenland but common to Labrador and Newfoundland Indian cultures of A.D. 1000, this small find indicates direct contact between Vikings and Native North Americans. Perhaps it was even brought to Greenland in the body of a Norseman.

aboriginal people, their boats, weapons, or ways of life were accurately preserved through generations of oral transmission. The annals and other accounts that record events during the thirteenth to fifteenth centuries were written shortly after the events that they reported, but their reliability may be distorted by political or religious considerations related to the motives for recording the events (see Sigurðsson, chapter 16). In general, the historical records deriving from the Norse colonies can only be considered as indicating when and where some contacts occurred between Norse and aboriginals and providing hints as to the nature of some of these meetings. We must assume that other unrecorded contacts did occur, and perhaps only encounters of a certain nature were thought worthy of record.

The Norse applied the term *skraeling* to all the aboriginal groups they met in the New World, including both those encountered during the early Norse voyages to Vinland and Markland and those who moved into Greenland between the twelfth and thirteenth centuries. One of the tasks of archaeology, therefore, is to determine which aboriginal populations encountered the Norse and the nature of the relationships that developed at different places and at different periods. The encounters are best summarized in terms of the four geographical areas the Norse occupied or explored in the northwestern Atlantic: Greenland, Helluland, Markland, and Vinland. Each of these areas had a distinct history of aboriginal contact, with encounters occurring at different periods in the history of Norse occupation, involving different peoples, and probably producing quite different results.

Markland and Vinland: Contact with Indians

The first recorded contact with Indians occurred around A.D. 1000 in the forested areas named Markland and Vinland during the early Norse voyages of exploration to the west and south of Greenland. The saga descriptions relate to meetings in the vicinity of the Norse stations in Vinland involving trade followed by skirmishes with the natives, and it is clear that the presence of a hostile native

force was an important element in the Norse decision to abandon settlement of the region. Archaeological evidence indicates that the *skraeling* of Vinland, as well as those whom the Norse encountered and fought in Markland, must have been Indians and probably ancestors of the Newfoundland Beothuk and the Labrador Innu. Norse exploration parties probably encountered other groups during voyages around the Gulf of Saint Lawrence. These would have included ancestral Micmac and Maliseet or even Iroquois encountered during summer hunting or trading journeys to the Strait of Belle Isle and the Gaspé. Indian populations around the Gulf of Saint Lawrence must have been significantly larger than those that would have been met along the subarctic coasts of Labrador and Newfoundland, and the Norse would have been extremely cautious in dealing with such groups.

Archaeological evidence relating to Indian-Norse contact is practically nonexistent. Although archaeological remains of Indian occupation have been found in the vicinity of the Norse settlement at the site of L'Anse aux Meadows, there is no indication that the people who left these remains lived there at the same time as the Norse. The only possible hint of contact comes from a stray archaeological find in Greenland; a stone projectile point, very similar in style and material to those used during this period by Indians of Newfoundland and Labrador, was found eroding in the Norse graveyard at Sandnes in the Western Settlement (fig. 17.2) (Roussel 1936: 106).

Perhaps the absence of archaeological evidence of contact in North American sites is not due to chance. As will be seen later, a relatively low-level relationship between the Norse and the Inuit in Arctic Canada resulted in the transfer of metal and other European artifacts into native hands, and this material has been wi-dely recovered from ar-

chaeological sites. If Norse-Indian encounters had been relatively extensive, a similar result would be expected. It therefore seems quite possible that Norse-Indian contact was no more extensive than that which was actually

17.3, 17.4 RICHMOND GULF PENDANT

17.3, 17.4 RICHMOND GULF PENDANT

This pendant (fig. 17.4) made from reworked Norse copper was found at a twelfth-century site on the east coast of Hudson Bay (fig. 17.3). One of the first Norse-related objects found in a Dorset site in the Canadian Arctic, it was probably transported to Hudson Bay through native trade networks from Labrador or Baffin Island, where Norse contacts would have been more likely to occur.

described in the *Vinland Saga* accounts: brief attempts to trade quickly undermined by misunderstandings and outbreaks of violence. Such situations would have been exacerbated by the fact that the Norse in Markland and Vinland were far from their Greenlandic home base. Norse exploration parties in these distant regions would have been small relative to the size of communities they would have encountered in Indian lands. In these lands, the Icelanders and Greenlanders would have found themselves in an alien forested environment, which must have contributed to their unease and insecurity. Contacts between Norse and Indians may have been limited to rare and cautious encounters, and the one archaeological hint of such contact—the projectile point from the graveyard at Sandnes—may be an accurate reflection of the nature of relations between the two peoples.

HELLULAND: CONTACT WITH DORSET PALEO-ESKIMOS

The slight historical evidence for later Norse voyages to North America is limited to an account of a small Greenlandic ship being storm-driven to Iceland in 1347 while on a voyage from Markland. It has been suggested that the motive for such voyages was most likely the acquisition of timber for Greenlandic construction needs (Seaver 1999). Logging expeditions would most likely have been directed to the most northerly forested

regions of the Labrador coast, adjacent to the tundra regions occupied at the time by Dorset peoples, that were probably a portion of the treeless country the Norse named Helluland. Contact between Norse and the Dorset occupants of these regions is evidenced by two archaeological finds of small objects made from smelted copper, products of a technology unknown to aboriginal peoples of northern North America. One object was recovered from a twelfth- or thirteenth-century Dorset site in Richmond Gulf on the eastern coast of Hudson Bay (fig. 17.4) (Harp 1974–75) and the other from a similar site on Hudson Strait (Plumet 1982: 262).

A coin recovered from an Indian settlement site on the coast of Maine was at first thought to be further evidence of Norse-Indian trade and possibly as evidence that the Norse had penetrated regions as far south as coastal New England. The Goddard site, where the coin was found, represents the remains of what may have been the largest coastal settlement in Maine at the time of the Norse voyages (Bourque and Cox 1981; Cox, sidebar, p. 206). The coin, however, probably does not represent evidence that the Norse traveled this far to the south of Greenland. The specimen is a Norse penny minted between 1065 and 1080, more than fifty years later than the Vinland voyages recorded in Icelandic sagas. Reexcavation of the Goddard site, which was probably occu-

PATRICIA D. SUTHERLAND

17.5

17.6

17.5, 17.6 WOODEN FIGURINES
This figure, which has been symbolically killed by having a hole gouged through its body, may have been made by a shaman to cause injury to the person or spirit represented. The horned figure (fig. 17.6) reveals the Dorset artist's ability to draw inspiration from raw material, in this case the potential of eroded driftwood.

pied during the thirteenth century as well as at other times according to radiocarbon dates, yielded evidence that the occupants of the site chipped some of their stone tools from Ramah chert, a particularly valuable type of stone that derives from a quarry in northern Labrador. At this time the region was in the hands of the Dorset, who must have traded local resources with their Indian neighbors to the south. The northern Labrador stone supplies, the Norse penny, and two distinctive Dorset artifacts also found on the site in Maine must have reached its occupants through an extensive trade network leading from the north (Bourque and Cox 1981). The penny probably reached North America on a Norse ship and passed into Dorset hands somewhere on the coast of Labrador, either through trade or as the result of a skirmish with a shore party. It then could have been traded southward to Indian groups, along with a shipment of stone.

Contacts between the Norse and the Dorset occupants of northern Labrador may have begun significantly earlier than the date of the Norse penny. A small soapstone lamp carved in a characteristically Dorset form (fig. 14.20), which was associated with the

Norse remains at L'Anse aux Meadows, provides evidence of such encounters. The Dorset people had deserted Newfoundland and southern Labrador several centuries before the arrival of the Norse in the region, and this lamp is most readily explained as an object the Norse obtained from the Dorset or from an abandoned Dorset site in northern Labrador or the eastern arctic prior to a visit to the Newfoundland settlement (Ingstad 1985: 92, 217).

Norse contact with Dorset people was not limited to Labrador. A nearly ten-foot (three-meter) length of yarn spun from the fur of arctic hare was recovered from a Late Dorset dwelling at a site on northern Baffin Island. Spinning was not a part of the technology of northern aboriginal peoples, suggesting that this specimen originated in a European community. This supposition is supported by the identification of several goat hairs in the yarn and by the discovery of very similar cloth made of yarn spun from hare fur and goat hair from Gård Under Sandet (Farm Beneath the Sand), a Norse farm site in the Western Settlement of Greenland (Rogers 1998, 1999; Berglund, this volume). The acquisition by the Dorset people of a length of spun yarn hints at a form of contact more complex than a simple trade in useful metal objects.

Far to the north, a piece of smelted iron appears to be associated with the Late Dorset occupation of a site on Axel Heiberg Island on the extreme northwestern fringes of Dorset habitation. Together with material of Norse origin recently recovered from a Late Dorset site in northwestern Greenland (Appelt et al. 1998), as well as the yarn from Baffin Island, this find suggests that contacts between the Norse and Dorset people, although probably infrequent, must have occurred over a wide area from Labrador to the High Arctic.

Another archaeological hint of such contact appears in the occasional representation of Europeanlike faces in the art of the Dorset. The Dorset people produced numerous small sculptures in ivory, antler, or wood representing a wide range of animals and humans or humanlike creatures (fig. 13.5). The art seems to have been intimately associated with their shamanistic religious beliefs and view of the world, and among their work are several forms of artifacts that may have been the equipment of shamanic

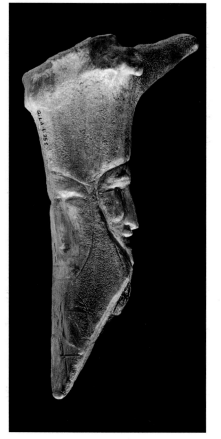

17.7

17.8

17.7, 17.8 DORSET FACES
Simply rendered human faces on bone, antler, and ivory are a common theme in Dorset art. This antler beam from a Bathurst Island site reveals an amusing Dorset profile (fig. 17.7), while the weathered bone from Axel Heiberg Island has a more typical stylized Dorset face (fig. 17.8).

practitioners. One such recurring artifact is in the form of a billet of antler, or occasionally of wood, containing relief carvings of human faces (figs. 17.6–17.8). The carvings on these batons depict a range of images, but a distinctive long and narrow face with a prominent straight nose and occasional hints of a beard appears on several specimens, one of which came from the same Baffin Island winter house that produced the piece of Norse yarn. It is tempting to suggest that these portrayals may represent the strangers who occasionally landed on the coasts inhabited by the Dorset people.

A possible early meeting with Dorset inhabitants of the barren east coast of Greenland may be described in *Saga of the People of Floi,* an account generally considered to incorporate much fictional material. There is also a possibility that some of the saga descriptions of *skraeling* whom the Norse encountered in Markland while on their Vinland voyages may refer to Dorset people. Aside from these, none of the encounters with *skraeling* mentioned in Norse sagas or annals can be convincingly interpreted as representing contact with Dorset

groups. Yet if the Norse made occasional visits to Labrador over a period of two or three centuries to obtain timber or other commodities, they would have sailed along the shores of Baffin Island and northern Labrador, areas occupied by Dorset people until the fourteenth century. Some communication with the Norse would seem to have been likely, and the archaeological finds noted earlier suggest that such contacts could have occurred sporadically from perhaps the eleventh to thirteenth centuries. These two peoples may have been more predisposed to establish a trading relationship than would the Norse and Indians. Both the Dorset and the Norse were comfortable in the tundra environments where such meetings would have occurred, and Dorset populations were sparse enough in many regions that they would not have threatened small Norse exploration or trading parties.

HELLULAND AND GREENLAND: CONTACT WITH THE INUIT

The most prolonged and probably the most extensive contact was to occur with the third group of aboriginals whom the Norse encountered, the Thule people who moved eastward from Alaska to occupy most of Arctic Canada and Greenland at about the same time that the Norse were venturing into the northwestern Atlantic.

The nature and timing of the Inuit expansion into the eastern Arctic is poorly understood. The process must have required a significant duration and comprised several distinct phases. Initially, it was thought that the ancestral Inuit must have moved quickly through the relatively unproductive channels of the central Arctic at some time between the eleventh and thirteenth centuries. Such a hazardous enterprise must have been propelled by a compelling motive, and it has been suggested that the Inuit of the western Arctic had learned that the eastern Arctic held a source of iron, which was an extremely valuable commodity in early Inuit culture (McGhee 1984c). If this hypothesis is correct, the attracting source may have been either the deposits of meteoritic iron deposits in northwestern Greenland or smelted metal that could be obtained by trade with the Greenlandic Norse. The Inuit of the western Arctic may have learned of either source, as well as of the rich sea-mammal resources of the eastern Arctic, from the Dorset Paleo-

17.9 HOUSE 4, SKRAELING ISLAND

Peter Schledermann's excavation team records the interior of one of the thirteenth-century Thule houses on Skraeling Iseland, off the east coast of Ellesmere Island, that contained Norse artifacts together with Thule-culture materials.

eskimo occupants of Arctic Canada.

The early Inuit migrants from the western Arctic are known to archaeology as the Thule people. Our views on the nature of relationships between these Thule people and the Dorset, Indian, and Norse peoples whom they encountered in the eastern Arctic are based on our reconstruction of early Inuit social and economic patterns. The Thule people probably lived year-round in small communities with an average population of approximately thirty to fifty people, although larger communities must have existed at locations where food was abundant. Most such communities may have supported at least ten to twenty hunters accustomed to working together and under the direction of an *umealik* (hunting captain). Armed with lances and with bows powered by a cable of twisted sinew, as well as with warlike traditions developed in the large competing communities of coastal Alaska, such a band of warriors would have been a formidable enemy. They could have easily displaced the small and poorly armed communities of Dorset people from prime hunting localities, forcing them to retreat to more marginal areas. They would also have been a fair match for the crews of Greenlandic Norse ships.

In their dealings with the Norse, the Thule people would not have been at any social, cultural, or technological disadvantage with the Norse communities in Greenland. The Norse left no known accounts of possible encounters with the Inuit in Arctic

Canada; the records of contact in Greenland are meager, report only a few instances of hostilities, and are difficult to interpret. In contrast, archaeological evidence demonstrates that material of Norse origin found its way into the hands and the trade routes of the Canadian Arctic Inuit. This evidence suggests that contact may have been considerably more extensive and complex than the few skirmishes mentioned in Norse accounts: discussions center on three quite different scenarios (Arneborg 1996, 1997). The first was the prevailing opinion among archaeologists during the first half of the century, when Inuit occupations had not yet been dated and when evidence of contact was limited to Inuit sites in Greenland. This view was based on the lack of historical records reporting contacts and suggested that Norse material in the hands of Inuit had been scavenged from the abandoned remains of the Norse colonies during the centuries after these colonies disappeared. This hypothesis assumed that Inuit sites containing Norse materials dated to later than the mid-fourteenth century, when historical accounts suggest a general Norse abandonment of the Western Settlement.

The past decades have yielded evidence for an Inuit presence in western Greenland significantly earlier than the disappearance of Norse occupation (Gulløv 1982), suggesting that Norse-Inuit relations must have been more complex than the simple looting of abandoned farms. Inuit sites in Arctic Canada at which Norse materials have been found have been dated to between the eleventh and thirteenth centuries, and the associated European objects were therefore most probably derived from direct contact between Norse and Inuit. This assumption leads to two alternative scenarios regarding the nature of such contact. On the one hand, it may be suggested that most or all Norse material in the possession of Inuit living far to the north and west of the Norse colonies was obtained as a result of a single event. Perhaps this was a successful attack by Inuit on a Norse ship's crew engaged in exploration or in the exploitation of a distant resource; perhaps the salvage of a wrecked Norse ship engaged in such activity; or perhaps a single major trading encounter occurring somewhere along the coasts of the eastern Arctic (see Schledermann, chapter 18). Alternately, the evidence can be inter-

17.10 a, b

17.11 a, b

17.10, 17.11 REFASHIONING
NORSE IRON

Both Dorset and Thule people used
meteoritic iron from the Cape York
meteor fall in northwest Greenland,
but small pieces of Norse iron and
copper—when they could be
obtained—were easier to make into
knives and points. Boat rivets were
especially easy to hammer into
blades and points.

preted as resulting from numerous minor encounters occurring over a period of centuries
and in several locations. The spatial and temporal distribution of materials of Norse origin, as well as the nature of such materials,
may allow us to assess the relative probability
of these alternate explanations.

Material of European origin that probably originated with the Greenlandic Norse
has been recovered from the archaeological
remains of Thule Inuit settlements across
much of the Canadian Arctic (figs. 17.10,
17.11). Unfortunately, precise dates are not
known for most of these sites, which have
generally been assigned to "Early Thule" or
"Classic Thule" phases assumed to have
existed between the eleventh and fifteenth
centuries A.D. A knife blade of smelted iron
has been recovered from a Thule winter

house on the Amundsen Gulf coast of the
western Canadian Arctic (David Morrison,
personal communication, 1999). This specimen may have been traded across the Bering
Strait from Siberia, but it seems equally likely
to have reached the area through trade routes
from the eastern Arctic. Three small specimens of smelted iron have been found in
Thule villages of similar age and located at a
similar distance from Greenland on the west
coast of Hudson Bay in the central Arctic
(McCartney and Mack 1973). To the north,
four early Thule winter villages on the southern coasts of Bathurst and Cornwallis islands
have yielded several pieces of bronze and
smelted copper (Franklin et al. 1981:16;
McGhee 1984b: 75-76). Smelted iron objects
have been found in Thule sites on Somerset
Island (Whitridge 1999), northern Ellesmere
Island, and eastern Axel Heiberg Island
(Sutherland 1989,1993).

The dispersion of these materials indicates the existence of widespread trade among
the Inuit groups who occupied Arctic Canada
during the Thule period, but tell us little
about the way in which the metal first came
into Inuit possession. The presence of specimens composed of meteoritic iron at most of
these sites indicates the existence of trade in
metal that originated in northwestern Greenland, the only known source of meteoritic
iron in Arctic North America. A parallel
route may have existed for the dispersion of
Norse materials, perhaps from a single High
Arctic source such as that described by
Schledermann, chapter 18. The Thule
culture sites located in the Bache Peninsula
region of Ellesmere Island, and related sites
in adjacent regions of northwestern Greenland, have produced the greatest concentration and widest variety of Norse materials
known from an Inuit context (fig. 17.9)
(Schledermann 1980, 1990). If this concentration is the result of a single event, as
Schledermann suggests, then this event may
also have provided the source for much of
the smelted metal found in Inuit sites elsewhere in Arctic Canada. On the other hand,
this diverse collection of metal objects may
have derived from a diversity of sources.

A few Inuit sites in Arctic Canada have
produced items that have greater potential
for information on the nature of Norse-
Inuit contact. One such item is a portion of
a cast bronze pot excavated from a Thule
winter house on the coast of Devon Island's

17.12

17.13

17.12 Bronze Pot Fragment

Scholars wonder how native people acquired bronze pot fragments because it is not likely that Norse would have traded such valuable materials. This example was found in a Devon Island Thule winter house; a fragment from a different vessel was recovered from a thirteenth-century Late Dorset site in northern Greenland (Arneborg and Gulløv 1998).

17.13 Folding Balance Arm

How did this fragment of a bronze trader's scale, found in a Thule site on the northwest coast of Ellesmere Island, reach this remote location? Why would a Norseman have carried—and parted with—such a valuable item on a trip into the ice-choked waters of northern Davis Strait? Could Norse have been engaged in formal European-style trade with Thule people? Like the valuables found at Thule sites on Skraeling Island and nearby Greenland, it was more likely obtained from the Norse by some act of violence or disaster than by trade.

Grinnell Peninsula (fig. 17.12) (McGhee 1984b: 17). This pot appears to be of northern European origin and of a type first produced during the late thirteenth or fourteenth centuries. If the incident of Norse contact in the High Arctic described by Schledermann occurred during the mid-thirteenth century, this pot may have come into Inuit hands as a result of a later episode and hints at a more complex history of contact with the Norse. Fragments of bronze vessels have also been reported from Thule (Holtved 1944) and Late Dorset (Appelt et al. 1998) occupations in northwestern Greenland.

A Thule site on the northwestern coast of Ellesmere Island provides a further hint at the nature of Norse-Inuit relations. This evidence is in the form of a portion broken from a bronze balance of the type used by traders throughout the Norse world (figs. 6.1, 17.13). The folding-arm design of this balance was in use throughout both the Viking Age and the Middle Ages, but the large size of this specimen is not typical of the earlier centuries of Norse culture. This is a type of artifact we would expect to find in the

possession of a medieval Norse trader and suggests the possibility of a more deliberate form of relationship between the two societies than that resulting from either a single shipwreck or the looting of abandoned farms.

More extensive contact is suggested by an object recovered from a Thule village on the south coast of Baffin Island (Sabo and Sabo 1978). This is a small figure carved from driftwood depicting a human figure in what is apparently European clothing (fig. 17.1). The style of the carving is typical of local Inuit representation, with a flat featureless face and arms reduced to short stumps, but the figure is clothed in a hooded ankle-length European-style cloak or gown split up the front to waist level. Lightly incised lines may represent a decorative edging, and a pair of similar lines seem to indicate a cross on the middle of the chest.

It has been suggested that the gown and cross represent the clothing of a Christian priest, perhaps seen by the Baffin Island Inuit while he was on a missionary visit to the area. Large pectoral crosses do not, however, appear to have been worn by medieval priests but by members of crusading orders (Rousselière 1982). In fact, the costume depicted on this carving could well represent that worn by Teutonic knights during the thirteenth and fourteenth centuries when the order flourished in northern Europe. As their crusading efforts in Palestine declined, the efforts of the Teutonic knights were concentrated on fighting the Baltic and Slavic peoples bordering their power base in Prussia. During this period, the order attracted itinerant warriors from across northern Europe and served a diversity of religious and political causes. The growing influence of the Hanseatic cities in Norwegian trade after the establishment of their base at Bergen in 1344 may have provided the opportunity for individuals of this order to become involved in Norse matters. It would not seem impossible that such individuals would be attracted to missions organized to defend or rescue Greenlandic Christianity, such as those hinted at in fourteenth-century records. It is generally thought that expeditions such as that called for in 1355 by King Magnus Eriksson did not actually occur (Jones 1986: 101; Seaver 1996:111). However, a possible representation of a Teutonic knight from the eastern coast of Arctic Canada may suggest that this view should be reconsidered.

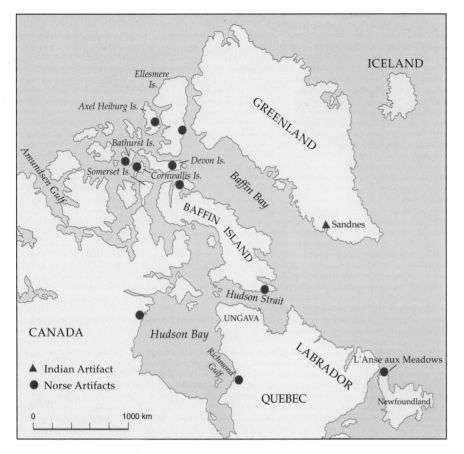

NORSE ARTIFACTS IN NORTH AMERICA

CONCLUSION

The sagas and other records written by early Icelandic historians make no distinction between the three quite different aboriginal populations whom the Norse met in northeastern North America. All are called by the disparaging term *skraeling*, and the sagas and annals refer only to occasional antagonistic encounters.

The archaeological evidence suggests a more complex series of relationships involving all three northern aboriginal populations and taking different forms in each of the regions the Norse occupied or visited at different times. The earliest contacts may have been with Indian inhabitants of Vinland encountered in the decades around 1000 during the early period of Norse exploration. Archaeological information relating to such contacts is practically nonexistent, providing slight confirmation for the saga accounts of brief and hostile meetings between Indians and Norse. No archaeological finds hint at Norse penetration of regions to the south or west of the Gulf of Saint Lawrence, and in fact the evidence for relatively dense Indian populations in these lands strongly suggests that the Norse would have been wary of visiting such regions.

Contact with the Dorset peoples of Arctic Canada may have begun during the early Vinland voyages and seems to have continued at least occasionally for the following two or three centuries. These encounters most likely took place along the eastern coasts of the Arctic Archipelago and the adjacent treeless regions of northern Labrador and may have been incidental to Norse expeditions in search of timber, bog iron, or other materials unavailable in the Greenlandic environment. The Norse may have been tempted to contact Dorset groups to trade small amounts of metal for walrus ivory, narwhal tusks, furs, or other products of value in Greenland and Europe. The small amount of Norse metal recovered to date from the remains of Dorset settlements suggests, however, that if such trade did occur, it was not significant to either party.

The most extensive and enduring relationships between the Norse and aboriginal Americans appear to have been those that developed with the Inuit who immigrated to Arctic Canada, and subsequently to Greenland, during the period of Norse occupation. These were the *skraeling* who were first mentioned in Icelandic records as newcomers to the Norse hunting grounds in the mid-thirteenth century and who later are reported to have moved southward to the vicinity of the Greenlandic Norse colonies. The archaeology of Inuit settlements confirms this general picture, although suggesting that the date of Inuit arrival in the eastern Arctic was earlier than is indicated by Norse accounts.

The first contact between Inuit and Norse may have occurred in the far north, as suggested by Norse historical records, and this event may have resulted in the concentration of Norse materials found in the thirteenth-century Inuit villages of northwestern Greenland and eastern Ellesmere Island. Inuit groups may have been attracted southward into Greenland by the opportunities to trade with the Norse inhabitants, and the most extensive relationships between the two groups must have occurred along Greenland's western coast during the fourteenth and fifteenth centuries. The widespread distribution of materials of Norse origin in the Inuit settlements of this period in Arctic Canada hints at another set of contacts, however, that may have occurred along the western coasts of Baffin Bay. Norse voyages to this region continued until at least the mid-four-

PATRICIA D. SUTHERLAND

Century	Norse/Indian	Norse/Dorset	Norse/Inuit
11?	Stone weapon point from graveyard		
11	at Sandnes, Greenland	Soapstone lamp at L'Anse aux Meadows	
11–13		Iron fragment, Axel Heiberg Island	
12–13		Copper amulet, east coast Hudson Bay	
12-13		Copper fragment, south coast Hudson Strait	
12–13			Norse coin at Goddard site, Maine
13			Norse material from Bache Peninsula sites
12–14			Iron knife blade, Amundsen Gulf coast
12-14			Iron fragments, west coast Hudson Bay
14?			Metal fragments, central High Arctic sites
13–14			Bronze pot fragment, Devon Island
13–14			Bronze balance fragment, Ellesmere Island
13–14			Iron specimens, extreme High Arctic sites
13–14			Carving of European, south coast Baffin Island

Summary of archaeological evidence of contact between Norse and Native North Americans, with an estimate of the century during which the contact probably occurred. Locations of North American finds are indicated on the map, p. 246. Date estimates are based on calibrated radiocarbon dates, stylistics, and literary records.

teenth century, and the occasional meetings the Norse had probably undertaken with the earlier Dorset occupants of this region may have been continued with their Inuit successors. The Inuit were accomplished sea-mammal hunters and had access to supplies of walrus ivory, walrus hides, and other materials extremely valuable to the Norse. Like their descendants of later centuries, they were probably willing to trade this material for small pieces of iron, bronze, or copper, which was a scarce and necessary raw material for the cutting tools and weapons of Inuit technology.

A regular and extensive trade probably never developed between the two peoples, but it seems likely that over a period of two centuries the Norse and the Inuit of the eastern Arctic came to know one another and took occasional opportunities to profit from a trade beneficial to both parties. The Greenlandic Norse must have known the *skraeling* of Arctic Canada as more than a threat to landing parties or prey for Norse attackers.

The Inuit must have appreciated the benefits of dealing with the strangers who arrived in wooden ships and whom they probably knew as *qadlunat*, a term universally applied to Europeans when they once again arrived in the Arctic. When Martin Frobisher's exploration parties visited Arctic Canada in the 1570s, probably little more than a century after the Norse colonies disappeared, the Inuit of Baffin Island appeared familiar with Europeans as either trading partners or coastal raiders (Seaver 1999).

The archaeological and historical records can do no more than hint at the nature of relationships between the Norse and the aboriginal peoples of northeastern North America. Yet these hints point in a consistent direction: toward a suggestion that over a period of several centuries these peoples knew one another and knew of both the dangers and the benefits of meeting with strangers whose cultures had developed on opposite sides of the world.

18 | ELLESMERE

Vikings in the Far North

BY PETER SCHLEDERMANN

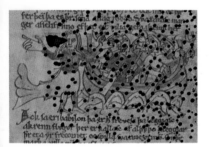

MEN IN ARMOR, *PHYSIOLOGUS*

F OR MORE THAN TWO CENTURIES, Nordsetur, thought by most scholars to be the greater Disko Bay region in western Greenland, had provided such indispensable commodities as walrus hides and tusks, narwhal turks, polar bear skins, the occasional live polar bear cub, and falcons (fig. 18.8). The Norsemen's very real need to seek better walrus and narwhal hunting grounds, combined with an enthusiasm for adventure, pushed their exploration farther and farther north along the west coast of Greenland. For generations the Nordsetur hunters had been unopposed in their quest for riches along the west coast of Greenland and had competed for the best hunting grounds only among themselves. In Markland (Labrador) large numbers of *skraeling* (Old Norse for native peoples) were always on hand to harass any Norse party looking for a load of timber. One portentous day, early in the thirteenth century, however, Norse hunters caught the first glimpse of foreigners in Nordsetur; the *skraeling* had arrived in the land the Norsemen thought to be exclusively their own. Whether in Vinland, Markland, or Greenland, the appearance of *skraeling* was not good news. Expert sea-mammal hunters, the newcomers chased and killed bowhead whales on the open sea using large skin boats called umiaks and hunted seals and walrus from sleek, skin-covered kayaks. When the seas froze and the land lay covered with snow, these *skraeling* traveled far and wide on sleds pulled by large teams of dogs.

Much like the Norsemen who had migrated westward and gradually settled the North Atlantic islands including southwest Greenland, the Inuit whale hunters were themselves part of an impressive migration process that had brought them eastward from the shores of the Bering and Chuckchi seas through the Canadian Arctic, all the way to Greenland in the north and to the coast of Labrador in the south. Today they are known as the Thule people because the first discoveries of their artifacts were made near present-day Thule in northern Greenland (fig. 18.7). Before the arrival of the Thule, who were ancestors of the modern Inuit (Eskimo), parts of Green-land were occupied by the Dorset people (fig. 18.4). There can be little doubt that occasionally the Thule encountered groups of Dorset people, although on this point the archaeological record is surprisingly inconclusive. From excavations on Ellesmere Island we know that the Dorset people in the High Arctic made good use of meteoritic iron from the Cape York area north of Melville Bay. The archaeological record from Ellesmere Island also suggests that the knowledge of this important iron source was transmitted to the pioneering Thule people who wasted little time crossing into Greenland in search of the iron stones

18.1 SNORRI IN ERIK'S FJORD
The reconstruction of Viking ships has not been left entirely to Scandinavian craftsmen. Hodding Carter built the *Snorri*, a knarr-style vessel, in Maine and sailed it from Greenland to L'Anse aux Meadows in 1998. Ice was a constant threat to Viking ships traveling west of Iceland; even a small chunk could create a hole large enough to sink a vessel.

18.2 SKRAELING ISLAND
This small island located off the east coast of Ellesmere Island was the site of a thirteenth-century Thule village. Among the items its occupants abandoned in their houses were Norse ship rivets, chain-mail armor, and wool fabrics. How the Thule people obtained these materials is a mystery.

have eyed the inset meteoritic iron blades with some interest—iron was a precious commodity in Norse Greenland. The impetus to set out on an expedition to explore unknown regions north of Melville Bay most likely came about as a result of early contact between Thule and Norse (fig. 18.1).

ARCHAEOLOGICAL EVIDENCE

In 1824 a runic stone was found in a cairn on Kingiktorssuaq Island north of present-day Upernavik, about thirty-six nautical miles (sixty-six kilometers) south of Melville Bay (fig. 24.2). The inscription states that three men—Bjarni Thorarson, Erlingur Sigvatsson, and Endridi Oddson—incised the runes and placed the stone in the cairn in late April. The three men undoubtedly spent the winter somewhere in the area. The dating of this event is generally accepted to be the middle to late thirteenth century (Stoklund 1982). If that date is correct, the first encounters between Inuit and Norse took place in Greenland. The three men who left the runic stone may have been part of a hunting expedition to the far north.

Between 1935 and 1937, the Danish archaeologist Erik Holtved began a series of archaeological excavations in the Thule district of northern Greenland (Holtved 1944). On Ruin Island, near the coast of Inglefield Land, Holtved excavated the ruins of seven Thule winter houses. Among the finds were a number of Norse artifacts that Holtved considered to be associated with the original use of the dwellings and placed the occupation to sometime in the thirteenth century. Radiocarbon dates on materials from the house ruins convinced later investigators that the Norse artifacts on Ruin Island had been deposited in the dwellings several hundred years following the initial Inuit occupation. The assumption that Thule-culture Inuit groups first arrived in Greenland around the middle of the tenth century—in other words prior to the Norse settlement of southern Greenland—remained fairly entrenched in scientific and popular writings about arctic prehistory until the 1970s.

Between 1977 and 1995 an extensive series of archaeological investigations were carried out on the central east coast of Ellesmere Island. The Buchanan Bay/Bache Peninsula region was chosen as a study area because of its close proximity to the Greenland coast and because it is the first

(Schledermann 1996). Shortly after 1200 the Thule people set out to cross the mighty Melville Bay, a barrier that seems to have been too formidable for the Late Dorset people to cross, perhaps explaining why southwestern Greenland was unpopulated when Erik the Red first arrived.

We will never know precisely where and when Norse Greenlanders first encountered Thule people, although it is reasonable to think that the meeting took place on the coast somewhere in the northern reaches of Nordsetur. The hunting prowess of the Thule probably impressed the Norse hunters, as did stories and indications, however transmitted, of excellent walrus and narwhal hunting far to the north. Norse hunters must also

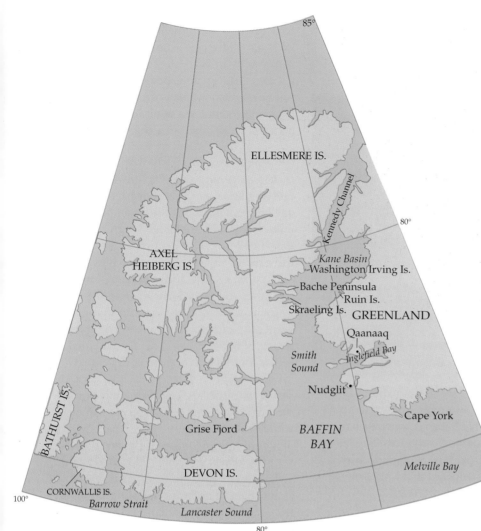

began in 1978 and by the end of the first season Sverdrup's choice of name seemed quite apt. Among the many exquisite Thule-culture artifacts, we also recorded a large chunk of rusted chain mail (fig. 18.12), an intact rivet from a Viking ship (fig. 18.10a), and a large section of an iron blade. The ship rivet was found in the bottom of an interior, stone-lined meat pit; the chain mail and the iron blade were on the floor nearby. A small piece of oak charcoal was found in the kitchen hearth. Just as significant was the discovery that the style of the Inuit houses and the associated artifacts reflected a strong and fairly recent connection to the original homelands in Alaska (fig. 13.2, 18.5). The Inuit inhabitants of the houses on Skraeling Island were themselves relative newcomers to the far north.

Between 1978 and 1995 the inventory of Norse artifacts from the east coast of Ellesmere Island grew steadily. By far the largest concentration of Norse finds came from house ruins on Skraeling Island (fig. 18.2). The finds included two pieces of woven woolen cloth (figs. 18.14, 18.15), ship rivets, knife and spear blades, iron wedges, a carpenter's plane (fig. 18.13), an awl, the chain mail, and several small individual chain-mail rings. The dwellings also yielded several pieces of meteoritic iron from Cape York in Greenland and sixty-two unanalyzed pieces of iron and copper most of which may very well be of Norse origin. Among the house ruins the greatest concentration of Norse items came from the *karigi* (large gathering house) (fig. 18.3).

The presence of meteoritic iron in these dwellings suggests that the Inuit newcomers had been either amazingly lucky to have discovered the Cape York meteorites so quickly or they had obtained the iron pieces from Dorset people encountered somewhere along the way. The radiocarbon-dated Late Dorset and Early Thule occupations in the Smith Sound region are statistically close enough to overlap and could support an argument for Dorset and Thule people having been contemporaneous in the far north.

Most of the Norse artifacts from the east coast of Ellesmere Island came from the earliest Thule-culture house ruins. In each case, there is no doubt about the association of the Norse and Inuit artifacts. A series of radiocarbon dates from the Skraeling Island site support a temporal sequence of events

place where it is possible to cross the ice-covered Kane Basin/Smith Sound in the winter. South of Smith Sound is a large polynia, the North Water, which never freezes over. During the summer, crossing the Smith Sound, which is twenty-eight miles (forty-five kilometers) wide, required only stamina and a spell of good weather (map).

On an early expedition Otto Sverdrup wintered in a small cove opposite Pim Island on the edge of Smith Sound (Sverdrup 1904). His expedition carried out extensive geographical surveys of the central east coast of Ellesmere Island, occasionally recording the remains of ancient camps along the way. Sverdrup named the largest of several islands at the head of Alexandra Fjord "Skraeling Island." In 1977 Tore Bjorgo and I visited the island to ascertain Sverdrup's reason for choosing this name. Almost immediately the answer lay before us: clusters of ruins of ancient Thule-culture winter houses built of sod, stone, and whalebone. Excavation of selected house ruins on Skraeling Island

18.3 **THULE TREASURE TROVE**
Because wood is scarce in the
treeless Arctic, Dorset and Thule
peoples dug their winter houses
into the ground, then raised
up walls of sod and stone and used
whalebone to put roofs over their
heads. When such houses collapsed,
the cultural materials became
permanently frozen—a treasure
trove for archaeologists.

that sees the Thule-culture Inuit arriving in
Ellesmere Island and Greenland nearly two
centuries following the Norse *landnám*
(McCullough 1989). Comparing the results
(house styles, artifact types, and Norse finds)
of excavations on Ellesmere Island with the
archaeological data from Holtved's excavations on Ruin Island shows that Holtved was
correct in his conclusion that the Norse finds
were associated with the original use of the
dwellings on Ruin Island, placing the occupation to sometime in the thirteenth century.
The concept of a later appearance of Thule
people in the Smith Sound region provides a
far more reasonable explanation for the timing of the first appearance of the Inuit in the
Disko Bay area of West Greenland around
1250, obviating the need to explain why it
should have taken Inuit families more than
two hundred years before they ventured
south of Melville Bay (Schledermann 1996).

In North Greenland five Norse artifacts
were located on Ruin Island (Holtved 1944:
Pl. 44), distributed in four houses, one of
which, House 6, was a *karigi*. Aside from a
Norse comb found in House 4, the Ruin
Island finds (woven cloth, game piece, and
lump of chain mail) are matched by the finds
from Skraeling Island. The radiocarbon date
of the woven cloth from Ruin Island (ca.
1260±100) and the date of the woven cloth
from Skraeling Island (ca. 1190±60) are
within acceptable range. The physical appearance and measurements of the chain-mail
rings from the two sites indicate that they
came from the same source. On both sites
the individual rings measure one-half inch

(between 11 and 12 millimeters) in outer
diameter and one quarter inch (between
6 and 7 millimeters) in inner diameter.

The appearance of the house ruins, the
radiocarbon dates, and the artifact styles
leave little doubt that the Norse artifacts
found on Ruin Island and Skraeling Island
are contemporaneous in the sense that they
derived from the same Norse voyage to the
High Arctic. The Norse items found on
Skraeling Island and not on Ruin Island—
that is, the unaltered and the reworked ship
rivets (fig. 18.10b), the wooden part of a
carpenter's plane, and the small wooden face
carving—may be the most crucial evidence
suggesting that the Inuit inhabitants of the
Skraeling Island dwellings had been in direct
contact with a party of Norse explorers on
the Ellesmere Island side of Smith Sound.
Although the ship rivets might have survived
intact as a trade item, one suspects that they
would have been mostly reworked if a long
trade route were involved. The fact that
some of the rivets are complete also suggests
that they were removed from joined sections
of ship's planks, perhaps salvaged from a
section of a ship's hull washed ashore after a
shipwreck. The relatively small number of
rivets in the artifact assemblage may also reflect limited Norse use of iron rivets and a
greater reliance on wooden pegs and cords of
baleen for fastening ship's planking, as mentioned by Nansen (1911: 305) and Nørlund
(1967: 68).

The complete carpenter's plane was cast
aside not far from the discarded piece of woven wool cloth. It is unlikely that the plane,
as a trade item, would have traveled very far
once the iron blade was removed. The small
carving of a face with non-Inuit features
(fig. 18.6) suggests that the Inuit artist on
Skraeling Island based his carving on an
encounter with Norsemen. It is also noteworthy that the hearth in the kitchen of
"the chain-mail house" on Skraeling Island
contained a small, charred fragment of oak,
dated to 1260±110, remarkably close to the
date of the woven cloth (1260±100) from
Ruin Island, and close to the date of the oak
member (dated to 1220±100) of the frame of
an ancient umiak discovered by Eigil Knuth
in Pearyland (Knuth 1984: 141). Perhaps all
these finds result from a single Norse expedition to northwestern Greenland.

Scattered Norse finds have come to
light beyond the Kane Basin/Smith Sound

region. Prior to 1978 excavations of Thule-culture sites in the Canadian Arctic produced a few items of Norse origin including pieces of iron from the west coast of Hudson Bay (McCartney and Mack 1973); a piece of smelted iron and a portion of a cast bronze bowl from Devon Island (McGhee 1976: 19); pieces of smelted copper and a bronze pendant from Bathurst Island (McGhee 1984: 15); a possible bronze balance arm (fig. 17.13) (Sutherland 1987); and a wooden figurine from the south coast of Baffin Island (fig. 17.1) (Sabo and Sabo 1978). These items are all believed to have reached their destinations through trade between Inuit groups and not as a result of direct contact with Norsemen.

Moving southeast from the Smith Sound region along the Greenland coast, in the direction of old Norse settlements, the trail of Norse finds, not surprisingly, is far more significant than to the west. Holtved's prolific excavations of thirty-seven house ruins on the Nugdlit site yielded two Norse iron blades from Houses 23 and 24B. His excavations of the Uummannaq site, south of Nugdlit, yielded seven pieces of Norse origin from Houses 16, 19, and 21West (Holtved 1944). One of the Norse items from the Uummannaq site, a chess piece, has a possible mate or counterpart in Inglefield Land where a similar chess piece was found in House 3 on the large Inuarfigssuaq site (Holtved 1944; pl. 44, p. 9). The chess piece from Inuarfigssuaq was not included with the Norse finds from Ruin Island because the configuration of House 3 could not be clearly identified as an early style of Thule dwelling.

At the southwestern end of northern Greenland, in the southern part of Melville Bay, five Norse artifacts were discovered in ruins of winter houses, thought to be from the earliest Thule-culture period (Grønnow 1981: fig. 6). The find consists of four chain-mail links and possibly a fragment of a ship rivet. Even though few details are available about their location, the Norse items seem to fit the assemblages from Skraeling Island and Ruin Island very well.

Timing, Cause, and Effect

The degree and the cultural effect of encounters between Norsemen and Inuit hunters have intrigued investigators over the centuries. Did the appearance of Thule people on the west coast of Greenland result in changes in the material, social, and spiritual nature of Norse society and vice versa? Although most arguments of this nature have rested principally on scarce documentary evidence and Inuit legends, archaeological data have occasionally been presented as evidence of such encounters. Based on the results of his excavations near Upernavik, Therkel Mathiassen (1931) proposed an Inugsuk phase of the Thule culture, which reflected a blending of Norse and Inuit material traits. Critical examination of the archaeological evidence from Mathiassen's work and other sites in western Greenland has been carried out by Jette Arneborg (1993). Arneborg concluded that the archaeological data alone does not reveal evidence of direct contact between the two peoples. Yet we know from much later Inuit accounts in Greenland that there was some contact, hostile or otherwise. Like the search for evidence of Dorset-Thule contact, providing convincing evidence of contact between two groups of people lies in the often-complex task of separating archaeological components. The argument for contact between the Inuit and the Norse in the far north is easier to support by confining the discussion to a time-restricted event, combined with the nature of the finds themselves, such as the carving of a non-Inuit face from Skraeling Island.

Broadening the discussion to include Norse finds from later Thule-culture sites on Ellesmere Island and in northern Greenland, we discover that such finds are scattered both in time and space. These items may have arrived in the far north through exchange between Inuit groups. Fifteen identifiably Norse items and sixteen unanalyzed or unidentified pieces of copper and iron have been located in later Thule-culture dwellings on the Sverdrup site, Haa Island, Eskimobyen, Inuarfigssuaq, Uummannaq, and Comer's Midden. The occupation of these sites appears to span a considerable time period, from about 1350 to 1700—from the time of the abandonment of the Western Settlement to a couple of decades before the arrival of the missionary Hans Egede on Haabets Island near present-day Nuuk.

For contact to be expressed in the archaeological record, elements must first of all

18.6, 18.7 IVORY FIGURE, WOODEN FACE

Only the initial outline of a figure has been carved into a walrus tusk by a Thule artist. The blank expression of this unfinished figurine contrasts the rough-hewn force of this wooden figure, whose visage, judging from its features and hair style, seems to be Norse.

18.6

18.7

18.8 SEAL HUNT

Olavus Magnus illustrated his description of northern cultures in 1555 with this woodcut showing Scandinavians hunting seals on the pack ice with boats and spears. Vikings also hunted seals, walrus, and polar bears with this method in Greenland. Dorset and Thule hunters had developed a more efficient method involving floats and toggling harpoons, but their techniques were not adopted by the Greenland Norse.

survive the passage of time. Items must pass from one group to the other through trade or simple exchange. Innovations, like boat types and hunting weapons and practices, could be copied. In terms of trade, the economic significance of particular items would have had to be recognized by both Inuit and Norsemen. Who had what to offer? The social and economic structure of Norse society in Greenland involved the payment of tithe and taxes to the church and the Norwegian crown, and the accumulation of valuable trade goods to sustain essential commerce between Greenland and Europe. Notwithstanding the value of the occasional live falcon and polar bear cub, the most valuable Norse trade commodities included walrus ivory, walrus hides for rope, and narwhal tusks. To satisfy the demands of the church, the crown, and local landlords and clergy, Norse hunters sought new hunting areas farther and farther north along the west coast of Greenland (Arneborg, chapter 23). Then came the Inuit competition for the same resources, although their presence could have provided an opportunity for trade, that is, if the Norsemen had something worthwhile to offer the Inuit.

The Norse Greenlanders most likely to have established regular and perhaps intimate contact with the Inuit were undoubtedly the Nordsetur hunters and possibly members from the major settlements who had been banished or outlawed for committing crimes. The Norse population of Greenland lived in a stratified society consisting of farmhands, cottagers, and tenants, whose lives were to a large extent controlled by powerful chieftains and church officials. Large estate owners and the church hierarchy constituted the controlling social forces within the Norse community. In contrast, Inuit society was far more egalitarian. In terms of lifestyle, one would think that the Nordsetur hunters could have appreciated the Inuit way of life, as least as far as hunting and boating skills were concerned. Given the difficulties of maintaining wooden boats, the Norsemen may have been impressed with the large skin-covered umiaks and sleek kayaks and the expert sea-mammal–hunting techniques of the Inuit. Norse hunters undoubtedly considered themselves to be expert hunters and may have been little inclined to learn from people considered (by some) to be inferior *skraeling*. Even if an

18.9

18.10c

18.11

a

b

18.12

18.9–18.12 Iron Treasures

Iron artifacts found at Skraeling Island suggest various Thule attitudes about their new acquisitions. Spikes, nails, and rivets (fig. 18.10a) from Norse boats were easily remade into points (fig. 18.10b), knife blades, and engraving tools used for decorating ivory objects like this brow band fragment (fig. 18.10c). The Norse iron wedge seems to have been used without modification for splitting bone and ivory. The lump of chain mail (fig. 18.12) was probably seen as a useless curiosity.

exchange of hunting technology was deemed of little value, information about hunting areas and sources of ivory must have been high on the Norse agenda. What did the Inuit have to gain by trading with the Norsemen? Iron and wood were both items of great value to the Inuit and the Norsemen; in fact, one might speculate about who had the greater need for these items. The Norse Greenlanders were almost completely dependent on imported iron (Buchwald and Mosdal 1985: 25), whereas the Thule-culture Inuit made good use of the meteoritic iron from Cape York, and, to a lesser extent, telluric iron from the Disko Bay area. No doubt wrought iron was of a better quality, but it might have been less easy to shape through cold hammering. Thin pieces of meteoritic iron easily fit into ivory or bone knife handles and provided sharp blades for harpoon heads and arrows. During excavations of a large inland farm, Nipaitsoq, in the Western Settlement, an arrowhead made of Cape York meteoritic iron was discovered, which seems to suggest that the Norsemen were aware of this iron source (Andreasen 1982: 186, Fig. 13). The artifact inventory from that farm also included several small iron rings, thought to have been part of chain mail.

The second item of great value to the Thule-culture Inuit in the far north was wood. It was, however, an equally treasured resource for the Norsemen, particularly by the thirteenth century when increasing masses of *storis* (pack ice) drifted southward along the east coast of Greenland in the summer, preventing driftwood from being deposited as easily on the shores of the Eastern Settlement as had been the case in earlier centuries (fig. 18.17). The sparse number of Norse finds on Inuit sites and vice versa may reveal that trade between the two peoples during their time of coexistence in Greenland was limited. In many ways the Norse Greenlanders had considerably more to gain from incorporating Inuit ways and technologies than the other way around. Considering the growing scarcity of wood for boat repairs and construction, the Norsemen might have benefited from adopting the Inuit umiak. With the colder environment and greater extent of fjord ice, copying the Inuit technique of breathing-hole hunting would also have improved the Norse hunter's ability to catch ringed seals (fig. 18.8). In most cultures, however, people's conservative

18.13 CARPENTER'S PLANE

One of the more remarkable finds at Skraeling Island was a small Norse hand plane, found without its blade. No doubt Thule people would have considered the blade a treasure, but the plane, so crucial to Norse technology, was summarily discarded. Analysis of its wood suggests it was made from tough Greenlandic birch.

18.14, 18.15 WOOLEN CLOTH

Of all the materials gathered from the Norse, woven cloth would have been the most surprising. Numerous pieces of wool fabric were recovered from the Skraeling Island permafrost. The piece, perhaps a sail fragment, being inspected in photo at right by Peter Schledermann, was probably woven on a Norse farm in southern Greenland.

nature and reluctance to incorporate new lifestyles often prevent acceptance of innovations. In the end, the Norse did not adopt these ideas.

Norse voyages to the far north were long and dangerous and probably deemed not worth the effort. Perhaps the evidence we have from Skraeling Island and the Greenland side of the Smith Sound region reflects one of the few such expeditions ever undertaken. Norse finds made in High Arctic Inuit dwellings from a later time period were most likely brought there through trade between Inuit populations along the coast. After the Norse disappearance from the Western Settlement around 1350, the Inuit could search the abandoned farmsteads for useful items. About a hundred years later,

they could do the same in the Eastern Settlement (Arneborg 1996).

Aside from the artifacts left in the hands of the Inuit, did the Norse explorers leave any other traces of their activities in the High Arctic? Two unusual hunting activities practiced by the Inuit living in the High Arctic prior to recorded western contact in 1818 have caught investigators' attention. One is the building of massive stone constructions for trapping polar bears (Schledermann 1977). The other is the prolific use of constructed stone nesting places for attracting eider ducks, a practice also known to the Norse in the North Atlantic region (Ingstad 1966). Both the Norsemen and the Inuit were eager to obtain polar-bear skins and since the High Arctic polar-bear traps are basically very large copies of Inuit stone traps for fox it is more likely that some enterpris-

ing Inuit hunters came upon the idea of trapping bears in a similar manner without input from Norsemen.

That leaves us in our search for evidence of contact with two cairns discovered by Captain George Nares on Washington Irving Island in 1875 (fig. 18.16). The island is located in the northwestern part of the Kane Basin about 130 miles (80 kilometers) north of Skraeling Island. In August of 1875, Nares and his men discovered and dismantled two ancient-looking cairns on the southern plateau of the island. They found no message but concluded that since no other known western explorer had built them, some long-forgotten voyagers had constructed the cairns. From our own investigations of the remains of the cairns on the island, we concluded that an Inuit origin was unlikely and that the cairns had been built most plausibly by members of the Norse expedition whose artifacts were so liberally distributed in house ruins not all that far away. The cairns may have marked the farthest north reached by the expedition. What happened to

18.16 Norse Landmarks?

This drawing depicts cairns discovered on the summit of Washington Irving Island (northwestern Kane Basin) by the 1875 Nares Expedition (Moss 1878). Since there is no record of other Europeans visiting this location, the cairns may have been made by the same thirteenth-century Norsemen whose artifact remains have been found at Skraeling Island. If so, they are probably the northernmost Norse landmarks in the world.

18.17 Barrels and Boxes

Norse wood was also found at Skraeling Island. Dorset and Thule people would have been curious about Norse carpentry and wood species, especially hardwoods like oak that are not present in arctic driftwood. Native North Americans may have learned from observing Norse examples how to make buckets and barrels from staves and hoops, because this technology is not present in earlier Dorset or Alaskan Thule culture.

the Norsemen who had brought their vessel into Kane Basin more than 1,050 miles (1,750 kilometers) north of the Western Settlement? Did they manage to get back home to southern Greenland or did they shipwreck and eventually perish in the far north? The Norse artifacts located in the Smith Sound region may provide a hint of an answer to these questions. The iron wedges and the carpenter's plane are items found in a shipwright's tool kit and not readily exchanged; the intact ship rivets may have been removed from ship's planking following a crushing of the vessel in ice. The gaming pieces, the chain-mail rings, the comb, and the many pieces of iron and copper are more likely to have been trade items in contrast to the sections of woolen cloth. But why, when the winter houses were abandoned in the spring, did the Inuit occupants leave behind so many Norse pieces? Perfect knife and spear blades, iron wedges, and ship rivets are useful objects. In some instances the Norse items were among very few artifacts found in a dwelling while others were mixed in with a large amount of debris. The overall impression is that the Norse items were of no particular value or interest to the Inuit. The pieces of woolen cloth, the carpenter's plane, the balance arm, and the chain-mail rings, were of little utilitarian value to the Inuit, fascinating only as items of curiosity. Items such as iron and copper blades had been attached to bone and wooden handles and added to the tool kit. Their presence in the abandoned winter dwellings may reflect the relatively easy access the Inuit had to meteoritic iron.

We may never know the fate of the Norse explorers in the High Arctic unless, like the Norsemen on Kingiktorssuaq Island, they left behind a runic message still waiting to be found.

19 | A WORLD IN TRANSITION
Early Cartography of the North Atlantic

BY DOUGLAS MCNAUGHTON

I N 1957 A RELATIVELY INSIGNIFICANT medieval book entitled *The Tartar Relation* was shown to a Yale University faculty member, Thomas E. Marston, along with a world map showing "Vinilanda Insula" bound inside it with the handwritten word "Speculi" inscribed at the top on verso. A few months later a manuscript labeled *Speculum historiali* appeared for sale from a related source, this time with parchment pages numbered in pencil in the same hand as the word "Speculi" on the map verso. A relationship was suggested by the book dealer who owned *The Tartar Relation*, and the Yale purchaser, Marston, between the map and the *Speculum,* but the inks of the map and the *Speculum* did not match, nor did the subject, nor anything except that the unexceptional coincidence that the pages of both the world map and the *Speculum* were made of parchment and not paper. Subsequently and secretly, both the books and the map were sold to billionaire Paul Mellon, an alumnus and major benefactor of Yale. Instead of following the normal process—presenting the map to the scholarly public for examination and scholarly review—it was kept secret. Eight years later a large book, *The Vinland Map and the Tartar Relation* (Skelton et al. 1965), appeared proclaiming the map's legitimacy before it had been seen by the cartographic community. The existence of the map was announced just before Columbus Day, October 11, 1965, as part of a worldwide publicity campaign for the book. The "revolutionary nature" of the Viking Map was proclaimed in newspapers and magazines around the world, and scholars who only then had heard about this fabulous discovery rushed to attend the elaborately staged news conference in New Haven and to acquire a copy of the book.

Over the past three decades the academic and public response to the announcement of the Vinland Map has been immense. Medieval researchers, archivists, map librarians, and scientists representing an array of conservation and analytical fields have spent a huge amount of time, energy, and funds since 1965 responding in various ways to the revelation of the Vinland Map. No other cartographic find in the twentieth century (Wallis et al. 1974) has created such a stir, and certainly no other controversial find relating to the Vikings has been given such widespread exposure and publicity since the "discovery" of the Kensington Stone (Wallace and Fitzhugh, this volume). Even the discovery in 1961 and scientific validation of the Norse site at L'Anse aux Meadows has been eclipsed, at least for the general public, by the Vinland Map and the controversy over its authenticity and origins.

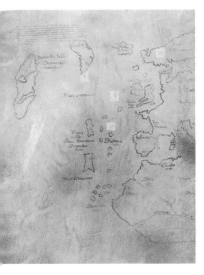

DETAIL OF THE VINLAND MAP
The Vinland Map, whose parchment and purported provenance suggest a date in the 1440s, has been a source of controversy since its existence was announced in 1965. If legitimate, it would prove that extensive knowledge about the northeasternmost regions of North America existed in Europe in the fifteenth century. Scientific and cartographic evidence indicates instead that the map is a modern forgery.

Vikings and Maps

At the outset it must be said that the Vikings and early medieval Norse did not make maps (Burden 1996), nor did they leave any artifacts that could be described as maplike. The so-called Vinland Map (Skelton et al. 1965) is not a Viking artifact and has never been considered as such by cartographic historians. The Norse voyages and settlements in the North Atlantic did, however, influence maps made by others, and those maps demonstrate how the European worldview was transformed to include what we now know as the North Atlantic region when the Norse moved westward away from Europe, first to the Faeroes and Iceland, and then to Greenland and Vinland. Before discussing the Vinland Map, which from a public perspective may be the best-known map of any purporting to represent early knowledge of the Americas, we need to understand what maps were like one thousand years ago and why they look so different from the Vinland Map and maps of the post-Columbian era.

With this information we may then be able to evaluate its significance and understand why cartographic historians today view it as a modern artifact masquerading as a medieval document.

Medieval Maps

Cartographic historians refer to the Viking Age, one thousand years ago, as the early medieval period. Medieval maps were based on concepts learned from the ancient Greeks and Romans directly or indirectly by way of the Islamic world and the Christian church. The classical Greeks valued balance and symmetry and viewed the world as a sphere. In its two-dimensional image, the world is shown as a circle with the three known "continents" of Asia, Europe, and Africa in the middle surrounded by a narrow circular ocean. This type of map style is called a "T-O" map (fig. 19.1) by cartographic historians because of the T-shape of the landmasses and the O-shaped ocean; they are also called "Ptolemaic" maps after the second-century Greek/Egyptian philosopher and chronicler Ptolemy. On Islamic maps of the period the circle is the dominant form, and Mecca, when shown, is located in the center of the map. On maps from Christian Europe, the worldview is almost always shaped as a circle, with Jerusalem in the center and east, rather

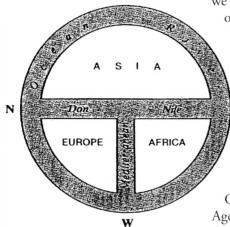

19.1 T-O–Style Maps
Medieval maps always surrounded the land by a world ocean, which forms an O, while the Mediterranean and the Nile and Tánais (or Don) rivers divide the land, which forms a T. This form was a schematic representation of God's ordering of the world; it was certainly not a cartographic instrument. The T shape reflected the points of the cross, with east, the location of Paradise, on top. Jerusalem is at the center, representing a city that was considered both secular and divine.

than north, at the top. The concept of location was borrowed in large part from the map images of Islam and the Greeks, but where Europeans located themselves on that framework is always interesting.

Most detailed, medieval European maps show locations of places from Bible stories, such as Jerusalem, Rome, the Garden of Eden, or Paradise (Campbell 1981). These were the places in the world that Europeans had heard of outside their own small villages, and which they expected to find on any map showing locations outside their homelands. The fact that no one could travel to the Garden of Eden was irrelevant because the importance of the map was not to give travel directions or distances but to show Europeans a world they accepted and could understand. All these locations would be illustrated with pictures, to aid those who read with difficulty or not at all. Rivers and mountains could be real or imaginary and frequently were used on maps to show how difficult travel might be to positions that were relatively close together on a map. Actual knowledge of global geography was almost nonexistent; what interested people were Bible locations, not Vinland, Paris, or Athens.

Saint Sever (Paris I) World Map of 1030

A beautiful example of such a medieval world is the Paris I version of the Saint Sever World Map held by the Bibliothèque Nationale (fig. 19.2); it is an elongated T-O–style map that was created in 1030 with east on top and an image of Adam, Eve, and the Serpent. The land is light colored and all the world's oceans or seas are blue and illustrated with fish and boats—all except the Tánais River, which runs to the left, and the Red Sea, which extends to the right and is colored red. The Mediterranean Sea forms the base of the T in the center, which is typical of maps from this period. To the right (south) of the Red Sea or Mare Rudrum (the equatorial ocean) is a strip of land representing the land of the mythical Antipodeans.

Although this map was made after Viking voyages into the Mediterranean and Rome and after the Viking settlement of Iceland and Greenland, Viking lands are not shown as part of this world nor is Scandinavia. Some later medieval maps show the latter as an island, but here Scandinavia does not appear even as a legend. The imaginary

Adam of Bremen

A great deal of the pseudogeographic information about the Norse world has been attributed in this century to the work of Adam of Bremen. Adam wrote a history of the See of Hamburg and the Christian missions in the north from 788 to 1072 titled *Gesta Hammaburgensis Eccliesiae Pontificum*, in which he mentions Greenland and what he called "Winland":

> Furthermore he [King Svend of Denmark] mentions an island found by many in that ocean. This island is called Winland, because grapevines grow there wild, yielding the finest wine. And that crops grow there in plenty without having been sown, I know not from fabulous report, but through the definite information of the Danes (Adam of Bremen, "Descriptio Insularum Aquilonis," Book IV, p. 38, *Gesta Hammaburgensis Ecclesiae Pontificum*, trans. by Arthur F. J. Remy).

The oldest known version of Adam of Bremen's work was made in the twelfth or thirteenth century from the Hamburg original, which was written about 1075, but it has not survived. A resurgence of interest in Adam's work at the beginning of the seventeenth century, which derived from the information it provided about the Norse, caused subsequent editions to be produced in Copenhagen in 1579. Andreas Severinus Velleius (Vedel) published an edition, which coincides with the appearance of the Stefansson Map. Adam's work was republished in 1595 and 1609 by Erpold Lindenbruch in Copenhagen; this publication corresponds with the first appearance (1605) of the Resen Map and perhaps explains its reference to Vinland.

In the late nineteenth and early twentieth centuries this work was rediscovered by German champions of the Viking (and hence Germanic) discovery of North America, and new translations into German were published in 1850 and 1898. In assuming that Adam of Bremen was relating actual geographic information about Greenland and Vinland and that his use of the term "islands" was consistent with modern concepts, researchers have not considered his medieval worldview or the fact that Adam never locates either Greenland or Winland anywhere except over the water or in the ocean. Adam identified Greenland as an island, just as any medieval scholar would have, sight unseen, using that term as a common reference to a far distant place. The title of his geographical appendix, "Descriptio Insularum Aquilonis," denotes that in the mind of Adam of Bremen all of the Danish lands were isolated and removed from his world. But his use of *insula* for these lands led to fantastic speculation that Vinland was a real island and that the Vikings must have circumnavigated Greenland (Fischer 1903)! We understand now that Adam's use of the medieval Latin word *insula* for both Greenland and Vinland did not mean that these locations had been circumnavigated, because that term did not solely or literally mean "land surrounded by water," but rather it meant "remote, wild, removed." Certainly Iceland was known to be an island. Indeed, Iceland is spelled "Is-Land" on most early English maps and later Norwegian maps; but "Grønland" (Greenland) is typically shown and conceptualized as a peninsula across the northern segment of the world circle. Records of northern Norse or Viking voyages in Greenland never suggest anything like a circumnavigation; they indicate instead that the northern limit of these voyages was somewhere up the island's west coast. Until the publication of the Vinland Map in 1965, in which "Vinilanda Insula" is figured as an island, there had never been a single reference that suggested that the Vikings voyaged around Vinland. In the absence of any distinguishing directions regarding coastal configurations of Vinland, we must assume that the phrase "Winland Insula" was again being used by Adam of Bremen in its common medieval form to mean a remote location, not a body of land surrounded by water.

land of the Antipodes in the far south is more interesting to the cartographer and is charted and described as a real place. In the west, Britain and Ireland are at the end of the world. There is no suggestion that the world might have oceans large enough to require long sea voyages to reach distant lands; anywhere one needed to go is accessible by land or by a very short day's crossing by small boat.

COTTONIANA MAP OF 995

The first map in which there is a suggestion of knowledge derived from Viking explorations is the Anglo-Saxon Map, also known as the Cottoniana Map (fig. 19.3) because its repository is the Cotton Collection at the British Museum (Barber 1999). It is a very different and remarkable map. Whereas most medieval maps of the world forced the cartographer to show the world within the formalized circle pattern, the Cottoniana does not use the circle or even the oval like the Saint Sever map: it is rectangular. Although the world is still primarily one large landmass surrounded by a small ocean, this map is unusual in showing a part of the world

that is normally on the small edge of the
world circle: the area of northwestern Europe
where Britannia lies. The Vikings, Celts, and
Anglo-Saxons knew more about the shape of
their coastlines than they knew about Jerusalem; the map was drawn to show Britain,
Ireland, and other places where the Vikings,
Celts, and Anglo-Saxons had traveled and
settled, and it includes Iceland for the first
time. The Cottoniana lists place-names associated with Viking activities in northern Europe during the eighth to tenth centuries.

Iceland and the Faeroes, Orkneys, and
Shetland islands, which were so important
to both Irish monks and early Norse seafarers, are represented. Iceland is shown here at
the time the Norse were traveling there to
explore and colonize. Iceland (written "Island" in early maps) is probably shown and
named on the Cottoniana because Vikings
had also settled in Ireland and the northern
British Isles. Their successful move into Iceland with male and female slaves of Celtic
blood had possibly been at the expense of
Irish monks who had allegedly already colonized Iceland. Thus the Anglo-Saxons had

good reasons for learning about Iceland and
certainly would have been aware of its Viking
settlement. Indeed, many scholars assume
that the cartographer who drew the
Cottoniana Map was an Irish monk.

At a time when Vikings were displacing
the Irish monks from Iceland, the
Cottoniana Map records that changing world
for the first time. It is also the last detailed
view of the northern world in this form for
several hundred years. Surprisingly it includes no reference to Saint Brendan, the legendary Irish saint who is reported to have
sailed far west in the North Atlantic in the
sixth century, and whose travels were well recorded before the Cottoniana map was
drawn. If Irish monks drew the Cottoniana,
then the lack of references to the Brendan voyages or to Isles of Saint Brendan, which are frequently found on later maps, is mysterious.

The slightly more realistic style of cartography that the Cottoniana used to represent Britannia was not duplicated in other
contemporary maps where Britannia remains
an abstract form, usually at the frontier edge
of the world circle. The conventions that

DOUGLAS MCNAUGHTON

19.3 Cottoniana "Anglo-Saxon" World Map, 995

At the bottom left of this map is the northwestern corner of Europe, which is enlarged and remarkably detailed, especially the British Isles. The map may have been drawn by an Irish monk with special knowledge of his corner of the world. The small island at the corner is believed to be the first representation of Iceland on a map. But in other respects this map continues the tradition of Roman maps by showing features from classical mythology such as the Pillars of Hercules (Gibraltar) at the entrance to the Mediterranean.

determined every aspect of medieval life were too rigid to be changed just because of a single Irish monk's map. The formal cartographic conventions of a circular world image were maintained and repeated for the next five hundred years.

THE CLAUDIUS CLAVUS MAP OF 1427

Gronlandie insule cheronesus dependet a terra inaccessibili a parte septentrionis uel ignota proper glaciem. Veniut tamen Kareli infideles, et vidi, in gronlandiam cum copioso exercitu quottidie et hoc absque dubio ex alterera parte poli septentrionalis. [The peninsula of Greenland extends from an inaccessible northern land, unknown on account of the ice. The Kareli infidels, every day, invade Greenland with a sizable army, and come from the other side of the North pole.]

One of the early Danish contributors to geographic knowledge about Greenland was an ecclesiastic writing in the early fifteenth century who was known by the latinized name of Claudius Clavus, for Claudius Clausson Svart (the Black), and who was also known as Nicholas Niger. He derived his knowledge of Greenland and Iceland in part from Norse people who still resided in

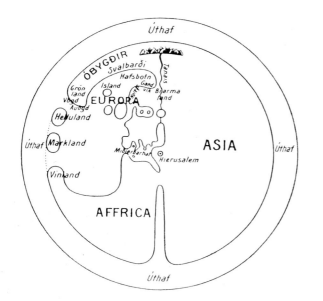

19.4 BJØRNBO RECREATION OF A CLAVUS MAP

In 1912 A. A. Björnbo drew a map to illustrate how information about northern lands, including Greenland, contained in fifteenth-century descriptions and in the sagas might have appeared in a fifteenth-century map of the world. Vinland would most likely have been interpreted as a northern peninsula of Africa or as an island. Greenland would certainly have been a peninsula descending from the northern lands.

Greenland and from information about them related in Iceland. Although he was not himself a cartographer, maps were based on his descriptions and literary references to locations throughout the Norse world, including the Ptolemaic manuscript commissioned by Cardinal Filiaster, which is also known as the Nancy Map of 1427, and the later maps of Martellus (Shirley 1983; Kejlbo 1971).

Clavus clearly identified Greenland as a remote peninsula connected by a frozen unknown land north of Europe to Asia (northwestern Russia). He also calls the people coming into Greenland from the far north "Kareli infideles" (Karelian infidels), which may be an allusion to the *skraeling* of the Norse sagas. Around the turn of the last century, A. A. Björnbo found two Clavus codices dealing with the Norse in the Imperial Library of Vienna and used these descriptions with other earlier maps to replicate or create a "Clavus Map" (fig. 19.4) (Björnbo 1912). Skelton (Skelton et al. 1965) and others did not believe that Clavus ever made a map. Josef Fischer, who is suspected by some (Seaver 1996) as the author of the Vinland Map, believed that a Clavus Map had existed and was the source for every map of Greenland made after the Filiaster or Nancy Map in 1427. He considered the purported Clavus Map to be one of the most influential maps ever made and called Clavus "the first cartographer of America" (Fischer 1913). That is an exaggeration to be sure, but the Martellus Map and another famous fake map, the Zino

Map, probably were influenced by the descriptions of Clavus. The Zino Map, which was forged to show a pre-Columbian discovery of America by Zino (Burden 1996; Shirley 1983), used the Clavus names for towns around the Greenland coast, but these names were not real and came from an old Danish folk song of which Clavus was fond (Kejlbo 1971).

THE BIANCO MAP OF 1436

Another map of the world that is important to the history of cartography because it shows a transition from a T-O–style map to maps that extend the world into new areas, is a Ptolemaic-style map that was made in Venice in 1436 by Andrea Bianco, a famous cartographer and former seaman. The Bianco Map (fig. 19.5) has become better known in recent years because the author of the Vinland Map used it to draw an antiquarian image of the world, as we shall see later. The Bianco Map shows the world as a single, large landmass surrounded by a circle of water that is not divided into oceans but as one continuous body. There is no suggestion of North America, South America, Greenland, or Australia. The Madeira Islands, the Canaries in the eastern Atlantic, and some of the Azores further out in the Atlantic reveal the extent of Bianco's knowledge of exploration to the west. Although the Europeans were not great sailors at this time, the English and others certainly traveled frequently to Iceland for the cod fishery, but nothing suggests they had any knowledge of Vinland, Helluland, or Markland of the Viking sagas. Because it was believed there was nothing across the ocean, there was no motivation to consider a long sea voyage. There is not the slightest indication in 1436 that Bianco knew of the Norse settlements in Greenland and Iceland.

THE CANERIO MAP OF 1503–1505

One of the world's most beautiful and important maps was made by the Genovese cartographer Nicolo Canerio (also known as Caverio) around 1503 to 1505 and is archived at the Bibliothèque Nationale in Paris. The Canerio Map (fig. 19.6) gives a startling view of the entire world as the Portuguese and Spanish had recently discovered it. It was not the Old World of Christendom or Islam, but a mathematical and cartographic reconstruction. This exciting and unsuspected New World pictured at the dawn of the Re-

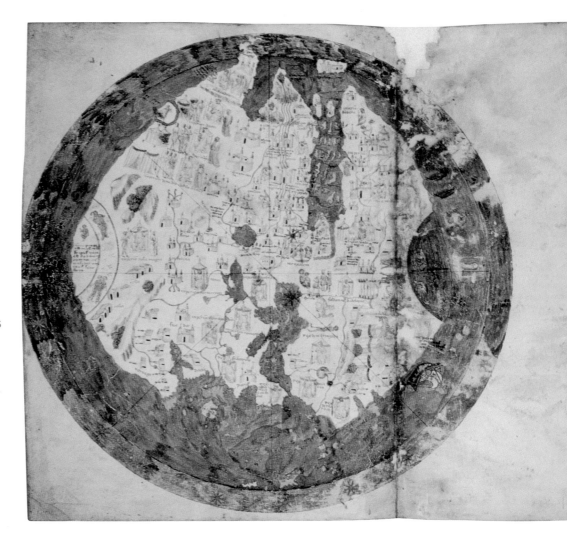

19.5 BIANCO WORLD MAP, 1436
The world map drawn by Andrea Bianco shows the flowering of cartography in the late medieval period. By stretching the conventions of the T-O–style map, greater geographic information was brought to maps. Here Spain and the Mediterranean have assumed outlines far more accurate and familiar to the modern viewer. Whoever produced the Vinland Map probably used this map as the basis for the shape of lands east of the Atlantic Ocean.

naissance carried a startling discovery: there were huge unknown lands and peoples on Earth that were not mentioned in the Bible and that had never before been shown on any earlier maps.

In the Canerio Map, the world no longer ends at Britannia with a narrow ocean encircling the land. Rather the North Atlantic is fully depicted, including North America; Greenland is also shown for the first time, when the last of the Norse colonists were dying or emigrating. Ironically, the Portuguese who claimed Greenland in 1500 had no idea that there had been Viking and Norse settlers in Greenland since 1000; they thought Greenland was the furthest part of eastern Asia (Harrisse 1892). In addition to showing Greenland, Canerio clearly indicates an outline of the east coasts of North and South America. It was slowly dawning on European cartographers that this was not Asia, as Columbus had declared, but a different land altogether—something new and unknown.

After Columbus sailed for the Spanish crown, claiming to have reached Asia by sailing west across the Atlantic in 1492, Vasco de Gama navigated east around Africa for the Portuguese crown to India. The Portuguese did not believe Columbus had reached Asia at the latitude he claimed, for his descriptions did not match previous knowledge about the Indies, its goods, or people. By 1496 the competing Portuguese and Spanish claims for dominion over lands in both Asia and what later became the Americas prompted the Pope to announce a demarcation line west of the Cape Verde Islands in the Atlantic, dividing the world outside Europe and the Mediterranean between the Spanish and the Portuguese. The demarcation line was set in the Treaty of Tordesillas in 1496: everything east of the line belonged to Portugal; everything to the west went to Spain. Obviously, some ability to determine longitude must have been required for this task. The Canerio Map, which was largely based on secret cartography of the Portu-

19.6 CANERIO MAP, 1503–1505

The Genovese cartographer Nicolo Canerio made this map showing the startling changes in geography that resulted from Portuguese and Spanish discoveries in America. Unlike most previous maps, this map is not based on religious precepts but on mathematical and cartographic observations. In addition to revealing advances in cartography, its political import was in showing the existence of huge unknown lands and people that were not mentioned in the Bible.

guese, demonstrates that they were extremely adept in determining both latitude and longitude. For the first time in the history of cartography, a latitude scale is included in the margin to help in locating new lands. This revolutionary feature is now common on all world maps. Knowledge of northern lands in North America is also demonstrated in a remarkable way on the Canerio Map, indicating clearly the changes in cartography and navigation that were required for successful ocean voyaging. The use of the compass and the astrolabe, as well as the mathematics of geometry and algebra, allowed coasts to be charted according to their latitude and, to a certain extent, longitude (Cortesão 1965).

The image of North America on the Canerio Map shows considerable knowledge about this new land only a few years after Columbus's voyages. So too is the image of the large island west of Greenland in the North Atlantic a significant addition. It is shown with strange tree shapes, all positioned in a line with the labels of locations on the Newfoundland and Labrador coast to the west. This island, which represents the Portuguese claim to the Newfoundland and Labrador area, has been moved east and is shown as an island in order to be on the proper side of the demarcation line of the Treaty of Tordesillas. The Portuguese flag is shown here, as well as on Greenland, but

both islands have been relocated on the chart to conform to the terms of the treaty.

The large island in the North Atlantic was largely misunderstood to be a pseudo-Labrador/Newfoundland or Mystery Island in the nineteenth century. Recent studies by cartographic historians show that both Greenland and this island were located east of the Tordesillas demarcation line as it would be repositioned after it was renegotiated in 1506, moving it further west to meet Portugal's demands. These positions are exactly placed, which suggests that contrary to early interpretation by cartographic historians (Harrisse 1892), this schematic may have expressed the Portuguese negotiating position of the day. Earlier suggestions that the island was positioned in error reflect an overwhelming bias against the Portuguese and the belief that they were incapable of conducting accurate navigation. Some even believed that the placement of the island was based on an earlier unknown map that placed Newfoundland in the mid-Atlantic. This lost-map hypothesis was later resurrected in the attempt to justify the origins of the Vinland Map (Skelton et al. 1965). Ironically, there is a relationship in detail between the Canerio and its sister map, the Cantino, which betrays the Vinland Map's modern origin (Sigurðsson 1965). Whoever drew the Vinland Map took advantage of this Mystery Island theme and on it labeled

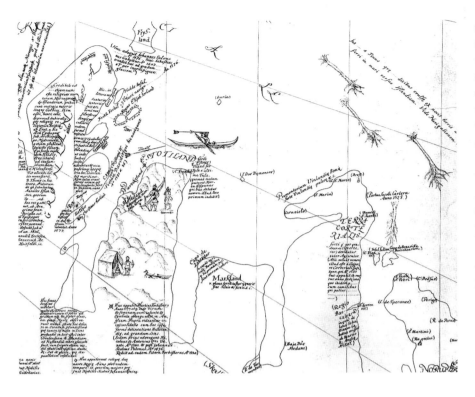

the mystery island "Vinilanda [or Winilandia] Insula" in keeping with a very popular twentieth- century idea that the Vikings had discovered America.

That Greenland is in the same location on both the Canerio and the Vinland Map indicates that the charting of the latter is based on Renaissance Portuguese cartography. Consequently, the Vinland Map cannot be medieval in origin. The shapes of Greenland and Portuguese Newfoundland have not been slavishly copied onto the Vinland Map anymore than the Bianco Map was slavishly copied onto the Vinland Map, but the locations for Greenland and the island labeled "Vinilanda Insula" were copied. Vinilanda on the Vinland Map is exactly the same distance from Greenland, Africa, Spain, and England as the Mystery Island is from those points on the Canerio Map. Greenland, Great Britain, and the Mystery Island form a distinct triangle on the Canerio Map because of the Treaty of Tordesillas, and this triangle is duplicated on the Vinland Map.

POST-COLUMBIAN MAPS OF THE SAGA LANDS

The voyages of Columbus and those of the Portuguese João, Diaz, and Vasco de Gama radically changed cartography forever. Modeling and presenting a new worldview that included landmasses that had never been charted before was a tremendous intellectual

and social challenge. The formalized medieval map styles were too confining for cartographers to show these new discoveries, and the demands from kings, popes, merchants, and traders to show the world in a useful manner changed the purpose of cartography from religious illustration to one of practical geography and navigation.

It is a curious phenomenon that although the Vikings did not draw any maps, the impact of the Columbus voyages and the subsequent claims to the Americas made by the Spanish and Portuguese created a desire by later generations in northern Europe to produce maplike images showing Helluland, Markland, and Vinland of the Viking sagas. These were not based on earlier Viking maps, which we know did not exist, but on the imagination of the authors that created them and the conventions of their own generations and cultures about what such maps should entail. They are rather remarkable in that they are not maps of geographic locations but composites of map images and the imaginary locations drawn from the sagas. What is interesting to historians is how these images of the saga lands became more elaborate as the view of the world's geography became more complex and detailed.

Eighty or more years after the Columbus voyages, maps began to be made to document a northern European claim to discovery, specifically a Viking or Norse claim. The Stefansson Map (fig. 15.3), whose first version dates to 1570, and the more developed and detailed of Resen Map (fig. 19.7) of 1605 are well-known examples of such attempts. Stefansson's map, which appeared shortly after the works of Adam of Bremen were published in Copenhagen, was the first to present the saga names as part of a maplike image. The Stefansson Map, a woodcut image with a very simplistic attempt at cartography, claimed legitimacy through literary illusion. Because it includes information from English and French explorers who ventured to North America in the late sixteenth century, the Resen Map has a more developed cartographic sense.

Until recent times most people believed that the Vikings had never sailed to North America, but the archaeological discoveries at L'Anse aux Meadows in the 1960s confirmed a Viking presence in North America around one thousand years ago (Ingstad 1977). As others have pointed out, the site at

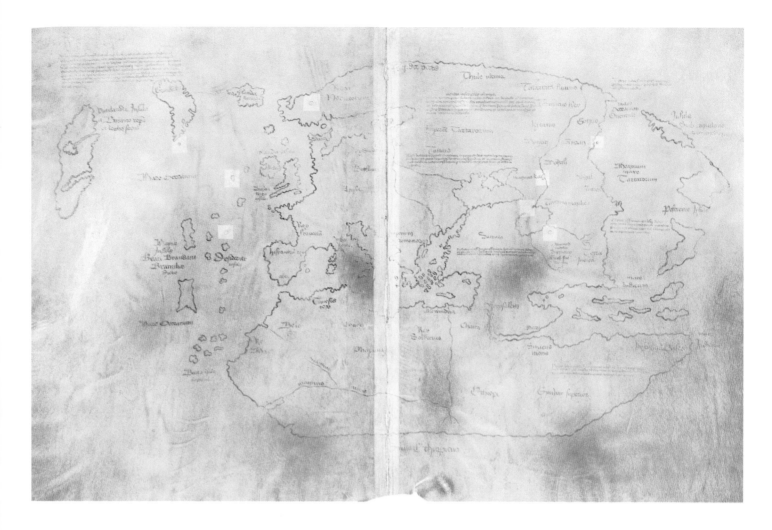

19.8 THE VINLAND MAP

A review of medieval European maps made before Columbus clearly shows numerous stylistic inconsistencies in the Vinland Map. It is anachronistic in not being a classic T-O style, and it is not oriented to the east. Instead, the Vinland Map appears to have been made by compiling information from both the Bianco and Canerio Maps at the same time, a situation that could not have occurred until the twentieth century when modern libraries, travel, and reproduction made such a comparison practical. Finally, scientific studies suggest that the map was produced with a twentieth-century printer's ink. The fugitive nature of this ink, which renders the reproduction faint, is part of the argument against its authenticity.

L'Anse aux Meadows does not fit the details of Vinland very well; exactly where Vinland was located consequently remains a matter of debate and mystery for nothing in the sagas reveals this information (Sigurdsson, Wallace, this volume). Because of the importance of North America in modern history, historians have for the last 150 years focused on sites in North America as the location of Vinland. Not knowing the location of Vinland has not stopped dozens of people from creating maps of where they believed Vinland might have been. Cartographers living in the Protestant countries of northern Europe first began making maps mentioning Vinland in the late sixteenth century, some eighty years after the voyages of Columbus. The message behind these new maps was Protestant and ethnic: they appeared after the Reformation and coincide with the rise of the Protestant church in the north of Europe. Most of these maps, which were made for publication only in Protestant Bibles, repudiate the predominately Catholic maps that had been made previously, refusing to accept a world defined

by Papal treaties and demarcation lines (Shirley 1983). Nor did these Protestant Bible maps accept Spanish and Portuguese discoveries shown on earlier maps as proof of ownership of the New World or that it was to be controlled from Rome.

The split from the Catholic church and the appearance of maps showing Vinland may seem coincidental, but it is not. The revolutionary idea that perhaps this semi-mythical place called Vinland in the old sagas might be somewhere in America, and not a part of Africa, is first expressed by Protestant mapmakers in the late sixteenth century. To illustrate this position with a convincing argument, "Vinland" and other names from the sagas were added to contemporary maps where their designers thought they might fit in a "New World" context. The lack of cartographic accuracy was not an issue because these first maps were published to stake a claim to a territory, not as a navigational tool. These crude new maps showing Vinland began to appear in northern countries that had no recognized legal claims of exploration in the area, except from the distant old sagas, and even those had been practically forgotten.

THE RESEN MAP

For some rather confusing reasons, in the mid-twentieth century the Resen Map has been mistakenly presented as independent cartographic support for the validity of the Vinland Map. The original map, drawn in 1605 by Danish Bishop Hans Poulsen Resen, is not shown in *The Vinland Map and the Tartar Relation*. The original map did not refer to Vinland at all (Dupont, pers. comm., April 1999); the map, dated 1605, that does appear in *The Vinland Map and the Tartar Relation* is not from 1605 but is instead a nineteenth-century reproduction, which was taken from a facsimile made in 1889 and published in volume 9 of *Meddelelser om Grønland*. K. J. V. Steenstrup has shown that three different hands (probably at three very different points in history) wrote the various legends on the nineteenth-century Resen Map (fig. 19.7). None of the names relating to Vinland on the map were in the well-known handwriting of Bishop Resen; they were added later, sometime between 1605 and 1889. Under the circumstances, it is extremely difficult to understand the mistaken assessments made by Painter and Skelton (1965) that the Resen Map somehow supports the legitimacy of the Vinland Map.

THE VINLAND MAP

The Vinland Map (fig. 19.8) is a world map built in part to suggest the outline of the medieval landmass with an added view of part of the North Atlantic. Its surprising features, considering its alleged early fifteenth-century date, are found in its representations of Greenland as an island and its depictions of the geography of northeasternmost North America. Even if we accept the remote and unlikely possibility that a medieval map could somehow show Vinland cartographically rather than abstractly, the map does not resemble the medieval worldview. The most telling error is the modern concept of the world, which is seen in the absence of an ocean band that delineates Heaven and Earth surrounding the world landmass. This delineating border was critical in true medieval maps. The absence of such a border or delineating edge indicates that the map is a modern construct.

The Vinland Map is best considered as two pages rather than one. It is not very large and its two separate leaves are held together by a binding strip that runs north/south at the longitude between Italy and Greece. No one knows who put the binding strip on or when, but it appears to be from the twentieth century as the adhesive is in better condition than anything else on the map. A number of small square patches are found on the map; previously it was thought that these covered wormholes; but the patches in two places are located in areas that match the cartographic location of mythical islands shown on sixteenth-century maps (such as the Canerio) and even seventeenth-century maps. The location of the large island in the mid-Atlantic on the left page of the Vinland Map, labeled "Winilanda Insula" or possibly "Vinilanda Insula," matches the position of a similar Mystery Island on sixteenth-century Portuguese charts. The name "Vinland" does not appear anywhere on the Vinland Map.

Professionals, except for the original authors of *The Vinland Map and the Tartar Relation* (Skelton et al. 1965), have been severe and negative in their opinions about the map (Seaver 1995, 1997, 1998). Even an inexperienced observer easily notices that something is very wrong with this document. The reproduction shown from *The Vinland Map and the Tartar Relation* is heavily enhanced to show a map that existed only briefly in the mid-1960s. The actual map today has no black ink lines left, as the black pigment has been falling off at a highly abnormal rate since its purchase in 1957 (Moller 1985). This is at variance with all the other maps we have examined in this chapter that are far older and far more detailed. Ink lines may be lost over centuries, but on the Vinland Map all the ink pigment has fallen away in the few decades since it was revealed. None of the major cartographic publications cataloging maps of the world or North America (Shirley 1983; Burden 1996; Harley and Woodward 1987) have accepted the Vinland Map for inclusion as a legitimate map of even minor significance. It has been called a fake since it was first seen by cartographic historians. Nothing about the map style, the ink, the lack of provenance (Wallis 1991), or its unknown date of production suggests otherwise. While its cartographic value appears to be nonexistent, its value is declared by Yale

University to be twenty million dollars.

Only one major cartographic historian supported the Vinland Map: the late and well-liked R. A. Skelton of the British Museum. He spent at least eight years working in secret, from 1957 to 1965, trying to authenticate the map for Mellon, the anonymous purchaser of the Vinland Map. Skelton put a remarkable amount of work into his research, examining every medieval map known. But his position ultimately was not the logical conclusion based on cartographic or scientific evidence supporting of the map; in fact, he totally discounted the technical and scientific evidence against the map. The entire defense that Skelton composed to support his opinion that the map *might be* legitimate rested on his proposed belief that because the map did not match any medieval map ever known, it must have been copied from an unknown and lost medieval original but that it is only a poor copy of that hypothetical map. Such a wildly antihistorical theory, without any technical or cartographic support to bolster it, has not been accepted.

There are no true medieval maps that show Vinland. The entire argument and all the publicity proclaiming the Vinland Map legitimate is without evidence and relies utterly on the ignorance of the general public. Unless one shares Skelton's faith that the map is a copy of an unknown medieval map of Vinland, there is no reason to consider it as anything but a forgery.

The Vinland Map has been considered a forgery because of a very large number of reasons that do not rest on belief at all, but on the evidence and facts. It was drawn on antique vellum, and it was then rebound by an unknown party using an eighteenth-century binding that placed the map inside a book, *Tartar Relation*, dating to 1440. The binding could have been done anytime after the eighteenth century and before its sale in 1957 because it is possible to purchase old bindings to rebind even modern books (Goldstein 1971).

The ink used in the book, which is a typical medieval type, does not match the ink on the map, which contains modern commercial components (Baynes-Cope 1974). *Tartar Relation* does not refer to the map at all, yet the supposed proof that the map is fifteenth century is largely based on its being found inside a book of that era. No effort has been made to determine when the book was rebound. Where the book or the map came from is unknown. The eastern North Atlantic view shown on the map is based on sixteenth-century Portuguese maps that only gained public attention in the late nineteenth and early twentieth centuries. The worldview of the Vinland Map is a distorted image of Bianco's 1436 map, which has always been kept locked up in Venice and was never on public display. Even today, few people in the world have ever seen the Bianco Map or any of the maps used to create the Vinland Map, and perhaps no more than a dozen people, in all of history, have ever seen all of them in one lifetime. Modern communications and reproductions have given us only recently the ability to see these maps together. The author of the Vinland Map must therefore have come from a very small pool of people with the knowledge to have created it.

Scientific Studies of the Vinland Map

The Icelandic archivist Haraldur Sigurðsson was the first researcher to recognize that the locations of Vinland and Greenland on the Vinland Map at Yale University were based on Portuguese charts from the sixteenth century. Sigurðsson pointedly remarked that the creator of the Vinland Map must have either copied or had copies of sixteenth-century maps like the Canerio in front of him when drawing the Vinland Map. Although it correctly refuted the claim that the Vinland Map was pre-Columbian, Sigurðsson's article (1965) was published in Icelandic in an Icelandic journal far removed from the media storm and did not have the impact it deserves.

In time, virtually all other major cartographic historians also expressed severe reservations about the legitimacy of the map. The scientific staff of the British Museum were the first to announce technical and scientific evidence that the Vinland Map was a fake (Baynes-Cope 1971). Even the simplest examination demonstrated that the ink did not match European medieval inks, including those inks in the books it was said to be a part of, and that the map parchment itself appeared to have been treated or scrubbed.

In 1974 Walter McCrone examined the map ink and announced that it contained modern twentieth-century commercial titanium dioxide (TiO_2, anatase, anatase form; McCrone 1974, 1978). The dark pigment in the ink, which had also been questioned by the British Museum, was identified as being composed of iron and chromium. McCrone was not aware that the compound of iron and chromium in the form of the mineral chromite had also been specifically used as a commercially milled ink pigment in the early twentieth century (McCrone 1998). He focused solely on the titanium dioxide, arguing that any map drawn with twentieth-century anatase ink, even if it was found in a fifteenth-century book, was a forgery.

The commercial production of titanium dioxide for paints, inks, and varnishes began concurrently in Niagara Falls, New York, and Norway in 1916 to 1917 (McNaughton 1999). TiO_2 is common in nature, but the commercial production process created an easily identifiable product. Today it is widely used as a whitening agent in plastics, paints, printers inks, and even some chewing gums for whitening teeth. Independently, Ken Towe (1975) of the Smithsonian examined McCrone's data for Yale and determined that McCrone actually did have X-ray diffraction data and images from the Vinland Map ink that were clearly commercial anatase (TiO_2). He confirmed McCrone's conclusion: the ink was composed with twentieth-century commercial anatase, and so the map was a fake.

A number of laboratories are currently working to identify the specific modern ink that was used to draw the Vinland Map (McNaughton 1999). The current theory is that the Vinland Map was drawn on a fifteenth- or early sixteenth-century parchment with a modern commercial ink, probably a specialty ink made for use in printing onto paper, not parchment, and certainly not on very old dry parchment. Data from all the studies to date points to a common varnish-based printer's ink used to produce raised glossy black lettering. Such inks have a very old history, going back to the early European printing and are still used today. In the early twentieth century commercial anatase (TiO_2) was added to such inks to improve their opacity. From the late nineteenth century until World War II milled chromite was used in Europe to produce a bright, metallic black letter that could be quickly trapped in place by the varnish on paper during machine printing. This type of ink is normally heated to about 200° F before being added to the printing machine. The pigment must be hot to trap properly in the varnish, consequently this type of ink is not made for application by hand.

The forger of the Vinland Map was probably not aware of this requirement for the ink application. Nor was he apparently aware that the drying oil in the varnish (linseed) would immediately be absorbed by the old vellum, leaving only the resin, chromite, solid drying agents, and TiO_2 on the surface. It probably looked very good—and old—when completed, but the insoluble elements left on the surface react variously to ultraviolet light and temperature. Attempts were probably made to dry the varnish after the linseed oil passed into the vellum because the resin would have appeared tacky as it was not drying properly. These efforts to dry the ink probably accelerated the breakdown of the pigments from the varnish matrix and hastened the oxidation and crystallization of the resin. The hard chromite particles found by Moller (1985) would naturally be the first to break free of the thin resin shell that held them together. Examination of the mineral pigment particles found in the crease of the map shows this to be true.

Within decades of even the most careful conservation practices, the normal oxidation and crystallization of the abietic acid in the resin caused the entire ink structure to crumble and fall away. What is left today is only the smallest particles of the ink that followed the linseed oil into the map's vellum. Thus there is no need to hypothesize, as McCrone had done, that the map lines had originally been sketched in light yellow ink; this yellow line is simply the stain created by the absorption of the linseed oil that carried the original ink.

20 | UNANSWERED QUESTIONS

by KIRSTEN A. SEAVER

THE STORY OF THE NORSE OUTPOST in Greenland is closely tied to that of Norse voyages to North America. This chapter provides an overview of what we now know about Norse activities in Greenland and North America over half a millennium and considers future inquiries that might bring the picture into better focus. The history of the medieval Norse will always involve places and a period for which records are scarce and for which historians must often depend on archaeology and other disciplines for information.

HOW THE NORSE LOCATED NORTH AMERICA

Erik the Red founded the Western Settlement of Greenland, located in the inner part of the Nuuk region some 300 miles (500 kilometers) north of the Eastern Settlement, at about the same time that he established the main colony to the south. The inner fjords of the Western Settlement, which Erik

ASSEMBLY GATHERING, *REYKJABÓK*

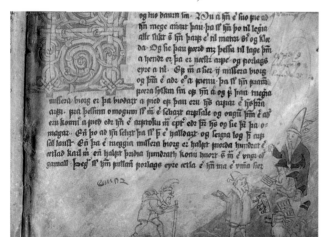

clearly had also investigated during his explorations in 984 to 992, offered pastures and sheltered farm sites but were also decidedly tougher environments for stock farming. Yet Erik must have considered the settlement's advantages important because he staked out a family claim to the best and most strategic farm site there. Inland were large herds of caribou (fig. 20.2), while the adjoining waters abounded in seals and fish,

just like farther south. Equally important was the Western Settlement's situation midway between the Eastern Settlement and Disko Island, the center of rich marine-hunting grounds. Reducing travel time during the relatively short northern summer hunting season would have increased the odds of profit.

Those northern hunts put extra food on the table, but their chief value lay in the accumulation of non-farm goods long assured of a market in Europe. Walrus ivory in particular provided a reliable and handsome return for the hunter's trouble. Profit considerations would likewise have been a key factor in the Norse Greenlanders' voyages westward to Arctic North America and, eventually, farther south. Where the Davis Strait narrows to two hundred miles (320 kilometers) at Cape Dyer before widening into Baffin Bay to the north, it creates a bottleneck that, in the earlier part of the summer season, traps drift ice from the north to form a barrier of dense ice. Walrus welcome such ice for their haul-outs (Born et al. 1994), but in hunting them, the Norse Greenlanders would have had to steer west to stay in open water. During such pursuits,

20.1 NORTHERN VISTA—NEW HORIZONS

Scenes such as this luminous view from Skye evoke vistas the Vikings saw. The search for knowledge of the Viking past now extends beyond sagas and recorded history. Scholars now probe bogs, ocean sediments, and glacier ice; seek evidence in the chemistry of jasper and iron; and investigate native sites and old Norse kitchen middens. Data accumulates; questions are raised and debated, but few are settled forever.

20.2 ARCTIC RESOURCES

The Greenland Norse learned quickly to use the natural resources of their newfound lands. Wild animals such as caribou, seals, seabirds, and fish supplemented the Norse diet, while polar bear and walrus were hunted for fur, hides, and ivory for European markets.

some early Norse hunters would inevitably have gone far enough west to discern Baffin Island on the other side, and it would not have taken them long to link that distant coast with Bjarni Herjolfsson's story of the far western regions he had spotted while drifting off course on his first voyage out to Greenland, as told in the *Greenlanders' Saga*. Bjarni's tale would have given the Norse every reason to expect that they would find forests—an all-important resource lacking in Greenland—if they kept going south (fig. 20.3). Investigating the economic potential of that other coast required an organized expedition.

The *Vinland Sagas* make it clear that the first deliberate westward expeditions involved sailing up the west coast of Greenland toward the narrowing of the strait, where the ships cut across and proceeded south along the North American coast. The leaders of these expeditions, which originated at Brattahlid, probably used Sandnes farm in the Western Settlement as an entrepôt. Erik's three sons Leif, Thorstein, and Thorvald would have done so and also the Icelander Thorfinn Karlsefni, who married Thorstein Eriksson's widow Gudrid, making him presumably a part-owner of Thorstein's farm. Karlsefni's connection with Gudrid would have been reason enough to entrust him with a colonizing expedition to an overseas region; Erik and his sons clearly intended to control profits to be garnered from this outpost.

The initial Norse voyages to North America were, in short, tightly organized ventures by those who already held power back in Greenland. Birgitta Wallace is likely correct in supposing that the L'Anse aux Meadows site represents Leif Eriksson's choice of a safe and strategic "gateway to Vinland" and to North American produce (Wallace 1991b, 1993, 1996, this volume). But while the site constitutes indisputable evidence of an actual Norse presence in North America, the debate still rages about how far south the Norse went—in other words, where Vinland in fact lay—and about the very name of Vinland.

Nobody worries much about the geographical definition of Helluland and Markland—the other two American regions

20.3 THE MARKLAND FOREST
The Greenlandic and Icelandic Norse needed fresh-cut timber for boat building and repair. The large forests bordering Hamilton Inlet, Labrador, and Sandwich Bay, or possibly the forest fringe in southern Ungava Bay, must have supplied some of these needs. Parties of Norse might also have remained in Markland or Vinland long enough to build new ships, because sailing home with a heavy load of timber would have been hazardous.

Leif gave name to—as these names are easy to associate with known stretches along the Canadian east coast. In the case of Vinland, however, the focus is still on pinpointing an exact location. The saga information has been mined and sifted without making us any the wiser (Sigurðsson; Wallace, this volume), and so any further information here can come only from future archaeological excavations on both sides of the Davis Strait or from the miraculous discovery, somewhere, of a revealing document.

WHAT IS IN A NAME?
In the course of their westward quests, the Norse usually indicated a prominent characteristic of a given region, not of a well-defined location. Any feature singled out for naming purposes did not exclude other characteristics; the name merely served to tell other Norse where a new place fit in their economic ranking system. When Erik the Red named his own fledgling colony Greenland to attract settlers, he did not know either the shape or the size of the place. It did not matter either to him or to his followers. In keeping with this medieval Norse practice, Leif Eriksson named each of three American regions for its economic potential, according to the *Greenlanders' Saga*. His fellow Greenlanders would have interpreted Helluland as "So-So Land," Markland as "Useful Land," and Vinland as "Luxury Land."

Even the saga reference to grapes in Vinland seems dubious to some, however, despite both modern archaeological evidence and recent linguistic research. The *Green-*

landers' Saga is quite specific about the reason why Leif named the southernmost region he explored Vinland. Common sense alone should suffice to take the saga at its word here. The Norse knew very well what kind of "berries" made wine. Norsemen had been trading with the Continent for several hundred years by A.D. 1000, during which time the Vikings had wintering places in France and on the Iberian Peninsula, where their drink of choice probably was not sour milk or whey. Modern scholars assume that both "wheat" and "self-sown crops" refer to the wild rice in the Saint Lawrence region.

NORSE EXPLOITATION OF NORTH AMERICAN RESOURCES
Far from being a short-lived and failed experiment made while riding the last exuberant crest of westward expansion, the Norse voyages to North America in the early eleventh century established a route and provided information about vital resources. Judging from sagas, historical sources, and modern archaeological evidence, the Norse Greenlanders apparently continued making voyages to the west for several hundred years.

Those first Europeans who explored North America would have given the rocks and slabs of Helluland short shrift and assigned a low priority to homesteading among the belligerent North American natives who had threatened the safety of Karlsefni's would-be Norse colonizers in an area far enough south to allow for stock farming. The perishable grapes of Vinland would not in themselves have been worth the risks of a voyage, and furs and other important resources available south of the Saint Lawrence could also be found farther north in the Markland region.

To Leif and his company, the pleasant surprise of wild rice and grapes would not have been nearly as important as the discovery of large stands of trees—which suggests a mainland site. Only Markland—"Useful Land"—would have been worth future crossings from Greenland. It would have made poor sense to risk ships and men, much less their families and animals, on continued expeditions farther south than necessary for the produce they originally went in search of: lumber and, most likely, iron. We know from L'Anse aux Meadows that they had found both of these resources during their earliest forays, and we know that they had reached

20.4 NORSE AXE

Norse who visited Markland for timber would have used axes like this one, found at a site in the Eastern Settlement in Greenland. Yet only one Norse axe has been reported from North America, and that one from Ungava Bay (p. 195), is now lost and was never authenticated.

forests well before arriving at Leif's wintering site at L'Anse aux Meadows.

Archaeological information suggests that later visits were to more northerly sites, within a region whose resources promised the best return on the investment any such voyage would have represented in a sparsely populated country such as Greenland. Shortage of manpower, with attendant safety concerns, is also the likely reason why these later voyages appear to have been seasonal ventures. A party of just one or two dozen men would have been vulnerable to attack, and the erection of permanent winter houses in areas already inhabited by Dorset, Thule or American Indians would have represented an unnecessary challenge.

The Norse Greenlanders were as dependent on ships as their other North Atlantic cousins (fig. 20.5). It is therefore not surprising that archaeological remains confirm that they built their own vessels (Seaver 1996). The ships on which the Norse depended for ocean sailing were traditionally constructed from flexible planks, cut with an axe from the center of carefully selected, knot-free tree trunks, each tree yielding one perfect plank of heartwood after finishing (Seaver 1999: 528–29). Although planks cut from radially split tree trunks (preferably oak) were common elsewhere in Europe prior to the use of sawed planks, in western Norway—the source of the shipbuilding techniques practiced in medieval Greenland—tangentially split pine planks evidently were in general

use (Crumlin-Pedersen 1989: 30–33). The trees found in the southwestern Ungava Bay region would therefore have been adequate to their requirements.

Recent wood analyses performed on ten ship's parts from two Norse Greenland settlements revealed six specimens of larch, which is native only to North America and Siberia (Andersen and Malmros 1992; Seaver 1996: 28). Had these samples not been specifically from ships, one might concur with this study's conclusion that the larch was most likely driftwood from Siberia (fig. 20.6). A simpler and more likely explanation, however, is that the Greenland Norse availed themselves of North American lumber for their shipbuilding. A wider sampling of Norse Greenland ship remains—one that includes comparisons with North American tree species—would help clarify this issue.

Fastening flexible boards into overlapping strakes while shipbuilding required iron nails or rivets. The Norse Greenlanders did their own blacksmithing, producing tools, ornaments, and weapons (fig. 20.4), as well as nails and rivets for ship construction. The latter were also fashioned at their L'Anse aux Meadows site. The one element in the ironworking process for which there is no evidence in Norse Greenland ruins, but which we know was a process the settlers mastered from the beginning of their time there and made use of at L'Anse aux Meadows, was smelting bog iron to form blooms shaped somewhat like a round loaf of peasant-style bread. These slag-rich blooms then had to be processed a second time to expel slag and produce serviceable ingots or tools.

There is plenty of evidence that the Greenland Norse worked slag out of crude iron blooms in their home smithies, so they must have obtained this material somewhere. That "somewhere" is unlikely to have been Iceland, where fuel was, if anything, more scarce than in Greenland and where they needed the locally produced bog iron themselves. Although the *King's Mirror* (a Norwegian work from about 1260) advised that iron would fetch a good price in Greenland, it is unlikely that exported iron would have been in the form of crude blooms rather than as finished products or the spatulate iron bars (fig. 2.7) typical of Norwegian semimanufactured iron throughout the entire Middle Ages (Seaver 1996: 233–34).

There was no local bog iron in

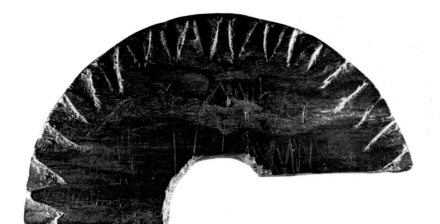

20.5 THE UNARTOQ "SUN COMPASS"

In 1948 Christian Vebek found part of a notched wooden disk while excavating a Norse ruin in southern Greenland. Several years later Carl V. Sølver decided this piece was part of a sun compass that could be used as a bearing dial to determine direction based on the sun's shadow thrown by a pointed shaft in the center of the dial. The disk has since become a controversial object. Supporters (Thirslund 1987) have argued that the disk works, while detractors argue that it was probably a toy top or buzz-spinner and that its notches are too irregular to have mathematical precision.

20.6 ARCTIC TIMBER

Greenland lacked timber, but driftwood (shown in this Olavus Magnus illustration) carried by the polar currents from Siberia, northern Scandinavia, and Alaska could be put to use.

Greenland, just as there were no forests supplying timber for ships. Norwegian merchants were probably ready to remedy the Greenlanders' domestic shortages whenever an opportunity offered (figs. 20.10, 20.11), but lumber and iron would have been very expensive after coming such a long distance. The Greenlanders would have preferred to use their own trade goods for articles that were otherwise unobtainable, such as grain, malt, honey, pottery, and silk and linen cloth.

In the sheltered southwest corner of Canada's Ungava Bay, within the Markland region and only a few hundred miles from the Norse Greenland settlements, the forest of black spruce and larch reaches practically down to the shore. High-grade bog iron from the Labrador iron trough also runs down to the shore, close to or on the surface, and could have been easily smelted with charcoal made from green (freshly cut) wood, as the Norse method required. Another advantage, from the Greenland Norse point of view, would have been the absence of Indians and Eskimos in this area at that time; the Norse would have had less resistance from the Dorset Eskimo people who were

living here between 1000 and 1300 (Lee 1968; Plumet 1985, 1994).

Going to Ungava Bay in the late summer, they would have had a fairly ample working season. Even today, when the climate is evidently much as it was before the Little Ice Age, the bay does not freeze over until November, and Hudson Strait is usually ice-free from the end of July until October.

EVIDENCE OF LATER CROSSINGS

No traces of Norse settlements (Contra Lee 1968; p. 195) have been found in Ungava Bay even after extensive surveys by Patrick Plumet in the 1970s and 1980s (Plumet 1985, 1994). If the Norse Greenlanders availed themselves of resources there or elsewhere in Markland, most of their activities would likely have taken place right on the shore to guard against native attacks. It would also have facilitated the launch of a finished ship if they built their ships there rather than hauling the lumber home.

Inventio fortunata—said to have recorded the experiences of an English Minorite friar who sailed to Norse Greenland around 1360 and continued north into the Davis Strait on a voyage of exploration—appears to have described such Norse activity on the western shore of the strait, along a stretch the medieval English voyager is likely to have considered a continuation of the Greenland coast as it veered northwest with a solid belt of ice to the north. The friar encountered Eskimos ("pygmies") in a land where no people lived, except "on the last side where in that narrow land [isthmus] there were 23 people not above 4 feet tall ... whereof 16 were women." Correlated with modern archaeological knowledge of medieval Eskimo sites, the description suggests southeast Baffin Island for this sighting. In two places farther inland, the Minorite found "a great piece of ship's planking and other balks which had been used in big ships, besides many trunks of trees which at some earlier date had been hewn down" (Taylor 1956; Seaver 1996: 122–26, 132–36). A well-traveled friar could surely distinguish between driftwood and deliberately logged trees, and we know for certain that he could not have seen logging activities anywhere in Greenland or north of Hudson Strait.

It was also at a thirteenth-century Thule site on the south coast of Baffin Island

20.7 INUIT OR NORSE WALRUS RITUAL?

Alignments of walrus mandibles at two Inuit sites in outer Frobisher Bay have suggested possible rituals and cultural relationships. These configurations have been found at historic-period Inuit walrus-hunting sites where ritual or children's play might account for such treatment. The Norse also buried caches of walrus heads in a churchyard in Greenland, which raises questions needing further study.

20.8 NORSE OR ENGLISH IRON?

In 1862 Charles Francis Hall found several large lumps of iron at a site on Kodlunarn Island in Frobisher Bay that held the remains of the Martin Frobisher expeditions of 1577–78. Although the iron has been firmly associated with the Frobisher site and has been dated to the time of the Frobisher voyages, some believe the Kodlunarn iron might have a Norse provenance and be related to the Willows Island walrus mandibles. (See fig. 2.8)

that in 1977 the archaeologist Deborah Sabo found a driftwood carving representing a European dressed in the style of the period (fig. 17.1) but not as a fisherman-farmer. Clearly made by a Thule-culture Inuit, it depicts a person wearing a one-piece, long tunic with a split in front and a cross carved on the chest. There is no scholarly agreement that this figure specifically represents a Norseman (Seaver 1996: 39), nor should we take it for granted that it represents a male.

In a surer indication that Norse Greenlanders did not just wait for expensive shipments of lumber from Norway, three entries from 1347 in the *Icelandic Annals* note that a small ship with seventeen or eighteen Greenlanders on board had made it to safety in Iceland after drifting off course on its way home to Greenland from a voyage to Markland (Storm 1977: 213, 353, 403). There was no elaboration, which suggests that to the Icelandic contemporaries of the annalists, both the place-name and the purpose of the trip would have been self-explanatory.

Evidence for contacts and travel to the west may also be seen in a chert projectile point found in the churchyard cemetery at Sandnes in the Western Settlement (fig. 17.2). The material suggests an origin around Ramah Bay or Ungava Bay, and the style is, according to Robert McGhee and William Fitzhugh, associated with the Indians of southern Labrador and Newfoundland in the period between 1000 and 1500. The projectile point may have accompanied a Norseman—who had been shot by a Native North American—to his burial at home. The fact that this artifact turned up in a churchyard context that postdates the formal introduction of Christianity in Greenland—well after the voyages described in the sagas—suggests the projectile point has associations with the Labrador-Ungava Bay region.

Excavations of a twelfth-century Indian village on the coast near Brooklin, Maine, turned up both Dorset artifacts and a Norwegian coin (fig., p. 206) minted during Olaf Kyrre's reign (1065–80), while Dorset sites along the coasts of Hudson Bay and Hudson Strait have yielded small fragments of smelted metal likely to have come from contact with the Norse. William Fitzhugh found the most interesting one of these metal pieces in 1967, an amulet made of reworked, European-derived copper (fig. 17.4), in the late Dorset site at Gulf Hazard -l in Richmond Gulf, radiocarbon dated to between A.D. 1095 and 1315 (Harp 1974–75; Fitzhugh 1980: 30).

The discovery of bison hairs and fibers from pigmented (brown or black) bears in the late culture layer at Gård Under Sandet (Farm Beneath the Sand), the Western Settlement site that was abandoned in the mid-fourteenth century, may be evidence of continued Norse crossings to North America. These non-Greenlandic animal hairs are not likely to be of European origin (Arneborg and Gulløv 1998:81–82; Berglund, this volume).

Baffin Island sites recently investigated in connection with Martin Frobisher's voyages (1576–78) in search of the Northwest Passage also contained items that may be related to Norse voyages in those parts. Two carefully placed alignments of walrus mandibles with the teeth extracted (one mandible radiocarbon dated to between 1460 and 1520) were found on Willows Island in outer Frobisher Bay, Baffin Island (fig. 20.7). On Kodlunarn Island and other sites around the Countess of Warwick Sound, the discovery of several medieval-type iron blooms has given rise to much speculation (fig. 20.8) (Fitzhugh 1993; Fitzhugh and Olin 1993). The Willows Island mandible displays appear to be unique among Canadian finds. Dorset and Thule inhabitants of the Baffin Island region are not known to have had rituals associated with alignments of walrus mandibles, and formal arrangements of this sort have not been found in Dorset or Thule sites on the Greenland side. What *has* been found in Greenland are walrus mandibles buried right outside the Norse cathedral wall at Gardar in soil that the Norse themselves had brought in to provide sufficient fill for a graveyard (Nørlund 1930; Arneborg, this volume). The Baffin mandibles may also be of Norse origin.

There is general agreement that the iron blooms found at the Frobisher sites have characteristics consistent with bog ore and medieval hearth-pit origins, but no hearth-pit furnace has been located in conjunction with them. Indeed, it appears that Baffin Island is as devoid of bog ore as Greenland. Disagreement begins with dating the blooms and deducing their provenance. The physical and chemical analyses and the radiocarbon datings of a couple of these blooms have been described in considerable detail and by several experts (Fitzhugh and Olin 1993; Fitzhugh 1997). Some of these data contradict each other, but as far as we can tell, the blooms predate the Frobisher expeditions and fall within the period when the Norse were still functioning in Greenland. To the degree that it has been possible to analyze charcoal fragments in one of these blooms, there are identifications of four wood species the Norse would have been likely to use if smelting bog iron in the southern Ungava Bay region: spruce, larch, birch, and alder.

The Canadian geologist Normand Goulet, long familiar with the iron deposits in southwest Ungava Bay, noted in a personal communication that hematite, jasperlite, and magnetite characterize the local iron ore. He suggested that iron samples from Greenland Norse excavations should be examined for the presence of olite, which occurs in small, red, circular accretions in Leaf Bay iron from the Labrador iron trough. A similar analysis of the Baffin Island iron blooms should also be made. Without such tests, there is little hope of settling the uncertainties over this issue.

Whatever the origin of the Frobisher

blooms and the Willows Island mandible alignments, the evidence from medieval Dorset, Thule, and Norse sites far northward from Baffin Island on both sides of the Davis Strait suggests neutral or even friendly relations, with occasional barter, as the Norse went in search of trade and tithe goods in the region they called Nordsetur (Sutherland, this volume). This region appears to have included the Lancaster Sound area in Arctic Canada (at about 75° north) and the coast of western Greenland at least up to 73° north, but Norse artifacts have been found even farther north (Schledermann, this volume). Future excavations in Arctic Canada and Greenland will no doubt fill the holes in our present knowledge of Norse travel and interaction with people from the Dorset and Thule cultures.

VOYAGES TO NORDSETUR

Much of our information about Norse Greenland exports comes from Norwegian church records. Greenland's first official bishop, Arnald, arrived at his see in 1126, and the Greenland Church reached its zenith during the thirteenth and early fourteenth centuries (Seaver 1996: 61–66). Thus it is probably not a coincidence that most Norse finds in the High Arctic have been assigned to the thirteenth century. It was also in the early- to mid-thirteenth century that three intrepid Norse Greenland hunters carved the small runestone (fig. 24.2) the Greenlander Pelimut discovered in 1821 in a cairn on Kingiktorssuaq Island, at about 73° north (Seaver 1996: 37).

Discoveries made by Robert McGhee while excavating Thule winter houses at Brooman Point on Bathurst Island in the Canadian High Arctic, however, indicate even earlier contacts (McGhee 1984a). Though quite far inland, Bathurst Island is accessible from Lancaster Sound. The excavation site, which had clear associations with a brief Thule occupation in the late eleventh or early twelfth centuries, exhibited some pre-Dorset and Dorset features and yielded several Norse artifacts. McGhee interpreted these Norse objects as signs of direct contact between the Norse and North American arctic natives long before Nordic written sources hint of such meetings; he does not view them as evidence of circuitous Eskimo trade routes or of pilfering from Norse Greenland farm sites. Later excavations else-

20.9 New Data From Archaeology
Research on Norse activities in the western North Atlantic continues, often with surprising results. Peter Schledermann's Norse finds in Thule sites on Skraeling Island, shown here, and recent Danish finds in late Dorset sites in the Thule District confirm that there were thirteenth-century Norse expeditions to northern Davis Strait. They also show that Dorset people lived in the area longer and the Thule arrived later than previously thought.

where in the High Arctic lend weight to McGhee's reference to the Arabic geographer al-Idrisi, working for King Roger II of Sicily around 1150, whose description of a people living on the "innermost isles" of the North Atlantic suggests that stories about the Thule people had reached Europe by that time (McGhee 1984a: 11).

The late-twelfth-century work *Historiae Norvegiae* reports that Greenland hunters in the far north had encountered small people they called *skraeling*—quite possibly the Dorset people, who seem to have overlapped with the incoming Thule people for at least a century in the extreme north and who left behind tantalizing "multiple head" sculptures (fig. 13.7) showing distinctly European faces. On the Greenland side of the Smith Sound region, in a Late Dorset ruin from about the end of the thirteenth century, Hans Christian Gulløv and his team found a fragment of a European bronze pot (Arneborg and Gulløv, eds. 1998: 151–71). A complete metallurgical analysis of the pot fragment might also reveal where in Europe the pot was made and thus add to our general knowledge of northern trade in the Middle Ages.

Among more than fifty items of Norse origin discovered off the east coast of Ellesmere Island in thirteenth-century Thule ruins by Peter Schledermann and his team (fig. 20.9) was evidence of chain mail—an unlikely garment for fishermen and hunters going about their business (fig. 18.12) (Schledermann, this volume). At least one of two northern expeditions around 1266, which a Greenland priest reportedly described in a letter to a colleague, may have

gone all the way up to Melville Bay before returning to Gardar (Seaver 1996: 42, 72). These were clearly not regular hunting voyages, and their object may well have been to subject the indigenous people to taxation, in the manner of Scandinavian Norse taxation of the Saami in northern Norway. If so, chain mail is likely to have been worn by those wealthy enough to possess it (Seaver 1996: 42).

While chain mail indicates anticipated hostilities, even in the Davis Strait in the Middle Ages it should not be taken for granted that such armor had a Norse origin. On the Western Settlement farm V48 (Nipaitsoq), links associated with chain mail were found along with several examples of a circa 1330 version of the Campbell clan's coat of arms, one of them engraved on a small silver shield (fig. 23.10). If the friar who wrote *Inventio fortunata* found his way to Greenland from Britain around 1360, it is not surprising that a link with the British Isles existed thirty years earlier. Nor does the British connection stop there.

A pewter cross (undated) found at Hvalsey has an alloy suggesting English origins, and a manufactured table knife found in a late stratum at Gardar has a counterpart in a late-fourteenth-century find made in London. Fifteenth-century European clothing styles found in Herjolfsnes graves reveal outside contacts well after Norse Greenland's rupture with Norway and the Roman church (fig. 23.16). Among late-medieval artifacts retrieved from the shoreline here was a small crucifix made of jet (figs. 23.20, 23.21), which is reminiscent of finds from around Whitby Abbey in England. Four pieces of unworked iron found at farm +71 (a late-phase Eastern Settlement farm) point to a connection similar to that which the English had with Iceland in the fifteenth century and which had its roots firmly in the codfish business (Seaver 1996: 171–74, 229–35). Only a detailed metallurgical analysis can determine the origin of these four iron pieces, and such an investigation might also illuminate the circumstances under which the Eastern Settlement was abandoned.

The Final Phase

In the absence of incontrovertible datings, modern scholars assume that the Western Settlement ceased to exist before 1400 and that the Eastern Settlement cannot have been viable past 1500.

Why and how either of the two settlements was abandoned is unknown, but the reasons for leaving were clearly cumulative and complex in both cases. Nor is it yet possible to determine the relationship between the cessation of voyages to Nordsetur and the demise of the Western Settlement, or between the effective end of the Eastern Settlement and English and Portuguese expansion into the North Atlantic in the last decades of the fifteenth century.

Investigations at the Farm Beneath the Sand (Berglund, this volume) indicate that a worsening climate in the middle of the fourteenth century led the Norse to give up farming in their northernmost community; they do not support the notion that their departure was caused by the effects of isolation. At some point, however, this small community clearly decided that the advantages of proximity to the northern hunting grounds no longer outweighed the disadvantages of farming at that latitude. When they chose to leave, one option was relocation to the Eastern Settlement.

Like their northern cousins, the inhabitants of the Eastern Settlement are likely to have had opportunities for emigration over time. There is little reason to take literally the Icelandic bishop Gísli Oddsson (1593–1638), however, who noted that in 1342 the Greenlanders willingly abandoned their Christian faith and joined with "the folk of America" (Seaver 1996: 86). In the Eastern Settlement, the Norse were still around in the fifteenth century and buried their dead in a Chris-

20.10, 20.11 TRADE WITH NORWAY

Greenland's links with Europe occurred largely through trade with Bergen. Contact between the two locations is suggested by this comb from Bergen, which is similar to Greenland combs (fig. 23.18) and, like them, is marked with runes to indicate who owned this object.

In the fifteenth century, when Europe was in economic crisis and the Black Death was rampant, Greenland became increasingly isolated. Under these circumstances, Greenlanders who still had boats might have taken new interest in Vinland, but no conclusive proof of Greenlandic emigration has been revealed so far.

Wood tags identifying property—this one from Bergen says "Thorgrim's pile"—continued to be used in Labrador into the twentieth century.

20.11

tian manner to the end, as the graveyard at Herjolfsnes testifies.

Recent research nevertheless indicates that Eastern Settlement farming suffered a sharp decline after about the middle of the fifteenth century. There is convincing evidence of pastures reverting to wild meadows around that time and of inclement weather that may at least in part have been owing to a massive 1453 volcanic eruption in the southwest Pacific, which caused worldwide cooling and unstable weather for three or four years. In Greenland, unstable weather would certainly have taken a toll, but the Norse Greenlanders had ridden out periods of bad weather before, and climatic changes would not in themselves have caused an entrenched population to die off within two or three decades while there was still plenty of food in the sea. Medieval Icelanders with similar or worse problems recovered from every disaster, including from the Black Death, which did reach Iceland in 1402 but is unlikely ever to have reached Norse Greenland (Seaver 1996).

There is no evidence that late-fifteenth-century Greenlanders had less ability to cope, or less will to live, than either the Icelanders or their own ancestors who had accompanied Erik the Red. Lynnerup's research has shown that these people suffered from neither genetic deterioration nor malnutrition (Lynnerup 1998). Nor is there any reason to believe that either Eskimo hostility or European pirates caused the desertion of the Norse farms in Greenland as has previously been claimed (Arneborg; Gulløv, this volume). The archaeological evidence firmly suggests that the withdrawal from the Eastern Settlement was orderly and nonviolent and therefore voluntary. But what made these people decide that their own country was no longer worth living in?

Future research needs to focus both on the signs of renewed prosperity in the first half of the fifteenth century (evidenced by the building of three impressive festal halls), which is likely to have been fueled by trade and contact with the outside world and related to the changing economic circumstances in Iceland during the same period. The strong possibility that the last decades of the fifteenth century brought unprecedented economic decline and isolation to the Greenlanders is also worthy of further study.

KIRSTEN A. SEAVER

Both developments would have had the same likely cause, namely the European demand for the wind-dried cod known as stockfish—which became a crucial source of protein as European populations began recovering from the Black Death. The English became the middlemen for the trade to the Iberian Peninsula in stockfish from the North. English fishing doggers went ever farther west in search of new fishing grounds and were probably fishing off North America by the middle of the fifteenth century. They dominated the approaches to Iceland and Greenland from about 1420 onward and may soon have made it dangerous for the Greenlanders to sail beyond their own coasts. Further datings of the remains of Greenland Norse ships might show whether such a blockade prevented further trips to Markland and therefore left the Eastern Settlement denizens without oceangoing ships by the last quarter of the fifteenth century.

The English worked out a direct route from Britain to Labrador and Newfoundland by around 1480 and were no longer dependent on imported fish. While the Icelanders were now selling their wares through Hanseatic merchants, the same would not have been true of the Greenlanders. With their traditional farm economy replaced by an export economy, Icelanders even had to import butter. If the demonstrated decline in farming indicates that Greenlanders also had grown dependent on English trade in marine products, and then in the last couple of decades of the fifteenth century they lost practically all their customers to more direct trading partners, the effect would have been devastating.

If an offer to relocate was accompanied by the promise of transportation, the Greenlanders may well have decided the time had come to act (Seaver 1996). Any such inducement would also have had to provide a place with room for several households. The Norse were accustomed to group hunting and fishing, and a group exodus is indicated by the fact that they seem to have taken both church relics and personal valuables with them—both church and farm ruins mostly contain misplaced or discarded items. Any inducement would also have had to promise sufficient independence and land ownership to people accustomed to both. These criteria narrow the field considerably.

Although land ownership in Iceland went through upheaval because of the Black Death, there is no documentary indication that rich heirs to innumerable farms gave up ownership to Greenlandic Norse strangers in the first part of the fifteenth century; in the second half, Iceland would have been no more inviting to a group of newcomers than Norway was, for political and economic reasons. No collection of Greenlandic artifacts pointing to such immigration has turned up in either Iceland or Norway; furthermore, in both countries representatives of the Dano-Norwegian crown were so thick on the ground that word would have spread if it became obvious that the Greenland colony was now extinct. Archbishop Valkendorf and Christian II would then have had no reason for an expedition to the old Norse colony in Greenland in the early sixteenth century.

This leaves the possibility that the Norse Greenlanders lent their presence and their fishing skills to a colonizing venture on the American side. Any search for evidence of their presence should probably start above Newfoundland, because English and Portuguese entrepreneurs were required to establish fisheries far enough north (and east) to avoid running into Spanish territory as defined by the Treaty of Tordesillas. The Norse may have joined the fate of untold others whose hopes and lives have vanished there without a trace.

INTRODUCTION
FROM VIKINGS TO NORSEMEN

BY JETTE ARNEBORG AND KIRSTEN A. SEAVER

GEOLOGICALLY, GREENLAND IS A PART of North America, to which it is also geographically closer than to any other territory in the North Atlantic. Only the narrow Smith Sound separates the bleak, but beautiful wilderness of Canada's Ellesmere Island from Greenland. This close relationship was of no concern even to educated Europeans, however, until the early sixteenth century, when it became clear that a huge and as yet unexplored continent lay between western Europe and the east Asian coast at which Christopher Columbus thought he had arrived in 1492.

It took longer still before explorers and geographers established that the American continent was unconnected to Asia in the far north, and that Greenland was neither a westward protrusion from the Scandinavian Peninsula nor an eastward extension of Arctic America. For at least two centuries after the recorded voyages of John and Sebastian Cabot, the Corte Real brothers, and many others who ventured into the Davis Strait in the years around 1500, these remote regions were, to most educated Europeans, as much mental constructs as geographic realities.

Greenland is immense, covering almost 840,000 square miles (1,350,000 square kilometers) as it reaches from 59 degrees latitude north at Cape Farewell in the south all the way to 83 degrees latitude north, even farther north than Arctic Canada. While the inner southwestern fjords where the Norse settled are verdant, the country has great natural barriers to exploration, including mountains and glaciers inland and menacing drift ice along both coasts. It was not completely circumnavigated by Europeans until early in the twentieth century.

The cultural isolation and geographical remoteness of these northern regions have never stood in the way of public interest in them, however. Around 1075 Adam of Bremen wrote about Greenland and other areas recently settled by the Norse during their relentless westward quest for land and profit. To this day authors draw on the popular fascination with medieval Norse exploration in the northwestern Atlantic and with the extraordinary lives of the Dorset and Thule people who preceded the modern Inuit in Greenland and Arctic America by some three thousand years. Fortunately, as various chapters in this volume show, our knowledge of all three peoples has been greatly expanded in the last few decades.

When interest in Iceland and its ancient literature was rekindled in Denmark and Norway in the sixteenth and early seventeenth centuries and people became fascinated with Norse exploits in Greenland and North America, no one thought the Norse Greenlanders were extinct. During the years 1514 to 1516, the Norwegian Archbishop Erik Valkendorf had tried to organize an expedition to Greenland to hug that province to the Dano-Norwegian bosom once more and to reclaim it for the Catholic church, after a communication gap of well over a century. This expedition did not take place, but the bureaucracy ground on, one example being Pope Leo X's appointment of the Danish Minorite Vincent Petersson as yet another nonresident bishop of Gardar in 1519. From time to time after that, there was still talk of sending a royal expedition to Greenland, suggesting that the Danish crown was not immune to recent European excitement over the economic and strategic potential of the North

---

GREENLAND

When Erik the Red sailed for Greenland in 982, the island was not entirely unknown, but he was the first to explore its west coast and identify the two most promising settlement areas. Although conditions for farming were better in the Eastern Settlement, the Western Settlement had more wild game and was closer to the walrus-hunting grounds, known to later Greenland Norse as the Nordsetur. The American-built replica Viking vessel *Snorri* visited some of these locations in 1998.

CRUCIFIX

From a large farm complex in the Western Settlement, well-preserved wooden wall panels, a six-foot (two-meter) long loom head stave, and this wooden crucifix were recovered. The adoption of Christianity in Iceland and Greenland in A.D. 1000 brought an end to the old "Viking" way of life. Thereafter the residents of Greenland and Iceland are more appropriately known as "Norse," and the European Vikings as Scandinavians.

American landmass to which they believed Greenland was geographically connected.

When King Christian IV sent out the first of two expeditions to West Greenland in 1605, he was still convinced that the Norse Greenlanders were alive and just needed to be tracked down. They proved so elusive, however, that after a second futile expedition in 1606, a third one sent out in 1607 had orders to search for the Eastern Settlement in eastern Greenland. The expedition was unable to reach shore because of the wide belt of sea ice that commonly blocks this coast, and some crew members may have been relieved, because they had been warned to exercise great care when confronting the fierce Greenland Norse.

Despite its name, the Eastern Settlement, the main Norse Greenland colony, was actually located on the southwest coast, where the stock farming settlers exploited the grazing potential of the relatively fertile inner fjords first explored in the 980s by Erik the Red, a feisty Norwegian-turned-Icelander. The much smaller Western Settlement lay some four hundred miles (six hundred fifty kilometers) to the north, at the heads of fjords in the present-day Nuuk region. It was founded at about the same time as the main colony to the south, and the reason is not hard to find. Although a decidedly tougher environment for stock farming, the region was rich in land and marine game, and it formed a convenient midpoint for the northern hunts that featured so prominently in the Norse Greenlanders' export economy. Soon, the Western Settlement became central to planned expeditions to North America.

The Western Settlement's advantages were evidently not sufficient to offset a deteriorating climate (and other problems), however, and the colony became extinct in the mid-fourteenth century. The Eastern Settlement is believed to have closed down around 1450 for reasons that are even more widely debated. Scholars now believe, however, that climatic fluctuations, which affected the resources available both on land and at sea, played an important part in the history of the Greenland Norse, just as they did in the migrations of the prehistoric Dorset and Thule peoples. In the case of the Norse, the severity of the sea ice blocking their shores during cold periods is also likely to have had an effect on shipping as well as on hunting.

With the approval of the Danish authorities, the Norwegian missionary Hans Egede arrived in the outer part of the former Western Settlement region in 1721, just like Valkendorf hoping to bring the wayward Norse back into the Christian fold. But he found no Norse and no trace of Norse habitation. Instead, he was greeted by groups of Inuit in an atmosphere of mutual suspicion and curiosity. Relations improved over time, and with the benefit of Inuit knowledge, Egede expanded his understanding of Greenland's geography and located several deserted Norse farms.

Egede had only the vaguest idea of the country to which he had brought his family and of its inhabitants past and present. Like other Norwegians and Danes of his era, he thought that the Eastern Settlement lay on the east coast

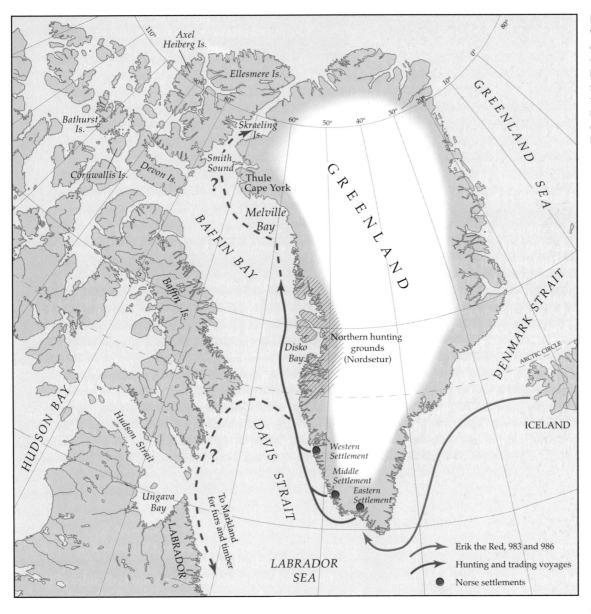

EXPLORING NEW LANDS
With Erik the Red's discovery in 983 of the West Greenland fjords, new land became available for Norse settlement. Greenland was the richest territory of the Norse expansion, far exceeding the Faeroes and Iceland in wild game.

Erik the Red, 983 and 986

Hunting and trading voyages

● Norse settlements

of Greenland. The knowledge gained by the Greenland Norse during almost five centuries of occupation was truly lost, even to the Norwegians, and scholars have been working for more than two hundred and fifty years to retrieve it. This task has not been made easier by the fact that much of our approach has been shaped by nineteenth- and early twentieth-century scholars with notions about the power of temporal and ecclesiastical authorities and nonindustrial and non-European societies that would not be acceptable today.

For a long time, scholarly effort concentrated on tracing the Greenland Norse, whose ancient farms in both settlements were gradually being located and excavated. The study of medieval Dorset and Thule sites added fresh perspectives to the archaeological and anthropological quest. The years 1960 to 1965 constitute yet another watershed, when the Norse site at L'Anse aux Meadows in northern Newfoundland Island was discovered by Helge and Anne Stine Ingstad and subsequently excavated, with results that forever put to rest the discussion of whether the Norse had reached North America during the so-called Vinland voyages.

The first systematic investigation of the Norse in Greenland began in the early 1830s at the initiative of members of the newly created Kongelige Nordiske Oldskriftselskab for Oldkyndighed (Royal Nordic Society for Ancient Manuscript Research), chief among them the Danish-Icelandic scholar Finnur Magnusson and the Danish philologist C. C. Rafn, whose published belief in the Norse origins of the Newport Tower in Rhode Island created a sensation (Wallace and Fitzhugh, this volume).

Although Norway was at that time under Swedish hegemony, both Iceland and Greenland were still Danish colonies. Requests went out from Copenhagen to Danish civil servants and missionaries stationed in Greenland to collect information about the ancient Norse there; local Danish clergymen and traders undertook excavations of several prominent Norse ruin sites; and the native

Greenlanders were promised rewards for new information about ruin sites, especially ones with runestones.

With archaeology still in its infancy, written information, whether from runes or from sagas, was considered of paramount importance. The major Icelandic saga manuscripts had long since been transferred to Copenhagen, where they were now subjected to systematic scrutiny. The preliminary result of all this activity was the compilation of virtually everything known about the history of the Greenland Norse in the three-volume work *Grønlands Historiske Mindesmaerker* (Greenland's Historical Monuments). It was published between 1838 and 1845 and is still used today.

From the time the first volume appeared, a main scholarly concern was with what had caused the demise of the Norse colony in Greenland after half a millennium of presumably successful tenure at the edge of what was then considered the civilized world. The deserted ruins of big and small farms, of churches and of summer farms in the mountains, spoke of a Christian peasant society much like that known from medieval Iceland and Norway.

Although they still thought of Greenland as remote, scholars had now learned that the Eastern Settlement had been on the southwestern coast, and they had gained a window on the medieval Norse Greenlanders' lives, but they knew very little else. It was generally assumed that the immediate ancestors of the modern Inuit, who were then living throughout these regions, must somehow have been responsible for either killing or displacing the Norse. Therefore, when the Danish officer Daniel Bruun undertook his archaeological expedition to the Western Settlement in 1903, he saw it as his task to collect evidence not only of the Norsemen's domestic economy but also about their relationship with their Thule Inuit neighbors. Had he lived another hundred years, he would no doubt have been pleased to know that not only do the two cultures appear to have coexisted in a relatively peaceful manner, but (as Petersen, this volume, suggests) modern Greenlanders accept the possibility that their ancestors learned from their Norse neighbors.

In the Eastern Settlement, excavations at Ikigaat (Herjolfsnes) in 1921 by the Danish historian Poul Nørlund under the aegis of the Danish National Museum produced the first major breakthrough in modern Norse Greenland archaeology. The medieval clothing Nørlund found in the churchyard there, as well as the human remains themselves, greatly advanced knowledge of medieval Norse life in Greenland, right up to what may have been its final stage. We know, for example, that the Norse Greenlanders kept up with fifteenth-century clothing styles even after they were supposedly cut off from outside contact. The burial practices noted here and in other Norse Greenland graveyards, along with bones and other remains, have furnished modern scientists with invaluable material for study, as noted in the following chapters. These new analyses suggest that neither malnutrition and genetic deterioration, nor assimilation with the Thule people, caused the end of the Norse Greenland colony. A number of other eventualities remain on the table, however, ranging from changes in climate and economic dispositions to the possible part played by the proximity of North America and by fifteenth-century English and Portuguese probes in the North Atlantic. There is, however, a general scholarly agreement that the disappearance of the Norse Greenlanders is unlikely to have had a single, traumatic cause.

A century ago, Captain Bruun believed that only a multidisciplinary approach would solve the complex problems facing those who wanted to reconstruct the fate of a community that had vanished so mysteriously several hundred years earlier. Modern researchers fully embrace his view and have brought to bear not only techniques unknown to both Bruun and Nørlund but also a multicultural and international approach whose fruits are evident in the chapters appearing in this section. We have, for example, the culmination of the investigations of the deep-frozen Farm Beneath the Sand, discovered in 1990, where new evidence is rapidly changing our view of this supposedly isolated community. Its denizens were clearly not isolated from either their fellow Norse in the Eastern Settlement or from the greater Norse Atlantic community nor indeed from the North American continent, with which it appears that they maintained contact for several hundred years after the Vinland voyages.

Other archaeological evidence from both sides of the Davis Strait corroborates this story. It has also become clear that this continued American contact included occasional trade with the Dorset and Thule people, whose tenure in the farthest north overlapped much more than we knew only a few years ago, and whose relations with the Norse appear to have been such that they cannot be blamed for the end of the Norse colony in Greenland. Instead, the surviving evidence of this cross-cultural contact is likely to furnish evidence of lives in both cultures that were more complex, more tolerant, and with a wider geographical reach than hitherto has been imagined. And we have already learned that far from being at the end of the world, medieval Greenland and arctic North America constituted the meeting grounds of European and Asian cultures long before Renaissance navigators explored the world.

21 | LIFE AND DEATH IN NORSE GREENLAND

BY NIELS LYNNERUP

GOD SPEAKING TO JOSHUA, *STJÓRN*

ALONG THE SHORES OF THE DEEP fjords in southwest Greenland and inland in the valleys between them, usually on some of the choicest patches of land, stones placed in quadrangular patterns mark the ruins of old Norse churches and churchyards. The bones of many thousands of the old Norse lie tightly packed in these churchyards, silent witnesses of Viking Age expansion and the medieval way of life. They lie in possibly the most remote place settled by the European medieval society (fig. 21.1).

Abandoned for almost five hundred years, the Norse churchyards have since become the focus of many archaeological excavations, and the bones of the Norse men and women have been rediscovered. Most of the known old Norse burial sites have been excavated. The physical anthropological material covers many Norse burial sites, including material from a cathedral church at Gardar; a probable monastic church at Narsarsuaq; major parish churches at Sandnes, Undir Høfda, and Herjolfsnes, and perhaps even the very first church in Greenland, Thjodhild's Church. Most types of churches are thus represented in the material, a fact which in conjunction with the well-defined geographical setting and the limited time span of the settlements, makes the Norse skeletal material unique as a source of biological data on the medieval period.

SKELETAL CHRONOLOGY AND BURIAL CUSTOMS

Burial in consecrated earth was important for the Christian Norse. The grave of Gudveg may serve as an illustration. When excavating at Herjolfsnes, the archaeologist Poul Nørlund found a rune stick in a coffin (Nørlund

1924: 61–62) with the inscription: "This woman, whose name was Gudveg, was laid overboard [buried] in the Greenland Sea" (Jónsson 1924). As human remains were observed in this coffin—not bones but apidocire, remnants of fatty tissue—Nørlund believed that the rune stick had been carved in memory of Gudveg and laid in the coffin with another body, perhaps that of her husband.

Recent radiocarbon dating analyses made on twenty-eight carefully selected bone samples have established a chronological framework covering not only the bones but also the churches and churchyards (Lynnerup 1998). Although several archaeologists were able to give approximate dates for the church buildings using architectural styles (Roussell 1941; Krogh 1982), these cannot be taken to be representative of the anthropological material because the churchyard often antedates the church building; indeed, faint traces of older churches often appear upon excavation (for example, at Gardar and Brattahlid). Several skeletons were found below the actual foundations of the church at Herjolfsnes and Gardar.

In earlier anthropological studies, church dates were taken to be representative of the human remains. An important reason

When Erik the Red explored Greenland, the verdant landscape inspired him to call it Greenland, because, as recorded in *Erik the Red's Saga*, "people would be attracted to go there if it had a favorable name." Erik's farm at Brattahlid is still one of the best farming locations in Greenland. Its location at the inner end of Eriksfjord protects it from the cold foggy weather and arctic waters of the outer coast. Thjodhild's church was located to the right of the houses on the left.

for this was that until recently, it was not possible to date the skeletal material itself. Because of Christian burial practices, grave goods and artifacts were very rarely found with the interred individuals that would give clues about the age of the bodies. Nor was stratigraphy in use at the time of most of the Norse excavations, which were made before World War II or shortly thereafter. The results of the radiocarbon analyses of the skeletal remains did corroborate the previous interpretations. We now know Thjodhild's Church was an early church, and Herjolfsnes was from the Late Settlement, as had been surmised by the archaeologists' analysis of the buildings.

Interestingly, the radiocarbon dating seems to indicate that the Norse observed the changing burial customs of northern Europe throughout the medieval period even though it was once believed that the Greenlanders were isolated completely from European society at the time. Based on a large study of Danish and Swedish medieval cemeteries, it has become apparent that the position of the arms in the grave changed throughout the period. In early Christian times the arms were usually laid down by the side of the corpse in the grave. Later, the arms were placed slightly bent so that the hands would meet across the lower abdomen. Later, the arms were placed across the abdomen crossing each other, the elbows being bent in right angles. Finally, by the fourteenth and fifteenth centuries, the arms were placed across the breast, folded as if the deceased were praying (Kieffer-Olsen 1993). The reasons for this shift are not clear, but perhaps it is

related to a shift in the perception of the afterlife. During the earlier stages of medieval Christianity, the afterlife was assured, but later on purgatory became a focus of what happened at death, and thus the more pious posture in the grave. When the data on the Norse arm positions are compared to the data from the Danish and Swedish medieval period, there is a good accordance between them and the radiocarbon analyses. This seems to indicate that the Norse, throughout the settlement period, adjusted their burial customs to the prevailing customs in northern Europe, which again may indicate that although remote, the Norse colonies were not completely isolated.

THE MASS GRAVE AT THJODHILD'S CHURCH: REFLECTIONS OF A VIOLENT SOCIETY?

The Norse churchyards furnish other interesting glimpses of a bygone way of life. At the small Thjodhild's Church (fig. 21.4-21.6), probably one of the earliest churches built by the Norse in Greenland (see Arneborg, this volume), an unusual mass grave was discovered when the church and churchyard were excavated in the 1960s (fig. 21.2, 21.3). Thirteen individuals, all male, and a nine-year-old child, whose age was determined by tooth eruption sequences, were found in a mass grave situated in the southern part of the cemetery. Not only were all these individuals buried at the same time in the same grave but their skeletons were completely disarticulated, with the crania neatly arranged lined up along the grave's eastern side.

Knud Krogh, the excavating archaeolo-

Church might constitute a ship's crew. Indeed, such a burial might reflect two passages in the saga literature (Krogh 1982: 46–47). The first is the story told in the *Greenlandic Annals* (*Grønlands Historiske Mindesmaerker* II: 663) of Lig-Lodin (literally "Corpse-Lodin"), a nickname apparently earned because its bearer sailed in the northern areas and brought back the bodies and remains of the deceased, shipwrecked, and so on. The second passage, also from the *Greenlandic Annals*, is the story of Einar Sokkason. Einar and his men, landing in the *utbyggðir* (literally "outposts," probably the areas north of the settlements) on an expedition, found a shipwreck and a small cabin. Several decomposed bodies were found in the cabin, and Einar ordered his men to "put the bodies in boiling water using the boilers which belonged to the dead men, so that the flesh can be separated from the bones, which then will be easier to bring to church" (*Grønlands Historiske Mindesmaerker* II: 691). While the mass grave may not exactly corroborate these accounts, it may perhaps corroborate the existence of such customs (that is, the securing of skeletal remains). There are other accounts of the finding of corpses in the sagas (for example, the *Saga of the Sturling Family* mentions a ship's crew found in a cave *Grønlands Historiske Mindesmaerker* II: 755, although there is no specific mention of whether they were brought back for interment).

Judging from the saga, the transportation of bodies from the place of death to the home churchyard seems to have been quite commonplace among the Norse settlers. In *Erik the Red's Saga*, Erik's third son, Thorstein (*Grønlands Historiske Mindesmaerker* I: 231) sailed to Vinland to find his brother's body and bring it back because his brother Thorvald had been slain in a confrontation with the indigenous people and had been buried there. When they were wintering in the Western Settlement, a fatal disease killed many of his crew. He then commanded that coffins be made and the bodies put on the ship, so that they could be brought back to the Eastern Settlement.

A shipwreck is not the most likely explanation of the mass grave at Thjodhild's Church. Three of the thirteen individuals sustained fatal cranial injuries inflicted by a sharp instrument, for example, an axe or sword. One male in the mass grave had an older, healed cut wound. These injuries do not suggest crushing, as they would if the individual had been smashed against rocks in a shipwreck, or the use of blunt instruments. In the light of the burial circumstances, these wounds might suggest a warrior or a clan group who had been in combat. Blood feuds and family revenge were certainly not unknown to the Norsemen. The sagas regularly give examples of such feuds (Byock 1988) and of the use of axes and swords in such conflicts (for example, *Grønlands Historiske Mindesmaerker* II: 325, 337, 353). As if to underscore this view of the Norse, a knife blade was found stuck between the ribs of a male in another grave at Thjodhild's Church (Krogh 1982). It therefore seems plausible that the mass grave represents a clan party that lost a feud, with all members of the party cut down and killed. This could have taken place at some more remote place, hence they were transported to the churchyard as bones.

Aside from such episodes of violence between clans or groups of people, the Norse had their share of domestic brutality, for instance, as recorded by a female skeleton's fractured hyoid. The hyoid bone is embedded in the organs of the throat, and fracture of this small bone is taken as highly indicative in forensic medicine of attempts at manual strangulation. Such a healed fracture suggests that she was choked with some force, but survived.

EARLY THEORIES

The remains of at least 457 individuals are represented in the Norse physical anthropological collections from Greenland. Although this may seem a high number, it is really hardly enough to give a general physical anthropological description of the Norse. The material is also very fragmented. It is enough, however, to dispel the notion of the Greenland Norse as a population that had degenerated into a small and sickly people. This misconception was the result of the first physical anthropological examination of Norse human bones in 1924 by the Danish anatomist F. C. C. Hansen. The first observations were based on the study of the Herjolfsnes material, where Hansen (1924) concluded that there had been a "striking decrease...of the size of their skulls." Since many saw cranial size, and hence cranial capacity, as directly related to brain size, and brain size as directly related to mental capacity, this meant that the Norse

21.2 MASS GRAVE
In addition to individual graves, excavators found thirteen males in a mass grave near the south wall of Thjodhild's Church. Most of the skulls had been placed at the west end of the pit, but the rest of the bones were jumbled and not in anatomical position. Possibly they had been brought here for Christian burial from a pagan cemetery or retrieved from a shipwreck, a hunting disaster in the Nordsetur, or a battle site.

"race" experienced a "reduction of the extent and capacity of intellectual life" (Hansen 1924: 434), ultimately paving the way for the Norse extinction. Implicit in Hansen's conclusion is the idea that the Norsemen, at the beginning of the settlement period, were tall and powerfully built. Indeed, Hansen considered that a decrease in stature had taken place: "The tall Northern race degenerated into small, slight, and delicate women, and correspondingly slightly taller men" (Hansen 1924: 465). This belief was further fueled by Roussell's (unpublished) remarks on Undir Høfda, when he found that a shallower-buried skeleton was shorter than four skeletons buried beneath it.

Later, the material from Herjolfsnes was generally discredited, and Fischer-Møller stated concerning his observations on the Sandnes material: "There is all the less reason for talking of degeneration, inasmuch as the extremity bones, although they exhibit somewhat shorter lengths than Norwegian medieval bones, are certainly no less massive or less well-developed" (Fischer-Møller 1942: 79). This was seemingly supported by the finds at Gardar, where Bröste and associates concluded that the stature was "also quite considerable" (1941: 58).

The bones from the Norse churchyards were to differing degrees subjected to postmortem changes, lying in humid earth for many hundreds of years. The material from Herjolfsnes is now recognized to be warped due to such changes and its usefulness for inferring direct measurements has been discredited. Still, a comprehensive study of all the Norse bones, excluding those with diagenetic or postmortem changes, show that of all the investigated Scandinavian samples, including Icelandic, Danish, and Norwegian crania, the Greenlandic Norse specimens differed most from all others and were the smallest (Hanson 1986, Scott et al. 1991). Fischer-Møller attributed this either to environmental causes (comparing the Norse with the Iceland horse or the Shetland pony) or to "racial peculiarities" due to the probable isolation of the Norsemen (Fischer-Møller 1942: 79). It must be borne in mind that the notion of the Vikings as especially tall and powerful is, however, somewhat unfounded. Actually, the people of the Viking Age were smaller than later medieval populations (Bennike 1985).

MEETING THE INUIT

The possible admixture of Inuit (Eskimos) in the population has nearly always been addressed in anthropological studies of the Norse: "none of the skulls showed characters, not even in the jaws or facial regions, that indicated a possible intermixture of Eskimo blood" (Hansen 1924: 430)! "It has not been possible to demonstrate the presence of Eskimo elements in the Gardar finds as a sign of mixture....In this connection it must be borne in mind that the Gardar finds belong to the first centuries of the colonization, when the possibilities of bastardization were perhaps not so obvious" (Bröste et al. 1941: 57); "Even though there might have been low levels of Inuit gene flow into the medieval Greenlandic populations, this is not revealed in their pattern of crown and root frequencies" (Scott et al. 1991: 198). Only Fischer-Møller proposed, on the basis of his study of the material from Sandnes, that three Norse crania exhibited Inuit traits: "there are several skulls on which the Eskimo stamp is so pronounced that we can only believe that we have before us mixtures of the Nordic and Eskimo races...[but]...this blood mingling is relatively limited" (Fischer-Møller 1942: 79). However, more recent reexamination of the material, using more sophisticated morphometrical and statistical means has failed to demonstrate this. Moreover, no Norse traits have been found in the pre-sixteenth-century Thule Inuit skeletal material (Balslev-Jørgensen 1953; Meldgaard 1965).

21.4

21.5

21.4–21.6 THJODHILD'S CHURCH

The sagas report that Erik's wife Thjodhild, who had converted to Christianity, wished to have a church built. Erik, though still pagan, agreed. The Greenland native artist Jens Rosing drew a reconstruction of the small church from archaeological evidence and knowledge of Norse building techniques (figs. 21.4, 21.6). The foundations of the church that was found at this site (foreground, above) is almost certainly Thjodhild's. It dates to about A.D. 1000, and so it is the first Christian church in the New World. (A modern church stands at the site today, in the background of this photo.)

21.6

The preoccupation with this question, especially in the earlier anthropological studies, is a reflection of the anthropological science of the times when racial typing was common. Fridtjof Nansen was a main proponent of a theory of assimilation: namely that the Norse were peacefully assimilated into the Inuit population. In support of this, Nansen had claimed that the Inuit were essentially a peaceful people. Nansen was probably also influenced by his own visits to Greenland, where he saw how rapidly intermixture had already taken place between the European settlers and the Inuit (Fyllingsnes 1990). However, this hypothesis is now completely abandoned. There have been very few finds of items that suggest a mixture of Norse and Inuit culture. For example, the clothes found at Herjolfsnes (figs. 21.12, 23.16) from the late settlement period are all distinctly European in fashion, and Nørlund used this to argue against the assimilation theory (Nørlund 1934). In this connection, it must also be remembered that the Norse Greenlanders saw themselves as agriculturalists (figs. 21.8, 21.9): social status and wealth were directly linked with land ownership (Arneborg 1993). The idea of becoming nomadic as the Inuit was undoubtedly far from their minds.

PATTERNS OF DISEASE

Just as the Norse have become infamous in the physical anthropological literature for a perceived racial degeneration and slightness of stature, so have many thought that their skeletons might be racked with signs of malnutrition and changes reflecting a lifetime of hardship and toil. Again, this seems to be caused by an overreliance on some of the first physical anthropological analyses of the Norse. Too little attention was paid to the detrimental effects of the forces of decomposition, and sample sizes were small. Living in medieval times, especially in such a remote place as Greenland, did have its consequences in terms of health, however. For example, the presence of more females in the younger adult age groups and more males in the older adult age groups, a pattern repeatedly found for all the major sites, indicates a higher mortality for females at a younger adult age than for males. A high mortality rate for younger females is traditionally explained as due to the risks of childbearing, especially postpartum infections, and the

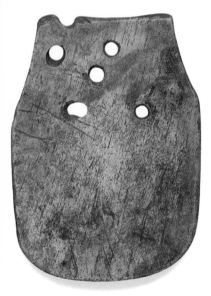

21.7 Whalebone Blade

Food crops could not be grown even in the warmest locations in Greenland. This blade from a Norse site at Nipaitsoq was probably lashed to a wooden handle and used to dig trenches, muck out stables, cut turf, and dig snow.

21.8 Wild Food and Nutrition

Hooks like this from the Norse farm at Kilaarsarfik were used to hang meat or other stored materials. Wild game provided much of the nourishment for the Greenland Norse. Early theories that poor nutrition contributed to Norse decline and extinction are not supported by new research, which shows local stature was only slightly smaller than other Norse populations. Another theory, that genetic mixing with Inuit took place, is also not supported.

risks of such infections could be exacerbated by poor health.

No signs of malnutrition have been identified, except two cases of poroctic hyperostosis. This condition displays a netlike bone formation especially in the roof of the eye sockets and is often taken as indicative of iron deficiency anemia. Only two examples hardly make the case for general nutritional deficiency. Another condition often used to indicate the health level of a population is dental enamel hypoplasia. This condition results from periods of ill health during early childhood, when the tooth enamel is being formed. The enamel is formed improperly, leaving a linear scar usually seen as a thin horizontal line across the teeth. These enamel defects can be counted and thereby reveal how often a particular individual was sick or ill fed. For the Norse, no trends could be discerned, meaning that their health probably did not deteriorate during the settlement period (Scott et al. 1991).

Isotope Studies: Dietary and Climatic Changes

While direct study of the physical remains may reveal some characteristics of the Norse, much can be learned by analyzing only minuscule amounts of bone. Radiocarbon analyses seem to indicate a dietary shift from a predominance of terrestrial resources to a more marine diet (Lynnerup 1998; Arneborg et al. 1999). These results accord generally with the results of studies of house refuse material, which indicate over time shifts as well as differences between the Western and Eastern Settlement (McGovern 1992). What would induce such a shift (figs. 21.7, 21.10, 21.11)? Animal husbandry was integral to the Norse way of life. Having to supplement one's diet with more and more marine input could mean that the Norse simply could not sustain their livestock production adequately. Livestock production was in turn dependent on the carrying capacity of the land. Reduction of output in terms of feed for the animals would be detrimental, and one obvious reason for such a reduction might be a colder climate. Indeed, ice-core borings in the Greenland ice shelf have indicated such a change, even of such a magnitude that the period is termed the Little Ice Age. It seems that the colonization of Greenland coincided with slightly warmer temperatures and that later, in the thirteenth century, the Little Ice Age arrived, substantially lowering temperatures. Proving climatic changes in the Greenland ice shelf does not, however, immediately translate to climate changes of the same magnitude in the deep and well-protected fjords of South Greenland, which also owe their relatively mild climate to the effects of the warm sea currents.

The skeletons, however, have borne testimony to such events. Small amounts of dental enamel were taken from the teeth of several Norse skeletons. The proportion of an isotope of oxygen, ^{18}O, was determined. Some of the oxygen atoms in water, H_2O, will be of the isotopic ^{18}O form. Just how many atoms reflects the temperature conditions at which water was formed in the atmosphere. After forming in the atmosphere, the water falls as rain or snow, ultimately passing through the soil and becoming springs, at which point the water will be drunk by humans. Thus, the proportion of ^{18}O in body tissue reflects the climate. Tooth enamel is used because it will reflect specifically the point in time around which this tissue was formed, which is in early infancy. The results agreed with the ice-core borings: the temperatures had dropped over a span of several hundred years (Fricke et al. 1995). The Norse were directly affected by a colder climate.

The Norse Population Size

How big was the Norse population in Greenland? This is a central question when reconstructing a past society. Explanations on the demise of the Norse settlements very much hinge on how big the population was. If it was small, then even slight perturbations may have rapidly brought the population below sustainable levels, whereas a large population would have a better buffering effect. Estimating the population size may be done, for example, by analyzing the number and size of farms and correlating this with a population size. Indeed, several archaeologists have done this, and estimates have ranged from an average population of about three thousand (Gad 1984) to four thousand (Berglund 1986), four thousand to five thousand (Meldgaard 1965), and five thousand to six thousand (McGovern 1979). Very few farms have been dated, however. Because the

21.9 COOPERED TUB AND LADLE
Wooden barrels, pails, and tubs were crucial to Greenland Norse domestic economy and were used for storing foods, making cheese, holding urine needed for bleaching and dying wool, and other tasks. Most of these implements, like this tub and ladle recovered from the Norse farm at Austmannadal, were made of Siberian/Alaskan driftwood. Similar containers appear in Greenlandic Inuit sites after 1500, which suggests that they borrowed the technique from the Norse.

Norse Greenlanders probably used the shieling system, that is, they moved their livestock to outlying grasslands for part of the grazing season (Berglund 1986), there could be two seasonal farm sites for each family. This means that the archaeological values probably represent maximum figures. If these figures do not seem very big, it must be remembered that the figures represent the population number at a given point in time. Such population levels accumulate into much bigger figures when the total number of deaths over the settlement period is calculated. For example, a population of around five thousand people will over a five hundred-year period produce as many as seventy thousand deaths. Is it plausible that the Norse churchyards contain so many skeletons? Based on calculations of the churchyard sites that have been thoroughly excavated, and then calculating an average burial density, it is possible to extrapolate from the known churchyard areas to a total inhumed population. This figure is much lower, pointing at an average population of some fifteen hundred to two thousand people.

Another way to analyze this would be to look at the biological framework for such a population. Was an increase from a starting population of four to five hundred individuals to at least two thousand individuals possible within a three hundred-year period without having to assume extreme values for life span, mortality, and fertility? And, consequently, could a population of this size pass into extinction?

A starting population was set arbitrarily at five hundred individuals. This was based on historical research, drawing on the accounts in the *Greenlanders' Saga* and *Erik the Red's Saga*, saying that "25 ships sailed for Greenland...but only 14 made it there" (*Grønlands Historiske Mindesmaerker* I: 179, 207). Allowing for a capacity of about thirty individuals per ship—it has been estimated that some of the larger Viking cargo ships in 1000 had a cargo capacity of 40 tons (Crumlin-Pedersen et al. 1992), this means that about three to four hundred people could have settled in Greenland in the first wave (Meldgaard 1965). Keller has mentioned that the capacity of the ships may have been smaller, but that there was more regular immigration, leading to a starting population of about three to eight hundred people (Keller 1986). A minimum starting population of some five hundred people would fit with the accepted minimum levels for sustainable populations of about four to five hundred (Geist 1978; Dyke 1984). Using an exponential model, a rate of increase of 0.62 percent would have to be assumed for the population level to increase to about two thousand within about two hundred years. This rate actually parallels a calculated population increase in Iceland in the period 970 to 1095 (using population figures from Thórarinsson 1961) and fits with rates calculated for many other populations in ethnographical analyses (between 0.15 and 0.40 percent). A slight continuing immigration would probably also be realistic. This rate probably dropped to zero (or rather the net rate of immigration and emigration was zero) between 1100 and 1200. This, along with a slowing of population increase as the population approached carrying capacity and thus began to strain resources, could be consistent with a leveling out by 1200.

Given a positive growth rate, emigration remains a possible explanation of a decreasing population. Emigration may occur when a population exceeds its optimum level in relation to living conditions (Hasan 1981). This could be because the Norse population reached the carrying capacity of their habitat, which may itself have been decreasing. Allowing for a decreasing rate of growth (since the young tend to emigrate, thereby not only counting themselves out of the population but also removing their potential offspring), this means that the emigration rate based on

21.10

21.10, 21.11 Culinary and Dietary Change

DNA testing has revealed that the Greenland Norse diet changed dramatically from dairy products and meat (caribou and livestock) in the earliest years to a diet largely based on fish, sea mammals, and marine birds in the last settlement phase (mid-fifteenth century). In addition to its use as food, which was eaten from bowls like this (fig. 21.10), marine-mammal oil also became the predominant fuel for heating and lighting Norse homes. This soapstone lamp (fig 21.11) is encrusted with charred seal oil. As elsewhere in the Norse world, fires were started by striking iron strike-a-lights against flinty rocks such as jasper, chert, or quartz.

a peak population of two thousand people would have to be about eight individuals per year. For a small population like the Norse, such a level of emigration would certainly have a massive effect. Are such rates realistic? We must first remember that these rates represent averages; that is, emigration would probably have taken place in waves of one hundred people every ten years. Furthermore, there can be stochastic variation: once the population is sufficiently small it becomes vulnerable to fluctuations in fertility and mortality (Weiss and Smouse 1976). Incipient decline could thus have been precipitated, and the population could have fallen sharply, perhaps with short periods of relative stability (fig, 21.14).

The size difference between the Western and Eastern Settlements must also be taken into account. Judging by the number of farmhouses (west 80, east 250; Gad 1984) and by the number of churches, there seems to be a 1:3 ratio between the settlement population sizes. Viewed in isolation, the Western Settlement would rapidly approach the minimum population size of five hundred. Indeed, given the preceding emigration rates and lowered fertility rates, the population would fall below this level after just twenty years. It is thus possible that decline set in around 1300. Fifty years later, most people would have emigrated from the Western Settlement, leaving perhaps only a few, mainly old, settlers. The Western Settlement could thus have been completely depopulated during the fourteenth century. Perhaps the Eastern Settlement then experienced some immigration that for some years offset the rate of decline, but then decline proceeded at the same rate as in the Western Settlement. This would leave the Eastern Settlement depopulated in the mid-fifteenth century.

A population may also become extinct due to exceptionally high mortality rates. High mortality rates are usually linked with war and epidemics. However, even rates of up to 10 percent of young adults killed in warfare would not substantially decrease birthrates. This leaves only highly lethal epidemics as the cause of a dramatic reduction in the population within a short time span. Plague struck both Iceland and Norway in the fourteenth and fifteenth centuries, and total mortality rates of between 30 and 50 percent have been suggested. Clearly, a halving of the Norse population in Greenland in just one or two years would be disastrous for such a small population and on the basis of the numbers alone could quite plausibly explain the population reduction.

Assuming the preceding rates and populations levels, an accumulated population size of 26,500 was calculated, equivalent to an average population size of 1,377. These figures are very close to the figures arrived at in the preceding section based on the number of interments. This does not constitute proof but points to the fact that the Norse population could have reached reasonable levels and conversely pass into extinction within the five hundred-year span of Norse settlement, without assuming undue biological parameters.

Where Did All the Norse Go?

On the basis of the skeletal material, some theories of extinction may be rejected: admixture with the Inuit, eradication by Inuit or pirates (no consistent signs of trauma during the later settlement periods) and "degeneration." Other theories seem more plausible; that is, the biological data might "fit" the theories (although not specifically proving them). As McGovern wrote (1992): "it seems probable that all the models [of the Norse society] advanced are at least partly correct (some perhaps more relevant to certain periods than others)." In this context, it is also important to consider developments in the other Scandinavian countries and the rest of the European continent not to infer direct, specific societal similarities, which, as mentioned previously, may be erroneous because of the probable uniqueness of the Norse Greenlandic society, but to place medieval Greenland in a wider framework.

21.11

In the first place, there seems to have been massive depopulation in most European countries at that time. As mentioned earlier, a 60 percent decrease in population has been projected for northern Norway, and at least a 30 percent decrease for Iceland. This massive depopulation, usually ascribed to the great plague epidemics, had enormous demographic, economic, and social repercussions. In the wake of the plague, there was large-scale population resettlement, where inhabitants of the more unproductive areas left for the better, "vacant" areas. Whether Norse Greenland was directly affected by plague, it would most certainly have been affected by the indirect effects of plague. For instance, the export prices of several Icelandic commodities fell dramatically (Keller 1986), and this may well also have had economic consequences for Greenland. Since it seems that the decline in population levels had already started before the plague epidemics reached the northern European countries, we could assume from paleoclimatic and zooarchaeological results that there was a climatic change in the years after 1300. This shift stressed the population, probably resulting in a trend toward ever harsher living conditions. Adaptive responses would include increasing reliance on marine foodstuff and efforts to increase land yield, the former evidenced by the radiocarbon analyses and the latter perhaps reflected by irrigation systems and the buffering capacity of the local community, headed by large farmsteads, which could redistribute food in times of need (fig. 21.13).

Perhaps after some internal resettlement, however, emigration accelerated in the fifteenth century. Better land became available in Iceland, a larger community, and it is even possible that old family claims could be invoked. The marginal land of Greenland no longer held the same attraction. The population pressure of the Viking times that had led to emigration had now reverted to an involution. Because of the size of the Western Settlement, with a projected population just above the minimum level for sustaining a community, the emigration of young adults would soon leave it in a state of irreversible decline, perhaps within twenty to thirty years. Thus, even without causes such as widespread famine, Inuit or pirate attacks, or epidemics, such a scenario may have led to swift decline. This resettlement may have been to Iceland and perhaps also to Norway. Such a scenario of "slow and quite undramatic emigration from the Norse settlements in Greenland" has also been proposed on the basis of cultural and historical research (Arneborg 1993). Such an ordered resettlement would also explain the lack of finds of precious items in the Norse settlements. An emigration rate of ten per year would depop-ulate the settlements within a two hundred-year period, assuming a peak population of some two thousand to twenty-five hundred people.

If this scenario does present something like the true picture of the past, it would also serve to eliminate some of the mystery of the settlement's demise. The Norse moved to Greenland because of a perceived gain and the possibility of land ownership, perhaps pushed to some extent by population pressure and the rapid exploitation of Iceland. They moved back when this possibility arose elsewhere. It would be surprising, in the light of the almost universal demographic changes and overall depopulation in Norway, Iceland, England, and so on, if a remote and already economically vulnerable settlement such as the Norse settlement in Greenland did not decline.

What then becomes of the apparent historical indifference to the fate of the Norse settlements in Greenland? Written accounts of the demise of the populations in Greenland are scarce, and surely such an influx to Iceland would have been noticed. The peak population of the Greenland settlements, probably at most twenty-five hundred people, must be compared with the Icelandic population size, which has been estimated at seventy thousand people (pre-plague). Even allowing for a 30 to 50 percent

21.12 Health and Clothing
Greenland Norse continued to keep up with European clothing fashion even in the final decades of the Eastern Settlement. By this time they had made contact with the Inuit, but rather than adopting the warmer and drier native skin dress, local wool clothing continued to be produced on looms frequently fitted with soapstone pot fragments refashioned as warp weights.

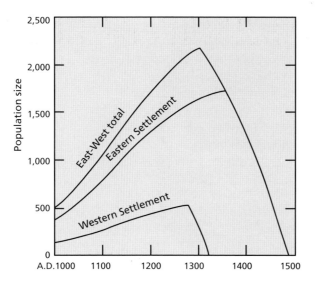

Data from the Norse cemeteries allow minimum population levels to be reconstructed. The Western Settlement began with a population of two hundred people, peaked at four hundred about A.D. 1300, and was abandoned by A.D. 1350. The Eastern Settlement began with a population of four hundred, peaked at 1,700 about A.D. 1380, and was probably abandoned by A.D. 1450. The highest total population, between two and three thousand, existed about A.D. 1300.

decrease due to plague, an influx of perhaps ten people a year would hardly be noticeable especially if there was some concurrent turmoil in the midst of plague and internal resettlement. Indeed, the marriage in Greenland in 1408 of a young couple who then moved to Iceland furnished the last written testimony about the Greenland Norse (see Arneborg, this volume) and might conceivably reflect young Norse Greenlanders resettling in Iceland.

Finally, much earlier Norse research presupposes a clear identification of Greenland as an isolated entity. The Norsemen may not have held such a view themselves. To them, Greenland was probably an extension of habitable lands and fjords stretching from Norway over the Shetlands, Orkneys, Faeroes, and Iceland all the way to Labrador and Newfoundland. For example, the Norse were not aware of having discovered a new continent when they arrived in Vinland; they had simply set out to look for exploitable land. This they found, but probably as a result of a decrease in population pressure and the uneconomically long distances, they never formed a proper settlement there. It is perhaps unmistakably modern (or at least postmedieval) to see Greenland as a distinct entity. In other words, perhaps the Norse did not give up Greenland—they gave up some land and fjords that had become less and less profitable for their way of life and moved back to more auspicious shores where new opportunities had arisen.

21.13 Sickle Blade

Greenland's climate never permitted the growth of food crops, only grass and hay for fodder. Small iron sickles like this one from Austmannadalen were used to cut hay from the infield near the farm. Grass growth was enhanced at some farms by irrigation channels that led run-off to choice fields.

22 | THE FARM BENEATH THE SAND

BY JOEL BERGLUND

FOR THE PAST SEVERAL YEARS RE-search at an unusually well-preserved Norse inland farm site in Greenland's Western Settlement has provided many fascinating new details about Norse life in Greenland. New excavation and conservation techniques and new scientific approaches have led to new conclusions about life on an inland farm that was occupied for nearly the entire period the Norse lived in Greenland from the eleventh to the fifteenth centuries. This site, called the "Farm Beneath the Sand" (*Gård Under Sandet*, or GUS), had been nearly perfectly preserved beneath frozen river sands.

HISTORY AND LOCATION
In the early autumn of 1990 two Inuit caribou hunters from Nuuk, hunting about fifty-five miles (eighty kilometers) east of town, noticed some large pieces of wood sticking out at the foot of a river bluff. Wood does not occur naturally in Greenland, and when they discovered that the wood had been worked, the hunters immediately notified the Greenland National Museum and Archive in Nuuk. They had found the remains of a Norse building, and the unusual piece of timber turned out to be part of a weaving loom (Berglund 1998a: 7).

The hunting area is on a plateau near Nipaitsoq, and just under six miles (ten kilometers) from the edge of Greenland's ice cap. This huge sand plain now lies as barren as a desert, with meandering meltwater rivers flowing through it. The land near the site consists of terraces of sand and gravel deposited by the water and is covered with arctic heath vegetation. Higher up one sees a more varied landscape with vegetation ranging from grass and hillside flowers to bushes and small trees. This scrub provides shelter for ptarmigan, arctic hare, arctic fox, and small birds, and is also part of the habitat of the wild caribou.

This part of West Greenland belongs to the subarctic zone (map), and because of its inland situation the climate is continental, that is, cold and dry. The proximity to the inland ice has a beneficial effect on the climate, which is favored by the stable high pressure that forms over the inland ice. This means that the summers are reasonably warm and the winters are rather cold. In the summer months it is not unusual to record a temperature of 79° F (26° C), while the temperature in the coldest winter months can drop to -58° F (-50° C) (Berglund 1998a: 11).

FIELD WORK
It was evident at the outset that the remains of the building lay in permafrost with an average of fifty inches (160 centimeters) of

THE GOAT HEIÐRÚN, *SNORRA EDDA*

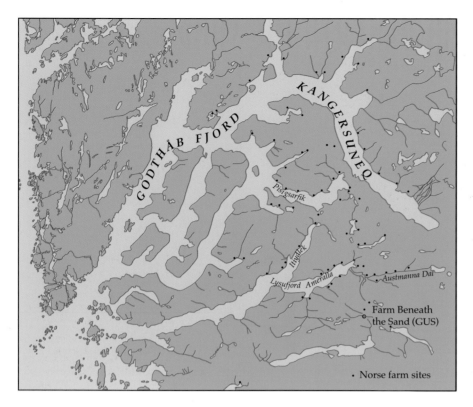

FARM BENEATH THE SAND,
SITE LOCATION MAP

22.1 SEA OF GLACIAL SAND
The Farm Beneath the Sand or *Gård Under Sandet* (GUS), located in Nipaitsoq fifty-five miles (eighty kilometers) east of Nuuk, is only six miles (ten kilometers) from a melting lobe of the inland ice sheet. This view over-looking the riverside site (lower left) shows the extensive glacial sand deposits that during high-water episodes wash down over the site covering and preserving its archaeological remains.

sand deposited on top (fig. 22.1). Traces of buildings were evident in the river bluff over a stretch of a good sixty-five yards (sixty meters). In the winter the river is frozen, and the water volume only reaches a maximum during the summer months. At low water a number of building stones were revealed in the river, which could mean that the whole front of the building complex had already been eroded away, and what was left was the interior of one or more buildings. It was also quite evident that it was only a matter of time before the small point on which it all

lay would disappear into the river. The cultural layer was not directly washed away, but the river had undermined the permafrost subsoil, and the cultural layer and the sand above it were collapsing into the river. After considering possible ways to divert the river or stabilize the site it was decided that an archaeological rescue excavation was the only suitable course of action (Arneborg 1998: 3).

The excavation proved to be extremely labor intensive and difficult. Before the actual cultural layer could be excavated a sterile sand layer fifty inches (160 centimeters) thick had to be removed; in one particular year, about a thousand tons of sand were shoveled away! The cultural layer was frozen into compact ice that had to be thawed before it could be excavated. The maximum thaw rate was about four inches (ten centimeters) a day, and this turned the upper layers into a morass of mud and water. The water, in particular, was a problem because it could not seep away, but lay in the excavation field as small lakes. The permafrost turned out to be a blessing in disguise because it had stopped all the processes of decay, creating the best possible preservation conditions for organic material.

It took four seasons before the excavation had reached the original ground surface. The farther we dug down, the closer we came to the level of the river, and new technical problems were encountered. As the water level of the river rose, water also began to seep up from below. We built a wall of sand-bags against the river and a bridgehead of excavated fill to change the direction of the current so that it did not flow directly into the excavation field. This helped somewhat, but only with the use of a motorized pump was it possible to keep the water in check. One year there was a disastrous water discharge from the inland ice: in the course of thirty minutes the water level rose three feet (one meter) and flooded the whole excavation area (fig. 22.2). The work had to be stopped, but fortunately the season was almost over anyway and little damage was done.

EXCAVATION RESULTS
After the covering sand layer had been removed and the permafrost had been thawed, the cultural layer appeared as a black deposit. The top layer was characterized by great amounts of timber in different sizes, which we interpreted as bearing elements for the

JOEL BERGLUND

The more we uncovered, the more complex the interior of the building became, with more than thirty rooms (fig. 22.3)! Because the building process stretched from the mid-eleventh to at least the early fourteenth century, and perhaps into the fifteenth century, as determined by geological data (see below), not all the rooms and passages were in use at the same time. This building was a living organism that changed throughout its lifetime: new rooms were added, and others were torn down. Almost all the rooms had changed both size and function in the course of the building's use, usually from living or storage space to stalling space for animals, but there were also proper animal sheds with stall partitions and stone paving. Filled-in doors and openings in walls for new doors indicated a restructuring of the interior circulation pattern. There also seems to have been a tendency to make the rooms smaller over the course of time.

The walls had a cofferwork construction with timbers and fill, in some cases resting on a stone sill. In a few other cases stone was used as an alternative to turf in cofferwork walls, but no pure stone walls were found. The turves were cut from the surrounding terrain in the specific sizes that were needed to build up the wall in a herringbone pattern with short, diagonally opposite turves separated by long, horizontally placed turves, a technique that is also seen in Iceland (fig. 9.8). The walls appeared in different thicknesses from about twenty to forty inches (half a meter to more than one meter).

The chronological framework of the buildings ranges from the first half of the eleventh century to possibly as late as the end of the fifteenth century, which covers most of the Norse period in Greenland. Around the mid-eleventh century the Norse settlers took over land at the edge of the plateau, which at that time was a fertile wetland with meadows and sediment-free watercourses. Like the later complex, the facade of this first house was oriented toward the plain, as was the custom among Norse farmers. The remains of the house were excavated during the last two seasons and lay below the later complex on the original ground surface. All that remained was a leveled hearth, but the traces of walls, hearth, entrance, and roof posts were still clear. It had been a smallish three-aisled longhouse or hall (Albrethsen and Ólafsson 1998: 19ff) with inside dimensions

collapsed roof. There was no apparent scarcity of wood, as one might normally expect: some of the wood was riddled with holes made by shipworms and could be identified as driftwood but other wood was undamaged and may have come from Vinland or Norway. Wood occurred from the youngest (top) layer to the oldest (bottom) of the site, but most of it was in the more recent layers, which suggests that this precious resource was recycled as rooms were changed or new ones were added. The timber was usually formed into objects such as poles, planks, and laths. Its preservation was better the farther one penetrated down through the layer, which indicates that the sanding over of the site did not happen all at once, because the wood in the top layers had been exposed to freezing and thawing in the open air for several years.

We can only guess at the structure of the roof, but in the latest occupation of the site large quantities of small branches were found in every room, in and above the floor layer. This has been interpreted as collapsed roofing material from a pitched roof whose underside was covered with branches while the exterior surface was covered with a thin layer of turf.

The earliest phase of the complex was identified as a centralized farm, which means that all the rooms and functions were in the same building. This building type is particularly well known from the Western Settlement and seems to have been a special Greenlandic development of the turf house (Roussell 1941: 159ff). At least eight to ten rooms, perhaps more, seem to have been associated with this phase with interconnected rooms and passages.

22.3 THE FARM COMPLEX

After three years of excavation, the Farm Beneath the Sand site began to take shape as rooms and passageways were revealed. It became clear that the front of the farm (to the right) had been eroded by the river; fortunately, the river sands that covered the site had sealed it from the air and caused permafrost to preserve everything.

of forty by sixteen feet (twelve by five meters) and with turf walls between four and six feet (1.2 and 1.9 meters) thick; benches along the walls, on either side of a long hearth, provided seating. The building material was wood for the bearing parts and furnishings like benches, and turf for the walls and roofing. To make the walls of this hall alone, turf would have had to be peeled from an area of about 1,100 square yards (1,000 square meters). The entrance, on the long northern side of the building, had been furnished with slab rocks and a threshold. The first room was an antechamber separated from the main room by a thin plank wall, in which there were traces of a storage barrel and a small cooking pit.

The hall was used for only a short period as a dwelling before it was adapted as an animal shed. This is revealed by the thin floor layer at the bottom, which was covered by a thicker layer of sheep manure mixed with fragments of bones and chopped branches that had been used for animal feed or floor covering. In this phase a couple of smaller side buildings were added, but because they were poorly preserved not much can be said about them; in one, the impressions of several storage barrels were observed. At some point after it was adapted for animals there was a fire, and all the wood and turf in the building burned. A compact layer of charcoal was visible at the floor and above this a red-colored ash layer from the completely burned roof turf. The whole building perished on this occasion, and several of the sheep also seem to have died in the fire.

The hall represents a building type that was quite common in the North Atlantic

area during the late Viking Age and the beginning of the Norse medieval period; however, this building differs from most in not having the curved long sides that were so common. The ground plan is generally the same, with a single room framing the centrally placed long hearth. This tradition of arranging spatial elements had endured more than a thousand years but it changed in the course of the Middle Ages.

GEOLOGICAL STUDIES

Investigations of the local geology, in profiles as well as the excavation, suggests that there was a gap in settlement between the time the hall burned down and the later central complex was built. The lifetime of the hall has been radiocarbon dated to the period between circa 1020 and 1200 (Albrethsen and Ólafsson 1998: 26). At some point close to 1200 new building resumed, and construction began on the complex that would in time develop into the centralized farm.

Geological evidence suggests that there was an attempt to improve the home field (*tún*) by spreading waste over the areas around the building to improve fertility and retain moisture. This is the first time that presumed soil-improvement measures have been recorded in a Norse context. This surface differs from those before and after the settlement, precisely in having a larger quantity of various waste remains. The movement of domestic animals around the building could be seen in small depressions from hooves that were filled with sand (Schweger 1998: 14ff). Otherwise the presence of domestic animals was evident from bones and above all from their manure, which when the permafrost layer thawed could be distinguished by the eight hundred-year-old stable smell. Those sensitive to such things could distinguish between the smell of cattle and that of sheep or goats.

FAUNAL ANALYSIS

The people who participated in the *landnám*, or original parceling of land to settlers, and their descendants were primarily farmers with domestic animals as their specialization. The preliminary identifications of bones from the excavation indicate that the animals included cattle, horses, sheep, and goats. The proportions of each kind of bones show that the stock was mostly sheep or goats and to a lesser extent cows and horses. A few bones

22.4, 22.5 TABLEWARE
Among the innumerable remains preserved by frost on the floor of the main dwelling room were a well-used wooden bowl and a decorated triangular wooden trencher or platter whose surface shows the cut marks of metal knives. Like most of the utensils recovered, these lack the wormholes that are usually found in Siberian driftwood, so it is presumed that they were made of wood imported from Europe or Markland.

from a long-legged spitz-type of domestic dog were found, which may have been used as a sheepdog. The many textile remains that were found spread all over the complex indicate that some sheep were kept for wool; impressions of barrels suggest that other sheep and goats as well as cows supplied milk for the occupants of the farm.

The type of animal bones can indicate the attitude toward local wild animal resources, which sometimes reflects economic necessity. A preliminary review showed that most bones came from such game as hare, seal, and caribou, confirming that the domestic animals were kept for milk and wool. The area was a habitat for the same animals then as now; it was not unusual during the excavation to see a herd of twenty caribou wandering over the plain and up over the low mountains, indeed, even through the archaeologists' camp. Larger predators such as the arctic wolf and polar bears would also have been hunted when the opportunity arose, but finds of these animals were rare, as were those of walrus. Perhaps these bones are evidence of long-ranging hunting trips up along the west coast to

Disko Bay, which was presumably the inexhaustible hunting grounds of the sagas, called the Nordsetur (Berglund 1986: 113). The biggest bones that were found were whale vertebra used to sit on or for use as worktables! They were probably isolated finds from skeletons of beached whales.

As in other excavations of Viking and early Norse sites, there were only a few fish bones. This is surprising because it contrasts strongly with the maritime emphasis of later Norse economics. Although early people must have exploited the rich stocks of salmon, trout, and cod, because the bones are small and easily soluble they have not left many traces. The fish refuse may also have been eaten by dogs or gathered to use as a dietary supplement for stabled animals during the winter. More fish bones were found during this excavation than in earlier ones, which suggests that the absence of this data resulted from poor preservation.

The imported domestic animals were alien to the natural Greenland fauna and, except for the sheep, could not survive without coexisting with human beings. The same is true of a much smaller animal that came with the immigration—the house mouse, which is not rare in Norse excavations (McGovern 1992: 96) and was found in Farm Beneath the Sand too. The interior of the building complex with heat and animal and human waste provided very favorable conditions for the small rodent, which always appears with settled human beings. Building complexes can in fact be regarded as a man-made micro-landscape with different biotopes or niches conditioned by factors like heat, animal species, humans, and waste. During the excavation regular samples of the cultural layer were taken, among other reasons to identify the species of parasites that would inevitably have lived in this landscape. Certain parasite species are specific to certain environments, and the identification of a species can reveal the use of rooms and areas in the building. Body lice parasitical on humans were found as well as lice that are exclusively parasites on sheep (Buckland et al. 1998: 74 and this volume). The many much-worn combs that were found everywhere indicate clearly the presence of this nuisance.

FUNCTION AND FINDS
More than thirty rooms were identified in the complex as a whole, but a function could

22.6 GREENLAND GOTHIC?

This small wood fragment with interwoven floral designs carved in relief was once part of a larger panel. It is one of the few pieces found in Greenland bearing this type of decoration. A similar decoration is found on a spoon box cover from Sermermiut (fig. 24.11).

22.7 DECORATED BOX LID

This five-inch (thirteen-centimeter) long sliding box lid has interlaced foliage and cross-braid designs cut deeply into its surface. The underside (not illustrated) has a stylized dragon head and runes for a female name, Bjørk.

be assigned to only a few of them. Perhaps the most intriguing room that could be identified without hesitation was a place where textiles were made (Østergård 1998: 65). The remains of an upright loom, probably the oldest in the medieval North Atlantic area, were found there. They were a beam and a lease board on which one can see the marks the warp had cut in the course of time. The highest concentration of warp weights—that is, weights used to weigh down the warp—was also found in this room: about eighty of them, as well as a number of spindle whorls and spindles used to spin yarn. The spindle whorls and warp weights were made of soapstone: often the warp weights were simply shards from a broken vessel in which holes had been bored (fig. 21.12), while the spindle whorls were always made for the purpose and were sometimes finely decorated with line patterns. Both warp weights and spindle whorls were found all over the complex, but never in such high density as in this room. It was the largest room and had been built during the older phase of the complex, but it seems to have been used until the end of the life of the building—indicating the ongoing importance of weaving. This is the only place in the complex where a kind of furniture was found, that is, a niche for keeping small objects. In this niche there was a bundle of raw wool and one of the oddest objects from the excavation: a braided chain of hair from a fair-haired person that was worn as a bracelet or necklace. Use of braided hair as jewelry has continued in Scandinavia right up to our own times (Østergård 1998: 61).

The making of textiles would have been a very important activity in the small community. Certainly it was necessary to make clothing, but wadmal, a coarse but warm homespun wool, may also have had a commercial function.

Icelandic sagas indicate that it was used as a criterion of value or even simply as currency. Most of the textiles were made from animal wool, but one textile based on plant fiber, probably cultivated flax (*Linum usitatissimum*), was found in the hall—that is, from the oldest phase. An example of shaggy-pile weave, otherwise only known from one other *landnám* farm, was also found here; this technique can be traced back to the early Bronze Age in Denmark (Østergård 1998: 63). All the cloth remains found were of high quality and quite in keeping with the medieval tradition in Iceland and southern Scandinavia.

The wool was primarily supplied by sheep, but analyses of its origin demonstrated a variety of other species. Not surprisingly, hair from domestic animals such as sheep, goats, and oxen is present in the wool; but caribou, polar bear, arctic fox, and possibly musk ox also contributed fibers. It was rather surprising to find fiber from animals that neither live nor have lived in Greenland such as brown bear and bison. The latter finds give rise to speculation about direct links with Canada, where trade with Inuit cannot be excluded, or that it was wool from the Scandinavian bear and European bison, or wisent (Rogers 1998: 71).

The textile finds are unfortunately only small fragments of clothing, but one can get an idea of how the clothes looked by comparing these pieces with a unique collection of medieval everyday garments that was excavated from Herjolfsnes in southernmost Greenland in 1921; today these finds from Norse Greenland are on display at the Danish National Museum in Copenhagen (Nørlund 1924: 91ff). It is clear that the textiles were expertly made in accordance with the European taste of the day (fig. 23.16).

The weaving room also had a hearth consisting of flat flagstones set on edge to form an open box. The hearth was movable and thus was not an architectural fixture but an item of furniture. In several rooms there were traces of hearths that had been taken down or moved. A total of five hearths were found; they all had the same basic shape, built up against a wall, but the fire chamber varied in size. The most complex one was three hearths built together in a row. At least some of the fuel was wood, which could be seen from small pieces of charcoal; but animal manure was probably used also.

22.8 CHRISTIANITY IN GREENLAND
Small devotional crosses are often found at Norse farm sites and graves in Greenland. Christianity was present at the beginning of the colony in the late tenth century, and by 1126 Greenland received its own bishop. Crosses such as this were designed with pointed bases so they could be moved and staked into the ground or turf walls.

22.9 OWNER'S MARKS
This wooden scoop was photographed in the field before conservation. The handle was split and had been mended by the Norse with clamps. The bottom is marked with an incised X whose upper and lower quadrants have small, embellished Christian crosses, the owner's personal identification mark.

Dwelling Room

In the center of the complex was a space that can only be interpreted as a living room, which was later used as an animal shed. It was not particularly big, about ten by seventeen feet (three by five meters), and had two entrances, including one door that we found intact. The room belonged to the last building phase. The floor was partly covered with pieces of board and small, flat paving stones on which people walked so as not to sink into the mud on the floor. Another door had been added later at the opposite end of the room when it changed status from living room to animal shed and when the hearths were removed. The preserved door lay flat in the opening among the stones that formed the foundation of the doorframe. The door consisted of three flat-cut planks joined together with a tongue-and-groove system, fixed by two wooden crosspieces riveted on with wooden dowels. It has been repaired with baleen lashings and a preserved band or strap of caribou antler. The door was made of worm-eaten Siberian driftwood that had been brought to Greenland by sea currents.

The floor layer in this room was rich in finds. Household articles such as bowls, ladles, and cutting boards made of wood and soapstone were found (figs. 22.4, 22.5), as were horn spoons, tools for spinning wool, warp weights, and combs. Other pieces included a shoe last (fig. 22.11), a decorated box with lid (fig. 22.7), and a panel with a carved plant motif in the early Gothic style (fig. 22.6). A surprising find was two smallish, very beautifully worked wooden devotional crosses (fig. 22.8) of a type otherwise only known from grave finds (Berglund 1998b: 48ff). Bones were found everywhere in the layer; they were clearly the remains of meals, and a large number had been broken open to get at the marrow. It appears that the remains were simply thrown on the floor, where they gradually disappeared into the mud.

Animal Sheds

It was most obvious that the function of a room had changed when it was converted to an animal shed. Some rooms in the oldest part of the complex had been intended as animal sheds from the beginning. Several purpose-built animal sheds were excavated, and they were distinctive in having stone paving, sometimes a central dung trough, and flagstones set on edge to partition off stalls for individual larger animals. These stalls show the presence of larger as well as smaller animals, while the rooms made into stalls seem to have been used only for smaller animals. The number of artifact finds in the sheds was as expected minimal, and usually they were objects that naturally belonged there—for instance, a manure spade made from the shoulder blade of a whale lashed to a wooden shaft. Sometimes these rooms contained small crudely carved blubber lamps. Enough shards from the biggest soapstone vessel known from Norse Greenland were recovered; when intact it would have held ten gallons (forty-five liters). Its many metal repair clamps attest to careful stewardship of this valuable receptacle. A burned crust in the vessel suggests that it was used to heat organic material, perhaps a kind of extra fodder for the animals during the winters.

Without knowing how many animal sheds were in use at the same time, it is impossible to calculate how many animals there were. All rooms in the complex became smaller with time, so it is likely that there were fewer domestic animals toward the end of the life of the farm and that only the smaller ones—sheep and goats—were given space in the newly converted rooms while larger ones remained in the dedicated stalls. The practice of housing animals and humans under the same roof extends back into Norse prehistory; the benefits of such coexistence meant that the heat from their bodies helped to maintain a tolerable temperature indoors during the extremely cold winters.

Storage Rooms

Impressions from large barrels in the floor layer identify rooms that were used for storage. In several rooms circular impressions up to three feet (one meter) in diameter were recorded; but no remains of the barrels themselves were found. These rooms may have been later converted and the barrels moved elsewhere. Many finds of small staves and barrel bottoms in the complex showed that the occupants were very familiar with the

22.10

SHOE LAST

This wooden shoe last, used to size and form shoes and boots, is similar to many such finds from Greenland. Its shape and pointed toe appear quite stylish. A family would need a number of lasts for different-sized individuals, but only one per size—there were no rights or lefts!

22.11 MEASURING DIVIDERS

This compasslike tool of wood and iron was used to measure distances and inscribe circles. One possible use might have been for marking out decorative carvings on wood. Similar tools are used today by navigators, carpenters, and engineers. It is one of the most complex mathematical instruments recovered from a Norse site.

22.12 POLAR-BEAR TOOTH PENDANT

Among the thousands of finds recovered at the Farm Beneath the Sand only one—a perforated polar-bear canine—has a hole suggesting use for wearing as decoration or as an amulet. Perforated canine teeth are common in Thule Inuit sites.

22.12

technique of coopering; in one of the later rooms a whole coopered vessel was found. The large barrels probably held sour-milk products that are known from the sagas to have been important in the Norse Greenland economy.

Crafts

Time and time again during the excavation the occupants' skill and expertise as craftsmen was revealed. They worked in wood, horn, soapstone, bone, and iron. Many of their tools were found, mostly scrapped fragments, but enough to piece together a toolbox with several knives, a bore, an auger, a plane, an axe, a marking gauge (fig. 22.11), and several grindstones as well as pieces of pumice that had been used for polishing. Fragments of building timber and other materials that show traces of working testify to the sharpness of the tools. Finger-thick cut branches often show an even, smooth cut surface with no stepping, which reveals that the branches were cut with a single stroke. These long unbroken cuts are most easily made with long-bladed knives, but the knives recovered in the excavation had short blades. Larger items, for example, the planks in the door, had been given an even surface finish with an adz, while the building timbers were often rather crudely finished.

The few finds of carved ornamentation were cut with a carving technique that involves making notches with the point of a knife along a pattern and that has persisted to the present; in fact, neither the toolbox nor woodworking techniques have changed much since the Middle Ages.

THE LAST PHASE OF THE FARM

At some time late in the 1200s there was a marked change in the living conditions for the people at Nipaitsoq. Climatologists believe the average temperature dropped probably as a prelude to the Little Ice Age, which dates from the mid-1300s to the mid-1800s. Colder conditions meant that the inland ice grew, glaciers advanced, and the amount of summer meltwater increased. The earlier clear watercourses that

22.11

flowed through the plateau changed to sediment-rich, milky-colored streams whose waters had to be settled before drinking. The pastures sanded up, and little by little it became impossible to farm the area. By the late fourteenth to early fifteenth centuries, the farm had to be abandoned (Schweger 1998: 14ff).

There is nothing to suggest that the place was abandoned in a panic; for example, about 90 percent of the found objects seem to have been discarded naturally. Whatever the occupants could use and take with them, they took. It is striking, however, that no large objects—benches, beds, and other large furnishings—were found, so these items may have been removed to use somewhere else where the occupants settled. Not many objects bore owners' marks, which again suggests that people packed their personal possessions in a calm and orderly fashion (fig. 22.8).

When the occupants left the Farm Beneath the Sand, where did they go—to neighbors, to the more southerly Eastern Settlement, or away from Greenland? We do not know the exact year, but the geology studies suggest that the farm was abandoned at the end of the fifteenth century. This dating is surprising, because many scholars believe the lifetime of the Western Settlement ended in the mid-1300s (Schweger 1999). The investigations are not yet over; we may see further explanations of this difference between literary and scientific datings. What we know about the personal life of these people is limited: that they were Roman Catholic, that the West Norse language was spoken, and that they thus belonged to the North Atlantic Norse cultural sphere. We come closest to them in rune carvings (fig. 22.7) that include the names of two men and one woman who were associated with the house in some way: Thor, Bardur, and Bjork (Stoklund 1998: 55). There were children at the farm, and finds of toys such as a miniature shoemaker's last (fig. 22.10) and wooden model knives reveal that play was part of their life and that simulation of grown-up life was, then as now, an important part of children's play.

One written source (Roussell 1936: 10) tells us that around the middle of the 1300s the cleric and civil servant Ivar Bardarson was sent to the Western Settlement to contact the people there, since in the more southerly and larger Eastern Settlement no one had heard from them for many years. He found no people, only empty farms and stray farm animals. The quantities of animal manure that lay in all rooms in this abandoned farm appear to confirm the story of untethered domestic animals. They would have been unable to take all their animals with them, and those that were left behind would have stayed near the farm for shelter until it disappeared. In the previously mentioned living rooms there were smaller quantities of animal dung, because the door kept the animals out for a certain time until it fell in. One of the last creatures to live on the farm—a goat, its skeleton with skin and hair preserved more or less intact in the permafrost—was found under a collapsed wall (fig. 22.13).

Animals were not the only living creatures to visit the abandoned farm. A very small number of finds in the upper layers suggest that Thule Inuit caribou hunters used it overnight during hunting trips inland. Objects associated with the Thule culture show that these people, during their migrations from the north, reached the area around the fjord complex at Nuuk during the 1300s (Gulløv 1997: 435). In addition to the few objects found, traces of a small fire lit on a floor suggest that the caribou hunters contributed to the ultimate collapse of the building. There were traces of fire all over the building in the last phase, but not of an overwhelming, all-consuming fire. The traces of burning were sporadic, never complete combustion. Perhaps sparks from the caribou hunters' fire jumped into the turf wall, where they lay smoldering until a draft made the fire flare up, only to die down again when the wind calmed. This could have gone on for some time, until the upper structures of the building became so weak that they collapsed into the house. Movements of the animals in the house would have contributed to the decay, among other ways by keeping openings such as doors and any holes in collapsed walls open to wind and weather.

Little by little the decay progressed. Studies of the house remains show that there was no sudden, catastrophic collapse; on the contrary, it seems to have happened at different rates in the different parts of the building. The final destruction of the farm came from quite a different quarter—the inland ice. The increasing meltwater gradually flooded the whole plain, and in the end water rose above the farm. When it receded again the sand completely covered the farm and the traces of the medieval Norse farm on the plain disappeared from view, only to be discovered five centuries later by Inuit hunters.

22.13 THE END OF THE FARM BENEATH THE SAND

The final part in the dramatic history of the Farm Beneath the Sand was reserved for a goat. Ivar Bardarson's mid-fourteenth-century *Description of Greenland* tells of his visit to the Western Settlement, which he found abandoned, with animals wandering wild in the fields. His report appears confirmed at the Farm Beneath the Sand, where animal dung lay thick on the floors of the living rooms and the last occupant, a goat (below), lay frozen where he died beneath a collapsed wall.

BY JETTE ARNEBORG

It happens in Greenland…that all that is taken there from other countries is costly there, because the country lies so far from other countries that people rarely travel there. Every item, with which they might help the country, they must buy from other countries, both iron and all the timber with which they build houses. People export these goods from there: goatskins, ox-hides, sealskins and the rope…which they cut out of the fish called walrus and which is called skin rope, and their tusks…The people have been christened, and have both churches and priests…. (King's Mirror, Hellevik 1976)

THIS PASSAGE FROM THE NORWEGIAN *King's Mirror* describes Norse Greenland's contacts with the rest of the world at the beginning of the thirteenth century. The book, written in the mid-1200s, is structured as a father's reply to his son's questions about why people traveled to Greenland despite the risk to life involved and whether the population there was Christian as it was in the rest of Europe.

SCARCE GOODS AND TRADE

The father in the *King's Mirror* tells his son that the Greenlanders imported iron and timber, while they exported skins, hides, rope, and walrus tusks. On the face of it, it seems logical that timber for house and ship construction had to be imported to the sparsely wooded Greenland. The few analyses made so far of wood finds from the Greenlandic settlements show that Greenlanders made extensive use of the large quantities of driftwood from the Siberian and North American forests that accumulated in skerries near their settlements; this confirms the provenance suggested by visible traces of shipworm on the wood used. Analysis of ship wood from

HANGING A THIEF, *JÓNSBÓK*

The better rooms were often furnished with wood paneling, and light partition walls and doors were made of wood (Roussell 1936: 163, fig. 178; Roussell 1941: 179ff). All the larger pieces of wood found in the Farm Beneath the Sand site (Berglund, this volume) bear the characteristic traces of shipworm. Practically all the wood—whether used in house construction or to make household utensils—is driftwood. Smaller objects were made of such local woods as birch (*Betula*), willow (*Salix*), and juniper (*Juniperus*). In this respect the Farm Beneath the Sand differs little from the previously excavated farms in the Western and Eastern Settlements.

In 1347 a Greenlandic ship with eighteen men came to Iceland. The ship had come from Markland (which scholars today agree refers to Labrador), which is described as flat and forested. The Greenland ship may have been in Markland to get timber, perhaps to compensate for insufficient supplies from Norway. To date, archaeological investigations of the Norse settlements have not corroborated that much wood was imported, and so far none can be assigned positively to the American continent.

The trade goods of the Greenlanders, according to the information in the *King's Mirror*, were goatskins, ox hides, sealskins, skin rope, and walrus tusk. The same group of goods is mentioned in the few written sources that record Greenlandic tithe payments to the church. In 1282 Pope Martin IV wrote to Archbishop Jon of Nidaros in Norway that the Greenlandic tithes, which had been paid in ox hides, sealskins, walrus

the Norse farms—often in secondary use, for example, as benches and floor covering—shows that ships were built with larch (*Larix*) and spruce (*Picea*), both of which are found in Greenland as driftwood from Siberia (Andersen and Malmros 1993).

The buildings in the later settlement period were either pure stone constructions or were built of cut turves and stone. The walls were roof-bearing, but not much wood was used in their construction, apart from what was absolutely essential to the structure.

tusks, and ropes made of walrus hide, should be converted to silver or gold. The next record of Greenlandic tithe payments is from 1327, when a papal tax collector submits accounts for a large quantity of walrus ivory from Greenland.

The consumption of skins and hides, used in the production of garments, shoes, and belts, was high during the Viking Age and the Middle Ages. Skins and hides were so highly regarded that they became de facto currency and were accepted as a valid means of payment. Pope Martin IV's 1282 letter reveals that the manufactured rope with which the Greenlanders paid their tithes was the most valuable. Because skins and hides were also produced by northern Scandinavians, the walrus products, which were unique to Greenland at that time, commanded the greatest interest on the Scandinavian and European markets. Walrus rope, one of the strongest types available, was particularly in

demand as ship's rope. Walrus tusk—and narwhal tusk, which is not mentioned in the written sources—were very costly raw materials used in the production of luxury articles (fig. 23.1) for both secular and ecclesiastical purposes (Roesdahl 1998). More exotic and prestigious goods such as hunting falcons and polar-bear skins also found their way from Greenland to Europe. In 1338 Bishop Haakon in Bergen sent four hounds, seven walrus tusks, and a polar-bear skin as a gift to a certain Aegidius Correnbitter in Bruges.

Walrus Tusk and Hunting Trips to Nordsetur

Most of these trade commodities were acquired on dangerous hunting trips to the north. While there may have been a colony of walruses in the Western Settlement area when the Norse settlers arrived, the most important hunting grounds comprised Nordsetur, in Disko Bay and farther north,

JETTE ARNEBORG

23.3 COUNTING STICKS

Trade transactions were tallied using counting sticks, so called for the notches carved along the long sides, and wooden tags carved with runic messages of ownership (fig. 20.11). This unusual fish-shaped counting stick may have also had a religious purpose, such as tracking the recitation of the rosary. It bears a runic inscription that begins with "Maria," but the rest is undecipherable, probably written in bastardized Latin.

where besides walrus, hunters could also catch equally valuable narwhals and polar bears. The Nordsetur hunting region was as important to the Norse colonists as their actual settlement areas in southern Greenland (figs. 24.4–24.6). That the area was regarded as Norse territory is expressed in a treaty between the Norwegian king and the Greenlanders from 1261, where the Greenlanders agree to pay fines for homicide, whether the killing takes place in the settlements or "in the northern summer camps up to just under the Pole Star."

Other fourteenth-century records (Halldórsson 1978: 259ff) show that important farmers in Greenland owned ships to sail to the northern hunting grounds and that the farmers often went personally on the hunting trips. Archaeologically, Nordsetur hunting is evident from artifacts and the remains of walrus bone found in farm middens. Polar-bear bones and teeth are very rare and narwhal bones are almost only known from the literature (Pingel 1833: 319). Most of the walrus bones are skull fragments, indicating that hunters only brought back skulls with valuable tusks on the long journey from the hunting grounds. In the Western Settlement limb bones from walrus have also been found, indicating that walrus was also used for meat (Degerbøl 1936: 7). The quantity of walrus bones varies from farm to farm, but there is a clear tendency for the biggest concentrations of walrus bones to be found at the big farms such as the bishop's farm at Gardar, Erik the Red's farm Brattahlid in the Eastern Settlement, and Sandnes in the Western Settlement (Degerbøl 1930:181ff, Degerbøl 1934: 150ff; McGovern 1983). The concentration of finds must be viewed as vestiges of payments to big farmers. The Gardar finds are remarkable in that twenty to thirty walrus skulls were found buried both in the churchyard and inside the church itself. Out in the churchyard the skulls lay in rows side by side (Nørlund 1930:138), and four or five narwhal skulls were buried in the

eastern part of the chancel (Pingel 1833: 310). The purpose of these burials is unknown, but the skulls may have been regarded as a kind of hunting trophy (see Seaver, p. 276).

FARMERS AND TRADERS

The Icelandic sagas hint at a decentralized trading structure in the Greenlandic settlements: foreign traders moored their ships near the large farms and traded directly with local farmers (fig. 23.3). There would undoubtedly have been a harbor or a sheltered anchorage at all the big farms because the major farmers played a central role in Greenlandic trade. Through their ownership of the hunting boats and taxation of goods they controlled the local trade; the foreign traders brought the goods from Europe to their farms and from their farms the goods were distributed further in Greenlandic society (figs. 23.3, 23.10). Often the merchants also lodged with the farmers while they were in Greenland. According to both the *Greenlanders' Saga* and *Erik the Red's Saga*, for example, the Icelandic merchant Thorfinn Karlsefni lived with Erik the Red at Brattahlid before he and Gudrid went to Vinland (Magnusson and Pálsson 1965).

The inquisitive son of the *King's Mirror* wanted to know what induced people to travel to Greenland despite such dangers as frequent storms and sea ice in both summer and winter. The answer was clear: the profitable trade with the Greenlanders was the attraction. Indirectly, the source tells us that it was the foreign traders who went to Greenland; from other sources too we have information about Icelanders and Norwegians who voyaged to Greenland (Magerøy 1993). Only one account of the Greenlanders who went on trading journeys to Scandinavia is preserved. At the beginning of the 1190s Greenlanders are mentioned among the many different people (Icelanders, Englishmen, Germans, Danes, Swedes and Gotlanders), who came to the trading place in Bergen (fig. 23.2) (Magerøy 1993: 34).

23.4

23.5

23.6

23.7

23.4–23.7 Games from the Western Settlement
Located close to the source of valuable trade goods such as walrus and polar bear, the Western Settlement, though smaller than the Eastern Settlement, was a prosperous community. A toy boat found in a sauna (top), dice (right), a chess piece (fig. 23.6), and a whalebone playing piece for the newly introduced game of backgammon (bottom) all testify to available leisure time. Undoubtedly this was in the winter, when both farming and hunting were impossible.

The trade and exchange pattern in Iceland shows that in the first centuries after the initial settlements, or *landnám*, Icelanders participated on an equal footing with foreigners. In the course of the twelfth to thirteenth centuries Icelanders lost their role in trade, and Norwegian merchants in particular came to dominate the Icelandic trade from the thirteenth century on (Magerøy 1993: 60ff). This process should be viewed in the context of trade policy developments that took place during the Middle Ages, not only in Norway but throughout northern Europe, and that led to centralization, monopolies, and the specialization of trade. The islands in the North Atlantic were dependent on the foreign merchants, and the changes in northern European trade patterns also affected the societies in Iceland and Greenland. As the specialization of trade developed, the farmer-traders were displaced and professional merchants assumed control of trade either as independent entrepreneurs or financed by the big landowners, the aristocracy, the crown, or the big ecclesiastical institutions, who owned the merchant ships. In the course of the fourteenth century German merchants, known as the Hanseatic League, took over the Norwegian foreign trade, while the Norwegians themselves dealt with the regional trade (Blom 1956–78).

For the Norwegian kings the taxation of the goods landed in Norway was a lucrative source of income. As early as the beginning of the eleventh century the Icelanders signed a treaty with the Norwegian king, which among other things meant that Icelandic trade took place in the name of the king. Because trade was under the protection of the king, Icelanders enjoyed the king's protection when they were in Norwegian harbors. In return the merchants had to pay taxes on their

23.9

23.8–23.10 STATUS THROUGH CONNECTIONS

The Greenland Norse signaled high status through items made of rare imported metals from Europe. This large iron and bronze key (right) is similar to keys found throughout Scandinavia. The gold finger ring (top) is one of two found in Greenland; interestingly, both were found at the bishop's seat at Gardar. One was found in a bishop's grave; this one was found in the choir of the church and dates to the eleventh or twelfth century. The silver shield (bottom) bears a striking resemblance to the coat of arms of the Campbell clan of Scotland (Seaver 1996), though what it is doing in Greenland or what it signifies is uncertain.

23.8

23.10

trading goods. The king could exploit his rights by transferring his trade levies to others: for example, to fund the establishment of an archiepiscopal see in Nidaros in 1152–1153 the king granted the archbishop the right to import flour to Iceland and to keep the profits on sales. Later, in 1170, the see was granted further rights to customs duties on goods from an Icelandic ship (Thorsteinsson 1985: 44 f; Magerøy 1993: 30ff).

The information in *Historia Norvegiae* from the first half of the twelfth century may indicate that at this early phase of the Norse Greenlandic settlements Greenlanders—unlike Icelanders—remained free of the sovereignty of the Norwegian king. *Historia Norvegiae* describes Iceland as a Norwegian tributary, but not Greenland (Ekrem 1998: 30). Formally the Greenlanders were perhaps able to avoid coming under the sway of Norway until as late as 1261, when, according to the *Saga of King Haakon Haakonsson,* they joined the Norwegian kingdom. In practice the trade with Greenland was probably subject, both before and after the treaty of 1261, to the same conditions as the Icelandic trade: the Norwegian king would have taxed the Greenland voyagers like the Icelandic voyagers when they landed in a Norwegian harbor, and could have transferred some percentage of the taxes to the church.

One of the most valuable Greenland commodities in Europe was walrus ivory, which was used as a substitute for elephant ivory in decorative art; from Greenland it was much in demand in periods when it was difficult to obtain elephant tusks from Asia or Africa. In northwestern Europe this was the case from the ninth century until the last quarter of the thirteenth century after the Crusades had ended. The number of carvings in walrus ivory held in the museums of Europe and the United States dating to after the year 1000 increases concurrently with the Norse settlement of Greenland. Increased supplies to the western European market from Greenland may explain the large number of ivory artifacts that have been preserved (Roesdahl 1998: 18). Decorative art and craft products in walrus ivory were produced first and foremost at the courts of princes and other magnates and at ecclesiastical centers (fig. 23.11). Walrus ivory was carved at the royal castle in Sigtuna in Sweden around the year 1000, and groups of carvings from 1100 until the beginning of the 1200s are

23.11 GUNHILD'S CROSS

Greenlandic walrus ivory was in high demand for ecclesiastical art in European churches. The back of this cross, carved in Denmark for Princess Gunhild (d. 1157) out of Greenland walrus ivory, depicts biblical scenes. In the center, Christ stands in judgment of mankind, with the blessed to his right and the damned to his left. Above is Lazarus in Abraham's bosom, and below is the rich man with the devil. A crucified Christ, originally affixed to the front, has been lost.

ascribed to workshops in western Norway, presumably Trondheim; to Zealland—more specifically Roskilde—in Denmark; to Canterbury in England; and to Cologne in Germany (Roesdahl 1998: 26ff). At the end of the thirteenth century, with the retaking of the Holy Land by the Crusaders, it again became possible to obtain elephant ivory in western Europe. Importation of ivory, probably from east Africa, increased rapidly in the course of the fourteenth century, but by the fifteenth century ivory carving went out of fashion, and production seems to have almost ceased (Roesdahl 1998: 40f).

For Greenlanders changes in economic conditions in Europe from 1300 on must have been a catastrophe. The plentiful supply of skins and hides from Scandinavian markets would tempt fewer merchants to make the long and dangerous journey to Greenland. The lack of demand for Greenlandic walrus tusks made Greenlanders increasingly dependent on trade with the king, even if it was no longer as profitable as it had once been. As a result, the official Norwegian trade with Greenland decreased and seems to have ceased completely at the beginning of the fifteenth century (Magerøy 1993: 228). The last record of Icelandic ships returning from a trade voyage to Greenland is 1410.

INTRODUCTION OF CHRISTIANITY IN GREENLAND

If we are to believe *Erik the Red's Saga* (see Magnusson and Pálsson 1965) it was Leif the Lucky who, on behalf of the Norwegian King Olaf Tryggvason, introduced Christianity in Greenland. This was around the year 1000. Leif's father, Erik the Red, was not particularly enthusiastic, but Leif's mother, Thjodhild, adopted the new faith and had a church built at Brattahlid, just far enough away from their home so as not to irritate Erik.

So far no remains of heathen Norse burials have been found in the Norse settlements, but in 1961 during the erection of a new building in the sheep-farming settlement of Qassiarsuk, workers found the remains of a very small church, only a few hundred yards from Erik the Red's farm, which has been identified as the church mentioned in *Erik the Red's Saga* (Krogh 1971; but see also Krogh 1982a). The identification is problematical, but whether this is the church

23.12 FURNISHING GREENLAND'S
CHURCHES
The Greenland Norse considered
themselves as equals in the wider European, Catholic world. They imported expensive and often finely
decorated bronze church bells to
hang in their churches, though only a
few fragments remain today, such as
this piece recovered recently by a
Greenland native farmer in Ikigaat. To
its left is a fragment of glass found
near the bishop's church at Gardar.
The pattern of chipping on its sides
indicates that it might have been part
of a stained-glass window.

Thjodhild had built at Brattahlid, the remains of the little church building can be
seen today in Qassiarsuk (figs. 21.3–21.6).
The church was very small, about seven by
eleven feet (two by three and one-half meters),
with a wood-clad interior, surrounded by a
thick, insulating turf wall. The two long walls
were slightly convex, like the houses of the
Viking Age known from Scandinavia, and inside along the walls there were low benches.
Outside the church was a small churchyard
containing 144 graves—twenty-four children,
sixty-five men, thirty-nine women, and sixteen unidentified. Radiocarbon dating of the
skeletons excavated from around the church
show that the churchyard was in use from the
end of the tenth century until the end of the
twelfth century (Arneborg et al. 1999). Ari
the Wise wrote in his *Book of the Icelanders*
that the *landnám*, first settlement, of
Greenland took place fourteen or fifteen winters before Christianity was introduced in
Iceland (A.D. 1000), which indicates that
Greenland must have been settled around the
year 985. The building style and radiocarbon
dating thus suggest that Thjodhild's Church
and the churchyard were built at more or less
the same time as the Norse settled in
Greenland, which suggests that they had converted to Christianity before they arrived.

THE GREENLANDERS' BISHOPS

The Tale of the Greenlanders (see Jones 1986:
236ff) recounts that the farmer at Brattahlid,
Sokki Thorisson, sought and won the support

of other farmers for the idea of Greenlanders
having their own bishop. Sokki's son Einar
was chosen to take the request to the Norwegian King Sigurd Jorsalfar. Loaded with walrus tusks, a polar bear, and skins, Einar sailed
to Norway, and the king appointed Norwegian priest Arnald the first bishop of the
Greenlanders. Icelandic chronicles placed the
event in 1124.

There is no evidence that Bishop Arnald
ever went to Greenland. The Icelandic
chronicles say that he was in Iceland in the
1120s; and he is mentioned the next time in
1152, when he is appointed first bishop of the
Norwegian town of Hamar. The first record
of a bishop *in* Greenland is in 1210 or 1212,
when Bishop Helgi arrived. For the next 170
years or so the Greenlanders had a bishop in
their midst, but with long vacancies and long
periods when the bishop was traveling in
Scandinavia. The longest period without a
bishop was from 1348 until 1368, when
Bishop Alf arrived in Greenland. Alf died in
1378 and was the last bishop to reside in
Greenland (Arneborg 1991).

All the Greenlandic bishops mentioned
in the written sources came from outside the
island, presumably from Norway. In this respect too the experience of Greenlanders differed from that of Icelanders: the first bishop
there, Isleifur Gizurarson, belonged to the
circle of Icelandic farmer-magnates. Isleifur
had himself appointed in 1056; in the subsequent centuries, control of the bishopric
played a central role in the internal power

23.13, 23.14 Power of the Church
Christianity became deeply imbedded
in the economic, social, and political
life of Greenland. The church at
Hvalsey was an impressive stone
church (fig. 23.14), one of two in
the Eastern Settlement. But the most
powerful church in Greenland was the
church at Gardar, the bishop's seat.
The importance of this church was
confirmed when this walrus ivory
crosier (fig. 23.13) was found there,
along with a gold ring, in what is
thought to be the grave of Bishop
Helgi (d.1230), Nikolas (d.1240), or
Olaf (d.1280).

politics of Iceland (Thorsteinsson 1985: 45f
and 109; Sigurðsson 1999: 185ff).

THE BISHOP'S SEAT AT GARDAR

"The Bishop established his seat at Gardar,
and moved in there," according to *The Tale of
the Greenlanders.* The bishop's seat has been
identified by the many ruins—including
those of a large stone church—at Gardar (the
modern Greenlandic sheep-farming settlement
of Igaliku). Except that the church, dwelling,
and cow sheds were larger, the farm did not
differ substantially from other farms in the
Norse settlements. The site was confirmed as
the bishop's seat with great probability in
1926 when the Danish archaeologist Poul
Nørlund uncovered in the northern chapel
of the church the remains of a bishop who
lay buried with crosier and ring (fig. 23.13).
The skeleton has later been radiocarbon-dated
to 1272 (with statistical deviation giving it a
range 1223 to 1290) (Arneborg et al. 1999).
The deceased must have been one of several
bishops who are thought to have died in
Greenland during this period: Helgi, who
died in 1230; Nikolas, who died about ten
years later in 1240; and Olaf, who died in
1280 or 1281 (Arneborg 1991: 144).

Gardar was the biggest Norse farm in
Greenland. It was centrally situated in the
Eastern Settlement on a tongue of land be-
tween what was then Einar's Fjord (today
Igaliku Fjord) and Erik's Fjord (today
Tunnuliarfik) where Brattahlid lay. About

23.15 PROTECTING THE DEAD
More than thirty-five wooden crosses, all remarkably well preserved, were found with the dead at Herjolfsnes. The one at the right above bears the runic inscription, "God the Almighty guard Gudleif well."

Other small buildings scattered both inside and outside the home field wall had functioned as dwellings, a smithy and other workshops, storage buildings, stables, and barns.

The size of the cow sheds indicates that it was possible to procure enough fodder for the many animals that were stabled during the long winter months. Some grass was gathered on the large home field, which was irrigated during the summer to get the optimum yield from the field. Water was conducted through irrigation canals that can still be seen in the terrain, down to the home field from dammed-up lakes in the mountainous country behind the farm (Krogh 1974).

GREENLANDIC CHURCHES

Seventeen church ruins have been registered in the Eastern Settlement and two, perhaps three, in the Western Settlement. The ruins are roughly divided into three main groups according to their basic form (see Krogh 1976). The first group has a smallish chancel and a wider nave; the west gable is open. The other churches are rectangular buildings, and two of these (from the ruin groups E149 and E66) have an open west gable. The third group, which includes Thjodhild's Church at Brattahlid (figs. 21.4–21.6), is less homogeneous, but the recurring feature is small size. Most churches in this group were built of stone and turf. Only the Hvalsey Fjord Church (figs. 23.14, 25.1), the latest church at Brattahlid (Brattahlid III) in the Eastern Settlement, and the church in Anavik, in the northernmost part of the Western Settlement, stand today as true stone churches.

The interpretation of the church ruins is closely connected with the problems of dating and cultural contacts. At the beginning of this century the Hvalsey Fjord Church (fig. 23.14), Brattahlid III and Anavik were thought to be among the first churches built in Greenland, under the direct or indirect cultural influence of Ireland through Great Britain (Clemmensen 1911: 315ff; Nørlund and Stenberger 1934: 38). The theory remained unchallenged for some decades, until the Danish architect and archaeologist Aage Roussell (1941: 122ff) established that the rectangular stone churches, not only in Greenland but in the entire North Atlantic area, had been built after 1250 to 1300, with inspiration from contemporary Norwegian church building. Before these, Romanesque churches with a

forty ruins have been discovered on the large fertile grassy plain toward Igaliku Fjord, with a church, residence, and the most important utility buildings centrally located within the stone wall that enclosed the home field area. The church, thirty-five yards by nineteen yards (thirty-two by sixteen meters), had a nave, a narrow chancel, and two side chapels. Its most recent form was built in the thirteenth century, but archaeological investigations revealed that it had at least two predecessors (fig. 23.9). The church building is surrounded by a smallish churchyard, and south of this, almost built into the churchyard wall, archaeologists uncovered a large stone structure interpreted as the foundations of the bell tower (Nørlund 1930: 47ff). The fifty-five yard (fifty meter) long residence south of the church featured an impressive hall of 172 square yards (143 square meters) that was only used for prestige functions and on festive occasions. In the immediate vicinity of the residence lay two animal sheds and barn complexes with room for more than one hundred cows—a very large number in comparison to most farms, which had stalls for very few animals.

23.17

23.19

23.18

23.17–23.19 Buttons, Buckles, and Combs

The Greenlandic Norse kept close ties to European society, but they had to improvise to maintain that link. These buttons are made from walrus teeth, the buckle from whalebone, and the comb from caribou antler. Only the two animal heads at the top of the belt buckle suggest a link with Viking artistic tastes; otherwise, these items are purely European in design.

nave and smaller chancel had prevailed, as in Scandinavia. Krogh (1982b: 272) dates the Romanesque churches from the eleventh until slightly into the thirteenth century.

The third group of churches, which was recognized as early as Nørlund's and Roussell's time, only really came into focus with the finding of Thjodhild's Church in 1961. Thjodhild's Church has been dated to the 1000s to 1100s, and some scholars argue that the entire group of small churches is older than the Romanesque churches (Vebæk 1991: 9). The existence of circular churchyards surrounding a few of the small churches has been adduced as support for the early dating, because circular churchyards reflect early Christian influence from the British Isles. In both Iceland and the Faeroes there are churches with circular churchyards that are ascribed to later periods (Simún Arge, personal communication), and so circular churchyards do not necessarily prove that a church is from the earliest Christian period. Knud Krogh thinks (1976: 308) that large and small churches were used concurrently but with different functions: the large churches would have served the surrounding farms indiscriminately as a kind of public church, while the small churches were the exclusive domain of the occupants of the farm as private prayer-houses (*baenhús*).

North Atlantic *Eigenkirche*

The organization of the Greenlandic church was one of the key issues in the development of

23.16 SLAVES TO FASHION?
The churchyard in Herjolfsnes contained more than 120 burials. When excavated in 1921, well-preserved wool clothing, which forms the basis of much of our knowledge about Greenland Norse costume, was found. The hood shown here is in the same style and pattern as contemporary Europeans fashion, although the Greenland Norse were thousands of miles away and in a vastly different environment.

the Norse Greenlandic community. Although churches apparently have different statuses, all Greenlandic churches were built in connection with a farm, as in Iceland of the same period. Presumably the churches in Greenland—as in Iceland—were *eigenkirche*, or private churches, which roughly speaking meant that the farmer who owned the land on which the church lay was entitled to the income that came to it in the form of tithes and duties (fig. 23.12). The *eigenkirche* system in Iceland is described in the Icelandic lawbook *Grágás* from the beginning of the twelfth century and in the *máldagar*, a register of churches that listed the rights and properties of each. The churches were categorized according to the rights they enjoyed and especially the size of the tithe basis (Smedberg

1973: 15–23). A few churches received tithes from several farms; others only from the farm at which the church lay. Mass could be said in a *baenhús*, or the *baenhús* could be the farm's private devotional chapel. Greenlandic churches are identified archaeologically on the basis of the presence of a churchyard and burials, but only a few churches appear to have had burial privileges (fig. 23.15). Only the bishop could consecrate churches and grant permission for the saying of masses in the prayer-houses. The bishop decided which farms were to pay tithes to which churches and selected which churches were to have baptism and burial rights—and thus the economic advantage of charging payment for these services (Smedberg 1973: 17ff). This may be what motivated the big Icelandic farmers to fight to keep power over the bishoprics.

The established church, which was struggling for independence from the church-owners of the individual farms, found the situation in the North Atlantic unacceptable. The pressure on the Icelandic church-owners increased in the course of the thirteenth century as the church and the Norwegian king stood together in this struggle. In 1297 the church-owners were forced to accept a settlement, in which valuable property was transferred to the ecclesiastical administration; the power of once so mighty farmer-magnate families was weakened by this agreement (Thorsteinsson 1985: 98ff).

Exactly what happened in Greenland, we do not know. The official church policy in Norway was that the privately owned churches in Greenland had to be eradicated. The Greenlandic farmer-magnates and church-owners, whose power was based on their control over those resources of society that were essential to the maintenance of cultural contacts with the outside world, had much at stake. King and church acted together, and the Greenlanders' accession to Norwegian rule in 1261 probably created even greater pressure on the Greenlandic church-owners. Only two sources show that the Greenlanders —all of them to some extent—paid dues to the Pope. One of these records crusade tithes the Pope received in 1282 from Greenland; the second, from 1327, is an official papal receipt for six yearly tithes from Greenland.

In 1341 the Bishop of Bergen issued a passport to the Norwegian priest Ivar Bardarson to travel to Greenland on his behalf. The reason for his voyage is not specified in the *Description of Greenland*, which Ivar must have drawn up after he returned to Norway, but that work includes a topographical description of the Eastern Settlement with a thorough account of its churches and their ownership. This has prompted scholars to suggest that Ivar's task was to register the Greenlandic church system (Andersen 1982: 169), perhaps with a view to its reorganization. If this was the intention, not much seems to have come of it.

THE TWILIGHT OF GREENLAND

In the autumn of 1408, Sigrid Bjornsdottir and Thorstein Olafsson were married in the church at Hvalsey Fjord in Greenland. Both seem to have been Icelanders, and they took back to Iceland a certificate that the marriage had been celebrated in the church with the three preceding statutory proclamations of the banns required by the church. The certificate had been drawn up at Gardar in 1409 by the priest Sire Paul Hallvardsson and by Eindrid Andreasson, both presumably Greenlanders. Eindrid described himself as *officialis*, that is, a church official who mainly

dealt with the legal issues of the diocese.

In 1414 some of the wedding guests—Brand Haldorsson, Thord Jorundsson, Thorbjorn Bardarson, and Jon Jonsson—had to testify in Iceland that they had been present in the church in Hvalsey when the marriage was celebrated. Ten years later in 1424, also in Iceland. Saemund Oddsson, who was kin to the bride, testified that he had been present in the church both when the wedding had taken place and previously when the banns had been read. The letters do not tell us why it was necessary for Saemund Oddsson and the other wedding guests to swear to the certificate the Greenland priests had drawn up in 1409, but the account of the wedding celebration in Hvalsey Fjord Church is the last sign of life that exists from the Norse settlements in Greenland.

The costumes of the people buried in the churchyard in Herjolfsnes (fig. 23.16) show that there was life at the Greenlandic Norse settlements until the mid-1400s. The cut of the clothing does not suggest isolation; in fact, to the contrary, the clothes follow the latest fashions in Europe. The Norse Greenlanders viewed themselves as European

23.20, 23.21 CROSSING THE OCEAN While most evidence points to contact between Greenland and Norway, there is also evidence of contacts with England (figs. 23.9, 23.10). These two remarkably similar small jet crosses, possibly worn as amulets, were found thousands of miles apart. The one at the right was found on the beach alongside the Herjolfsnes cemetery; the one at the left is from York (fig. 23.21), the bustling Viking trading town in England. Jet was quarried nearby in Whitby and must have been imported to Greenland from England.

23.21

23.20

23.22 END OF AN ERA

From the ninth century until the last quarter of the thirteenth century, Europeans used walrus ivory for artistic carvings. But when the crusaders took the Holy Land, elephant ivory became available and was more desirable because of its larger size. This mirror back was made of elephant ivory in Paris in the early fourteenth century. Appropriately, it shows a couple playing chess; after the 1300s, chess pieces were less likely to be made of Greenland walrus ivory (fig. 23.1).

and maintained those ties, through the church and through trade. Written accounts, however, paint a picture of an unfortunate combination of conservative Greenlandic society and waning European interest. The demand for the Greenlanders' most important trading commodity, walrus tusk, more or less disappeared in the course of the fifteenth century (fig. 23.22); official sea trade seems to have ceased at the beginning of the 1400s; and the church neglected to send a successor for Bishop Alf. From that time until the definitive depopulation of the Norse settlements in Greenland, the small society was only of interest to the inhabitants—probably in time very few—who held out to the end.

BY HANS CHRISTIAN GULLØV

I N 1721 THE DANISH/NORWEGIAN King Frederik IV recolonized Greenland. At this point Greenland was considered part of the Danish kingdom even though it had not been inhabited by Europeans since the reign of Queen Margrete I (1375–1412). During this period, the three Nordic countries—Denmark, Norway, and Sweden—entered into a union that linked Norway and its North Atlantic possessions with Denmark for more than four hundred years.

Hans Egede, a Moravian Lutheran minister from northern Norway, was placed in charge of this colonization in 1721, establishing a small trade and mission station at 64 degrees north latitude. After having been in Greenland for fifteen years, he wrote that the Norsemen had not been the first and original inhabitants there, that priority belonged instead to the "savages" on Greenland's west coast. They were descended from the "Americans" (Native Americans) who lived north of Hudson Bay and whom they resembled in appearance, ways of life, and dress. These Americans came from the north down along the west coast of Greenland, where they "often had wars with the Norwegians" (1818: 315). Egede knew the historical source material dating from John Davis in the 1580s to Lourens Feykes Haan in 1720 that mentioned the native people on the other side of Davis Strait. His supposition of an immigration to North Greenland still holds true.

Egede was, however, mostly concerned with the fate of the Norse, and he never changed his view that it was the *skraeling* who had driven his forefathers from the country. This chapter draws on linguistic, documentary, and recently uncovered archaeological

evidence to discuss Norse contacts with indigenous Dorset and Thule peoples in Greenland and the circumstances of the European abandonment.

Egede found evidence for his belief in the many Norse settlement ruins, which he thought had been destroyed by the savages. His view of conflict-induced Norse extinction presupposes culture contact of a hostile nature, but critical analysis of the evidence does not lend credence to this theory today (Arneborg 1997). Egede himself never used the word *skraeling*, which only appeared in the medieval written sources where it was synonymous with "weakling" or "scrawny." Instead, he was told that the native Green-landers called themselves *Kalals,* an early form of the modern Greenlandic Inuit word *Kalallit.*

THE *KALALS* IN GREENLAND

After he had been in Greenland for a year, Egede wrote in his diary that the people in his church settlement, known as Hope Colony, had returned from the fjord and told him that a number of the savages were there now. "They said that our people were not to go in there, because the Kalals, as they called themselves, wanted to go hunting and fishing; but if our

ZOOMORPHIC FIGURE, *JÓNSBÓK*

people still wanted to go there, they were not to do them harm or hinder them in their occupation" (1818: 48). Egede also referred to the Greenlanders as *Kalals* in 1723:

> [There] were a number of Greenlandic strangers with us, who had many fox skins to trade...and had first and foremost come here in order to visit us...in addition to what I spoke to them about and asked them about, I was also told that in the south, where they live, there are many abandoned stonebuilt houses in which the Kablunachs [*Qallunnaarsuit*] i.e., the Norwegians, had dwelt, but they are now deserted, so the Kalals, as they call themselves, now again live in many of these abandoned dwellings… (1818: 86).

We know that in 1654 the Greenlanders from Ball's Rivier (Godthåb Fjord) called

24.1 RUIN NEAR UMIATSET

When the Danes returned to Greenland in 1721 with the mission of Hans Egede, sent to re-Christianize the lost Norse colony they expected to find, native Greenlanders showed them the ruins of former Norse farms and churches. Artists such as Andreas Kornerup, who made this watercolor of a stone storehouse at Umiatset in 1876 for the Greenland Geological Survey, recorded some of these sites scientifically.

themselves *Inuit* and the Europeans *Qallunnaarsuit* (Resen 1987). This information came from the kidnapped Inuit who were brought to Denmark and who still had family and friends living in the area seventy years later when Egede began to study the Greenlandic language. Egede also noted that Inuit means "people" (Egede 1818: 386).

In part because *Kalals* are only mentioned in southwestern Greenland, the appellation has been suggested to derive from the Norse word *skraeling*, which Egede also knew (Thalbitzer 1904: 36). Because this suggestion has no phonetic justification, it has been rejected (Petersen 1961). Another source that had been suggested was the Karelians, whom

the Danish cartographer Claudius Svart said in the 1420s were the inhabitants of Karelia and northern Scandinavia (see McNaughton, this volume). On maps of the time, Karelia was connected to the arctic regions, and it was said that the Karelians would go "ever down in Greenland in large hosts" (Gad 1967: 212). However, this source was first brought to light in 1904 (Bjørnbo 1912: 89), suggesting we need to look elsewhere for the origin of the term back in the eighteenth century.

The two appellations, *Inuit* and *Kalal*, were used simultaneously in South Greenland in the Middle Ages (Kleivan 1984a: 620). Thus, it must be presumed that Egede asked the Greenlanders what they were called and was told *Kalal*. This name is included in the dictionary prepared by Hans Egede's son, Poul Egede, with the comment that "they say the appellation was introduced by the old Christians who earlier lived in their country" (1750: 68). We do not know whether the name was originally confined to the south Greenlanders, who visited in the Nuuk district and Disko Bay on their travels, or whether it was remembered by Inuit in the whole of southwestern Greenland. It seems reasonable to assume that the Norse and Inuit used the names *Kalal* and *Qallunnaarsuit* to refer to one another. It has also been suggested that *Kalal* is derived from the Icelandic word *klaedast* (skin), meaning those who wear skin clothing. This does not carry the same negative meaning as the derogatory term *skraeling*, which is found only in Norse sources (Collis 1988: 259; *Grønlands Historiske Mindesmaerker* III: 33). Together with a few other words of probable Norse origin (Egede 1818: 36; Thalbitzer 1904: 36), *Kalal* constitutes an ethnohistorical source that tells of a meeting of cultures (fig. 24.7; Petersen, this volume).

SKRAELING IN THE WRITTEN NORSE SOURCES

Between the seventeenth-century description of the Greenlanders as *Kalal* and the time of the medieval Norse disparagement of the natives as *skraeling* lies a gap of both of time and attitude. The natives are indirectly mentioned in the *Book of the Icelanders,* which is thought to have been written by Ari the Wise at the time of Erik the Red's settlement in Greenland during the eleventh century: "In both the eastern and the western parts of the country they found human dwellings, frag-

24.2 KINGIKTORSSUAQ RUNESTONE

In 1823 a Greenland Inuit found this small runestone in a cairn on an island north of Disko Bay. Its inscription tells of three Norse hunters at the end of the thirteenth century: "Erlingur Sigvatsson, Bjarni Thordarson, and Enridi Oddsson built Saturday before Rogation Day a cairn." This is the only authentic runestone known in North America and is conclusive proof that Norse visited far northern Greenland.

24.3 WALRUS HUNT

This Olavus Magnus illustration from 1555 shows hunters grappling with a walruslike beast in arctic Scandinavia. Magnus imagined a tusked beast very different from a real walrus. Harpoon hunting is incorrectly shown here as a line tied through the beast's skin. Norse hunters in Greenland did not use harpoons, but took walrus with spears and clubs, a very inefficient method compared with the Inuit toggling harpoon.

ments of boats of skin, and stone artifacts, from which it appears that the same kind of people had passed that way as those who inhabited Vinland, whom the Greenlanders [i.e., the Norsemen] call *skraeling*" (Jansen 1972: 28–29). Whether this is a direct observation or a later addition, as the reference to Vinland suggests, cannot be determined. One must assume that at a fairly early stage the Norse were aware of the fact that the new land had previously been inhabited.

Written in the late eleventh century, *Historia Norvegiae* (History of Norway) is the second earliest known Norse source on Greenland. In the fragment of it that has been preserved is the following remark:

> On the other side of Greenland, toward the North, hunters have found some little people whom they call Skraelings; their situation is that when they are hurt by weapons their sores become white without bleeding, but when they are mortally wounded their blood will hardly stop running. They have no iron at all; they use missiles made of walrus tusks and sharp

stones for knives. (Jansen 1972: 35)

This quotation is thought to describe the first meeting between the Norse and the natives whom they called *skraeling*. This meeting took place on the west coast, north of the Norse settlements from which hunting expeditions were frequently sent north to collect ivory from narwhal and walrus, among other things (figs. 24.3–24.6). How far north these expeditions went cannot be determined from this source alone, but the summer expeditions along the west coast were so widely known in the early period of the Icelandic/Greenlandic commonwealth (1000–1200), that long songs were composed about them (*Grønlands Historiske Mindesmaerker* II: 419–575; III: 234–246).

Lawman Haukur Erlandsson's early fourteenth-century *Hauk's Book* contains the following geographical description of the north-going expeditions:

> This summer people arrived from the Nordsetur [the northern hunting grounds], who had traveled further north than earlier accounts mentioned. They found no signs that the *skraeling* had settlements with the exception of Krogsfjordshede [The flat and waste heath by the Crooked Fjord]....After that the priests therefore sent a ship northward to investigate how things were even further north than the remote localities they earlier had visited. However, they sailed from Krogsfjordshede with the coastal line out of sight. At nightfall a southern wind blew up and not being able to navigate in the dark, they let the wind carry them away. But when the storm had faded out and it again became light, they saw many islands and all kinds of catch such as seals, whales and a large number of bears. They entered Havbugten ["Ocean" or Melville Bay], and

The rich Nordsetur hunting grounds around Disko Bay were important to the Greenland Norse for food and exports to Europe. Although the Norse did not typically create animal sculptures as did the Dorset and Thule Inuit, these tiny ivory carvings of a gyrfalcon or peregrine (fig. 24.4), a walrus (24.5), and a polar bear (fig. 24.6) found at Sandnes and Austmannadal in the Western Settlement represent these animals as finely as any examples of Inuit art.

24.4

then the land rose in front of them, both the southern coastal line and the glaciers, but south of them glaciers too were also to be seen as far as the eye could see. They found some indication that the *skraeling* in former times had settled in these places, but because of the bears they could not go ashore. Later on they sailed back in three days, where they found remains of the *skraeling* on some islands south of Snefjeld [Snow Mountain]. Thereafter they returned south to Krogsfjordshede.... (*Grønlands Historiske Mindesmaerker* III: 241)

The description contains several details that suggest that this is a reliable source. The quotation starts when people arrived from the northern hunting grounds and found no *skraeling*, which most likely can be dated to 1266, as noted under that year in the *Icelandic Annals*, which therefore is the year for this specific expedition. Even though no *skraeling* were found, their existence was known. Presumably meetings might have taken place in the northern hunting grounds at Krogsfjordshede, which is the area around the northern part of Disko Bay, where Vaigat (north of Disko Island) could have been the "Crooked Fjord." Later on, the expedition reached the "Ocean Bay" (Melville Bay), the shores of which were covered by ice from the inland glaciers.

In the same description Erlandsson notes that "all Greenlandic farmers of a high rank had large ships and vessels built to send these on hunting in the northern settlements and were equipped with all kinds of hunting implements and trimmed timber, and sometimes they even participated.…These so-called Nordsetur men had their booths or huts in both Greipar and some in Krogsfjordshede" (*Grønlands Historiske Mindesmaerker* III: 243). Greipar, which means the space between the fingers, lies somewhere south of Disko Bay and is most convincingly located in the region approximately 67 degrees north latitude, where the Norse settlements end. North of this area lie the hunting grounds, where a number of Norse place names have been located.

The only concrete evidence of

24.5

24.6

Norse presence in the northernmost reaches of West Greenland is from Kingiktorssuaq, an island on approximately 73 degrees north in the Upernavik district. In 1823, a Greenlander found a small runic stone made of phyllite, a locally available mineral, in a cairn on top of the island (fig. 24.2). The inscription, which was read by the linguistic researcher Rasmus Rask, lists the names of three Norse hunters who had been in the area at the end of the thirteenth century: "Erlingur Sigvatsson, Bjarni Thordarson, and Enridi Oddsson built Saturday before Rogation Day a cairn."

Until the middle of the fourteenth century there are no sources at all, after which time the *skraeling* are mentioned in quite a different way than they had been previously. For example, in reverend Ivar Bardarson's *Description of Greenland*, thought to have been written while he was principal at the Episcopal residence at Gardar during the last half of the fourteenth century, there is mention of the *skraeling*. Bardarson's main task was to collect taxes for the king from the settlers, who, according to a memorandum from the Episcopal residence of Skálholt, Iceland, may have abandoned Christianity (Arneborg 1988). With regard to his voyage north, Bardarson reported: "Now the *skraeling* have the whole of the Western Settlement, there are only horses, goats, cattle, and sheep all wild, but no inhabitants, neither Christian nor Heathen" (*Grønlands Historiske Mindesmaerker* III: 259). According to this quotation, which is the only historical source to date the demise of the Western Settlement, the *skraeling* had occupied the region by that time, that is, the late fourteenth century. New research suggests, however, that the quotation might more correctly be taken to mean that there are no longer Norse taxpayers left in Greenland's northern settlement

24.7 MULTIFACED CARVING

This six-inch (sixteen centimeter) wood carving was found in an Inuit grave in the Upernavik district and was sent to the Danish National Museum in 1889 without documentation. For many years it was attributed to a Dorset artist who had portrayed Inuit and European faces, suggesting contact between Dorset and Norsemen in northern Greenland. Recently, however, the wood has been radiocarbon dated to the 1700s, raising questions about its Dorset origin.

(Arneborg 1988; Seaver 1996: 110). Whether some Norse still resided in the Western Settlement around year 1400 remains an open question (Arneborg 1988; see Berglund, this volume).

The last source that should be mentioned here comes from the *Icelandic Annals*, which note in 1379 that "the *skraeling* made a hostile attack on the Greenlanders, killed 18 men and captured two boys and made them slaves" (*Grønlands Historiske Mindesmaerker* III: 33). Because the flow of information from the Western Settlement had terminated at this stage, we assume that this incident took place in the Eastern Settlement. We cannot, however, exclude the possibility that the assault took place in the northern hunting grounds.

No documentary sources of later date about the *skraeling* are known from the Norse Middle Ages. In approximately 1420, the cartographer Claudius Svart maintained that he had seen pygmies (Inuit) who had been caught in their kayaks and that one of these boats together with an umiak was hanging in Trondheim Cathedral (Bjørnbo 1912: 109). In 1505 Olavus Magnus mentions that he has seen a couple of "these small skin vessels fastened to the wall above the west entrance of Oslo Cathedral" (*Grønlands Historiske Mindesmaerker* III: 465).

Written sources, however, do not cast much light on the demise of the Norse settlements in Greenland. As a result, there has been no lack of hypotheses on why a whole population disappeared. Among the most tenacious lines of reasoning is that the Inuits' superior adaptation to the ever-changing arctic environment, coupled with inadequate supplies from Europe and dwindling demand for the country's products left the Norse increasingly unable to resist the advancing natives. The myth about the *skraeling* having driven out Hans Egede's Norse ancestors was formed on this basis. At that time it was acceptable to admit that the defeat of the Norse resulted from an unequal struggle over resources, but not to admit the impossible thought of Inuit cultural superiority.

Recent research has focused on the different attitudes toward resources that characterize mobile Inuit hunting societies and sedentary Norse agricultural society. As a consequence, the Norse emigration from Greenland is now seen as a gradual movement that took place beginning in the thirteenth century due to climatic changes that resulted in a decrease in agricultural areas and livestock. According to this view, it was not a question of cultural impoverishment but of cultural adjustment. Inuit expansion was interpreted in the same way: as an adjustment to the increased occurrence of sea mammals along the west coast (Albrethsen and Keller 1986; Berglund 1986; Gulløv 1997; Lynnerup 1998; McGovern 1983). Both groups were only modifying their cultural systems to conform to new environmental conditions without engaging in aggressive activities.

GEOGRAPHIC DETERMINATION

All the Norse sources that mention the *skraeling* after the twelfth century take place in Greenland with the exception of the *Book of the Icelanders*, which mentions *skraeling* in Vinland. The hunting expeditions to the Nordsetur are mentioned prominently in these records. The hunting huts were erected in Greipar at 67 degrees North Latitude and at Krogsfjordshede in northern Disko Bay at approximately 70 degrees north latitude. Sailing directly west from Greipar is the shortest way to Baffin Island, which the sagas call Helluland (the Slab Rock Land).

Disko Island is mentioned as Bear Island; to its north lies Eysunes, literally, "glowing or smoldering" peninsula, a name that refers to the coal and oil-bearing slate strata on the Nuussuaq Peninsula, which catch fire spontaneously when sparks are cast during rockfalls. On the western point of Nuussuaq lies the only known Norse building in the Nordsetur, the so-called bear trap, where tusks from narwhal and walrus are thought to have been stored (*Grønlands Historiske Mindesmaerker* III: 881–885; Meldgaard 1995).

North of this area lies Melville Bay, which the find of the small runic stone at Kingiktorssuaq (discussed earlier) suggests that the Norse must have visited in the thirteenth century. There are no written sources about territories north of Melville Bay; archaeological

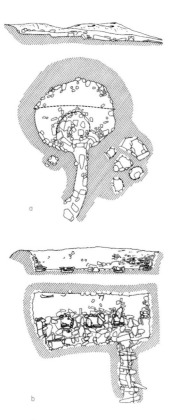

24.8 CHANGES IN INUIT HOUSES
In the two centuries following their colonization of eastern Canada and Greenland, Thule Inuit people lived in round single-family houses of turf, stone, and whalebone. After 1450, Thule dwellings began to increase in size to accommodate extended families in larger rectangular communal houses. Increasing house size has been attributed to cooling climate and social factors relating to European contact.

24.9 BRONZE BELL FRAGMENT
Inuit sites often contain pieces of bronze from the bells that had been mounted in Norse churches. At first, when bell metal fragments began to be found in Inuit sites, it was thought that the Inuit had overrun the Norse settlements and taken the bells as raw materials for making other tools. It now seems likely that bell metal was only a curiosity to the Inuit. But how the bells came to be broken and not taken away by the Norse as they abandoned their settlements remains unknown.

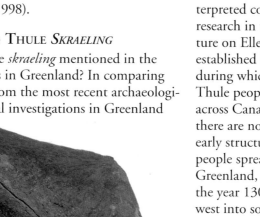

finds provide the only evidence of possible Norse northern voyages.

In the Thule district some Norse artifacts (chain mail, iron blades) have been found in Thule-culture house ruins from the thirteenth and fourteenth centuries (Schledermann, this volume), but their implications for a Norse presence in the area are unclear: the artifacts may have been brought north by Norse or Thule Inuit from Nordsetur or might have originated from a shipwreck. For example, the same type of chain mail has been found in ruins of Inuit houses in Melville Bay, in the Thule District at approximately 79 degrees North Latitude, and on Ellesmere Island (Holtved 1944; Meldgaard 1995). However, finds of meteoritic iron from the Cape York meteorite fall south of Thule and musk ox hair in Norse farms of the Western Settlement suggest that trade with the *skraeling* took place in the Nordsetur, unless the Norse themselves reached the Thule District to trade with natives there (Arneborg and Gulløv, eds. 1998).

The presence of the Norse in the Thule district is suggested by recent archaeological observations. During the excavation of a Dorset house ruin, a fragment of a bronze pot was found. A similar piece of bronze pot has been found in nearby Canada (fig. 17.12). Pots of this particular type were manufactured in northern Europe beginning in the late thirteenth century, and the house ruin also dates to that century. The Dorset people are not known to have been traveling or living south of Melville Bay at this time. The possibility cannot, however, be excluded that the piece came from trade with the Thule people, who by this time had arrived in Greenland (Appelt et al. 1998).

DORSET AND THULE *SKRAELING*

Who are these *skraeling* mentioned in the Norse sources in Greenland? In comparing results from the most recent archaeological investigations in Greenland

with the written sources discussed previously, the *skraeling* must have represented both the Dorset and Thule cultures. The Late Dorset culture first appeared at Smith Sound in the eighth century. Prior to that time, the region had been uninhabited for more than five centuries. Dorset settlements after this date have only been found in Greenland along the coasts of the Nares Strait in the Thule District. In addition, there was a stray find of a Late Dorset harpoon head in Disko Bay, and a few radiocarbon dates from northeasternmost Greenland and Scoresby Sound suggest the presence of Late Dorset in those areas as well. Today it has been established that the core area of Late Dorset culture in Greenland lay in the Thule District.

Comparisons with objects from Danish excavations in Canada dated Late Dorset culture in Greenland to the period between 700 and 900 (Meldgaard 1960). This dating was confirmed by radiocarbon dates from the contemporary Late Dorset phase on Ellesmere Island at the west side of Smith Sound (Schledermann 1990); however, a few dates also lay in the tenth century (Schledermann 1990). Dates from one of the recently examined Dorset sites fell in the ninth to tenth centuries as expected, but none of the new dates from the main Dorset site in the Thule District are before 1000. The structures there had been in use several times during a couple of centuries, first in the period between 1050 and 1150 and then in a terminal Dorset phase that ended around 1300.

In the 1960s the arrival of Thule-culture Inuit in Greenland was thought to have taken place around the year 900. Recent research indicates that these dates were not interpreted correctly. This became clear when research in the 1980s on the Early Thule culture on Ellesmere Island (McCullough 1989) established its appearance at 1200 to 1400, during which there was continual flow of Thule people immigrating from Alaska across Canada to Greenland. In addition, there are now a number of dated objects and early structures that demonstrate that Thule people spread around the north end of Greenland, reaching Scoresby Sound around the year 1300 and continuing south and west into southwestern Greenland later in the fourteenth century (Gulløv 1997).

It is now certain that both Late Dorset and Early Thule people were present at the so-called Gateway to Greenland, the Nares

24.10 ANTLER COMB

Contacts between cultures are often recorded archaeologically in exchanges of material culture. To the extent that quantities exchanged reflects extent of contact, Inuit culture had little impact on the Norse. Only a few Dorset or Thule objects have been found in Norse sites, one being this Thule antler comb found at Austmannadal.

24.11 SPOON BOX LID

This wooden lid for a box made to hold spoons is decorated with early Gothic floral designs similar to those found on a panel from the Farm Beneath the Sand (fig. 22.6). It was found in a Thule house at Sermermiut, Greenland, in 1955, and a box it may have covered was found several hundred miles from there, also in a Thule site.

Strait/Smith Sound region in northwest Greenland, in the period 1200 to 1300. Archaeological evidence shows that these two distinct cultures met and that there was also a third population in Greenland at this time: the Norse, who had been in that country for almost two centuries before the Thule culture arrived.

A cautious evaluation of the accounts of the meetings contained in the written sources, together with the recent archaeological results from the gateway region sites, seem to point to the thirteenth century as a period of particular historical interest. In this period *skraeling* are no longer present at their previously known (Dorset) sites, but thereafter (as Thule) suddenly became numerous. It seems probable that the archaeologically demonstrated transition from Dorset to Thule in the thirteenth century may have removed the *skraeling* from the Norse's field of vision for a time. Thereafter the mobile people of the Thule culture, having replaced the Dorset people, occupied the scene of action, which then shifted from northwestern to southwestern Greenland.

The presence of the Neo-Eskimo Thule culture in Greenland around the year 1200 demonstrates the changes from the previously known Paleo-Eskimo (pre-Dorset and Dorset cultures) way of life, which had occurred in the eastern Arctic for three and a half millennia. Most important was the introduction of new means of transport—dogsleds and large skin boats called umiaks—which allowed the Neo-Eskimo Thule to follow migrating animals far more effectively than the Dorset ever could. Their larger boats allowed them to hunt baleen whales unobtainable by Late Dorset people, whose primary and largest game animal was the walrus.

There must have been a certain amount of coexistence between the two populations at the Thule District gateway in the thir-

teenth century, with members of the two groups able to learn from one another. Local knowledge of raw materials such as meteoritic iron and soapstone was transmitted to the newcomers, who also seem to have adopted the use of snow knives, bone knives that were used to cut snow blocks for snow houses. One impact of the newcomers is reflected in the changed form of domestic architecture: the Dorset dwelling is replaced by a Thule type with rear sleeping platforms (fig. 24.8).

Evidence from the written sources and the objects found in population centers suggests that the Norse met Dorset people on their hunting trips to Nordsetur in the eleventh and twelfth centuries; and we assume that the Dorset transmitted their knowledge of these foreigners to the recently arrived Thule people in the thirteenth century. This period of coexistence can be dated to the middle of the Norse era. Accounts of the *skraeling* in the Norse sources point to two periods of contact: one before 1200, when the Late Dorset culture still occupied northeast Greenland, and one after 1300, when the Thule culture was dominant there.

Whether the Norse obtained walrus ivory from the earlier Dorset residents or from the Thule newcomers, we can be sure that ivory became an even more valuable commodity to the Norse after 1261 when the Greenland settlements became subject to the Norwegian crown and particularly after 1281 when, together with Iceland, they received new laws and were forced to pay new taxes (*Grønlands Historiske Mindesmaerker* III: 130–142).

THE NORSE ARTIFACTS

Although it is difficult to prove trade contacts, the appearance of Norse and *skraeling* (either Dorset or Thule) artifacts in each other's sites is probably indicative of trade. On the one hand, very few artifacts of Inuit

24.12–24.14 Norse Goods: Scavenged or Traded?

Nearly two hundred Norse artifacts have been found in late Thule and early historic (Inugsuk) culture sites in Disko Bay and the Nuuk region. Most of these objects, such as this knife, wool shears, chess piece, and fire-starter (bottom) were objects that the Inuit could make use of and were collected by Inuit from abandoned Norse sites rather than being the result of trade or direct contact.

origin have been found in Norse sites (fig. 24.10). Arneborg (1997) has suggested that materials the Norse received in trade from the *skraeling*, such as tusks and hides, were meant for export, and therefore are not likely to be found in Norse sites in Greenland. On the other hand, a much larger number of artifacts of European origin or inspiration have been found in excavations of Inuit house ruins, especially in the Disko Bay-Nordsetur region (figs. 24.11–24.14). In all, Norse artifacts amount to approximately 170 pieces. Then there are pieces inspired by Norse objects, including 167 ornamental pins for which the prototypes are thought to be styluses (medieval writing utensils) and which have been found in Greenland but nowhere else in the Inuit world. There are also wooden staves for boxes and containers, which are thought to be of Norse inspiration although the construction technique is also known from Late Dorset culture. Most of these seem to have come from early Inuit contexts that predate contact with European whalers in the seventeenth century (Gulløv 1997: 426–433). Finally, there are nine carvings interpreted as Inuit portraits of Norsemen (figs. 24.15, 24.16).

Not all of these artifacts are necessarily evidence of direct contact between these cultures. Excavations and seventeenth-century written sources reveal that Thule built their own houses inside of deserted Norse ruins (Gulløv 1997: 426–433). A considerable number of artifacts that probably came into the possession of the *skraeling* while the Norse still inhabited the country were found in early Thule sites in northern Greenland (Holtved 1944; Buchwald and Mosdal 1985).

The 170 Norse artifacts found in Thule sites in Greenland have an interesting geographic distribution. In southern Greenland, where the Eastern Settlement was located, fifty-seven artifacts have been found. In the southwestern part of the country from the Western Settlement to Greipar, thirty-eight artifacts have been recovered. In the Nordsetur, along the northern west coast from Disko Bay to the Upernavik District, twenty-three artifacts have been found. From Melville Bay, the Thule District, and the land to the north, come thirty-two artifacts. East Greenland, on the opposite side of the peninsula, is less well endowed. In the northern part of East Greenland, between 80 and 83 degrees North Latitude, six artifacts have

24.15, 24.16 Images of the Norse
Figures that represent the Norse have been found in Greenland Inuit sites, as they have on Baffin Island (fig. 17.1). The carved portrait (fig. 24.15) can be identified as Norse by facial structure and hairdo; the reverse side has carving of a Norse knot motif. The figurine wears a Norse hooded cape (fig. 24.16). But were these objects made by the Norse and later scavenged from abandoned sites by Inuit, or are they Inuit representations of Norsemen? The face and knot carving is more likely Norse in content and style but has eyes made with baleen insets, an Inuit technique; the figurine appears wholly Inuit. Both pieces were found in Upernavik in a fifteenth-century Inugsuk-culture midden.

been found, while in southeastern Greenland, the number is ten artifacts (Buchwald and Mosdal 1985).

Norse artifacts found in Thule settlements in the southwestern part of the country are considered to have arrived there after the Norse settlements were deserted (Mathiassen 1931, 1936). On the other hand, we have to account for the thirty-two artifacts from the Thule District as an expression of some kind of coherent circumstance as they are all found in house ruins from the thirteenth and fourteenth centuries based on recalibrated radiocarbon datings (Gulløv 1997: 429–30). The same goes for the ninety artifacts of Norse origin found on Ellesmere Island (McCullough 1989).

Metal is the dominant material in the total finds, consisting of forty-four pieces of iron; twenty-four pieces of copper, bronze, or tin; and thirty-three pieces of bell metal (fig. 24.9) for a total of 101 metal artifacts. In addition to these come seventy-seven pieces of iron and nine pieces of copper from Ellesmere Island (McCullough 1989). If the distribution of these metal artifacts is depicted in accordance with the Norse cultural geography, then forty-six pieces have been found in the Norse core area up to Greipar; from Nordsetur ten pieces have been found; and from the land north of Melville Bay come twenty-three objects. Lastly can be added the eighty-six metal objects from Ellesmere Island; so, the total number of metal objects from the gateway region is 109. To put these numbers in perspective, these 218 metal pieces would have constituted 22 percent of the total number of European metal pieces from the eighteenth-century house ruins at Nuuk, when metal had become an everyday commodity (McCullough 1989). It is clear that metal was in great demand, as it constituted 70 percent of all Norse material found in Inuit sites from the period.

We have reason to believe that it was from Nordsetur that most contact activities took place. From there, Norse objects were taken north by Thule-culture people to Melville Bay. Seven of the nine known Inuit portraits of Norsemen originate from Nordsetur, while the other two originate from the Nuuk District (the Western Settlement) and from the Thule District (the land

north of the Melville Bay), respectively (McCullough 1989).

Unfortunately, the written sources, with very few exceptions, are strikingly quiet about these activities, which appear to have taken place over a period of three hundred years. Whether Norse and native cultures engaged in significant trade and economic activities and whether the Inuit played a decisive hand in the demise of the Norse colonies is still unclear, but recent research demonstrates that archaeological evidence, not documentary sources, will provide the answers.

Kalaallit Nunaat

In the eighteenth century, a permanent European settlement was again seen in Greenland three centuries after the last signs of Norse life from the country were received in Europe. In 1492, Pope Alexander VI had recommended that a bishop be appointed to Gardar at the end of the world in Greenland, as there had been no word from there for eighty years (Walløe 1927: 3–4). The old tributary country, however, no longer existed. According to Egede, the only inhabitants were the *Kalal*. The question of the fate of the Norse would thereafter engage researchers for subsequent centuries, and the Norse ruins were the only visible remains after nearly half a millennium of early European occupation.

The descendants of the *skraeling* lived primarily in the southwestern part of Greenland and had only sporadic contact with the Inuit in northern West Greenland and southeastern Greenland. In response to the European questions about the fate of the Norse, an imaginative oral tradition took form among the Inuit. Being confronted with the allegations of the missionaries that their Inuit ancestors had exterminated the Norse was a serious concern for the native Greenlanders in the eighteenth century, for blood revenge was still in use as a means of sanction by the Inuit at that time (Gulløv 1997:371). To avoid being charged with murder, therefore, they shifted the blame onto their evil ancestors, stressing that they, the living descendants, were blameless (Egede 1778: 33). Sheep are again grazing on the old Norse agricultural areas from the Middle Ages in the country that is now called Kalaallit Nunaat, the Land of the Kalal.

25 | THE DEMISE OF NORSE GREENLAND

BY THOMAS H. MCGOVERN

DURING THE FOURTEENTH AND fifteenth centuries the peoples of Atlantic Europe suffered the hardships of widespread famine, war, and plague. In the first half of the fourteenth century a series of cold, wet summers caused widespread crop failure, hunger, and some cases of mass starvation in the Atlantic climate zone, which stretches from the hill farms of Scotland to the rich cloth towns of Flanders. Urban food riots and rural farm abandonment were widespread, and it is now recognized that the contraction of an early medieval peak in settlement and population began well before the onset of the Black Death in 1348. All over Norway and northern Britain upland farms on hills and moors that had been pioneered in the Viking Age or early Middle Ages were being given up forever. Increased disease, warfare, and religious intolerance throughout Europe both reflected and intensified the agony of a once-confident civilization entering a period of deep distress.

Only in Greenland, however, did that crisis become a catastrophe of total cultural and biological extinction. While northern Europe suffered, Norse Greenland died. As Europe struggled with its own problems, contact with the Greenland colony faded and documentary records become more scattered and unreliable. By the mid-fifteenth century the fate of Norse Greenland had slipped into legend and speculation. The last definite record dates to 1408, when travelers record that a proper Christian marriage was performed in the church at Hvalsey Fjord in the Eastern Settlement (fig. 25.1) and mention that a fellow named Kolbein was burned to death for witchcraft at the same place a few years before. Our last view is of a functioning late medieval society, complete with stone churches, monks, nuns, good Christians, and a few sternly punished unbelievers. A generation before, a record left by the Norwegian cleric Ivar Bardarson had

outlined the extent of church property in Greenland but also recorded the end of the Western Settlement in these few, cryptic words: "*Skraeling* [a perjorative term for native populations] have destroyed all the Western Settlement. There is an abundance of horses, goats, bulls, and sheep all wild, and no people neither Christian nor heathen." (transl. Astrid Ogilvie in Barlow et al. 1997). Bardarson's account was probably first written down in about 1364 but survives only in seventeenth-century manuscripts.

EARLY EXTINCTION THEORIES: INUIT CONFLICT, ISOLATION, INBREEDING

It only gradually dawned on Europeans that the Norse Greenlanders were indeed all gone. When the Norwegian missionary Hans Egede traveled to Greenland in 1721 he expected to find living Norse people to convert from medieval popish idolatry to enlightenment Lutheranism. It was only

25.1 Hvalsey Church

Following the demise of the Western Settlement in the mid-fourteenth century, the Eastern Settlement continued for another one hundred years. In 1408 a wedding was recorded at the Hvalsey Church, but that was the last word to come from Greenland; after that was silence. The church stands today as a reminder of the perils of living too close to the edge in an unpredictable world.

after exploring the inner fjords and carrying out some protoarchaeological survey of the medieval ruins that Egede realized that no Norsemen survived and he must turn his conversion efforts on the Inuit Greenlanders. Speculation on the fate of the Norse Greenlanders began immediately upon Egede's confirmation of their demise, and over the next two hundred years a number of theories were constructed. Stories collected by Egede and his sons from the Inuit appeared to include credible tales of interaction with medieval Norse, in which the clumsy, violent Norsemen regularly lose out to the clever, cooperative Inuit (fig. 25.3). Inuit raiding, climate change, disease, and isolation from Europe were all proposed as executioners at one time or another prior to the beginning of professional archaeology in Greenland by the Danish Captain Daniel Bruun at the turn of the twentieth century (fig. 25.2).

Bruun's archaeological work in Iceland and the Faeroes as well as Greenland provided him with a wide perspective on later medieval settlement in the North Atlantic; and he was aware of the massive population losses of late medieval Iceland and the severe contraction of settlement there (Bruun 1902). Bruun suggested that only a broad, multidisciplinary approach would solve the mystery of the end of Norse Greenland, and he made some of the first archaeological collections of animal bone, plant, and pollen samples from the Norse sites to promote such work. This tradition, continued by later researchers, provides the basis for

modern understanding of the lost settlements.

The patient work of bone and pollen counting was overshadowed, however, by spectacular finds of frozen garments of late medieval style found wrapped about skeletons excavated from the Eastern Settlement site of Herjolfsnes and published by Nørlund in 1921 (fig. 23.19). The Herjolfsnes garments were used to date stylistically the end of the Eastern Settlement to around 1500 through the presence of two well-preserved examples of a cylindrical hat, which Nørlund identified as a late fifteenth-century "Burgundian Cap." This identification was to set the official end of the settlements for the next seventy years until new historical research by Jette Arneborg (1996) of the Danish National Museum revealed that this stylistic attribution was incorrect: the caps are probably women's headdresses similar to those illustrated in late medieval Icelandic sources, and the radiocarbon dates of the cloth and the skeletons now cluster in the early to mid-fifteenth century. On this basis most scholars now date the end of the Eastern Settlement to no later than around 1450. This redating scuttles some colorful theories of Norse extinction, which saw the last survivors carried off by English, Basque, or even Moorish pirates in the late fifteenth or early sixteenth centuries (see Seaver, this volume).

The initial analyses of the human bones excavated from Herjolfsnes created an equally long-lived misunderstanding. The physical anthropologist F. C. C. Hansen,

who carried out the initial examinations in 1924, concluded that these late medieval Greenlanders represented a "degeneration" from the fine physical specimens of the Viking Age (see Lynnerup, this volume). In 1942, while Denmark was occupied by the Nazis, K. Fischer-Møller bravely published a refutation of Hansen's thesis, demonstrating that the Herjolfsnes bones were too soft and badly preserved to allow for detailed measurements and so there was no clear evidence of disease or degeneration (Fischer-Møller 1942). Subsequent research on teeth and the bone supporting them by G. R. Scott (Scott et al. 1991) demonstrated that while the Norse Greenlanders showed few of the signs of childhood malnutrition sometimes manifested in teeth, they all had massive bony ridges around the base of their teeth that were not present in medieval Icelandic and Norwegian skulls. The most likely explanation is similar biomechanical stresses operating on the Inuit and Norse Greenlanders, suggesting that the Norse Greenlander's diet was tougher and less easily chewed than that of their relatives in Iceland and Norway. A comprehensive project by Niels Lynnerup (1995) and his colleagues in Copenhagen suggests that the Norse diet became more and more reliant on marine species as time passed. Only the skeleton of a bishop (buried with ring and crosier) was inconsistent with this analysis: he clearly had far more beef and cheese in his diet than most of his flock (Arneborg et al. 1999).

Separation from Europe was an often-cited cause for the end of Norse Greenland, and it is certainly true that connections grew more tenuous in the later Middle Ages. It took the Pope three years to get a letter carried by the most rapid post available, and the number of transatlantic crossings clearly declined rapidly after the devastation wrought by the plague in the port of Bergen in the mid-fourteenth century. There is, however, little reason to think that the basic year-to-year subsistence economy could have been dependent on imported goods. Given the small size of early medieval cargo craft, there is no possibility that significant amounts of food could have been imported at any time. From settlement onward Greenland had to be self-sufficient in basic supplies, and while beer, new swords, and fine garments may have been sadly missed by recent immigrants and the lonely clerical administrators sent from Norway, the majority of the Norse Greenlanders indeed had probably "never seen bread" as claimed in the thirteenth-century *King's Mirror*, a Norwegian pedagogical treatise. The lack of imported bread was not likely to have triggered the collapse of this self-sufficient society.

Other theories blossomed as archaeology began to uncover the ruins of Norse Greenland. The distinguished pollen specialist Johannes Iverson witnessed an outbreak of *Agrotis occulta* caterpillars in the Western Settlement one summer and speculated that similar outbreaks in the past could have devastated the Norse hay fields and precipitated a catastrophe (Iverson 1935). While caterpillars and pirates excited some imaginations, decades of patient work by pollen specialist Bent Fredskild and his students uncovered an unexpected threat to Norse survival in Greenland—the impact of their own imported cattle, pigs, sheep, and goats (Fredskild 1992; Jakobsen 1991). Numerous pollen cores in both settlement areas uncovered a common pattern of rapid decline of willow and birch pollen, followed by an increase in grass-sedge pollen, and then followed by rapid erosion of exposed ground. These records also reveal a recovery of vegetation and soil after the Greenland Norse had disappeared and then a return to deforestation and erosion with the reintroduction of sheep farming in the area of the Eastern Settlement in the 1920s. In Iceland, pollen and soil science research combined with the datable volcanic tephra (ash layer)

clearly document the impact of Norse grazing animals, first evident in the higher elevations, but spreading down to valley floors by the fourteenth century in many areas (Dugmore and Buckland 1991). Deforestation, followed by overgrazing, followed by irreversible erosion, followed by farm abandonment was the grim sequence of events in much of Iceland in the later Middle Ages, and much evidence suggests a similar chain of events in Greenland (fig. 25.4). In modern Greenland and Iceland, erosion control is a major concern, and levels of animal stocking have been repeatedly reduced to conserve vegetation and soil.

CLIMATE IMPACTS

Of all the single-cause explanations for the death of Norse Greenland, climate change has been the most durable. Noting that the Herjolfsnes graves had been dug down into what in the 1920s was permanently frozen ground, Nørlund speculated on the possibility of a warmer medieval climate. In the 1930s to 1940s excavators regularly noted large cattle byres and other agricultural buildings, suggesting far richer pastures and a warmer climate than they were currently experiencing. Early paleoclimatic data from ice cores and other sources of indirect evidence of past temperature indicated a prolonged Medieval Warm Period of around 800 to 1300 that was followed by a Little Ice Age of around 1300 to 1850, apparently providing a neat climatic execution for the Norse colonies (fig. 25.5). Most scholars were content to show temporal correlation between climate change and the Norse extinction, and the basic argument can be fairly summarized as "it got cold and they died." To researchers today, this example of classic climatic determinism—even if literally true as a description—is far too simple as an explanation.

Work on ice cores from Greenland's central ice cap provides detailed climate records that can be correlated with sea sediment cores and tree-ring evidence to provide indirect evidence of past temperature, sea ice, and global circulation patterns down to the annual and even seasonal scale. These human-scaled climatic data have been applied to the problem of the end of Norse Greenland by climatologists and climate historians Lisa Barlow, Paul Mayewski, Anne Jennings, and Astrid Ogilvie in a remarkable combination of geophysics and social science (Barlow et al. 1997, Buckland et al. 1996, Mayewski et al. 1994, Ogilvie 1991, Jennings and Weiner 1998). The newly detailed climate records reveal that the Medieval Warm Period was heavily sprinkled with cold periods and that the Little Ice Age was far from universally cold. The Norse in Greenland survived cold spells in the Viking Age and did not perish the first time they encountered sustained climatic cooling.

Climate change remains the most probable immediate cause for the end of Norse Greenland, but we are now far from simple deterministic explanations. Not everyone in Greenland died when it got colder: the Inuit flourished and spread in this same period of supposedly stressful cold. This uneven outcome suggests that culture had as much to do with the Norse extinction as did nature and that we need to be more rigorous in our search for causes.

Explaining that the total extinction of a small but hardy population that had survived almost five hundred years in its arctic home is a complex problem of historical ecology.

25.5 DRIFT ICE

Sea ice is a major hazard to navigation during the summer in southern Greenland, as seen in this photograph taken in Anodliuitsog in 1995. Summer drift ice comes largely from East Greenland and is carried north along the west coast by currents and wind. Paleoclimatic and documentary evidence indicates that summer ice was rare or absent during the Viking period. Modern drift ice conditions probably began in South Greenland around 1300.

Human action and intention operating over different time scales (single lives, generations) interacts with longer-term history (rise and fall of kingdoms, economic cycles) and natural processes (erosion, climate change), each with its own rhythms and dynamic. Such interlinked series of causation are not well understood by single scholars or effectively described by single disciplines. In recent years this understanding has brought us back to Bruun's vision of a multidisciplinary collaboration as the best way to approach such events as the death of Norse Greenland. Some combination of climate change, culture contact, and subsistence failure are the probable major factors.

THE NORSE ECONOMY IN VIKING AND MEDIEVAL GREENLAND

Thanks to work by archaeologists and zooarchaeological specialists, we now have evidence for the spread of Norse economy from mainland Scandinavia into the Atlantic Islands (Amorosi 1992, 1996; McGovern 1981, 1991, 1992; Perdikaris 1990). Figs. 25.6 and 25.9 compare the bones of domestic animals from early sites in southern Norway, southern and northern Iceland, and Greenland. The chieftain's farm of Aaker in southern Norway probably represents a high-status ideal that colonizing chieftains dreamed of equaling in their new island homes. By the tenth century, even rich farms in the northeast and eastern interior of Iceland had reduced their cattle herds and nearly eliminated pig keeping. This trend was to continue throughout the rest of Iceland's history, even in the warmer south.

When late-tenth-century chieftains set out from Iceland to settle Greenland, they rather optimistically imported the homeland's ideal farmyard rather than the mix of domestic animals then more common in contemporary Iceland (McGovern et al. 1996). Pigs briefly colonized Greenland as well as Iceland and probably did their share of rooting up dwarf willow and birch stands before succumbing to the rigors of an arctic landscape without significant forest cover. Our overall picture is of colonizing farmers with an optimistic attitude toward introducing temperate-zone animals further and further into the arctic. While they may also have attempted to spread barley cultivation into Greenland, most years were simply too cold for grain agriculture, even in the warmer climate of Erik the Red's day one thousand years ago. Much of our understanding of these events today is a result of modern and historical studies of climate and farming practice in Iceland, where the Nordic society used farming methods similar to those of the Norse Greenlanders but survived into the modern day.

25.6 VIKING PERIOD DOMESTIC STOCK

Comparison of domestic mammal bones recovered from Viking Age sites in the North Atlantic are illustrated in this chart. Aaker, a chieftain's farm in southern Norway, probably had the mix of animals that an aspiring North Atlantic colonizer would have preferred. The slightly later ninth-century sites of Tjarnagata and Herjólfsdalur in southern Iceland reflect this ideal in their large numbers of cattle and pig remains. The roughly contemporary sites of Hofstadir and Granastadir in northern Iceland have the same mix of animals, but the smaller number of animals, especially pigs, suggest a compromise with the more arctic conditions there. Two later Icelandic sites directly contemporary with the settlement of Greenland in A.D. 985 to 1050 illustrate general trends in later Icelandic farming—more sheep, fewer cattle, and no pigs. However, the early Greenlandic colonists brought a mix of domestic animals more similar to those found in ninth-century Iceland or Norway and eleventh-century Iceland. The ideal of a cattle and pig–rich farm-yard was not easily shattered.

25.7 VIKING AGE HUNTING AND FISHING

The North Atlantic colonizers were flexible in their use of whatever wild species were locally abundant. The large numbers of bird bones from Viking Age sites in southern Iceland probably reflect unwary colonies not used to human predation and include some bones of the extinct great auk. While seals were taken in many parts of the North Atlantic, none of the other colonies made such heavy use of them as the Norse Greenlanders.

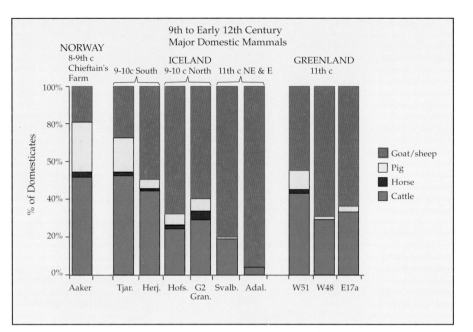

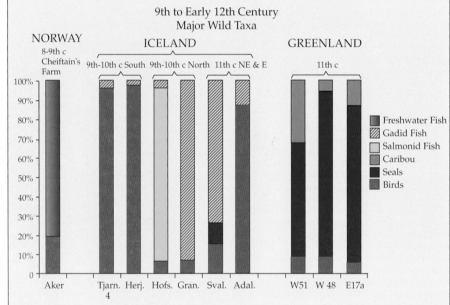

While these North Atlantic colonists may have had a fondness for their traditional mix of domesticates, they showed great flexibility in exploiting the very different wild resources of their new environments. Fig. 25.7 illustrates the proportions and mix of wild birds, fish, and mammals that supported the farming component of the Norse economy from the same sites illustrated in fig. 25.6. Southern Iceland was clearly rich in migratory birds unused to human predation in the ninth century, and later Icelandic texts recall that at first animals were unafraid of humans. Freshwater and marine fish were of varied importance in early Iceland, but cod and haddock came to dominate the diets of

Icelanders in the later Middle Ages. In the Greenland Viking Age, fish played a very minor role, but seals and caribou bones regularly exceeded those of domestic stock. While seals were taken in many parts of the Norse North Atlantic, only in Greenland do they dominate the bone collections. Thus the Greenlandic economy was different from that of Iceland or the Nordic homelands from the very beginning.

As time passed, the differences between the Icelandic and Greenlandic economies became more marked. Fig. 25.8 compares stratified bone collections from two rich farms, the chieftain's farm at Sandnes on the Ameralla Fjord in the Greenlandic Western

25.8 ICELAND-GREENLAND COMPARISON

This graph compares bones from the stratified layers of the midden heaps of two farms of similar size and status in northeast Iceland (Svalbard, SVB) and in the Western Settlement of Greenland (Sandnes, W51). In Iceland, fishing was always more important than in Greenland, and as time passed and climate changed the Icelanders expanded fishing both for food and export. The Greenlanders continued to focus on walrus hunting, despite a declining demand for ivory in Europe after the fourteenth century. While Icelanders and Greenlanders shared a common Nordic heritage, the economies of the two communities were diverging by the early Middle Ages.

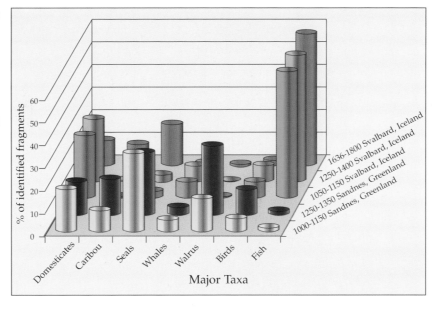

25.9 SMALL AND LARGE GREENLANDIC FARMS

As time passed, most farms appear to have followed the route of a very small and poor farm, V48, which reduced the number of cattle, eliminated most domestic animals, and became increasingly dependent on seal meat for survival. A few large farms such as Sandnes W51 maintained Viking Age patterns into the fourteenth century but expanded their consumption of caribou. The larger farms also had disproportionately large cattle byres and storage buildings, suggesting that increasing social ranking and economic differentiation had taken place before significant Inuit contact or major climate change occurred.

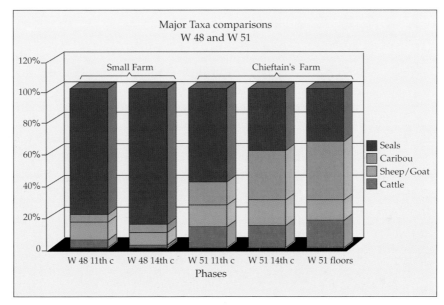

Settlement and a wealthy church farm at Svalbard in Thistil Fjord in northeast Iceland (McGovern et al. 1996, Amorosi 1992). While the Icelandic farm follows the broader Icelandic pattern of increasing use of marine fish for both subsistence and export between the eleventh and eighteenth centuries, the Greenlandic site retains its old Viking Age pattern of seal and walrus hunting down to the fourteenth-century extinction.

Differences within the Greenlandic economy between the few prosperous farms and the large number of poor farms also widened in the later Middle Ages. Fig. 25.9 contrasts the Viking Age and mid-fourteenth-century deposits at the chieftain's farm

Sandnes and the very poor farm W48 a few kilometers away. While the chieftain's farm maintained a fair cattle herd and consumed increasing amounts of caribou meat, the smallholders at W48 struggled to maintain any domestic stock at all and clearly relied increasingly on seal flesh.

Part of this economic differentiation was ecological, for the distribution of pasture plant communities was the key to Norse farming in Greenland, and these communities are restricted to a few pockets in the inner fjords of the Eastern and Western Settlements. Even within these environmental pockets, long-term farming success was tied to the possession of the best patches. Since

Erik the Red's day, the chieftains' farms always occupied the richest pastures in the most sheltered valley bottoms (fig. 25.12). The lesser colonists had to be content with less-sheltered and productive grass-sedge pastures, often at higher elevation (fig. 25.13). These poorer pastures were considerably more vulnerable to overgrazing, climate change, or even caterpillar attack than the protected holdings of the chieftains. Computer simulations have underlined the difficulties that mid-ranking farmers would face in maintaining long-term prosperity based on these sorts of pasture resources. Over time middle-ranking households tend to "lose" in the simulation and decline to become poor tenants, much as many real, historically documented Icelandic farmers did during the same period. Thus ecology combined with politics to produce increasing economic distance between higher- and lower-ranking farmers in Norse Greenland, as reflected in both the animal bones discarded in middens and the dietary trace elements remaining in the Norse colonists' skeletons. In Greenland as in contemporary Europe, stone churches, stained glass, and other trappings of high medieval civilization were coupled to increasing social and economic divisions by the early fourteenth century (figs. 25.10, 25.11).

Seasonal Round and Seasonal Vulnerabilities

By making use of both archaeology and historical documents, we can reconstruct the broad outlines of the seasonal round of the Norse Greenlanders. Summer was brief and filled with activities. This was the sailing season, when visitors from Europe might appear. It was also the season for the annual trip up the coast of Greenland to the "northern hunting ground" or Nordsetur (see Arneborg, Gulløv, this volume). It would appear that most Norse households participated in some way in this remarkable long-distance hunt aimed at acquiring the arctic treasures that could lure European merchants.

Other summer tasks were focused more directly on subsistence. Sheep and goats as well as cattle were milked, and the production of cheese and yogurtlike *skyr* to provide storable winter food was a vital task. In late summer, the hay harvest was equally critical, as every bit of potential fodder had to be collected, dried, and stored to allow the domestic animals to survive the long winter. When

the haymaking was done, intensive exploitation of nesting seabird colonies probably began. Murre and guillemot bones dominate the Norse bird collections, and these species are most vulnerable during their late-summer flightless phase. As winter set in and the majority of the domestic stock was brought indoors to be penned up for the winter, another hunt was organized to take caribou migrating in from their coastal summering range. Lines of cairns, possibly first built by ancient Paleo-Eskimo hunters, were definitely used by the Norse colonists as elements in several well-developed drive systems. Large dogs were kept on most farms (even poor ones) and these most resembled the long-limbed Irish wolfhound or Norwegian elkhound. These great hunting dogs may have been able to run down caribou or aid in driving them into prepared ambush sites. A few caribou skulls with holes punched by crossbow bolts and some evidence of communal distribution of the hunt in the frequencies of bones have been recovered from different farms.

Winter seems to have been a relatively quiet time, with people and animals living off stored food and keeping indoors. Many chess pieces and several gaming boards have been found (figs. 23.4–23.7), but no indicators of extensive winter-season hunting are known. By May to June, most households would be checking fodder stores and human food reserves, as a long winter or a poor harvest or hunt in the previous summer could turn spring into a time of hunger for humans and domestic stock alike. The arrival of migratory harp seals coming up the coast from their pupping grounds off Newfoundland must have been eagerly awaited. What appear to be seasonal Norse sealing stations have been identified in two outer-fjord locations in the Western Settlement, both well positioned to harvest migrating seals by stringing nets between islands. Netting seals in the water or clubbing them on land or ice were the traditional Norse hunting methods; they never adopted Inuit harpoon-hunting techniques.

This seasonal round provided basic subsistence and even a modest export surplus in walrus products and the occasional polar bear, and it clearly worked well enough for nearly five hundred years to allow the Greenlanders not only bare survival but also the resources to build churches and monasteries and to copy the latest fashions from Europe. Unlike the grain-based economies

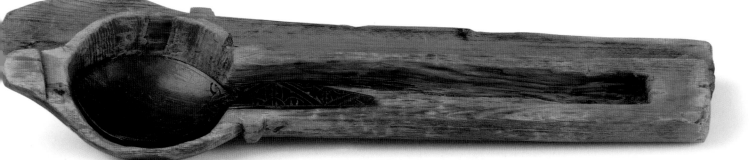

25.10 CARVED CHAIR OR TILLER ARM

One of the finest pieces of wood carving found in Greenland is this chair arm from an eleventh-century chieftain's farm at Sandnes in the Western Settlement. A Viking-style dragon head and three cat faces are executed in a variant of the Oseberg or Borre styles (chart, p. 66), making it undoubtedly a long-lived heirloom of high-status individuals. A runic inscription reading "Helgi" is scratched on the side of the arm.

25.11 HORN SPOON IN BOX

A finely decorated horn spoon from Austmannadal, seen here in its protective box, provides further evidence of social ranking in the larger Greenlandic farms.

of contemporary Europe, however, the herding and hunting Greenlanders had little ability to store surpluses accumulated in good years to offset hardship in bad. Unlike their relatives in Iceland, the Norse Greenlanders did not come to participate in the expanding commercial fisheries of the later Middle Ages, instead retaining their traditional emphasis on the Nordsetur and its hunting products. The Greenlandic seasonal round was something of a balancing act, in which fodder production, domestic animal consumption, caribou hunting, and sealing were the major factors that had to be juggled successfully each year. While the Viking Age and early Middle Ages may have been periods of comparative prosperity, this closely balanced economy was by the early fourteenth century increasingly operating at the long-term expense of the smallholders and was drawing down the accumulated natural capital of soil fertility and pasture viability (Fredskild 1992).

CLIMATE CHANGE, CULTURE CONTACT, AND CRISIS

The new detailed paleoclimate evidence from sea and ice cores and careful culling of the Icelandic medieval records have provided an unprecedented understanding of the sort of climatic challenges that this precariously balanced economy faced beginning around 1300 and becoming more serious in the fourteenth and fifteenth centuries. Ivar Bardarson's account mentions that newly abundant sea ice caused changes in navigation between Iceland and Greenland, and

Icelandic sources investigated by Astrid Ogilvie indicate sea ice reaching Iceland in 1306, 1319 to 1320, 1321, around 1350, and 1374, and on numerous occasions in the fifteenth century (Barlow et al. 1997). This documentary record is supported by analysis by Anne Jennings and Nancy Weiner (1998) of sea cores taken from Nansen Fjord in southeastern Greenland, which indicates circulation changes bringing in polar water and sea ice in the fourteenth century, locally peaking around 1370. The temperature-sensitive deuterium isotope record of the new central Greenland ice cores studied by Lisa Barlow (Barlow et al. 1997) show yearly low-temperature periods in 1308 to 1319, 1324 to 1329, 1342 to 1362, and 1380 to 1384. Breaking this record down into a summer and winter signal, Barlow noted that while the 1308 to 1319 cold period was mainly a winter phenomenon, the twenty-year cold period of 1342 to 62 was marked primarily by unusually cold summers. Work with a range of chemical climate indicators for atmospheric circulation on the same ice core by Paul Mayewski's team at the University of New Hampshire indicates that a shift in values for the Polar Circulation Index (a measure of the intensity of polar atmospheric circulation) around 1400 to 1420 was the most marked change in the past eight thousand years (Mayewski in Barlow et al. 1997). Something significant does seem to have happened to the Northern Hemisphere climate in the fourteenth and fifteenth centuries.

The twelfth to fifteenth centuries saw not only climate change but also growing contact between the Norse residents and the southward-migrating ancestors of the modern Inuit Greenlanders. These Thule people had begun their migration eastward from Alaska around 800, close to the beginning of the westward migrations of the Vikings. In Greenland, the two cultures met sometime

25.12 BRATTAHLID: A RICH FARM
Wealth in cattle and other domestic animals ultimately rested on possession of rich pastures. Pasture plant communities in Greenland are restricted to the inner fjords of the southwest—exactly the areas settled by the Norse farmers. Within these inner-fjord pastures are spotty and excellent meadows like this at Brattahlid, Erik the Red's old farm site, are rare.

after 1150, and this time it was the Norse who played the role of settled native and the Inuit who were the expanding newcomers. The late thirteenth to early fourteenth century *Historia Norvegiae* briefly notes violent contact between Norse hunters in the Nordsetur and new people who "used walrus teeth for missiles and sharpened stones for knives" (Gad 1971: 88). Despite intensive research, we still know few details of the nearly three-hundred-year contact between Norse and the people they dismissively called *skraeling,* something like "wretches." Besides Bardarson's assessment that the *skraeling* had destroyed the Western Settlement, few other documentary records of contact and conflict survive in the *Icelandic Annals*. For 1379 it is stated that: "The *skraeling* attacked the Greenlanders and killed eighteen men and took two boys into slavery" (transl. Astrid Ogilvie in Barlow et al. 1997).

Archaeological evidence indicates that occasional conflict did not prevent the Inuit from expanding their winter settlements down the west coast, first into the Norse Nordsetur hunting grounds and then into outskirts of the Norse settlement areas (Gulløv 1997). By 1300, Inuit settlements probably occupied the outer fjords of the Western Settlement, close to the seasonally important harp-sealing stations. Archaeology also reveals a wide range of Norse objects in Inuit sites, ranging from salvaged metal for harpoon end blades and knives to Norse gaming pieces reworked into Inuit-style spin-

ning tops (Gulløv, this volume). The Inuit were clearly interested in the Norse, and the legends collected in the eighteenth century do mention both friendly and hostile encounters. On the Norse side, Inuit artifacts and technology are conspicuously absent. The Norse did not adopt Inuit skin boats or clothing styles. More seriously, they did not acquire the highly developed Inuit harpoon-hunting technology. As animal-bone collections demonstrate, both the Norse and the Inuit were accomplished seal hunters, and by 1300 seal meat probably played a critical role in Norse subsistence (especially in the early spring). Because the Norse lacked harpoons and ice-hunting gear, however, they were effectively restricted to the two species of migratory ice-riding seals (harp and hooded seals) and to the localized harbor seals. These species were present or vulnerable mainly in spring and early summer, and could be hunted without using a complex of specialized gear centered on the toggling harpoon in the winter ice. Inuit animal-bone collections are full of ringed seal bones, and harpoon heads are common enough finds to be used for dating, whereas Norse collections from Greenland lack harpoons entirely and only rarely contain any ringed-seal bones. Ring seals are generally hunted at breathing holes on the winter ice. Had the Norse acquired harpoons and winter ice-hunting capacity, the vulnerable gap in their subsistence round would have been closed by ring seals. But the Norse did not choose to widen their subsistence base by

25.13 A POOR FARM
Most farms in Greenland were small and had access to relatively poor and exposed pastures, such as these just an hour's walk uphill from Sandnes W51. Sheepherding and caribou hunting in the uplands were carried out from small shelters like the one in the foreground.

taking up Inuit-style winter hunting, and some evidence suggests that the late winter gap eventually proved fatal, at least to some communities.

Several generations of archaeological work in the southern third of the Western Settlement gives us a unique picture of a small medieval community. While excavations of middens and buildings have provided an invaluable view of normal subsistence economy and daily life, there has always been something strange about the final floor deposits. Everywhere that soil conditions allowed for wood preservation, excavators have found large fallen roof beams, supporting posts, even whole doors still lashed together with baleen left behind along with wooden bowls, trenchers, wooden crosses, and crucifixes. In the modern North Atlantic, building timber was still expensive and wood from abandoned structures is quickly recycled by neighboring farms, yet this structural timber was left to rot. It is also hard to understand why scarce and portable wooden artifacts (secular or holy) would be left behind by farmers abandoning their holdings to move elsewhere. The spectacularly preserved, buried Farm Beneath the Sand (Gård Under Sandet, GUS) excavated between 1992 and 1997 by teams led by Joel Berglund and Jette Arneborg (see Berglund, this volume) produced a host of wooden artifacts and structural timbers, as well as the fully articulated skeleton of a goat that died there

sometime after abandonment (fig. 22.13). Perhaps a few domestic animals did survive the end of the Western Settlement, at least for a while.

This eerie echo of Bardarson's short account is matched by analysis of excavations carried out between 1976 and 1977 by Claus Andreasen on the W54 farm directly adjacent to the Farm Beneath the Sand site (McGovern et al. 1983). The interior of this farm contained the usual collection of food waste, lost artifacts, and accidentally imported European mice, beetles, and flies in the brushwood mat that formed the floor of most Greenlandic farms. On the top layers of this richly composting floor, some less typical remains were found: in the larder were the hooves of five cattle, mixed in with the feet of nearly a dozen grouselike ptarmigan and some feet of arctic hare. Hare and ptarmigan are both present in winter, but Inuit rightly regard the scrawny winter hare and grouse as last-ditch famine food. In the hallway outside the larder was the partial skeleton of one of the great hunting dogs, with cut marks on some of its bones. The insect distribution (Buckland et al. 1996) also suggested grim times; the lower, normal floor layers of the human living areas were rich with the pupae and adults of warmth-loving flies that had been imported with the Norse and thrived in the warm organic-compost layers of the interior floors. The upper layers, which held the foot bones and the butchered dog, showed a different distribution: the warmth-dependent flies had become nearly extinct, carrion-eating flies had expanded their range from the larder to the sitting hall and sleeping room, and native Greenlandic flies had also entered from the outside. This farm had not just been abandoned, it had died.

Reanalysis of older excavations from the 1930s indicate a similar fate may have befallen several of the other neighboring farms in this district. At the chieftain's farm at Sandnes, no fewer than nine partial skeletons of hunting dogs lay on the floors of stables and dwelling houses, buried beneath the collapsed roofing timbers that no survivor had claimed. While more work in this and other communities of Norse Greenland is required, it seems that at least one whole parish of the Western Settlement did not survive one long winter in the mid-fourteenth century. Did the survivors attempt to reach the Eastern Settlement prior to the relief expedition led

25.14, 25.15 Spindle and Whorl
Women twined yarn with simple spindles fitted with soapstone or ceramic whorl weights. The sheep used by the Norse produced lanolin-rich wool that was ideal for clothing and sailcloth, but the animals created great stress on local ecology. Because of declining temperatures, overgrazed pastures, and a human population that had overgrown its limits, catastrophe was only a stone's throw away. Runes mark this soapstone whorl, which was found in an Inuit site, but had probably been scavenged by those who had adapted to arctic conditions.

by Bardarson, only to perish at sea or in conflict with the Inuit? Did some go to live with the Inuit, who were by this time nearby? If starvation was rampant, and precious cattle and family dogs were being eaten on at least some farms, where did the loose animals described by Bardarson and documented by the Farm Beneath the Sand excavators come from? We still have many questions to answer about the end of this district and of Norse Greenland as a whole, but it is clear that the patient multidisciplinary cooperative research effort begun by Daniel Bruun nearly a hundred years ago has borne fruit.

Until Death Take Us or the World End

Why did the Norse die while the Inuit prospered? While Bardarson blamed the Inuit for the sudden end of the Western Settlement, the long climate record available to us would suggest that climate had shifted decisively against farmers tied to the few pockets of pasture capable of supporting domestic animals in the fourteenth century (figs. 25.14–25.17). While Inuit sea-mammal hunters could readily shift their settlements north or south along Greenland's long coastline to follow shifting concentrations of seals and whales, the Norse were tied to the only two substantial pockets of pasture vegetation in all of Greenland. For the Inuit, Greenland was thus a far bigger place than for the Norse, and their economy and lifeways allowed a more flexible response in settlement location. The perspective provided by long-term soil and vegetation analyses likewise inform us of the threat of erosion and pasture-productivity loss that could be only dimly perceived by any single generation of Norse farmers. The continuing concentration on walrus products during the late medieval period—when European taste was turning away from ivory decorations and when other North Atlantic communities were shifting to large-scale commercial fishing—also looks like a mistake. Some of the last recorded visitors to Greenland complained about being forced to take unwanted Greenlandic goods with them when they departed. By the fourteenth century, the Greenlanders were beginning to lose their small place in the evolving European market economy, just as drift ice may have made the long trip increasingly dangerous.

With twenty-first-century hindsight, we also can recognize that the Norse would have been better off reducing their investment in elaborate stone churches and increasing their efforts to borrow critical arctic technology from the Inuit. We can criticize the Norse for maintaining a conservative, stratified, Eurocentric outlook that valued cattle over seals and allowed cattle-rich chieftains to stifle the voices of the seal-dependent smallholders in vital subsistence and settlement choices. We can also point to the multicultural society that has evolved in modern Greenland since recontact in the eighteenth century as a historical alternative to the preservation of ethnic purity at the expense of survival by the medieval Norse. The Norse society in Greenland failed in part because of climate change, in part because of Inuit contact and competition, in part from soil erosion caused by the grazing of their own imported stock; even caterpillar attack may have played a role as well. On the larger scale, however, it was a series of decisions made and enforced by particular people at critical moments that turned Norse Greenland down its fatal road to extinction. While archaeology, history, and environmental science cannot name the people or date the critical decision points, we can certainly track an outcome fatal to the whole society.

From our well-informed and comfortable position in the late twentieth century, it is easy (and not totally incorrect) to blame the Norse demise on their own leadership. We must wonder why no Greenlandic bishop or bishop's steward was ever a native Greenlander (while virtually all Icelandic bishops came from Icelandic families) and what effect this management by outsiders born in the temperate zone had on the quality of decisions made in an increasingly arctic environment. The tremendous economic power of the later bishops is apparent in the scale of the ruins of the manor and cathedral at Gardar. While a contemporary chieftain's farm had space for twenty or thirty cattle, and a smallholder might have two to five, the huge byres of the bishop at Gardar offered space for as many as 150 cattle. With this sort of economic power concentrated in the bishop's hands, and massive ecclesiastical investment in imported cattle and high-quality pasture, it is not hard to see a probable source for the single-minded concentration on European-style stock-raising strategies. Many authors (Berglund 1991; McGovern 1981) have commented on the disproportionately

25.16, 25.17 BONE NEEDLE AND SCISSORS

Greenlandic Norse women crafted clothing with tools that are remarkably similar to those we use today, as shown by this decorated embroidery needle recovered from excavations at Brattahlid and pair of scissors from Austmannadal.

large size of the stone churches of the Eastern Settlement: a building program begun in the twelfth century produced a score of well-designed stone church buildings apparently well furnished with stained glass, church bells, and vestments by 1300 (fig. 23.12). Given contemporary attitudes toward non-Christians and possible heretics prevalent in Europe in the fourteenth and fifteenth centuries, the economic and political dominance of imported churchmen and their agents may have had a great deal to do with the clear barrier to the adoption of Inuit technology and skills. The leaders of Norse society in Greenland fatally misunderstood the changes of the fourteenth and fifteenth centuries, overvalued cattle and the pasture they required, and invested in churches and intensified political control instead of showing the flexibility that might have preserved their whole society. Was ethnic purity and domestic order preserved at the cost of extinction? Did the Norse managers in Greenland defend their privileged position so well that they reserved for themselves the privilege of starving last?

The Norse were victims of a short span of observation as much as a failure of individual perception. Without the millennium-long record of environmental change assembled by scientists over the past three decades, we would have no better chance of separating short-term weather fluctuation from long-term climate shift than did the medieval Norse. The economic constraints of the Norse Greenlanders were firmly founded in their European homeland both in the Viking Age and in the high Middle Ages. The basic patterns of culture, settlement, land-holding, power, and belief in Norse Greenland were formed within a specific environmental and social context. When faced with multiple challenges to the basic environmental and social framework of their economy and society, the Norse Greenlanders chose to avoid innovation, to emphasize and elaborate their traditions, and ultimately to die rather than abandon what they must have seen as core values. A common form of the feudal oath of fealty that would have been familiar to many medieval Greenlanders pledged a vassal's service "until death takes me, or the world end." This small medieval society remained true to its roots right up to the end of its world.

The author wishes to acknowledge contributions by Sonia Perdikaris, Thomas Amarosi, and Clayton Tinsley.

26 THE NORSE LEGACY IN GREENLAND

BY HANS CHRISTIAN PETERSEN

BARTERING, *JÓNSBÓK*

WHEN THE VIKINGS CAME FROM Iceland to Greenland under the leadership of Erik the Red a thousand years ago, they found evidence that people had once lived in western Greenland. "They found there, both eastward and westward in the country, dwelling places for people, as well as pieces of boats and worked stone objects," according to the priest Ari Thorgillson, as quoted and translated in *Grønlands Historiske Mindesmaerker* (1976, vol. 1: 169) (fig. 26.1). Archaeologists call the people who left these traces the Dorset people and believe their culture reached back twenty-five hundred years in Greenland's history. Dorset people are also known from the Hudson Bay and other Canadian arctic and subarctic regions. The Dorset were preceded by the Pre-Dorset culture, people who originally came from Alaska and Siberia and who crossed the narrow Nares Strait between the Canadian Ellesmere Island and Greenland's present-day Thule Municipality as early as forty-five hundred years ago. Today native Greenlanders (Inuit) call the Dorset people *Tornit* (pronounced "dornit") or *Tunit* (pronounced "dunit").

The Norse lived in Greenland for four to five hundred years in two settlements the Western and Eastern settlements, until they mysteriously disappeared (see McGovern, this volume). For some of this time, the Norse lived in proximity to the Dorset people. Around the fourteenth century another Eskimo group, the Thule Inuit, came into Greenland from Canada (see Gulløv, two volume). The Norse and the Inuit established contact along Godthåb Fjord in present-day Nuuk municipality (Western Settlement) and in southern Greenland near present-day Cape Farewell (Eastern Settlement). As an East Greenlander once told me, "we East Greenlanders have three ancestors: Inuit, *Tornit*, and Norse" (fig. 26.11). This paper is about how these three ancestors interacted—best known from oral traditions—and how all three continue to influence modern Greenland.

THE *TORNIT*

Saga of the People of Floi tells the journey of the Icelander Thorgils Scar-legs to visit his friend Erik the Red in Greenland in the winter of 998–999 or 999–1000. Unfamiliar with conditions around Greenland, he started his voyage too late in the autumn to reach his destination. He stopped in eastern Greenland at the onset of winter and was abandoned by some of his crew who stole his ship and fled. In the course of the winter the Norse met some of the local *Tornit* population, one man and three women, whom they attacked and wounded. Toward spring Thorgils built a skin boat and sailed south. During this voyage he again met some local people, who borrowed the skin boat and brought it back again. A few days later the Norse travelers reached their goal, the Norse Eastern Settlement. This story indicates that

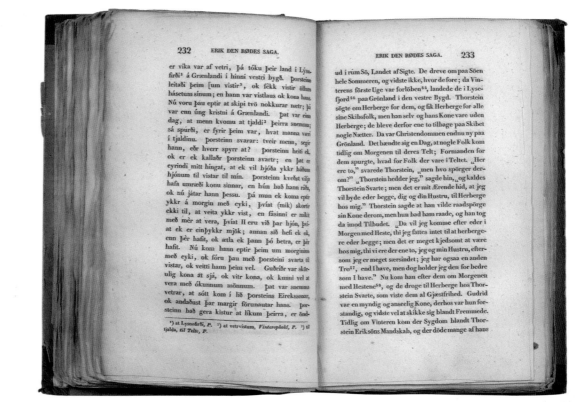

26.1 GRØNLANDS HISTORISKE MINDESMAERKER
Volume one of the three-volume *Grønlands Historiske Mindesmaerker* (Greenland's Historical Monuments), included a translation of *Erik the Red's Saga*, which is shown here. The compilation of this set between 1838 and 1845 was a major effort of the intellectual elite in Copenhagen to gather all the documentary evidence on Greenland—from sagas to church records—into one place. This publication led to greater interest in Greenland and inspired later archaeological investigations. It also helped strengthen Denmark's claim of sovereignty over Greenland by emphasizing historic ties.

the *Tornit* and Norse had very little interaction, and when they did interact it was intermittently friendly and hostile.

Descendants of the *Tornit* people in East Greenland had more extensive interaction with the Inuit. In East Greenland, where the *Tornit* remained longer, the two groups intermarried, making East Greenlanders distinctive. This combination can be seen clearly in East Greenlandic art, which retains the skeleton ornamentation of the *Tornit* culture.

DISAPPEARANCE OF THE NORSE

The records of Ivar Bardarson, a cleric from Trondheim Cathedral in Norway who came to Greenland in the 1340s to administer the church in Greenland from the bishop's seat at Gardar, indicate approximately when the Norse left the Western Settlement. He returned to Trondheim in the 1360s and published a report on Greenland, which has been preserved. He wrote that one summer in the mid-1350s the Eastern Settlement (in southern Greenland) had heard nothing from the Western Settlement in the Nuuk area (Bruun 1918: 131ff). The next summer he went on an expedition to investigate. The ship sailed to Ameralik Fjord where they found the farms abandoned and farm animals that had become half-wild, but saw neither Christians nor heathens. The expedition then sailed

home to the Eastern Settlement. This story provides an intriguing clue about the ending date of the Western Settlement, but gives very little other information. The ending date of the larger Eastern Settlement is also unknown, although we do have records from a wedding that took place in the Eastern Settlement in 1408. That settlement must have lasted until at least 1450.

DANISH REDISCOVERY

When the Danish crown took renewed interest in Greenland in the seventeenth century, they did not realize that the Norse had disappeared. Toward the end of the 1600s the Danish King Friedrich Wilhelm IV asked an Icelandic historian, Thormod Thofaeusson, to collect old stories about Greenland. His book, which appeared in 1707, is called both *Det Gamle Grønland* (Ancient Greenland) or *Det Gamle Grønlands Beskrivelse* (Description of Ancient Greenland). One of the readers of the book was a young pastor from northern Norway named Hans Egede. The book piqued his interest in the fate of the Norse settlers, and his brother-in-law, Niels Rasch, who had visited Greenland during his voyages as a ship's mate, provided tantalizing new information. Egede thought the people that his brother-in-law told him about must be descendants of Norse who had forgotten

26.2, 26.3 EUROPEAN REDISCOVERY
Hans Egede, the Norwegian minister who first confirmed the disappearance of the Norse Greenlanders, drew this map (fig. 26.2) of the Gothåb Fjord area around 1723. Dutch incursions into Greenlandic waters prompted the Danish crown to reassert its claim to Greenland. Shortly after Hans Egede's mission was established in Greenland, missionaries from the Moravian Church (fig. 26.3) were sent by the Danish crown to assist him in the difficult task of converting the skeptical Greenlanders.

their Christianity. Interpreting his own interest as a vocation from God, he petitioned the king to start a mission, but the state's coffers had been depleted by wars, and he was unable to get financial help. So Egede established a trading company in Bergen and managed to sail to Greenland with his family in 1721 (fig. 26.2). There he met a quite different people than he was expecting, and his vocation from God became missionary work among the heathen native Greenlanders. They showed him ruins left by Norse pioneers who had lived along Godthåb Fjord in what had once been the Western Settlement. In 1723 he traveled along the coast from Nuuk to Cape Farewell and confirmed that the Norse had disappeared from Greenland (Egede 1925: 74). This was a surprise to the

Danes, and scholars became very interested in what had become of the Norse.

When the missionaries learned Greenlandic, they heard traditional oral tales about the Norse of the Western Settlement that the Inuit had remembered from before 1350. In the spring of 1858, the scholar and South Greenland government superintendent, H. J. Rink, posted a notice all over west Greenland urging people to write down Greenlandic legends and asking those who could draw to illustrate them. One of the first responses Rink received came from Aron, a local catechist from Kangeq, a settlement near Nuuk, who sent stories with illustrations. A collaboration was quickly established. Rink provided Aron with paper and watercolors, and when a graphic artist visited Nuuk, Aron was trained in the techniques of woodcut and lithography. *Atuagagdliutit*, the Greenlandic cultural periodical that first appeared in January 1861, also published Aron's texts and illustrations over the years.

Rink received many written legends from throughout western Greenland. At Rink's initiative, some missionaries and traders had also collected legends, which Rink compiled. Rink's collection included stories about the Norse of the Western Settlement such as their first meeting with the Inuit:

> In former times, when the coast was less peopled than now, a boat's crew landed at Nuuk (Godthåb). They found no people, and traversed the fjord to Kangersunek. Half-way up to the east of Kornok, near Kangiusak, they came upon a large house; but on getting closer to it, they did not know what to make of the people, seeing that they were not Inuit. In this manner they had quite unexpectedly come across the first Norse settlers. These likewise for the first time saw the natives of the country (Rink 1974: 317).

Rink's collection tells of the fear and uncertainty the Inuit had of the Norse, such as this excerpt from "Ungortok, the chief of Korkortok":

> A girl was sent out to draw water in the evening, but while she was filling the pail, she noticed the reflection of something red down in the water. At first she thought it to be the reflection of her own face; but turning round, she was horrified at seeing a great crowd of Kavdlunait (Norse). She was so confounded that she left the pail behind, and hurried into the house to tell what had happened (Rink 1974: 310).

26.4

26.5

26.4, 26.5 THE BEGINNING OF THE TALE: ARCHER'S MOUNTAIN

The best-known Native Greenland folktale dealing with the Norse and the Greenlanders is based on a series of tales collected by Henrik Rink and illustrated by Aron of Kangeq in the 1850s. It begins with the Norse and the Greenlanders meeting and establishing friendly relations (fig. 26.4), especially two young men, one Greenlandic and one Norse, who loved to play together. One day the Norse boy challenged the Greenlandic boy to hit a target in the sea from the top of a mountain, with the condition that whoever missed would be pushed off the mountain. The Norse boy missed and was pushed off (fig. 26.5). Because this was his idea, the incident did not damage the relationship between the Norse and the Greenlanders.

Similarly, another tale tells of the Norse fear of the Inuit:

A kayaker one day went to the bay of Iminguit to catch thong-seals. Arriving there he observed a tent belonging to some Kavdlunait. He heard them jesting and prating inside, and was strongly minded to go and look in upon them. Accordingly he left his kayak, went up to the place, and began to strike on the sides of the tent. This made them apprehensive, and they now became quiet, which only encouraged him to continue all the more, until he succeeded in silencing them altogether. Then he took a peep in at them, and behold! They were all dead with fear (Rink 1974: 319).

A CONTINUING TRADITION

Three stories written down in the Rink collection about the Norse of the Western

Settlement—*Pisissarfimmik* (about *Pisissarfik*, the Archer's Mountain); *Navaranaamik* (about Navaranaaq); and *Uunngortoq*—have become the basis for a composite legend of the Norse read by all modern Greenlandic schoolchildren. [Editor's note: The three tales summarized by Petersen appear in Rink with significant differences in details and without being linked to one another. Readers interested in comparing the folklore about the Norse from the nineteenth century with the modern, abbreviated version told here should see Rink 1875, 1974.]

PISISSARFIMMIK

In the old days, when Greenland was still sparsely populated, an umiak (a large wooden boat) sailed from the south and came to the region of present-day Nuuk where it sailed into the northern fjord. When it reached the inmost part of the fjord the crew saw large stone houses built in several places. There they met foreign people whose language they did not understand and whose customs were different from theirs. Then the boat sailed out of the fjord, and they told their experiences to other Greenlanders they met.

After this many umiaks sailed into the fjord to see the foreigners. The meeting between the two peoples took place in peaceful circumstances (fig. 26.4). When they could speak together, friendships were forged between the two peoples. In the settlement of Kapisillit two young men, a Greenlander and a Norseman, became very close friends. They were always together for hunting or sport. They were equally matched in many contests of archery, running, and so forth.

One day the Norseman said to his friend: "Let's stretch out a hide on a small island, and go up on the high mountain, and shoot at the hide as a target from above. The one who doesn't hit the target will then be pushed over the cliff." The Greenlander answered: "I won't agree to that. We are best friends, neither of us should die." The Norseman persisted, but his friend still would not accept the suggestion. When the Norseman insisted, other Norsemen said to the Greenlander: "Let him have his way. We all know that it is his idea. If it is he who has to be pushed over, it will not spoil the relationship between our peoples." In the end the Greenlander, under protest, had to agree to the proposal.

26.6

26.7

26.6, 26.7 The Situation Worsens:
Navaranaamik

The good relations between the Norse and the Greenlanders continued for some time, and Greenlandic girls worked at Norse farms. One girl named Navaranaaq created animosity between the Norse and the Greenlanders by claiming that one side was going to attack the other. Believing her claims, the Norse decided to attack the Greenlanders first (fig. 26.6), killing the women and children of a nearby village. In retaliation, the Inuit built a magic umiak that allowed them to sneak up on and burn down the Norse chieftain's home (fig. 26.7).

A large caribou skin was stretched out on the small island. Many people, both Greenlanders and the Norse, went with them up the mountain (fig. 26.5). The Norseman shot first and missed; the Greenlander hit the skin. Then the Norseman went out to the edge of the cliff, since among the spectators were also several Norse chiefs who knew about his proposal. He was pushed off.

Since then the mountain has been called *Pisissarfik*, that is, the Archer's Mountain, as a Greenlander and a Norseman had competed there to see who shot best. The legend emphasizes that the incident had no consequences for the two peoples.

Navaranaamik

Later, a young Greenlandic girl, Navaranaaq, was engaged as a housemaid by a Norse family. After some time had passed she began to say to her own family, when she was visiting, "the Norsemen want to slaughter you," and to the Norse, "the Greenlanders are very angry at you!" At first no one took her seriously, but when she persisted in saying this, the Norsemen decided it would be wisest to strike first. One summer's day, while the Greenlandic men were hunting caribou inland, the Norsemen attacked the camp and massacred the women and children (fig. 26.6). Only one woman, who hid among fallen stones, escaped the massacre. When the men came home, she told them what had happened.

Uunngartoq

The Greenlanders were very angry, especially a man called Qasapi, whose wife and only child were among those killed. The couple had previously had several children, all of whom had died in infancy, but it seemed that their last child, who was thriving in its mother's *amaat* (large parka hood), would have survived.

Qasapi traveled around and looked for a shaman who was good at singing incantations. At last he found the one he was looking for, and he organized a raid in revenge. For this he built a specially designed umiak, consisting of several sections that could be assembled into a boat and stripped down again. Some sections he covered with dark skins; others he covered with white skins so that the boat looked like a dirty iceberg.

When they went into the northern Nuuk Fjord, they found only abandoned Norse farms. They were told that the Norse had gathered at the chieftain Uunngortoq's farm in the southern fjord. (The chieftain's Greenlandic name, Uunngortoq, seems to be the Norse name Yngvardur in Greenlandic pronunciation.) There they had camouflaged the buildings so that they would be more difficult to see. (Later the fjord was named Ameralla after the Greenlandic word for camouflaging skin. The fjord bears that name today.)

Qasapi and his party paddled to this fjord and found that the Norse had gathered at the chieftain's farm. There were guards outside the farmhouse. People were coming and going all the time. The Greenlanders set the umiak adrift with the wind blowing into

26.9

26.9

26.8, 26.9 THE END OF THE TALE: QASAPI

After the raid, the Greenlanders discovered that the Norse chieftain had fled the house. Qasapi, a Greenlandic man whose wife and only child had been killed in the earlier Norse raid, pursued the Norse chieftain, finding him running south carrying his son in his arms. As Qasapi got closer, the Norse chieftain threw his son into a nearby lake and escaped. After this, there were no more Norse in the Western Settlement, according to the tale. The Greenlanders were not pleased with the turn of events, and punished the girl Navaranaaq by dragging her until she died.

the fjord toward the house. The Norse saw it, and many of them went out to watch it drift (fig. 26.7). The crew of the boat could not be seen, but through holes in the skin they could watch the Norse. Qasapi asked the shaman to sing a magic song that would keep the Norse inside the house. He gave orders for the boat to be split. The different sections floated apart and drifted with the wind. The Norse assumed what they saw was a calving iceberg, so they went into the house without leaving a guard outside. The umiak sections drifted onto the beach, and the men went ashore with their weapons. The shaman continued singing his spell song.

In this way the men reached the chieftain's farm without being seen. When

Qasapi carefully looked in through a little window, he saw that the men were sitting around a table playing poker. The chieftain had Qasapi's wife's head, which had a stick stuck through a hole in the skull. They were gambling for it. Qasapi ordered his men to fill the entrance with fuel and set it on fire. Only now did the Norsemen realize that something was wrong. Everyone who tried to escape from the burning house was slain with arrows.

They had not seen the chieftain Uunngortoq, however. Suddenly he jumped out from the burning house. He had his little son in his arms and started running. Qasapi followed him. The chieftain ran very fast, and Qasapi overtook him slowly. Then Uunngortoq kissed his little son and threw him into a lake he was passing (fig. 26.8). After that he began running fast and could not be overtaken. And so he escaped.

Only after these events did the Greenlanders realize how the friendship had actually been destroyed. They became very angry with the young woman who had ruined the precious friendship between the two peoples. They took her and tied her hands and topknot with a rope, then dragged her behind them on the ground (fig. 26.9). Again and again they asked her "Navaranaaq, are you happy now?" "You'd better believe I'm happy," she answered. In the end they wore away her back, and she answered no more. Thus they punished and killed her without using weapons (Knuth 1968: 64ff). After this there were no more Norse in the Nuuk fjords.

COMMENTARY

A close reading of the legend reveals its intention. It is meant to show how much the Greenlanders appreciated the friendship between themselves and the Norse. Several examples are given of conflict that could have spoiled the friendship, but it survived because there was mutual respect between the two peoples. A duplicitous girl, Navaranaaq, who sowed strife between the two peoples, eventually spoiled this friendship. She was believed, and open war broke out. There are very few tales about the end of the Norse, and though this is thought to be one of them, it is more about the relationship that developed between the Norse and Inuit.

The legend of *Navaranaaq* is well known not only in Greenland but also among the Canadian Inuit. As mentioned earlier, Superintendent Rink published the first samples of his legend collection in four bilingual volumes in the period 1860 to 1865. Later he published *Grønlandske Myter og Sagn* (Greenlandic Myths and Legends), volumes 1 and 2, in Danish in 1866 and 1872. In it he included two legends, one from Greenland written down by Amos Davis, the other from Labrador, which the Moravian missionary Albrecht had collected in Okak. Both legends were about an event involving a Canadian Inuk girl named Navaranaaq and the Indians. The legend thus originated in Canada, in the context of Inuit and Indians, but became a well-known folktale in Greenland. A similar event probably happened in Greenland between the Inuit and the Norse, or such an event was taken as symbolic for the tense and changing relationships between the Norse and the Inuit. At any rate, the composite legend told here captures the modern understanding of the relationship between the Norse and the Inuit in the Western Settlement.

TALES FROM SOUTH GREENLAND

Rink also received legends about the Norse in South Greenland, the Norse Eastern Settlement (Rink 1974: 197ff). The legends are scattered and inconsistent, but they do continue the tale of Qasapi's hunt for the chieftain Uunngortoq. The legend says among other things that Uunngortoq had killed Qasapi's brother and cut off one of his arms. So Qasapi cut off one of Uunngortoq's arms, lifted it up, and said: "As long as I live, and as long as you live, your arm will not be forgotten!" Aron made a famous illustration of this episode (fig. 25.3).

These legends mostly speak of strained relations between the two peoples and of random attacks by both sides. Between the Eastern and Western Settlements there is a coastal stretch of two hundred and forty miles (four hundred kilometers) with scattered Norse ruins. Our knowledge of the Norse's use of the area is limited. As far as I know there is no oral tradition concerning the Norse among the Greenlanders of this coastal area (Fischer-Møller 1942: 79).

One of the stories about the Norse in South Greenland comes from Niels Egede, the son of the missionary Hans Egede, who managed the trading post in Sisimiut. He recorded his experiences and tales that he heard. One spring a group of several umiaks was passing through Sisimiut on the way from southernmost Greenland to the meeting place of Taseralik toward the north. A man from this company visited Niels Egede. Niels Egede wrote down one of his stories, and it was printed in the *Meddelelser om Grønland* 120, *Continuation af Hans Egedes Relationer* 1938: 268. The man explained that his tale was something his family had told from generation to generation and that the events had happened in South Greenland, where the family lived. It can be summarized as follows:

The time was over when there had been hostility between Greenlanders and the Norse. The Greenlanders lived as sealers out by the coast, and the Norse lived farther inland up the fjord in their settlement with their domestic animals. In the summer, when the Greenlanders were on their way up to the head of the fjord, they would visit the Norse.

One summer, while the Greenlanders were visiting, three ships were seen making their way up the fjord to the settlement. It turned out that it was foreign pirates who were trying to attack the settlement. The Norsemen resisted, and killed several pirates. One ship was set on fire, another was taken, and the rest of the pirates fled on the third ship.

The next summer, when the Greenlanders were visiting again, the Norsemen said that they were expecting another attack. So they asked the Greenlanders whether they would take the women and children up the fjord. The Greenlanders could hand back their guests on their way home. Before the Greenlanders sailed on, they noticed that a lot of small ships were on their way. The Greenlanders took the women and children and sailed on to their summer hunting grounds.

Toward autumn, the hunters went home and steered toward the Norse settlement to deliver their guests, but, alas, the whole settlement had been laid waste. Not one living Norseman met them, and the animals were also gone. Since they could not just leave the Norse women and children, they took them back to their winter settlement. They were then assimilated with the Greenlanders. Some of the women married Greenlanders and the boys were brought up as hunters.

A FOREIGN BOY FROM INLAND

This is similar to the story of the foreign boy from the inland reaches of Sisimiut/

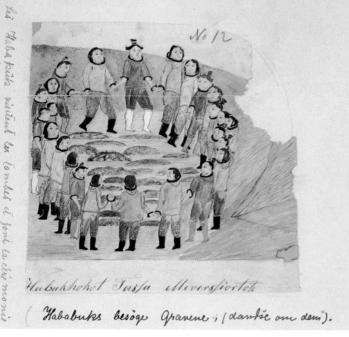

The Habakuk-party visit the graves and dance around them. (Funeral ceremony).

No 12

Habakkohot Tasfa Meversfiortek

(Hababuks besöge Qravene ; (dantse om dem).

26.10 Ring Dance

The ring dance was a medieval tradition that the Norse Greenlanders followed. Today's Greenland Inuit also have a ring dance, and it is likely they learned it from the Norse and continued to dance it after the Norse disappeared. The ring dance acquired a peculiar form in one district in Greenland, where a Christian cult leader and his wife encouraged their followers to dance in a ring around graves. This painting by Jens Kreutzmann was made in 1858, some sixty years after the height of the cult.

Holsteinsborg that I heard as a boy. Later when I lived in Sisimiut I asked if the tale was still remembered, and it turned out that it was. When I tried to date the story by talking to people who still remembered the tale, the only thing I could learn was that the event had happened before Hans Egede's time. Here is the story:

> Up the northernmost arm of the Sisimiut Fjord, people gathered in summer at a caribou-hunting and trout-fishing camp. One summer they heard that a child was on his way in from the countryside. When he came to the camp he turned out to be a boy of ten to twelve. He was not a Greenlander but a fair-haired boy whose language no one understood. He was eager to explain something and pointed enthusiastically inland, but no one understood. A childless elderly couple took him in and adopted him. Everyone was curious to find out what he would say about his origins once he could speak Greenlandic; his adoptive father in particular looked forward to the tale. At the end of the summer people went home to the winter settlements. The boy had begun to understand Greenlandic and gradually began to talk. Before he could say what he wanted to say, the boy was killed by a madman, which made the rest of the settlement sorry, because they would have liked to hear the boy's account of his origins. "Was he a Norse boy?" people asked.

A Norse Family among Greenland Sealers

Up the Sisimiut Fjord at Ikereteq, there is a place on the northern bank of the fjord where the grass was very green, indicating a ruin. Its place-name, Qallunaannguit, means "the dear Danes." To investigate the origin of the name, I visited an old couple in the nearest settlement. "Yes, there's a story that explains the name," the man began. "In the old days a Norse family lived there by hunting like Greenlanders. The man was a great hunter. Over on the other side of the fjord, at Anngarsuit, there is a similar house ruin. It is said that a great Greenlandic hunter lived there with his family. The two families were very close friends. When one family caught something that could be shared, they would not dream of cheating their friends. That's how they lived."

I realized that "the dear *qallunaat*" were not Danes, but Norse settlers who preferred to live by hunting like the Greenlanders. (The Norse were once called *qallunaat,* "the pale ones.") After the Danes colonized the country, the term was then used for them, after which the original Norse were called *qallunaatsiaat.* This Norse family cannot have been the only one to follow its inclinations by hunting and eventually being assimilated with the Greenlandic hunting families. Recent blood group studies also suggest that there has been mingling between the Norse and the modern Greenlanders (Persson 1969).

Mutual Influences

Though the oral tales provide the most extensive information about the relationship between the Norse and the Inuit, modern Greenlanders are still interested in investigating the history of their country and how it is linked with that of the Norse. I have been gathering evidence of this mutual influence over the years. Almost always, unfamiliar things are quickly interpreted as the work of the Norse. For example, in the hinterland of Sisimiut/Holsteinsborg there is a cairn in a conspicuous position. It has been built so that one can rock it from side to side without toppling or weakening it. "The Norsemen must have built it," people say.

Bjorn Thorleifsson, the lord lieutenant of the Danish king Christian I in Iceland, who was caught by the field ice and had to winter in South Greenland in the fifteenth century, spoke of Inuit women and children among the Norse

26.11 *"We Have Three Ancestors"*
Modern Greenlanders are experiencing a cultural rebirth. After years under Danish colonial pressures to assimilate to European ways, Greenlanders are now asserting their own rights, while maintaining their links, both economic and political, with the outside world. By drawing on their Dorset, Thule, and Norse past, modern Greenlanders are building a distinct identify that differs from that of the Danes.

(*Grønlands Historiske Mindesmaerker* 1976, vol. III: 408). We should therefore expect to find cultural influences going both ways. In the *Saga of the Foster Brothers*, we can read about special sealing harpoons that seem to have been unknown to the Icelanders and Norwegians (Seaver 1996: 62). In our own day archaeologists have found parts of Inuit seal harpoons at Norse archaeological sites.

Cultural Traces among Greenlanders

Some evidence for contact and mutual influence can also be found in everyday cultural practices of the Greenlanders. There is a wood joining method—the "hook-scarf" technique—which was used both in east and west Greenland to lengthen wood for making boat frames and hunting implements. A whaling umiak of the Alaska type, a type unknown in the rest of Greenland, was found on the eastern side of Peary Land far to the north. A close examination of its construction shows that the hook-scarf technique was not used but more primitive lengthening techniques, instead. It is thus very likely that the Greenlanders had learned the hook-scarf technique from the Norse, who had been using it since prehistoric times in Scandinavia.

The ring dance that Hans Egede illustrated in his book *Det gamle Grønlands nye Perlustration eller Naturel Historie,* 1741 (Egede 1925: 376ff, illustration, p. 85), and which we children danced, might come from the Norse chain and ring dance (fig. 26.10). Otherwise tangible cultural influences that we can trace to the Norse are few.

There is evidence of linguistic influ-

ences, as seen in examples of Norse loan words. The flower *Angelica archangelica* grows in the southern part of west Greenland. An edible plant, it is called *kuanneq* in Greenland. Its Norse name is *kuan/kvan.* The common porpoise *(Phocaena phocaena)* is an Atlantic species that frequents the west Greenland Atlantic current in the summer. Its name in Greenlandic is *niisa,* in Norwegian *nisse.* The earliest missionaries in south Greenland noticed that the word *kuuna* (Norse *kone/kona*) was used for wife there instead of the Greenlandic *nuliaq. Kuunara* means "my wife." It is even possible that the Greenlanders' ethnic name for themselves, *kalaaleq,* comes from the Norse. Poul Egede wrote that the Greenlanders called themselves Inuit. When they speak of themselves in South Greenland to foreigners, however, they use *kalaaleq.* We know that the Norse called Inuit and Native Americans *skraeling.* The sound combination *skrael* was impossible for the Greenlandic tongue to get around in those days. It is possible that *kalaaleq* was a Greenlandicization of *skraeling* (See Gulløv, this volume).

A New Norse Influence

The settlement by the Norsemen and their use of Greenland has again come to influence the Inuit Greenlanders. Basing their farming on livestock breeding, with cows, sheep, and goats, the Norsemen grew fodder and vegetables. Hunting was also an important part of their economy. Archaeological investigations conducted in the 1980s in the Ameralla settlements showed that some 70 percent of the food of the Norse families came from the local animals they hunted (*Forskning i Grønland/tusaat,* 1977, 2: 3). The Norse thus knew that farming with sheep, goats, and cows was feasible in Greenland when it was supplemented by the exploitation of local resources.

The Norse once lived by sheep breeding in South Greenland. For the Inuit, livestock farming is an alien idea, but for those of mixed descent, it is not as strange. In 1915 the Danish government offered the South Greenlanders the opportunity to establish themselves as sheep farmers. In connection with the offer a consultancy scheme was established, as well as practical training as sheep farmers for young people, with the possibility of establishment loans.

Today Greenlandic farmers have been

26.12, 26.13 Eastern and Western Settlements Today

In South Greenland, where the large Norse Eastern Settlement was located, small rural communities dot the landscape near the important hunting and fishing grounds. Nuuk, in the area of the former Norse Western Settlement, is now the capital of Greenland in the new Home Rule Government established in 1979.

working at their occupation for seventy to eighty years. Greenlandic farming began on old Norse fields and has now been in progress for two or three generations. A beginning has been made in agriculture, which is important now that the hunting of wild animals is subject to stricter and stricter limitations. Besides the imported domestic animals, which now form the basis of Greenlandic farming, the country also has its caribou and musk oxen, which can be incorporated into domesticated breeding. We must assume that by studying the Norse way of working, we can find good farming patterns from which our own farmers can benefit in the future.

VI VIKING LEGACY

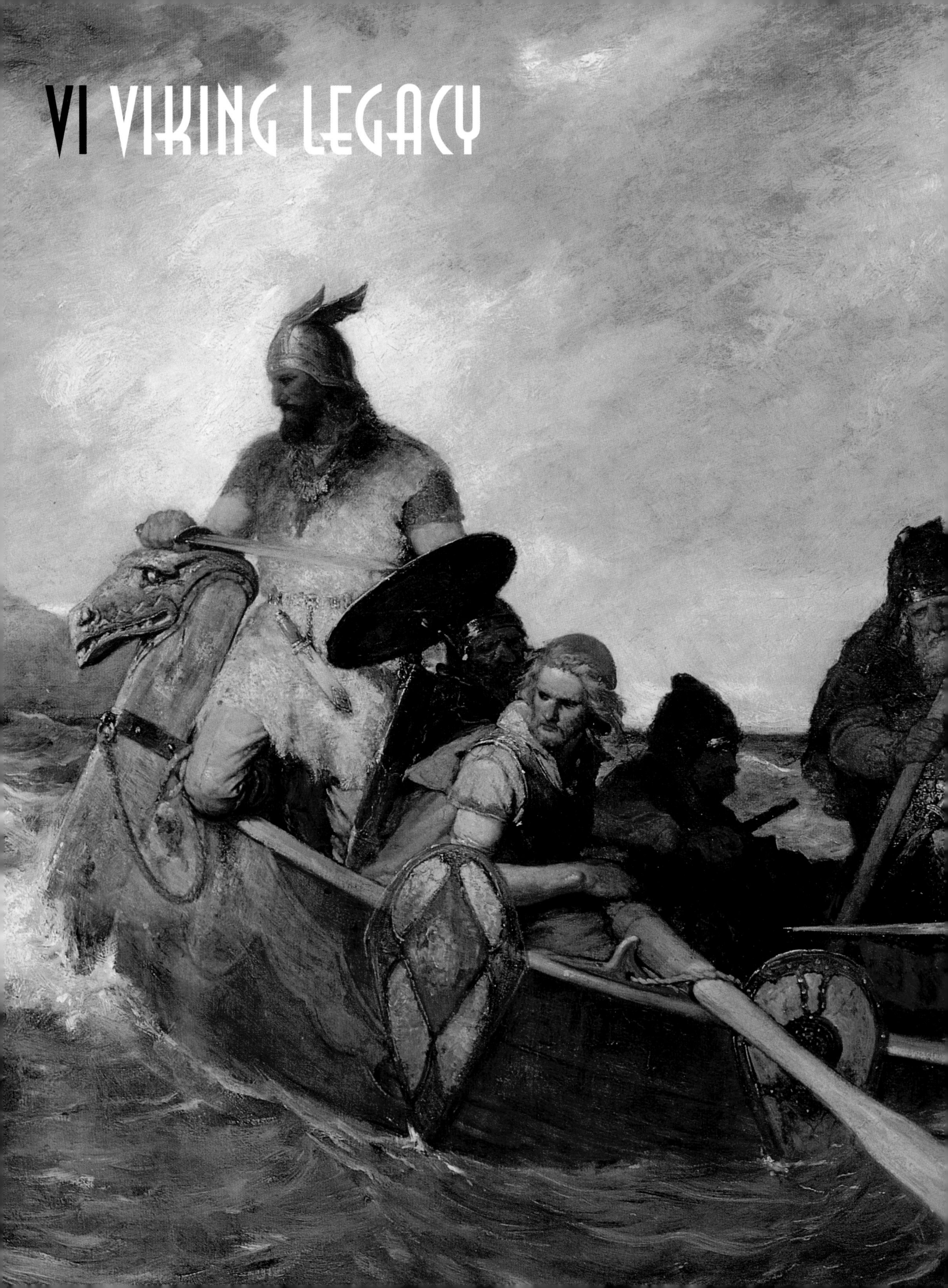

CELEBRATING THE VIKING PAST

A VIKING MILLENNIUM IN AMERICA

BY WILLIAM W. FITZHUGH AND ELISABETH I. WARD

S OON AFTER THE GREENLAND SETTLEMENTS were abandoned in the mid-fifteenth century, a dashing young Genovese explorer, Christoval Colon, was currying favor with the Queen of Spain to fund an expedition to find the fabled water passage to India. The rest is history we all know, but this version of the discovery and exploration of North America obscures the contributions of another group. Scandinavian-Americans, whose Viking ancestors had preceded Columbus to the New World by five hundred years, have been frustrated by the lack of recognition of their special contributions to the history of the New World. For more than a hundred years Columbus Day has been recognized and celebrated as a holiday in the United States. Columbus Day in 1992, supposedly the quincentenary of the European discovery, was marked by nationally televised programs, exhibitions and lecture series, books and other forms of educational programming intended to revolutionize how the European settlement of North America was interpreted. As the first Columbian anniversary to focus on historical and cultural interactions between Europe and North America as its principal theme, the 1992 Quincentennial broke new ground and changed how Americans perceive the "discovery" of the New World. Many of the themes that Quincentennial programs explored were based on new research and changing views: the effect of European society on indigenous cultures, landscapes, and biota is now seen to be at least equally positive and negative, and the relations between Native American peoples and successive waves of European, African, and Asian immigrants are more disturbing than inspiring (Axtell 1985; Crosby 1972; Dobyns 1966; Thomas 1989; Krech 1998). The word "celebration" was rarely heard in connection with this anniversary; Americans—better educated, more interested in history, more sensitive to ethnic and cultural diversity—had entered a more reflective era.

In the midst of this public Quincentennial colloquy, another group strained for recognition. Some of the Nordic population in the United States hoped to bring attention to their history and heritage in the New World by sponsoring a Viking ship and an exhibition. Inevitably, however, programming and media focused on 1492 and its aftermath. Scandinavian-Americans have had to compete for attention in a cacophonous national debate over how to represent the diverse strands of immigration to America.

The Viking heritage remains relatively invisible to most Americans, except perhaps on days when the Minnesota Vikings play. At the national level, knowledge of Viking and Norse contributions is almost nonexistent, except in Scandinavian-American communities. Most Americans remain uninformed about Vikings as a culture and are only vaguely

NORWEGIANS LANDING ON ICELAND, IN THE YEAR 872 Norwegian artist Oscar Wergeland completed this oil painting in 1877, when romantic nationalism was at its peak in Norway. Many details of dress, armament, and ship construction are inaccurate because excavation of Viking sites had not yet taken place. Today we have an opportunity to replace this romantic view of the Vikings with one based on history and science.

aware of their historical presence in the Americas or of their contributions to its history. No one interviewed by Elisabeth Ward during our informal canvassing of opinion about the Vikings at the start of our exhibition planning responded to the question, "Who were the Vikings?" with the answer, "Vikings were the first discoverers of North America around 1000." Very few identified Leif Eriksson as the first European to land on the mainland of North America. Although scholars in the United States have expanded knowledge of the Vikings through archaeological and historical studies, the average American probably identifies Vikings with theme parks and commercial projects or recalls the arguments of those who have promoted claims of ancient Viking inscriptions and monuments in New England and the Midwest.

As an historical and cultural achievement, the Viking Age and its North Atlantic medieval extension stand out as one of the most remarkable periods in human history. Within the span of three hundred years, seaborne Viking warriors, traders, and farmers redefined the shape of Europe, established trade networks reaching from Greenland to Baghdad, colonized Greenland and other North Atlantic islands, brought Christianity to Scandinavia and Greenland, and explored northeastern North America. Even as Vikings segregated into Christianized nationalities in Sweden, Denmark, and Norway after 1100, and others assimilated into local populations in Normandy, Brittany, and the British Isles, Nordic populations that had become established in the Faeroes, Iceland, and Greenland maintained Viking biological, linguistic, and cultural features to the modern day. The Icelandic language still retains many characteristics of Old Norse, and the local genotype, which has likewise been preserved over the centuries by geographic isolation, has become both a national treasure and an important asset to global medical research. With such obvious legacies, why are the Viking contributions to the modern world not recognized? Does Viking history—revolutionizing early Europe, transforming Scandinavian culture, settling the North Atlantic, and reaching North America—not speak for itself?

In Scandinavia, the Viking legacy is commemorated in countless museum exhibitions, festivals, reenactments, and touristic enterprises. Even the countries that were terrorized by the "heathen Viking hordes," like France, England, and Ireland, often celebrate the Viking past rather than ignore it. In 1911 the Scandinavian settlement in Normandy celebrated its millennial anniversary with banquets and festivals, where copies of Scandinavian archaeological discoveries were presented as commemorative gifts to Normandy from the Nordic countries. In Scandinavia, where ethnic and national identities have found common ground in their shared Viking heritage, celebrations of the Viking past have been an overt and powerful force in Nordic national identity for more than two hundred years. Today the Viking legacy lives on in the daily lives, recreation, and education of every Scandinavian.

Why has the Viking discovery of North America failed to penetrate the national consciousness? Perhaps because the location and activities that took place in Vinland, recounted primarily in the Icelandic sagas, have remained a source of speculation. The thirteenth-century sagas asserted the existence of new lands southwest of Iceland and recounted efforts to explore and settle Markland and Vinland. But interpreting the information in the sagas has been hampered by its vagaries and led to a string of speculative locations for Vinland, leaving the average American to assume that there is no fact behind the fiction. Various proponents—beginning in 1837 with Carl Christian Rafn, who mistakenly identified the Newport Tower as Norse rather than colonial, and including the Smithsonian curators and Scandinavian scholars who erroneously accepted the validity of the Kensington Stone—have added to the public uncertainty about Viking explorations of North America. One small example of the changing scholarly findings might suffice: after Rafn's identification of the Newport Tower as Norse, a Native American burial was found that contained a great deal of copper plating. The finds were sent to Denmark for inspection, with the assumption that this burial was of a Norseman. The burial and the Tower generated an overwhelming certainty that Vikings were in New England, which inspired Henry Wadsworth Longfellow's poem of 1841, "A Skeleton in Armor." What a disappointment it was for Scandinavian-Americans and New Englanders when the Tower was reidentified as colonial and the burial was determined to be Native American.

Many finds advanced at various times during the past one hundred and fifty years as proof of Viking explorations deep into the hinterlands of North America—including the Newport Tower, the Kensington Stone, the Beardmore relics from Ontario, the Heavener carvings from Oklahoma, the Spirit Pond runestones from Maine—have suffered the same fate: after an initial blush of excitement, they have been invalidated by scholars. This endless cycle has proven frustrating to both scholars and the general public. Scholars have long believed that these fakes are perpetrated by strange and dangerous individuals; throwing sand into the gears of history is not appreciated by professional historians or archaeologists. But the scholars themselves have not understood this popular phenomena for what it is—an expression of commitment to Nordic legacies by a special interest group that feels divorced from its homelands and its past. For a century scholars have battled with the demons of "fantastic archaeology"—that brand of amateur enthusiasm for imagining the past (Williams 1991)—without enough consideration of its sociological source in Scandinavian-American immigrant communities.

Until the 1960s, when the Ingstads, and later Birgitta Wallace, uncovered archaeological remains of indisputably Scandinavian origin and convincing antiquity at L'Anse aux Meadows, the Viking legacy in North America was

SÓLFARIÐ

Erected in 1974 to commemorate the eleven-hundred-year anniversary of the Vikings' arrival in Iceland (A.D. 874), this sculpture along the harbor of downtown Reykjavík is a modern expression of the Viking legacy. Icelanders feel close ties to their Viking past, which is frequently symbolized as a boat. The title means "Path of the Sun" and evokes Viking westward expansion.

Viking legacy in the United States. The exciting new scientific discoveries made since 1961 at L'Anse aux Meadows and Viking finds at Native American sites elsewhere in Canada and in the northeastern United States coincide with the millennial anniversary of Leif Eriksson's discoveries in 1000. These studies reveal the western Viking world as a fascinating one of challenge and response, of human ingenuity and bravery, and of sophistication and civility. Despite the devastating impact of climate change on Norse settlements in the North Atlantic and Greenland, Nordic settlers found ways to survive and even prosper in relatively unforgiving lands at the edge of the European world. Although these intrepid settlers were only dimly aware of the native residents in neighboring lands, they did recognize the importance of these discoveries sufficiently to record them in the sagas. Comments attributed to the Viking explorers of these lands in the eleventh century persisted in Nordic tradition, but the Greenland settlers were unable to fully integrate that discovery into their culture. It took another five hundred years and a new cast of characters from a different part of Europe to realize its potential.

mired in uncertainty, with Scandinavian-Americans searching for proof and scholars roundly dismissing their efforts. Part of the reason it took so long to find an actual Viking site is that energy was expended looking for the Vikings from New England to the Chesapeake Bay. As early as the late sixteenth century, the geographic concepts of Vinland, Markland, and Helluland were committed to paper by Sigurgeir Stefansson in the Stefansson Map (fig. 15.3); these features were elaborated on another map drawn by Bishop Resen, which contains notations and drawings of natives (fig. 19.7). The accuracy of the landforms and the images of natives suggests that the knowledge of the voyages from 1000 lived on in Nordic cultural memory. Interestingly, the name "Promontorium Winlandiæ" appears on a northward-jutting peninsula exactly where, four hundred years later, Helge and Anne Stine Ingstad found what most specialists agree is Leifsbuðir, Leif Eriksson's base camp for his Vinland explorations.

A greater appreciation of the Viking legacy in North America, both by scholars and a broader, non-Nordic population, can be found in the Canadian model. Canada, especially attentive to its Viking history after the discovery of the Viking site at L'Anse aux Meadows and its reconstruction and designation as a World Heritage Site, has vigorously promoted Canadian Viking legacy in school curricula, publications, and museums exhibitions, and has devoted huge resources to the development of "Viking Trail" heritage tourism featuring the L'Anse aux Meadows site in northern Newfoundland.

The "Viking Millennium" programming now underway presents an opportunity for suitable recognition of the

Science and history have increasingly illuminated what Vikings did and sometimes did not do in the western North Atlantic and North America, but this information does not dispel the romance of the Viking past, which is firmly planted in the souls of Scandinavian-Americans and Scandinavian-Canadians. The true legacy of Viking explorations in North America may supplant the long-cherished myth of the Vikings roving freely across the continent. One can easily imagine new Norse sites, as well as highly significant Norse artifacts, coming to light as future archaeological discoveries. L'Anse aux Meadows may not be the only Viking settlement ever built on North American soil; the quest continues.

American popular culture continues to respond to the curiosity and romance of a Viking presence in North America, but the image has been recast. No longer the marauding Viking plunderers of European monasteries and villages, a new hero more in the American style has been identified in the dramatic figure of Leif Eriksson. As a lone male explorer-warrior, he epitomizes how the Viking heritage in North America has become abstracted into a set of human ideals that serve as inspirational motifs for the new millennium. Vikings have captured an iconic role in North American popular culture but their role in North American history has now been bolstered by valid science; with any luck, this time they are here to stay.

27 | THE OLD NORSE DREAM

BY CARIN ORRLING

(AST YOUR MIND BACK FIVE
hundred years, to the Renaissance in Europe. For the previous four hundred years,
the Catholic church had been the main scholarly and intellectual agent in Europe.
The church, centered as it was in Rome, had absorbed many classical ideas of
the Greek and Roman empires into its doctrine. With Protestant movements desta-
bilizing the power of the Catholic church, Renaissance thinkers began to reevaluate
the ideas of the church but remained heavily influenced by classical thinking.
During this period university-trained scholars first began to explore the Nordic past,
in some ways as an alternative to the classic Greek and Roman models. Their perceptions and ideas about the north and the Nordic people filtered down through
the ages, changing slightly and adapting to political changes, from the Renaissance
to the Romantic period, and played a role in the rise of nationalism and of Nazism.
Great thinkers, artists, and authors—many, but certainly not all, of them Scandinavian—have brought the Vikings back to life for Europeans during the last five
hundred years and continue to explore this topic today.

ODIN, *SNORRA EDDA*

THE INSPIRATION

An important factor in the long-term interest
in Old Norse culture and history is the large
corpus of medieval literature that exists
about the Vikings. When the classic Old
Norse sagas and skaldic poems were written
down in Iceland during the twelfth and thirteenth centuries, the authors already considered the Viking era to be the "golden age"
of Iceland, a period of glory and heroism.
These Icelandic records have formed the
basic view of every aspect of the Vikings and
their achievements. Yet the sagas themselves
do not separate historical facts from narrative
fiction, which makes any understanding of
the Vikings based on the sagas subject to the
same ambiguity. Although factually problematic, the heroic sagas (*fornaldar sögur*),
recorded as late as the fourteenth century,

became favorites of learned Scandinavians
during the seventeenth century and have
ever since been an important part of popular
movements to rediscover and celebrate the
Viking past.

Because of their intricate rhyming patterns, some of the Old Norse poems
recorded in the twelfth and thirteenth centuries are believed to date back to a time
before the Vikings. The delightful poems in
the *Hávamál* ("Words of the High One" in
the *Poetic Edda*), for example, are composed
in a sophisticated metaphoric and musical
language, which makes its verses easy to remember, just as the old laws were. Their
structure made it possible to consider these
poems as evidence of a pre-Viking, proto-
Germanic past, which appealed to a wider
Germanic audience. Other works of interest

27.1 THOR'S BATTLE WITH THE GIANTS
The Norse gods—powerful, exciting, and with deep cultural resonance—were common motifs in nineteenth-century romantic nationalistic paintings. In this work painted between 1866 and 1872 by Márten Eskil Winge, the Norse god of thunder, Thor, wields his mightly hammer, Mjolnir, and frightens off the giants who seek to destroy the world.

as the rulers of the Roman empire and have them accepted by Christendom as honorable pagans (Lundstrøm and Orrling 1972).

The two brothers Johannes (1488–1544) and Olavus (1490–1557) Magnus, exiled to Rome by the Swedish king Gustav Vasa for not abandoning their Catholic faith in favor of Lutheranism, both wrote histories of Sweden. Johannes's *Historia de omnibus gothorum sveonumque regibus* (History of All the Gothic and Swedish Kings), written in Latin, lists more than a hundred Swedish kings, with names and dates. His glorification of the Swedes and his argument that the Goths came from Sweden introduced a nationalistic element into Swedish literature of the time. His younger brother Olavus wrote *Historia de gentibus septentrionalibus* (A Description of the Northern Peoples), in which the daily life of noble Scandinavians is described. These two later works show a movement away from the king-focused state that Snorri and Saxo had emphasized earlier toward a national identity, which formed partially because of the collapse of the Catholic church during the Reformation.

NORDIC ROMANTICISM IN EUROPE

These works led to new efforts in the seventeenth and eighteenth centuries, which became more widely available with the adoption of the printing press and inspired an interest in the Nordic Viking past not only among Scandinavians but also throughout Europe (Karlsson 1992). The Icelanders Thorlak Skulsson and Magnus Olafsson translated Icelandic literature for Danish and Swedish scholars in the seventeenth century. In 1646 the Latin version of the *Poetic Edda* arrived in Paris. Later the Swiss historian Paul-Henri Mallet (d. 1807) of Geneva, who was a professor of French at the University of Copenhagen in the 1750s and 1760s, translated Nordic mythological poems found in the *Poetic Edda* into French. In 1763 his work was translated into English and later into German. Mallet also translated Snorri Sturluson's *Prose Edda*, a handbook of poetics, into French in 1756.

A series of works published at the end of the eighteenth century established the modern understanding of Nordic history and mythology (Mjöberg 1967). *Nordiska Kämpadater* (Deeds of the Nordic Heroes) was edited by Eric-Julius Biörner (1696–1750) and Johan Göransson published a commen-

were the histories written about the Viking kings of Denmark, Norway, and Sweden. The Danish cleric Saxo Grammaticus (died circa 1220), whose Latin history of Denmark, *Gesta Danorum,* had great influence, wrote of the glory and noble conduct of the early Danish kings. Later, the Icelandic chieftain Snorri Sturluson (d. 1241) wrote the history of the Norwegian kings in *Heimskringla* ("Orb of the World"), a collection of kings' sagas compiled in the first half of the thirteenth century and written in the vernacular. The most famous and popular saga, the story of King Olaf Tryggvason (d. 1000), is still read in Norway, often in the original Old Norse. Both Saxo and Snorri wanted to elevate their pagan ancestors to the same level

27.2, 27.3 *FRIÐJOF'S SAGA*
Much romantic Viking-themed literature in Scandinavia and Europe drew on the sagas as sources of inspiration. *Friðjof's Saga*, a sixteenth-century Icelandic courtly romance (27.3), was one such work. Between 1820 and 1824, the Swedish author Esaias Tegner retold this saga as an illustrated heroic poem that became an international success. Fig. 27.2 shows an illustration by August Malmström for an English version.

tary on Snorri Sturluson's *Prose Edda* and *Voluspá* (Prophecy of the Seeress). Olof von Dahlin (1708–1763) wrote *Svea rikes historia* (History of the Swedish Kingdom). In 1808 N.F.S. Grundtvig's (1783–1872) *Nordens mytologi* (Northern Mythology) was published in Denmark; in this work, individual myths are retold in the form of a chronology of religious sagas.

The original purpose for these works was to heighten the status of Scandinavia within Europe, not to foster nationalism within these countries. The most extreme example of this seventeenth- and eighteenth-century trend can be seen in Sweden, where Professor Olof Rudbeck (1630–1702) of Uppsala University wrote his four-volume masterwork *The Atlantica* (1679–1702), which expressed extreme Gothic chauvinism and a grandiose conception of Scandinavia as the womb of nations, equating Sweden with Atlantis, the sunken island paradise described by Plato.

During the seventeenth and eighteenth centuries, paintings produced about the Viking Age conformed to the heroic aesthetic of the day. Norsemen and the pagan gods were depicted with the beauty of Greek gods and heroes in an attempt to elevate the status of northern Europe (Wilson 1997). In seventeenth-century Scandinavian pictures of Viking Age people and buildings, the artists equip gods and men with the status symbols of the time. In an annotated edition of Saxo's *Gesta Danorum*, the god Thor is shown with a crown and scepter, symbols of kingship in the seventeenth century, while Odin has been attired in a full suit of armor and a plumed helmet.

Outside Scandinavia, Norse literature often became combined with Celtic literature, in a general romantic antiquarianism for things northern (Roesdahl et al. 1996). In particular, the series of poems known as the Ossian cycle, which James Macpherson composed in 1808, though claiming he was transcribing the work of a legendary third-century Irish bard, Ossian, was often confused with Nordic poems, creating a generalized Celtic-Scandinavian style. This hybridization also became popular among the French. Anne-Louis Girodet (1767–

27.2

27.4 Drinking Horn
Reliving the glorious Viking past was a favorite pastime of learned Scandinavians, especially for members of the Gothic Society in Sweden. Author, poet, and university professor Erik Gustaf Geijer, one of the leaders of this movement, was presented with this magnificent drinking horn decorated with scenes from the *Poetic Edda* by his students in 1817. The silver mounting was designed by Bengt Erland Fogelberg and made by the silversmith Johan Petter Grönvall.

1824), on orders from Napoleon, decorated Malmaison with wall painting inspired by the Ossian poems, which depicted the Norse creator god Odin in Valhalla receiving Napoleon and his generals.

ROMANTIC NATIONALISM

The romantic and antiquarian interest in a nonclassical past took on a decidedly nationalistic tone in the nineteenth century owing to political changes in Scandinavia. By 1814, when the Napoleonic wars were finally over in Europe, a patriotic historical romanticism arose in every country affected by those wars. The German countries turned toward the medieval period, while the authors from each of the Scandinavian countries began to romanticize the period and the Vikings, when the Scandinavian kingdoms had held great power over Europe. The Swedish poets Erik Gustaf Geijer (1783–1847) and Esaias Tegner (1782–1846), wrote literary works about heroic gods and heroes from Nordic prehistory.

In the Scandinavian academies of art, the traditional themes found in the Bible or in Greek mythology were used. By the beginning of the nineteenth century, artists instead sought motifs in the Nordic sagas. Although the new themes were Nordic, the style and look of the human figures remained classi-

cal—that is, Greek—for the early part of this movement. One example of the antique ideals of beauty that persisted was Bengt Erland Fogelberg's (1758–1854) three colossal statues of Odin, Thor, and Balder. Although they carry icons that signify their identity— Thor's hammer and Odin's spear— their appearance mimicked classical style. These statues once stood in the entrance hall of the Stockholm Museum of National Antiquities. In the mid-nineteenth century the classical Greco-Roman image of the Vikings was replaced by a more Nordic one. By this time archaeology had become a source of inspiration for Scandinavian artists who sought to portray the Nordic past, but the basic chronology of this new science had not yet been well established. In many works of art from the mid-nineteenth century, objects that date to different periods of the past are nevertheless shown together (fig. 27.1).

Theatrical performances followed a similar pattern, with an increasing number of Nordic themes. As early as the eighteenth century, in the reign of Gustaf III (1771–1792), theatrical productions with Old Norse names had been presented. Gustaf III himself wrote *Odin and Frigga*. During the nineteenth century, many operas and theatrical spectacles with ancient Nordic themes were performed. In 1808, *Hakon Jarl*, a play about the confrontation between paganism and Christianity during the Viking Age written by the Dane Adam Oehlenschlager (1779–1850) had its premiere on the birthday of the Danish king. Oehlenschlager had also written the poem *Guldhornene* (Golden Horn),1803, which recounts the archaeological discovery in Denmark of two remarkably large, Migration Period (A.D. 500) gold horns decorated with mysterious pictures that were thought to represent pagan gods. Stolen soon after their discovery, the horns were melted down by the thieves, but Oehlenschlager's nationalistic poem about them has been read by generations of Danish schoolchildren.

THE GOTHIC SOCIETY

This assertion of a unique Nordic identity in the nineteenth century coincided with rising nationalistic political movements. One of the earliest nationalistic organizations was the

27.5, 27.6 From Stone to Fabric
A society called Handarbetets Vänner (Friends of Textile Art Association), founded in 1874, taught its members to sew interlaced dragon patterns like the one above, designed by Hanna Winge (fig. 27.5). In 1877 Signe Sohlman designed a more complex pattern for handwoven linen damask. It continued to be produced by the Almedal Company until the beginning of the 1970s (fig. 27.6).

Götiska förbundet (Gothic Society), established as a men's organization in Sweden in 1811, whose purpose was to encourage patriotic spirit and advance Nordic archaeological research. The members of the Gothic Society were eminent representatives of art and science who participated in meetings at which everyone sang the anthem, "In Ancient Times Goths Drank from Horns" and drank mead out of his own horn. Many of these horns are preserved today in the collection of the Nordic Museum in Stockholm. The members were given different Viking names, such as Skoglar Toste or Einar Tambaskälve. The Gothic Society promoted greater Nordic representation in the arts through lectures on such topics as how to use the Nordic myths in fine art. It also published a magazine, *Iduna*, named after the Norse goddess who carried the life-sustaining apples of the gods. The content of *Iduna* was mainly literary, but archaeology was also featured prominently; as such, the magazine became Sweden's first journal of antiquities. Among the works published under the influence of the Gothic Society were Geijer's "Vikingen" (The Viking) and "Odalbonden" (The Yeoman Farmer), poems that soon became the stereotypical expression of a perceived Viking spirit and recited during patriotic gatherings. *Friðjof's Saga* by Tegner (fig. 27.2), a pastiche built on the model of an original Icelandic saga about courtly activities in Europe (fig. 27.3), came out in 1825 after parts of it had first been published in *Iduna*. *Friðjof's Saga* was translated into several different languages and influenced romantic movements in Germany, England, and even France.

Drinking Horns and Scandinavianism

During the 1830s students and poets created the concept of a shared common culture in Scandinavia, based on the combination of a shared Viking past and modern circumstances. They congregated in meetings where men sang and read Old Norse songs and poems. According to the ancient Icelandic *Snorra Edda,* real skalds or poets must drink of Odin's magic mead—stolen in ancient times from the giants—in order to create great poetry. Naturally, mead flowed copiously from drinking horns at these meetings. In 1817 students in Vaermland residence hall of Uppsala University presented the writer Erik Gustav Geijer with a splendid drinking horn (fig. 27.4) ornamented with silver that was fashioned by Johan Petter Grönvall (1771–1843). Three of these silver-ornamented drinking horns were made from Bengt Erland Fogelberg's design by Grönvall, including one ordered by King Karl XIV Johan. During the nineteenth century thousands of drinking horns made of various materials and designs were used by clubs and societies and as honorary presentations to individuals. Drinking horns were given a central place of honor in middle-class dining rooms, where they stood among ceramic and stoneware tankards and steins.

The notion of a common Scandinavian past and future, supported by the closely related Scandinavian languages, created a feeling of solidarity that led to a movement called "Student Scandinavianism." At these festive student meetings, people competed in singing grandiloquent, patriotic Nordic songs and giving high-flown speeches. At a student meeting in 1862 Norse gods were chosen as the official mascots. Norwegian students chose Thor, the Danes chose Heimdall, and the Swedes from Uppsala chose Odin. Participants at these meetings petitioned their universities to establish chairs in ancient Nordic languages. As a result of such popular interest a professorate in Nordic languages was set up at Uppsala in 1859. The early Nordic languages were taught in some secondary schools; for example, during the 1860s and 1870s, classes in Old Icelandic were given at Skara High School.

Nationalism and Archaeology

At the midpoint of the nineteenth century, Scandinavia confronted the great demographic adjustment of industrialization and urbanization. Between 1830 and 1870 the population of Sweden increased from 3 million to 4.2 million. During this process, the proportion of farm owners shrank, although

27.7

27.8

27.7, 27.8 Aristocratic Dragons
The Gothic revival movement was enthusiastically supported by the aristocracy. This impressive marble case with dragon-shaped gilt and silver mountings made by Torolf Prytz of Oslo was presented to King Oscar II of Sweden by the Norwegian court on the occasion of the twenty-fifth year of his reign. The impressive summer house of the Curman family (fig. 27.8) at Lysekil was similarly embellished with dragon-head finials.

27.9 Runes for a King
Scandinavian royalty embraced the romantic infatuation with the Vikings. This wooden chair with runes was the nursery chair used by King Gustav Adolph (born 1892 and Swedish king 1950–1973). The translation of the runes reads, "best is one's own nest, however small; you are master in your own house," inspired by a romantic view of independent-minded Vikings.

70 percent of the population was engaged in agriculture. This created an agricultural proletariat of tenant farmers and servants, and many of those who owned no property abandoned farm life for industrial opportunities in the cities and in the sawmills of the northern provinces. Communications were improved, new markets opened up, and development accelerated. The new city dwellers began to identify themselves less by the local districts from which they came and more on a national level as Swedes. Burgeoning expansion produced optimism about the future until the end of the 1870s when the pressure of increasing social problems caused a steep drop in public confidence.

It was no coincidence, then, that during the 1860s and 1870s, the popularity of neo-Gothic ideological currents (that is, those connected in various ways with ancient Scandinavia) surged in Sweden. In the sixteenth and seventeenth centuries, historians had invented a glorious past for Sweden. Archaeology as a field of study began to develop in the early nineteenth century, concurrent with changes in agricultural technology and land divisions that led to large tracts being plowed with better and deeper-cutting plows than before; as a result, many antiquities were uncovered and collected. Although objects were still valued mostly for their artistry and the most striking pieces were collected, sold, or exhibited, many remarkable objects entered Swedish archaeological museums during this period.

Discussions and meetings between archaeologists and other intellectuals brought these antiquities into the larger cul-

27.10 DAILY-USE VIKING TABLEWARE
The Scandinavian middle class also embraced the romantic celebration of the Viking past. An array of items decorated with dragonesque meanders were mass produced, including porcelain tableware. This piece by Erik Hugo Tryggelin made in 1878 has dragon handles and medallions illustrating Viking scenes within a dragonesque pattern.

tural realm: during the 1850s and 1860s two artists, Mårten Eskil Winge and August Malmström, achieved popularity with their archeological realism and revived the Gothic tradition in the pictorial arts. Both men were active book illustrators, and the history and mythology of the remote past was prominent in their art. Malmström illustrated Tegner's *Friðjof's Saga* in an edition first published in 1868 (fig. 27.2). He also designed furniture and household furnishings, porcelain, textiles, and building ornamentation, as well as costumes and scenery for tableaux and masquerades. Winge's paintings *Loke och Sigyn* (Loki and Sigyn) and *Tors Strid med Jättarna* (Thor's Battle with the Giants) were reproduced in schoolbooks.

DRAGONESQUE MEANDERS

The neo-Gothic movement is seen most definitively in the decorative arts as the "dragonesque meander," a form of ornamentation adapted from runestones and objects of the Viking Age (fig. 27.9). Introduced in the 1870s on utilitarian objects, these images, ascribed to remote Nordic antiquity, have obdurately survived all changes in fashion and are still in use today. The dragonesque meander became the symbol of the independence, originality, and power of the Nordic countries. Its originality and distinctness was especially important at the newly popular world's fairs, where countries competed to assert national character and identity. The Scandinavian arts and industries exhibition in Stockholm in 1866 was organized around an Old Norse theme. At the world's fair in Paris in 1867 Sweden showed Old Norse–inspired wooden architecture ornamented with dragonesque meanders in a pavilion designed by Fredrik W. Scholander. The

design of the pavilion combined peasant architecture with what were considered Old Norse designs, bringing together an agrarian past and a heroic past.

At the London Exposition of 1871, porcelain by Swedish designers incorporated Old Norse elements and themes. Gustavsberg Works mass-produced porcelain, such as the service decorated in the "Dragon Pattern" drawn by August Malmström, which was printed in blue on an existing rococo-style service. The Nordic collection, with medallions showing Old Norse saga themes and decorations of dragons and dragonesque meanders, did not have great commercial success—even though Gustavsberg received a Gran Prix at the world's fair in Paris in 1878 and the pattern sold well. A few of the motifs persisted in catalogs into the twentieth century, but most disappeared much earlier.

The great success of Swedish textiles at the Vienna exhibition of 1873 was among the reasons for the founding in 1874 of the organization called Handarbetets Vänner (Friends of Textile Art Association), which worked up pattern pages in the dragon style. The dragon style sparked a reform movement in textiles led by Friends of Textile Art, who championed ancient Nordic symbols as something primitive that had been long forgotten (fig. 27.5). A dragon pattern that was applied by the artist Signe Sohlman to damask tablecloths displayed at the Amsterdam exhibition of 1877 was still being reproduced in the 1970s (fig. 27.6).

The dragonesque meander ornamented every conceivable material and object, including those that had no prototypes in Norse culture, for example, coffee pots, cream pitchers, and sugar bowls in porcelain and silver (figs. 27.7, 27.10). Table settings in silver were decorated with dragonesque meanders as were candlesticks and beer tankards. The pattern could be found on bread boxes and hairbrushes. From 1916 to 1932, the weekly magazine *Allers Family Journal* published jigsaw patterns in which the dragonesque meander appeared on lamps, egg cups, fruit baskets, bookends, and other items.

The enthusiasm for neo-Gothicism was also evident in the performing arts. Masquerades, dances, and little theatricals in the Old Norse spirit were organized—with participants dressed as Vikings frequently wearing garments decorated with dragonesque meanders (fig. 27.12). At salons in Stockholm,

27.11 Brünnhilde
The cultural, linguistic, and historic
ties between Scandinavia and
Germany were of great interest to the
intellectuals of the Romantic period. The
best-known product of this milieu is the
three-part opera *Ring of the Nibelungs*
by Richard Wagner. Its characters were
drawn from Old Norse religion,
including the female lead Brünnhilde,
who was Odin's daughter and beloved
of the hero, Siegfried. Between 1935
and 1952, Kirsten Flagstadt (seen here),
a famous Norwegian soprano, appeared
in the role of Brünnhilde at the
Metropolitan Opera in New York City.

27.12 Viking Balls
Some Swedish social clubs required
participants to don Viking costumes
for the annual Military Society ball
held in 1869. The participants were
photographed with their costumes,
which were probably not seen as
strange but as a kind of national
costume.

discussions, readings, and lectures on art, literature, music, and natural science were attended
by Oscar Montelius, Hans Hildebrand, Arthur
Hazelius, and other celebrities of Swedish
culture.

As early as the Nordic artists' meeting in
Gothenburg in 1869, the possibilities of developing an independent architecture based
upon old Nordic building techniques had
been discussed. The Old Norse home, which
became the symbol of the patriarchal ideal,
reflected anxiety over the pace of change in a
rapidly industrializing society. The intellectual elite had country houses built for themselves and their families with dragonesque
elements: Axel Key had his mansion Bråvalla
built in Gustavsberg in 1870; Carl Curman's
house in Lysekil on the west coast was erected
in 1873 (fig. 27.8); and in Djurgården in
Stockholm in 1874 Lorentz Dietrichson had
his Solhem showplace built. Many middle-
class homes had a room that was decorated in
dragonesque style or furnished with porcelain
or silver in dragonesque style. Toward the end
of the nineteenth century several public
buildings were built in dragonesque style, for
example, the Biological Museum in
Djurgården in Stockholm, designed by Agi
Lindgren and erected in 1893. In 1894 in the
town of Boden in northern Sweden, the dedication of a wooden railroad station decorated
with dragon heads was attended by King
Oscar II who made a patriotic speech.

Families in the Nordic countries and in
Germany began to give children such Old
Norse names as Gunnar, Sigurd, Harald,
Frithiof, Gunborg, Gudrun, Ingegerd,

Ingeborg, and Valborg. The writer Viktor
Rydberg contributed a list of 258 names he
had compiled from the Icelandic *Book of
Settlements*, from the Norse sagas, and other
sources. Boats, locomotives, streets, and city
blocks were also given Old Norse names.
Interest was also shown in the sports of the
forefathers: gymnastic societies and sporting
associations were formed and given Old
Norse appellations, as were student associations, choirs, and temperance societies.

Nationalism in Norway
The Swedish-Norwegian political union,
started in 1814 after Norway split from
Denmark, was dissolved in 1905. Finland
became independent of Russia in 1917; and
in 1918 Iceland, which had been an independent nation from 874 to 1264, regained
a measure of sovereignty, although its last ties
to Denmark were broken only in 1944. The
newfound independence of Finland, Iceland,
and Norway helped fuel nationalistic flames.
Snorri's *Heimskringla,* the history of the Norwegian kings, was read by every Norwegian
during this period and illustrated by prominent artists like Christian Krogh (1852–
1925), Erik Werenskiold (1855–1938), and
others (fig., p. 350). Early stories and plays
by the popular writers Henrik Ibsen (1828–
1906) and Bjørnstjerne Bjørnsen (1832–
1910) also utilized Viking themes. The
discovery of the Viking ships at Tune in
1867, Gokstad in 1880, and Oseberg in
1903 contributed to a growing Viking fever.
Copies of the Gokstad ship, which revealed
details of ship construction, were produced,

27.13 "FOR DENMARK! AGAINST BOLSHEVISM!"
Viking romanticism also had a dark chapter. Nationalistic pride in a Nordic past fit easily with the racist thinking of the Nazi party. When the Nazis invaded Denmark during World War II, posters such as this encouraged Danes to join the Germans, their Viking "brothers" of old. It was perhaps this extreme example of Viking nationalism that led to the decline of the Vikings as a major influence in modern Scandinavian culture.

until 1905, Norway had been part of the Danish kingdom, and Danish was the language of all official transactions. In the rural communities, dialects that had greater affinity with Icelandic and Old Norse continued to be spoken but not written. Ivar Aasen carried out field studies in the Norwegian countryside, recording these dialects, and in 1848 and 1850 he published a grammar book and a dictionary of the Norwegian language. These rural dialects, which were linguistically more archaic than written Norwegian, were offered as proof of the greater Norwegian affinity with the Viking heritage than that of either the Danes or the Swedes. The effort to construct a distinct Norwegian language out of the diverse rural dialects garnered support from the early Norwegian state because it was seen as essential to Norwegian identity. Interest in the Viking past and in the nationalistic affirmation of a distinct Norwegian identity both came to focus on the Norwegian language. Today, Norwegian children learn two written languages, *bokmål*, which is based largely on the old official Danish, and *nynørsk*, which is based on the work of Aasen and others, but at home they most likely speak a third type of Norwegian, based on their local dialect.

NAZISM AND THE VIKINGS

The German and Scandinavian cultures affected each other and occasionally even fused together in a worldview that was expressed as an intense interest in the cultural heritage of the heroic past. For the Germans it was not a very big step to consider themselves the descendants of the Vikings, given the linguistic ties and the close geographic relationship. In the 1880s, the structure of the German kingdom became the model for the reigns of King Oscar and King Oscar II in Sweden. So many Scandinavian artists made pilgrimages to Dresden and Düsseldorf for training that Scandinavian art and literature did not break out of the bounds of German influence until near the end of the century. German artists, too, sought inspiration in Scandinavia, especially in the untouched and pristine Nordic landscape. The German brothers Jacob and Wilhelm Grimm published songs from the *Poetic Edda*; when Jacob wrote *Den Tyska Mytologin* (German Mythology), he started a trend throughout Germany and Scandinavia for collecting folktales from rural districts.

and a full-scale copy was sailed from Norway across the Atlantic in 1893 and became an attraction at the World Columbian Exposition in Chicago (fig. 28.3). Viking ships captured the imagination of artists who rendered fantastic images, some resembling Roman galleys. The artist Jenny Nyström, who illustrated a translation of Snorri Sturluson's *Heimskringla* in 1894, had her Viking ship described as a "fantastiske sjøuhyrer" (fantastical sea monster) by a Norwegian critic.

The reawakening of interest in Old Norse language throughout Scandinavia was particularly nationalistic in orientation in Norway. Before joining Sweden from 1814

27.14 MODERN VIKING DESIGN
Today the wave of interest in the Vikings has settled into a simpler commercial manifestation. But the desire to have emblems of a Viking past adorn homes is still evident in such items as this trivet made by the Swedish artist Lisa Larsson in the image of a picture stone (figs. 3.1, 3.2).

Richard Wagner's (1813–1883) *Ring of the Nibelungs* (1852–74), which is based on old Germanic and Nordic mythology, both expressed the interest in the Germanic cultural heritage and strengthened it (fig. 27.11). Germans championed the work, which was considered a magnificent presentation of the Germanic spirit. Toward the end of the nineteenth century the Wagnerian mystique fused with Nietzsche's elitist concept of the superman and the master race in the form of a nationalism too sinister to be labeled romantic.

In 1899 H. S. Chamberlain expressed that the German people belonged to the highly gifted people "we usually call Aryans." Chamberlain's followers took the next step by equating Aryans with Norsemen, the pure Germanic type. This concept eventually reached its culmination in the National Socialist Party's idealization of blond, blue-eyed beings and their extreme prejudice again any other racial types. After the Germans were defeated in World War I, these racist concepts were transformed into party politics by Adolf Hitler and his followers, who in 1933 initiated a crusade against "decadent modern culture." Celebrating the Vikings was part of that effort to regain a pure, Ger-

manic past. Excavations of the Viking town of Hedeby, which is now in Schleswig, the German portion of the Danish peninsula, were assigned by the German government in the 1930s to Heinrich Himmler, SS Reichsführer. The close identification between the ideal of the pure German and the Vikings, which had been fueled by romantic antiquarianism, found its most extreme expression in the militant nationalism of the Third Reich, which sought to bring within its power and borders all those lands sharing a perceived Germanic past. One overt manifestation of this was that the regiment of Norwegian Nazi sympathizers who were sent to attack the Russians at the end of World War II was named Viking. Propaganda posters of Nazi Germany emphasized this common heritage: for instance, one shows a German soldier in the foreground and a Viking warrior in the background (fig. 27.13). The connection between Nazism and the romantic idealization of the Vikings that was expressed in the neo-Gothic movement is still being evaluated in Scandinavia, but in discussing the Old Norse dream one cannot escape this particular nightmare.

VIKINGS TODAY

The public's image of the Vikings today is not greatly different from what prevailed at the end of the last century. The Vikings are considered to have been brave, blond warriors, inspired poets and artists, and daring seafarers (fig. 27.14). The Viking world that was portrayed during the nineteenth century has been broadly diffused and has persisted as the base of the Nordic population's image of its history, though with modifications. *Röde Orm* (The Long Ships), by Frans G. Bengtsson (1894–1955), is a humorous depiction of Vikings that was published in 1941 and became very popular; it has been translated into nineteen languages and is still read worldwide, with new editions continuing to appear.

With the end of the World War II, interest in Viking heritage waned not only in Germany but also in Scandinavia. The Vikings themselves became more and more popular as a kind of antihero: for example, Asterix, the central figure in a French comic of the 1970s, and Hagbardt Handfaste (Hagar the Horrible in English, Olafó in Spanish), a comic strip launched by the American cartoonist Dik Browne in 1973

27.15, 27.16 VIKING KITSCH
Horned-helmeted figurines are prevalent in Viking kitsch, shown here as a shaving cream brush and an egg timer! The egg timer was made in West Germany and was bought in São Paulo, Brazil, demonstrating the international appeal of the Vikings.

that now appears in thirteen hundred newspapers, have made Vikings known all over the world. In Browne's comic series, masculine failings of a generic kind are ridiculed and Hagar, the Viking symbol of masculinity, wears a horned helmet. Archaeologists regard this helmet with perplexed amusement, because no material dated to the Viking Age includes a horned helmet or even a nonhorned helmet. The single Viking grave in which a helmet was found, the rich grave in Germundbu, Norway (fig. 7.5), has many archaic features, and so may have been an heirloom when it was deposited in the grave some time in the tenth century. How did later images of the Vikings come to acquire horned helmets? The answer is complex, but the antiquarian

stylings of nineteenth-century artists is the most likely source of Viking helmets with wings or horns; composer Richard Wagner and his costume and set designers are also strongly suspected of having a hand in it.

The symbol of the Vikings surfaces in modern Scandinavia now and then in the form of souvenirs (fig. 27.15), trademarks, advertising, and in pop music, where the horn-helmeted Viking is often used in advertising campaigns (fig. 27.16). Places named after the pagan gods are many: Torsby, Torshälla, Odensvi, Odensala, Ulltuna, Ullevi, and so on. Local governments use Viking imagery in their coats of arms. For instance, the shield established in 1928 for the town of Lidingö consists of a Viking ship in gold on a background of blue. In many cities and communities in Scandinavia there are streets named for the Nordic gods. And of course, Thursday is Thor's day, Wednesday is Odin's day, Tuesday is Tyr's day, and Friday is the day of Frey. Looking at the evidence, one might be tempted to think the old gods are still worshipped in Scandinavia!

Today the Vikings are probably more popular than ever. Viking festivals and Viking markets are being organized, Viking villages are being built, and Viking boats are being copied as never before. Copies of their weapons and their dress are being sold, people are cooking Viking menus and presenting plays with Viking themes. *Vikings: The North Atlantic Saga* will keep the spirit alive well into the twenty-first century.

28 REFLECTIONS ON AN ICON

Vikings in American Culture

BY ELISABETH I. WARD

BATTLE OF STIKLASTAÐIR, *FLATEYARBÓK*

WHEN THE U. S. NATIONAL Football League granted a franchise to Minnesota in 1961, the general manager of the new team, Bert Rose, suggested that the team be nicknamed "The Vikings." The logo commissioned to represent the new team was a square-jawed warrior with long blond hair and a handlebar mustache, wearing a horned helmet. The uniforms are similarly decorated; stylized horns appear on the sides of the helmets (fig. 28.1). The mascot on the field is a man dressed in leather and fur, wearing a horned helmet, and carrying a battle-axe (fig. 28.2). The official fan Web site explains, "The Vikings are named after Norsemen, the Scandinavian warriors that settled modern-day Minnesota." Any scholar would find this statement preposterous, but a large number of the Americans of Scandinavian descent who live in Minnesota do not. Because the football team is so well known, this pairing of the name "Viking" with a warrior in a horned helmet is perhaps the most prevalent image of ancient Scandinavians in American culture, reinforced for hundreds of thousands of viewers across the United States every Sunday afternoon during football season.

Bert Rose could have chosen another image for the team's logo: a longship. Like the horned helmet, the longship is an iconic image that is readily associated with Vikings. Though both icons are male and aggressive, the horned helmet is associated with a fearsome warrior, while the ship evokes the idea of heroic exploration. These two competing images are the surface manifestation of a deeper debate about how we want to understand the Vikings today: were they berserker warriors, heroic adventurers, or something else entirely? Do we see the Vikings as a historic culture or as a mythic creation? A review of the ways Vikings have been defined and represented in American popular culture reveals a dynamic and contradictory picture of this distinct group.

The competing and changing visions of Vikings are not a product of lack of knowledge; in scholarship there is also a range of interpretations, which is apparent in the confusion over what to call them. The term "Viking" (Old English *wicing*) is found in medieval history books, as well as "Northmen," "heathens," and "Danes." Historians, especially British historians, have preferred the term "Viking" and have understood this term to mean ferocious warriors (Marsden 1995). The sagas use a different set of terms; the explorers are referenced by geographic place of origin: Norwegians, Icelanders, Greenlanders. This makes sagas especially well suited for nationalistic interpretation. Archaeologists also use various terms for the Vikings at home; late Iron Age Scandinavian is one term, as is Norse, though Norse is more of a linguistic term with a western regional

28.1, 28.2 FOOTBALL HELMETS AND HORNED HELMETS
In their modern popular-culture manifestations Vikings still conjure visions of barbaric warriors. The power of this imagery was tapped by the Minnesota NFL franchise in 1969 when they chose the name Vikings for their team. To emphasize the ferocious stereotype of Vikings, the logo and team helmet uses the well-known icon of the horned helmet. This imagery is so popular that many fans come to games in Viking regalia; one fan was so impressively outfitted that he was hired as the team's mascot.

distribution. This struggle over a definitive term is not just philological fancy; it encapsulates a scholarly debate about how to perceive and conceptualize the Vikings.

SCANDINAVIAN-AMERICANS AND THE VIKINGS

Although scholars may have a professional interest in the definition of Vikings, Scandinavian-Americans have a deeply personal one. Though immigration and emigration records are spotty, between 1850 and 1875 alone, approximately 370,000 Scandinavians emigrated from Sweden, Norway, and Denmark to the United States (Ljungmark 1971). Finland's emigration surge came a bit later but was equally dramatic, and today there are almost as many Icelandic-Americans as there are Icelanders (250,000). These immigrants brought a nationalistic pride in a Nordic past with them (see Orrling, this volume). In the United States, that past is the central marker of their Nordic ethnicity; white and Protestant like the dominant Anglo culture, Scandinavian-Americans rely on their cultural traditions and Viking past as a means to define themselves. Scandinavian-American newspapers—such as *Den Danske Pioneer* published in Chicago and the *Scandinavia-USA News (SUN)* published in Denver—actively maintain the link between Scandinavia and the United States, while also providing a crucial network within the United States for all Scandinavian-Americans. The Scandinavian-American community is a vibrant and well-organized ethnic group that is actively concerned with how the Vikings are portrayed and understood.

SHIP SAILINGS

In the summer of 1893, The World Columbian Exposition was held in Chicago at the time of the U.S. celebration of the four-hundred-year anniversary of Christopher Columbus's discovery of America. The Norwegian contribution to the Exposition was the replica of the Gokstad ship that, along with the impressive ship burials at Tune and Oseberg, had created a public sensation when they were excavated in the late nineteenth and early twentieth centuries. New research on Viking boat-building techniques led to a surge of interest in Viking ships. The aptly named *Viking* (Anderson 1996) was built in Norway and sailed to New York as testament to Leif Eriksson's voyage five hundred years *before* Columbus (fig. 28.3). This brazen bit of ethnic one-upmanship, designed to flaunt their precedence in America, was a memorable moment for many Scandinavian-Americans. Since that sailing, several other replicas have been sailed across the Atlantic to North America, including *Saga Siglar* in 1992, on the occasion of the five-hundred-year anniversary of Columbus's voyage. In the summer of 2000, a fleet of Viking ships is scheduled to sail to North America from all over Scandinavia as part of the Viking Millennium.

These ship sailings strongly associated the image of the Vikings with the idea of exploration. While the Viking longship in Europe still evokes the idea of the Viking raids, the image of a Viking ship in the United States is more apt to prompt an association with sea voyaging, heroic exploits, and long-distance contacts (fig. 28.4). Scandinavian-Americans highlighted this heroic aspect of their Viking heritage as a defining characteristic of their identity. These well-publicized events were powerful statements by the Scandinavian-American community that Vikings should be understood as heroic explorers who reached America five hundred years before Columbus.

The ship icon has become incorporated into the logos of groups interested in portraying Vikings as explorers. For example, "Nordic America," an amusement park being built in Minnesota, has a logo of a ship drawn in profile, while the "Leif Ericson Millennium Committee" logo has a ship at a slight angle, as if dramatically cutting through the waves. The logos for many

WORLD'S COLUMBIAN EXPOSITION, 1893

COPELIN PHOTO

306 DEARBORN ST. CHICAGO

28.3 ARRIVAL OF THE *VIKING*
The arrival of a replica Gokstad ship—the first replica Viking ship to cross the Atlantic—in the United States in 1893 ignited Scandinavian-American interest in the Vikings. The *Viking* voyaged to Cape Cod, New York, through the Erie Canal to the Great Lakes, and to the World. Columbian Exposition in Chicago, where this photograph was taken. The purpose of the trip was to "propagandize Leif Ericson as the true discoverer of North America" (Andersen 1996).

Scandinavian-American companies also incorporate ship images (fig. 28.5). Some of these businesses have "Viking" explicitly in their titles (fig. 28.8); a survey of the telephone directory revealed more than three hundred such business names in Minnesota alone. But in most cases the ship alone is enough to invoke the Vikings and the idea of long-distance travel through billowing sails on sturdy ships; these logos thereby also represent Vikings as successful traders.

KENSINGTON STONE

For Scandinavian-Americans, Leif Eriksson's voyage to North America is not just a fact of history; it is a point of pride related to their own migration. There is also, I would suggest, a complex, widely held feeling of unease among Scandinavians about why the voyage did not have a more lasting impact. One expression of this unease has been the plethora of Viking finds—from mooring holes, halberds, and the Newport Tower, to, most famously, the Kensington Stone—during the nationalistic immigrant period (see Wallace and Fitzhugh, this volume). The Kensington Stone, found in 1898 near the Red River in Minnesota on the farm of a Swedish immigrant, Olof Ohman, is universally considered a hoax by scholars today, but it remains an important icon to Scandinavian-Americans. In

Alexandria, Minnesota, the Runestone Museum has been built to house the stone, and nearby an enormous replica, a dozen times larger than the original stone, stands in Runestone Park (Gilman 1993). Its text purports to describe an "exploratory journey from Vinland" (Nielsen 1999) in 1362, which ventured deep into the heartland of North America but was attacked by Indians. To the nineteenth-century immigrants, the idea of subsequent voyages deep into North America made perfect sense; if Vikings could reach the shores of North America, then the descendants of Vikings naturally went even further. The text also explained why the various voyages did not have a lasting impact: aggressive Native Americans stood in their way. This must have seemed a fitting reversal of history for immigrants living on land that once belonged to Native Americans. Although scholars can easily debunk these various finds, many fail to realize that however dubious they are as historic artifacts, such finds have an important and persistent psychological role in Scandinavian-American folk culture. For Scandinavian-Americans, forwarding the Vikings as heroic explorers is closely tied to nationalism and self-perception (fig. 28.6).

POP GO THE VIKINGS!

During the summer of 1976, the Viking Mission to Mars, the National Air and Space Administration (NASA) project to search for life on Mars, was hot news. Coverage of the Viking landing on Mars appeared on the front pages of papers across the country, from the *Los Angeles Times* to the *New York Times*. The success of the mission captured the attention of the populace from young to old and made Viking a household word. When the mission was named in 1966, the archaeological site at L'Anse aux Meadows, Newfoundland, had just been confirmed as the first and only Viking site in North America—other than Greenland. The heroism of the Vikings to go beyond the horizon one thousand years ago was an appealing concept to mission planners (fig. 28.7) seeking to characterize the voyage to Mars as the next great step in space exploration (Biemann 1977).

This media event solidified Vikings as a fixture in American popular culture. The strong, white, and independent Viking male

28.4

28.6

The Viking ship icon appears in an array of items associated with the Scandinavian-American community. Such memorabilia as plates and mugs bearing a ship riding the waves signals pride in a Viking past. The ship icon has also become an effective marketing tool for Scandinavian and Scandinavian-American products; it has been incorporated into hundreds of company logos, including this one for Viking brand sparkling water.

put forward vigorously by Scandinavian-Americans had been gradually incorporated into American popular culture and became especially resonant for post-World-War II America proud of its own independence and strength and struggling with race relations. Popular culture latched onto the Vikings as a convenient icon upon which cultural ideas, particularly about the role of men, were projected. In this process, the Vikings as a concept in the U.S. became disassociated with concrete facts about Viking culture, and the inaccurate horned helmet icon (fig. 28.9), as opposed to the Viking ship, came to the fore.

The changing ways Vikings are portrayed in American popular culture—in juvenile literature, novels, movies, and comic books—says something about how Vikings are understood but also about major issues in American culture.

JUVENILE LITERATURE

American youths have gleaned ideas about the Vikings from juvenile fiction beginning in the 1950s in such works as *The Road to Miklagaard* (Treece 1957) and *The Land the Ravens Found* (Mitchison 1955), which were aimed at boys as aids in forming their male identities. Since the 1960s, juvenile literature, which is closely tied to the educational system, has represented an intersection between popular culture and scholarly thinking about the Vikings. One of the earliest examples of this is *Eric, the Tale of a*

Red-Tempered Viking, which came out in 1968 just as the discovery of a Viking site at L'Anse aux Meadows was receiving wider notice. While inspired by the exciting new information being uncovered by archaeology, Vikings are nevertheless seen primarily as warriors and every character in the story wears a horned helmet. The text puts a positive spin on Vikings' male aggressiveness by suggesting that the Viking expansion across the North Atlantic was caused by Erik the Red losing his temper.

Today juvenile literature focuses more on the Vikings as a living culture and forwards the conception of the Vikings primarily as traders. Four cultures that show up with astounding regularity in the educational series that publishing companies create for children and preteens are the Romans, Greeks, Egyptians, and Vikings. The first three are conventional birthplaces of civilization, which reflect a continued focus on Mediterranean history. The Vikings are the only representatives of northern European societies, which may account for their inclusion. In the eighteenth century, Viking-inspired art was put forward as a counter-example to classical Greek and Roman art (see Orrling, this volume) and the same tendency is seen here in juvenile literature two hundred years later.

One organization that has contributed with astounding regularity to the growing body of juvenile literature and the new image of the Vikings as traders is the York Ar-

28.7

28.8

28.6 ETHNIC PRIDE

Although all members of the Scandinavian-American community share a sense of pride in a Viking past, it is not a unified, single group. It is comprised of five different nationalities—Danish, Finnish, Icelandic, Norwegian, and Swedish—who carried the long-standing rivalry of the Nordic countries with them to North America. Here they settled near one another and often inter-married, but still one can choose to either "Do it like a Dane," join a "Super Swede," or cruise with "Norwegian Power." Whichever pin you wear, you'll be "Taking a Viking to Lunch!"

28.7 MARTIAN VIKINGS

NASA's naming of the 1974 Mission to Mars established the Vikings as far more than an ethnic symbol. Once in the realm of popular culture, Viking iconography became infinitely mutable. The decorations on the T-shirts of two members of Mission Control team show a Viking warrior with Martian antennae "horns"!

28.8 VIKINGS IN CALIFORNIA?

As Scandinavian immigrants settled in North America, they lost some elements of their Scandinavian ethnicity, but identification with the Vikings was not entirely lost. In the small town of Solvang, settled by Danish immigrants in central California, where farming and baking are the claim to fame far more than raiding and pillaging, businesses tout the Vikings on every street.

chaeological Trust. It runs the Jorvik Viking Center, an innovative interpretive museum that opened in 1984 in York, England. It presents the impressive archaeological finds that had been unearthed by the York Archaeological Trust during the construction of a shopping center in an accurate, educational, and entertaining interpretive site that 11.7 million people have visited since its opening (Richard Hall, pers. comm.). Because Viking raiders captured York, an emphasis on the Vikings as warriors might be expected, but in actuality, the center focuses on the Vikings as traders and craftsman. The site was the center of bowl making and leather working in the Viking Age; the museum shows and explains these processes in detail. The Center's location in a shopping mall gives even greater resonance to the conception of Vikings as traders.

In keeping with the museum's emphasis, the many juvenile literature books that the York Archaeological Trust has consulted on or written about the Vikings focus on the Vikings as productive workers—building ships, milking cows, forging iron, spinning wool, and trading goods. The children's book *History as Evidence: The Vikings* (1986) has, out of thirty-six pages, only two pages on raiding, and that image is presented without any bloodshed. Portraying the Vikings as savvy traders is a concept that children in modern, capitalist economies can relate to their own world, and so juvenile literature highlights that aspect of Vikings culture.

VIKING NOVELS

More than eighty novels with Viking themes or characters have been written in English. One of the earliest mass-produced novels about the Vikings was Sir George Webbe Dasent's *The Vikings of the Baltic*, published in 1875. A retelling of *Saga of the Ancestors*, this three-volume set goes far beyond the narrative of the original saga. In an extended introduction Dasent defends using the sagas and liberalizing historic facts, with the justification that since the Vikings are basically narrative constructs of the sagas, one can freely project one's imagination upon them.

In 1928 Arthur Loring Mackay wrote *The Viking Prince*, based on the adventures of Harold Tryggvason, a fictionalized character who did not realize he was the brother of Olaf Tryggvason, king of Norway. It draws on the sagas and several other works, including Henry Wadsworth Longfellow's poem *The Skeleton in Armor* about a Viking warrior far from home (fig. 28.10a). That poem, published in 1841 in the popular New York magazine *Knickerbocker*, made quite a stir in New England because it alluded to two New England antiquarian features, the Newport Tower and a nearby Indian burial (see Wallace and Fitzhugh, this volume). To draw on a poem, rather than just the sagas, was a further step in fictionalizing the Vikings; the four gold-leaf winged helmets adorning the cover is an iconic representation of the fictionalized Viking depicted in the book.

28.9 HORNED HELMETS GALORE!
The erroneous association between Vikings and horned helmets continues, despite protests from scholars. But the crazed, animalistic warrior image of the Vikings embraced by popular culture is captured perfectly in a pair of horns protruding from a helmet. The blond pigtails suggest the origin of this icon: Wagner's opera had most characters in winged helmets, including a pigtailed Brünnhilde.

Frans G. Bengtsson was published to critical acclaim and has since been republished almost twenty times and widely translated. It was first translated from Swedish into English in 1954, just as the popular conception of the Vikings as the ideal independent male warrior was firmly taking root in the United States. While this work of fiction does draw on historic or saga characters and battles, the book captures not historic fact but the author's perception of the warrior spirit of the Viking period. Its cover image underscores this: a single horned-helmeted warrior storms a European beach, with his sword raised above his head.

Other works such as the *The Winter Serpent* (1958) by Maggie Hill Davis and Michael Crichton's *Eaters of the Dead* (1976) also draw on historical and saga-based accounts but remain clearly within the realm of fiction by emphasizing the warrior aspect of the Vikings. *Eaters of the Dead* (fig. 28.10b) is a creative retelling of *Beowulf* (which is an Old English, not a Viking, poem) combined with the account of the Arab historian Ibn Fadlan. Told from Ibn Fadlan's point of view as a devout Muslim, it highlights the uncleanliness, superstition, and stoicism of the Vikings. The novel's cover shows a gold skull wearing a golden horned helmet. Through all of these novels, the horned helmet is paired with the idea of Vikings as warriors.

In the latest trend, novels have retreated from heroic epics and warrior aspects of the Vikings and toward a more realistic understanding of daily life. Jane Smiley's epic novel *The Greenlanders* and a more recent release from Joan Clark, *Eiriksdottir* (fig. 28.10c), both made use of archaeological research, as well as the sagas, for their narrative base. Thomas McGovern, founder of the North Atlantic Biocultural Organization (NABO), consulted with Smiley on *The Greenlanders*, while Clark's *Eiriksdottir* benefited from the advice of Birgitta Wallace, the head archaeologist of L'Anse aux Meadows. Befitting this new emphasis, the cover image of *Eiriksdottir* is the face of Freydis, the female title character, shadowed by the face of her father, Erik the Red.

MOVIES

Viking novels have inspired several Hollywood productions. Unbeknownst to early moviegoers, they had already been privy to Viking culture through the highly popular stock westerns that movie studios churned out. Örnólfur Thorsson suggests that it was a well-known trade secret that the writers of westerns turned to the sagas for plot lines and character ideas. Sagas, like westerns, revolve around self-made justice in a remote and newly inhabited region and express the cultural belief that violence may be sanctioned and even necessary in extreme circumstances.

Vikings moved into the limelight with the 1958 movie *The Vikings*, which was based on the novel *The Viking* by Edison Marshall. Notice the switch from the singular, heroic "Viking" in the novel's title to the plural, ill-defined, and animal-like "Vikings" in the movie's title. Starring Kirk Douglas, Tony Curtis, and Janet Leigh, the movie told "the saga of the loves and lusts of the fierce Norse raiders who swept over Europe bringing death and destruction," according to its poster. The cover shows Kirk Douglas in a nail-studded leather shirt standing next to the prow of a Viking ship and two dragon boats on gray sea (fig. 28.11). Instead of depicting heroic adventurers, the movie relies upon a bizarre mistruth that Vikings were afraid of fog and dared not travel beyond what they could easily see. The movie also highlights the viciousness of the Vikings, especially Douglas's character, who ultimately loses both love and life to a British slave played by Curtis. Though a popular movie for its rambunctiousness and lustiness, the overall conception of the Vikings that it forwards is a strange pairing of ruthless warrior with fearful explorer.

Since then, this portrayal of the Vikings has been repeated in other movies. In 1974

a · b · c

28.10 LITERARY VIKINGS
English authors used the sagas as references for their works as early as the nineteenth century. American authors such as Henry Wadsworth Longfellow followed suit, publishing *The Skeleton In Armor*, a poetic book devoted to Vikings in Rhode Island in 1841(a). The popularity of Vikings as literary subjects has actually increased in the last fifteen years, when the two books shown here were written, one a macho stereotyped view of the Vikings by Michael Crichton and the other an archaeological interpretation by Joan Clark.

Disney released *Island at the Top of the World*, a live-action film that involved a dangerous voyage by an Englishman, Frenchman, and American to an island near the Arctic Circle; the explorers discover that Vikings had made it there first and were still living on the island one thousand years later. While acknowledging the Vikings as adventurers, the film undermines that perception by having these Vikings isolated on the island for one thousand years, becoming more and more fearful of outsiders, unwilling to travel beyond the mountains, and extremely hostile to the newcomers.

In 1989, the comedy *Erik the Viking*, written and directed by Monty Python's Terry Jones and starring Tim Robbins and John Cleese, also uses the "fierce warrior who is afraid of the fog (unknown)" conception of Vikings. Robbins plays a soft-hearted Viking who has trouble raping and pillaging; the opening scene shows him trying to get to know the maiden rather than raping her. This same sensitive Viking is the only one brave enough to recover the sun from the witch who stole it from the sky, a folktale motif in both Saami and Native American cultures. The recently released film entitled *The Thirteenth Warrior*, starring Antonio Banderas and based on Michael Crichton's novel *Eaters of the Dead*, again portrays Vikings as fearful of the fog, though in a less cartoonish manner.

The origins of this idea of the Vikings as superstitious and afraid of falling off the earth is quite mysterious. The sagas do speak of Vikings invoking Thor when in dangerous waters, and their culture was imbued with expressions of religious belief. But Viking mariners certainly navigated through fog and storm, often out of sight of land. Rather than drawing on fact, this narrative device serves to undermine the idea of the heroic male warrior. Perhaps after the conflict in Korea and the Vietnam War, Americans were more willing to embrace a conception of Vikings as frightened warriors rather than as fearless heroes.

COMICS

The comic series *Thor*, begun in 1965, takes the tradition of fictionalizing the Vikings one step further, making the Vikings mythical. The action of this comic series is sometimes set in the mythical home of the Norse gods, *Ásgarð*, where Thor always wears a winged helmet, while some of the other Norse gods such as Odin and Loki appear with horned helmets (fig. 28.12). Thor himself is a big, strong, blond-haired, square-jawed warrior, outfitted in leather with spiked boots. Though not attaining the popularity of Superman, Thor shares a central characteristic with this superhero; he chooses to be mortal most of the time, until he grabs his hammer and transforms into Thor. His hammer cannot only transform him from mortal to god but also transport

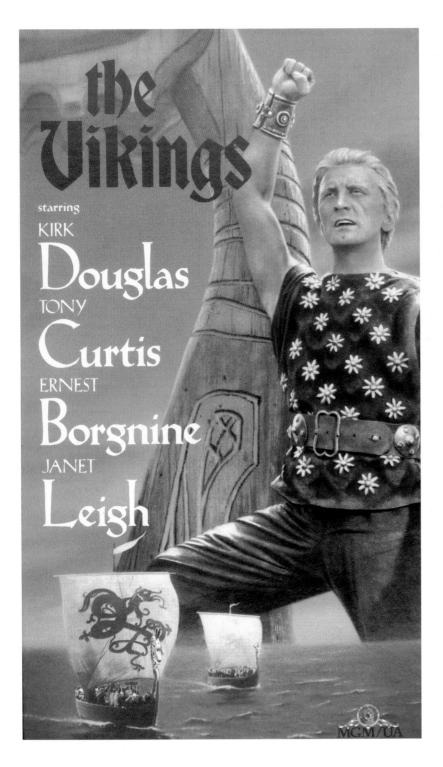

28.11 VIKINGS AT THE MOVIES
The epic, big-screen adventure starring Kirk Douglas, Janet Leigh, and Tony Curtis of 1954 remains one of the most influential cinematic works in the formation of the popular conception of the Vikings. Violent, wanton, and lusty, its Vikings act tough but cower in the face of unknown seas and fog. This is hardly the image of heroic voyagers embraced by Scandinavian-Americans. However divorced from reality, it resonated in popular culture.

him to any time or place. The Thor of the comic books is a fantastic character, disassociated from reality or a living culture of the Vikings. Instead, the narrative of the comic draws heavily on Thor as a mythical warrior, able to defeat any enemy at any time or place. This fictionalized and idealized image of the Vikings likely influenced the Americans who read this series in their youth.

Also Viking-inspired but with a far different attitude is the comic strip *Hagar the Horrible*, started by Dik Browne in 1973. *Hagar the Horrible* makes a very close association between Hagar and his Viking roots; his ship has a pronounced dragon head and his house has dragon heads over the doorway modeled after the dragon-headed wooden tent posts found in the Gokstad burial. Hagar himself wears a horned helmet, and he is frequently seen leading Viking raids. Far from the idealized Viking hero, however, Hagar is short and overweight, his band of warriors are incompetent, and he often returns home from battle with torn clothes and scars. The comic strip is far more about his life at home with his hardworking wife, beautiful daughter, and bright son. Hagar is a modern man set in the Viking Age. Unable to reconcile the expectations of his home life with his warrior vocation, he ends up failing at both. While comical, Hagar is symbolic for the contradictory roles males are expected to play in modern society. Between Thor and Hagar, the comic-reading public is left to choose between two competing visions of the Vikings: either they are mythical heroes or mundane failures.

TROLL DOLLS
The recent trend of depicting Vikings as less than ideal can also be seen in the wholly unrealistic (and often grotesque) troll-like Viking dolls which can be bought in gift shops in Scandinavian population centers in the U.S. and Canada and all over Scandinavia (fig. 28.13). The troll as an icon has a close association with Scandinavian, particularly Norwegian, nationalism. Trolls are recurrent characters in Scandinavian folktales such as the Norwegian tales collected in the late nineteenth century by Peter Christen Asbjørnsen and Jørgen Moe. The illustrations by Erik Werenskiold and others depicted large, lumbering trolls with long noses, bulbous faces, and round, dark eyes (Asbjørnsen and Moe 1982). These trolls were produced as dolls in the 1960s by the Troll Company of Denmark and have since been widely copied.

The Viking troll dolls capture two of the most salient Scandinavian nationalistic images of the nineteenth century; though robbed of their overt potency through humor, they have become more accessible to a wider non-Scandinavian audience. Perhaps these dolls are a reaction against the overly idealized Viking explorers embodied in the

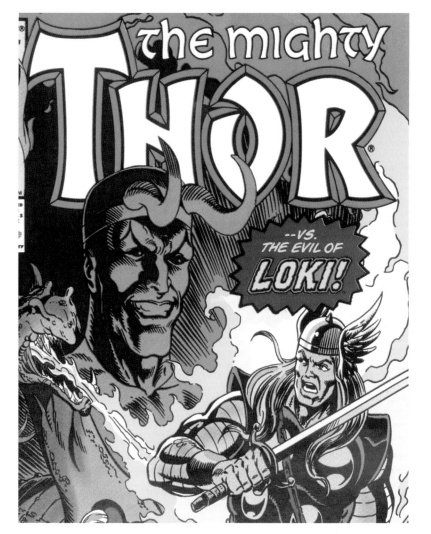

movie or book was about not the Vikings but the Anglo-Saxons, the Celts, or medieval knights. These historic cultures lack a well-defined icon and appear to have become subsumed under the umbrella of the horned-helmeted Viking. With greater understanding of the Vikings as a specific historic people in whom they take pride, the Scandinavian-American community represents them by the more accurate longship icon. In American popular culture, Vikings in horned helmets seem to have become symbolic for all of northern European medieval and earlier peoples.

During a survey of what visitors to the National Museum of Natural History knew about the Vikings, I was twice told they lived in caves, indicating that Vikings could

28.12 THE MIGHTY THOR
The comic book caricature of an undefeatable super warrior named Thor is the latest in a thousand-year romance with the Norse god of strength. In the thirteenth century, Thor was featured in the Icelander Snorri Sturluson's retelling of the pagan Norse myths. Those heroic stories of battling evil giants continue to inspire the modern romance with the Vikings. This idealized male figure is central to the power of the Vikings as an icon in American popular culture.

28.13 DOLLS AND TROLLS
Colorful Viking souvenir dolls testify to the international appeal and commercial success of Vikings as a stereotyped, humorous icon. This sampling includes (left to right) Russian-inspired Vikings, an American Campbell soup can–style Christmas ornament, and an imitation Danish Viking troll doll. The late Magnus Einarsson, an Icelandic-Canadian, collected pop memorabilia, which he bequeathed to the Canadian Museum of Civilization.

ship icon. The enthusiasm for Viking troll dolls by Scandinavians and Scandinavian-Americans suggests that the fictional horned-helmeted Viking icon of popular culture has been adopted by Scandinavians to some extent, but only when retaining a core of nationalistic symbolism.

A FINAL THOUGHT

This brief survey hardly does justice to the Vikings in popular culture; to say, for example, that a Viking theme appeared in such and such a book or movie fails to capture the wider phenomena. I am struck by the fact that many people seem to have had a personal experience to relate about a book they had read as a child, a scene in a movie they remembered, a comic strip they particularly loved, or a memory from school about the Vikings. In many cases, the remembered

be symbolic for all "precivilized" peoples. The potency of the horned-helmet image could reflect the deep cultural schism we feel between the past and the present. As we today go about driving, working in air-conditioned offices, eating packaged foods, and feeling more and more civilized, we relish the otherness of the horned-helmeted Vikings whose experiences were more brutal. In this imaginary past that has been projected onto the Vikings, one could also do what one wanted: take violent action as vengeance for a wrong, satisfy sexual urges at any time or place, and steal whatever caught the eye. This is why the Vikings football team makes such cultural sense; in competitive sports, our culture allows that violent, aggressive male "uncivilized" behavior to be celebrated for a few hours on a Sunday afternoon.

29 | STUMBLES AND PITFALLS IN THE SEARCH FOR VIKING AMERICA

BY BIRGITTA LINDEROTH WALLACE AND WILLIAM W. FITZHUGH

As Americans, we are particularly susceptible to this species of newly awakened interest. It is but the other day . . . that we began to look around the northern parts of the continent for objects of antiquarian interest. Every thing in our own history and institutions is so new and so well known that . . . it appears refreshing to light on any class of facts which promises to lend a ray of antiquity to our history. (Schoolcraft 1853–1857, 1: 109)

. . . hardly a year passes unsignalized by the announcement of the discovery of tablets of stone or metal, bearing strange and mystical inscriptions. (Squier and Davis 1848: 274)

IN THE 1830S, THE IDENTIFICATION of an old stone tower in Newport, Rhode Island, as a Viking monument created a wave of speculation about pre-Columbian discoveries in North America. Such tangible proof of early European contacts in the New World was especially enticing to north European and Nordic immigrants for whom the tower served as convincing proof of a Viking presence on American soil five hundred years before Columbus.

HARALD THE FINEHAIR AND DOFRI,
FLATEYJARBÓK

The Newport Tower (fig. 29.1 and p. 376) is not the only icon of Nordic deeds in North America. Similar claims have been made about the Kensington Stone from Minnesota, the Heavener rock carvings in Oklahoma, the Beardmore relics from Ontario, the Spirit Pond Runestones from Maine, and many other sites, monuments, and objects. Most of these finds and claims were made in the late nineteenth and early twentieth centuries when archaeology and historical scholarship in North America was in its infancy and when little was known about the Vinland sagas or Norse archaeology in Greenland. Given the lack of geographic precision in the sagas (Sigurðsson, Wallace, this volume), it has always been possible to imagine that Vikings traveled widely in North America, even deep into the Midwest and to the Gulf of Mexico. Recently, however, advances in linguistics, history, and archaeology have enabled scholars to evaluate claims of Viking sites and contacts south of Newfoundland. With the single exception of an eleventh-century Norwegian penny found at an Indian site in Maine (Cox, this volume; fig., p. 206), all such claims have been rejected by archaeologists.

Unfortunately, the allure of a pre-Columbian Viking presence in mainland North America persists—in fiction, in the movies, and in the minds of ardent believers (see Ward, this volume). Scholars have been reluctant to take on the time-consuming task of debunking frauds, which yield scant new knowledge; as a result, a gulf has emerged between scientific and popular opinion of what Vikings did and did not do in North America. The contested ground between scholarship and popular or folk culture has been a constant and problematic feature of the social side of American archaeology.

This chapter reviews some prominent assertions for Viking finds south of the arctic regions of North America. Many of these claims have become so ingrained in American popular culture that a Viking presence in the United States is often taken for granted, as seen for example in the Web site of the Minnesota Vikings football team, which remarks in a matter-of-fact way about

29.1 NEWPORT TOWER
During the 1830s the Danish scholar Carl Christian Rafn became convinced that the area around Narragansett Bay matched the saga descriptions of Vinland. His search led him to an unusual structure of mysterious origins in Newport, Rhode Island, seen here in an anonymous mid-eighteenth-century work. Rather than being a Viking monument, as claimed by Rafn and many others since, the tower was probably built as a windmill by Rhode Island's Governor Benedict Arnold, who referred to the structure in 1677 as "my stone built wind miln [sic]."

29.2 CARL CHRISTIAN RAFN
Carl Christian Rafn (1795–1864) revolutionized conceptions of the American past when he presented a scientific case for Vikings reaching the coast of New England five hundred years before Columbus in his magnum opus *Antiquitates Americanae* (1837). His original "discovery" of a New England Vinland, though discounted by scholars today, continues to inspire debate about the location of Vinland and fuels the Italian-Scandinavian rivalry about the history of North America.

the Viking settlement of Minnesota. The notion that Vikings explored and settled in southern Canada and the eastern and northern United States appears to be a widely held belief, especially among people of Nordic heritage—even though this view has no basis in fact.

ANTIQUARIAN BEGINNINGS

Speculation about Viking presence in the New World began in the early 1600s when the Icelandic sagas became known in Scandinavia. When the Danish scholar Carl Christian Rafn (fig. 29.2) published an English version of his *Antiquitates Americanae* (1837), with translations of parts of the *Vinland Sagas* and descriptions of possible Viking sites and finds in North America, people in North America began to search in their own lands for Norse sites and finds. Rafn's publication found fertile ground in seafaring New England. Local antiquarians began studying architectural monuments such as the Newport Tower, searching for mythical cities like Norumbega (fig. 29.7) (Baker et al. 1994), investigating rock carvings, and studying Native American languages for Viking linguistic clues. Reviews of Viking history and relevant finds in the Americas were given prominence in early historical reviews published by the Smithsonian (Haven 1856; Babcock 1913). Since then, more than fifty sites, one hundred inscriptions, and seventy-five artifacts found in southern Canada and the United States—consisting of swords, halberds, spears, shield bosses, runic inscriptions, fortified sites, architectural monuments, mooring holes, boat sheds, and other remains—have been attrib-

uted to the Norse. Most of these claims originated before scholarly knowledge or scientific techniques were available to evaluate them.

During the twentieth century historians, archaeologists, and linguists studied these claims periodically, applying new dating and analytical methods as they became available and making detailed investigations of the circumstances of the finds, the finders, and their promoters—all with negative conclusions (Wallace 1971, 1982). Scholars have also pointed out the unlikely distribution of purported Viking finds, many of which are inaccessible by boat and required extensive overland travel, which entailed the risk of Indian attack, all for no apparent reason. Besides problems with the basic motivation for such excursions, scholars have found the coincidence of such purported finds with areas of nineteenth-century Nordic immigrant settlements disturbing, since some of these immigrants owned Norse artifacts and had knowledge of and interest in runic writing.

During the past two decades, the expansion of general archaeological knowledge has provided a better context for interpreting claims of Norse finds. One of the most striking discoveries is the distance between the disputed early finds from southern regions, none of which was professionally excavated, and those recently excavated by professional archaeologists in northern regions whose authenticity has never been an issue. In areas of southeastern Canada and the eastern United States where Viking claims have been advanced but are disputed, only one find—the Norwegian penny from Maine noted above—has been accepted. By contrast, archaeological investigations in the Canadian arctic and northern Greenland have produced a large number of undisputed Norse artifacts from Dorset or Thule sites: fragments of iron, copper, and bronze; pieces of chain mail; boat planks with iron rivets; pieces of woven wool cloth; and native-made figurines possibly depicting Norsemen. Fragments of woven cloth appear to have been kept as curiosities or were used as ornamentation; copper fragments and silver coins were made into amulets; and iron was employed as superior to stone tools for knives and harpoons (McGhee 1984b; Sutherland, Gulløv, this volume). All appear to have arrived at native sites by trade or by direct or indirect contacts between native peoples and Norse travelers.

The Newport Tower BY JOHANNES HERTZ,

In 1837 Carl Christian Rafn, a Danish philologist, published a major work, *Antiquitates Americanae*, in which he attempted to demonstrate that the "Vinland" mentioned in Icelandic sagas and other medieval written sources was situated in the areas that now make up the states of Massachusetts and Rhode Island. Amidst the stream of information about suspected Norse finds flowing in as a result of Rafn's work his attention was drawn to a ruined tower in Newport, Rhode Island. The building was known to have belonged to Governor Benedict Arnold, who, in 1677, referred to it as "my stone built wind miln [sic]."

For a mill, however, it has an extremely unusual structure: a cylindrical upper part supported by eight round pillars (fig. 29.1). On the basis of drawings that had been sent to him by Thomas Webb, Secretary of the Rhode Island Historical Society, Rafn interpreted the building as originally being a baptistry built by Norse settlers in the twelfth century—making it the earliest church and the first European building in the New World. Inspired by Rafn's theory, the poet Henry Wadsworth Longfellow's ballad *The Skeleton in Armor* (1841) made the tower famous by referring to it as the home of a supposed Viking found in a warrior's grave at nearby Fall River.

Rafn's theory acquired many followers while others maintained that the tower had been built as a mill by Governor Arnold. After a century of heated debate, it was decided to solve the riddle by excavation, which was carried out in 1948 to 1949 by William S. Godfrey, a graduate student at Harvard University. Among the thousands of fragments found, none were older than the colonial period. In a hollow space in one of the pillar footings Godfrey found a small piece of a clay pipe, and in another footing a piece of a gun flint. Beneath an impression of a hob-nailed boot or shoe with a flat toe and a square heel found at the bottom of a foundation ditch Godfrey uncovered a fragment of a decorated stem of a mid-seventeenth-century clay pipe. For the excavators, the case was closed: either Governor Arnold of one of his contemporaries built the tower.

The excavation results were strongly disputed, however, by local supporters of the Norse settler theory. Besides, several new theories had been advanced about the original construction, claiming it had been a watch-

tower, a warehouse, a lighthouse, a fortified refuge, or even an astronomical calendar. Fissures in the stones of the tower's masonry were interpreted as runes. Nordic Vikings, Irish monks, Portuguese sailors, and Dutch or English colonists were all proposed as its builders. To replace wishful thinking with facts, the Committee for Research in Norse Activities in North America, 1000–1500, mainly sponsored by Marvin Howe Green, Jr., had the tower photogrammetrically surveyed in 1991 by staff of the Danish Technical University. In 1993 staff from Helsinki University, Finland, and the Danish National Museum, studied the evidence, and it is now possible almost with certainty to exclude a pre-Columbian dating of the tower. Because the structure existed in 1677, it probably dates from the seventeenth century and in fact from around the middle of that century—in complete accordance with Godfrey's conclusion. These facts, taken together with considerations about the context of the prestige features of the tower's architecture, allow us to conclude that the Newport Tower was constructed by Governor Benedict Arnold as a windmill. At Chesterton in Warwickshire, England, stands a mill of similar pillared construction (illustrated abouve). It was built in 1632 in the Palladian style. Benedict Arnold (1615–1678) came to America in 1635 and in 1651 settled in Newport. In 1663 he was appointed the first Governor of Rhode Island. By taking a fashionable architectural innovation in the old country as a model for his own mill he may have wished to give a special contribution to the creation of a New England on foreign soil. A report on this research has been published in *Newport History* (Hertz 1997).

CHESTERTON WINDMILL
Circumstantial evidence points toward the Chesterton windmill, Warwickshire, England, as the model Governor Arnold had in mind when he built his mill. Arnold left England at age 20, three years after the Chesterton mill was completed not far from his birthplace. This structure, which was designed either by Inigo Jones or by his pupil John Webb, created great local interest in England and would have been known to Arnold. "It is difficult to believe that there is no connection between the only two windmills in the world with this construction and of about the same date" (Hertz 1997: 88).

"Speak! speak! thou fearful guest!
Who, with thy hollow breast
Still in rude armor drest,
Comest to daunt me!
Wrapt not in Eastern balms,
But with thy fleshless palms
Stretched, as if asking alms,
Why dost thou haunt me?"

29.3 LONGFELLOW'S *THE SKELETON IN ARMOR*
Rafn's *Antiquitates Americanae* (1837) was the first serious scholarly work to substantiate a pre-Columbian discovery of the New World. These discoveries, publicized widely in New England, stimulated Henry Wadsworth Longfellow's romantic reconstruction of the Viking discovery in an epic poem titled *The Skeleton in Armor* (1841). A lavish edition of 1877, illustrated with Viking motifs drawn in Viking-Celtic style, began with this plate featuring the Newport Tower.

29.4 MISTAKEN "ARMOR"
In addition to the Newport Tower, Rafn was impressed with a burial found in Fall River in which a skeleton was buried with "armor" plates on its chest. Local antiquarians believed it was a Viking buried in armor, but later archaelogists determined the find to be typical of seventeenth-century Indians buried with copper trade goods. Some of the finds are illustrated (d, h, e) in Charles Willoughby's *Antiquities of the New England Indians* (1935). The finds were sent to be analyzed by Viking experts at the Danish National Museum and remain there today.

The message from this distributional pattern is clear. Given the widespread occurrence of Viking finds in native sites in the north, it is impossible to imagine Vikings having left monuments or artifacts in so many southern locations without leaving Viking settlement sites (like L'Anse aux Meadows) or without Viking artifacts being found in native sites in these regions also. The pattern seen in the northern Viking finds is what archaeologists have learned to expect when Europeans make contact with native groups. Norse visitors would not have repeatedly left isolated Viking finds in areas where no other evidence of Vikings exists.

During the past century, divisions between professionals and interested sectors of the public appeared as science began to contradict popular folk interpretations based on sagas, oral history, literature, and local lore. With little common ground between the scientific establishment and the general public, and with the popular media relatively uninterested in serious historical education, Viking studies took on a life apart from historical reality, and the Viking America myth took form.

THE AMERICAN VIKING MENAGERIE
The disputed evidence—a veritable menagerie of finds—from the southern zone comes from two areas: New England and the Upper Midwest, especially Minnesota. Not surprisingly, until modern archaeological work be-

gan in the Arctic after World War II, these were the areas where people were most actively searching for Norse remains. The New England evidence is generally associated with the Vinland voyages of the eleventh century, while that in the Midwest is linked with a putative Norwegian expedition of 1354 to Greenland. Claims from New England and the Canadian Maritimes have been associated with literary scholars, amateur historians, and antiquarian societies; those of the Midwest began with the Swedish immigrant community.

Claims of ancient Nordic ancestry in America cover the gamut from scholarly treatises, to serious amateur history and science, or even quasi-religious tracts (for amateur works, see Anderson 1996; Hall 1982, 1984; Nilsestuen 1995; and several works by Holand, Nielsen, and Pohl). The latter include approaches that Stephen Williams has termed "fantastic archaeology" (Williams 1991; Gilmore and McElroy 1998), which flourishes where there is an absence of concrete information regarding a topic that is of great interest to a special-interest group. Such views are most prevalent in cases where literary sources create an illusion of reality. The *Vinland Sagas* are a prime candidate for imaginative historical reconstruction because Vikings did not make maps; because the saga texts are geographically unspecific in their location of Vinland (allowing different readers to come to different conclusions from the same texts); and because their subject matter, involving seamanship, ethnology, geography, linguistics, astronomy, botany, and others, is of interest to many different people. The remainder of this discussion presents some of the more famous building blocks of this shaky but astonishingly durable conception of Viking America.

THE FALL RIVER SKELETON
In addition to identifying the Newport Tower as a Norse construction (see Hertz sidebar) Rafn also cited human physical remains that he identified as those of a Viking explorer. One of the sites brought to his at-

29.5 SPIRIT POND RUNESTONES
In 1971, a few years after the public announcement that an "English" penny had been discovered at the Goddard site in Brooklin, Maine (p. 206), three stones bearing runic inscriptions and a "map" of the find location were found on a beach in Popham, Maine. Like other "Viking" discoveries, the Spirit Pond runestones created a sensation in the press—including a story in *The New Yorker* by Calvin Trillin (5 February 1972)—but were later determined to be frauds.

29.6 THOR'S HAMMER
This bronze hammer is one of three in the estate of B. M. Crandall, whose father is supposed to have found them in 1924 while dredging Smith's Cove in Niantic, Connecticut. This one is unusually large and has an a typical suspension ring, little corrosion for such an ancient specimen, and higher nickel content than most Viking bronze. Its closest similarity is with a Swedish Viking Thor's hammer that appeared in the April 1970 issue of *National Geographic* (vol. 137, no. 4) in an illustration that lacked an accompanying scale bar.

tention was a burial found near Fall River, Massachusetts, on the Rhode Island border. The body of a man was buried in a sitting position in a deep pit and had copper sheeting, copper and brass beads, and copper arrowheads on his chest (fig. 29.4). The find caused a sensation and inspired poet Henry Wadsworth Longfellow to write his 1841 poem, *The Skeleton in Armor,* which read in part (fig. 29.3):

> I was a Viking old!
> My deeds, though manifold,
> No skald in song has told,
> No saga taught thee!
> Take heed that in thy verse
> Thou dost the tale rehearse,
> Else dread a dead man's curse!

The contents of the burial were shipped to Rafn for analysis in Copenhagen, where it has remained. For a long time people seriously believed it was a Norseman buried in armor, but it was later identified as a colonial-period Narragansett Indian buried with trade goods cut from copper kettles dating from the late sixteenth or early seventeenth century (Putnam 1901).

INSCRIPTIONS

Looking back at European archaeology, where runestones and inscribed monuments provided a literary link with the distant past, it seemed likely that runic inscriptions might also be found to document Viking presence in the Americas. At the time of Rafn's work, Indian rock carvings and pictographs were imperfectly known and were believed to be the work of mysterious Old World visitors. The Dighton Rock on the Taunton River in Berkley, Massachusetts, was covered with such carvings. Thomas Webb had drawings made and sent to Rafn, who distinguished a mix of runic and Latin forming the phrase CXXXI NAMTHORFINS, which he interpreted as Thorfinn [Karlsefni]; a date and in the pictographs he saw representations of Karlsefni's bull, his wife Gudrid, and son Snorri, figures described in the *Vinland Sagas.* A few years later, however, Henry Schoolcraft, who on behalf of the Smithsonian's Bureau of the American Ethnology had investigated Indian customs and culture throughout the United States, decided that the Dighton carvings were the work of local Algonquian Indians. Even

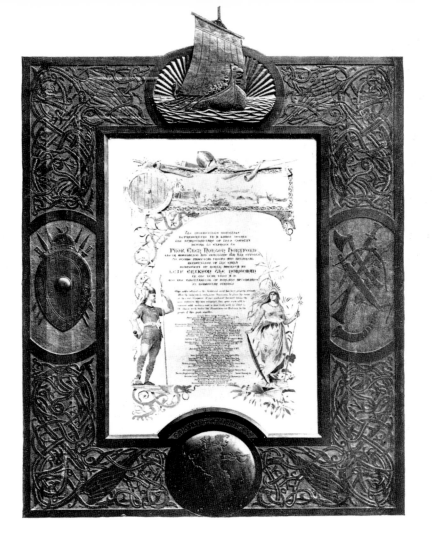

though this has since been confirmed by many later researchers, Dighton Rock continues to attract those who believe it has Norse inscriptions. A similar belief exists about an engraving found on a boulder at No Man's Land on Martha's Vineyard, reading "L.E. MI" in runes, interpreted as "Leif Eriksson, 1001." The engraving marks appeared recent; the find has been discredited and is now lost, but lives on as local lore.

In 1971 a third find, consisting of three engraved stones—two slate slabs and a cobble— bearing runic inscriptions and a map were found by Walter J. Elliott at Spirit Pond near Popham Beach at the mouth of the Kennebec River in Maine (fig. 29.5). Being the first runic inscriptions to appear in the northeastern United States in more than one hundred years, the engraved stones created a considerable stir in the media. A detailed linguistic analysis by Einar Haugen of Harvard University, however, showed the text and its accompanying "map stone" to be a modern fraud (Haugen 1972). The perpetrator was later identified, but engraved works thought to have been produced by this individual continued to appear periodically, reportedly made with the same steel engraving tool that cut the Spirit Pond finds (Alaric Faulkner, pers. comm.).

THE CRANDALL HAMMERS
Potentially the most diagnostic of all Viking finds from New England, three bronze Thor's hammers—amulets that are commonly found in graves of the Viking period in Scandinavia—were reportedly found by the father of the late B. M. Crandall while dredging Smith's Cove near Niantic, Connecticut, in 1924. The hammers first came to the attention of Jørgen Siemonsen, a Danish businessman who for the past ten years has been involved in stimulating research on Viking issues and helping to resolve some of the many mysteries revolving about Viking claims in North America. Through Siemonsen's help one of the three hammers (fig. 29.6) was delivered to Denmark for analysis by Lars Jørgensen, curator of Viking collections at the Danish National Museum. Jørgensen's report to Siemonsen notes that the hammers are larger than others known in Scandinavia or northern Germany, which are often found in Viking graves but are usually made of silver or iron rather than bronze. The Niantic finds were also unusual in the method of closing the ring loop and in their lack of wear and corrosion. One specimen also had an unusually high nickel content. Jørgensen reported that the closest parallel to the Niantic finds is a little over one inch (2.7 cm) hammer of silver found in Sweden before 1780 which had been published, without a scale or measurements indicated, in volume 137 of *The National Geographic Magazine* in 1971 (p. 497), and it was this image that alerted Crandall to the identity of the find. In a report to Jørgen Siemonsen (30 July 1998), Jørgensen noted the coincidence that the proportions of the Crandall hammer he studied were identical to the Swedish hammer but one and a half times larger, implying that the hammers may have been modeled after the unscaled image in *The National Geographic*.

FOLLINS POND
Follins Pond near Bass River, Cape Cod, has been identified as the site of Leif Eriksson's Vinland by the English teacher and science fiction writer, Frederick J. Pohl, who described two rectangular pits that he believed were the remains of Leif's house and that of

The best-known "Viking" artifact in North America is the Kensington Stone. A Swedish immigrant farmer named Olof Ohman found this stone slab near Kensington, Minnesota, in 1898. Its runic inscription, dated on the stone to 1362, tells of party of "8 Goths and 22 Norwegians on an exploration journey from Vinland to the west ..."

These photographs of the inscription were taken in 1899 by John F. Steward in Evanston, Illinois, for Professor George Curme, a Nordic language expert at Northwestern University. Curme examined the stone soon after it was found and declared it to be modern. He sent these photos to Prof. L. D. A. Wimmer at the Danish National Museum in Copenhagen in October 1899. They provide the best evidence for the condition of the stone and its carvings soon after its discovery in November 1898.

his companion explorers, Helgi and Finnbogi. He also identified a palisade and a ship-shaped gully with post emplacements (Pohl 1952, 1961, 1966, 1972). The Massachusetts Archaeological Society tested the site, and the posts were later radiocarbon dated and found to be from the eighteenth century. Other investigations by the Society showed that the house sites were cranberry bogs and the palisade of an old fence line (George Wilbur, pers. comm., 19 September 1964). Documentary evidence indicated that the gully had been used for repairing boats not by Vikings but by local fishermen (Smith 1953).

VIKINGS IN THE MIDWEST

Most so-called Viking finds from the Midwest have been linked to a single putative medieval Norwegian expedition by Paul Knutson who—according to a lost letter of 1354 known from a poor Danish translation of 1600—was instructed by King Magnus of Denmark to command an expedition to Greenland to preserve Christianity there. This missionary zeal has been used (Holand 1940) to explain why the expedition continued beyond Greenland to Rhode Island in its search for the missing Norse from the Greenland Western Settlement. After searching here, the expedition traveled into Hudson Bay and up the Nelson River to Lake Winnipeg and then followed the Red River into Minnesota, where an attack by Indians left ten expedition members dead (Holand 1919, 1940, 1956, 1962; Pohl 1961, 1966, 1972). The total distance covered from Greenland would have been 8,760 miles (13,900 kilometers) as the crow flies and much farther by ship. This elaborate theory has been used to link the finding of two runic inscriptions, nineteen axes, seven halberds, four swords, twelve spears, five steel fire-strikers, and thirty-eight "mooring-hole" sites (fig. 29.12). A recent study of the Knutson documents reveals that the expedition was not sent out for missionary purposes, if it indeed ever did take place; identifying such a role is a mistranslation in the Danish copy. Instead the letter simply identifies Knutson and confirms that he has the king's protection (Knirk 1997: 105). Rather than a holy mission to uphold Christianity, the expedition was in all likelihood a royal attempt to collect taxes from the Greenlanders.

From an archaeological point of view it is very unlikely—implausible, say the skeptics—that we would find such a multitude of sites and objects from a single expedition traveling across the landscape. Search for remains of Hernan DeSoto's 1541 march through the southeastern United States, for example, has produced few verifiable archaeological traces. Furthermore, with the exception of the fire-starters, all the metal objects recovered are weapons. If all these weapons were indeed from the fourteenth century and Norse, the chance recovery of so many scattered pieces would suggest the presence of an army. And why should we find only weapons? Even warriors use household objects for cooking and eating, personal items such as combs and knives, clothing articles, and other objects of daily life. Why

It was around this time, in 1879, that a Swedish emigrant named Olof Ohman, a stonemason from Forsa, Hälsingland, arrived in Minnesota and in 1891 bought a farm just outside Kensington near Alexandria. According to affidavits he signed, in November 1898, while digging out stumps on his land (fig. 29.9), Ohman came across an unusual tabular stone clasped in the roots of a tree. On it he found a runic inscription reading (fig. 29.8):

> 8 Goths and 22 Norwegians on an exploration journey from Vinland to the west. We had camp by 2 skerries one day's journey north from this stone. We were [out] to fish. One day after we came home [we] found 10 men red of blood and dead. AVM Save [us] from evil. [We] have 10 men by the sea to look after our ships 14 day's travel from this island [In the year] 1362.

The stone created a sensation. It was exhibited at a local bank in Alexandria, and newspaper articles publishing translations of the text appeared in local newspapers. A transcription said to have been made by Ohman was sent to Professor Olaf Breda at the Department of Scandinavian Languages at the University of Minnesota. Breda concluded that it was modern, because it contained numbers that were not proper runic numbers. Arrangements were then made to have the actual stone inspected for authentication at the Germanic Department of Northwestern University. The Chicago *Daily Inter Ocean* noted that "if authentic [the inscription] is destined to revolutionize previous researches of archaeologists" (21 February 1899), and the *Chicago Tribune* reported that it could be "the oldest record of American history" (20 February 1899).

One of the professors at Northwestern, George Curme, however, told the media that the text was clearly modern. Copies and photographs of the inscription were also sent to the leading runologists and philologists in Sweden, Norway, and Denmark. All declared both the text and the runes modern. These results seem to have been accepted without protest by Ohman, and the stone was returned to him.

This might have been the end of the matter had it not been for a young Norwegian-born amateur historian named Hjalmar Holand who became interested in it while traveling through Minnesota giving lectures on Norwegian history. He obtained the

were such items only found in Minnesota? It is striking that, with the exception of one mooring hole at Lake Winnipeg, not a single object has been found on the long way from Labrador to the Midwest, although many of these areas are as well surveyed archaeologically as interior Minnesota. In addition to the implausibility of the expedition itself, the provenance or authenticity of all the finds has been questioned.

THE KENSINGTON STONE

The most famous piece of purported evidence from this 1354 mission is a runestone found on a farm near Kensington, Minnesota. The Kensington Stone provides a fascinating and complex example of a romanticized Viking past. Nordic fascination with Vikings and their explorations in North America began with the emigration from the Nordic countries that took place during the height of a period of romantic nationalism in the late 1850s and 1860s. The 1874 work *America Not Discovered by Columbus,* by Rasmus B. Anderson, professor of Scandinavian languages at the University of Wisconsin, became exceedingly popular even outside academic circles. *The Wineland Voyages,* both in its Norwegian and English editions, were widely discussed in Midwestern Scandinavian newspapers. Interest in things Norse culminated in 1893 with the arrival in Chicago of captain Magnus Andersen's *Viking,* a replica of the Gokstad ship that had sailed across the Atlantic, proving for the first time that the Viking voyages were technically possible (Blegen 1968: 110–111).

29.10 Kensington Stone at the Smithsonian
Early specialists dismissed the Kensington Stone as a fraud, but a campaign by its later owner, Hjalmar Holand, brought public support. With a push from the Wisconsin congressional delegation, the Smithsonian put the stone on exhibit from 1948 to 1953, describing it as possibly "one of the most significant historical objects ever found in the New World." Those present at the opening included (left to right) Waldo R. Wedel, Curator of Archaeology at the Smithsonian, Representative Andersen of Minnesota, Sidney Dean Sarff of the Minnesota State Society, and John E. Graf, Acting Secretary of the Smithsonian. Today the Smithsonian sides with the majority of Nordic language scholars who believe the stone is a modern creation.

29.11 Ulen Sword
The Ulen sword is supposed to have been found in 1911 three miles west of Ulen, Minnesota. Although advanced as a Viking find by Hjalmar Holand, it bears no resemblance to Viking or medieval European swords, which are much larger and often have two-handed hilts. The prototype for this sword was designed by Louis David for the École de Mars in Paris in 1794, and its maker's mark indicates manufacture in Philadelphia in the early 1800s.

stone from Olof Ohman on the condition that he deposit it on Ohman's behalf in the Minnesota Historical Society. Instead, Holand kept the stone (even carving his own initials in it) and declared it authentic, dismissing Olaf Breda's and George Curme's analyses. Insisting it was a Nordic runestone from 1362, he skillfully linked the inscription to the Paul Knutson expedition and built it into an emotionally satisfying narrative.

Holand's vigorous campaigning led the Minnesota Historical Society to look further into the matter, and in late 1909 and early 1910 they sent State Geologist Newton H. Winchell to investigate. Winchell's diary indicates that hostility existed between Holand and Ohman. His written report was heavily influenced by Holand, who was hired by Winchell to translate, because Ohman did not speak English and Winchell did not speak any Scandinavian language. The report indicates that Ohman denied having carved the inscription but established that he knew runic writing and had an interest in history. Winchell concluded that the inscription might be genuine but that the lack of patina on the runes on the otherwise well-patinated stone indicated that the runes were recent. The governors of the Minnesota Historical Society concluded that the inscription was in all probability a fake and that Ohman was probably the perpetrator.

Spurred by the investigation, Holand offered to sell the stone to the Minnesota Historical Society for $5,000, but the society declined because Ohman insisted that he was the rightful owner and was willing to part with it for $100. The society soon lost interest, and Holand kept the stone until he parted with it for $4,000 paid by the Alexandria Chamber of Commerce, which is still its current owner. Holand went on to write several books and numerous articles and gave many lectures, always insisting that the stone's inscription was authentic. Careful reading reveals numerous flaws in his analyses, as Nordic scholars have always main-

tained (Bronsted 1951, 1954; Glosecki 1998; Ingelsang 1993; Jansson 1949; Knirk 1997; Liestøl 1966, 1968; Nielsen 1951, 1987; Wahlgren 1993a, 1993b). Despite nearly universal scholarly disdain, the Kensington Stone continues to be promoted by a few defenders (Landsverk 1961; Hall 1994; Nielsen 1986, 1987, 1988, 1989; Nilsestuen 1995) whose most successful argument against these Scandinavian conclusions is that specialists on runes and Nordic languages are prejudiced against laymen and refuse to believe Vikings could have traveled to Minnesota. Another favorite argument is that the tree growing over the stone was at least seventy years old. On the contrary, contemporary descriptions noted that the tree was judged to be only five to twelve years old and that the root around it was small (*Minneapolis Tidende*, 3 October 1911; letter from Cleve Van Dyke, 19 April 1910, Minnesota Historical Society).

The Kensington Stone might have remained a matter of local interest and probably would never have gained national recognition had it not been for its display at the Smithsonian Institution in Washington, D.C., between 1948 and 1953 (fig. 29.10). How the stone came to be put on display involved a convergence of influence applied by the Minnesota congressional delegation and the feeling of some Smithsonian curators that the stone—whether authentic or not—was important enough that it should be seen by the public. The display opened on March 12, 1948, accompanied by a Smithsonian Institution press release: "A stone carved with Norse runes, the authenticity of which now is widely accepted by archeologists…is now on exhibition in the foyer of the National Museum of Natural History….Even if it cannot be indisputably authenticated, the confirming evidence that the stone constitutes a genuine record is so strong that this relic is regarded by Smithsonian archeologists as one of the most significant historical objects ever found in the New World." A disclaimer was, however, included in the same release: "Smithsonian archeologists reserve judgment on the authenticity of the Kensington Stone," revealing perhaps the staff's divided opinions. The stone was exhibited from February 17, 1948, through February 25, 1949, when it was returned to its owners in Alexandria, Minnesota, and was replaced by a plaster cast, which re-

mained on exhibition for several more years.

As a result of the ensuing controversy in which many archaeologists and linguists criticized the Smithsonian for mounting a misleading display, the Institution commissioned a new study of the stone by the Danish ethnologist William Thalbitzer. Thalbitzer was a highly respected elderly scholar, but his specialty was Eskimo ethnology, not archaeology or runes. His study (1951) gave qualified support for the authenticity of the runes, but the Institution, by now somewhat gun-shy, failed to give it unqualified support and, in a news release of September 23, 1951, noted that "the Smithsonian has taken no position with regard to its authenticity, but felt that its presence in Washington would provide runic scholars a further opportunity to study it." Given this rather supportive stance and the fact that many viewers were unable to read runes or evaluate the age of the chisel work, it is not surprising that many people had the impression that the Smithsonian had in effect "authenticated" the stone a second time.

The Smithsonian's ambivalent position stimulated still more controversy in the academic community, which was by this time solidly against authenticity. The continuing controversy soon led to the appearance of a critical review (Brønsted 1954), published by the Smithsonian, and two books (Moltke 1953; Wahlgren 1958) all of which took decisive stands based on detailed studies of the history and circumstances of the find. Eric Wahlgren's (1958) analysis in particular makes a plausible case for the appearance in the late nineteenth century of a runestone in a Scandinavian-settled area of Minnesota, given a probable perpetrator (Ohman) with an interest in history, folk knowledge of runes, and a sense of humor.

Knowledge of runes was not an esoteric academic discipline in the nineteenth century. Runic script was alive and well, especially in remote rural areas of Norway and Sweden (Boethius 1906; Jansson 1963). Ohman's mother came from Orsa in Dalecarlia, a community where runes were still being used in the 1920s (Boethius 1906). Ohman himself came from Forsa in the neighboring province of Hälsingland, where runes were also still understood.

Although many rural people were illiterate in regular reading and writing, knowledge of runes was widespread. Runic forms changed from one generation to another, and it is revealing that some of the runes on the Kensington Stone are of an eighteenth- to nineteenth-century variety used in Dalecarlia, the province of Ohman's mother. Ohman admitted knowing runes and had been seen carving runes on sticks during his early years in Minnesota.

Among the articles found pasted into Ohman's scrapbook, now in the Minnesota Historical Society, is one from the Swedish newspaper *Post och Inrikes Tidningar* dated December 13, 1867. It describes a runestone of 1612 found in Vadstena, Sweden, clasped by the roots of an ash tree. The article mentions how the stone was shown to be one hundred and fifty years old by a count of the tree's growth rings. According to a neighbor of Ohman's, Jonas P. Gran, the runic inscription was planned long in advance of its finding and may have been inspired by this newspaper story. In tape recordings (also held by the Minnesota Historical Society), Gran said that the inscription had been composed by Ohman and his friend, Sven Fogelblad, a former Lutheran minister, and that Ohman and Gran did the actual chiseling. Ohman and Gran buried the stone under the roots of a small ash and then waited for a good opportunity to retrieve it. Both Gran and Ohman enjoyed pranks and, according to Gran, they enjoyed the commotion that resulted.

Today, the National Museum of Natural History continues to receive public inquiries about the Stone and the Smithsonian's current position. The Department of Anthropology answers these inquiries with a statement written in unambiguous terms saying that scholarly opinion has judged the Kensington Stone to be a nineteenth-century creation.

The Kensington Stone has been an intriguing and successful mystery. More than one hundred years after its finding, the inscription is still the subject of debate, one of whose most interesting arguments is that its "errors" result from purposeful "encryption" (Mongé and Landsverk 1967; Landsverk 1969). While cryptographic runes are known from Scandinavia, they adhere to consistent criteria, which the American examples do not (Wallace 1982). Such sidetracks divert attention from the real significance of the Kensington Stone, which is as a memorial to the creativity of Scandinavian immigrants

29.12 "MOORING HOLES"
Small holes drilled into bedrock have often been advanced as evidence of mooring Viking ships and have been found in large numbers in New England and Minnesota. Vikings used mooring posts and a similar technique employing mooring rings anchored in rock, as illustrated in Olavus Magnus's *Description of Northern Peoples* (1555). Most "mooring holes" are associated with rock quarrying and home foundation building and are far from coasts and Minnesota waterways.

and the living tradition of runic knowledge they brought with them to the New World. It is a remarkable example of early Nordic-American folk culture, but it is not a milestone in American archaeology.

In its aftermath the Kensington Stone prompted a rash of Scandinavian finds in Minnesota and nearby regions of the Upper Midwest. The "fortifications" on Mandan Indian sites on the Missouri River were thought to have been modeled after military structures typical of medieval Europe. It was even suggested that relict Vikings from past expeditions had joined native tribes to survive. A steady stream of purported Norse runestones, mooring holes (fig. 29.12), ring-bolts, and artifacts, including swords (fig. 29.11), halberds, spears, fire-strikers, and other materials began to surface as the indefatigable Hjalmar Holand continued to crisscross the territory speaking about the ancient Norse who had once passed through this region and inspecting and publishing finds people brought in for identification. The list is too long for detailed documentation here (see Wilfred Anderson 1996, Pohl 1961; Wallace 1971, 1982).

SUMMARY

Many will be disappointed to hear that the Knutson expedition was driven not by missionary zeal or that the Kensington Stone is the product of living history and that the many axes, halberds, and other weapons found in and around Minnesota are mementos of fur traders and settlers who have been present in this area from the seventeenth century onward. On the other hand, many will

refuse to believe this and will continue to cherish the thought that the Newport Tower was erected by the Vinland Norse; that the Beardmore relics from Ontario are an authentic Viking burial cache (Curran 1939, Currelly 1940) rather than an admitted hoax (Carpenter 1957, 1961); that the rock carvings from Heavener, Oklahoma, were made by wandering Vikings (Farley 1973) rather than being modern carvings made by a local Scandinavian enthusiast (Wykcoff 1973); that Viking explorers taught American Indians to smelt and work iron (Mallery 1951); or that the Ungava Bay "longhouses" of arctic Quebec were built by Celts (Mowat 1998) or by Norse (Lee 1968, 1974) rather than by Dorset people several hundred years before Vikings reached North America (Dekin 1972; Plumet 1985; Odess et al., this volume). The idea of the presence of Vikings and other pre-Columbian Norsemen in many quarters of the New World continues to fascinate, as it has for almost two hundred years. Now that education and knowledge have advanced to the point that claims for antiquities can be investigated more conclusively, we may hope that reason will begin to take precedence over speculation and unsubstantiated claims. Even without embellishments, the established facts of Viking finds in the New World as recounted in this volume are exciting, even if they do not document pre-Columbian Viking visits to New England, Minnesota, or Oklahoma.

On the other hand, history demonstrates that humans have a unique capacity for recreating and reshaping their past to suit social, political, or emotional needs. History suggests that new Norse "discoveries" will continue to be made by the ardent or the duplicitous. Despite the confusion such unwelcome "evidence" creates for professional linguists and archaeologists, credit must be given to the many committed amateur historians and archaeologists like Helge Ingstad, the discoverer of the L'Anse aux Meadows site, who have made important contributions to the history of Nordic peoples in the New World and probably will continue to do so in the future.

30 SAGAS AND SCIENCE

Climate and Human Impacts in the North Atlantic

BY ASTRID E. J. OGILVIE AND THOMAS H. McGOVERN

MARRIAGE PROCESSION, *REYKJABÓK*

Iceland: *It is high summer of the year 1000 in Iceland, and people are traveling home from the meeting of the Althing, the annual legislative gathering held beside the great lake of Thingvellir in the south of Iceland. This year's meeting was an unusually exciting—a decision had been made to accept Christianity as the official religion; pagan Viking beliefs would be tolerated but would no longer play a leading role in society. The change occurred when Thorgeir, the* lögsögumaður *(law speaker and chief parliamentarian) and a former pagan priest, from Ljósavatn in the north of Iceland, committed to Jesus Christ in a dramatic episode, reconciling opposed blocks in the assembly. After pondering the future of Iceland from under his cloak where he remained for a whole day and a night, in a trancelike state, he spoke profound words: "Let us all have one law and one faith. If we tear law asunder, we tear peace asunder." He rode out filled with the zeal of a convert and resolved to cast his wooden images of the old gods over the falls near his home. This dramatic act would leave the cataract with the name Goðafoss (Waterfall of the Gods) for the next thousand years.*

One of Thorgeir's neighboring chieftains is also riding north, probably in a less exultant mood. We do not know his name or lineage, for we know him only through the archaeological excavations of his large farm at Hofstaðir near Lake Mývatn. He has just completed what he now realizes must be the final expansion of a great feasting hall—many times larger than the average Viking Age longhouse—having decorated the outside with the horned skulls of cattle he has slaughtered in sacrificial feasts. Somehow, in the face of these Christian changes, he must find a way to keep his supporters and his status. As he rides, he travels through green pastures, and his path skirts thickets of birch and willow trees. Ptarmigan fly up from the grass, and he wonders for a moment if it would be worth settling one of his retainers in a small cot up here where he could do some hunting and keep the pigs a bit further from the home fields. As he nears the lake, smoke from a charcoal-burning pit drifts across his path. Well, old gods or new, it will be good to get home and see how much ale can be brewed up from the barley he is bringing home.

Greenland: *That same summer, a much newer settlement is growing along the fjords of southwestern Greenland. Smoke also drifts through the air here, this time from a line of fire working its way across a distant hillside where a new farm is being cleared from the brush lands at the head of the fjord. A red-haired man sits by the shore, his leg propped out stiffly on a board. Scowling blackly, he watches some young boys rolling in the dirt, scuffling instead of tending the goats. About to call out a sarcastic correction, he sees a line of horses winding down from the mountain and his face brightens as he counts the caribou slung over the saddles. Let the young men have their fun in Vinland, he thought, this new holding will be a rich place for as long as I need riches. Erik the Red settles back complacently and begins thinking about the roast caribou haunch he will soon have for dinner.*

Vinland: *Across the sea in Vinland, a small band of Erik's men are a long way from home. Their ship is drawn up on a beach at a small bay at the northern tip of an island later European explorers will call Newfoundland. Tired after a day of repairing their ship, they brush wood chips from their beards and eat some of the tasty butternuts they collected on the last voyage across the big bay to the southwest. They talk about the new lands they have seen and their chances of getting a farm of their own, someplace with lots of pasture, a good salmon stream, and a forest full of prime timber. They also talk about the strange* skraeling *and the daunting number of boats that swarmed out to meet them at some places. Although the natives they encountered had no swords or longships, they were good bow marksmen, and they were so aggressive that the Norsemen always had to post a watch, and no one felt comfortable with his weapons more than a few steps away. Vinland is indeed a rich land, but it is not empty.*

THAT SUMMER ONE THOUSAND years ago, the western North Atlantic seemed a place of endless bounty and opportunities for pioneering Nordic chieftains and their followers. Iceland was by now fully settled and was taking on its own identity; the Greenland colony was well started, and Vinland seemed to have great promise. Individually and collectively, Norse settlers were making plans and decisions that they expected would sustain a future for themselves and their descendants. Yet in all three cases imagined here, the sum of these plans and decisions was not long-term economic and environmental security, but long-term disaster—for both these new lands and their inhabitants. Unlike Greenland, Vinland was to die in infancy before it even got a start, a casualty of Native American resistance and its distance from Europe. Norse Greenland was to endure four hundred fifty years more, but eventually would wither and die. Icelanders, one hundred times as numerous as the Norse Greenlanders in their prime, survived, but at the price of terrible suffering and ecological damage in the later medieval and early modern periods. The promise of that bright summer of 1000 could not be kept, and none of our imagined actors realized their dream of long-term sustainability of their way of life.

The causes for these unforeseen and unhappy historical outcomes are too many to enumerate in a brief discussion (see McGovern, this volume); we wish instead to draw attention to a recurrent factor in archaeological and historical investigations—the cumulative effects of human interaction with the local and regional environment. While the human actors of 1000 played out roles that were selectively recorded years later by the saga authors, northern nature was undergoing equally dramatic changes. This chapter considers human-environment interaction and explores the lessons of these increasingly well-documented "natural sagas" of human impact, climate change, and fluctuating fisheries for modern humans who are today facing situations distressingly similar to those of one thousand years ago. While our perspective derives from the entire North Atlantic environment and settlement region, our primary focus is on the island of Iceland, where human settlement has persisted without a break since early in the ninth century and where there has been continuity in Nordic language, culture, and tradition (fig. 30.3).

CLIMATE, ENVIRONMENT, SEA ICE, AND ICE CORES

This servant of God was Bishop of that country which the books call Thile, but which northmen call Iceland. It must certainly be said that this is an appropriate name for the island, as there is plenty of ice both on land and sea. On the sea there is sea ice, which fills up the northern harbors in great quantity, and on the high mountains of the country there are permanently frozen glaciers....From under these mountainous glaciers sometimes pour torrential streams in great floods....There are no woods apart from birch and they are small. Corn grows in a few places in the south, but only barley, fish from the sea, and milk forms the basic diet of the ordinary people....The country is most widely settled along the coast, but least in the east and west. (From *The Saga of Bishop Gudmundur*, circa 1350, translated from Sigurðsson et al., *Biskupa Sögur* I–II 1858–78:2:5)

The island of Iceland is, geologically speaking, very young. It was created largely by volcanic activity and its ecosystem was fragile from the outset (fig. 30.1). The greater part of the landmass consists of an uninhabited central region. The most fertile areas are the coastal lowland and valley regions, and human settlement is concentrated there. Because of the cool climate, soil forms very slowly and is susceptible to erosion. From the Commonwealth period of early Norse settlement to the end of the nine-

30.1 FIRE AND ICE
Life in Iceland has been strongly shaped by its dynamic volcanic history. Eruptions spewing ash and lava over the countryside have periodically forced the abandonment of whole settlements. Soil stratigraphy, ash-fall chemistry, and new dating techniques provide keys to unlocking Iceland's settlement history. This view shows Hekla erupting in 1980.

30.2 SUMMER DRIFT ICE
As in southwest Greenland, the proximity of drift ice in waters off Iceland has a major climatic impact. During cold periods the arctic pack—"the country's ancient enemy" according to a famous nineteenth-century Icelandic poem—appears, bringing seals and polar bears but creating havoc for fishermen, farmers, and traders. Many of these effects are documented in dated church records. Absent during the Little Climatic Optimum (900–1250), drift ice began to appear regularly in Greenland and Iceland after 1300.

teenth century, the population varied but tended not to exceed around fifty thousand; the population today is approaching three hundred thousand. Prior to about 1860, Icelandic society was almost entirely rural in character with no towns or villages; everyone lived either on isolated farmsteads or in a few fishing settlements on the coast.

The history of the climate of Iceland over the past thousand years can be traced through a wide variety of written annals, reports, letters, and diaries (Thórarinsson 1956; Ogilvie 1991; 1992; Jónsson and Garðarsson n.d.; Jónsdóttir et al. n.d.). These data have been carefully evaluated to produce a long record of climate variations (figs. 30.6, 30.7; Ogilvie 1991, 1992) that have been compared with data that approximate climatic records from the North Atlantic region, such as atmospheric and environmental history obtained from long-accumulating, annually stratified ice cores taken from various sites in the Greenland ice sheet (see, for example, Dansgaard et al. 1975; Robin 1983; Barlow et al. 1997a) and from sediment cores taken from deep sea deposits (see, for example, Jennings et al. n.d.). By analyzing chemical composition (especially the changes in oxygen isotope ratios) and frequency of airborne inclusions like volcanic dust and sea salt and by dating the cores by their annual layers, radiocarbon dating, or other means, scientists have been able to piece together a detailed record of climatic history and environmental change that extends thousands of years into the past and shows the considerable and increasing imprint of human intervention.

One of the most important determinants of climatic and environmental changes in Iceland is the sea ice that drifts southward

out of the arctic toward Iceland in the East Greenland Current (fig. 30.2). The proximity of sea ice can have a severe and negative effect on human economies by lowering temperatures on land, reducing forage and grazing potential for animal husbandry, and preventing or restricting fishing, marine mammal hunting, and trade. During the twentieth century, sea ice has been comparatively rare in Icelandic waters, but in earlier times it was a frequent and dreaded visitor: "the country's ancient enemy," according to a famous nineteenth-century Icelandic poem. It has also been demonstrated that there is a close correlation between land temperature on Iceland and presence of sea ice in the Icelandic records (fig. 30.6) (Bergthórsson 1969; Ogilvie 1984a, 1992).

One of the standard methods for studying past climate is by reference to modern conditions, and here the detailed twentieth-century Icelandic climate records help provide an important perspective on the past. Typical winter temperatures for Reykjavík, for example, during this century, are around 32° F (0° C) and summer temperatures are around 52° F (11° C). The suggestion that climate was relatively mild (similar to that during much of the twentieth century) when the Norse first settled Iceland and Greenland has been largely supported by scientific and historical studies (Ogilvie 1991; Ogilvie et al. n.d.; see also Hughes and Diaz 1994). Oxygen-isotope records from two ice cores, the Crête core in northern Greenland (Dansgaard et al. 1975) and the GIS P-2 core in southern Greenland (Fisher et al. 1995; Barlow et al. 1997b), suggest that the periods between 700 and 1100 and between 900 and 1350 in these

30.3 ICELANDIC LEGACY
Iceland's population has been resident there for twelve hundred years—more than sixty generations. During this time the land and its people and animals have undergone major historical and climatic changes. Nevertheless, geographic isolation and careful management have resulted in preservation of a unique genetic and linguistic heritage. Today Icelanders and other North Atlantic societies can benefit as never before from knowledge accumulated by combining history and science.

respective regions were relatively warmer than the present. The founding of the Eastern Settlement in Greenland circa 985 may therefore have been especially favored by conditions facilitating animal husbandry. The isotopic signal of deuterium from the GISP-2 ice core suggests that the fourteenth century was the period of the lowest temperature in Greenland during the last seven hundred years (fig. 30.6). It therefore seems extremely likely that harsh climate was an important factor in the collapse of the Western Settlement in Greenland, which archaeologists and historians believe occurred in the mid-fourteenth century (Buckland et al. 1996; Barlow et al. 1997b).

Marine sediment cores from Nansen Fjord off the eastern coast of Greenland also indicate a warm and very stable climate from the eighth through the twelfth centuries, with little possibility that sea ice would hinder boat travel between Iceland and Greenland (Jennings and Weiner 1996; Jennings et al. n.d.). This marine record also suggests that lower temperatures on Iceland, which are usually associated with encroaching arctic waters or sea ice, were not frequent at this time. The core record from Nansen Fjord supports the widespread belief, based on earlier studies of fossil pollen and vegetation records from Scandinavia and northern Europe, that Norse expansion across the North Atlantic to Iceland and Greenland occurred during an interval when climate was relatively mild, perhaps similar to the present day, but perhaps more stable than at present. The Nansen Fjord record suggests that much more ice was present in the eighteenth and nineteenth centuries. Written

records maintained in Iceland also document a high frequency of sea ice off the coasts of Iceland at this time (Ogilvie 1991; Ogilvie and Jónsdóttir 1996; Jónsdóttir et al. n.d.).

FARMING, FISHING, AND FAMINE

On top of the very poor fishing last summer the hay harvest was a failure because the greater part of the hay rotted on account of long-lasting sleet and rain. The hay is thus of little use as winter fodder for the livestock and as the ordinary people only use fish and milk products for their subsistence they have had to suffer hunger and dearth during the previous winter and spring. As a result of this five people have died here in the district. Many of the people have subsisted on roots from the earth and seaweed from the shore. (1753 letter from Sheriff Brynjólfur Sigurðsson in Árnessýsla, translated in Ogilvie 1982)

From the time of the earliest Norse settlers to the late nineteenth century, farming—especially animal husbandry—has been the most important economic activity in Iceland (Ogilvie 1982; 1984b). The preoccupied Hofstaðir chieftain that we posited at the beginning of this chapter would have maintained a mix of domestic stock that included pigs and goats as well as the horses, cattle, and sheep that were to dominate the later Icelandic farm economy. This early mix of *landnám* species was a significantly greater threat to the stability of Icelandic flora and soils than the later domesticates. Goats can eat bark and twigs, and pigs root up vegetation and consume roots, destroying the ground cover and upper soil layer, so that these two species would have been very effective in eliminating the forest cover and shrub patches that existed in Iceland during the *landnám* period. It is probably significant therefore that pig and goat remains are extremely rare in archaeological site remains in Iceland dating after 950 to 1000. Pollen studies indicate that the scrub forests had been largely eliminated from Iceland by this time, a result of the combined effects of human use of wood for fuel and construction materials and agricultural activities. As Icelandic farmers gained experience and adjusted their stock mix, the rate of damage may have slowed, but the legacy of this early agricultural heritage remained in a damaged ecosystem (fig. 30.8).

Many different types of climatic cir-

30.4

30.5

30.4 Skálholt
The Christianization of Iceland promoted the writing of histories and sagas as early as the twelfth and thirteenth centuries. Annals and church records provide documentation of important events including climatic observations that can be linked to environmental history from glaciers, sea cores, and terrestrial sediments. Skálholt and other church centers have been instrumental in new multidisciplinary research into North Atlantic history.

30.5 Cod, by God!
In the late thirteenth century, fishing began to dominate Iceland's subsistence and trade economy. As economic and political power became concentrated in fewer hands, offshore interests emerged to dominate trade, and fishing became Iceland's major cash industry by the eighteenth century. In Icelandic context, the Christian emblem of the fish has been transformed into its commercial product, a split and dried codfish, on the pulpit of the Skálholt Church.

cumstances could have negative effects on farming practices in Iceland. A severe winter with snow and ice that lasted into the spring and early summer would delay the growth of grass, making for poor forage and a scarcity of winter fodder. Rain that fell excessively during the harvest or when the grass was reaped could cause it to rot and spoil. Scarcity of rain restricted grass growth, as did the presence of large amounts of sea ice off the coast, which lowered temperatures, reduced growth, and hindered the harvest. A combination of such circumstances—a rainy summer followed by a severe winter and the presence of sea ice late in the spring—could spell disaster. If it seemed impossible to feed all the livestock through the winter, many of them might be slaughtered in the autumn. People were often reluctant to reduce their herd, however, believing that conditions would improve or that the winter would be mild; but too often many of the cattle died of starvation. For example, historical documents indicate that livestock died from hunger and cold in at least twenty-four of the thirty-six years between 1730 and 1766 (fig. 30.4).

Fishing was also an important component of the Icelanders' diet, particularly in the form of dried cod (fig. 30.4). From the fourteenth century onward dried cod, as well as wool, was a principal export item to Europe. Fishing did not become a major industry in Iceland until the late nineteenth century, however, and, as in Norway, it was rarely carried on as a commercial enterprise or as an individual's sole means of support but was rather a part of the farming-fishing subsistence base. Because timber was not available locally, fishing boats were generally owned only by the wealthier farmers and were

crewed by the poorer people. In this regard, boat ownership in the medieval and later periods was not much different from that of the early Viking period. The lack of boats certainly was one reason why the Icelanders' fisheries industry took so long to develop.

Certain crisis years in Iceland in the seventeenth and eighteenth centuries appear to have been precipitated primarily by a failure of the fisheries. In 1732, for example, there were deaths from hunger in the south, and contemporary accounts indicate a lack of fish as the cause. Any difficulties brought about by a failure of the agrarian economy were doubtless intensified by poor fishing catches. The exceptionally poor catches during the years of scarcity in the 1750s must have greatly intensified the hardship experienced throughout Iceland during this decade.

SOCIAL STRUCTURE AND ECONOMIC STAGNATION

The only thing of importance that I have to recount concerns the past severe winter which has caused great misery to the inhabitants here in the district as they have lost almost all their livestock and means of subsistence and they were not able to buy flour and foodstuffs from the merchants, let alone obtain them on credit, the monopoly's control being what it is. This year the behavior of the merchant has been even more absurd and contrary than in previous years; in this time of dearth they have let people travel to the trading places two or three times. Sometimes they were turned away with scornful words, on other occasions made to wait there for no reason at all, as it suited the merchants, only to be finally refused unless they had goods to pay with at once. However, their woolen goods were rejected and they were rudely forced to give up the few remaining cattle they had to live off as payment. (1754 letter from Sheriff Bjarni Halldórsson in Húnavatnssýsla, translated in Ogilvie 1982)

Environmental change tends to produce winners and losers in any human society: to respond effectively to major changes in the natural environment requires alterations in daily life and social structure that often are not popular or politically acceptable. In both Greenland and Iceland, the rulers, who were often direct descendants of Viking Age chieftains, lived on large farms with comparatively rich pastures that supported large cattle herds. In addition, the devaluation of pasture by climate and erosion threatened the social and political position of the rulers of what had become essentially stratified societies based on cattle and other forms of animal husbandry (McGovern 1981, 1992; McGovern et al. 1988, 1996). It is not surprising that these rulers probably chose to ignore the early signals of climate change despite its long-term threats to Icelandic society as a whole: then as now, politics and ecology seem to have been closely interconnected.

As climate varied and the consequences of erosion caused by deforestation and over-grazing became more severe, one response was the intensification of fishing and sea-mammal hunting that had been practiced on a smaller scale since the Viking settlement period. Favorable fishing stations and sealing grounds were, however, often far from the pastures of the wealthiest farmers, and so it would have been difficult for them to control these activities. It is probably for this reason that sixteenth- to eighteenth-century Icelandic agrarian elites were generally opposed to the formation of permanent fishing villages, for they feared that this would weaken their control over seasonal laborers, as well as over general economic and political affairs.

HUMAN IMPACTS AND NATURAL CAPITAL

> In those days Iceland was clad with trees and bushes between shore and sea. *(Book of the Icelanders)*

The environmental historian William Cronon called the soils, plants, and wild animals present in Iceland when it was first settled a reserve of "natural capital" (1991)

that financed the early expansion of the settlement and growing prosperity during the early Commonwealth period. Without implementing management strategies to sustain these resources, such a natural "bank account" would be progressively depleted. Some of the practices associated with human settlement—such as manuring the home fields immediately around the farms and installing small-scale irrigation works—were intended to replenish this natural capital. Farther from the home fields, negative impacts of the imported agrarian economy became evident soon after settlement, however, and in many districts the positive effects of human intervention were overshadowed by the unintended negative impacts.

Over the course of several hundred years after *landnám* the rich grasslands of the Icelandic interior shrank and disappeared along with the scrub woodlands. Small farms that were established circa 1000 to 1100 in the less-resilient interior for access to grazing and hunting brought rapid environmental disaster rather than long-term prosperity. By 1100 more than 90 percent of the original Icelandic forest had been destroyed, and by 1700 nearly 40 percent of Iceland's soils had been washed or blown away, leaving northern "deserts" near Hofstaðir so barren that NASA astronauts used them for lunar training in the 1960s (Arnalds et al. 1987). As the hillside vegetation mat destabilized and began to shed soil, massive landslides wiped out whole farms and choked once-rich valley bottoms with rock slides and fans of gravel debris (fig. 30.8). Drainage patterns changed dramatically as watersheds shifted from dense brush and grasslands to bare rock and erosion desert, once-quiet rivers periodically became rushing torrents, and the water-retention capabilities of the soil declined. The massive amounts of soil transported downstream filled in lowlands and created vast gravel-covered *sandur* plains seasonally reworked by braided streams that wandered over the newly created outwash deltas.

Were our hypothetical tenth-century chieftain from Hofstaðir to return in the late twentieth century to ride through his former farmlands and uplands south of Lake Mývatn, he would be hard put to recognize his homeland. Although this is still an area of outstanding natural beauty and a program for reforestation has been initiated, the pastures and trees that he knew are largely gone. In

30.6 A SMOKING CLIMATE GUN? High-resolution isotopic data from the GISP-2 Greenland ice core suggest a period of lower temperatures in central southern Greenland between 1343 and 1362. Seasonal data indicate summers were particularly cool. Such weather may have had an adverse impact on Norse settlements in Greenland at about the time the Western Settlement disappeared.

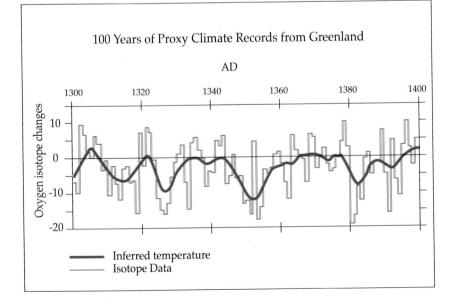

100 Years of Proxy Climate Records from Greenland

A. E. OGILVIE AND T. H. McGOVERN

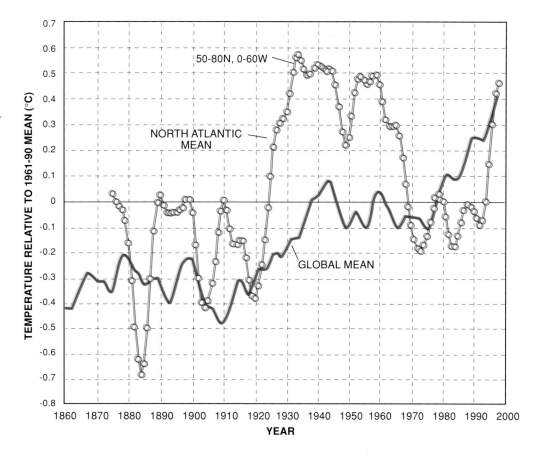

their place, the landscape has been reduced to bare gravel with archaeological sites surrounded by scraps of smelting debris the only sign of human settlement. As the human population grew, the small herding and hunting stations that he had anticipated establishing in the interior were often upgraded to full-scale small farms, but most of these failed disastrously when soil and vegetation were consumed after a few years. The ruins of a small tenth- to twelfth-century farm site of Sveigakot, just south of Mývatn on the edge of the modern erosion desert, may represent just this sort of settlement (fig. 30.9). The trash middens of this small farm, which was excavated in 1998 and 1999 by teams from the Icelandic Archaeological Institute and North Atlantic Biocultural Organization, contain the bones of the full range of early Icelandic domestic animals, including cattle and horses as well as sheep and goats, both freshwater and marine fish, bird bones, and masses of smithing slag. Such a range of activities seems incredible given the site's modern surroundings, but it was these very activities that helped create the eroded surroundings. The site appears to have been occupied only briefly before being permanently abandoned in the early medieval period. An understand-

ing of this type of destructive settlement and exploitation practice was anticipated nearly thirty years ago by Sigurður Thórarinsson (1956), who recognized a widespread pattern of settlement "overshoot," with hopeful farmers pushing too far inland before 1100, only to trigger a permanent contraction of the habitable zone a generation later. Farming decisions made in the Viking Age actually reduced the options and prospects of their descendants by leaving a degraded landscape for later generations.

THRESHOLDS AND BOOBY TRAPS

> There are other mountains in this country which produce terrible eruptions of fire and stones such that the crashing and crackling noise is heard all over the country . . .
> (*The Saga of Bishop Gudmundur*, circa 1350, translated from Sigurdsson et al., *Biskupa Sögur* I–II 1858–78:2:5).

Iceland had several features that would have surprised (and terrified) early settlers. With little warning, volcanic eruptions could destroy vegetation and human settlements, melt portions of glaciers, and deposit thick layers of ash (fig. 30.1). Other environmental traps were more subtle. In some areas, thick layers of powdery tephra—pumicelike

30.8 FARMING'S DOWNSIDE
Animals sustained Viking society in Iceland for several centuries, but eventually the cumulative ecological damage of overgrazing began to take its toll. This photograph from Thorsmörk, Iceland, shows the difference between grazed lands (right) and land protected by fencing (left). Without proper care, soils formed over thousands of years can be stripped away by wind, water, and hoof in a few years.

30.9 SVEIGAKOT: PARADISE DESTROYED
The northern Iceland ecosystem, like Greenland's Western Settlement, was more sensitive to changes in climate and human exploitation. Archaeological remains being inspected here show that in Viking times Sveigakot was a productive farm holding cattle, sheep, goats, and pigs, and its surrounding woodlands supported iron smelting and charcoal-making. Today this area is an eroded wasteland whose middens, furnace remains, and slag heaps document short-sighted human exploitation.

material ejected during volcanic eruptions—often lay a few centimeters below the deceptively green turf. Penetration of the sod layer above such a deposit often led to sudden, catastrophic destabilization of the whole farm field (Dugmore and Buckland 1991). Other, more stable Icelandic soils also presented unexpected problems. Because Icelandic soils are very fine and highly mineralized, they are extremely vulnerable to wind erosion (Arnalds et al. 1987). Erosion of such soils at the edges of streams, blowouts, and ledges are subject to rapid undercutting by wind at their exposed faces. Such erosion fronts can run for miles. Whole landscapes can cross critical erosional thresholds before stress on the community is clearly apparent, and once small-scale threshold crossings merge, the product is a fully eroded surface dotted by a few relict eroded ridges, mesalike structures known locally as *rofbarðs* (fig. 30.10).

LESSONS OF HISTORY

Ecologists and environmental historians have begun to study sequences of historical and environmental events recognizing the importance of the long interaction between humans and the natural environment and how each is contingent upon the other (see, for example, Parry 1981). We now recognize that the Viking Age colonists in the North Atlantic probably benefited from a period of variable, but generally mild climate unlike that of the twentieth century. The colonists of the Faeroes, Iceland, and Greenland also profited initially from soils and vegetation that had accumulated for hundreds if not thousands of years without human intervention; none of these landscapes had ever experienced domestic livestock, and in Iceland large herbivores were entirely absent. The historical conjuncture of favorable climate

and unexpended natural capital that the Viking voyagers found was critical to the success of the initial Viking *landnám*. The early choice of settlement sites and subsistence strategies were based on experience in other islands like the Shetlands, Orkneys, and Faeroes, or in their homeland regions, whose history and ecology were subtly but critically different and far more stable and resilient. In Norway or the northern British Isles, sheep could be grazed at high elevations and left out on these pastures late into the fall and early winter without undue damage to animals or vegetation. In Iceland and Greenland, a similar strategy would gradually reduce the resilience and reproductive capacity of the same plant communities, leaving the pastureland vulnerable to drastic decline from climate cooling or subsequent grazing pressure. Recent studies involving computer-based land-use simulations have suggested that only a few weeks of additional upland grazing in the autumn might be enough to trigger early erosion in the highlands of Iceland (Simpson 1999). Poorly informed about the long-term effects of their early settlement and subsistence choices, those first generations of Norse settlers, who had been blessed by benign weather for many years and a full natural resource "bank account," unwittingly set the stage for later tragedies experienced by their descendants, who found themselves struggling to respond to a less-favorable climate regime and an overdrawn natural capital account.

If this degradation of landscape in Iceland and the North Atlantic were unique, their importance for the wider world would be limited, but many characteristics of these island ecosystems and insular human populations may be widely applicable to "island Earth." Islands have provided scale models

30.10 Soil Loss in South Iceland
Even in warmer southern Iceland, human-induced changes have resulted in massive soil erosion when surface vegetation has been lost from overgrazing or cutting forest. Raised mesalike structures known as *rofbarð*s show that several meters of soil have been lost here since a benchmark was established in 1830.

for conceptualizing human societal and natural environmental change, and the historical ecology of islands is an active field today (Kirch and Hunt 1997).

In the late twentieth century, peoples around the world face some of the same problems of human-environmental interaction that the Norse faced a thousand years ago. Iceland's problems of deforestation, soil erosion, and massive landscape change are mirrored in modern ecosystems from the Sahel to the American Southwest. The same factors that made sustainable management of pastures and soils difficult for the medieval Icelanders apply in large areas of the world today, and the same mix of unanticipated results of past management climate fluctuation, and local and global politics that resulted in stripped pastures and dissipated natural capital is evident in many parts of the modern world. The steady worldwide contraction of the local farming populations holding long-term, fine-scale knowledge of the potentials and vulnerabilities of fields and flocks combined with rapid globalization of ownership and management, raise some of the same issues of managerial detachment and out-of-phase responses that appear in medieval Greenlandic and Icelandic land-holding patterns. As climates shift through a combination of natural and ever-increased human-induced pressures, present-day populations, like the medieval Icelanders, are faced with hard choices and difficult options. The fragile nature of the Icelandic ecosystem

mirrors that of the entire Earth. Although the twentieth-century Icelandic economy has prospered because of industrialization, reduced energy costs, and careful management of its fisheries, the current global fisheries crisis is a matter of serious concern for Icelanders and for all of us (McGoodwin 1990; Pálsson 1991; Vilhjálmsson 1997).

If current projections prove accurate, we face climate change over the next decades on a scale not seen since the cooling of the medieval period, which could possibly be associated with the kind of interseasonal variability that made life so uncertain for the people of the North Atlantic in the past (Wigley 1996). Some regions are likely to become unsafe or prohibitively expensive locations for farms, factories, and homes, as floodplains, valleys, and coastal margins become impacted by increasingly violent and unpredictable weather patterns. Clean water supplies, crop surpluses, energy supplies, and communication systems are all still profoundly affected by environmental variability, and so our ability to predict the direction and magnitude of change becomes an important resource for human survival. In separating short-term weather from a long-term threshold-crossing climate change, modern planners are better equipped to face some of the same problems that in the past confronted the chieftains of Norse Greenland and Iceland. We would do well to listen to and learn from what archaeology, natural science, and history have to tell us about our past and our future. The twelve-hundred-year Norse occupation of the North Atlantic can provide useful case studies for developing more rational policies for sustainable exploitation. Although recent research has emphasized the agrarian side of the Norse North Atlantic economic equation, an equally important area to study is the even more vulnerable northern fisheries, which sustain a far greater population and whose ecological basis is the entire North Atlantic marine system. Our increasingly small and hungry planet needs careful attention.

31 | TRAVEL THE VIKING TRAIL

Tourism and the Viking Heritage

BY IAN A. MORRISON

T HE VIKINGS HAVE A REMARKABLE grip on our imagination. People with little interest in other cultures of a millennium ago are intrigued by them, for the popular image embodies a frisson of sheer excitement. This reputation now extends all the way from Holy Island, England, to Hollywood, California, having persisted from the righteous horror of Lindisfarne monks to the tongue-in-cheek personification by Kirk Douglas in the 1958 movie *The Vikings*.

HERE I LIE, DEAD DRUNK, *HEYNESBÓK*

Tours and cruises that offer opportunities for recreational learning about the Vikings attract those who are simply keen to visit places associated with Viking history. Often, however, those who participate in tours with a Viking theme do have Scandinavian roots. These include people not only from the mainland Viking homelands in Denmark, Norway, and Sweden, but also from parts of the British Isles and the North Atlantic islands, and not least from among the descendants of the many generations of Scandinavians who have settled in recent centuries in the United States, Canada, and Australia. Feelings can run surprisingly strongly and are sometimes expressed with the laconic humor characteristic of the Viking sagas. Thus, in 1992, when Italian-Americans celebrated the quincentennial of Columbus's "discovery" of the New World, a Leif Eriksson faction took up spray cans and graffiti appeared, declaring "Columbus was a FINK." It is not an accident that Leif Ericson Day falls on October 9, three days before Columbus Day.

While some sign up for tours with initial acceptance of the popular image, others are very conscious of the simplistic stereotyping of the Vikings and are keen to explore what is now known of the actual archaeological and historical reality. Some are professional academics or well-informed amateur scholars, who wish to see Viking archaeology and the settings of the sagas firsthand. The great majority of the participants, though enthusiastic, tend to lack prior knowledge of the Norse world. To many, the Vikings are just part of a wide range of interests. Some of these global travelers do four or more trips a year, visiting places as diverse as Bali, Peru, Egypt, and Antarctica.

The emergence of tourism based on special-interest themes is part of the remarkable growth of tourism in general. During the last third of the twentieth century, despite wars, rising fuel prices, and currency upheavals, the tourist industry has grown 1 to 2 percent faster than the global economy. According to the World Travel and Tourism Council, by the close of the 1990s one job in ten is linked to travel and tourism. The World Tourist Organization estimates that by 2010 the number of vacation travelers could top one billion, with spending perhaps exceeding one and a half trillion dollars. Bill Gates of Microsoft has identified tourism as one of three key industries for the twenty-first century. Within this overall pattern, despite the continuing popularity on a massive scale of traditional beach, bar, and disco vacation packages, thematic holidays and study tours are becoming increasingly important, and it is in this context that Viking-based tourism has emerged.

Economic impetus has been given to the development of the Viking theme through the Council of Europe project called Cultural Routes. This project has the political aim of drawing the attention of European citizens to the existence of common cultural heritages that transcend the national boundaries that define the modern countries now grouped within the European Union. The Vikings were selected to be one of several major European ethnocultural entities in which the Council invests considerable sums for researching and publicizing tour routes. While resembling other "Viking trail" enterprises, the priorities in the selection of sites and interpretative centers strictly reflects the goal of creating itineraries that encourage travel across national boundaries for recreational learning.

The Viking Routes project arose from internal political goals within the European Union. A complementary outward-looking ethos is embodied in Viking Heritage, a network administered from Gotland in Sweden. Using both print and electronic media, this network seeks to coordinate the distribution of up-to-date and academically reliable information on the Vikings, not just within the European Union but from Russia to Canada. Since participation in this cooperative venture is open equally to organizations and individuals, it offers a useful resource for study-tour operators and for people who prefer to devise their own itineraries.

The assets upon which Viking-theme tourism is based include the legacy of original features such as archaeological sites, scenery and landscapes with saga associations, and modern presentations that offer additional and complementary attractions. These include museums and heritage centers with reconstructions and sometimes quite colorful reenactments of Viking lifestyles and events. These presentations bring the Vikings to life in a way that undoubtedly contributes a great deal to enhancing the appeal of Viking-based tourism and its capacity for generating revenue.

ROMANTIC ROOTS

One might legitimately ask where this fascination comes from and why it has such a grip on the modern recreational traveler. The answer is linked to the legacy of Viking impacts on Europe during the four hundred years from 750 to 1100, the time known as the Viking Age. Whether as raiders, traders, explorers, or colonizers, the Vikings altered the history and cultures of many areas of the western world and part of northeastern North America. Through history, but especially during the past two decades of the twentieth century, the Viking theme has grown many branches, like Yggdrasil, the tree upon which the Norse god Odin hanged himself to win the magic power of runes. With its trunk central to the mythological world of the Norse, Yggdrasil is indeed deeprooted.

As the eighteenth century moved into the nineteenth, interest in the Vikings was beginning to grow under the stimulus of the Romantic era in the Scandinavian countries and elsewhere. For example, in the British Isles, "Jarlshof" is one of the best-known Viking sites (see Batey and Sheehan, this volume) despite the fact that its name was devised in 1814 by Sir Walter Scott to give color to a scene in his historical novel *The Pirate*. The Viking houses at the site were not excavated until after Scott invented the name.

Among Scandinavians, the "dragon ship" became the quintessential symbol for the Vikings, and in Britain any clinker-built ship remains have long been excitedly ascribed as having Viking origin. As early as 1820, remains of a barge now known to date to the sixteenth century were taken all the way from Kent to London to draw crowds and raise money when exhibited as a "Viking" ship.

Nineteenth-century Norwegian archaeologists can take most credit for developing what have remained two of the key assets contributing to the success of Viking-based tourism: the effective presentation of genuine Viking ships to the general public and the use of replicas to catch popular imagination. The Norwegians set the pace in modern archaeology, at a time when all too many sites were being "excavated" without regard to the stratigraphic relationships of artifacts recovered from them, and only the most durable of finds survived to furnish "cabinets of antiquities." This was still so even late in the century, and even on major projects.

When partially preserved ship remains

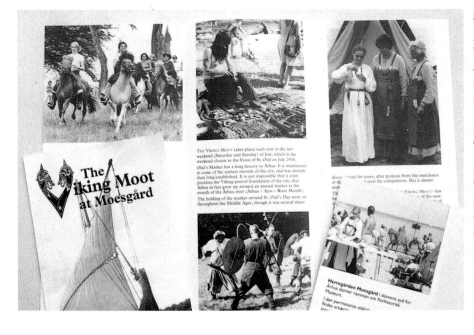

31.1 THE VIKING MOOT AT MOESGÅRD Since 1977 a local Viking Moot (Festival) has been held at Moesgård in Jutland, Denmark, to reenact the Market of St. Olaf's Feast. Replica Viking ships arrive with goods; sporting events, demonstrations, and theatrical events are staged; and reenactments provide entertainment for visitors and participants.

were discovered in a mound at Tune in the Olso Fjord in 1867, however, they were meticulously excavated by Professor Oluf Rygh. He not only recorded the find for academic purposes but also set the precedent from which Viking-based tourism has benefited ever since. He had the remains reinforced so that they could be taken to Oslo for exhibition to the public in a special building. Despite being incomplete, the remains caused a sensation.

The Tune vessel was supplanted in the public eye when the Gokstad and Oseberg ships, which had been much more fully preserved, were skillfully excavated in 1880 and 1904 under the direction of Nicolay Nicolaysen and Gabriel Gustafson. Their names should be better known, since again contemporary state-of-the-art excavation, conservation, curatorial, and display techniques were used not only to comply with academic ethics but also to stimulate and maintain public interest. Providentially, this policy was continued. Earlier displays were consolidated in 1930, when all three ships were exhibited as leading attractions in a marvelous architectural masterpiece, the Oslo Viking Ship Museum.

The use of replicas to catch popular imagination also had an early and impressive start. During the last hundred years, more than thirty Viking ships have been reconstructed. As long ago as the 1890s, a full-sized replica of the Gokstad ship was built and was sailed across the Atlantic by Captain Magnus Andersen, where it became a leading attraction at the 1893 World Columbian Exposition in Chicago (fig. 28.3). Recently this vessel was purchased by a Scandinavian-American group in hopes of exhibiting it on the shore of Lake Michigan on the campus of the Field Museum of Natural History.

MODERN MANIFESTATIONS

Today, ship replicas are built for many purposes, varying from technical research to commercial trips for tourists. Whatever the particular rationale underlying their construction, they still attract public attention and media coverage because of their visual impact and exciting associations. Vessels like the *Gaia*, which undertook a tour of nearly the entire Atlantic Ocean in 1992, sailing from Norway to North America and to South America promoting global environmental values at the time of the Earth Summit in Rio de Janeiro, have served a variety of functions as modern-day Vikings carried messages of exploration, endurance, and self-sufficiency.

In the latter half of the twentieth century, public interest in the Vikings through ship discoveries and activities with replicas received a very significant boost with the recovery of the Skuldelev ships in 1962 and the Danes' subsequent construction of their Viking Ship Museum at Roskilde. Created not only to display the remains but also to provide a center for experimentation and reconstruction, this enterprise has expanded the scope of museum learning. Besides having become a major tourist destination in itself, its influence is now intercontinental through multilingual publications, television coverage, and Internet programming.

Ship remains and replicas are just part of an extensive range of institutions, exhibitions, and events that can help generate income by attracting visitor. Some of the most successful attractions are, however, run efficiently by enthusiasts who celebrate their Viking heritage without seeking any personal profit whatsoever. For more than twenty years (since 1977) at Moesgård in Jutland, Denmark, an annual Viking Moot (Festival) has reenacted the Market of St. Olaf's Feast (fig. 31.1). Accurate longship replicas (from the Århus Viking-ship Guild) sail in bearing exotic goods. Fighting skills are demonstrated, including feats by a group of Danes who breed Icelandic horses and school them to reenact events of kinds described in the

31.3

31.2 CRUISE SHIP AT BRATTAHLID
Each year cruise ships deliver
thousands of tourists to out-of-the-
way Viking sites from Norway to
Newfoundland. A favorite stop is
Brattahlid, Erik the Red's farm site in
Narsarssuak, southwestern Greenland,
where visitors can see the foundations of his longhouse and the
reconstructed church similar to that
he built for his Christian wife
Thjodhild.

31.3 GREENLANDERS IN TRADITIONAL
COSTUME
Tourists visiting Viking locations in
Greenland usually call at towns and
villages where they meet people and
learn about local history and modern
life—with a heavy slant toward the
exotic. These young Native
Greenlanders pose after performing a
traditional dance in Nanortalik,
southwest Greenland, in 1995. In
keeping with tradition, the women
wear elaborately beaded costumes
and the young man wears dark
trousers and a simple white anorak
(parka).

sagas. During the Moot, Viking-design craft
goods are made in demonstrations of authentic
techniques and then traded as souvenirs. Appropriate food and drink is consumed. Admis-
sion is free, and the profits from booths go
entirely toward materials and equipment.

TOURISM AND ARCHAEOLOGY

There is a wide spectrum of styles used to
present the resource base for Viking tourism.
This extends from theme park–like interpretations with much use of replicas and electronic media but no original structures or
artifacts at all to actual archaeological sites
and locations associated with sagas, at some
of which artificial enhancement is minimal
or absent. Many of these approaches are
extremely effective, as in York, England, in
Hvalsey, Greenland, and in L'Anse aux Meadows, Newfoundland.

The results of the archaeological excavations at Jorvik, the Viking town and trading
center at York in northern England are presented in ways designed to cater to tourists
with different interests. The techniques used
include sophisticated interactive electronic
databases giving access to the actual details of
structures and finds excavated as well as a
very popular tram ride through a dramatic,
full-scale village reconstruction, replete with
talking mannequins, sound effects, and even
appropriate smells. The Jorvik Museum,
which is built inside the excavation site
beneath a basement in downtown York, has
received 11.7 million visitors since it opened
and currently draws more than half a million
visitors each year (fig. 31.4). It raises enough

income in tickets and sales to support a major
archaeological research and education program that has become a model for archaeological heritage programs throughout the
world. Overall, Jorvik ranks in effectiveness
with similarly holistic presentations in
Scandinavia, for example, at Ribe, Firkat, or
Lindholm Høje in Denmark; Bryggen or
Bigdoy in Norway; or Birka in Sweden.

Hvalsey, a ruin of a medieval church in
southwest Greenland, is very different.
Without any inhabitants, let alone tourist
hotels, it cannot be reached by road. Because
there is no airfield and the bay is too shallow
for cruise ships, landings are made via inflatable boats, which sometimes encounter the
whales after which the settlement was
named. There is no heritage center, yet this
can be one of the most evocative sites for
those on a Viking tour simply because of its
untouched state. Here, some of the last
Norse people in Greenland survived into the
fifteenth century and arguably into the lifetime of Columbus. Their church looms full
height through the mist, its masonry essentially intact because it was of no interest to
the Inuit, and no later European settlers
came to recycle the stonework.

Nearby, Brattahlid draws many more
visitors because it was Erik the Red's farm,
and it is undoubtedly an economic asset for
Viking-based tourism (fig. 31.2). Despite the
increase in visitors during the final decades
of the twentieth century, however, little was
reinvested in the site itself to clarify what is
there, either by research or presentation.
Well-informed travelers know that fresh

31.4 THE JORVIK VIKING MUSEUM
One of the most popular Viking attractions anywhere is the museum built upon and into the old Viking settlement of Jorvik in downtown York, England. Jorvik has received twelve million visitors since opening and attracts about half a million people each year, young and old. Once inside, the visitor experiences a time warp and travels through the reconstructed Viking village, replete with smells and sound effects. The proceeds from the museum and shop finance a world-class research and educational program.

excavations using modern techniques are necessary if major questions about the nature of Erik's original settlement are to be answered. The attention of those who come as less-knowledgeable tourists is caught by substantial stone-built structures, but these date to two centuries after Erik's time. The on-site museum does not explain this: it commemorates not Erik, but a twentieth-century sheep farmer. Not all tourist groups get time to visit the meager display about the Vikings, since it is not at the site itself but lies on the far side of Erik's Fjord, in a hut left over from World War II. Recently a plan for the development of the site as a historic place has been initiated. Reconstructions by Icelandic architectural historians of the longhouse and tiny church that the pagan Erik built for his Christian wife, Thjodhild, were installed at the site in the summer of 1999.

L'Anse aux Meadows provides a contrasting example of how a World Heritage Site may be managed to propagate Viking-based tourism. Because it is the only definitely accepted Norse settlement in America, the remains have not been overbuilt by reconstructions. They have been left in the state in which they appeared when discovered by Helge and Anne Stine Ingstad in 1960, accessible for future archaeological work as new questions and techniques evolve. Immediately adjacent to the site, however, is a full-size reconstruction of characteristic buildings in which local Newfoundlanders reenact domestic lifestyle and crafts based on archaeological finds. This reconstruction is updated as research proceeds. A combined museum and interpreta-

tive center exhibits the key finds and has models and videos that illustrate the results of scientific and historical studies (fig. 31.8). The center is built unobtrusively into a hill that gives the visitor a view of the site's relationship to the surrounding landscape.

TOURISM BOOM

Modern Viking tourism benefits from the wide variety of modern transport facilities now increasingly available even in remote regions of the North Atlantic. Air travel allows increasingly affordable worldwide commuting to join land tours or cruises. Local sightseeing by helicopter is sometimes an option in most of the countries where Viking tours are run because helicopters are now in routine use by the local communities. In the Faeroes, for instance, helicopter services are listed in the same integrated time-table booklet as buses and ferryboats. Cruise ships have proliferated. Some are purpose-built, but many of those used in Viking seas are converted Russian vessels hired or sold off after the Soviet Union disbanded. The use of fleets of inflatable boats in conjunction with the cruise ships now gives access to many coastal and island Viking sites that it would otherwise be impracticable for tourists to reach. This is true for some Viking sites in Scotland's Hebrides and in Greenland. Land transport has developed too, with small groups getting access to off-road sites by means of sport utility vehicles. Stöng, one of the more famous Viking archaeological sites in Iceland, lies in a valley covered in ash by an eruption of Hekla, preserving the site remarkably. This major Viking site is unfortunately located in the middle of a deserted, hostile environment accessible only to four-wheel-drive vehicles. To rectify the situation, the Icelandic government built a reconstruction of this Viking longhouse a few miles from the original site in a friendlier environment. It was inaugurated in 1974 to commemorate eleven hundred years of Viking settlement in Iceland. This reconstruction appears on the routes of some regular tour buses, and so an ample parking lot is provided at the base of the site. At the L'Anse aux Meadows site on the west coast of Newfoundland, huge streams of tourists now visit by car and busloads over the highly publicized Viking Trail travel route, with numbers climbing from five thousand to fifteen thousand in the past several years.

31.5 Up-Helly-Aa Boat Burning
One of the more spectacular Viking reenactments is the annual Viking boat burning staged each year in Lerwick in the Shetland Islands. As festivals go, this one has almost ancient roots: it dates to the nineteenth century when it was inspired by the adventures of Earl Rognvald in Joseph Anderson's translation of the *Saga of the Orkneys.*

Tourism and Local Identity

Viking heritage is not merely something that interests people of an antiquarian turn of mind, but it can mean much to present-day fishermen and midwives, bank managers, and children. One of the most spectacular of such assertions of identity is Up Helly Aa, an annual festival during which a full-size replica of a longship is burnt at Lerwick in Shetland (fig. 31.5). Until 1468 to 1469, when the king of Norway pawned the isles to Scotland, Shetland had been an integral part of Scandinavia. Even today many Shetlanders still talk of "going to Scotland" with disdain. Although it does embody elements from traditional midwinter fire festivals, the burning of the dragon ship only dates from the late nineteenth century, when it was inspired by Joseph Anderson's translation of the *Saga of the Orkneys.* This translation caught the imagination of the Shetlanders with its graphic account of the wrecking of Earl Rognvald near Lerwick. Despite its relative recency, this is not a pageant staged to make money from tourists. Few come north in the darkness of January (Shetland is on the same latitude as

Greenland's Cape Farewell). The eagle-winged helmets may not be authentic, but the Shetlanders' passion is. Much money is spent not only on the longship, but also on the costumes, which often cost several thousand dollars each. Each year's videotape of the Guiser Jarl's procession and the burning of the ship is ordered by families of Shetland lineage from Seattle to Sidney.

While this festival is the most spectacular manifestation of the Shetlanders perception of their identity, it is by no means the only one. The *Shetland Times* in Lerwick, for example, not only stocks a comprehensive range of international material on the Vikings but produces a notable list of its own publications. This pattern is repeated very impressively by other island communities whose small populations assert their identities by emphasizing their Viking lineage. Hafna Fjord in Iceland, not far from downtown Reykjavík, hosts an annual Viking festival on the grounds of a Viking museum. Though not a museum in the sense of a collection of verified archaeological pieces, it does try to capture the essence of the Vikings. While the local townspeople have given it an honored location in the center of the harbor, other Icelandic communities view it as commercialization of a rather proud and dignified tradition of Viking law and literature. Until recently, this tourist location was one of the few easily accessible and understandable Viking destinations in Iceland. With the onslaught of attention revolving around the year 2000 in Iceland, a new Viking interpretive park is being planned in Thingvellir, presumably more dignified than the events at Hafna Fjord but more lively than the current lack of Viking-based interpretation there. Similar events are staged on the other side of the ocean as well, seen in such local events at the annual Viking Parade in the small town of Brooklin, Maine, in which residents become revelers celebrating their concocted visions of a truly mythical Viking past. Many more such events are staged in villages and towns between here and northern Newfoundland; most have the purpose of luring and entertaining motorized visitors interested in Viking and other attractions (fig. 31.3).

Viking Publications

The local publishing achievements of Shetland and Orkney, the Faeroes, Iceland, and

31.6 Museum Replicas
The spectacular Lewis Chessmen (fig. 23.1) are also reproduced in facsimile, so almost everyone can have some Viking art in their own home or on their chessboard!

31.7 VIKING REENACTORS
Several years ago Parks Canada began to use reenactors to help interpret the L'Anse aux Meadows Viking site in northern Newfoundland to the growing numbers of visitors attracted to the only confirmed Viking site in North America. In former years, this reconstruction greeted the travel-weary visitor in silence. Today one encounters homespun humor as local Newfoundlanders bring Vikings to life at the site where they began—and may have ended—their North American adventure one thousand years ago.

31.8 "IN-YOUR-FACE" VIKINGS
The L'Anse aux Meadows site is literally at the end of the road—the northeasternmost location on the North American continent that can be driven to by car. Getting there is part of the fun. Upon arriving visitors are transported back to a time that was very different from today. L'Anse aux Meadows is not only a world-class archaeological site; it is a state of mind. Parks Canada and their staff shake visitors by the shoulders and say, "Hello, Leif! You've come a long way! Welcome to America!"

Greenland are truly remarkable in light of the economic constraints to which they are subject. Their books, journals, and less formal publications on the Vikings and their legacies command respect for their sheer range of coverage, their high academic standards, and their production quality.

Viking-oriented foreigners benefit, because many of these local publishers seek to supplement income from their dedicated home markets by targeting visiting tourists through multilingual editions and by circulating mail-order catalogues worldwide (contact addresses are available through their consulates and via the Internet). The viability of small publishers with this degree of idealism is surprising, not least in a world where the emotions of identity are rather more commonly focused on sports allegiances than on affinities for Viking roots. Interest in Viking literature hardly registers on the American side; here, myth, kitsch, and entertainment value override any latent tourist interests in Viking history (Ward, this volume).

The specialist publishing achievement of these small countries is certainly impressive, but in sheer volume of output it is far outstripped by the countries of mainland Scandinavia, the British Isles, and North America. Linked in international conglomerates and with powerful marketing organizations, their publishers are able to finance a wide range of often sumptuously illustrated books on the Vikings in the confidence that they can sell massive print runs. That this confidence has proved justified in hard economic times confirms the strength of the grip the Vikings exert on our imagination.

This grip is twofold. On the one hand, there is the undeniably exciting stereotype of seafaring adventurers who salted ruthlessness with laconic humor. On the other hand, paradoxically, there is the attraction of the richly creative antithesis to their destructiveness. This creativity is seen in their literature, in the technical sophistication and aesthetic quality of their artifacts (fig. 31.6), and in their development of long-distance trade routes with urban mercantile centers. The Cultural Routes project highlights this development of trade routes as an enduring Viking legacy relevant even to the cohesion of the present-day European Union.

Even a millennium after Leif Eriksson sailed west, his exploits and those of his countrymen still command our attention and fire our imagination, which is why Viking-based tourism continues to burgeon.

Contributors

SÍMUN V. ARGE
Faeroese Historical Museum, Tórshavn

JETTE ARNEBORG
Danish National Museum, Copenhagen

COLLEEN E. BATEY
Glasgow Art Gallery and Museums, Scotland

JOEL BERGLUND
Greenland National Museum and Archives, Nuuk

PAUL C. BUCKLAND
University of Sheffield, England

ARNE EMIL CHRISTENSEN
Viking Ship Museum, Oslo

STEVEN L. COX
Maine State Museum, Augusta

TORSTEN EDGREN
National Board of Antiquities, Finland

WILLIAM W. FITZHUGH
National Museum of Natural History,
Smithsonian Institution

ANNE-SOFIE GRÄSLUND
University of Uppsala, Sweden

HANS CHRISTIAN GULLØV
Danish National Museum, Copenhagen

LOTTE HEDEAGER
University of Oslo, Norway

JOHANNES HERTZ
Danish National Museum, Copenhagen

LARS JØRGENSEN
Danish National Museum, Copenhagen

SIGRID H. H. KALAND
University of Bergen Museum, Norway

STEPHEN LORING
National Museum of Natural History,
Smithsonian Institution

NIELS LYNNERUP
The Panum Institute, Copenhagen

IRMELIN MARTENS
University Museum of National Antiquities, Oslo

THOMAS H. McGOVERN
Hunter College, City University of New York

DOUGLAS McNAUGHTON
Independent Scholar, Catharpin, Virginia

CHRISTOPHER D. MORRIS
University of Glasgow, Scotland

IAN A. MORRISON
University of Edinburgh, Scotland

DANIEL ODESS
National Museum of Natural History,
Smithsonian Institution

ASTRID E. J. OGILVIE
University of Colorado, Boulder

HARALDUR ÓLAFSSON
University of Iceland, Reykjavík

CARIN ORRLING
Museum of National Antiquities, Stockholm

HANS CHRISTIAN PETERSEN
Independent Scholar, Nuuk, Greenland

NEIL S. PRICE
University of Uppsala, Sweden

PETER H. SAWYER
University of Leeds, England

PETER SCHLEDERMANN
University of Calgary, Alberta

KIRSTEN A. SEAVER
Independent Scholar, Palo Alto, California

JOHN SHEEHAN
National University of Ireland, Dublin

GÍSLI SIGURÐSSON
Árni Magnússon Institute, Reykjavík

KEVIN P. SMITH
Buffalo Museum of Science, Buffalo

PATRICIA D. SUTHERLAND
Canadian Museum of Civilization, Hull, Québec

HELGI THORLÁKSSON
University of Iceland, Reykjavík

ORRI VÉSTEINSSON
Institute of Archaeology, Reykjavík

BIRGITTA LINDEROTH WALLACE
Parks Canada, Halifax

ELISABETH I. WARD
National Museum of Natural History,
Smithsonian Institution

BIBLIOGRAPHY

compiled by
Erin M. Sweeney

Abels, Richard

1997 English logistics and military administration, 871–1066: The impact of the Viking wars. In *Military aspects of Scandinavian society in a European perspective, A.D. 1–1300: Papers from an international research seminar at the Danish National Museum, Copenhagen, 2–4 May 1996*, edited by Anne Nørgård Jørgensen and Birthe L. Clausen, 257–265. Studies in Archaeology and History 2. Copenhagen: Danish National Museum.

Aðalsteinsdóttir, Silja, and Helgi Thorláksson (eds.)

1983 *Förändringar i kvinnors villkor under medeltiden: Uppsatser framlagda vid ett kvinnohistoriskt symposium i Skálholt, Island, 22-25 juni 1981* (Changes in the role of women during the Middle Ages: Papers presented at a symposium with a women's historical perspective in Skálholt, Iceland, 22–25 June 1981). Ritsafn sagnfraedistofnunar 9. Reykjavík and Sagnfraedistofnun háskóla Íslands: Agentur, Sögufélag.

Aðalsteinsson, Jón Hnefill

1978 *Under the cloak: The acceptance of Christianity in Iceland with particular reference to the religious attitudes prevailing at the time.* Studia Ethnologica Upsaliensia 4. Stockholm: Almqvist & Wiksell International.

Adam, von Bremen

1959 *History of the archbishops of Hamburg-Bremen.* Records of Civilization, Sources and Studies 53. Edited and translated by Francis J. Tschan. New York: Columbia University Press.

Aðils, Jón J.

1926–27 *Den danske monopolhandel på Island 1602–1787* (The Danish trade monopoly on Iceland 1602–1787). Copenhagen: Dansk-Islandsk samfund med støtte fra Grossersocietetet og Dansk-Islandsk Forbundsfond.

Albaugh, William A.

1960 *Confederate edged weapons.* New York: Harper.

Albrethsen, Svend E., and Christian Keller

1986 The use of the saeter in medieval Norse farming in Greenland. *Arctic Anthropology* 23 (1–2): 91–107.

Albrethsen, Svend E., and Gudmundur Ólafsson

1998 A Viking age hall. In *Man, culture, and environment in ancient Greenland*, edited by Jette Arneborg and Hans Christian Gulløv, 19–26. Danish Polar Center Publication 4. Copenhagen: Danish National Museum and Danish Polar Center.

Almgren, Bertil

1987 *Die Datierung bronzezeitlicher Felszeichnungen in Westschweden.* (The dating of Bronze-Age petroglyphs in western Sweden). Acta Musei antiquitatum septentrionalium Regiae Universitatis Uppsaliensis 6. Uppsala: Uppsala Universitets Museum för Nordiska Fornsaker.

Alonso-Núñez, J. M.

1987 Jordanes and Procopius on northern Europe. *Nottingham Medieval Studies* 31: 1–16.

1988 Roman knowledge of Scandinavia in the Imperial period. *Oxford Journal of Archaeology* 7(1): 47–64.

Alsford, Stephen (ed.)

1993 *The Meta Incognita Project: Contributions to field studies.* Mercury Series Directorate Paper 6. Hull, Québec: Canadian Museum of Civilization.

Ambrosiani, Björn, and Bo G. Erikson

1994 *Birka. Vikingastaden* (Birka. The Viking town). Vol. 4. Höganäs: Wiken.

Amorosi, Thomas

1992 Climate impact and human response in northeast Iceland: Archaeological investigations at Svalbarð 1986–1988. In *Norse and later settlement and subsistence in the North Atlantic*, edited by Christopher D. Morris and D. James Rackham, 103–138. Glasgow: University of Glasgow, Department of Archaeology.

1996 Icelandic zooarchaeology: New data applied to issues of historical ecology, paleoeconomy, and global change. Ph.D. diss., City University of New York.

Amorosi, Thomas, Paul C. Buckland, Guðmundur Ólafsson, Jon P. Sadler, and Peter Skidmore

1992 Site status and the palaeoecological record: A discussion of results from Bessastaðir, Iceland. In *Norse and later settlement and subsistence in the North Atlantic*, edited by Christopher D. Morris and D. James Rackham, 169–192. Glasgow: University of Glasgow, Department of Archaeology.

Amorosi, Thomas, and Thomas H. McGovern

1995 A preliminary report of an archaeofauna from Granastaðir, Eyjafjarðarsðsla, northern Iceland. In *The settlement of Iceland; A critical approach: Granastaðir and the ecological heritage*, edited by Bjarni F. Einarsson, 181–188. Reykjavík: Hið IslenskaBókmenntafélag.

Andersen, Erik

1995 The use of wood in boatbuilding. In *Shipshape: Essays for Ole Crumlin-Pedersen: On the occasion of his 60th anniversary, February 24th 1995*, edited by Olaf Olsen, Han Skamby Madsen, and Flemming Rieck. Roskilde, Denmark: Viking Ship Museum.

Andersen, Erik Langer

1982 De norrøne stednavne i Østerbygden (The Norse place-naming [toponym] of the Eastern Settlement). *Grønland* 5/6/7: 163–176.

Andersen, Erik, and Claus Malmros

1993 Ship's parts found in the Viking settlements in Greenland. Preliminary assessments and wood-diagnoses. In *Viking voyages to North America*, edited by Birthe L. Clausen, 118–122. Roskilde, Denmark: Viking Ship Museum.

Anderson, Rasmus B.

1883 *America not discovered by Columbus.* 3d ed. Chicago: S.C. Griggs and Company.

1910 Draw your own conclusions. *Minneapolis Journal,* 2 June.

1920 Another view of the Kensington rune stone. *The Wisconsin Magazine of History* 3(4): 413–419.

Anderson, Wilford R.

1996 *Norse America: Tenth century onward.* Evanston, Ill.: Valhalla Press.

Andreasen, Claus

1982 Nipaitsoq og Vesterbygden (Nipaitsoq and the Western Settlement). *Grønland* 5/6/7: 177–188.

Andrén, Anders

1985 *Den urbana scenen: Städer och samhälle i det medeltida Danmark* (The urban scene: Cities and societies in Middle Age Denmark). Acta Archaeologica Lundensia 13. Bonn, Germany: R. Habelt.

1989 The early town in Scandinavia. In *The birth of Europe: Archaeology and social development in the first millennium A.D.*, edited by Klavs Randsborg. Analecta Romana Instituti Danici. Supplementum 16. Rome: L'Erma di Bretschneider.

Anthony, David W.

1990 Migration in archaeology: The baby and the bathwater. *American Anthropologist* 92(4): 895–914.

Appelgren-Kivalo, Hjalmar

1907 *Suomalaisia pukuja myöhemmältä rautakaudelta. Finnische Trachten aus der jüngeren Eisenzeit* (Finnish costumes from the late Iron Age). Helsinki: n.p.

Appelt, Martin, Hans Christian Gulløv, and Hans Kapel

1998 The gateway to Greenland: Report on the field season 1996. In *Man, culture, and environment in ancient Greenland*, edited by Jette Arneborg and Hans Christian Gulløv, 136–137. Danish Polar Center Publication 4. Copenhagen: Danish National Museum and Danish Polar Center.

Åqvist, Cecilia, with Lena Flodin

1992 Pollista and Sanda—two thousand-year-old settlements in the Mälaren region. In *Rescue and research: Reflections of society in Sweden 700–1700 A.D.*, edited by Lars Ersgård, Marie Holmström, and Kristina Lamm, 310–333. Skrifter 2. Stockholm: Riksantikvarieämbetet.

Arbman, Holger

1937 *Schweden und das karolingische reich* (Sweden and the Carolingian Empire). Stockholm: Wahlström & Widstrand.

1940–43 *Birka. Die Gräber* (Birka. The graves). Kungliga Vitterhets Historie och Antikvitets Akademien. Uppsala: Almqvist & Wiksells.

1969 Armes scandinaves de l'époque Viking en France (Scandinavian weapons from the Viking Age in France). *Meddelanden från Lunds Universitets Historiska Museum* 1966–68/1969: 163–202.

Arge, Símun V.

1991 The landnám in the Faroes. *Arctic Anthropology* 28(2): 101–20.

Arge, Símun V., and Niels Hartmann

1992 The burial site of við Kirkjugarð in the village of Sandur, Sandoy. *Fróðskaparrit: Annales Societatis Scientiarum Færoensis* 38/39: 5–22.

Armitage, Peter

1991 *The Innu (The Montagnais-Naskapi).* New York: Chelsea House Publishers.

Arnalds, Olafur, Asa L. Aradóttir, and Ingvi Thorsteinsson

1987 The nature and restoration of denuded areas in Iceland. *Arctic and Alpine Research* 19(4): 518–525.

Arneborg, Jette

1988 Nordboerne i Grønland. Et bidrag til diskussionen om eskimoernes rolle i Vesterbygdens affolkning (The Norse in Greenland. A contribution to the discussion on the role of the Eskimos in the depopulation of the Western Settlement). *Hikuin* 14: 297–310.

1989 Nordboarkæologiens historie—og fremtid (Norse archaeology's history—and future). *Grønland* 37: 121–137.

1991 The Roman church in Norse Greenland. *Acta Archaeologica* 61: 142–51.

1993 Contact between Eskimos and Norsemen in Greenland (in Danish). In *Beretning fra tolvte tværfaglige vikingesymposium Aarhus Universitet 1993*, edited by Else Roesdahl and Preben Meulengracht Sørensen, 23–35. Aarhus, Denmark: Hikuin.

1996a Burgunderhuer, baskere og døde nordboer i Herjolfsnæs, Grønland (Burgundian caps, Basques, and dead Norsemen at Herjolfsnæs, Greenland). In *Nationalmuseets arbejdsmark*, edited by Steen Hvass, 75–83. Copenhagen: Danish National Museum

1996b Exchanges between Norsemen and Eskimos in Greenland. In *Cultural and social research in Greenland 95/ 96: Essays in honour of Robert Petersen*, edited by Birgitte Jacobsen, 11–21. Nuuk: Ilisimatusarfik/Atuakkiorfik.

1996c Greenland, the Norse colonies at the end of the world. In *Margrete I: Regent of the North*, edited by Poul Grinder-Hansen, 196–200. Copenhagen: Danish National Museum.

1997 Cultural borders: Reflections on Norse-Eskimo interaction. In *Fifty years of arctic research: Anthropological studies from Greenland to Siberia*, edited by Rolf Gilberg and Hans Christian Gulløv, 41–46. Ethnographical Series 18. Copenhagen: Department of Ethnography, Danish National Museum.

1998a The High Arctic "Utmark" of the Norse Greenlanders. In *Outland use in preindustrial Europe*, edited by Hans Andersson, Lars Ersgard, and Eva Svensson, 156–166. Lund Studies in Medieval Archaeology 20. Lund: Institute of Archaeology, Lund University.

1998b The Farm Beneath the Sand, summary. In *Man, culture, and environment in ancient Greenland*, edited by Jette Arneborg and Hans Christian Gulløv, 208–209. Danish Polar Center Publication 4. Copenhagen: Danish National Museum and Danish Polar Center.

Arneborg, Jette, and Hans Christian Gulløv (eds.)

1998 *Man, culture, and environment in ancient Greenland.* Danish Polar Center Publication 4. Copenhagen: Danish National Museum and Danish Polar Center.

Arneborg, Jette, Jan Heinemeier, Niels Lynnerup, Henrik L. Nielsen, Niels Rud, and Árnð E. Sveinbjörnsdóttir

1999 Change of diet of the Greenland Vikings determined from stable carbon isotope analysis and 14c dating of their bones. *Radiocarbon* 41(2): 157–168.

Asbjørnsen, Peter Christen, and Jørgen Moe

1982 *Norwegian folk tales: From the collection of Peter Christen Asbjørnsen and Jørgen Moe.* Translated by Pat Shaw Iversen and Carl Norman. New York: Pantheon Books.

Atkinson, T. C., K. R. Briffa, and G. R. Coope

1987 Seasonal temperatures in Britain during the past 22,000 years, reconstructed using beetle remains. *Nature* 325(6105): 587–592.

Auger, Réginald, Michel Blackburn, and William W. Fitzhugh

1993 Martin Frobisher's base camp on Kodlunarn Island: A two-year time capsule in the history of technology. In *The Meta Incognita Project: Contributions to field studies*, edited by Stephen Alsford, 55–80. Mercury Series Directorate Paper 6. Hull, Québec: Canadian Museum of Civilization.

Axtell, James

1985 *The invasion within: The contest of cultures in colonial North America.* New York: Oxford University Press.

Babcock, William H.

1913 *Early Norse visits to North America.* Smithsonian Miscellaneous Collections v. 59, no. 19. Washington, D.C.: Smithsonian Institution.

Balslev-Jørgensen, J.

1953 The Eskimo skeleton. *Meddeleser om Grønland* 146(2): 1–154.

Barber, Peter

1999 *Catalog for the Hereford exhibit.* Hereford, England: Hereford Cathedral.

Barka, Norman F.

1965 Historic sites archaeology at Portland Point, New Brunswick, Canada, 1631–c. 1850 A.D. Master's thesis, Harvard University.

Barlow, L. K., J. C. Rogers, M. C. Serreze, and R. G. Barry

1997a Aspects of climate variability in the North Atlantic sector: discussion and relation to the Greenland Ice Sheet Project 2 high-resolution isotopic signal. *Journal of Geophysical Research* 102(C12): 26.333–344.

Barlow, L. K., Jon P. Sadler, Astrid E. J. Ogilvie, Paul C. Buckland, Thomas Amorosi, J. H. Ingimundarson, P. Skidmore, Andrew J. Dugmore, and Thomas H. McGovern

1997b Interdisciplinary investigations of the end of the Norse Western Settlement in Greenland. *The Holocene* 7(4): 489–500.

Bates, David

1982 *Normandy before 1066.* London: Longman.

Baudou, Evert

1995 Norrlands forntid: ett historiskt perpektiv (The prehistory of Norrland: A historical perspective). Bjästa: Sweden: CEWE-förlaget.

Baynes-Cope, Arthur D.

1974 The scientific examination of the Vinland Map at the research laboratory of the British Museum. *The Geographical Journal* 140(2): 208–211.

Bengtsson, Frans G.

1973 *The long ships: A saga of the Viking Age.* Translated by Michael Meyer. Geneva: Editor-Service.

Bencard, Mogens, Lise B. Jørgensen, and Helge B. Madsen

1991 *Ribe excavations 1970–76.* Vol. 4. Esbjerg, Denmark: Sydjysk Universitetsforlag.

Bendixen, K.

1985 Skandinaviske fund af sceattas (Sceattas found in Scandinavia). *Hikuin* 11: 33–40.

Bennike, Pia

1985 *Paleopathology of Danish skeletons: A comparative study of demography, disease, and injury.* Copenhagen: Akademisk Forlag.

Berglund, Joel

1981 Vinlandsspil (Vineland arrow). *Skalk* 1: 28–30.

1986 The decline of the Norse settlements in Greenland. *Arctic Anthropology* 23(1–2): 109–135.

1988 *Herjolfsnæs: Kirken ved havet* (Herjolfsnes—the church by the sea). Nanortalik: Nanortalik kommune.

1991 Displacements in the building-over of the Eastern Settlement, Greenland. *Acta Archaeologica* 61: 151–157.

1998a The excavations at the Farm Beneath the Sand, introduction. In *Man, culture, and environment in ancient Greenland*, edited by Jette Arneborg and Hans Christian Gulløv, 7–13. Danish Polar Center Publication 4. Copenhagen: Danish National Museum and Danish Polar Center.

1998b Christian symbols. In *Man, culture, and environment in ancient Greenland*, edited by Jette Arneborg and Hans Christian Gulløv, 48–54. Danish Polar Center Publication 4. Copenhagen: Danish National Museum and Danish Polar Center.

Bergthórsson, Páll

1969 An estimate of drift ice and temperature in Iceland in 1000 years. *Jökull* 19: 94–101.

1997 *Vínlandsgátan* (The Vinland riddle). Reykjavík: Mál og menning.

Bertelsen, Reidar

1979 Farm mounds in North Norway: A review of recent research. *Norwegian Archaeological Review* 12: 48–56.

1985 *Lofoten og Vesterålens historie* bd. 1 (The history of Lofoten Islands and Vesterålen, vol. 1). Oslo: Kommunene i Lofoten og Vesterålen.

1997 Kystfolket i jernalder og mellomalder. Fiskebønder eller bondefiskere? (The coastal dwellers in the Iron and Middle Ages. Fishing farmers or farming fishermen?). In *Arkeologi og kystkultur: foredrag ved seminaret* (Archaeology and coastal culture: Lecture from the seminar), edited by Helge Sørheim. Ålesund: Sunnmøre Museum.

Biemann, Hans-Peter

1977 *The Vikings of '76.* Cambridge, MA: Biemann.

Bigelow, Gerald F.

1991 The Norse of the North Atlantic conference. *Acta Archaeologica* 61: 1–5.

Bjørgo, Tore

1986 Mountain archaeology. Preliminary results from Nyset-Steggje. *Norwegian Archaeological Review* 19(2): 122–127.

Bjørnbo, Axel A.

1912 Cartographia Groenlandica. *Meddelelser om Grønland* 48: 1–332.

Björnsson, Björn Th.

1984 *Thingvellir, staðir og leiðir* (Thingvellir, places and paths). Reykjavík: Bókaútgáfa Menningarsjóðs.

Blair, Claude

1962 *European and American arms, c. 1100–1850.* New York: Crown Publishers.

Blegen, Theodore C.

1968 *The Kensington runestone: New light on an old riddle.* St. Paul: Minnesota Historical Society.

Blom, Grete Authén

1956–78 Köpman (Merchant). In *Kulturhistorisk leksikon for nordisk middelalder fra vikingetid til reformationstid 10* (Cultural encyclopedia for the Nordic Middle Ages to the Reformation 10), 118–20. Copenhagen: Rosenkilde og Bagger.

Bobé, Louis (ed.)

1936 *Diplomatarium groenlandicum 1492–1814* (Documents pertaining to Greenland 1492–1814). Copenhagen: C.A. Reitzel.

Böcher, Jens

1998 Insect remains from Asummiut. In *Man, culture, and environment in ancient Greenland*, edited by Jette Arneborg and Hans Christian Gulløv, 133–135. Danish Polar Center Publication 4. Copenhagen: Danish National Museum and Danish Polar Center.

Böcher, Jens, and Ole Bennike

1996 Early Holocene insect and plant remains from Jameson Land, East Greenland. *Boreas* 25(3): 187–194.

Boëthius, Johannes

1906 Dalska runinskrifter från nyare tid (Dalecarlia runic inscriptions from modern times). *Fornvännen* 1: 63–69.

Bolin, S.

1952 *Skattpenning och Plogpenning* (Tax money and plow money). Lund: Nordiska historikermötet i Göteborg.

Bonde, Niels, and Arne Emil Christensen

1993 Dendrochronological dating of the Viking Age ship burials at Oseberg, Gokstad, and Tune, Norway. *Antiquity* 67(256): 575–583.

Born, Erik W., Mads P. Heide-Jørgensen, and Rolph A. Davis

1994 The Atlantic walrus (*Odobenus rosmarus rosmarus*) in West Greenland. In *Meddelelser om Grønland: Bioscience* 40: 1–33.

Bourque, Bruce J.

1989 Ethnicity on the Maritime peninsula, 1600–1759. *Ethnohistory* 36(3): 257–284.

Bourque, Bruce J., and Steven L. Cox

1981 Maine State Museum investigation of the Goddard site, 1979. *Man in the Northeast* 22: 3–27.

Breckenridge, R. W.

1955 Norse halberds. *American Anthropologist* 57: 129–131.

Brett, Michael

1978 The Arab conquest and the rise of Islam in North Africa. In *The Cambridge history of Africa*, vol. 2, 490–555. Cambridge: Cambridge University Press.

Broadbent, Noel D.

1987 *Iron Age and medieval seal hunting sites: Archaeological investigations at Bjuröklubb, Västerbotten, Northern Sweden.* Research Reports 5. Umeå: Center for Arctic Cultural Research, Umeå University.

Brøgger, Anton W., Hjalmar J. Falk, and Haakon Shetelig

1917 *Osebergfundet: Utgit av den Norske stat* (The Oseberg excavation). Kristania: Universitetets Oldsaksamling.

Brøgger, Anton W., and Haakon Shetelig

1951 *The Viking ships, their ancestry, and evolution.* Oslo: Dreyer.

Brøndsted, Johannes

1951 Problemet om nordboer i Nordamerika før Columbus. (The question of the Norsemen in North America before Columbus). *Aarbøger for Nordisk Oldkyndighed og Historie* 1950: 1–152.

1954 Norsemen in North America before Columbus. In *Annual Report of the Board of Regents of the Smithsonian Institution*, 367–405. Washington, D.C.: Smithsonian Institution.

Brooks, Charles T.

1851 *The controversy touching the Old Stone Mill, in the Town of Newport, Rhode Island.* Newport, R.I.: C. E. Hammett, Jr.

Brooks, Nicholas P.

1979 England in the ninth century: The crucible of defeat. *Transactions of the Royal Historical Society* 29: 1–20.

Brèoste, Kurt, Knud Fischer-Møller, and P. O. Pedersen

1941 The mediaeval Norsemen at Gardar; anthropological investigation. *Meddelelser om Grønland* 89(3): 1–62.

Brumfiel, Elizabeth M., and Timothy K. Earle

1987 Specialization, exchange, and complex societies: An introduction. In *Specialization, exchange, and complex societies*, edited by Elizabeth M. Brumfiel and Timothy K. Earle, 1–9. Cambridge: Cambridge University Press.

Bruun, Daniel

1902 *Det høje Nord, Færøernes, Íslands og Grønlands udforskning* (Exploration of the High North, Faeroes, Iceland, and Greenland). Copenhagen: E. Bojesen.

1918 The Icelandic colonization of Greenland and the finding of Vineland. *Meddelelser om Grønland* 57: 1–28.

Buchwald, Vagn Fabritius, and Gert Mosdal

1985 Meteoritic iron, telluric iron, and wrought iron in Greenland. *Meddelelser om Grønland: Man & Society* 9: 1–49.

Buckland, Paul C.

1987 North Atlantic faunal connections—introduction or endemics? *Entomologica Scandinavica Supplements* 32: 7–30.

1992 Insects, man, and the earliest settlement of the Faroe Islands: A case not proven. *Fróðskaparrit: Annales Societatis Scientiarum Færoensis* 38/39: 107–114.

Buckland, Paul C., Thomas Amorosi, L. K. Barlow, Andrew J. Dugmore, P. A. Mayewski, Thomas H. McGovern, Astrid E. J. Ogilvie, Jon P. Sadler, and P. Skidmore

1996 Bioarchaeological and climatological evidence for the fate of the Norse farmers in medieval Greenland. *Antiquity* 70(267): 88–96.

Buckland, Paul C., Allan C. Ashworth, and Don W. Schwert

1995 By-passing Ellis Island: Insect immigration to North America. In *Ecological relations in historical times*, edited by Robin A. Butlin and Neil Roberts, 226–244. Cambridge, Mass.: Blackwell Publishers Inc.

Buckland, Paul C., P. I. Buckland, and P. Skidmore

1998 Insect remains from GUS, an interim report. In *Man, culture, and environment in ancient Greenland*, edited by Jette Arneborg and Hans Christian Gulløv, 74–79. Danish Polar Center Publication 4. Copenhagen: Danish National Museum and Danish Polar Center.

Buckland, Paul C., and Mark H. Dinnin

1998 Insect faunas at landnám: A palaeoentomological study at Tjørnuvík, Streymoy, Faroe Islands. *Fróðskaparrit: Annales Societatis Scientiarum Færoensis* 46: 277–286.

Buckland, Paul C., Andrew J. Dugmore, and Jon P. Sadler

1991 Faunal change or taphonomic problem? A comparison of modern and fossil insect faunas from south east Iceland. In *Environmental change in Iceland past and present*, edited by Judith K. Maizels and Chris Caseldine, 127–146. Glaciology and Quaternary Geology 7. Dordrecht: Kluwer Academic Publishers.

Buckland, Paul C., Kevin J. Edwards, J. J. Blackford, Andrew J. Dugmore, Jon P. Sadler, and Guðrún Sveinbjarnardóttir

1995 A question of *landnám*: Pollen, charcoal, and insect studies on Papey, Eastern Iceland. In *Ecological relations in historical times*, edited by Robin A. Butlin and Neil Roberts, 245–264. Cambridge, Mass.: Blackwell Publishers Inc.

Buckland, Paul C., Kevin J. Edwards, and Jon P. Sadler

1998 Early holocene investigations at Saksunardalur and the origins of the Faroese biota. *Fróðskaparrit: Annales Societatis Scientiarum Færoensis* 46: 259–266.

Buckland, Paul C., J. J. Gerrard, G. Larsen, Dave W. Perry, Diana R. Savory, and Guðrún Sveinbjarnardóttir

1986 The Holocene paleoecology at Ketilsstadir in Myrdalur, South Iceland. *Jökull* 36: 41–55.

Buckland, Paul C., Thomas H. McGovern, Jon P. Sadler, and P. Skidmore

1994 Twig layers, floors, and middens: Recent palaeoecological research in the Western Settlement, Greenland. In *Twelfth Viking Congress: Developments around the Baltic and the North Sea in the Viking Age*, edited by Björn Ambrosiani and Helen Clarke, 132–143. Birka Studies 3. Stockholm: Birka Project.

Buckland, Paul C., and Dave Perry

1989 Ectoparasites of sheep from Stóraborg, Iceland, and their interpretation. Piss, parasites, and people, a palaeoecological perspective. *Hikuin* 15: 37–46.

Buckland, Paul C., Dave Perry, and Guðrún Sveinbjarnardóttir

1983 *Hydraena britteni* Joy (Coleoptera, Hydraenidae) fundin á Íslandi í setlögum frápví seint á nútíma. (*Hydraena britteni* Joy [Coleoptera, Hydraenidae] found in Icelandic sediments from prehistory to the present). *Náttúrufræðingurinn* 52: 37–44.

Buckland, Paul C., and Jon P. Sadler

1989 A biogeography of the human flea, *Pulex irritans* L. (Siphonaptera: Pulicidae). *Journal of Biogeography* 16(2): 115–120.

1990 Ballast and building stone: A discussion. In *Stone quarrying and building in England A.D. 43–1525*, edited by David Parsons, 114–125. Chichester, Sussex: Phillimore & Co. Ltd.

1997 Insects. In *Scotland: Environment and archaeology 8000 B.C.–A.D. 1000*, edited by Kevin J. Edwards and Ian B. M. Ralston, 105–108. New York: John Wiley & Sons.

Buckland, Paul C., Jon P. Sadler, and David N. Smith

1993 An insect's eye-view of the Norse farm. In *The Viking Age in Caithness, Orkney, and the North Atlantic: Select papers from the proceedings of the Eleventh Viking Congress, Thurso and Kirkwall, 22 August–1 September 1989*, edited by Colleen E. Batey, Judith Jesch, and Christopher D. Morris, 506–527. Edinburgh: Edinburgh University Press.

Buckland, Paul C., Jon P. Sadler, and Guðrún Sveinbjarnardóttir

1992 Palaeoecological investigations at Reykholt, Western Iceland. In *Norse and later settlement and subsistence in the North Atlantic*, edited by Christopher D. Morris and D. James Rackham, 149–168. Glasgow: Department of Archaeology, University of Glasgow.

Buckland, Paul C., and P. Wagner

N.D. Is there an insect signal for the Little Ice Age? *Climatic Change*. Forthcoming.

Burden, Philip D.

1996 *The mapping of North America: A list of printed maps, 1511–1670*. Rickmansworth, Herts.: Raleigh Publications.

Busvine, James R.

1976 *Insects, hygiene, and history*. London: Athlone Press.

Byock, Jesse L.

1988 *Medieval Iceland. Society, sagas, and power*. Berkeley and Los Angeles: University of California Press.

Byrne, Francis J.

1973 *Irish kings and high-kings*. London: Batsford.

Callmer, Johan

1991 Territory and dominion in the late Iron Age in southern Scandinavia. In *Regions and reflections: In honour of Märta Strömberg*, edited by Kristina Jennbert et al., 257–274. Acta Archaeologica Lundensia 20. Stockholm: Almqvist & Wiksell.

1992 Interaction between ethnical groups in the Baltic region in the late Iron Age. In *Contacts across the Baltic Sea: During the late Iron Age (5th–12th centuries): Baltic Sea Conference, Lund October 25–27, 1991*, edited by Birgitta Hårdh and Bozena Wyszomirska-Werbart, 99–108. Report Series 43. Lund: University of Lund.

Campbell, Tony

1981 *Early maps*. New York: Abbeville Press.

Carlson, Catherine C.

1988 "Where's the salmon?" A reevaluation of the role of andromous fisheries to aboriginal New England. In *Holocene ecology in northeastern North America*, edited by George P. Nicholas, 47–80. New York: Plenum Press.

1996 The (in)significance of Atlantic salmon. *Federal Archaeology* 8 (3–4): 22–30.

Carpenter, Edmund S.

1957 Further evidence on the Beardmore relics. *American Anthropologist* 59: 875–878.

1961 Frauds in Ontario archaeology. *Pennsylvania Archaeologist* 31(2): 113–118.

Carus-Wilson, E. M.

1967 The Iceland venture. In *Medieval merchant venturers, collected studies*, edited by E. M. Carus-Wilson, 2d ed., 98–142. London: Butler & Tanner Ltd.

Chandler, Milford G.

1971 Appendix, the blacksmith shop. In *American Indian tomahawks*, Harold Leslie Peterson. New York: Museum of the American Indian, Heye Foundation.

Christensen, Arne Emil

1968 *Frø vikingskip til motorsnekke* (Boats of the north. A history of boatbuilding in Norway). Oslo: Samlaget.

1982 Viking Age ships and shipbuilding. *Norwegian Archaeological Review* 15(1–2): 19–28.

Christensen, Arne Emil, and G. Leiro

1976 *Klåstadskipet* (The Klåstad ship). Tønsberg, Norway: Trykt. Also published in *Vestfoldminne*. Eiere, Norway: UHS.

Christensen, Tom

1991 Lejre beyond legend: The archaeological evidence. *Journal of Danish Archaeology* 10: 163–185.

Christiansson, Hans

1959 *Sydskandinavisk stil; studier i ornamentiken pø de senvikingatida runstenarna* (Style in southern Scandinavia). Uppsala: n.p.

Christophersen, A.

1989 Kjøpe, selge, bytte, gi. Vareutveksling og byoppkomst i Norge ca. 800–1100: en modell (Buy, trade, exchange and give away. A model for the exchange of goods and the development of towns in Norway ca. 800–1000). In *Medeltidens Födelse* (The birth of the Middle Ages), edited by Anders Andrén. Nyhamnsläge: Gyllenstiernska Krapperupstift.

Chronicles of Oklahoma

1966–67 Recent data on the Heavener runestone. *The Chronicles of Oklahoma* 44(4): 444–446.

Clark, Joan

1994 *Eiriksdottir: A tale of dreams and luck: A novel*. Toronto: Macmillan Canada.

Clarke, Helen, and Björn Ambrosiani

1991 *Towns in the Viking Age*. Leicester: Leicester University Press.

Clarke, Howard B., Máire Ni Mhanaigh, and Raghnall Ó Floinn (eds.)

1996 *Ireland and Scandinavia in the early Viking Age*. Blackrock, Ireland: Four Courts.

Clausen, Birthe L. (ed.)

1993 *Viking voyages to North America*. Roskilde, Denmark: Viking Ship Museum.

Clemmensen, Mogens

1911 Kirkeruiner fra nordbotiden m.m. i Julianehaab distrikt, undersøgelsesrejse i sommeren 1910 (Church ruins from the Norse era in Julianehaab district). *Meddelelser om Grønland* 47: 283–358.

Collins, Henry B.

1961–62 The L'Anse aux Meadows archeological site in northern Newfoundland. *National Geographic Society Research Reports* 1961–62: 39–49.

Collins, Roger

1994 *The Arab conquest of Spain, 710–797*. 2d ed. New York: B. Blackwell.

1995 *Early medieval Spain: Unity in diversity, 400–1000*. 2d ed. New York: St. Martin's Press.

Collis, Dirmid Ronán F.

1988 Kalaaleq < (skinn) Klædast? (Does "Kalaaleq" derive from "klaedast" [dressed in skins]?) *Études Inuit Studies* 12(1–2): 259.

Columbus, Fernando

1986 *Christophe Colomb raconté par son fils*. Translation and notes by Eugène Muller. Preface by Jacques Heers. Paris: Perrin.

Cook, Ramsay (ed.)

1993 *The voyages of Jacques Cartier*. Toronto: University of Toronto Press.

Coope, G. R.

1986 The invasion and colonization of the North Atlantic islands: A palaeoecological solution to a biogeographical problem. *Philosophical Transactions of the Royal Society of London* B314: 619–633.

Cortesão, Armando

1935 *Cartografia e cartógrafos portugueses dos séculos XV e XVI*. Lisbon: Ediçâo da Seara nova.

Coupland, Simon

1991 The fortified bridges of Charles the Bald. *Journal of Medieval History* 17: 1–12.

1995 The Vikings in Francia and Anglo-Saxon England to 911. In *The New Cambridge Medieval History*, vol. 2, edited by Rosamund McKitterick, 190–201. Cambridge: Cambridge University Press.

Cox, Steven L.

1978 Palaeo-Eskimo occupations of the north Labrador coast. *Arctic Anthropology* 15(2): 96–118.

Crichton, Michael

1976 *Eaters of the dead: The manuscript of Ibn Fadlan relating his experiences with the Northmen in A.D. 922*. New York: Knopf. (republished as *The Thirteenth Warrior*)

Cronon, William

1991 *Nature's metropolis: Chicago and the Great West*. New York: W.W. Norton.

Crosby, Alfred W.

1972 *The Columbian exchange; biological and cultural consequences of 1492*. Westport, Conn.: Greenwood Publishing Co.

1986 *Ecological imperialism: The biological expansion of Europe, 900–1900*. Cambridge: Cambridge University Press.

Crozier, Alan

1998 The Vinland hypothesis: A reply to the historians. *Gardar* 29: 37–66.

Crumlin-Pedersen, Ole

1978 *Sovejen til Roskilde* (The sea route to Roskilde). Roskilde: Viking Ship Museum.

1991a Ship types and sizes. In *Aspects of maritime Scandinavia: A.D. 200–1200: Proceedings of the Nordic seminar on maritime aspects of archaeology, Roskilde, 13th–15th March, 1989*, edited by Ole Crumlin-Pedersen. Roskilde: Viking Ship Museum.

1991b Bådgrave og gravbåde på Slusegård (Ship burials and burial ships at Slusegård). In *Slusegårdgravpladsen 3: Gravformer og gravskikke, bådgravene* (The gravesite at Slusegård 3: Grave forms and burial traditions: The ship graves), edited by Søren H. Andersen, Birgit Lind, and Ole Crumlin-Pedersen. *Jysk Arkaeologisk Selskabs Skrifter* 14: 3. Copenhageni kommission hos Gyldendal.

1997 *Viking-Age ships and shipbuilding in Hedeby/Haithabu and Schleswig*. Ships and boats of the north 2. Schleswig: Roskilde.

Crumlin-Pedersen, Ole, and Merete Binderup (eds.)

1996 *Atlas over Fyns kyst i jernalder, vikingtid og middelalder*

(Atlas for the coast of the island Fyn in Iron, Viking, and Middle Ages). Odense: Odense Universitetsforlag.

Crumlin-Pedersen, Ole, and F. Rieck

1993 The Nydam ships. In *A spirit of enquiry. Essays for Ted Wright*, edited by John Coles, Valerie Fenwick, and Gillian Hutchinson. WARP Occasional Paper 7. Exeter: Wetland Archaeology Research Project.

Crumlin-Pedersen, Ole, Mogens Schou Jørgensen, and Torsten Edgren

1992 Skibe og Samfærdsel (Ships and travel). In *Viking og Hvidekrist* (From Viking to crusader: The Scandinavians and Europe 800–1200), edited by Else Roesdahl and David M. Wilson, 42–51. Uddevalla, Sweden: Bohusläningens Boktryckeri AB.

1992 Scandinavian society. In *From Viking to Crusader: The Scandinavians and Europe 800–1200*, edited by Else Roesdahl and David M. Wilson, 120–125. Uddevalla, Sweden: Bohusläningens Boktryckeri AB.

Curran, J. W.

1939 Here was Vinland. *Sault Daily Star Newpaper*. Sault Ste. Marie, Ontario.

Currelly, Charles T.

1940 Viking weapons found near Beardmore, Ontario. *Antiquity* 14: 200–204.

Da Silva, Manuel Luciano

1967 Finding for the Portuguese. *Medical Opinion and Review*, March, 42–51.

Dahl, Sverri, and Jóannes Rasmussen

1956 Víkingaaldargrøv í Tjørnuvík (Viking age graves from Tjørnuvík). *Fróðskaparrit Annales Societatis Scientiarum Færoensis* 2: 153–167.

Dansgaard W., S. J. Johnsen, N. Reeh, N. Gundestrup, H. B. Clausen, and C. U. Hammer

1975 Climatic changes, Norsemen, and modern man. *Nature* 255: 24–27.

Dasent, George Webbe, Sir

1875 *The Vikings of the Baltic; a tale of the north in the tenth century*. London: Chapman & Hall.

Davidson, Hilda Roderick Ellis

1969 *Scandinavian mythology*. London: Hamlyn.

1993 *The lost beliefs of northern Europe*. London: Routledge.

Davis, A. M., J. H. McAndrews, and Birgitta Linderoth Wallace

1988 Paleoenvironment and the archaeological record at the L'Anse aux Meadows site, Newfoundland. *Geoarchaeology* 3(1): 53–64.

Degerbøl, Magnus

1930 Animal bones from the Norse ruins at Gardar. *Meddelelser om Grønland* 76: 181–192.

1934 Animal bones from the Norse ruins at Brattahlid. *Meddelelser om Grønland* 88(1): 149–155.

1936 Animal remains from the West Settlement in Greenland, with special reference to livestock. *Meddelelser om Grønland* 88(3): 1–54.

Dekin, Albert A., Jr.

1972 Review of three Ungava reports by Thomas E. Lee. *American Anthropologist* 74(6): 1501–1503.

Delabarre, Edmund B., and Charles W. Brown

1935 The runic rock on No Man's Land, Massachusetts. With geological notes. *The New England Quarterly* 8: 365–377.

Dennis, Andrew, Peter Foote, and Richard Perkins (trans.)

1980 *Laws of early Iceland: Grágás, the Codex Regius of Grágás, with material from other manuscripts*. Winnipeg, Canada: University of Manitoba Press.

Det Kongelige Nordiske Oldskrift Selskab (eds.)

1833 *Nordisk Tidsskrift for Oldkyndighed* (Nordic times for antiquarianism). Vol. 2. Copenhagen: J. D. Qvist.

Dicuil

1967 *Dicuili Liber de mensura orbis terrae* (Dicuil's book on the measure of the sphere of the earth), edited by J. J. Tierney. Scriptores Latini Hiberniae 6. Dublin: Dublin Institute for Advanced Studies.

Djupdræt, Martin

1998 *Billeder af vikingen* (Images of the Viking). Copenhagen: Skoletjenesten.

Dobyns, Henry F.

1983 *Their numbers become thinned: Native American population dynamics in eastern North America*. Knoxville, Tenn.: University of Tennessee Press.

Dugmore, Andrew J., and Paul C. Buckland

1991 Tephrochronology and late holocene soil erosion in south Iceland. In *Environmental change in Iceland past and present*, edited by Judith K. Maizels and Chris Caseldine, 147–161.

Glaciology and Quaternary Geology 7. Dordrecht: Kluwer Academic Publishers.

Dupont, Ernst (trans.)

1970 *The history of Greenland*. London: C. Hurst.

Durrenberger, E. Paul

1989 Anthropological perspectives on the Commonwealth period. In *Anthropology of Iceland*, edited by E. Paul Durrenberger and Gísli Pálsson, 228–246. Iowa City: University of Iowa Press.

Dyke, B.

1984 Migration and the structure of small populations. In *Migration and mobility: Biosocial aspects of human movement*, edited by Anthony J. Boyce, 69–82. London: Taylor & Francis.

Edgerton, J.

1955 Sculptor [John Daniels] argues for the rune stone. *Minneapolis Star*, 1 July.

Edgren, Torsten

1968 Zu einem Fund von Gussformen aus der jüngeren Eisenzeit in Finnland (Archeological mold finds from the early Iron Age in Finland). *Suomen Museo* 75: 37–51.

1993 Den förhistoriska tiden (The prehistoric era). In *Finlands historia 1* (The history of Finland, vol. 1), edited by Torsten Edgren and Märtha Norrback, 11–270, 427–432. Esbo: Schildt.

1995 Kyrksundet i Hitis: Ett arkeologiskt forskningsprojekt kring en av 'det danska itineariets' hamnar i sydvästra Finlands skärgård (The Hiitti church sound: An archeological research project around one of the ports along the Danish route in the archipelago of southwestern Finnish). *Budkavlen* 74: 48–66.

Edwards, Kevin J., Paul C. Buckland, Robert Craigie, Eva Panagiotakopulu, and Steffen Stummann Hansen

1998 Landscapes at landnám: Palynological and palaeoentomological evidence from Toftanes, Faroe Islands. *Fróðskaparrit: Annales Societatis Scientiarum Færoensis* 46: 229–244.

Egede, Hans

1818 *A description of Greenland*. London: T. & J. Allman.

Egede, Poul

1741 *Continuation af Relationerne betreffende den grønlandske Missions Tilstand og Beskaffenhed: forfattet i Form af en Journal fra Anno 1734 til 1740* (Continuation of the account concerning the character and condition of the Greenland Mission written in the form of a journal covering the years 1734 to 1740). Copenhagen: Trykt hos Johann Christoph.

1750 *Dictionarium grönlandico-danico-latinum, complectens primitiva cum suis derivatis, qvibus interjectæ sunt voces primariæ è Kirendo Angekkutorum*. Havniæ: n.p.

1787 *Efterretninger om Grønland, 1721–1788* (Greenland information, 1721–1788). Copenhagen: H. C. Schroeder.

Egilsson, Olafur

1991 Columbus in Iceland—did knowledge of Leifur Eiríksson's journey guide Columbus to the New World? *Iceland Review* 3: 34–35.

Ekrem, Inger

1998 *Nytt lys over Historia Norwegie: Mot en løsning i debatten om dens alder?* (New light on the Historia Norwegiae: towards a reconciliation in the debate over its age). Bergen: Universitetet i Bergen, IKKR.

El-Hajji, Abdurrahman A.

1970 *Andalusian diplomatic relations with western Europe during the Umayyad period (A.H. 138–366/A.D. 755–976); an historical survey*. Beirut: Dar al-Irshad.

Eldjárn, Kristján

1956 *Kuml og haugfé úr heiðnum sið á Íslandi* (Graves and antiquities from the heathen period in Iceland). Reykjavík: Norri.

1961 Bær í Gjáskógum í Þjórsárdal (Settlements in Gjáskógum in Thjorsardalur). *Árbók hins Islenzka Fornleifafélags* 1961: 7–46.

1989 Papey. Fornleifarannsóknir 1967–1981 (Papey. Archeological research 1967–1981). *Árbók hins Islenzka Fornleifafélags* 1988: 35–188.

Eldjárn, Kristján, and Gísli Gestsson

1952 Rannsóknir á Bergþórshvoli (Research at Bergþórshvolur). In *Árbók hins Islenzka Fornleifafélags* 1951–52: 5–75.

Eliade, Mircea

1964 *Shamanism: Archaic techniques of ecstasy*. New York: Bollingen Foundation.

Eliade, Mircea (ed.)

1977 *From primitives to Zen: A thematic sourcebook of the history of religions*. London: Collins.

d' Entremont, Clarence J.

1982 *Nicolas Denys, sa vie et son oevre* (Nicolas Denys, his life and work). Yarmouth, Nouvelle-Ecosse: Impr. Lescarbot.

Espelund, Arne

1995 *Iron production in Norway during two millennia: From the ancient bloomery to the early use of electric power: A presentation with many questions and some answers*, edited by Arne Espelund. Trondheim: Arketype.

Fagnan, Edmond

1901 *Ibn al-Athir: Annales du Maghreb et de l'Espagne* (Annals of the Magreb and Spain). Algiers: n.p.

Farbregd, Oddmunn

1972 *Pilefunn frå Oppdalsfjella* (Arrow finds from the Oppdal mountains). Miscellanea 5. Trondheim: Norske Videnskapers Selskab.

Farley, Gloria

1973 The Oklahoma runestones are authentic. *Popular Archaeology*, August, 4–7.

Fell, Barry

1982 *Bronze Age America*. Boston: Little, Brown.

Fell, Christine, Peter Foote, James Graham-Campbell, and Robert Thomson (eds.)

1983 *The Viking Age in the Isle of Man: Select papers from the Ninth Viking Congress, Isle of Man, 4–14 July 1981*. London: Viking Society for Northern Research, University College.

Fellows-Jensen, Gillian

1984 Viking settlement in the northern and western Isles—the place-name evidence as seen from Denmark and the Danelaw. In *The northern and western isles in the Viking world: Survival, continuity, and change*, edited by Alexander Fenton and Hermann Pálsson, 148–168. Edinburgh: J. Donald Publishers.

1993 Place-names. In *Medieval Scandinavia: An encyclopedia*, edited by Phillip Pulsiano, 501–504. Vol. 1 of Garland Encyclopedias of the Middle Ages. New York: Garland Publishing, Inc.

Fenger, Ole

1992 Scandinavian Society. In *From Viking to Crusader: The Scandinavians and Europe 800–1200*, edited by Else Roesdahl and David M. Wilson, 120–125. Uddevalla, Sweden: Bohusläningens Boktryckeri AB.

Fernald, M. L.

1910 Notes on the plants of Wineland the Good. *Rhodora* 12(134): 17–38.

1915 The natural history of ancient Vinland and its geographic significance. *Bulletin of the American Geographical Society* 47: 686–687.

Fischer, Joseph

1903 *The discoveries of the Norseman in America with special relation to their cartographical representation*. Translated by Basil H. Soulsby. London: H. Stevens, Son & Stiles.

1913 Claudius Clavus, the first cartographer of America. *The Catholic Encyclopedia*. New York: The Encyclopedia Press, Inc.

Fischer-Møller, Knud

1942 The mediaeval Norse settlements in Greenland; anthropological investigations. *Meddelelser om Grønland* 89(2): 1–82.

Fisher, David A., Roy M. Koerner, Karl Kuivinen, Henrik B. Clausen, Sigfus J. Johnsen, Jorgen-Peter Steffensen, Niels Gundestrup, and Claus U. Hammer

1996 Inter-comparison of ice core $\delta^{18}O$ and precipitation records from sites in Canada and Greenland over the last 3,500 years and over the last few centuries in detail using EOF techniques. In *Climatic variations and forcing mechanisms in the last 2000 years*, edited by Philip D. Jones, Raymond S. Bradley, and Jean Jouzel, 297–330. Global Environmental Change 41. Berlin: Springer.

Fiske, John

1917 *The beginnings of New England, or, the Puritan theocracy in its relation to civil and religious liberty*. Boston: Houghton Mifflin Company.

Fitzhugh, William W.

1972 *Environmental archeology and cultural systems in Hamilton Inlet, Labrador; a survey of the central Labrador coast from 3000 B.C. to the present*. Smithsonian Contributions to Anthropology 16. Washington, D.C.: Smithsonian Institution Press.

1978 Winter Cove 4 and the Point Revenge occupation of the central Labrador coast. *Arctic Anthropology* 15(2): 146–174.

1980 A review of Paleo-Eskimo culture history in southern Quebec-Labrador and Newfoundland. *Études Inuit Studies* 4(1–2): 21–31.

1988 Persistence and change in art and ideology in western Alaskan Eskimo cultures. In *The late prehistoric development of Alaska's native people*, edited by Robert D. Shaw, Roger K. Harritt, and Don E. Dumond, 81–106. Alaska Anthropological Association Monograph Series 4. Anchorage, Alaska: Aurora.

1993 Field surveys in outer Frobisher Bay. In *Archeology of the Frobisher voyages*, edited by William W. Fitzhugh and Jacqueline S. Olin, 99–136. Washington, D.C.: Smithsonian Institution Press.

1994 Staffe Island 1 and the northern Labrador Dorset-Thule succession. In *Threads of arctic prehistory: Papers in honour of William E. Taylor, Jr.*, edited by David Morrison and Jean-Luc Pilon, 239–268. Archaeological Survey of Canada Mercury Series Paper 149. Hull, Quebec: Canadian Museum of Civilization.

1997 Iron blooms, Elizabethans, and politics: The Frobisher Project, 1974-1995. *The Review of Archaeology* 7(2): 12–21.

Fitzhugh, William W., and Jacqueline S. Olin (eds.)

1993 *Archeology of the Frobisher voyages*. Washington D.C.: Smithsonian Institution Press.

Foote, Peter G. (trans.)

1987 *Thingvellir: Iceland's national shrine, a visitor's companion*. Reykjavík: Örn og Örlygur.

Foote, Peter G., and David M. Wilson

1970 *The Viking achievement: A survey of the society and culture of early medieval Scandinavia*. New York: Praeger Publishers.

Franklin, Ursula M., E. Badone, R. Gotthardt, and B. Yorga

1981 *An examination of prehistoric copper technology and copper sources in western arctic and subarctic North America*. Archaeological Survey of Canada Mercury Series Paper 101. Ottawa: National Museums of Canada.

Fredskild, Bent

1981 The natural environment of the Norse settlers in Greenland. In *Proceedings of the International Symposium, Early European Exploitation of the Northern Atlantic, 800–1700*, 27–43. Groningen, Netherlands: Arctic Centre, University of Groningen.

1992 Agriculture in SW Greenland in the Norse period (ca. 982–ca. 1450). *PACT* 31(5): 39–45.

Fricke, Henry C., James R. O'Neil, and Niels Lynnerup

1995 Oxygen isotope composition of human tooth enamel from medieval Greenland: Linking climate and society. *Geology* 23(10): 869–872.

Fridriksson, Sturla

1959 Korn frá Gröf í Öræfum (Pollen from a grave in Oraef). *Arbók hins íslenzka fornleifafélags* 1959: 88–91.

1960 Jurtaleifar frá Bergthórshvoli á Söguöld (Saga age plant remains from Bergthorshvoli). *Arbók hins Íslenzka Fornleifafélags* 1960: 64–75.

Fritzner, Johan, Carl R. Unger, and Sophus Bugge

1886–96 *Ordbog over det gamle norske sprog* (Dictionary of Old Norwegian). Chicago: J.T. Relling & Co.

Fugelsang, Signe

1993 Runes and runic inscriptions. In *Medieval Scandinavia: An encyclopedia*, edited by Phillip Pulsiano, 550–553. Vol. 1 of Garland Encyclopedias of the Middle Ages. New York: Garland Publishing, Inc.

Fyllingsnes, Frode

1990 *Undergongen til den norrøne bygdene på Grønland i seinmellomalderen: eit forskingshistorisk oversyn* (The fall of the Norse settlements in Greenland in the late Middle Ages: Overview of the research history). Middelalderforum 2. Oslo: Middelalderforum.

Gad, Finn

1965 Sjældent farer mænd did (Man rarely goes there). *Grønland* 3: 81–91.

1967 *Grønlands Historie, I. Indtil 1700* (The history of Greenland, I. Up to 1700). Copenhagen: Nyt Nordisk Forlag.

1984 History of colonial Greenland. In *Handbook of North American Indians, Vol. 5, Arctic*, edited by David Damas, 556–576. Washington, D.C.: Smithsonian Institution Press.

Gaimster, Märit

1991 Money and media in Viking Age Scandinavia. In *Social approaches to Viking studies*, edited by Ross Samson, 113–122. Glasgow: Cruithne Press.

Galliou, Patrick, and Michael C. E. Jones

1991 *The Bretons*. Oxford: B. Blackwell.

Garmonsway, George N. (trans.)

1953 *The Anglo-Saxon Chronicle*. London: Dent.

Gathorne-Hardy, Geoffrey M.

1921 *The Norse Discoverers of America, the Wineland Sagas*. Oxford: Clarendon Press.

de Gayangos, Pascual (trans.)

1840–43 *The history of the Mohammedan dynasties in Spain; extracted from the Nafhu-t-tíb min ghosni-l-Andalusi-r-rattib wa táríkh Lisánu-d-Dín Ibni-l-Khattíb, by Ahmed ibn Mohammed al-Makkarí, a native of Telemsán*. London: W.H. Allen and Co.

Geist, Valerius

1978 *Life strategies, human evolution, environmental design: Toward a biological theory of health*. New York: Springer-Verlag.

Gelting, Michael H. (trans. and ed.)

1979 *Roskildekrøniken* (The Roskilde chronicle). Højbjerg: Wormianum.

Gestsdóttir, Hildur

1998 The palaeopathological diagnosis of nutritional disease: A study of the skeletal material from Skeljastaðir, Iceland. Master's thesis, University of Bradford.

Gillmor, Carroll

1988 War on the rivers: Viking numbers and mobility on the Seine and Loire, 841–886. *Viator* 19: 79–109.

1989 The logistics of fortified bridge building on the Seine under Charles the Bald. In *Anglo-Norman Studies 11, Proceedings of the Battle Conference 1988*, edited by R. Allen Brown, 87–106. Woodbridge, Suffolk: Boydell Press.

Gilman, Rhoda

1993 On the Viking trail. *Roots* 21(2): 4–9.

Gilmore, Donald Y., and Linda S. McElroy (eds.)

1998 *Across before Columbus? Evidence for transoceanic contact with the Americas prior to 1492*. Edgecomb, Maine: New England Antiquities Research Association, NEARA Publications.

Glosecki, Stephen O.

1998 The Kensington rune-stone: Authentic and important. *Language* 74(2): 437–438.

Godfrey, William S., Jr.

1949 The Newport puzzle. *Archaeology* 2: 146–149.

1950 Newport tower II. *Archaeology* 3: 82–86.

1951 The archaeology of the Old Stone Mill in Newport, Rhode Island. *American Antiquity* 17: 120–129.

Goldstein, Thomas E.

1971 Some reflections of the origins of the Vinland Map. In *Proceedings of the Vinland Map Conference*, edited by Wilcomb E. Washburn, 47–56. Chicago: University of Chicago Press.

Graham-Campbell, James

1983 The Viking-Age silver hoards of the Isle of Man. In *The Viking Age in the Isle of Man: Select papers from the Ninth Viking Congress, Isle of Man, 4–14 July 1981*, edited by Christine Fell, Peter Foote, James Graham-Campbell, and Robert Thomson, 53–80. London: Viking Society for Northern Research, University College.

Graham-Campbell, James (ed.)

1992 *Viking treasure from the north west: The Cuerdale hoard in its context: Selected papers from the Vikings of the Irish Sea Conference, Liverpool, 18–20 May 1990*. Occasional Papers Liverpool Museum 5. Liverpool, England: National Museums and Galleries on Merseyside.

Graham-Campbell, James, and Colleen E. Batey

1998 *Vikings in Scotland: An archaeological survey*. Edinburgh, Scotland: Edinburgh University Press.

Graham-Campbell, James, Colleen Batey, Helen Clarke, R.I. Page, and Neil S. Price (eds.)

1994 *Cultural atlas of the Viking world*. Abingdon, Oxfordshire: Andromeda Oxford Limited.

Graham-Campbell, James, and Dafydd Kidd

1980 *The Vikings*. Exh cat.: The British Museum, London, The Metropolitan Museum of Art, New York. New York: W. Morrow.

Granberg, Beatrice

1966 *Förteckning över kufiska myntfynd i Finland* (Overview of findings of cufic coins in Finland). Studia orientalia 34. Helsinki: Finska orientsällskap.

Grandien, Bo

1987 *Rönndruvans glöd: nygöticistiskt i tanke, konst och miljö under 1800-talet* (The glow of the rowanberry grape: Neogothic thought, art, and milieu during the eighteenth century). Stockholm: Nordiska Museet.

Gräslund, Anne-Sofie

1986–87 Runstenar, bygd och gravar (Runestones, settlements, and graves). *Tor* 21: 241–262.

1987 Pagan and Christian in the age of conversion. In *Proceedings of the Tenth Viking Congress: Larkollen, Norway, 1985: Festskrift for Charlotte Blindheim on her 70th birthday July 6th 1987*, edited by James E. Knirk. Universitetets Oldsaksamlings Skrifter 9. Oslo: Universitetets Oldsaksamling.

1988–89 "Gud hjälpe nu väl hennes själ"; om runstenskvinnorna, deras roll vid kristnandet och deras plats i familj och samhälle ("May God help her soul"; The runestone women and their role in the conversion, and their place in family and society). *Tor* 22: 223–244.

1994 Rune stones: On ornamentation and chronology. In *Twelfth Viking Congress: Developments around the Baltic and the North Sea in the Viking Age*, edited by by Björn Ambrosiani and Helen Clarke, 117–131. Birka Studies 3. Stockholm: Birka Project.

1997 Adams Uppsala—och arkeologins (Adam's Uppsala—and the archeology). In *Uppsala och Adam av Bremen* (Uppsala and Adam of Bremen), edited by Anders Hultgård, 101–115 Lund: Nya Doxa.

Grenfell, Wilfred T., Sir

1934 *The romance of Labrador*. New York: The MacMillan Company.

Griffiths, David

1992 The coastal trading ports of the Irish Sea. In *Viking treasure from the north west: The Cuerdale hoard in its context: Selected papers from the Vikings of the Irish Sea Conference, Liverpool, 18–20 May 1990*, edited by James Graham-Campbell, 63–72. Occasional Papers Liverpool Museum 5. Liverpool, England: National Museums and Galleries on Merseyside.

Grønlands Historiske Mindesmærker (GHM)

1976 *Grønlands Historiske Mindesmærker*, I–III (Historic memorials of Greenland), edited by Det kongelige nordiske oldskriftselskab. 1838-45 ed. Reprint, Copenhagen: Rosenkilde & Bagger.

Gronnow, Bjarne

1981 Den store slaedevej: Traek af Melvillebugtens forhistorie (The big sleigh route: The prehistory of Melville Bay). *Tusaut* 1/2: 2–9.

Grønvik, Ottar

1983 Runeinskriften steinen (Runic inscribed stones). *Maal og minne* 1983: 101–149.

Grönvold, Karl, Níels Óskarsson, Sigfús J. Johnsen, Henrik B. Clausen, Claus U. Hammer, Gerald Bond, and Edouard Bard

1995 Ash layers from Iceland in the Greenland GRIP ice core correlated with oceanic and land sediments. *Earth and Planetary Science Letters* 135: 149–156.

Gulløv, Hans Christian

1982 Eskimoens syn på europæerenda såkaldte nordbodukker og andre tvivlsomme udskæringer. (The Eskimo impression of the European). *Grønland* 30: 226–234.

1997 From Middle Ages to Colonial times: Archaeological and ethnohistorical studies of the Thule culture in southwest Greenland 1300–1800 A.D. *Meddelelser om Grønland: Man & Society* 23: 1–501.

Guttesen, Rolf (ed.)

1996 *The Faeroe Islands, topographic atlas: 31 articles with maps and descriptions*. Copenhagen: Det Kongelige Danske Geografiske Selskab.

Hakluyt, Richard

1965 *The principal navigations, voyages, traffiques, and discoveries of the English nation; made by sea or over-land to the remote and farthest distant quarters of the earth at any time within the compasse of these 1,600 yeares*, vols. 1–9, 1589–1600. Reprint, New York: AMS Press.

Hall, Richard A.

1984 *The Viking dig: The excavations at York*. London: Bodley Head.

1994 *English heritage book of Viking Age York*. London: B.T. Batsford/English Heritage.

Hall, Robert A., Jr.

1982 *The Kensington rune-stone is genuine: Linguistic, practical, methodological considerations*. Columbia, S.C.: Hornbeam Press.

1994 *The Kensington rune-stone: Authentic and important: A critical edition*. Edward Sapir Monograph Series in Language, Culture, and Cognition 19. Lake Bluff, Ill.: Jupiter Press.

Halldórsson, Ólafur

1978 *Grænland í miðaldáritum* (Greenland in Middle Age literature). Reykjavík: Sögufélag.

1986 Lost Tales of Guðríðr þorbjanardóttir Sagnaskemmtun. *Studies in honour of Hermann Pálsson on his 65th birthday, 26th May 1986*, edited by Rudolf Simek, Jónas Kristjánsson, and Hans Bekker-Nielsen, 239–246. Vienna, Cologne, Graz: Hermann Böhlaus.

Halldórsson, Ólafur (ed.)

1985 *Eiríks saga rauða: Texti Skálholtsbókar* (Erik the Red's saga: Skálhoit's book text). Reykjavík: Hiðíslenzka Fornritafélag.

Hallsdóttir, Margrét

1987 Pollen analytical studies of human influence on vegetation in relation to the landnám tephra layer in southwest Iceland. *Lundqua Thesis* 18.

1996 Frjógreining. Frjókorn sem heimildir um landnámið (Pollen analysis: Grain particles as evidence of *landnám*). In *Um landnám á Íslandi: fjórtán erindi* (*Landnám* in Iceland: Lecture fourteen), edited by Guðrún Ása Grímsdóttir, 123–134. Ráðstefnurit 5. Reykjavík: Vísindafélag Islendinga.

Hannon, Gina E.

1999 The use of plant macrofossils and pollen in the palaeoecological reconstruction of vegetation. Ph.D. diss., Swedish University of Agricultural Sciences, Alnarp.

Hannon, Gina E., Margrét Hermanns-Auðardóttir, and Stephan Wastegård

1998 Human impact at Tjørnuvík in the Faroe Islands. *Fróðskaparrit: Annales Societatis Scientiarum Færoensis* 46: 215–228.

Hansen, Frederick C. C.

1924 Anthropologia medico-historica Groenlandae Antiquae I. Herjolfsnes (Historical medical anthropology of Ancient Greenland). *Meddelelser om Grønland* 67: 291–547.

Hansen, Steffen S.

1988 The Norse landnam in the Faeroe Islands in the light of recent excavations at Toftanes, Leirvík. *Northern Studies* 25: 58–84.

1991 Toftanes: A Faeroese Viking Age farmstead from the 9–10th centuries A.D. *Acta Archaeologica* 61: 44–53.

1996 Aspects of Viking society in Shetland and the Faeroe Islands. In *Shetland's northern links. Language and history*, edited by D. J. Waugh, 117–136. Edinburgh: Scottish Society for Northern Studies.

Hanson, C. L.

1986 Biological distance in medieval western Scandinavia based on craniometrics. Ph.D. diss., Arizona State University.

Harley, John B., and David Woodward (eds.)

1987 *Cartography in prehistoric, ancient, and medieval Europe and the Mediterranean.* Vol. 1 of *The history of cartography.* Chicago: University of Chicago Press.

Harrisse, Henry

1892 *The discovery of North America: A critical, documentary, and historic investigation.* London: Henry Stevens and Son.

Harp, Elmer

1974–75 A Late Dorset copper amulet from southeastern Hudson Bay. *Folk: dansk etnografisk tidsskrift* 16/17: 33–44.

Hartz, G.

1987 Der Handel in der späten Wikingerzeit zwischen Nordeuropa (insbesondere Schweden) und dem Deutschen Reich nach numismatischen Quellen (Early Viking age trade between northern Europe (especially Sweden) and Germany from numismatic sources). *Untersuchungen zur Handel und Verkehr der vor-und frühgeschichtlichen Zeit in Mittel-und Nordeuropa* 4: 86–112.

Hasan, Fekri A.

1981 *Demographic archaeology.* New York: Academic Press.

Hastrup, Kirsten

1985 *Culture and history in medieval Iceland: An anthropological analysis of structure and change.* Oxford: Oxford University Press.

Haugen, Einar

1972 The runes stones of Spirit Pond. *Man in the Northeast* 4: 62–80.

Haven, Samuel F.

1856 *Archaeology of the United States.* Smithsonian Contributions to Knowledge 8. Washington, D.C.: Smithsonian Institution.

Haywood, John

1995 *The Penguin historical atlas of the Vikings.* London: Penguin Books.

Hedeager, Lotte

1988 Oldtid. Jernalderen (Prehistory. The Iron Age). In *Det danske landbrugs historie I. Oldtid og middelalder* (The history of Danish farming volume 1. Prehistory and Middle Ages), edited by Claus Bjørn. Odense: Landbohistorisk Selskab.

1992 *Iron-Age societies: From tribe to state in northern Europe, 500 B.C. to A.D. 700.* Oxford: Blackwell.

1997 *Skygger af en anden virkelighed: oldnordiske myter* (Shadows of another reality: Old Norse myths). Haslev: Samlerens Universitet.

Helberg, B. H.

1997 Nordnorsk fiske i jernalder og middelalder. Teknologiutvikling som grunnlag for romlig strukturering og eksluderende atferd (The fisheries in northern Norway in the Iron and Middle ages. The development of technology as a platform for spatial organization and excluding behavior). In *Arkeologi og kystkultur: foredrag ved seminaret* (Archaeology and coastal culture: Lecture from the seminar), edited by Helge Sørheim. Ålesund: Sunnmøre Museum.

Hellevik, Alf (ed.)

1976 *Konungs skuggsjá Norsk Kongsspegelen* (The King's Mirror). Oslo: Samlaget.

Hermannsson, Halldór

1936 *The problem of Wineland.* Islandica 25. Ithaca, N.Y.: Cornell University Press.

Hertz, Johannes

1997 The history and mystery of the Old Stone Mill. *Journal of the Newport Historical Society* 68(235): 54–111. Newport, R.I.

Hill, David

1981 *An atlas of Anglo-Saxon England.* Toronto: University of Toronto Press.

Hill, Peter

1997 *Whithorn and St Ninian: The excavation of a monastic town, 1984–91.* Stroud, Gloucestershire: Whithorn Trust/ Sutton Pub.

Hiorns, R. W.

1984 Selective migration and its genetic consequences. In *Migration and mobility: Biosocial aspects of human movement*, edited by Anthony J. Boyce, 111–122. London: Taylor & Francis.

Hodges, Richard, and David Whitehouse

1983 *Mohammed, Charlemagne, and the origins of Europe: Archaeology and the Pirenne thesis.* London: Duckworth.

Holand, Hjalmar Rued

1919 The Kensington rune stone: Is it the oldest native document of American history? *The Wisconsin Magazine of History* 3(2): 153–183.

1940 *Westward from Vinland: An account of Norse discoveries and explorations in America, 982–1362.* New York: Duell, Sloan & Pearce.

1946 *America, 1355–1364: A new chapter in pre-Columbian history.* New York: Duell, Sloan & Pearce.

1956 *Explorations in America before Columbus.* New York: Twayne Publishers.

1962 *A pre-Columbian crusade to America.* New York: Twayne Publishers.

Hollander, Lee M. (trans.)

1964 *Heimskringla: History of the kings of Norway.* Austin: University of Texas Press.

Holm, Gösta

1997 Vinrankorna gav Vinland namnet (Fruit of the grapevines gave Vinland its name). *Svenska Dagbladet*, 24 March. Stockholm.

Holtved, Erik

1943 The Eskimo legend of Navaranâq: An analytical study. *Acta Arctica* 1: 1–42.

1944 Archaeological investigations in the Thule district. *Meddelelser om Grønland* 141(1–2): 1–308.

Hovgaard, William

1914 *The voyages of the Norsemen to America.* New York: The American-Scandinavian Foundation.

Howley, James P.

1915 *The Beothucks or Red Indians, the aboriginal inhabitants of Newfoundland.* Cambridge: University of Cambridge Press.

Hreinsson, Viðar (ed.)

1997 *The complete sagas of Icelanders, including 49 tales.* Reykjavík: Leifur Eiríksson Publishing.

Hughes, Malcolm K., and Henry F. Diaz

1994 Was there a "Medieval Warm Period," and if so, where and when? *Climatic Change* 26(2–3): 109–142.

Hvass, Steen

1993 Settlement. In *Digging into the past: 25 years of archaeology in Denmark*, edited by Steen Hvass and Birger Storgaard, 187–194. Copenhagen: Aarhus Universitetsforlag

Ingstad, Anne Stine

1977 *The Discovery of a Norse Settlement in America: Excavations at L'Anse aux Meadows, Newfoundland, 1961–1968.* Oslo: The Norwegian University Press.

1985 *The Norse discovery of America.* Oslo: The Norwegian University Press.

Ingstad, Helge

1966 *Land under the Polestar: A voyage to the Norse settlements of Greenland and the saga of the people that vanished.* New York: St. Martins Press.

1969 *Westward to Vinland: The Discovery of Pre-Columbian Norse House-sites in North America.* New York: St. Martin's Press.

Iversen, Mette (ed.)

1991 *Mammen grav: Kunst og samfund i vikingetid* (Mammen grave: Art and societies in the Viking era). Jysk Arkæologisk Selskabs Skrifter v. 28. Aahus: Jysk Arkæologisk Selskab.

Iverson, Johannes

1935 Nordboernes undergang paa Grønland i geologiske belysning (The decline of the Norse in Greenland seen in a geological perspective). *Den Grønlands Arbok* 20: 5–16.

Jakobsen, Bjarne Holme

1991 Soil resources and soil erosion in the Norse settlement area of Østerbygden [Eastern Settlement] in southern Greenland. *Acta Borealia* 8: 52–64.

James, Edward

1997 The militarisation of Roman society, 400–700. In *Military aspects of Scandinavian society in a European perspective, A.D. 1–1300: Papers from an international research seminar at the Danish National Museum, Copenhagen, 2–4 May 1996*, edited by Anne Nørgård Jørgensen and Birthe L. Clausen, 19–24. Studies in Archaeology and History 2. Copenhagen: Danish National Museum.

Jankuhn, Herbert

1976 *Haithabu: ein Handelsplatz der Wikingerzeit* (Hedeby: A trading post in the Viking era). Neumünster: Wachholtz.

Jansen, Henrik M.

1972 A critical account of the written and archaeological sources' evidence concerning the Norse Settlements in Greenland. *Meddelelser om Grønland* 182(4): 1–158.

Jansson, Ingmar

1997 Warfare, trade or colonization? Some general remarks on the eastern expansion. In *The rural Viking in Russia and Sweden*, edited by Pär Hansson, 9–64. Örebro, Sweden: Örebro Kommuns Bildningsförvaltning.

Jansson, Sven B. F.

1945 Sagorna om Vinland. Handskrifterna till Erik den Rodes Saga (The Vinland sagas: the manuscript of Erik the Red's saga). *Kungliga Vitterhets-Historie och Antikvitets Akademiens Handlingar* 60(1).

1949 Runstenen från Kensington, Minnesota (The runestone from Kensington, Minnesota). *Nordisk Tidskrift för Vetenskap, Konst och Industri* 72(7–8): 377–405.

1963 *Runinskrifter i Sverige* (Runic texts in Sweden). Stockholm: Almqvist & Wiksell.

1987 *Runes in Sweden.* Stockholm: Central Board of National Antiquities.

Jenness, Diamond

1928 *People of the twilight.* New York: Macmillan.

Jennings, Anne E, S. Hagen, J. Harðardóttir, R. Stein, Astrid E. J. Ogilvie, and I. Jónsdóttir

N.D. Oceanographic change and terrestrial human impacts in a post A. D. 1400 sediment record from the southwest Iceland shelf. *Climatic Change*, Special issue, The *"Little Ice Age" in North Atlantic and European regions*, edited by Astrid E. J. Ogilvie and T. Jónsson. Forthcoming.

Jennings, Anne E., and Nancy J. Weiner

1996 Environmental change in eastern Greenland during the last 1,300 years: Evidence from foraminifera and lithofaces in Nansen Fjord, 68 Degrees N. *The Holocene* 6(2): 179–191.

Jensen, Stig

1991 *The Vikings of Ribe.* Ribe, Denmark: Den Antikvariske Samling.

Jesch, Judith

1991 *Women in the Viking Age.* Woodbridge, Suffolk: Boydell Press.

Jóhannesson, Jón

1956 Aldur Graenlendinga sögu (The date of the composition of the *Greenlanders' saga*). In *Íslendinga Saga* (Icelanders' Sagas), edited by Jón Jóhannesson, 149–158. Reykjavík: n.p.

Jóhansen, Jóhannes

1979 Outwash of terrestric soils into Lake Saksunarvatn, Faroe Islands. *Danmarks Geologiske Undersøgelse Årbog* 1977: 31–38.

1985 Studies in the vegetational history of the Faroe and Shetland Islands. *Annales Societatis Scientiarum Feroensis.* Supplementum 11. Tórshavn: Føroya Fróðskaparfelag.

Jones, Gwyn

1984 Appendix II, the Danelaw. In *A history of the Vikings*, 421–424. Rev. ed. Oxford: Oxford University Press.

1986 *The Norse Atlantic saga: Being the Norse voyages of discovery and settlement to Iceland, Greenland, and North America.* Oxford: Oxford University Press.

Jónasson, Pétur M.

1992 *Ecology of oligotrophic, subarctic Thingvallavatn.* Denmark: Oikos.

Jónsdóttir, I., Astrid E. J. Ogilvie, and S. Kristjánsdóttir

N.D. Diaries, letters, and sea-ice charts: Eighteenth- and nineteenth-century documentary sources of sea-ice data from Iceland. In *Climate and climate impacts through the last 1,000 years*, edited by P. D. Jones, T. D. Davies, Astrid E. J. Ogilvie, and K. R. Briffa. Cambridge: Cambridge University Press. Forthcoming.

Jónsson, Finnur

1911 *Erik den Rødes Saga og Vinland* (Erik the Red's saga and Vinland). Historisk Tidsskrift 5. Oslo: Universitetsforlaget.

1924 Interpretation of the runic inscriptions from Herjolfsnes. *Meddelelser om Grønland* 67: 271–290.

1930 *Det gamle Grønlands beskrivelse* (Description of the old Greenland). Copenhagen: Levin & Munksgaard.

Jónsson, Jón

1877 *Jón Jónsson's saga. The genuine autobiography of a modern Icelander*, edited by G. R. Fitz-Roy Cole, *Frazer's Magazine*, new series, 15(85).

Jónsson, T., and H. Garðarsson

N.D. Early meteorological observations in Iceland. *Climatic Change*, Special issue, *The "Little Ice Age" in North Atlantic and European regions*, edited by Astrid E. J. Ogilvie and T. Jónsson. Forthcoming.

Jørgensen, Lars

N.D. The Viking Age manor at Tissø. *Journal of Danish Archaeology* 14. Forthcoming.

Jørgensen, Lise Bender, and Torben Skov

1979 Trabjerg. A Viking-Age settlement in north-west Jutland. *Acta Archaeologica* 50: 119–136.

Kaalund, Bodil

1983 *The art of Greenland: Sculpture, crafts, painting*. Berkeley and Los Angeles: University of California Press.

Kaland, Sigrid H. H.

1987 Viking/Medieval settlement in the Heathland area of Nordhordland. In *Proceedings of the Tenth Viking Congress, Larkollen, Norway, 1985*, edited by James E. Knirk, 171–190. Universitetets Oldsaksamlings Skrifter, Ny rekke 9. Oslo: Harald Lyche & Co.

Karlsson, Lennart

1983 *Nordisk form: om djurornamentik* (Nordic design: Animal ornamentation). Studies 3. Stockholm: Museum of National Antiquities

Karlsson, Stefán (comp.)

1967 *Sagas of Icelandic bishops: Fragments of eight manuscripts*. Copenhagen: Rosenkilde and Bagger.

Karlsson, Svenolof (ed.)

1992 *The source of liberty: The Nordic contribution to Europe: An anthology*. Stockholm: Nordic Council.

Kejlbo, Ib Rønne

1971 Claudius Clavus and the sources of the Vinland Map. In *Proceedings of the Vinland Map Conference*, edited by Wilcomb E. Washburn, 77–84. Chicago: University of Chicago Press.

Keller, Christian

1986 Nordboerne på Grønland 985–1350. Bidrag til en demografisk økologisk diskusjon (The Norse in Greenland 985–1350. A contribution to a demographic ecological discussion). *Universitetets Oldsaksamling Årbok* 1984/1985: 145–157.

1989 The Eastern Settlement reconsidered. Some analyses of Norse Medieval Greenland. Ph.D. diss., University of Oslo.

Kelsey, Vera

1951 *Red River runs north!* New York: Harper.

Kenward, H. K., and A. R. Hall

1995 Biological evidence from 16–22 Coppergate. *Archaeology of York* 14(7: 435–797. York: Council for British Archaeology for York Archaeological Trust.

Kieffer-Olsen, J.

1993 Grav og gravskik i det middelalderlige Danmark. 8 kirkegårdsudgravninger (Graves and grave traditions in Middle Aged Denmark. 8 Churchyard excavations). Ph.D diss., Afd. for Middelalder-arkæologi og Middelalderarkæologisk Nyhedsbrev, Moesgård, Aarhus, Denmark.

Kirch, Patrick V., and Terry L. Hunt (eds.)

1997 *Historical ecology in the Pacific Islands: Prehistoric environmental and landscape change*. New Haven: Yale University Press.

Kivikoski, Ella M.

1964 *Finlands förhistoria* (Finland's Prehistory). Stockholm: Almqvist & Wiksell.

1965 Magisches Fundgut aus finnischer Eisenzeit (Magical grave findings from the Finnish Iron Age). *Suomen Museo* 72: 22–35.

1967 *Finland*. London: Thames & Hudson.

1973 *Die Eisenzeit Finnlands: Bildwerk und Text* (The Iron Age of Finland, drawings and text). Helsinki: Weilin & Göös.

Kjartansson, Helgi Skúli

1997 Landnámið eftir landnám (Settlement after landnám). *Ný Saga* 9: 22–34.

Kleivan, Inge

1984a History of Norse Greenland. In *Handbook of North American Indians, Vol. 5, Arctic*, edited by David Damas, 549–555. Washington, D.C.: Smithsonian Institution Press.

1984b West Greenland before 1950. In *Handbook of North American Indians, Vol. 5, Arctic*, edited by David Damas, 595–621. Washington, D.C.: Smithsonian Institution Press.

1996 Inuit oral traditions about Tunit in Greenland. In *The Paleo-Eskimo cultures of Greenland: New perspectives in Greenlandic archaeology*, edited by Bjarne Grønnow, 215–236. Danish Polar Center Publication 4. Copenhagen: Danish National Museum and Danish Polar Center.

Knirk, James E.

1997 Review essay: The Kensington runestone. *Scandinavian Studies* 69(1): 104–108.

Knuth, Eigil

1968 *Âlut Kangermio. Aron fra Kangek 'Aron of Kangek' (1822–1869). Kávdlunâtsianik. Nordboer og skrælinger* (Aron of Kangeq: The norsemen and the skraeling). Nuuk, Greenland: Det Grønlandske Forlag.

1984 *Reports from the musk-ox way*. Copenhagen: Eigil Knuth.

Krech, Shepard III

1999 *The ecological Indian: Myth and history*. New York: W. W. Norton & Company.

Kristjánsdóttir, Steinunn

1995 Klaustureyjan á Sundum. *Árbók hins Islenzka Fornleifafélags* 1994: 29–52.

Kristjánsson, Jónas

1996 Ireland and the Irish in Icelandic tradition. In *Ireland and Scandinavia in the early Viking Age*, edited by Howard Clarke, Máire Ni Mhanaigh, and Raghnall Ó Floinn, 259–276. Blackrock: Four Courts.

Krogh, Knud J.

1971 *Vikingernes Grønland* (Viking Greenland). Copenhagen: Danish National Museum.

1974 Kunstvanding—hemmeligheden bag Grønlandsbispens hundrede køer (Irrigation—the secret of the hundred cows of the Bishop of Greenland). In *Nationalmuseets Arbejdsmark* 1974: 71–80.

1975 Seks kirkjur heima á Sandi (The six churches on Sandur). *Mondul* 1975(2): 21–54.

1976 Om Grønlands middelalderlige kirkebygninger (The church buildings on Greenland in the Middle Ages). *Minjar og Menntir: Festskrift til Kristján Eldjárn*, 294–310. Reykjavík: n.p.

1982a *Erik den Rødes Grønland* (The Greenland of Erik the Red). Copenhagen: Danish National Museum.

1982b Bygdernes Kirker: Kirkerne i de middelalderlige norrøne grønlandske bygder (The village churches). *Grønland* 30: 263–274.

1993 *Gåden om Kong Gorms grav: historien om Nordhøjen i Jelling* (The mystery of the grave of King Gorm. The history of the north mount in Jelling). Copenhagen: P. Kristensen.

Lamm, Jan Peder, and Hans Åke Nordström (eds.)

1983 *Vendel period studies: Transactions of the Boat-Grave Symposium in Stockholm, February 2–3, 1981*. Studies 2. Stockholm: Museum of National Antiquities.

Landsverk, Ole G.

1961 *The Kensington runestone, A reappraisal of the circumstances under which the stone was discovered*. Glendale, Calif.: Church Press.

1967 Norse medieval cryptography in American runic inscriptions. *The American Scandinavian Review* 55(3): 252–263.

1969 *Ancient Norse messages on American stones*. Glendale, Calif.: Norseman Press.

1973 The Spirit Pond cryptography. *Man in the Northeast* 6: 67–75.

1974 *Runic records of the Norsemen in America*. New York: E. J. Friis.

Lang, James T.

1976a Sigurd and Weland in pre-conquest carving from northern England. *The Yorkshire Archaeological Journal* 48: 83–93.

1976b The sculptors of the Nunburnholme cross. *Archaeological Journal* 133: 75–94.

Larsen, Anne-Christine

1991 Norsemen's use of juniper in Viking Age, Faroe Islands. *Acta Archaeologica* 61: 54–59.

Larsen, Gudrun

1984 Recent volcanic history of the Veidivötn fissure swarm, southern Iceland—an approach to volcanic risk assessment. *Journal of Volcanology and Geothermal Research* 22: 33–58.

Larsson, Lars (ed.)

1996 *The earliest settlement of Scandinavia and its relationship with neighbouring areas*. Acta Archaeologica Lundensia 24. Stockholm: Almqvist & Wiksell.

Larsson, Mats G.

1992 The Vinland sagas and Nova Scotia: A reappraisal of an old theory. *Scandinavian Studies* 64(3): 305–335.

Larsson, Sven G., and Geir Gígja

1959 Coleoptera. *The zoology of Iceland* 3 (46a, 46b).

Lárusson, Magnús Már

1956–78 Félag (Society). In *Kulturhistorisk leksikon for nordisk middelalder fra vikingetid til reformationstid 4* (Cultural encyclopedia for the Nordic Middle Ages 4), 212–213. Copenhagen: Rosenkilde og Bagger.

Laxness, Halldór

1946 *Independent people, an epic*. New York: A.A. Knopf.

Lee, Thomas E.

1968a *Archaeological discoveries, Payne Bay region, Ungava, 1966*. Travaux divers 20. Québec: Université Laval.

1968b Summary of Norse evidence in Ungava, 1968. *Anthropological Journal of Canada* 6(4): 17–21.

1971 *Archaeological investigations of a longhouse, Pamiok Island, Ungava, 1970*. Collection nordicana 33. Québec: Université Laval.

1972 *Archaeological investigations of a longhouse ruin, Pamiok Island, Ungava, 1972*. Collection Paléo-Québec 2. Québec: Centre d'études nordique de l'Université Laval.

Lehtosalo-Hilander, Pirkko-Liisa

1980 Common characteristic features of dress—expressions of kinship or cultural contacts. *Fenno-Ugri et Slavi, Stencil* 22: 243–260. Department of Archaeology, University of Helsinki.

1982 *Luistari*. Suomen muinaismuistoyhdistyksen aikakauskirja 82. Helsinki: Suomen muinaismuistoyhdistys.

1984 *Ancient Finnish costumes*. Helsinki: The Finnish Archaeological Society.

1985 Viking Age spearheads in Finland. Society and trade in the Baltic during the Viking Age. *Acta Visbyensia* 7: 237–250.

1990 Le Viking finnois (The Finnish Vikings). *Finskt Museum* 97: 55–72.

1994 Bijoux et modes vestimentaires en Finlande à l'époque viking (Jewels and clothing styles in Finland during the Viking Age). *Proxima Thule: Revue d'Études Nordiques* 1 (Autumn): 111–121.

Leppäaho, Jorma

1964 *Späteisenzeitliche Waffen aus Finnland: Scwertinschriften und Waffenverzierungen des 9.–12. Jahrhunderts: ein Tafelwerk* (Iron-Age weapons from Finland: Sword inscriptions and decorations on weapons from the ninth through twelfth centuries: An index). Suomen muinaismuistoyhdistyksen aikakauskirja 61. Helsinki: Suomen Muinaismuistoyhdistys.

Liestøl, Aslak

1966 The Bergen runes and the Kensington inscription. *Minnesota History* 40 (2): 59.

1968 Cryptograms in runic carvings: A critical analysis. *Minnesota History* 41(1): 34–42.

Líndal, Sigurður (ed.)

1990 *Saga Íslands: samin að tilhlutan þjóð hátíð arnefndar 1974*. Reykjavík: Sögufélagið.

Lindkvist, Thomas

1989 Royal taxation and the state in Sweden. In *The birth of Europe: Archaeology and social develolpment in the first millennium A.D.*, edited by Klavs Randsborg, 171-184. Analecta Romana Instituti Daninci. Suplementum 16. Rome: L'Erma di Bretschneider.

Lindqvist, Sune

1936 *Uppsala högar och Ottarshögen* (The Uppsal mound and Ottars mound). Stockholm: Kunglige. Vitterhets Historie och Antikvits Akademien.

Lindroth, Carl H.

1957 *The faunal connections between Europe and North America*. New York: Wiley.

Lindroth, Carl H., Hugo Andersson, Högni Bödvarsson, and Sigurdur H. Richter

1973 Surtsey, Iceland, The development of a new fauna 1963–1970, terrestrial invertebrates. *Entomologica Scandinavica Supplementum* 5: 1–280.

Lindsay, Charles

N.D. The L'Anse aux Meadows radiocarbon dates. Manuscript on file, Halifax Regional Office, Parks Canada.

Ljungmark, Lars

1971 *For Sale—Minnesota; Organized promotion of Scandinavian immigration, 1866–1873*. Chicago: Swedish Pioneer Historical Society.

Lönnroth, Erik

1996 The Vinland problem. *Scandinavian Journal of History* 21(2): 39–48.

Loring, Stephen

1988 Keeping things whole: Nearly two thousand years of Indian (Innu) occupation in northern Labrador. In *Boreal forest and sub-arctic archaeology*, edited by C. S. (Paddy) Reid,

157–182. Occasional Publications 6. London, Ontario: London Chapter, Ontario Archaeological Society.

1997 On the trail to the caribou house: Some reflections on Innu caribou hunters in Northern Ntessinan (Labrador). In *Caribou and reindeer hunters of the northern hemisphere*, edited by Lawrence J. Jackson and Paul T. Thacker, 185–220. World Archaeology Series 6. Aldershot, Hampshire: Avebury.

Lund, Niels (ed.)

1984 *Two voyagers at the court of King Alfred: The ventures of Ohthere and Wulfstan, together with the description of northern Europe from the Old English Orosius.* York, England: Sessions.

Lundström, I., and Carin Orrling

1972 *Viking-Viking: Exhibition catalogue.* Stockholm: Statens Historiska Museum.

Lynnerup, Niels

1995 The Greenland Norse: A biological anthropological study. Ph D. diss., University of Copenhagen.

1998 The Greenland Norse. A biological-anthropological study. *Meddelelser om Grønland: Man & Society* 24: 1–149.

Madsen, Jan Skamby, and Ole Crumlin-Pedersen

1989 *To skibsfund fra Falster* (Two ship excavations from Falster). Roskilde: Viking Ship Museum.

Magerøy, Hallvard

1993 *Soga om austmenn: nordmenn som siglde til Island og Grønland i mellomalderen* (Sagas about the men from the East). Skrifter 19. Oslo: Norske Samlaget.

Magnus, Bente

1986 Iron Age exploitation of high mountain resources in Sogn. *Norwegian Archaeological Review* 19(1): 44–50.

Magnus, Olavus

1996–98 *A Description of the Northern Peoples*, edited by Peter Foote. Hakluyt Society, 2d series 182, 187, and 188. London: Hakluyt Society.

Magnusson, Gert

1965 *Lågteknisk järnhantering i Jämtlands län* (Traditional iron working in Jämtland). Stockholm: Jernkontorets.

Magnusson, Magnus, and Hermann Pálsson (trans.)

1986 *The Vinland sagas, the Norse discovery of America.* Baltimore: Penguin Books.

Mahler, Ditlev L. D.

1991 Argisbrekka: New evidence of shielings in the Faroe Islands. *Acta Archaeologica* 61: 60–72.

1998 The stratigraphic cultural landscape. In *Outland use in preindustrial Europe*, edited by Hans Andersson, Lars Ersgard, and Eva Svensson, 51–62. Lund Studies in Medieval Archaeology 20. Lund: Institute of Archaeology, Lund University.

Mallery, Arlington H.

1951 *Lost America; The story of Iron-Age civilization prior to Columbus.* Washington, D.C.: Overlook Co.

Malmer, Brita

1993 Är Ribe Danmarks äldsta myntort? Om detaljanalys kontra holism (Is Ribe Denmark's earliest royal mint?). *Nordisk Numismatisk Unions Medlemsblad* 1: 12–13.

Malmros, C.

1994 Exploitation of local, drifted and imported wood by the Vikings on the Faeroe Islands. *Archaeobotany, Botanical Journal of Scotland* 46(4): 552–558.

Marcus, Geoffrey. J.

1980 The conquest of the North Atlantic. In *Meta incognita: A discourse of discovery; Martin Frobisher's arctic expeditions, 1576–1578.* 2 vols. Mercury Series. Woodbridge, Suffolk: Boydell.

Margeirsson, Ingólfur

1994 *Þjóð á þingvöllum* (A nation at Thingvellir). Reykjavík: Vaka-Helgafell.

Marsden, John

1995 *The fury of the Northmen: Saints, shrines, and sea-raiders in the Viking Age, 793–878.* New York: St. Martin's Press.

Marshall, Ingeborg

1996 *A history and ethnography of the Beothuk.* Montreal: McGill-Queen's University Press.

Martens, Irmelin

1988 *Jernvinna på Møsstrond i Telemark: en studie i teknikk, bosetning og økonomi* (Iron working at Møsstrond in Telemark: A study of daily life and economy). Norske oldfunn 13. Oslo: Universitets Oldsaksamling.

Mathiassen, Therkel

1931a Inugsuk, a mediaeval Eskimo settlement in Upernavik district, West Greenland. *Meddelelser om Grønland* 77: 145–340..

1931b Ancient Eskimo settlements in the Kangâmiut area. *Meddelelser om Grønland* 91(1): 1–149.

Mathiassen, Therkel, and Erik Holtved

1936 The Eskimo archaeology of Julianehaab district, with a brief summary of the prehistory of the Greenlanders. *Meddelelser om Grønland* 118(1): 1–140.

Mauss, Marcel

1954 *The gift; forms and functions of exchange in archaic societies.* Glencoe, Ill.: Free Press.

Maxwell, Moreau S.

1984 Pre-Dorset and Dorset prehistory of Canada. In *Handbook of North American Indians, Vol. 5, Arctic*, edited by David Damas, 359–368. Washington, D.C.: Smithsonian Institution Press.

Mayewski, P.A., L. D. Meeker, S. Whitlow, M. S. Twickler, M. C. Morrison, P. Bloomfield, G. C. Bond, R. B. Alley, A. J. Gow, P. M. Grootes, D. A. Meese, M. Ram, K. C. Taylor, and W. Wumkes

1994 Changes in atmospheric circulation and ocean ice cover over the North Atlantic during the last 41,000 years. *Science* 263: 1747–1750.

McCartney, Allen P., and D. J. Mack

1973 Iron utilization by Thule Eskimos of central Canada. *American Antiquity* 38(3): 328–339.

McCrone, Walter C.

1974 Chemical analytical study of the Vinland Map. Unpublished report, Yale University.

1988 The Vinland Map. *Analytical Chemistry* 60: 1009–1018.

McCullough, Karen M.

1989 *The Ruin islanders: Thule culture pioneers in the eastern High Arctic.* Archaeological Survey of Canada Mercury Series Paper 141. Hull, Québec: Canadian Museum of Civilization.

McGhee, Robert J.

1969–70 Speculations on climatic change and Thule culture development. *Folk: dansk etnografisk tidsskrift* 11/12: 173–184.

1967 Paleoeskimo occupations in central and High Arctic Canada. *Society of American Archaeology Memoirs* 31: 15–39.

1978 *Canadian arctic prehistory.* Toronto: Van Nostrand Reinhold.

1984a *The Thule village at Brooman Point, High Arctic Canada.* Archaeological Survey of Canada Mercury Series Paper 125. Ottawa: National Museums of Canada.

1984b Contact between Native Americans and the Medieval Norse: A review of the evidence. *American Antiquity* 49(1): 4–26.

1984c The timing of the Thule migration. *Polarforschung* 54(1): 1–7.

1985 Contributions to the paleoeconomy of Norse Greenland. *Acta Archaeologica* 54: 73–122.

1994 Disease and the development of Inuit culture. *Current Anthropology* 35(5): 565–594.

McGoodwin, James R.

1990 *Crisis in the world's fisheries: people, problems, and policies.* Stanford, Calif.: Stanford University Press.

McGovern, Thomas H.

1979a The paleoeconomy of Norse Greenland: Adaptation and extinction in a tightly bounded ecosystem. Ph.D. diss., University of Michigan.

1979b Thule-Norse interaction in southwest Greenland: A speculative model. In *Thule Eskimo culture: An anthropological retrospective*, edited by Allen P. McCartney, 171–188. Archaeological Survey of Canada Mercury Series Paper 88. Ottawa: National Museums of Canada.

1980 Cows, harp seals, and churchbells: Adaptation and extinction in Norse Greenland. *Human Ecology* 8(3): 245–275.

1980–81 The Vinland adventure: A North American perspective. *North American Archaeologist* 2(4): 285–308.

1981 The economics of extinction in Norse Greenland. In *Climate and history, studies in past climates and their impact on man*, edited by T. M. L. Wigley, M. J. Ingram, and G. Farmer, 404–434. Cambridge: Cambridge University Press.

1983 Contributions to the paleoeconomy of Norse Greenland. *Acta Archaeologica* 54: 73–122.

1991 Climate, correlation, and causation in Norse Greenland. *Arctic Anthropology* 28(2): 77–100.

1992a Bones, buildings, and boundaries: Palaeoeconomic approaches to Norse Greenland. In *Norse and later settlement and subsistence in the North Atlantic*, edited by Christopher D. Morris and D. James Rackham, 193–230. Glasgow: Department of Archaeology, University of Glasgow.

1992b The zooarchaeology of the Vatnahverfi. *Meddelelser om Grønland: Man & Society* 17: 93–106.

1998 Animal bone from Hofstaðir. Interim report. Bone Laboratory, Hunter College, New York.

McGovern, Thomas H., Thomas Amorosi, Sophia Perdikaris, and James Woollett

1996 Vertebrate zooarchaeology of Sandnes V51: Economic change at a Chieftain's farm in West Greenland. *Arctic Anthropology* 33(2): 94–121.

McGovern, Thomas H., Gerald Bigelow, Thomas Amorosi, and Daniel Russell

1988 Northern islands, human error, and environmental degradation: A view of social and ecological change in the medieval North Atlantic. *Human Ecology* 16(3): 225–270.

McGovern, Thomas H., Paul C. Buckland, Diana Savory, Guðrun Sveinbjarnardottir, Claus Andreasen, and Peter Skidmore

1983 A study of the faunal and floral remains from two Norse farms in the Western Settlement, Greenland. *Arctic Anthropology* 20(2): 93–120.

McGovern, Thomas H., Ingrid Mainland, and Thomas Amorosi

1998 Hofstaðir 1996-1997. A preliminary zooarchaeological report. *Archaeologia islandica* 1: 123–128.

McGrew, Julia H. (trans.)

1970–74 *Sturlunga saga.* New York: Twayne Publishers.

McKitterick, Rosamond

1983 *The Frankish kingdoms under the Carolingians, 751–987.* London: Longman.

McNaughton, Douglas

2000 What's new about the Vinland Map ink. *The Portolan* 46.

Meinander, C. F.

1980 The Finnish society during the 8th–12th centuries. *Fenno-Ugri et Slavi, Stencil* 22: 7–13. Department of Archaeology, University of Helsinki.

Meldgaard, Jørgen

1960 Origin and evolution of Eskimo cultures in the Eastern arctic. *Canadian Geographical Journal* 60(2): 64–75.

1961 Fra Brattalid til Vinland (From Brattahlid to Vinland). *Naturens Verden* 4: 353–384.

1965 *Nordboerne i Grønland; en vikingebygds historie* (The Norse in Greenland). Copenhagen: Munksgaard.

1995 Eskimoer og Nordboer i det yderste Nord (Eskimos and Norsemen in the farthest north). *Nationalmuseets Arbejdsmark* 1995: 199–214.

Metcalf, D. M.

1985 Danmarks ældste mønter (The oldest coins in Denmark). *Nordisk Numismatisk Unions Medlemsblad* 1.

Mikkelsen, Egil

1994 *Fangstprodukter i vikingtidens og middelalderens økonomi: organiseringen av massefangst av villrein i Dovre* (The economy of hunting in the Viking and Middle Ages: The organizing of the mass hunt for reindeer in Dovre). Universitetets Oldsaksamlings skrifter. Ny rekke 18. Oslo: Universitetets Oldsaksamling.

Miller, William Ian

1986 Gift, sale, payment, raid: Case studies in the negotiation and classification of exchange in medieval Iceland. *Speculum* 61 (1): 18–50.

1990 *Bloodtaking and peacemaking: Feud, law, and society in saga Iceland.* Chicago: University of Chicago Press.

Minnesota Historical Society Collections

1976 The case of the Gran tapes: Further evidence on the rune stone riddle. *Minnesota History* 45(4): 152–156.

Mitchison, Naomi

1955 *The land the ravens found.* London: Collins.

Mjöberg, Jöran

1967 *Drömmen om sagatiden* (The dream of the saga age). Stockholm: Natur og Kultur.

Moller, Gregory

1985 A preliminary report on the scanning electron microscope analysis of particles from the Vinland Map. Unpublished report, University of California, Davis.

Moltke, Erik

1953 The ghost of the Kensington stone. *Scandinavian Studies* 25(1): 1–14.

Mongé, Alf, and Ole G. Landsverk

1967 *Norse medieval cryptography in runic carvings.* Glendale, Calif.: Norseman Press.

Morison, Samuel Eliot

1971–74 *The European discovery of America.* New York: Oxford University Press.

Morris, Christopher D.

1982 British Isles. In *The Vikings*, edited by Robert T. Farrell. London: Phillimore.

1996 Raiders, traders, and settlers: The early Viking Age in Scotland. In *Ireland and Scandinavia in the Early Viking Age*, edited by Howard B. Clarke, Máire Ni Mhanaigh, and Raghnall Ó Floinn, 73–103. Blackrock: Four Courts.

Morrison, David
1989 Radiocarbon dating Thule culture. *Arctic Anthropology* 26(2): 48–77.

Moss, Edward L.
1878 *Shores of the polar sea: A narrative of the arctic expedition of 1875–76.* London: M. Ward and Co.

Mowat, Farley
1965 *Westviking; the ancient Norse in Greenland and North America.* Boston: Little, Brown.
1998 *The farfarers: Before the Norse.* Toronto: Key Porter Books.

Müller-Wille, Michael
1976 Das Bootkammergrab von Haithabu (The boat chamber grave in Hedeby). Berichte über das Ausgrabungen in Haithabu 8. Neumünster: K. Wachholtz.
1978 Das Schiffsgrab von der Ile de Groix (Bretagne): ein Exkurs zum Bootkammergrab von Haithabu (The ship burial from the Ile de Groix [Brittany]: A meditation on the boat chamber grave from Hedeby). *Berichte über das Ausgrabungen im Haithabu* 12: 48–84.

Munch, Gerd Stamsø, and Olav Sverre Johansen
1988 Borg in Lofoten: An inter-Scandinavian research project. *Norwegian Archaeological Review* 21(2): 119–126.

Munch, Gerd Stamsø, Olav Sverre Johansen, and Ingegerd Larssen
1987 Borg in Lofoten. A chieftain's farm in arctic Norway. In *Proceedings of the Tenth Viking Congress, Larkollen, Norway, 1985,* edited by James E. Knirk, 149–70. Universitetets Oldsaksamlings Skrifter, Ny rekke 9. Oslo: Harald Lyche & Co.

Munn, William A.
1914 *The Wineland Voyages; Location of Helluland, Markland, and Vinland.* St. John's, Newfoundland: The Evening Telegram Ltd.

Musset, Lucien
1971 *Les invasions: le second assaut contre l'Europe chrétienne (VIIe–XIe siècles)* (The invasions: The second assault on Christian Europe [7th–11th centuries]). Paris: Presses universitaires de France.
1974 La renaissance urbaine des Xe et XIe siècles dans l'ouest de la France: Problèmes et hypothèses de travail (The urban revival of the tenth and eleventh centuries in western France: Studies and theories about labor). In *Études de civilisation médiévale, IXe–XIIe siècles: melanges offerts à Edmond-René Labande à l'occasion de son départ à la retraite et du XXe anniversaire du C.É.S.C.M. par ses amis, ses collègues, ses élèves* (Studies of the Middle Ages [9th–12th centuries]), edited by Edmond R. Labande, 563–575. Poitiers: C.É.S.C.M.
1992 The Scandinavians and the Western European Continent. In *From Viking to Crusader: The Scandinavians and Europe 800–1200,* edited by Else Roesdahl and David M. Wilson, 88–95. Uddevalla, Sweden: Bohusläningens Boktryckeri AB.

Myhre, Bjørn
1992 Borre—et merovingertidssenter i Øst-Norge (Borre—Merovingian center in eastern Norway). *Universitetets Oldsaksamlings Skrifter* 13: 155–179.

Nansen, Fridtjof
1911 *In northern mists; arctic exploration in early times.* London: W. Heinemann.

Nares, George S.
1876 *The official report of the recent arctic expedition.* London: John Murray.

Narmo, Lars E.
1996 *Jernvinna i Valdres og Gausdal: et fragment av middelalderens økonomi* (Iron production in Valdres and Gausdal). Varia 38. Oslo: Universitetets Oldsaksamling.

Näsman, Ulf
1998 Sydskandinavisk samhällsstruktur i ljuset av merovingisk och anglosaxisk analogi eller i vad är det som centralplatserna är centrala? (South Scandinavian social structure in the light of Merovingian and Anglo-Saxon analogy, or what is central about central places?). In *Centrala platser, centrala frågor: samhällsstrukturen under järnåldern: en vänbok till Berta Stjernquist* (Central places, central questions: Social structure in the Iron Age: A festschrift for Berta Stjernquist), edited by Lars Larsson and Birgitta Hårdh, 1–26. Stockholm: Almqvist and Wiksell.

Nelson, Janet L. (trans.)
1991 *The annals of St-Bertin.* Manchester: Manchester University Press.

Nelson, Janet L.
1992 *Charles the Bald.* London: Longman.
1997 The Frankish empire. In *The Oxford illustrated history of the Vikings,* edited by Peter H. Sawyer, 19–47. Oxford: Oxford University Press.

Nicolaysen, Nicolay
1882 *Langskibet fra Gokstad ved Sandefjord* (The longship from Gokstad by Sandefjord). Kristiania: A. Cammermeyer.

Nielsen, K. M.
1951 Kensingtonstenens runeindskrift(The Kensington Stone's runic transcription). *Aarbøger for Nordiks Oldkyndiged og Historie* 1950: 73–88.
1987 The numerals in the Kensington stone. *Kungliga Vitterhets-, Historie-och Antikvitetsakademien Konferenser* 15: 175–183.

Nielsen, Leif C.
1979 Omgård. A settlement from the late Iron Age and the Viking period in West Jutland. *Acta Archaeologica* 50: 173–208.

Nielsen, Richard
1986 The Arabic numbering system on the Kensington rune stone. *Epigraphic Society Occasional Publications* 15: 47–61.
1987 Kensington runestone: Part 2, aberrant letters—new evidence from Greenland, Iceland, and Scandinavia. *Epigraphic Society Occasional Publications* 16: 51–83.
1988 The Kensington runestone. Linguistic evidence. *Epigraphic Society Occasional Publications* 17.
1989 The Kensington stone. Linguistic evidence for its authenticity. *Epigraphic Society Occasional Publications* 18.

Nilsestuen, Rolf M.
1995 *The Kensington runestone vindicated.* Lanham, Md.: University Press of America.

Nilsson, Bertil (ed.)
1992 *Kontinuitet i kult och tro från vikingatid til medeltid* (Continuity in religious belief from the Viking Age to the Middle Ages). Projektet Sveriges kristnande 1. Uppsala: Lunne Böcker.
1996 *Kristnandet i Sverige: gamla källor och nya perspektiv* (The conversion of Sweden: Old sources and new perspectives). Projektet Sveriges kristnande 5. Uppsala: Lunne Böcker.

Nordin, Andreas (trans.)
1997 *Getica: om goternas ursprung och bedrifter/Jordanes* (History of Gotland's origin and accomplishments). Stockholm: Atlantis.

Nordman, Carl A.
1921 *Anglo-Saxon coins found in Finland.* Helsingfors: H. Schildt.

Nørlund, Poul
1924 Buried Norsemen at Herjolfsnes; An archaeological and historical study. *Meddelelser om Grønland* 67: 1–270.
1967 *De gamle nordbobygder ved verdens ende: skildringer fra Grønlands middelalder* (The old Norse settlements at the world's edge: Description of Greenland's Middle Ages). Reprint, Copenhagen: Danish National Museum.

Nørlund, Poul, and Aage Roussell
1930 Norse ruins at Gardar, the episcopal seat of mediaeval Greenland. *Meddelelser om Grønland* 76: 1–170.

Nørlund, Poul, and Mårten Stenberger
1934 Brattahlid. *Meddelelser om Grønland* 88(1): 1-161.

Nute, Grace Lee
1930 Posts in the Minnesota fur-trading area, 1660–1855. *Minnesota History* 4(4): 353–386.

Nylén, Erik, and Jan Peder Lamm
1988 *Stones, ships, and symbols: The picture stones of Gotland from the Viking Age and before.* Stockholm: Gidlunds.

O'Brien, Elizabeth
1996 The location and context of Viking burials at Kilmainham and Islandbridge, Dublin. In *Ireland and Scandinavia in the early Viking Age,* edited by Howard B. Clarke, Máire Ni Mhanaigh, and Raghnall Ó Floinn, 203–221. Blackrock: Four Courts.

Odess, Daniel
1998 The archaeology of interaction: Views from artifact style and material exchange in Dorset society. *American Antiquity* 63(3): 417–436.

Ogilvie, Astrid E. J.
1982 Climate and society in Iceland from the medieval period to the late eighteenth century. Ph.D. diss., University of East Anglia.
1984a The past climate and sea-ice record from Iceland, part 1: Data to A.D. 1780. *Climatic change* 6(2): 131–152.
1984b The impact of climate on grass growth and hay yield in Iceland: A.D. 1601 to 1780. In *Climatic changes on a yearly to millennial basis: Geological, historical, and instrumental records,* edited by Nils-Axel Mörner and W. Karlén, 343–352. Dordrecht: D. Reidel Pub. Co.
1991 Climatic changes in Iceland A.D. c. 865 to 1598. *Acta Archaeologica* 61: 233–251.
1992 Documentary evidence for changes in the climate of Iceland, A.D. 1500 to 1800. In *Climate since A.D. 1500,* edited by Raymond S. Bradley and Philip D. Jones, 92–117. London: Routledge.

Ogilvie, Astrid E. J., Lisa K. Barlow, and Anne E. Jennings
N.D. North Atlantic climate ca. A.D. 1000: Millennial reflections on the Viking discoveries of Iceland, Greenland, and North America. *Weather.* Forthcoming.

Ogilvie, Astrid E. J., and I. Jónsdóttir
1996 Sea-ice incidence off the coasts of Iceland: Evidence from historical data and sea-ice maps. In *26th International Arctic Workshop, Alpine and Arctic Environments, Past and Present, Program with Abstracts,* 109–110.
N.D. "Life is saltfish": Sea ice, climate, and Icelandic fisheries in historical times. Forthcoming

O'Kelly, Michael J.
1956 An island settlement at Beginish, Co Kerry. *Proceedings of the Royal Irish Academy* 57(C): 159–194.

Ólafsson, Erling
1991 *Íslenskt skordýratal* (Icelandic insects). *Fjölrit Náttúrufræðistofnunar* 17.

Ólafsson, Erling, and S. H. Richter
1985 Húsamaurinn (*Hypoponera punctatissima*) (House ant: *Hypoponera punctuatissima*). *Náttúrufræðingurinn* 55: 139–146.

Ólafsson, Guðmundur
1991 Fornleifarannsóknir að Bessastöðum 1987-1989 (Archaeological excavations at Bessasðir). In *Landnám Ingólfs: Nýtt safn til sögu þess* (Ingolf's landnám: New information on an old story), 4d ed, 91–108. Reykjavík: Félagið Ingólfur.

Olsen, Olaf
1992 Christiany and churches. In *From Viking to Crusader: The Scandinavians and Europe 800–1200,* edited by Else Roesdahl and David M. Wilson, 152–161. Uddevalla, Sweden: Bohusläningens Boktryckeri AB.

Olsen, Olaf, and Ole Crumlin Pedersen
1959 The Skuldelev ships: A preliminary report on an underwater excavation in Roskilde Fjord, Zealand. *Acta Archaeologica* 24: 161–175.

Ó'Ríordáin, Seán P.
1950 Lough Gur excavations: Carraig Aille and the "Spectacles." *Proceedings of the Royal Irish Academy* 52: 39–311 Dublin: Hodges, Figgis & Co.

Orrling, Carin
1996 Antiquité nordique et fantasmes culturels (Nordic antiquities and cultural fantasies). In *Dragons et drakkars: le mythe viking de la Scandinavie à la Normandie XVIIIe–XXe siècles* (Dragons and dragonships: the myth of the Scandinavian Vikings in Normandy during the 19th and 20th centuries), edited by Lucien Musset, 37–48. Caen: Musée de Normandie.

Østergård, Else
1998 The textiles—a preliminary report. In *Man, culture, and environment in ancient Greenland,* edited by Jette Arneborg and Hans Christian Gulløv, 58–65. Danish Polar Center Publication 4. Copenhagen: Danish National Museum and Danish Polar Center.

Page, Raymond I.
1987 *Runes.* Berkeley and Los Angeles: University of California Press.
1990 *Norse myths.* Austin: University of Texas Press.

Pálsson, Gísli
1991 *Coastal economies, cultural accounts: Human ecology and Icelandic discourse.* Manchester: Manchester University Press.

Pálsson, Hermann (trans.)
1971 *Hrafnkel's saga and other icelandic stories.* Harmondsworth: Penguin.

Panagiotakopulu, Eva
1999 Insect remains from Tell el Amarna. Unpublished report.

Park, Robert W.
1993 The Dorset-Thule succession in arctic North America: Assessing claims for culture contact. *American Antiquity* 58(2): 203–234.

Parry, M. L.
1981 Climatic change and the agricultural frontier: A research strategy. In *Climate and history, studies in past climates and their impact on man,* edited by T. M. L. Wigley, M. J. Ingram, and G. Farmer, 319–336. Cambridge: Cambridge University Press.

Pastore, Ralph T.
1992 *Shanawdithit's People: The archaeology of the Beothuks.* St. John's, Newfoundland: Atlantic Archaeology, Ltd.

Pell, Herbert
1948 The Old Stone Mill, Newport. *Rhode Island History* 7(4): 105–119.

Perdikaris, Sophia
1990 Aaker: A zooarchaeological perspective on a Norwegian

Iron Age site. Master's thesis, Hunter College, City University of New York.

Perkins, Michael
1931 Acromegaly in the far north. *Nature* 128(3229): 491–492.

Persson, Ib
1969 The fate of the Icelandic Vikings in Greenland. *Man* 4(4): 620–628.

Petersen, Jan
1928 *Vikingetidens smykker* (Viking Age jewelry). Stavanger: Stavanger Museum.

Petersen, Robert
1961 Karelerne på Grønland (The Karelians in Greenland). *Grønland* 12: 462–468.

Pirenne, Henri
1939 *Mohammed and Charlemagne*. London: G. Allen & Unwin.

Plumet, Patrick
1982 Les maisons longues dorsétiennes de l'Ungava (Dorset Eskimo longhouses on the Ungava peninsula). *Géographie Physique et Quaternaire* 36(3): 253–289.
1985 Archéologie de l'Ungava: le site de la Pointe aux Bélougas (Qilalugarsiuvik) et les maisons longues dorsétiennes (Archaeology of the Ungava peninsula and Beluga Point). *Paleo-Quebec* 18: 1–471. Laboratoire d'Archéologie, Université du Québec à Montréal.
1994 Le Paléoesquimau dans la baie du Diana (Arctique québécois) (The paleo-Eskimo in Diana Bay). In *Threads of arctic prehistory: Papers in honour of William E. Taylor, Jr.*, edited by David Morrison and Jean-Luc Pilon, 103–144. Archaeological Survey of Canada Mercury Series Paper 149. Hull, Québec: Canadian Museum of Civilization.

Pohl, Frederick J.
1952 *The lost discovery; Uncovering the track of the Vikings in America*. New York: Norton.
1961 *Atlantic crossings before Columbus*. New York: Norton.
1966 *The Viking explorers*. New York: T.Y. Crowell.
1972 *The Viking settlements of North America*. New York: C.N. Potter.

Price, Neil S.
1989 *The Vikings in Brittany*. London: Viking Society for Northern Research.
1991 Viking armies and fleets in Brittany: A case study for some general problems. In *Beretning fra tiende trúrfaglige vikingesymposium* (Report from the tenth Viking symposium), edited by Hans Bekker-Nielsen and Hans Frede Nielsen, 7–24. Aarhus: Aarhus University Press.
1998 Different Vikings? Towards a cognitive archaeology of religion and war in late Iron Age Scandinavia. In *Cult and belief in the Viking Age: A period of change*, edited by Anne-Sofie Gräslund, 5366. Uppsala: EC Socrates Programme Papers.

Prins, Harald E. L.
1996 *The Mi'kmaq: Resistance, accommodation, and cultural survival*. Fort Worth: Harcourt Brace College Publishing.

Procopius
1919 *Gothic war*. Vol. 3 of *Procopius*. Translated by Henry B. Dewing. Loeb Classical Library. London: W. Heinemann.

Putnam, Frederick W.
1901 Skeleton in armor. *American Anthropologist* 3: 388–389.

Quaife, M. M.
1937 A footnote on firesteels. *Minnesota History* 18: 36–41.

Rafn, Carl Christian
1837 *Antiqvitates Americanæ sive scriptores septentrionales rerum ante-Columbianarum in America* (American antiquities or northern records of pre-Columbian events in America). Copenhagen: Edidit Societas regia antiqvariorum septentrionalium.
1838 *Discovery of North America*. New York: Jackson.
1839 Account of an ancient structure in Newport, Rhode Island; the Vinland of the Scandinavians, communicated by Thomas M. Webb, M.D., in letters to Professor Charles C. Rafn, with remarks annexed by the latter. *Mémoires de la Société Royale des antiquiares du Nord 1836–1839*: 361–385. Copenhagen.
1840–44 Accounts of a discovery of antiquities made at Fall River, Massachusetts, and communicated by Thomas H. Webb, M.D., in letters to Charles C. Rafn, with remarks by the latter. *Mémoires de la Société royale des antiquiares du Nord* 1840–44: 104–119. Copenhagen.
1844 Brief notices of a runic inscription found in North America, communicated by Henry R. Schoolcraft in letters to Charles C. Rafn, with remarks annexed by the latter. *Mémoires de la Société royale des antiquiares du Nord* 1844: 128–131. Copenhagen.

Renaud, Jean
1989 *Les Vikings et la Normandie* (The Vikings and Normandy). Rennes: Editions Ouest-France.

Resen, Peder Hansen
1987 Groenlandia, org. 1687 (Greenland, 1687). *Det Grønlandske Selskabs Skrifter* 28: 1–189.

Resi, Heid G.
1990 *Die Wetz—und Schleifsteine aus* Haithabu (The whetstones and grindstones from Hedeby). Berichte 28. Neumünster: K. Wachholtz.

Reuter, Timothy
1985 Plunder and tribute in the Carolingian empire. *Transactions of the Royal Historical Society*, 5th series, 35: 75–94.

Reuter, Timothy (trans.)
1992 *The annals of Fulda*. Manchester: Manchester University Press.

Richards, Julian D.
1991 *Book of Viking Age England*. London: B.T. Batsford.

Rink, Hinrich Johannes
1875 *Tales and traditions of the Eskimos, with a sketch of their habits, religion, language, and other peculiarities*. Edinburgh: W. Blackwood and Sons.
1974 *Danish Greenland: Its people and products*. Montreal: McGill-Queen's University Press.

Ritchie, Anna
1977 Excavation of Pictish and Viking Age farmstead at Buckquoy, Orkney. *Proceedings of the Society of Antiquaries of Scotland* 108 (1976–77): 174–227.

Robin, Gordon de Q.
1983 The climate record from ice cores. In *The climatic record in polar ice sheets: A study of isotopic and temperature profiles in polar ice sheets based on a workshop held in the Scott Polar Research Institute, Cambridge*, edited by Gordon de Q. Robin, 180–195. Cambridge: Cambridge University Press.

Roesdahl, Else
1982 *Viking Age Denmark*. London: British Museum Publications.
1992 *The Vikings*. London: Penguin Books.
1998 L´ivoire de morse et les colonies noroises du Groenland (Walrus ivory and the Greenland Norse colonies). *Proxima Thulé* (Ultima Thule) 3: 9–48. Paris.

Roesdahl, Else, and Preben Meulengracht Sørensen (eds.)
1996 *The waking of Angantyr: The Scandinavian past in European culture*. Acta Jutlandica Humanities Series 70. Aarhus: Aarhus University Press.

Roesdahl, Else, and David M. Wilson (eds.)
1992 *From Viking to Crusader: The Scandinavians and Europe 800–1200*, edited by Else Roesdahl and David M. Wilson. Uddevalla, Sweden: Bohusläningens Boktryckeri AB.

Rogers, Penelope Walton
1998 The raw materials of textiles from GUS—with a note on fragments of fleece and animal pelts from the same site. In *Man, culture, and environment in ancient Greenland*, edited by Jette Arneborg and Hans Christian Gulløv, 66–73. Danish Polar Center Publication 4. Copenhagen: Danish National Museum and Danish Polar Center.
1999 A plied yarn from Nunguvik, Baffin Island, PgHb-1: 14765. Manuscript on file, Canadian Museum of Civilization.

Roland, A. E.
1998 *Roland's flora of Nova Scotia*. 3d ed. 2 vols. Halifax, Nova Scotia: Nimbus Publishing & Nova Scotia Museum.

Rosenberg, G.
1937 Hjortspringfundet (The Hjortspring excavation). *Nordiske Fortidsminder* 2(1).

Rothschild, M.
1973 Report on a female *Pulex irritans* in a tenth century Viking pit. *Proceedings of the Royal Entomological Society of London* 38: 29.

Roussell, Aage
1936 Sandnes and the neighbouring farms. *Meddelelser om Grønland* 88(2): 1–222.
1941 Farms and churches in the mediaeval Norse settlements of Greenland. *Meddelelser om Grønland* 89(1): 1–354.

Rousselière, Guy Mary
1982 A Viking priest among the Eskimos? *Eskimo* 23: 3–7.

Rowlett, Ralph M.
1982 1,000 years of New World archaeology. *American Antiquity* 47(3): 652–654.

Russell, Carl P.
1967 *Firearms, traps, and tools of the mountain men*. New York: Knopf.

Russell, Franklin
1970 *The Atlantic coast*. Toronto: N.S.L. Natural Sciences of Canada, Ltd.

Rydving, Håkan
1990 Scandinavian-Saami religious connections in the history

of research. In *Old Norse and Finnish religions and cultic place-names: Based on papers read at the symposium on encounters between religions in old Nordic times and on cultic place-names held at Åbo, Finland, on the 19th–21st of August 1987*, edited by Tore Ahlbäck, 358–373. Åbo, Finland: Donner Institute for Research in Religious and Cultural History.

Sabo, Deborah, and George Sabo, III
1978 A possible Thule carving of a Viking from Baffin Islands, N.W.T. *Canadian Journal of Archaeology* 2: 33–42.

Sadler, Jon
1991 Beetles, boats, and biogeography: Insect invaders of the North Atlantic. *Acta Archaeologica* 61: 199–211.

Salin, Bernhard
1904 *Die altgermanische thierornamentik* (The old Germanic animal ornamentation). Berlin: Kommission bei A. Asher & Co.

Salmo, Helmer
1948 *Deutsche Münzen in vorgeschichtlichen Funden Finnlands* (German coins in Finland's prehistoric finds). Suomen muinaismuistoyhdistyksen aikakauskirja 47. Helsinki: Suomen Muinaismuistoyhdistys.
1956 *Finnische Hufeisenfibeln* (Finnish horseshoe brooches). Suomen muinaismuistoyhdistyksen aikakauskirja 56. Helsinki: Suomen Muinaismuistoyhdistys.

Salwen, Bert
1978 Indians of southern New England and Long Island: Early period. In *Handbook of North American Indians, Vol. 15, Northeast*, edited by Bruce G. Trigger, 160–176. Washington, D.C.: Smithsonian Institution Press.

Samson, Ross
1991a Economic anthropology and Vikings. In *Social approaches to Viking studies*, edited by Ross Samson, 87–96. Glasgow: Cruithne Press.
1991b Fighting with silver. In *Social approaches to Viking studies*, edited by Ross Samson, 123–133. Glasgow: Cruithne Press.

Sanger, David
1987 *The Carson site and the late Ceramic period in Passamaquoddy Bay, New Brunswick*. Archaeological Survey of Canada Mercury Series Paper 135. Ottawa: National Museums of Canada.

Sawyer, Peter H.
1971 *The age of the Vikings*, 2d ed. London: Edward Arnold.
1982a *Kings and Vikings: Scandinavia and Europe, A.D. 700–1100*. London: Methuen.
1982b The camps of the Viking Age. In *The Vikings*, edited by Robert T. Farrell. London: Phillimore.
1988 Da Danmark blev Danmark (When Denmark became Denmark). In *Politikens Danmarks-historie 3: Fra år 700–ca. 1050* (Denmark's political history 3: 700–ca. 1050), edited by O. Olsen. Copenhagen: Gyldendals.
1998a *From Roman Britain to Norman England*, 2d ed. London: Routledge.
1998b *Anglo-Saxon Lincolnshire*. Lincoln: History of Lincolnshire Committee.

Sawyer, Peter H. (ed.)
1997 *The Oxford illustrated history of the Vikings*. Oxford: Oxford University Press.

Scales, Peter C.
1994 *The fall of the caliphate of Córdoba: Berbers and Andalusis in conflict*. Leiden: E.J. Brill.

Schefferus, Johannes
1675 *De orbibus tribus aureis* (About three gold bracteates). n.p.

Schledermann, Peter
1977 Eskimo trappers on Ellesmere Island, N.W.T. *Western Canadian Journal of Anthropology* 7(1): 84–99.
1980 Notes on Norse finds from the east coast of Ellesmere Island, N.W.T. *Arctic* 33(3): 454–463.
1990 *Crossroads to Greenland: 3,000 years of prehistory in the eastern High Arctic*. Komatik 2. Calgary: Arctic Institute of North America of the University of Calgary.
1993 Norsemen in the High Arctic? In *Viking voyages to North America*, edited by Birthe L. Clausen, 54–66. Roskilde, Denmark: Viking Ship Museum.
1996 *Voices in stone: A personal journey into the arctic past*. Komatik Series 5. Calgary: Arctic Institute of North America of the University of Calgary.

Scholz, Bernhard W. (trans.)
1970 *Carolingian chronicles: Royal Frankish Annals and Nithard's Histories*. Ann Arbor: University of Michigan Press.

Schönbäck, Bengt
1983 The custom of burial in boats. In *Vendel period studies: Transactions of the Boat-Grave Symposium in Stockholm, February 2–3, 1981*, edited by Jan Peder Lamm and Hans Åke Nordström, 123–132. Studies 2. Stockholm: Statens Historiska Museum.

Schoolcraft, Henry R.

1851 *Historical and statistical information respecting the history, condition, and prospects of the Indian tribes of the United States*, vol. 1. Philadelphia: Bureau of Indian Affairs.

1853-57 *Information respecting the history, condition, and prospect of the Indian tribes of the United States collected and prepared under the direction of the Bureau of Indian Affairs per Act of Congress of March 3rd, 1847*. Illustrations by S. Eastman, Captain of the U.S. Army, I-VI. Philadelphia: Lippincott.

Schübeler, F.

1859 *Om den 'Hvede', som Nordmændene i Aaret 1000 fandt vildtvoxende i Vinland* (Concerning the wheat that the Norse found growing wild in Vinland in A.D. 1000). *Christiania Videnskabs-Selskabs Forhandlinger* 1858: 21–31.

Schück, Henrik, and Karl Warburg

1926-49 *Illustrerad svensk litteraturhistoria* (An illustrated history of Swedish literature). Stockholm: H. Geber.

Schweger, Charles E.

1998 Geoarchaeology of the GUS Site: A preliminary framework. In *Man, culture, and environment in ancient Greenland*, edited by Jette Arneborg and Hans Christian Gulløv, 14–18. Danish Polar Center Publication 4. Copenhagen: Danish National Museum and Danish Polar Center.

1999 Preliminary report on radiocarbon dates of paleosoils on GUS. Unpublished.

Scott, G. Richard, Carrin M. Halffman, and P. O. Pedersen

1991 Dental conditions of medieval Norsemen in the North Atlantic. *Acta Archaeologica* 62: 183–207.

Searle, Eleanor

1988 *Predatory kinship and the creation of Norman power, 840–1066*. Berkeley and Los Angeles: University of California Press.

Seaver, Kirsten A.

1995 "The Vinland Map": Who made it, and why? New light on an old problem. *The Map Collector* 70: 32–42.

1996 *The frozen echo: Greenland and the exploration of North America ca. A.D. 1000–1500*. Stanford, Calif.: Stanford University Press.

1997 The Vinland Map: A $3,500 duckling that became a $25,000,000 swan. *Mercator's World*, March/April, 42–47.

1998 The Vinland Map and Tartar Relation. *Speculum* 73(3): 896–899.

1999 How strange is a stranger? A survey of opportunities for Inuit-European contact in the Davis Strait before 1576. In *Meta incognita: A discourse of discovery*, edited by Thomas H.B. Symon, 523–552. Mercury Series Directorate Paper 10. Hull, Québec: Canadian Museum of Civilization.

Secher, Karsten

1998 Stone finds from the hall (XVII) and their functions—geological commentary. In *Man, culture, and environment in ancient Greenland*, edited by Jette Arneborg and Hans Christian Gulløv, 45–47. Danish Polar Center Publication 4. Copenhagen: Danish National Museum and Danish Polar Center.

Seligman, C. G.

1931 Acromegaly among the old Northmen. *Nature* 128(3223): 221.

Shetelig, Haakon

1917a Skibet (The ship). In *Osebergfundet: Utgit av den Norske stat* (The Oseberg excavation), edited by Anton W. Brøgger, Hjalmar J. Falk, and Haakon Shetelig, 283–364. Oslo: Universitetets Oldsaksamling.

1917b Tuneskibet (The Tune ship). Norske Oldfunn 2. Oslo: Universitetets Oldsaksamling.

Shetelig, Haakon, and Fr. Johannessen

1929 *Kvalsundfundet og andre norske myrfund av fartøier* (Finds from Kvalsund). Bergen: Bergens Museum.

Shirley, Rodney W.

1983 *The mapping of the world: Early printed world maps, 1472–1700*. London: Holland Press.

Sigurdsson, Haraldur

1965 Vinlandskortid, aldur þess og upprúni (The Vinland Map, its age and origin). Þoðviljanum. 24 December.

Sigurdsson, Jón Viðar

1999 *Chieftains and power in the Icelandic Commonwealth*. The Viking Collection 12. Odense: Odense University Press.

Sigurðsson, Jón, Gudbrandur Vigfússon, Thorvaldur Björnsson, and Eiríkur Jónsson (eds.)

1858-78 *Biskupa sögur I-III* (Bishop sagas I-II). Kaupmannahöfn: I prentsmidju S. L. Möllers.

Silliman, H.

1979 *The Newport tower*. Special Publication. N.p.: New England Antiquities Research Association.

Silverberg, Robert

1968 *Mound builders of ancient America; The archaeology of a myth*. Greenwich, Conn.: New York Graphic Society.

Simpson, I.

1999 Modelling grazing pressure and its impact on the North Atlantic region: Retrospect and prospect. Paper presented to Historical Dimensions of Human Adaptability and Environmental Change in North Atlantic Regions. International NABO meeting at the Stefansson Arctic Institute, 16–21 July, 1999.

Simpson, Jacqueline

1967 *Everyday life in the Viking Age*. London: Batsford.

Sjøvold, Thorleif

1974 The Iron Age settlement of arctic Norway: A study in the expansion of European Iron Age culture within the Arctic Circle. *Tromsø Museums Skrifter* 10(2). Tromsø: Universitetsforlaget.

Skaare, Kolbjorne

1979 An eleventh-century Norwegian penny found on the coast of Maine. *Norwegian Numismatic Journal* 2: 4–17.

Skelton, Raleigh A., Thomas E. Marston, and George D. Painter

1965 *The Vinland Map and the Tartar Relation*. New Haven: Yale University Press. (Rev. ed. 1995)

Skidmore, Peter

1996 A dipterological perspective on the Holocene history of the North Atlantic area. Ph.D. diss., University of Sheffield.

Smedberg, Gunnar

1973 Norden första kyrkor. En kyrkorättslig studie (The first Nordic churches). *Bibliotheca theologiae practicae* 32. Lund: Gleerup.

Smiley, Jane

1988 *The Greenlanders*. New York: Knopf.

Smith, Benjamin

1953 A report on the Follins Pond investigation. *Massachusetts Archaeological Society Bulletin* 14(2): 82–99.

Smith, Julia M. H.

1992 *Province and empire: Brittany and the Carolingians*. Cambridge: Cambridge University Press.

Smith, Kevin P.

1995 Landnám: The Settlement of Iceland in Archaeological and Historical Perspective. *World Archaeology* 26(3): 319–347.

Snæsdóttir, Mjöll

1991 Stóraborg—an Icelandic farm mound. *Acta Archaeologica* 61: 116–119.

1992 Jarðhúsið í Stóraborg undir Eyjafjöllum (Turfhouse in Stóraborg near Eyja mountain). *Árbók hins Islenzka Fornleifafélags* 1991: 53–58.

Snow, Dean R.

1978 Late prehistory of the East Coast. In *Handbook of North American Indians, Vol. 15, Northeast*, edited by Bruce G. Trigger, 58–69. Washington, D.C.: Smithsonian Institution Press.

Sølver, Carl V.

1954 *Vestervejen om vikingernes sejlads* (The western route of the Vikings). Copenhagen: I. C. Weilbach.

Sørensen, Palle Østergaard

1994 Gudmehallerne; Kongeligt byggeri fra jernalderen (The Gudme halls; royal construction from the Iron Age). *Nationalmuseets Arbejdsmark* 1994: 25–37.

Squier, Ephraim G., and E. Hiram Davis

1848 *Ancient monuments of the Mississippi Valley: Comprising the results of extensive original surveys and explorations*. Smithsonian Contributions to Knowledge 1. Washington, D.C.: Smithsonian Institution.

Steensby, Hans P.

1918 *The Norsemen's route from Greenland to Wineland*. Copenhagen: H. Koppel.

Stefansson, Vilhjalmur

1939 *Iceland, the first American Republic*. New York: Doubleday, Doran & Co.

1940 *Ultima Thule; further mysteries of the arctic*. New York: Macmillan.

Steinsland, Gro, and Preben Meulengracht Sørensen

1994 *Menneske og makter i Vikingenes verden* (People and power in the Viking world). Oslo: Universitetsforlaget.

Stibéus, M.

1997 Medieval coastal settlement in western Sweden. In *Visions of the past: Trends and traditions in Swedish medieval archaeology*, edited by Hans Andersson. Stockholm: Almqvist & Wiksell.

Stoklund, Marie

1982 Nordboruiner (The runes of the Norse). *Grønland* 5/6/7: 197–206.

1993 Greenland runes: Isolation or cultural contact? In *The Viking Age in Caithness, Orkney, and the North Atlantic: Select papers from the proceedings of the Eleventh Viking Congress, Thurso and Kirkwall, 22 August–1 September 1989*, edited by Colleen E. Batey, Judith Jesch, and Christopher D. Morris, 528–543. Edinburgh: Edinburgh University Press.

1998 Runes. In *Man, culture, and environment in ancient Greenland*, edited by Jette Arneborg and Hans Christian Gulløv, 55–57. Danish Polar Center Publication 4. Copenhagen: Danish National Museum and Danish Polar Center.

Storm, Gustav

1887 Studier over Vinlandsreiserne, Vinlands Geografi og Ethnografi (The studies of the Vinland voyages, the geography and ethnography of Vinland). *A arbøger for Nordisk Oldkyndighed og Historie*: 293–372.

1889 *Studies on the Vinland Voyages*. Copenhagen: Thiele.

1977 *Islandske Annaler indtil 1578* (Icelandic annals until 1578). Oslo: Norsk Historisk Kjeldeskrift Institutt.

Stoumann, Ingrid

1979 Sædding. A Viking-Age village near Esbjerg. *Acta Archaeologica* 50: 95–118.

Strandwold, Olaf

1948 *Norse inscriptions on American stones collected and deciphered*. Privately published.

Stratford, Neil

1997 *The Lewis chessmen and the enigma of the hoard*. London: British Museum Press.

Strömbäck, Dag

1935 *Seiður; textstudier i nordisk religionshistoria*. (Seiður: Textual studies in the history of Nordic religion). Stockholm: H. Geber.

Sutherland, Patricia D.

1987 Umingmaknuna: Its people and prehistory. *Inuktitut* 66: 46–54.

1989 An inventory and assessment of the prehistoric archaeological resources of Ellesmere Island National Park Reserve. Microfiche Report Series 4. Environment Canada Parks Service.

1993 Prehistoric adaptations to changing environments on western Ellesmere Island and eastern Axel Heiberg Island. Final Report on the 1992 Field Season. Manuscript on file, Royal Canadian Geographical Society.

Sveinbjarnardóttir, Guðrún

1992 *Farm abandonment in medieval and post-medieval Iceland: An interdisciplinary study*. Oxbow Monograph 17. Oxford: Oxbow Books.

1993 Vitnisburður leirkera um samband Íslands og Evrópu á miðöldum (Pottery evidence for the relationship between Iceland and Europe in the Middle Ages). *Árbók hins Islenzka Fornleifafélags* 1992: 31–50.

Sveinbjarnardóttir, Guðrún, and Paul C. Buckland

1983 An uninvited guest. *Antiquity* 48: 32–33.

Sveinsson Einar Ó., and Matthias Thórðarson (eds.)

1935 *Eyrbyggja saga: Brands þáttr örva. Eiríks saga rauða. Groenlendinga saga. Groenlendingaþáttr* (Saga of the people of Eyri: The tale of Brand the Generous, Erik the Red's saga, Greenlanders' saga, and the tale of the Greenlanders). Íslenzk fornrit 4. Reykjavík: Hið Islenzka Fornritafélag.

Svensson, E.

1998 *Människor i utmark* (People in the hinterlands). Lund Studies in Medieval Archaeology 21. Lund: Institute of Archaeology, Lund University.

Sverdrup, Otto N.

1904 *New land; four years in the arctic regions*. London: Longmans, Green.

Taavitsainen, Jussi-Pekka

1990 *Ancient hillforts of Finland: Problems of analysis, chronology, and interpretation with special reference to the hillfort of Kuhmoinen*. Suomen Muinaismuistoyhdistyksen aikakauskirja 94. Helsinki: Suomen muinaismuistoyhdistys.

1991 Cemeteries or refuse heaps? Archaeological formation process and the interpretation of sites and antiquities. *Suomen Museo* 1991: 5–14.

Talvio, Tuukka

1980a Coin imitations as jewelry in eleventh-century Finland. *Finskt Museum* 1978: 26–38.

1980b The Finnish coin hoards of the Viking Age. *Fenno-Ugri et Slavi, Stencil* 22: 171–178. Department of Archaeology, University of Helsinki.

1982 Finland's place in Viking-Age relations between Sweden and the eastern Baltic/northern Russia: The numismatic evidence. *Journal of Baltic Studies* 13(3): 245–255.

Taviani, Paolo Emilio

1985 *Christopher Columbus: The grand design*. 2d ed. London: Orbis.

Taylor, Alexander B. (trans.)
1938 *The Orkneyinga saga*. Edinburgh: Olive and Boyd.

Taylor, E. G. R.
1956 A letter dated 1577 from Mercator to John Dee. *Imago Mundi* 13: 56–67.

Thalbitzer, William
1904 A phonetical study of the Eskimo language based on observations made on a journey in North Greenland 1900–1901. *Meddelelser om Grønland* 31: 1–406.
1951 Two runic stones, from Greenland and Minnesota. *Smithsonian Miscellaneous Collections* 116(3): 1–67. Washington, D.C.

Thirslund, Søren
1987 *Viking navigation. Sun-compass guided Norsemen first to America*. Humlebæk, Denmark: Gullanders Bogtrykkeri.

Thomas, David Hurst (ed.)
1989 *Archaeological and historical perspectives on the Spanish borderlands west*. Washington, D.C.: Smithsonian Institution Press.

Thórarinsson, Sigurdur
1943 Thjórsárdalur och dess forödelse (Thjórsárdalur and its destruction). *In Forntida Gårdar i Island* (Early Farms in Iceland), Mårten Stenberger, ed. 1943: 9–52.
1956 *The thousand years struggle against ice and fire*. Museum of Natural History Occasional Papers 14. Reykjavík: National Museum of Iceland.
1961 Population Changes in Iceland. *Geographical Review* 51: 519–533.

Thorláksson, Helgi
1984 *Sautjanda oldin: þaettir ur drögum að Sogu Islands V, saminni að tihlutan Thjodhátidarnefndar 1974* (Seventeenth century: Excerpts from Saga Islands V, on the occasion of the 1100-year celebration of the nation). Reykjavík: Boksala studenta.
1991 *Vadmal og verdlag: vadmal i utanlandsvidskiptum og buskap Islendinga a 13. og 14. old* (Wool and worth: Wool exports and the Icelandic bishop in the thirteenth and fourteenth centuries). Iceland: n.p.

Thorsteinsson, Arne
1977 Heimildir um seyðamjólking í Føroyum (Evidence of grain growing in the Faeroes). *Fróðskaparrit: Annales Societatis Scientiarum Færoensis* 25: 84–94.
1981 On the development of Faeroese settlements. *Proceedings of the Eighth Viking Congress, Aarhus 24-31 August 1977*, edited by Hans Bekker-Nielsen, Peter Foote, and O. Olsen, 189–202. Odense: n.p.

Thorsteinsson, Björn
1965–67 Islands-og Grœnlandssiglinar Englendinga á 15. öld og fundur Norður-Ameríku (English sailors to Iceland and Greenland in the fifteenth century and the discovery of North America). *Saga* 4/5: 3–72.
1985 *Island*. (Iceland) *Politikens Danmarks Historie*. Copenhagen: Politikens Forlaget.

Thóðarson, Matthías
1945 *Thingvöllur; Alþingisstaðurinn forni* (Thingvellir: The ancient place of the Althingi). Reykjavík: Alþingissögunefnd.
1969 *Vínlandsferdirnar: nokkar athugasemadir og skýringar* (Journeys to Vinland: some observations and explanations). Reykjavík: Safn til sögu Íslands.

Time-Life Books
1993 *Vikings: Raiders from the north*. Alexandria, Va.: Time-Life Books.

Towe, Kenneth M.
1975 The Vinland Map revisited: An analysis of the McCrone reports and an evaluation of the problem of the map's authenticity. Manuscript on file, Yale University.

Treece, Henry
1957 *The road to Miklagard*. New York: Criterion Books.

Turville-Petre, Gabriel
1975 *Myth and religion of the north: The religion of ancient Scandinavia*. Westport, Conn.: Greenwood Press.

Uino, Pirjo
1997 *Ancient Karelia: Archaeological studies*. Suomen Muinaismuistoyhdistyksen aikakauskirja 104. Helsinki: Suomen Muinaismuistoyhdistys.

Vebæk, Christen L.
1991 The church topography of the Eastern Settlement and the excavation of the Benedictine convent in Uunartoq Fjord. *Meddelelser om Grønland: Man & Society* 14: 1–81.

Vebæk, Christen L., and Søren Thirslund
1992 *The Viking compass guided Norsemen first to America*. Humlebæk, Denmark: S. Thirslund & C. L. Vebæk.

Vésteinsson, Orri
1998a Íslenska sóknaskipulagið og samband heimila á miðöldum (Organization of Icelandic parishes and households in the Middle Ages). *Islenska söguþingið 28.–31. maí 1997, Ráðstefnurit* I (Conference journal I: Icelandic saga meeting 28–31 May 1997): 147–166.
1998b Patterns of settlement in Iceland: A study in prehistory. *Saga-Book of the Viking Society* 25: 1-29.

Vilhjálmsson, H.
1997 Climatic variations and some examples of their effects on the marine ecology of Icelandic and Greenlandic waters, in particular during the present century. *Rit Fiskideildar* 15(1): 153–181.

Vilhjálmsson, Vilhjálmur Örn
1996 Gård og kirke på Stöng i Thjórsárdalur. I: Nordsjøen Handel, religion og politikk (Farm and church at Stöng in Thjórsárdalur.I: The North Sea trade, religion, and politics). In *Karmøyseminaret 1994 og 1995* (Karmøy seminar 1994 and 1995), 119–140. Stavanger: n.p.

Vinding, Niels
1998 *Vinland 1000 år* (Vinland 1000 years). Copenhagen: Lindhardt og Ringhof.

Wahlgren, Erik
1958 *The Kensington stone, a mystery solved*. Madison: University of Wisconsin Press.
1986 *The Vikings and America*. New York: Thames and Hudson.
1993 Kensington stone. In *Medieval Scandinavia: An encyclopedia*, edited by Phillip Pulsiano, 352. Vol. 1 of Garland Encyclopedias of the Middle Ages. New York: Garland Publishing, Inc.
1993 Viking hoaxes. In *Medieval Scandinavia: An encyclopedia*, edited by Phillip Pulsiano, 700–701. Vol. 1 of Garland Encyclopedias of the Middle Ages. New York: Garland Publishing, Inc.

Wallace, Birgitta Linderoth
1982 Vikings hoaxes. In *Vikings in the west: Papers presented at a symposium sponsored by the Archaeological Institute of America, Chicago Society, and the Museum of Science and Industry of Chicago at the Museum of Science and Industry on April 3, 1982*, edited by Eleanor Guralnick, 53–76. New York: Archaeological Institute of America.
1991a L'Anse aux Meadows: Gateway to Vinland. *Acta Archaeologica* 61: 166–198.
1991b The Vikings in North America: Myth and reality. In *Social approaches to Viking studies*, edited by Ross Samson, 206–212. Glasgow: Cruithne Press.
1993 L'Anse aux Meadows, the western outpost. In *Viking voyages to North America*, edited by Birthe L. Clausen, 30–42. Roskilde, Denmark: Viking Ship Museum.

Wallace, Patrick F.
1985 The archaeology of Viking Dublin. In *The comparative history of urban origins in non-Roman Europe: Ireland, Wales, Denmark, Germany, Poland, and Russsia from the ninth to the thirteenth century*, edited by Howard B. Clarke and Anngret Simms, 103–146. International series 255. Oxford: British Archaeological Reports.

Wallis, Helen
1991 The Vinland Map. Genuine or fake? *Bulletin du bibliophile* 1.

Wallis, Helen, F. R. Maddison, G. D. Painter, D. B. Quinn, et al.
1974 The strange case of the Vinland Map. *Geographical Journal* 140(2): 183–214.

Walløe, Peder O.
1927 *Peder Olsen Walløes dagbøger fra hans rejser i Grønland 1739–53* (Peder Olsen Walløe's diaries from his travels in Greenland 1739–53). Grønlandske selskabs Skrifter 5. Copenhagen: G. E. C. Gad.

Wamers, Egon
1995 The symbolic significance of the ship-graves at Haiðaby and Ladby. In *The ship as symbol in prehistoric and medieval Scandinavia: Papers from an international research seminar at the Danish National Museum, Copenhagen, 5th–7th May 1994*, edited by Ole Crumlin-Pedersen and Birgitte Munch Thye, 149–159. Copenhagen: Danish National Museum.

Wamers, Egon, Hans Drescher, Egon Lietz, Herbert Patotzki, and Göran Possnert
1994 König im Grenzland: neue Analyse des Bootkammergrabes von Haithaby (The king in the border zone: The new analysis of the boat chamber graves from Hedeby). *Acta Archaeologica* 65: 1–56.

Washburn, Wilcomb E. (ed.)
1971 *Proceedings of the Vinland Map Conference*. Chicago: University of Chicago Press.

Webster, G., R.H.M. Dolley, G. Dunning
1953 A Saxon treasure hoard found at Chester. *Antiquaries Journal* 33: 22–32.

Weibull, Lauritz Ulrik Absalon
1948–49 *Nordisk historia: Forskningar och undersökningar*, vol. 1 (Nordic history, vol. I). Stockholm: Natur och Kultur.

Weiss, Kenneth M., and Peter E. Smouse
1976 The demographic stability of small human populations. *Journal of Human Evolution* 5(1): 59–73.

Welinder, Stig, Ellen A. Pedersen, and Mats Widgren
1998 *Jordbrukets första femtusen år* (The first five thousand years of farming). Det svenska jordbrukets historia 1. Stockholm: Natur och kultur/LTs förlag.

Whitehead, Ruth H.
1991 *The old man told us: Excerpts from Micmac history, 1500–1950*. Halifax, Nova Scotia: Nimbus Publications.

Whitelock, Dorothy (ed.)
1979 *c. 500–1042*. Vol. 1 of *English historical documents*, edited by David C. Douglas. 2d ed. London: E. Methuen; New York: Oxford University Press.

Whitridge, Peter James
1999 The construction of social differences in a prehistoric Inuit whaling community. Ph.D. diss., Arizona State University, Tempe.

Whittier, John Greenleaf
1904 The Norsemen. In *The complete poetical works of John Greenleaf Whittier*. Boston: Houghton, Mifflin & Company.

Wigley, Tom M. L.
1996 A millennium of climate. *Earth* 5(6): 38–42.

Williams, Stephen
1991 *Fantastic archaeology: The wide side of North American prehistory*. Philadelphia: University of Pennsylvania Press.

Williamson, Kenneth
1948 *The Atlantic islands*. London: Collins.

Willoughby, Charles Clark
1935 *Antiquities of the New England Indians, with notes on the ancient cultures of the adjacent territory*. Cambridge, Mass.: Peabody Museum of American Archaeology and Ethnology, Harvard University.

Wilson, David M.
1997 *Vikings and gods in European art*. Højbjerg, Denmark: Moesgård Museum.

Wilson, David M., and Ole Klindt-Jensen
1980 *Viking art*. 2d ed. Minneapolis: University of Minnesota Press.

Wyckoff, Don G.
1973 No stones unturned. Differing views of Oklahoma's runestones. *Popular Archaeology*, August, 16–31.

Zachrisson, Inger
1977 Varför samiskt? (Why "Saami"?). In *Möten i gränsland: Samer och germaner i Mellanskandinavien* (Meetings in border country: Saami and Germanics in central Scandinavia), edited by Inger Zachrisson et al., 189–220. Stockholm: Statens Historiska Museum.
1994 Archaeology and politics: Saami prehistory and history in Central Scandinavia. *Journal of European Archaeology* 2(2): 361–368.

ACKNOWLEDGMENTS

VIKINGS: THE NORTH ATLANTIC SAGA is a large, complex exhibition and publication project that had to be completed in a very short time; for this reason it had more than its share of setbacks and dramatic recoveries. This catalogue and the associated exhibition have seen the light of day only because of the extraordinary goodwill of a large number of people, only a few of whom can be noted here; to the many others who contributed we extend our thanks and appreciation for helping to bring *Vikings* to North America in time for the Leif Eriksson millennial.

At the very outset we thank those who first conceived of having a Viking exhibition in North America: Dag Sebastian Ahlander, Counsel General for Sweden in New York; Ove Joanson and Jørgen Grunnet, cultural ministers, respectively, of the Swedish and Danish Embassies in Washington, D.C.; Carl Henrick Svenstedt, Senior Advisor for the Nordic Council of Ministers (NCM); and Per Sörbom, then Chair of the NCM's Cultural Projects Abroad Committee. From then on the Nordic Council of Ministers played an essential role as the principal instigator and funder. The NCM staff who shouldered much of the later planning included Marianne Möller, Senior Advisor; Laufey Guðjónsdóttir, Chair of Cultural Projects Abroad; Søren Dyssegaard, Chair of the Viking project; Birgitta Schreiber, administrative assistant; and Ole Morten Orset, who served as Counselor and resided at the NMNH during the last year of the project. Among those involved in these preliminary discussions within the Nordic museums were Thor Magnusson, Director of the National Museum of Iceland; Ritva Wäre, Director of the National Museum of Finland and Curator Torsten Edgren; Egil Mikkelsen, Director of the University Museum of National Antiquities in Oslo and Curator Irmelin Martens; and Deputy Director Niels-Knud Liebgott of the Danish National Museum.

The project began in late 1996 when Ove Joanson and Jørgen Grunnet, acting on behalf of the NCM, asked Marjory Stoller, then Chief of the NMNH Special Exhibitions Office, if the Museum would be interested in undertaking a Viking exhibition. In the spring of 1997 NCM invited William W. Fitzhugh (NMNH), Patricia Sutherland of the Canadian Museum of Civilization (CMC), and Birgitta Wallace of Parks Canada to explore the exhibition concept with Scandinavian authorities, museum curators, and the NCM. We concluded that such an exhibition should feature the territorial expansion of Vikings across the North Atlantic into the New World rather than be a replay of European-focused art exhibitions like *The Vikings,* organized by James Graham-Campbell and David Wilson for the British Museum and the Metropolitan Museum of Art in 1980, or *Viking to Crusader*, an NCM exhibition curated by Else Roesdahl in 1992, which was one of the models suggested for our project. As the concept evolved, agreements developed between the principal North American players, the Canadian Museum of Civilization (thanks to George MacDonald, Sylvie Morel, and Stephen Inglis), Parks Canada (thanks to Christine Cameron), and NMNH (thanks to Robert Sullivan). We thank the CMC, Parks Canada, and the Government of Newfoundland and Labrador for providing artifacts that made it possible to explore thoroughly the themes of Viking settlement and Native contacts in North America. As the project matured under the direction of Robert Sullivan, the NMNH production team of Joseph Madeira, acting Chief of Special Exhibits; Deborah Wood, registrar; Kara Callaghan, administrative assistant; Anna-Lincoln Whitehurst, Development Officer; Randall Kremer, Associate Director of Public Affairs; and Laura McKie, Chief of the Education Office, safely guided us to completion.

Vikings never would have come to fruition without the financial support of the Nordic Council of Ministers and Volvo. Throughout, the fundraising effort was planned by NMNH in concert with the Nordic embassies, with assistance from the Department of State and the White House Millennium Council. The Cultural Group of the Nordic Embassies, consisting of representatives of all five Nordic countries in Washington, Ottawa, and New York, was led by three individuals during the course of the exhibition planning: Ove Joanson, Swedish Embassy; Lis Frederiksen, Danish Embassy; and Eivind Homme, Norwegian Embassy. Nordic Affairs Desk Officer Andrew Silski and his assistant, Kara Grimaldi skillfully handled coordination at the State Department. Thanks to the efforts of the Icelandic Foreign Minister, the project became a featured component of the joint U.S.-Icelandic Leifur Eiriksson Working Group on the Millennium chaired by Ellen McCulloch Lovell, co-chaired by Einar Benediktsson, Chairman of the Icelandic Leifur Eiriksson Millennium Commission, and vice-chaired by Caroline Croft, who also joined the NMNH Vikings Task Force and helped secure the interest of First Lady Hillary Rodham Clinton. Through these connections we obtained the assistance of Nancy Ruwe, widow of former U.S. Ambassador Ruwe to Iceland. Day

Olin Mount, then United States Ambassaor to Iceland, is due special thanks for his continued promotion of the project and for the hospitality he and Katherine Mount provided during curatorial visits to Iceland. Robert Fri, Director of the National Museum of Natural History, provided strong support within NMNH, and Marc Pachter, Counselor to the Secretary of the Smithsonian, provided crucial support from the Smith-sonian's central administration.

Outside the political and financial arena, William Fitzhugh, head curator, and Elisabeth Ward, assistant curator, were aided by a large international group of scholarly advisors. Several members of this team were official NCM appointees: Carin Orrling, Editor-in-Chief of the Museum of National Antiquities in Stockholm; Sigrid Kaland, Senior Curator at University of Bergen Museum; Torsten Edgren, Curator at the National Board of Antiquities, Finnish National Museum; Jette Arneborg of the Medieval Department of the Danish National Museum; Lilja Arnadóttir, Conservator of the National Museum of Iceland; and Joel Berglund, Vice-Director of Greenland National Museum and Archive (GNM). Equally important to the project were Colleen Batey, Curator of Archaeology at Glasgow Art Gallery and Museum, Kelvingrove; Tom McGovern, Hunter College; Peter Schledermann, Research Associate at the Arctic Institute of North America, University of Calgary; and Örnólfur Thorsson, Special Assistant to the President of Iceland. By far our greatest debt for continuing curatorial support and assistance is owed to Birgitta Linderoth Wallace of Parks Canada, who provided advice and assistance at every turn. Many others also provided assistance and hopefully will recognize their contributions. Special thanks, however, are due to Steen Hvass, Director of the Danish National Museum, who offered important Viking treasures and the expert curatorial services of several members of his staff.

The task of turning the exhibit plan into an exhibition was masterfully accomplished by MFM Design of Washington, D.C. The design team was directed by Richard Molinaroli, assisted by Beth Miles, Michael Lawrence, and Katherine Lenard. The script was written by Sue Voss; exhibition models, murals, and interactives were prepared by Hugh McKay and David Coldwell, and exhibition maps were prepared by Robert Pratt of National Geographic Society. The Smithsonian's Office of Exhibits Central, directed by Michael Headley, built exhibition cases and produced mannequins prepared by Lora Collins and Carole Reuter; Mary Bird produced the first exhibition floor plan before a design team was available.

Special thanks are due to all the lending institutions who helped with consultation, lending objects, and providing illustrations, including Christine McDonnell and Richard Hall of the York Archaeological Trust; Leena Soyrinki-Harmo, who assisted after Torsten Edgren's retirement; Hans Christian Gulløv, Anne Pedersen, and Lars Jørgensen of the DNM; David Morrison and Patricia

Sutherland of the CMC; Bruce Bourque and Steven Cox of the Maine State Museum; Heid Gjøstein Resi of the University Museum of National Antiquities, Oslo; Anne Stalsberg of the University Museum of Natural History and Archaeology, Trondheim; and Kevin McAleese of the Newfoundland Museum.

This book had to be produced simultaneously with the exhibition–always a daunting task! We thank our many authors for their willingness to undertake writing on short notice. Many were kind enough to write in English, but for those who did not, translation from Swedish was provided by David Mel Paul, from Danish by James Manley of Gronningen ApS, and from Finnish by Jarmo Kankaanpaa. Some authors took on extra or urgent assignments, including Jette Arneborg, Thomas McGovern, Chris Morris, Neil Price, Astrid Ogilvie, Peter Sawyer, and Kirsten Seaver. Birgitta Wallace and Gísli Sigurðsson allowed extensive reformulation of their saga and interpretation manuscripts. Örnólfur Thorsson helped secure permission to republish saga materials, and the *Journal of European Archaeology* permitted us to adapt from a paper previously published by Lotte Hedeager.

Many authors were also instrumental in supplying photography for the catalogue, either for their own articles (Símun Arge, Joel Berglund, Paul Buckland, Steven Cox, Torsten Edgren, Johannes Hertz, Lars Jørgensen, Stephen Loring, Niels Lynnerup, Thomas McGovern, Ian Morrison, Astrid Ogilvie, and Carin Orrling), or for arranging photography of loan objects from their own institutions for their papers or those of others (Jette Arneborg, Colleen Batey, Arne Emil Christensen, Hans Christian Gulløv, Sigrid Kaland, Patricia Sutherland). Carin Orrling deserves particular mention for her efforts to provide access to a large number of Swedish collections, many of which were on tour. Other lenders also made extraordinary efforts to meet our photography deadlines, among them the National Museums of Scotland (David Clarke), the Grosvenor Museum (Dan Robinson), the British Museum (Leslie Webster), York Archaeological Trust (Christine McDonnell), and National Museum of Iceland (Lilja Arnadóttir). Vesteinn Ólason and Gísli Sigurðsson arranged for the photography of illuminated manuscripts in the Arni Magnússon Institute. We also thank project photographers Carl Hansen of NMNH and Peter Harholdt for their superb efforts in photographing collections overseas and in Canada. All photographic and illustration credits are listed elsewhere.

For illustrations provided by the National Geographic Society we thank Bill Allen, Robert Poole, Prit Vesilind, Katherine Moran, and especially Sisse Brimberg, who allowed us to use her photographs in this book and in the exhibition. Icelandair provided travel support for object photography through the assistance of Deborah Scott, who also provided us with an introduction to skipper Gunnar Eggertsson, from whom we obtained the cover illustration.

New York photographers Judith Lindbergh and Russell Kaye provided photographs of scenic landscapes. Robert Humphrey drew the historical ecology cartoons.

In addition to object photographs, this volume uses illustrations provided by more than eighty institutions. Special thanks are due to the Danish Royal Library, the British Library, and the Bibliothèque Nationale de France, Paris. The task of invoicing, tracking, and ensuring that illustration payments were made was the principal duty of the Arctic Study Center's Sarah Ganiere, who also helped out with tracking down bibliographic and illustration research. Maps and line drawings required expert attention and became the responsibility of Daniel Odess, who worked closely with Anthropology Department illustrator Marcia Bakry, whose fine maps inform this book. Here and in many other areas, Dennis Stanford and Carolyn Rose provided crucial support. Zaborian Payne kept our financial records intact. We would also like to acknowledge project volunteers Jerry Salzberg, Karin Magnusson, Arthur Myhre Scott, and Hilkka Mälarstedt.

We relied yet again on the legendary talents of book designer Dana Levy and editor Letitia Burns O'Connor, proprietors of Perpetua Press in Los Angeles, to transform the manuscripts and graphic ideas into a book, which they did with great style and great speed. Tish organized all phases of the production and headed the team of skilled editors that also included Kathy Talley-Jones, who prepared the index, and Brenda Johnson-Grau, who cheerfully took on such tedious chores as editing the complex bibliography and proofreading. Erin Sweeney provided editorial assistance to the curators at NMNH in preparing the manuscript for publication. Tom Hummel coordinated the manufacturing for Toppan Printing Company. The Smithsonian Institution Press joined the project as publisher largely through the indefatigable efforts of Caroline Newman, Executive Editor, Museum Publications, with the help of Annette Windhorn, marketing manager, and publicist Matt Litts.

No project can be done without support from the home front. Elisabeth Ward thanks her parents, Bill and Greta Lange, for encouraging her interest in her Icelandic roots; John Lindow, professor at University of California at Berkeley for his instruction in Viking archaeology and saga literature; and Keith Ward, whose knowledge of medieval culture enriched *Vikings* and whose selfless willingness to shoulder an unfair amount of life's daily burdens allowed his wife to undertake this voyage of discovery. Elisabeth thanks Bill Fitzhugh for including her in every phase of this intellectual journey and for recognizing her efforts by honoring a junior colleague as coeditor. William Fitzhugh thanks Elisabeth Ward for her unstinting dedication, which pulled this project through many a tight spot; the Arctic Studies Center staff for support and assistance; and family and friends for enduring—hard on the heels of *Ainu*—yet another exhibition saga. He thanks his parents, whose stories of his ancestor, Thorpin the Dane of Orkney, initiated his interest in Viking history, and Lynne Fitzhugh, who kept the home fires burning bright to guide her husband back from his circumpolar wanderings, even while she produced her own first book on Labrador. Together we have revived the thousand-year-old connection between Labrador and Fitzhugh family history that parallels the westward course of the Vikings themselves. To all those above—and others—thank you!

Institutions Lending to the Exhibition

Antiquity Collection, Ribe, Denmark / Den Antikvariske Samling i Ribe (ASR)

Árni Magnússon Institute, Reykjavík, Iceland / Stofnun Árna Magnússonar á Íslandi (AMI)

Beinecke Library, Yale University, New Haven, Connecticut (BLY)

The British Museum, London (TBM)

Canadian Museum of Civilization, Hull, Québec (CMC)

Danish National Museum, Copenhagen / Danmarks Nationalmuseet (DNM)

Faeroese Historical Museum, Tórshavn / Føroya Fornminnissavn (FMS)

Glasgow Art Gallery and Museum, Scotland (GAGM)

Greenland National Museum and Archives, Nuuk / Grønlands Nationalmuseet og Arkiv (GNM)

Grosvenor Museum, Chester City Council, Chester, England (CHEGM)

Isle of Man Manx Museum, Douglas, Manx National Heritage (IOMMM)

Lindisfarne Priory Museum, English Heritage (LPM)

Maine State Museum, Augusta (MSM)

Metropolitan Opera, New York City (MO)

Museum of National Antiquities, Stockholm / Statens Historiska Museum (SHM)

National Board of Antiquities, Finnish National Museum, Helsinki / Museovirasto (FBA)

National Museum of Iceland, Reykjavík / Thjóðminjasafn Islands (NMI)

National Museum of Natural History, Smithsonian Institution, Washington (NMNH)

National Museums of Scotland, Edinburgh (NMS)

Newfoundland Museum, Government of Newfoundland and Labrador, Saint John's (NFM)

Parks Canada, Atlantic Region, Halifax (PC)

The Royal Library, Copenhagen / Det Kongelige Bibliotek (KB)

University of Bergen Museum / Universitet i Bergen, Historisk Museum (UBM)

University Museum of Cultural Heritage, Oslo / Universitetets Oldsaksamling (UOO)

University Museum of Natural History and Archaeology, Trondheim, Norway / Vitenskapsmuseet (VSM)

Viking Ship Museum, Oslo / Vikingsskiphalle (VSH)

Yorkshire Museum, City of York Council (YORYM)

Object Checklist
and Illustration
Credits

An asterisk following the collection number indicates an object that appears in the exhibition.

Any illustration commissioned for this publication is identified in the checklist with the acronym NMNH. This material may be available from the Arctic Studies Center.

All photographs from the Yorkshire Museum were provided by the York Archaeological Trust (YAT).

Page 10
Illumination from *Jónsbók,* c. 1350
Photograph by Jóhanna Ólafsdóttir, AMI
AMI Gks 3269a quarto*

Page 11
Fig. 1 Atlantic puffins, Iceland
Photograph by Judith Lindbergh, New York

Page 12
Fig. 2 Helge and Anne Stine Ingstad
Photograph courtesy National Geographic Society

Page 13
Map of the Norse North Atlantic
Prepared by Marcia Bakry, NMNH

Page 15
Fig. 3 Gokstad ship model
Wood, canvas; 4 m; modern re-creation
Photograph by Christer Åhlin, SHM
SHM 32584*

Page 16
Fig. 4 Finger ring
Gold; 2.7 cm; Viking Age
Isle of Skye, Hebrides, Scotland
GAGM 7919*

Page 17
Fig. 5 Penannular brooch
Silver, gold; 21 cm; 9th c.
Hatteberg, Hordaland, Norway
Photograph by Peter Harholdt, NMNH
UBM B8377*

Page 19
Fig. 6 Bronze brooch hoard
Ceramic, bronze, silver, glass; Viking Age
Photograph by Sisse Brimberg
Courtesy of National Geographic Society
DNM

Page 20
Fig. 7 Approaching Greenland from Iceland
Photograph by Judith Lindbergh, New York

Page 21
Fig. 8 Leif Eriksson statue, Reykjavík
Photograph by William W. Fitzhugh, NMNH

Page 22
Fig. 9 *Micmac Indians*
Oil painting; mid 19th c.
Courtesy The National Gallery of Canada, Ottawa, 6663

Page 23
Fig. 10 *The Skeleton in Armor*
Paper, leather, gold leaf; 23 cm; 1877
Photograph courtesy NMNH
Arctic Studies Center, NMNH*

Page 24
Fig. 11 U.S. Department of Justice building frieze, Washington, D.C.
Photograph by Carl Hansen, NMNH

Page 25
Fig. 12 *Snorri* replica Viking ship launching in Maine
Photograph by Russell Kaye, New York

SECTION I
Page 26
Fyrkat, Jutland, Denmark
Photograph by Sisse Brimberg
Courtesy National Geographic Society

Page 28
Map of Northern Europe and Scandinavia
Prepared by Marcia Bakry, NMNH

Page 30
Birka, Uppland, Sweden
Photograph by Ted Spiegel
Courtesy National Geographic Society

Page 31
Illumination from *Jónsbók* (*Skarðsbók*), c. 1363
Photograph by Jóhanna Ólafsdóttir, AMI
AMI AM 350 folio

Fig. 1.1 Holte Forest, Denmark
Photograph by William W. Fitzhugh, NMNH

Page 32
Fig. 1.2 Ålesund, Norway
Photograph by William W. Fitzhugh, NMNH

Map of geography and resources of Scandinavia
Prepared by Marcia Bakry, NMNH

Page 33
Fig. 1.3 Birka, Uppland, Sweden
Photograph by Jan Normann, RAÄ
Courtesy SHM

Fig. 1.4 Yttervik, Sweden
Photograph by William W. Fitzhugh, NMNH

Fig. 1.5 Fishing weight, spear, and hook
Stone, iron, iron; 16.6, 19.8, 7.6 cm; Viking Age
Uggestad, Buskerud, Norway; Fossesholm, Buskerud, Norway; Koltjønn, Telemark, Norway
Photograph courtesy UOO
UOO C-7201, C-1272, C-19724c

Page 34
Fig. 1.6 Axe
Iron; 11 cm; Viking Age
Fornby Äs, Västmanland, Sweden
Photograph by Christer Åhlin, SHM
SHM 1111*

Page 35
Fig. 1.7 Arrowheads
Iron; 11 cm; Viking Age
Birka, Uppland, Sweden
Photograph by Christer Åhlin, SHM
SHM 5208:276-277*

Fig. 1.8 Bone skates
Metatarsal bone; 22 cm; Viking Age
Birka, Uppland, Sweden
Photograph by Christer Åhlin, SHM
SHM 5208:1640*

Fig. 1.9 Woodcut from *Description of the Northern Peoples,* 1555
Reproduction permission from The Hakluyt Society, London

Page 36
Fig. 1.10 Oval brooches
Copper alloy; 10 cm; Viking Age; Norway
Photograph by Peter Harholdt, NMNH
UBM B6483 a,b*

Fig. 1.11 Oval brooches
Bronze; 12 cm; Viking Age
St. Ilian, Västmanland, Sweden
Photograph by Christer Åhlin, SHM
SHM 19732:2*

Page 37
Fig. 1.12 Round brooch
Bronze; 6.5 cm diam.; Viking Age
Kvalsta, Västmanland, Sweden
Photograph by Christer Åhlin, SHM
SHM 12300*

Page 38
Fig. 1.13 Penannular brooch
Iron; 7 cm diam.; Viking Age
Berg, Västmanland, Sweden
Photograph by Christer Åhlin, SHM
SHM 12475:15*

Fig. 1.14 Penannular brooch
Silver; needle length 20 cm; Viking Age
Vall, Gotland, Sweden
Photograph by Christer Åhlin, SHM
SHM 1399*

Page 39
Fig. 1.15 Box brooch
Silver and gilt; 6.5 cm; Viking Age
Boge, Gotland, Sweden
Photograph by Christer Åhlin, SHM
SHM 10654*

Fig. 1.16 Gotlandic ring brooch
Silver; 4.5 cm; 10th c.
Lau, Gotland, Sweden
Photograph by Christer Åhlin, SHM
SHM 32302*

Page 40
Fig. 1.18 Beaded necklaces
Sheet metal, glass; 60 cm; Viking Age
Birka, Uppland, Sweden
Photograph by Christer Åhlin, SHM
SHM 5208:2195*

Fig. 1.19 Fifty-bead necklace
Glass, crystal, carnelian chalcedony; 2.3 cm diam.; Viking Age
Gryta, Västmanland, Sweden
Photograph by Christer Åhlin, SHM
SHM 10974*

Page 41
Fig. 1.17 Forty-nine bead necklace
Glass, copper sheeting; 40 cm; Viking Age
Birka, Uppland, Sweden
Photograph by Christer Åhlin, SHM
SHM 5208: 2196*

Page 42
Illumination from *Jónsbók* (*Reykjabók*), c. 1600
Photograph by Jóhanna Ólafsdóttir, AMI
AMI AM 345 folio

Page 43
Fig. 2.1 Longhouse excavation at Borg, Lofoten, Norway
Photograph by Karsten Kristiansen
Courtesy Tromsø University Museum

Page 44
Fig. 2.3 Ard
Iron; 20.8 cm; Viking Age
Furnes, Hedmark, Norway
Photograph by Peter Harholdt, NMNH
UOO C-169a*

Fig. 2.4 Scythes
Iron; 21 cm; Viking Age
Rise, Sør Trøndelag, Norway
Photograph by Peter Harholdt, NMNH
UOO C-5267*, C-5268

Page 45
Fig. 2.2 Drawing of three views of wooden plow
Prepared by Darlene Hamilton

Page 46
Fig. 2.5 Nearly complete arrow, bifurcated arrow point, and arrow point
Iron, wood, resin, birch bark, tendons; 65 cm; 8th c.
Oppdal, Sør-Trondelag, Norway; Rundhøgda, Sør-Trøndelag, Norway; Atnosen, Hedmark, Norway
Photographs by Per E. Fredriksen, VSM
VSM T-17698h*, T-16477*, T-5930*

Fig. 2.6 Stone Age pitfall at Arjeplög, northern Sweden
Photograph by William W. Fitzhugh, NMNH

Page 47
Fig. 2.7 Iron Bloom
Iron, slag, charcoal; 19.5 cm diam.; Viking Age
Øyane, Telemark, Norway
Photograph by Peter Harholdt, NMNH
UOO C-34847*

Standard blank bars
Iron; c. 30 cm; Viking Age
Hverven, Buskerud, Norway
Photograph by Peter Harholdt, NMNH
UOO C-37551*

Fig. 2.8 Diagram of smelting furnace
Prepared by Darlene Hamilton

Fig. 8.1 Castle Esplanade Hoard
Silver, ceramic (not shown); c. 965
Castle Esplanade, Chester, England
Photograph courtesy Grosvenor Museum,
　Chester City Council
CHEGM coins #4, 36, 48, 51, 61a, 74-77,
　223, 264, 347, 372, 454, 448, 479, 494,
　517, 522, 524;
ingots #B, D, E; hacksilver #1-5, 7, 12, 14, 15,
　41-43, 54, 60, 72, 85, 105, 113*

PAGE 129
Fig. 8.2 Lindisfarne memorial, back
Stone; 42 cm; 9th c.
Lindisfarne (Holy Island), England
Photograph courtesy English Heritage
LPM 81077057*

PAGE 130
Figs. 8.3, 8.4 Arm rings
Silver; c. 7 cm; Viking Age; Irish Sea region
Photograph courtesy Trustees of TBM
M&LA 1854.12-27.62; M&LA 1851.7-15.9*

PAGE 131
Map of Viking Britain
Prepared by Marcia Bakry, NMNH

PAGE 132
Fig. 8.5 Shrine mounts
Copper alloy, gilt, amber; 7.5 cm; Viking Age
Carn a'Bharraich, Oronsay, Scotland
Photograph courtesy Trustees of NMS
NMS X.FC 163, 164

PAGE 133
Fig. 8.6 Human skull
Bone; 15.5 cm; c. 900
Ballateare, Isle of Man, United Kingdom
Photograph courtesy of Manx National
　Heritage
IOMMM 1966-0373/11

Fig. 8.7 Shield boss
Iron; 6.5 cm; 9th c.
Reay, Caithness, Scotland
Photograph courtesy Trustees of NMS
NMS X.IL 366*

Fig. 8.8 Spearhead
Iron; 37.6 cm; Viking Age
Tofta, Gotland, Sweden
Photograph by Christer Åhlin, SHM
SHM 12996:3*

PAGE 134
Fig. 8.9 Coppergate excavation, 1976, York,
　England
Photograph copyright YAT

PAGE 135
Fig. 8.10a Drawing of scabbard decoration
Prepared by Darlene Hamilton

Fig. 8.10b Scabbard
Leather; 18.9 cm; mid-10th c.
Coppergate, York, England
Photograph copyright YAT
YORYM 1980.7.7900*

Fig. 8.11 Shoe
Leather; 25.5 cm; 10-11th c.
Coppergate, York, England
Photograph copyright YAT
YORYM 1980.7.11013*

Fig. 8.12 Knife
Iron, brass; 11.7 cm; 12th c. (?)
Coppergate, York, England
Photograph copyright YAT
YORYM 1976.7.164*

PAGE 136
Fig. 8.13 Amber beads and pendants
Baltic amber; 2.5 cm; Viking Age
Coppergate, York, England
Photography copyright YAT
YORYM 1979.7.4021, 1976.7.302,
　1976.7.606, 1981.7.13038 1980.7.8978*

Fig. 8.14 Ring fragments
Jet; 1.2 cm; Viking Age
Coppergate, York, England
Photograph copyright YAT
YORYM 179.7.5732; 1980.7.8594;
　180.7.8396; 1977.7.1821*

Fig. 8.15 Skate
Metatarsal bone; 23.8 cm; Viking Age
Coppergate, York, England
Photograph copyright YAT
YORYM 1980.7.10993*

Fig. 8.16 Cup
Wood (yew); 11.5 cm diam.; late 10th c.
Coppergate, York, England
Photograph copyright YAT
YORYM 1977.7.1383*

PAGE 137
Fig 8.17 Textile fragment
Eastern imported silk; 24.5 cm; Viking Age
Coppergate, York, England
Photograph copyright YAT
YORYM 1981.7.14011*

PAGE 138
Fig. 8.18 Needles
Iron; 6.3 cm; Viking Age
Coppergate, York, England
Photograph copyright YAT
YORYM 1980.7.10854, 1980.7.8446*

Fig. 8.19 Candle holder
Iron; 10 cm; Viking Age
Coppergate, York, England
Photograph copyright YAT
YORYM 1979.7.7208*

Fig. 8.20 Tweezers
Iron; 16.2 cm; Viking Age
Coppergate, York, England
Photograph copyright YAT
YORYM 1980.7.9842*

Fig. 8.21 Grindstone
Gritstone; c. 14 cm; Viking Age
Coppergate, York, England
Photograph copyright YAT
YORYM 1980.7.9770*

Fig. 8.22 Pins and fish gorge (second from
　right)
Bird and animal bone; 0.9 cm; 10th c.
Drimore, South Uist, Scotland
Photograph courtesy GAGM
GAGM A7832:24-32*

Fig. 8.23 Cleaver
Whalebone; 15.2 cm; 10th c.
Drimore, South Uist, Scotland
Photograph courtesy GAGM
GAGM A7832:39*

PAGE 139
Fig. 8.24 Thorvald's cross
Slate; c. 35 cm; 10th c.
Andreas, Isle of Man, United Kingdom
Photograph courtesy of Manx National Heri-
　tage
IOMMM 128

Fig. 8.25 Pagan Viking boat burial in
　Westness, Orkney Islands, Scotland
Photograph by and courtesy of Sigrid H.H.
　Kaland

Fig. 8.26 Hogback burial markers
Stone; 136 cm; 10th c.
Brompton, Yorkshire, England
Photograph by Christopher D. Morris

PAGE 140
Fig. 8.27 Penannular brooch replica
Gold, glass (original material), copper alloy,
　amber (copy); 14.3 cm, replica of 8th-9thc.
　brooch
Kilmainham, Dublin County, Ireland
Photograph courtesy GAGM
GAGM A1901.120J*

Fig. 8.28 Crosier
Bronze, enamel; c. 10 cm; 8th c.
Helgö, Uppland, Sweden
Photograph courtesy SHM
SHM Replica 29750:475*

PAGE 141
Figs. 8.29, 8.30 Graffiti
Slate; 17.8 cm; 9th to 10th c.
Jarlshof, Shetland, United Kingdom
Photograph courtesy Trustees of NMS
NMS HSA 793*, HSA 790*

Fig. 8.31 Jarlshof ruins
Shetland, United Kingdom
Crown Copyright: Historic Scotland

SECTION III

PAGE 142
Lofoten Islands, Norway
Photograph by Sisse Brimberg
Courtesy National Geographic Society

PAGE 144
Map of the North Atlantic region
Prepared by Marcia Bakry, NMNH

PAGE 146
Illumination from *Jónsbók*, 14th c.
Photograph by Jóhanna Ólafsdóttir, AMI
AMI AM 127 quarto

PAGE 147
Fig. 9.1 Saksunardalur, Faeroe Islands
Photograph by Paul C. Buckland

Fig. 9.2 Graph of vegetation history
Researched by Margarét Hallsdóttir
Prepared by Marcia Bakry, NMNH

PAGE 148
Fig. 9.3 Ard blade
Iron; 38.5 cm; Viking Age
Stöng, Thjórsárdalur, Iceland
Photograph by Carl Hansen, NMNH
NMI 13560*

Fig. 9.4 Axe head
Iron; 16.8 cm; Viking Age
Búrfellsháls, Arnessysla, Iceland
Photograph by Carl Hansen, NMNH
NMI 10204*

Fig. 9.5 Sickle
Iron; 9 cm; 11–14th c.
Western Settlement, Greenland
Photograph by Erik Holm, GNM
GNM 1950x363*

PAGE 149
Fig. 9.6 Diagram of longhouse
Drawn by Phil and Paul C. Buckland
Prepared by Marcia Bakry, NMNH

Fig. 9.7 Soapstone pot
Steatite; 35.5 cm; Viking Age
Snaehvammur, Northern Iceland
Photograph by Carl Hansen, NMNH
NMI 3927*

PAGE 150
Fig. 9.8 Longhouse interior at Saudhusvellir,
　Iceland
Photograph by Paul C. Buckland

Figs. 9.9, 9.10 Needlecase and comb
Bronze, walrus ivory; 19.1 cm; 11th to 12th c.
Stöng, Thjórsárdalur, Iceland
Photograph by Carl Hansen, NMNH
NMI 13829*, 1983:25*

PAGE 151
Fig. 9.11 Ear spoon
Bronze; 7.5 cm; Viking Age
Birka, Uppland, Sweden
Photograph by Christer Åhlin, SHM
SHM 5208:172*

Fig. 9.12 Norse comb
Antler; 22 cm; 10th c.
Coppergate, York, England
Photograph copyright YAT
YORYM 1980.7.7870/8073*

Fig. 9.13-9.14 Combs
Antler; 13 cm; Viking Age
Birka, Uppland, Sweden
Photograph by Christer Åhlin, SHM
SHM 5208:720*, 5208:770*

Fig. 9.15 Shears and wool comb (with
　replica handle)
Iron, wood; 28 cm; Viking Age
Terum, Sogn og Fjord, Norway
Photograph by Peter Harholdt, NMNH
UBM B6846*, B8991*

PAGE 152
Fig. 9.16 Insect remains
Photograph by G. Dowling
Courtesy Paul C. Buckland

PAGE 153
Figs. 9.17, 9.18 Drawings of fleas and flies
Prepared by P. Skidmore

PAGE 154
Illumination from *Jónsbók* (*Skarðsbók*),
　14th c.
Photograph by Jóhanna Ólafsdóttir, AMI
AMI AM 350 folio

PAGE 155
Map of the Faeroe Islands
Prepared by Marcia Bakry, NMNH

PAGE 156
Fig. 10.1 Sandur Harbor, Sandoy, Faeroe
　Islands
Photograph by Símun V. Arge

PAGE 157
Fig. 10.2 Norse/Irish ringed pin
Bronze; 12.5 cm; 11th c.
Tjørnvík, Streymoy, Faeroes
Photograph by Per á Hædd, FMS
FMS 3718/p*

Fig. 10.3 Toftanes excavation
Photograph by S. Stummann Hansen, FMS

PAGE 158
Fig. 10.4 Pot hanger
Iron; 114 cm; Viking Age
Stokke, Sogn og Fjordane, Norway
Photograph by Peter Harholdt, NMNH
UBM B6743*

Fig. 10.5 Cauldron
Iron; 26 cm diam.; Viking Age; Norway
Photograph by Peter Harholdt, NMNH
UOO C.795*

PAGE 159
Fig. 10.6 Meat fork
Iron; 32 cm; 10th c.
Sekse, Hordaland, Norway
Photograph by Peter Harholdt, NMNH
UBM B-1201*

Fig. 10.7 Frying pan
Iron; 84 cm; Viking Age
Photograph by Peter Harholdt, NMNH
UBM B5030*

PAGE 160
Fig. 10.8 Norse line sinker
Basalt; 13.5 cm; Viking Age
Kvívík, Streymoy, Faeroes
Photograph by S. Stummann Hansen, FMS
FMS 3500/S1*

Fig. 10.9 Cordage, barrel top, and stave
Juniper root, Scots pine; 133 cm; Viking Age
Toftanes, Eusturoy, Faeroes
Photograph by S. Stummann Hansen, FMS
FMS 4666/1762*, 4666/1745, 4666/2157*

PAGE 304
Illumination from *Jónsbók*, 14th c.
Photograph by Jóhanna Ólafsdóttir, AMI
AMI AM 3269a quarto

Fig. 23.1 Chessmen (bishop, queen)
Walrus ivory; c. 10 cm; late 12th c.
Uig, Isle of Lewis, Scotland
Photograph courtesy NMS
NMS NS 25*, 29*

PAGE 305
Fig. 23.1 Chessmen (king, queen, knight, bishop)
Walrus ivory; c. 10 cm; 12th c.
Uig, Isle of Lewis, Scotland
Photographs courtesy NMS; TBM
NMS NS 23; TBM 80, 87, 106, 85*

PAGE 306
Fig. 23.2 Pot
Clay; 10cm; 13th to 14th c.
Bryggen Harbor, Bergen, Norway
Photograph by Peter Harholdt, NMNH
UBM

PAGE 307
Fig. 23.3 Runic tally stick
Wood; 10 cm; 12th to 14th c.
Austmannadal, Western Settlement, Greenland
Photograph by Carl Hansen, NMNH
DNM D12487*

PAGE 308
Fig. 23.4 Toy boat
Wood; 22.2 cm; 11th to 14th c.
Uumiviarssuk, Western Settlement, Greenland
Photograph by Carl Hansen, NMNH
DNM D12304*

Fig. 23.5 Game die
Walrus ivory; 1.1 cm; 11th to 14th c.
Farm Beneath the Sand, Western Settlement, Greenland
Photograph by Erik Holm, GNM
GNM 1950x2510*

Fig. 23.6 Chess piece
Walrus ivory; 2.5 cm; 11th c.
Kilaarsarfik (Sandnes), Western Settlement
Photograph by Erik Holm, GNM
GNM 4x401*

Fig. 23.7 Game disk
Whalebone; 5.4 cm; 11th to 14th c.
Kilaarsarfik (Sandnes), Western Settlement
Photographs by Carl Hansen, NMNH
DNM D11741*

PAGE 309
Fig. 23.9 Finger ring
Gold; 1.8 cm; 11th to 15th c.
Igaliku (Gardar), Eastern Settlement, Greenland
Photograph by Carl Hansen, NMNH
DNM D1157*

Fig. 23.8 Key
Iron, brass; 7.5 cm; 11th to 12th c.
Kilaarsarfik (Sandnes), Western Settlement
Photograph by Erik Holm, GNM
GNM 4x1109*

Fig. 23.10 Miniature shield
Silver; 1.6 cm; 14th c.
Nipaitsoq, Western Settlement, Greenland
Photograph by Erik Holm, GNM
GNM 991x109*

PAGE 310
Fig. 23.11 Reliquary cross
Ivory; 28.4 cm; Danish
Photograph by Carl Hansen, NMNH
DNM 9087

PAGE 311
Fig. 23.12 Church fragments
Bronze; glass, ceramic; 11.5 cm (bell); 1300
Igaliku (Gardar), Eastern Settlement, Greenland
Photographs by Carl Hansen, NMNH
DNM D12685, D11175*, D12687

PAGE 312
Fig. 23.13 Crosier (replica)
Walrus ivory; 14.1 cm; 13th c.
Igaliku (Gardar), Eastern Settlement, Greenland
Photograph by Carl Hansen, NMNH
DNM D11154*

Fig. 23.14 *Church of Hvalsey*
Watercolor by J. M. Mathiesen; mid 19th c.
Courtesy DNM Archives

PAGE 313
Fig. 23.15 Crosses
Wood; c. 15-20 cm; 14th c.
Ikigaat (Herjolfsnes), Eastern Settlement, Greenland
Photograph by Carl Hansen, NMNH
DNM D10670, D 10651, D10623 (with runes)*

PAGE 314
Fig. 23.17 Belt buckle
Whalebone; 10.2 cm; 12th c.
Kangersuneq, Western Settlement, Greenland
Photograph by Carl Hansen, NMNH
DNM D12561.528*

Fig. 23.18 Comb
Antler; 8.2 cm; 13th to 14th c.
Austmannadal, Western Settlement, Greenland
Photographs by Carl Hansen, NMNH
DNM D12356.257*

Fig. 23.19 Buttons
Walrus ivory; 1.5 cm; 12th to 14th c.
Nipaitsoq, Western Settlement, Greenland
Photograph by Erik Holm, GNM
GNM 991x623, 991x624*

PAGE 315
Fig. 23.16 Hood
Wool; 68 cm; 14th to early 15th c.
Ikigaat (Herjolfsnes), Eastern Settlement, Greenland
Photograph by Kit Weiss, DNM
DNM D10606*

PAGE 316
Fig. 23.20 Cross
Jet and silver; 1 cm; 10th c.
Ikigaat (Herjolfsnes), Eastern Settlement, Greenland
Photograph by Carl Hansen, NMNH
DNM D10626*

Fig. 23.21 Cross
Jet and silver; 1.1 cm; 12th to 14th c.
Coppergate, York, England
Photograph copyright YAT
YORYM 1976.7.500*

PAGE 317
Fig. 23.22 Mirror back
Elephant ivory; French; mid 14th c.
Photograph courtesy V&A Picture Library, Victoria and Albert Museum 803-1891

PAGE 318
Illumination from *Jónsbók*, early 14th c.
Photograph by Jóhanna Ólafsdóttir, AMI
AMI GKS 3270 quarto

PAGE 319
Fig. 24.1 *Ruin near Umiatset*
Watercolor by Andreas Kornerup; 1876
Courtesy DNM Greenland Archive

PAGE 320
Fig. 24.2 Runestone
Phyllite; 11.2 cm; 13th c.
Kingiktorssuaq, Upernavik, Greenland
Photograph by Carl Hansen, NMNH
DNM XCCII*

Fig. 24.3 Woodcut from *A Description of the Northern Peoples*, 1555
Reproduction permission from The Hakluyt Society, London

PAGE 321
Fig. 24.4 Gyrfalcon carving
Walrus ivory; 3.2 cm; 11th to 14th c.
Kilaarsarfik (Sandnes), Western Settlement
Photograph by Erik Holm, GNM
GNM 4x310*

Fig. 24.5 Walrus carving
Walrus ivory; 3.9 cm; 11th to 14th c.
Uumiviarssúk, Western Settlement
Photograph by Carl Hansen, NMNH
DNM D12364*

Fig. 24.6 Polar bear carving
Walrus ivory; 2.5 cm; 11th to 14th c.
Kilaarsarfik (Sandnes), Western Settlement
Photograph by Carl Hansen, NMNH
DNM D11793*

PAGE 322
Fig. 24.7 Inuit multifaced carving
Wood; c. 25 cm; Late Dorset or 18th c.
Upernavik, Greenland
Photograph courtesy GNM
GNM 3

PAGE 323
Fig. 24.8 Diagram of Thule house
Courtesy Arctic Studies Center, NMNH

Fig. 24.9 Church bell fragment
Bronze; 8.2 cm; 11th to 15th c.
Tuttutup Isua, South Greenland
Photograph by Carl Hansen, NMNH
DNM L15-20*

PAGE 324
Fig. 24.10 Comb
Antler; c. 12 cm; 11th to 14th c.
Austmannadal Western Settlement, Greenland
Photograph by Carl Hansen, NMNH
DNM D12358*

Fig. 24.11 Spoon-box lid
Wood; 22 cm; 11th to 15th c.
Sermermiut, Western Settlement, Greenland
Photograph by Carl Hansen, NMNH
DNM L6-1737*

PAGE 325
Fig. 24.12 Shears
Iron; 16.5 cm; 11th to 15th c.
Sermermiut, Western Settlement, Greenland
Photograph by Carl Hansen, NMNH
DNM L6-773*

Knife
Iron, walrus ivory; 13.4 cm; 11th to 15th c.
Uummannaq, Thule District, Greenland
Photograph by Carl Hansen, NMNH
DNM L3-6840*

Fig. 24.13 Chess piece
Walrus ivory; 3 cm; 11th to 15th c.
Uummannaq, Thule District, Greenland
Photograph by Carl Hansen, NMNH
DNM L3-5707*

Fig. 24.14 Fire-starter
Iron; 8 cm; 11th to 15th c.
Illutalik, West Greenland
Photograph by Carl Hansen, NMNH
DNM L15-491*

PAGE 326
Fig. 24.15 Inuit face carving
Wood; 8 cm; 15-16th c.
Inugsuk, Upernavik, Greenland
Photographs by Carl Hansen, NMNH
DNM L4-3058

Fig. 24.16 Inuit human figure
Wood; 5 cm; 15-16th c
Upernavik, Greenland.
Photograph by Carl Hansen, NMNH
DNM L4-3225*

PAGE 327
Illumination from *Helgastaðabók*
Photograph by Jóhanna Ólafsdóttir, AMI
AMI Perg quarto NR 16

PAGE 328
Fig. 25.1 Hvalsey Church in Greenland
Photograph by Judith Lindbergh, New York

PAGE 329
Fig. 25.2 *Brattahlid*
Watercolor by N. P. Jørgensen; 1894
Courtesy DNM Greenland Archive

PAGE 330
Fig. 25.3 Woodcut by Aron of Kangeq
Photograph courtesy NMNH

Fig. 25.4 Igaliku (Gardar), southwest Greenland
Photograph by Bent Fredskild, Copenhagen

PAGE 331
Fig. 25.5 Anodliuitsoq, southern Greenland
Photograph by Judith Lindberg, New York

PAGES 332–333
Figs. 25.6–25.9 Animal resource graphs
Research by Thomas McGovern
Prepared by Marcia Bakry, NMNH

PAGE 335
Fig. 25.10 Chair arm
Wood; 37.8 cm; 11th to 15th c.
Kilaarsarfik (Sandnes), Western Settlement
Photograph by Kit Weiss, DNM
DNM D12016*

Fig. 25.11 Horn spoon in box
Horn, wood; 31 cm; 11th to 14th c.
Austmannadal, Western Settlement, Greenland
Photograph by Carl Hansen, NMNH
DNM D12807, L6-1734*

PAGE 336
Fig. 25.12 Brattahlid, Eastern Settlement, Greenland
Photograph by Judith Lindbergh, New York

PAGE 337
Fig. 25.13 Western Settlement, Greenland
Photograph by Richard H. Jordan

PAGE 338
Fig. 25.14 Spindle shaft
Wood; 42.8 cm; 11th to 14th c.
Kilaarsarfik (Sandnes), Western Settlement
Photograph by Carl Hansen, NMNH
DNM D11878*

Fig. 25.15 Norse spindle whorl
Steatite; 2 cm; 11th to 15th c.
Illutalik, South Greenland
Photographs by Carl Hansen, NMNH
DNM L15-626*

PAGE 339
Fig. 25.16 Embroidery needle
Bone; c. 15 cm; 11th to 15th c.
Brattahlid, Eastern Settlement, Greenland
Photograph by Carl Hansen, NMNH
DNM D12206.927*

Fig. 25.17 Scissors
Iron; 16.5 cm; 11th to 14th c.
Austmannadal, Western Settlement, Greenland
Photograph by Carl Hansen, NMNH
DNM D12811*

PAGE 340
Illumination from *Jónsbók* (*Skarðsbók*), c. 1363
Photograph by Jóhanna Ólafsdóttir, AMI
AMI AM 350 folio

PAGE 341
Fig. 26.1 Detail of *Grønlands Historiske Mindesmaerker*, 1838
Photograph by Carl Hansen, NMNH
DNM Medieval Department Library

PAGE 342
Fig. 26.2 Map of Gothåb Fjord area
Drawn by Hans Egede; ca. 1723
Courtesy DNM

compiled by
Kathy Talley-Jones

Vikings: The North Atlantic Saga
was produced for the
Arctic Studies Center,
National Museum of Natural History
and the Smithsonian Institution Press
by Perpetua Press, Los Angeles.
Edited by Letitia Burns O'Connor,
Kathy Talley-Jones and Brenda Johnson-Grau
Design and typography by Dana Levy
Typeset in Adobe Garamond with Anna for display
by Theresa Velasquez, Spirit Dancer, Bisbee, AZ
Printed in Japan by Toppan Printing Co.